United States History II

1877 - Present

Michael Bellesiles I Charles Couch I Mark Angelos

CENGAGE
Learning™

Australia • Brazil • Japan • Korea • Mexico • Singapore • Spain • United Kingdom • United States

United States History II
1877 - Present

Michael Bellesiles | Charles Couch |
Mark Angelos

Executive Editor:
Maureen Staudt
Michael Stranz

Senior Project Development Manager:
Linda de Stefano

Marketing Specialist:
Sara Mercurio
Lindsay Shapiro

Senior Production/Manufacturing Manager:
Donna M. Brown

PreMedia Supervisor:
Joel Brennecke

Rights & Permissions Specialist:
Kalina Hintz
Todd Osborne

Cover Image:
Getty Images*

For product information and technology assistance, contact us at
Cengage Learning Customer & Sales Support, 1-800-354-9706

For permission to use material from this text or product,
submit all requests online at **cengage.com/permissions**
Further permissions questions can be emailed to
permissionrequest@cengage.com

Compilation Copyright © 2009 Cengage Learning

ISBN-13: 978-0-618-17008-1

ISBN-10: 0-618-17008-1

Cengage Learning

5191 Natorp Boulevard
Mason, Ohio 45040
USA

This book contains select works from existing Cengage Learning resources and was produced by Cengage Custom Solutions for collegiate use. As such, those adopting and/or contributing to this work are responsible for editioral content, accuracy, continuity and completeness.

Cengage Learning is a leading provider of customized learning solutions with office locations around the globe, including Singapore, the United Kingdom, Australia, Mexico, Brazil, and Japan. Locate your local office at:
international.cengage.com/region

Cengage Learning products are represented in Canada by
Nelson Education, Ltd.

For your lifelong learning solutions, visit **www.cengage.com/custom**

Visit our corporate website at **www.cengage.com**

Printed in the United States of America

Contents

1

Formation of the Knights of Labor (1878)

T E R E N C E   V .   P O W D E R L Y

The Noble Order of the Knights of Labor was the first national labor union. Originally organized by the garment workers of Philadelphia in 1869, the Knights of Labor began in 1876 to expand its membership to include other skilled workers. Terence V. Powderly, a machinist from Scranton, played a key role in making the Knights of Labor into a national organization. Along with Robert Schilling, Powderly wrote the preamble of the union's constitution, which served as the guiding document of the Knights until they were supplanted by the American Federation of Labor in the 1890s. Powderly perceived that workers suffered from a social stigma which minimized the value of their labor, and hoped that the Knights would give workers a sense of their own worth.

Questions to Consider

- Why was the Knights of Labor kept secret?
- What does Powderly think are the advantages of a union?
- What reforms were necessary and why?

On May 14, 1877, a conference was held in Pittsburg, but many of those who had signified a willingness to attend, failed to do so, and the MEETING FELL FAR SHORT of what was expected....

While D.A. [District Assembly] No. 3 [of Pittsburgh] had done excellent work and had made marvelous headway, it lost sight of the fact that the patient years of toil which were given to the laying of the foundation of the order by the parent assemblies of Philadelphia were necessary, and that without them no organization could be properly established. The feeling which existed after the closing of the Pittsburg conference was not satisfactory to those who had taken a part in the meeting.

No notice of the Philadelphia convention had been given to the Scranton assembly, in 1876, and although a

large and powerful district assembly flourished in the Lackawanna and Wyoming valleys when the Pittsburg conference was called, the officers of that district WERE NOT NOTIFIED until the proceedings of the conference were mailed to them by the corresponding officer of D.A. 3, who had by merest accident learned of the existence of the Scranton district.

When the secretary of D.A. No. 5, of Scranton [Powderly], received the report of the conference, he at once communicated with such members of the order as had taken a part in the various efforts to establish a national body, and at the same time corresponded with D.A. No. 3, advising that proceedings be stayed until a convention could be called that would be truly REPRESENTATIVE IN ITS CHARACTER...The result of the correspondence was to give to the recognized head of the order, D.A. No. 1, a record of such assemblies as were in existence so far as the addresses could be obtained.

Source: T. V. Powderly, *Thirty Years of Labor. 1859 to 1889* (Columbus, OH, 1890), pp. 234–254, 258–276, 279–283.

When this work was commenced D.A. No. 1 decided not to hold the convention in Pittsburg, as agreed upon in the Philadelphia meeting, and postponed the date until September, but a wave of political excitement swept over the order about that time, and it was decided to lay aside all differences and unite with the western part of the order in holding the meeting in January, 1878. In order that neither Philadelphia or Pittsburg would have cause for complaint, it was agreed that the meeting should be held in Reading, Pa....

On January 1, 1878, the representatives of the various parts of the order met in Reading, Pa. Richard Griffiths, of Chicago, who had been elected by the Chicago assembly, No. 400, was not present, owing to the fact that he was not PROVIDED WITH THE NECESSARY FUNDS by his assembly, and he could not afford to defray his own expenses. He had deputized T. V. Powderly to represent him should it be decided that representation by proxy would be legal....

When the delegates assembled in Crouse's Hall, 508 Penn street, Thomas King, Secretary of D.A. No. 4,...called the meeting to order, and nominated Uriah S. Stephens as temporary chairman....

It was voted to call the body, which was then in session, the GENERAL ASSEMBLY OF THE KNIGHTS OF LABOR OF NORTH AMERICA. The names by which subordinate bodies were designated previous to that time were continued. It was at this meeting that the subordinate assembly was first called Local Assembly, a term which has continued in use ever since.

Two district assemblies appearing, through their representatives, bearing the number five on their credentials, it was resolved to allow the one which had already procured a seal and other property to retain the number. The Scranton D.A. surrendered its right to the number, and accepted sixteen, by which number it has been known ever since.

To the titles by which the officers of local assemblies were designated was added the word grand. The chief officer of the general assembly was to be known as Grand Master Workman; the presiding officer of the D.A. was to be known as District Master Workman, and the executive of the L.A. was to continue in office as Master Workman.

Mr. Stephens was called home before the convention adjourned, but his true worth was known to the assembled representatives, and when the election of officers took place he was chosen G.M.W....

No nominations were made except in an informal way, each representative casting his ballot for that person whom he believed to be BEST QUALIFIED TO FILL THE POSITION. The first committee on constitution of the order of the Knights of Labor, appointed by Mr. Stephens, consisted of representatives Robert Schilling, Chairman; Ralph Beaumont, Thomas King, T. V. Powderly, and George S. Boyle...

Preamble

The recent alarming development and aggression of aggregated wealth, which, unless checked, will invariably lead to the pauperization and hopeless degradation of the toiling masses, render it imperative, if we desire to enjoy the blessings of life, that a check should be placed upon its power and upon unjust accumulation, and a system adopted which will secure to the laborer the fruits of his toil; and as this much desired object can only be accomplished by the thorough unification of labor, and the united efforts of those who obey the divine injunction that "In the sweat of thy brow shalt thou eat bread," we have formed the *****[1] with a view of securing the organization and direction, by co-operative effort, of the power of the industrial classes; and we submit to the world the objects sought to be accomplished by our organization, calling upon all who believe in securing "the Greatest good to the greatest number" to aid and assist us:—

I. To bring within the folds of organization every department of productive industry, making knowledge a stand-point for action, and industrial and moral worth, not wealth, the true standard of individual and national greatness.

II. To secure to the toilers a proper share of the wealth that they create; more of the leisure that rightfully belongs to them; more societary advantages; more of the benefits, privileges, and emoluments of the world; in a word, all those rights and privileges necessary to make them capable of enjoying, appreciating, defending, and perpetuating the blessings of good government.

III. To arrive at the true condition of the producing masses in their educational, moral, and financial condition, by demanding from the various governments the establishment of bureaus of Labor Statistics.

IV. The establishment of co-operative institutions, productive and distributive.

V. The reserving of the public lands—that heritage of the people—for the actual settler;—not another acre for railroads or speculators.

VI. The abrogation of all laws that do not bear equally upon capital and labor, the removal of unjust technicalities, delays, and discriminations in the administration of justice, and the adopting of measures providing for the health and safety of those engaged in mining, manufacturing, or building pursuits.

---

[1] The Knights of Labor was a secret organization until 1881, and even its name was kept confidential.—*Ed.*

VII. The enactment of laws to compel chartered corporations to pay their employee weekly, in full, for labor performed during the preceding week, in the lawful money of the country.

VIII. The enactment of laws giving mechanics and laborers a first lien on their work for their full wages.

IX. The abolishment of the contract system on national, State, and municipal work.

X. The substitution of arbitration for strikes, whenever and wherever employers and employes are willing to meet on equitable grounds.

XI. The prohibition of the employment of children in workshops, mines and factories before attaining their fourteenth year.

XII. To abolish the system of letting out by contract the labor of convicts in our prisons and reformatory institutions.

XIII. To secure for both sexes equal pay for equal work.

XIV. The reduction of the hours of labor to eight per day, so that the laborers may have more time for social enjoyment and intellectual improvement, and be enabled to reap the advantages conferred by the labor saving machinery which their brains have created.

XV. To prevail upon governments to establish a purely national circulating medium, based upon the faith and resources of the nation, and issued directly to the people, without the intervention of any system of banking corporations, which money shall be a legal tender in payment of all debts, public or private.

After adopting a constitution and the preamble given above, the General Assembly elected officers for the ensuing term, fixed upon St. Louis as the place to hold the next session, and adjourned with the following corps of officers:

Grand Master Workman—Uriah S. Stephens, of
    Pennsylvania.
Grand Worthy Foreman—Ralph Beaumont, of New
    York.
Grand Secretary—Charles H. Litchman, of
    Massachusetts.
Grand Assist. Secretary—John G. Laning, of Ohio....

The first session of the General Assembly was regarded somewhat in the light of an experiment, and the bodies of which it was made up were not as sanguine of success as the representatives. When the latter reported to their constituencies it was some time before they responded with sufficient enthusiasm to predict the successful continuance of the General Assembly as the head of the order of the Knights of Labor. The means provided by the General Assembly for the collection of revenue outlined in the following section:

"SECTION 1. The revenue of the G. A. of ***** shall be derived as follows: For charters to D.A., five dollars; for charters and A.K. to L.A.'s, five dollars; for each traveling, transfer, or final Card issued, ten cents; in addition, all D.A.'s shall pay, in advance, the sum of one cent and a half every three months for every member on the books of the L.A.'s represented therein."

But few of the representatives, when making their reports, endeavored to impress upon the minds of their constituencies the necessity for a PROMPT REMITTANCE OF FUNDS to headquarters in order that the work might be carried on as mapped out at Reading. The proceedings were to be published, constitutions, rituals, blank reports, and forms of all kinds were to be printed and mailed.

The salary of the Grand Master Workman was fixed at $200 per annum. The salary of the Grand Secretary was $800 per annum, and the salary of the Grand Treasurer was limited to $50 per annum. Without a dollar in the treasury the first corps of officers undertook the task of placing upon its feet an organization which aimed at the performance of more good to the cause of labor, more of reform and more educational facilities than any other organization that had ever taken up the cudgel in defense of the workingman. It was a herculean task, and none but strong, true men were wanted; none else were put at the head of the order.

The adoption of a seal for the use of the Assembly was left to the Grand Master Workman and the Grand Secretary. These officers, soon after the adjournment of the General Assembly, held a conference and adopted a design.... The inscription, which appears around the edge: "THAT IS THE MOST PERFECT GOVERNMENT IN WHICH AN INJURY TO ONE IS THE CONCERN OF ALL," was taken from the precepts of Solon, the Grecian sage and law-giver.

In the selection of this motto the grand officers were not actuated by mere sentiment, or a desire to make use of nicely worded phrases, or high sounding terms. They studied carefully and well before adopting that motto.

In accepting the preamble of the Industrial Brotherhood, the convention fully realized that for the most part the reforms which were asked for in that preamble must one day come through political agitation and action. The chief aim of those who presented the document to the convention was to place something on the front page of the constitution which, it was hoped, every workingman would in time read and ponder over. It was their hope that by keeping these measures, so fraught with interest to the people, constantly before the eye of the worker, he would become educated in the science of politics to that extent that he would know that those things that were wrong in our political system were wrong simply because he did not attend to his political duties in a proper manner;—that the righting of such things as were wrong should not be done by those who had the management of political affairs up to that time, but by himself. "Man, know thyself," is a good advice. Man, know thy rights; man, know thy wants; and man, know how to properly and temperately minister to these wants, and secure these rights, are WORDS OF ADVICE that should also be listened to....

In the ordinary affairs of labor, in the daily experiences of workshop life, action is often taken which at first may seem to be trifling, and to concern only those who are the immediate participants. It often develops that a trifling grievance in a workshop, if not carefully and judiciously handled, will involve others far removed from the scene of action. The experiences of the past, the many miserable failures which had attended the efforts of struggling labor organizations of former years, were before the eyes of the men who selected the inscription to place upon the outer edge of the seal, and they had in mind the duty which every workingman owed to his brother man....

Notwithstanding the fact that there were no funds in the treasury, and that the whole of the order was not represented at the Reading convention, the Grand Secretary, Mr. Litchman, PROCEEDED WITH THE WORK, and before the end of March every district assembly and local assembly in the order was provided with copies of the proceedings of the convention, and sample copies of the constitution. Blank forms were sent out at the same time on which to make application for charters for the various assemblies. Samples of traveling and transfer cards were also mailed by the Grand Secretary, and all of this was done before one dollar of revenue had been paid into the treasury.

When the different assemblies saw that the secretary was attending to his duty, they began to respond, and by the end of the year 1878 every assembly, whose whereabouts could be ascertained, was in possession of a charter and a sufficient number of constitutions to supply all members. Confidence in the order and the grand officers was at once established, and the work of organizing new assemblies was at once begun.

While the organization was working secretly, yet the stir in organizing soon attracted attention, and the first move from the outside against the association came from the church. The events which preceded the erection of the gallows in Schuylkill county, Pa., were still fresh in the minds of residents of that place, and one of the first fields that opened up to the organizer was the MIDDLE COAL REGION OF PENNSYLVANIA. Everything in the shape of a society, which was at all secret or new, was supposed to be the outcome of Molly Maguireism. It became necessary to allow the name of the order to become known, but the name was no shield from persecutions, misrepresentation, and misunderstanding, and soon a scathing denunciation of the association came from the altar of one of the churches in Schuylkill county. The members became alarmed; many

left the order at once; others withdrew temporarily, while others, knowing the justice of the principles, determined to make an effort to have objectionable features, if any there were, removed.

Grand Master Workman Stephens was written to, and after investigation a special session of the General Assembly was called to take action on the matter of placing the aims and objects of the order in a favorable light before the public. The request for this call came from the middle coal fields of Pennsylvania.

The workingmen of that region were sincerely desirous of having the features of the society properly understood by every body. They still held in dreadful remembrance the TERRIBLE LESSONS that were taught at the foot of the gallows, when men were strangled whose guilt was never proven, and whose innocence is to this day believed in by those who knew them best.[2] Whether the men who were hanged in Pennsylvania were all guilty of murder is not known, but it is known that men were hung on the testimony of those who were themselves murderers. It is known that that plague spot on American civilization, the Pinkerton detective, had entered the council chambers of the workingmen of Schuylkill county, and under the guise of friendship urged the men on to deeds of desperation and blood.

When the final day shall come, and the deeds of all men shall become known, the writer of this believes that no man's hand will be redder, no individual will be steeped more deeply in the guilt and crime for which men died upon the scaffold in Pennsylvania than the men who controlled the corporations which were operating the coal mines at that time. Justice no longer knew an abiding place in their hearts, honesty had given way to make room for the craze for gold; and with one ambition constantly before them, is it any wonder that they cared but little if one of their hired assassins of character swore away the lives of the innocent with the guilty? Men of influence, politicians, businessmen, clergymen, and professional men united in condemning the Molly Maguires, but the voice of him who condemned the outrageous system which made the Molly Maguires possible was never heard above a whisper. Men who had witnessed the terrible scenes of past years knew full well how easy men's lives could be sworn away; and when they saw the same men opposing organization in 1878, they naturally became alarmed, and urged that a special convention be called at once to set at rest the fears of those who were as yet uninitiated....

---

[2] Powderly is referring to the execution of ten Molly Maguires, a group of Irish coalminers who launched a violent counter-attack against the perceived injustices of management. A Pinkerton agent infiltrated the Molly Maguires and gave evidence against at the trial of twenty-four leaders in 1876.—*Ed.*

In order to successfully reach all who are engaged in "PRODUCTIVE INDUSTRY," it is necessary that the members of the order should know who may appropriately come under that head. The belief was prevalent until a short time ago among workingmen, that only the man who was engaged in manual toil could be called a workingman. The man who labored at the bench or anvil; the man who held the throttle of the engine, or delved in the everlasting gloom of the coal mine, did not believe that the man who made the drawings from which he forged, turned, or dug could be classed as a worker. The draughtsman, the time-keeper, the clerk, the school teacher, the civil engineer, the editor, the reporter, or the worst paid, most abused and illy appreciated of all toilers—woman—could not be called a worker. It was essential that the mechanics of America should know who were workers….

Not only did his employer and overseer believe that his dress, habitation, furniture, and living should be of the coarsest cheapest material or quality, but he also shared in that belief, and took it for granted that it was ordained of heaven; that the stay of the laborer on earth was only as a matter of convenience for his master, and that he must put up with every indignity, every insult, and privation rather than violate the rules of government, which were held up to him as being as sacred as the Ten Commandments. The holy Scriptures were quoted to show to the toiler that it was said in holy writ that he should be content with his slavish lot on earth in that he might enjoy an eternity of bliss in a future world, through the portals of which those who held him in subjection could not get a glimpse of the happiness beyond. "SERVANTS, OBEY YOUR MASTERS," was written on every wall in letters of fire for those who could read, and the story was told and retold to those who could not, until the worker believed that to ask for better things on this earth was almost a sacrilege. It would be flying in the face of Divine Providence to even remonstrate against the injustice which the employer practiced upon the poor laborer.

It was necessary to teach the laborer that it was not essential for him to grovel in the dust at the feet of a master in order to win his title deed to everlasting bliss in the hereafter; and it can not be wondered at that many who strove to better the condition of the toiler lost all respect for religion when they saw that those who affected to be the most devout worshipers at the foot of the heavenly throne, were the most tyrannical of task-masters when dealing with the poor and lowly, whose unfortunate lot was cast within the shadow of their heartless supervision. Men who kneeled before the altar of the Most High and asked for heavenly grace; men who prayed for their "daily bread," were to be found among those who denied the meanest privileges to the workman, and not only denied to him the right to worship his God in a decent manner, but actually took

from his mouth, from the fingers of his half-fed babes, the crust of bread on which they sought to sustain life itself.

It was no wonder that to many workingmen religion seemed to be but a parody when they contrasted their own condition with that of their employers….

As a recompense for the hours of misery and pain spent on earth, the toiler would have the happiness in the next world of seeing the rich man writhing in hell, while he roamed at will in the realms of eternal bliss. No creed taught this doctrine, no religion said to workingmen that they should look at these scriptural passages in the light in which I have portrayed them, but that these impressions were created on the minds of the workingmen every man who toils can testify.

It then became a question whether to acquire wealth was not a sin, and again the imitative qualities of man came to his rescue. He saw that the minister of the religion which he professed never made calls of a friendly nature on him; his neighbors, who worked where he did, never received a visit from the clergyman, but he saw that the man who could not get into heaven until the camel passed through the eye of a needle was often favored with a visit from the minister who preached poverty and humility as a means of acquiring grace on earth and happiness in heaven.

It became the duty of the workingman's friend to solve the camel question. How was it to be done? To make knowledge a standpoint for action, it was necessary to teach the toiler that it was THE USES, THE ABUSES OF RICHES, and the methods by which wealth was acquired that would be the test when the rich man would enter upon his race to eternity, with the camel as a competitor.

The deep-toned voice of many a minister of God rang out in denunciation of the workingman, who, in his poverty, in his agony, in his very despair often struck against the systems which crushed him to earth; and there were those in the ranks of toil, who, mistaking the false for the true, railed against religion because some of those who preached it and professed it failed most miserably in the practice of it. Knowledge for the workingman meant that he should be able to detect the difference between the real and the sham. Whenever a learned man said that which did not appear to be just to labor, he was to be questioned, publicly questioned, as to his base of actual facts.

….At the decree of Cleopatra, men, made in the same mould as men are made in to-day, wrought with hammer and chisel upon the surface of the stone that still survives to testify to the skill of past centuries. The name of Cleopatra still lives. We may go back among the dust-covered crooks and crevices of time and search for the name, the memory even, of the mechanic whose skill designed the huge stone; we may search for the name of the artisan whose hand in by-gone ages cut into the face of the solid rock the characters which still remain upon its surface. Oblivion, mystery, gloom, and everlasting death surround the names of the men who worked out the emblems whose import is as a sealed book to the man who to-day looks in wonder and awe at the imperishable monuments to the genius of the by-gone age....

In the city of Washington there stands a monument to the memory of the man who gave to the world a hope and to the toiler the right to enjoy political and re-ligious freedom. Ask of the guide who attends your visit to that magnificent, awe-inspiring pile, created in honor of "THE FATHER OF HIS COUNTRY" whose hand placed the first stone in its mortar-bed, and he will stand speechless as the marble itself.

...While the names of rulers have been handed down, the names of generals have been remembered for the lives they took, and the cities they destroyed, the names of those who ministered to the sum of human happiness in erecting cities and adding to the store of the world's greatness and wealth have been forgot-ten, the recollection of their deeds have passed away with the entombing of their lifeless clay. Those who de-stroyed have been remembered; those who constructed have been forgotten....

The rights of the people were usurped, their liberties were being gathered up in the strong hand of wealth, and the FINGERS OF DEATH were being circled around the constitution of the United States, when it was resolved to make "moral worth, not wealth, the true standard of individual and national greatness." Wealth had bought its way into senate chamber and council hall; it had seated its pliant tool upon the bench.... Politicians had made pledges only to break them, for they knew that to keep a promise and to break it would win the same reward from the toiler whose vote was cast for party and not for principle. The politi-cian knew that once seated in office he need not care for the opinion of the laborer; he need not exert himself to do that which was indicated in the platform of his party.... The Declaration of Independence said one thing, and the people practiced an entirely different thing. All men were declared to be born equal, yet the people of a nation stood by and saw millions born into servitude, the most damnable and revolting. This taught politicians to be dishonest, for honesty was ban-ished from the high places....

To make moral worth the standard of individual and national greatness, the men of toil had to be roused to a sense of duty; they had to be taught what their rights and duties were. To do this the hollow pretenses of the political parties, which every year came before the country and on platforms of "glittering generalities" appealed for the suffrages of the people, HAD TO BE EXPOSED AND SHOWN to the people in their true light.

Legislation for labor came through the halls of Congress and State Legislature as a bone comes through the fingers of a stingy master to a half-starved dog, with the meat picked from it...When tested before a tribunal of any kind, nearly all the legislation...would be declared unconstitutional. It was not...considered unconstitutional to grant a whole territory to a railroad company, or to grant a valuable franchise to a corpora-tion, but the moment the well-picked bone that was be-stowed upon the hungry dog,—Labor,—was taken to the Supreme Court, it was declared to be only a bone, nothing more. A knowledge of who his friends were in each Congress, in each session of the Legislature, was to be made the standpoint for action when the time rolled round to select new legislators,...and why should not the laborer do his own legislating, instead of letting it out to a second party?

...A change had to come, and with it the placing of the preamble of the Knights of Labor in every man's hand every day of the year, to be studied not one day in every four years, but every day in every year, so that those things that were pointed out in it would be care-fully bedded in the mind of man or discarded as untrue, and therefore worthless.

Parties would never provide the means of diffusing such an education as was here sought for. Something else had to be found to serve mankind, and that some-thing was presented to the American people when the order of the Knights of Labor was instituted....

To elect men on a third ticket at that time was a rea-son why members of the existing parties should unite against [them], and labor discovered that it was due to her to make use of the machinery already in existence before erecting new parties The measures of reform were all-important, and the name of the party of no consideration. This was the doctrine to teach the work-ingman.... It is being taught to him every day.

Parties are good only when they serve the best inter-ests of the majority of the people. The majority of all parties is made up of toilers, and their interests should RECEIVE FIRST CONSIDERATION. It was urged that inasmuch as the preamble of the Knights of Labor dealt with such questions as called for legislation, the order should at once be formed into a political party. Each of the old parties sought to convince the members of the Knights of Labor that there was no use for the order; that the party to which they belonged would effect all reform legislation if allowed to do so in its own way; but the workingmen who had carefully watched the history of the years which followed the close of the civil war, felt certain that party leaders cared nothing for the people, and they were right in many instances. The party leader saw that the people cared nothing for themselves, and why should he care for the people? The people took no interest in politics except during campaigns, why should the office-holder take any interest in the people except to get their votes? Political leaders STRONGLY URGED THE DISBANDING of the Knights of Labor. They asserted that the ordinary trade union was sufficient to take care of the interests of the wage worker. On that subject the General Master Workman of the Knights of Labor, in reply to a letter published by a prominent Democrat, in which the latter urged that all labor organizations affiliate with the Democratic party and give up their labor organizations, said in 1883:

"A great deal has been said of late concerning the dismemberment of the Knights of Labor, and the forming of a federation of trades. The principal reason given for the proposed action, summed up in a few words is, that each trade or craft in being organized for itself, can more easily and successfully engage in a strike…. One thing is certain, the originator of that idea was neither a Knight of Labor, nor a member of a trade union, for members of these associations know that the tendency of the times is to do away with strikes; that remedy has been proved by experience to be a very costly one for employer and employe.

"The trade union does not favor a strike; it is regarded as a *dernier resort* by every labor association in the land; and as no good can come of the dismemberment of an association which, among other things, aims at the perfecting of a system by which disputes between the laborer and capitalist can be settled without resorting to so costly an experiment as the strike,…why the Knights of Labor and the various labor associations of the country are in no great danger of being disbanded.

"I called the strike an experiment, and I would have every advocate of such a measure note these words. Strikes have been resorted to for centuries, and to-day, after hundreds of trials have been had, men can not embark in a strike with any assurance of success based upon a former precedent…. I will never advocate a strike unless it be a strike at the ballot-box, or such an one as was proclaimed to the world by the unmistakable sound of the strikers' guns on the field of Lexington. But the necessity for such a strike as the latter does not exist at present. The men who made the name of Lexington famous…were forced to adopt the bullet because they did not possess the ballot. We have the latter; and if the money of the monopolist can influence us to deposit our ballots in favor of our enemies; if we can not be depended on to go quietly to the polling booth and summon to our aid moral courage enough to deposit a little piece of paper in our own interest, how can it be expected of us to summon physical courage enough to do battle for our rights as did our fathers at Lexington?…

"What, then, is the duty of the hour? Men may argue from what I have said that I believe our cause to be hopeless; and did I not have faith in the Knights of Labor I would say, 'yes, the cause is lost.' Other men entertain different opinions, and positively assert that the panacea for all the ills we suffer will come through the adoption of such advice as they have to offer. For instance, 'Democrat' says in his letter of July 4th, that in order to secure the blessings we seek we 'have only to merge ourselves into the great Democratic party and help to swell the triumph of the plain people in 1884.' I must be pardoned for differing with him. I do not believe that it lies within the province of any party to protect the many against the unjust encroachments of the moneyed few, unless the many are properly instructed in the science of government….

"It may be inferred from the position I have taken in the foregoing lines, that the mission of the Knights of Labor is to become a political party, and that is intended to take precedence of the Democratic party. The inference would be wrong. The Knights of Labor is higher and grander than party. There is a nobler future before it than that which clings to its existence amidst partisan rancor and strife. The Knights of Labor is a friend to men of all parties, and believing that the moment it assumes the role of a political party its usefulness will be destroyed, it has refrained and will refrain from doing so….

"We have political parties enough. Every one of them in its early days was honest, and gave promise of good results, but the moment that success perched upon its banners, the vultures who feed upon spoils also perched upon its body, and to a certain extent frustrated the designs of its organizers.

"The same would be true of the Knights of Labor. If that order is not to become a political party, what good can it accomplish? This brings us to the root of the question, and gives the reason why there can be no dismemberment of the Knights of Labor. One reason why political parties degenerate is because the masses of the common people are not educated. We may be able to read and write, but we are not educated on the economic and social questions with which we are brought in contact every hour. If we were we could more easily discern the difference between good and bad legislation, and we would not be clamoring so often for the repeal of bad laws. The chief aim of the Knights of Labor is to educate, not only men but parties; educate men first that they may educate parties and govern them intelligently and honestly…."

To cause the worker to understand that to bring about reforms, which were political in their nature, without forming a new party, was a difficult undertaking…. There were honest men who insisted that a new party should be made up of Knights of Labor and industrial organizations. They failed to see that…a profitable field would be opened up to a new set of politicians who would naturally crowd to the front in a successful movement, no matter what its name might be. The duty of the Knights of Labor is to place citizenship above party.

… A labor party is not likely to become a success for the reason that it is not in accord with the genius of American institutions to form a party of any one class.

American citizens vote not for party, not for a class, but for the whole community; and that party through which the most people can be benefited is the one for whose candidates the people should vote, even though they become guilty of political apostasy every year. Class distinctions have wrought almost irreparable injury to the people of the United States. The workingmen are making an HONEST ENDEAVOR to rid the country of them by purifying parties and purging them of the evil tendency to lay everything at the feet of monopoly.

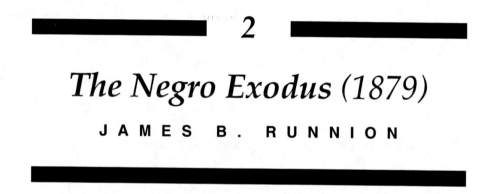

The Negro Exodus (1879)

JAMES B. RUNNION

As the Ku Klux Klan increased its terrorism campaign, many freed men felt that they could not truly enjoy their freedom unless they left the South. Many of these "Exodusters" settled in Kansas and established African-American communities in this relatively safer clime. The "Bourbons," who had reestablished white domination throughout the South, attempted to halt this exodus. Writing for the popular *Atlantic Monthly*, James Runnion offered a condescending perspective on the migration as well as a series of recommendations for solving the "race troubles" in the South.

Questions to Consider

- Why would the white elite object to the departure of so many of those very people they terrorized?
- What were the economic motivations of the Exodusters?

A recent sojourn in the South for a few weeks, chiefly in Louisiana and Mississippi, gave the writer an opportunity to inquire into what has been so aptly called "the negro exodus." The emigration of blacks to Kansas began early in the spring of this year. For a time there was a stampede from two or three

of the river parishes in Louisiana and as many counties opposite in Mississippi. Several thousand negroes (certainly not fewer than five thousand, and variously estimated as high as ten thousand) had left their cabins before the rush could be stayed or the excitement lulled. Early in May most of the negroes who had quit work for the purpose of emigrating, but had not succeeded in getting off, were persuaded to return to the plantations, and from that time on there have been only straggling

Source: *Atlantic Monthly* 44 (1879): pp. 222–230.

families and groups that have watched for and seized the first opportunity for transportation to the North. There is no doubt, however, that there is still a consuming desire among the negroes of the cotton districts in these two States to seek new homes, and there are the best reasons for believing that the exodus will take a new start next spring, after the gathering and conversion of the growing crop. Hundreds of negroes who returned from the river-banks for lack of transportation, and thousands of others infected with the ruling discontent, are working harder in the fields this summer, and practicing more economy and self-denial than ever before, in order to have the means next winter and spring to pay their way to the "promised land."

"We've been working for fourteen long years," said an intelligent negro, in reply to a question as to the cause of the prevailing discontent, "and we ain't no better off than we was when we commenced." This is the negro version of the trouble, which is elaborated on occasion into a harrowing story of oppression and plunder.

"I tell you it's all owing to the radical politicians at the North," explained a representative of the type known as the Bourbons; "they've had their emissaries down here, and deluded the 'niggers' into a very fever of emigration, with the purpose of reducing our basis of representation in Congress and increasing that of the Northern States."

These are the two extremes of opinion at the South. The first is certainly the more reasonable and truthful, though it implies that all the blame rests upon the whites, which is not the case; the second, preposterous as it will appear to Northern readers, is religiously believed by large numbers of the "unreconciled." Between these two extremes there is an infinite variety of theories, all more or less governed by the political faction to which the various theorizers belong; there are at least a dozen of these factions, such as the Bourbons, the conservatives, the native white republicans, the carpet-bag republicans, the negro republicans, etc. There is a political tinge in almost everything in the extreme Southern States. The fact seems to be that the emigration movement among the blacks was spontaneous to the extent that they were ready and anxious to go. The immediate notion of going may have been inculcated by such circulars, issued by railroads and land companies, as are common enough at emigrant centres in the North and West, and the exaggeration characteristic of such literature may have stimulated the imagination of the negroes far beyond anything they are likely to realize in their new homes. Kansas was naturally the favorite goal of the negro emigre, for it was associated in his mind with the names of Jim Lane and John Brown, which are hallowed to him. The timid learned that they could escape what they have come to regard as a second

bondage, and they flocked together to gain the moral support which comes from numbers.

Diligent inquiry among representative men, of all classes and from all parts of Louisiana, who were in attendance at the constitutional convention in New Orleans, and careful observation along the river among the land owners and field hands in both Louisiana and Mississippi, left a vivid impression of some material and political conditions which fully account for the negro exodus. I have dropped the social conditions out of the consideration, because I became convinced that the race troubles at the South can be solved to the satisfaction of both whites and blacks without cultivating any closer social relations than those which now prevail. The material conditions which I have in mind are less familiar than the political conditions; they are mainly the land-tenure and credit systems, and mere modifications (scarcely for the better) of the peculiar plantation system of slavery days.

The cotton lands at the South are owned now, as they were before the war, in large tracts. The land was about all that most of the Southern whites had left to them after the war, and they kept it when they could, at the first, in the hope that it would yield them a living through the labor of the blacks; of late years they have not been able to sell their plantations at any fair price, if they desired to do so. The white men with capital who went to the South from the North after the war seemed to acquire the true Southern ambition to be large land owners and planters; and when the ante-bellum owners lost their plantations the land usually went in bulk to the city factors who had made them advances from year to year, and had taken mortgages on their crops and broad acres. As a consequence, the land has never been distributed among the people who inhabit and cultivate it, and agricultural labor in the Southern States approaches the condition of the factory labor in England and the Eastern States more nearly than it does the farm labor of the North and West.

Nearly every agricultural laborer north of Mason and Dixon's line, if not the actual possessor of the land he plows, looks forward to owning a farm some time; at the South such an ambition is rare, and small ownership still more an exception. The practice of paying day wages was first tried after the war; this practice is still in vogue in the sugar and rice districts, where laborers are paid from fifty to seventy cents per day, with quarters furnished and living guaranteed them at nine or ten cents a day. In sections where the wages system prevails, and where there have been no political disturbances, the negroes seem to be perfectly contented; at all events, the emigration fever has not spread among them. But it was found impracticable to maintain the wage system in the cotton districts. The negroes themselves fought against it, because it reminded them too much of the slave-gang, driven out at daybreak and home at sundown. In many cases the planters were forced to abandon it, because they had not the means to carry on such huge farming, and they could not secure the same liberal advances from capitalists as when they were able to mortgage a growing "crop of niggers." Then the system of working on shares was tried. This was reasonably fair, and the negro laborers were satisfied as long as it lasted. The owners of the land, under this system, would furnish the indispensable mule and the farming implements, and take one half the product. The planters themselves relinquished this system. Some of them contend that the laziness and indifference of the negro made the partnership undesirable; many others admit that they were not able to advance the negro tenant his supplies pending the growth of the year's crop, as it was necessary they should do under the sharing system.

Now the renting system is almost universal. It yields the land owner a certainty, endangered only by the death, sickness, or desertion of the negro tenant; but it throws the latter upon his own responsibility, and frequently makes him the victim of his own ignorance and the rapacity of the white man. The rent of land, on a money basis, varies from six to ten dollars an acre per year, while the same land can be bought in large quantities all the way from fifteen to thirty dollars per acre, according to location, clearing, improvement, richness, etc. When paid in product, the rent varies from eighty to one hundred pounds of lint cotton per acre for land that produces from two hundred to four hundred pounds of cotton per acre; the tenant undertakes to pay from one quarter to one half—perhaps an average of one third—of his crop for the use of the land, without stock, tools, or assistance of any kind. The land owners usually claim that they make no money even at these exorbitant figures. If they do not, it is because only a portion of their vast possessions is under cultivation, because they do no work themselves, and in some cases because the negroes do not cultivate and gather as large a crop as they could and ought to harvest. It is very certain that the negro tenants, as a class, make no money; if they are out of debt at the end of a season, they have reason to rejoice.

The credit system, which is as universal as the renting system, is even more illogical and oppressive. The utter viciousness of both systems in their mutual dependence is sufficiently illustrated by the single fact that, after fourteen years of freedom and labor on their own account, the great mass of the negroes depend for their living on an advance of supplies (as they need food, clothing, or tools during the year) upon the pledge of their growing crop. This is a generic imitation of the white man's improvidence during the slavery times; then the planters mortgaged their crops and negroes, and where one used the advances to extend his plantation, ten squandered the money.

The negro's necessities have developed an offensive race, called merchants by courtesy, who keep supply stores at the cross-roads and steamboat landings, and live upon extortion. These people would be called sharks, harpies, and vampires in any Northwestern agricultural community, and they would not survive more than one season. The country merchant advances the negro tenant such supplies as the negro wants up to a certain amount, previously fixed by contract, and charges the negro at least double the value of every article sold to him. There is no concealment about the extortion; every store-keeper has his cash price and his credit price, and in nearly all cases the latter is one hundred per cent. higher than the former. The extortion is justified by those who practice it on the ground that their losses by bad debts, though their advances are always secured by mortgage on the growing crop, overbalance the profits; this assertion is scarcely borne out by the comparative opulence of the "merchant" and the pitiful poverty of the laborer. Some of the largest and wealthiest planters have sought to protect their tenants from the merciless clutches of the contrary merchant, who is more frequently than not an Israelite, by advancing supplies of necessary articles at reasonable prices. But the necessities of the planter, if not his greed, often betray him into plundering the negro. The planter himself is generally a victim to usury. He still draws on the city factor to the extent of ten dollars a bale upon his estimated crop. He pays this factor two and one half per cent. commission for the advance, eight per cent. interest for the money, two and one half per cent. more for disposing of the crop when consigned to him, and sometimes still another commission for the purchase of the supplies. The planter who furnishes his tenants with supplies on credit is usually paying an interest of fifteen to eighteen per cent. himself, and necessarily takes some risk in advancing upon an uncertain crop and to a laborer whom he believes to be neither scrupulous nor industrious; these conditions necessitate more than the ordinary profit, and in many cases suggest exorbitant and unreasonable charges.

But whether the negro deals with the merchant or the land owner, his extravagance almost invariably exhausts his credit, even if it be large. The negro is a sensuous creature, and luxurious in his way. The male is an enormous consumer of tobacco and whisky; the female has an inordinate love for flummery; both are fond of sardines, potted meats, and canned goods generally, and they indulge themselves without any other restraint than the refusal of their merchant to sell to them. The man who advances supplies watches his negro customers constantly; if they are working well and their crop promises to be large, he will permit and even encourage them to draw upon him liberally; it is only a partial failure of the crop, or some intimation of the negro's intention to shirk his obligations, that induces his country factor to preach the virtue of self-restraint, or moralize upon the advantages of economy.

The land owner's rent and the merchant's advances are both secured by a chattel mortgage on the tenant's personal property, and by a pledge of the growing crop. The hired laborer (for it is common for negroes to work for wages for other negroes who rent lands) has also a lien upon the growing crops second only to the land owner's; but as the law requires that the liens shall be recorded, which the ignorant laborer usually neglects and the shrewd merchant never fails to do, the former is generally cheated of his security. Among those who usually work for hire are the women, who are expert cotton pickers, and the loss of wages which so many of them have suffered by reason of the prior lien gained by landlord and merchant has helped to make them earnest and effective advocates of emigration. The Western farmer considers it hard enough to struggle under one mortgage at a reasonable interest; the negro tenant begins his season with three mortgages, covering all he owns, his labor for the coming year, and all he expects to acquire during that period. He pays one third his product for the use of the land; he pays double the value of all he consumes; he pays an exorbitant fee for recording the contract by which he pledges his pound of flesh; he is charged two or three times as much as he ought to pay for ginning his cotton; and, finally, he turns over his crop to be eaten up in commissions, if anything still be left to him.

It is easy to understand why the negro rarely gets ahead in the world. This mortgaging of future services, which is practically what a pledge of the growing crop amounts to, is in the nature of bondage. It has a tendency to make the negro extravagant, reckless, and unscrupulous; he has become convinced from previous experience that nothing will be coming to him on the day of settlement, and he is frequently actuated by the purpose of getting as much as possible and working as little as possible. Cases are numerous in which the negro abandons his own crop at picking time, because he knows that he has already eaten up its full value; and so he goes to picking for wages on some other plantation. In other cases, where negroes have acquired mules and farming implements upon which a merchant has secured a mortgage in the manner described, they are practically bound to that merchant from year to year, in order to retain their property; if he removes from one section to another, they must follow him, and rent and cultivate lands in his neighborhood. It is only the ignorance, the improvidence, and the happy disposition of the negro, under the influence of the lazy, drowsy climate, to which he is so well adapted physically, that have enabled him to endure these hardships so long. And, though the negro is the loser, the white man is not often the gainer, from this false plantation and mercantile system. The incidental risk may not be so large as the planter and merchant pretend, but the condition of the people is an evidence that the extortion they practice yields no better profit in the long run than would be gained by competition in fair prices on a cash system; and in leading up to a general emigration of the laboring population the abuses described will eventually ruin and impoverish those who have heretofore been the only beneficiaries thereof.

The decay of improvements inevitable under annual rentings, the lack of sufficient labor to cultivate all the good land, and the universal idleness of the rural whites have kept the land owners comparatively poor; the partial failure of crops and the unscrupulousness of the negro debtor, engendered by the infamous exactions of his creditor, have prevented the merchants, as a class, from prospering as much as might be supposed; and, finally, the uniform injustice to the laborers induces them to fly to ills they know not of, rather than bear those they have. It is a blessing to the negro that the laws do not yet provide for a detention of the person in the case of debt, or escape would be shut off entirely; as it is, various influences and circumstances appertaining to the system in vogue have been used to prevent the easy flight of those who desire to go, and have detained thousands of blacks for a time who are fretting to quit the country.

Political oppression has contributed largely to the discontent which is the prime cause of the exodus. "Bulldozing" is the term by which all forms of this oppression are known. The native whites are generally indisposed to confess that the negroes are quitting the country on account of political injustice and persecution; even those who freely admit and fitly characterize the abuses already described seek to deny, or at least belittle, the political abuses. The fact that a large number of negroes have emigrated from Madison Parish, Louisiana, where there has never been any bulldozing, and where the negroes are in full and undisputed political control, is cited as proof that political disturbances cut no figure in the case. But the town of Delta, in Madison Parish, is at once on the river and the terminus of a railroad that runs back through the interior of the State; thus Madison Parish would furnish the natural exit for the fugitives from the adjoining counties, where there have been political disturbances. It would be just as reasonable to contend that the plundering of the ne-groes has had no influence in driving them away, since many of those who have emigrated were among the most prosperous of the blacks, as to deny the agency of political persecution.

Families that had been able to accumulate a certain amount of personal property, in spite of the extortionate practices, sold their mules, their implements, their cows, their pigs, their sheep, and their household goods for anything they would bring,—frequently as low as one sixth of their value,—in order that they might im-prove an immediate opportunity to go away; it is evi-dent that there must have been some cause outside of extortion in their case. There are candid native whites who do not deny, but justify, the violent methods which have been employed to disfranchise the negroes, or compel them to vote under white dictation, in many parts of Louisiana and Mississippi, on the ground that the men who pay the taxes should vote them and con-trol the disbursement of the public moneys. The gentle-men who advance this argument seem to ignore the fact that the very Northerner whom they are seeking to con-vert to "the Mississippi plan" may himself be a tax-payer in some Northern city, where public affairs are controlled by a class of voters in every way as ignorant and irresponsible as the blacks, but where bulldozing has never yet been suggested as a remedy. For the rest, the evidences of political oppression are abundant and convincing. The bulldozers as a class are more impecu-nious and irresponsible than the negroes, and, unlike the negroes, they will not work.

There has been more of the "night-riding," the whip-pings, the mysterious disappearances, the hangings, and the terrorism comprehended in the term bulldoz-ing than has been reported by those "abstracts and brief chronicles of the time," the Southern newspapers, which are now all of one party, and defer to the ruling sentiment among the whites. The exodus has wrung from two or three of the more candid and independent journals, however, a virtual confession of the fiendish practices of bulldozing in their insistence that these practices must be abandoned. The non-resident land owners and the resident planters, the city factors and the country merchants of means and respectability, have taken no personal part in the terrorizing of the negro, but they have tolerated it, and sometimes en-couraged it, in order to gratify their preference for "white government."

The negroes have suffered the more because they have not resisted and defended themselves; now they have begun to convince those who have persecuted them that, if they will not strike back, they can and will run away. No one who is at all familiar with the freed-man can doubt that the abridgment of his political rights has been one of the main causes of the exodus. Voting is widely regarded at the North as a disagreeable duty, but the negro looks upon it as the highest privi-lege in life; to be frightened out of the exercise of this privilege, or compelled to exercise it in conflict with his convictions and preferences, is to suffer from a cruel in-justice, which the negro will now try to escape, since he has learned that escape is possible.

The women, though free from personal assaults, suf-fer from the terrorism that prevails in certain districts as much as the men. "We might as well starve or freeze to death in Kansas," they say, "as to be shot-gunned here." If they talk to you in confidence, they declare that the ruling purpose is to escape from the "slaughter-pens" of the South. Political persecution, and not the extortion they suffer, is the refrain of all the speakers at negro meetings that are held in encouragement and aid of the emigration. It is idle to deny that the varied injustice which the negroes have suffered as voters is account-able for a large part of their universal yearning for new homes, and it will be folly for the responsible classes at the South to ignore this fact.

As it is the negroes who are fleeing from the South, it is natural to look among the dominant class for the in-justice which is driving them away; but it would be un-fair to conclude that the blame rests entirely upon the whites, and still more so to leave the impression that there is no extenuation for the mistakes and abuses for which the whites are responsible. Much of the intimida-tion of the blacks has been tolerated, if not suggested, by a fear of negro uprisings. The apprehension is a legacy from the days of slavery, and is more unreason-able now than it was then; but still it exists. This is not an excuse, but an explanation. The Pharaohs of the time of Moses were in constant dread lest the Hebrews under their rule should go over to their enemies, and their dread doubtless increased the cruelty of the Egyptians; but, while this dread was an extenuation in the eyes of the persecutors, it did not prevent the Hebrews from fleeing the persecution. So the blacks are going without regard to the justification which the whites may set up for their treatment; the only differ-ence between the old and new exodus is that, as the writer heard one negro speaker express it, "every black man is his own Moses in this exodus."

The negro may be lazy; it seems impossible to be oth-erwise in the Southern climate. He may not be willing to work on Saturdays, no matter how urgent the neces-sity; the indulgence in holidays is said to be one of the chief drawbacks to the advancement of the emanci-pated serfs of Russia. The blacks are certainly extrava-gant in their way, though the word seems to be almost misused in connection with a race who live largely on pork and molasses, and rarely wear more than half a dollar's worth of clothes at one time. They have not the instinct of home as it prevails among the whites, but incline to a crude and unsystematic communism; the negro quarters of the old plantations are all huddled together in the centre, and, except where the land owners have interfered to encourage a different life, there is still too much promiscuousness in the relation of the sexes. The negro, as a rule, has no ambition to become a land owner; he prefers to invest his surplus money, when he has any, in personal and movable property. In most cases where the blacks have been given the opportunity of buying land on long time, and paying yearly installments out of the proceeds of their annual crops, they have tired of the bargain after a year or two, and abandoned the contract.

The negro politicians and preachers are not all that reformers and moralists would have them; the imitative faculty of the African has betrayed the black politician into many of the vicious ways of the white politician, and the colored preacher is frequently not above "the pomps and vanity of this wicked world." All this is the more unfortunate, as the blacks have a child-like confidence in their chosen leaders, founded partly on their primitive character, and partly on their distrust of the native whites. Both their politicians and their preachers have given abundant evidence of their insincerity during the excitement of emigration by blowing hot and blowing cold; by talking to the negroes one way, and to the whites another; and even to the extent, in some instances, of taking money to use their influence for discouraging and impeding emigration.

These are some of the faults and misfortunes on the part of the blacks which enter into the race troubles. The chief blame which attaches to the whites is the failure to make a persistent effort, by education and kind treatment, to overcome the distrust and cure the faults of the negroes. The whites control, because they constitute the "property and intelligence" of the South, to use the words of a democratic statesman; this power should have been used to gain the confidence of the blacks. Had such a course been taken, there would not have been the fear of reenslavement, which actually prevails to a considerable extent among the negroes. So long as a portion of the whites entertain the conviction that the war of the sections will be renewed within a few years, as is the case, the negroes will suspect and dread the class who would treat them as enemies in case the war should come, and will seek to escape to a section of the country where they would not be so treated. Perhaps, too, there would have been a voluntary political division among the black voters, had the whites used more pacific means to bring it about, and had they themselves set the example. And last, but not least, in making up the sum of blame that the whites must bear, is their own unwillingness to labor, which gives the rural population too much time for mischief and too little sympathy with the working classes.

As we have traced the causes that have led to the exodus, and described the conditions which warrant the belief that there will be a renewal of the emigration on a more extended scale next spring, and endeavored to distribute the responsibility for the troubles equitably among whites and blacks, remedies have naturally suggested themselves to the reader; in fact, they are more easily to be thought out than accomplished. A few general reflections may be added, however, in order to indicate the probable solution of the race troubles that have brought about the exodus, if, indeed, the whites and blacks of the South are ever going to live together in peace.

(1.) It is certain that negro labor is the best the South can have, and equally certain that the climate and natural conditions of the South are better suited to the negro than any others on this continent. The alluvial lands, which many persons believe the negroes alone can cultivate, on account of climatic conditions, are so rich that it might literally be said it is only necessary to tickle them with a hoe to make them laugh back a harvest. The common prosperity of the country—the agricultural interests of the South and the commercial interests of the North—will be best served, therefore, by the continued residence and labor of the blacks in the cotton States.

(2.) The fact stated in the foregoing paragraph is so well understood at the North that the Southern people should dismiss the idea that there is any scheming among the Northern people, political or otherwise, to draw the black labor away from its natural home. The same fact should also influence the people at the North not to be misled by any professional philanthropists who may have some self-interest in soliciting aid to facilitate negro emigration from the South. The duty of the North in this matter is simply to extend protection and assure safe-conduct to the negroes, if the Southern whites attempt to impede voluntary emigration by either law or violence. Any other course might be cruel to the negro in encouraging him to enter on a new life in a strange climate, as well as an injustice to the white land owners of the South.

(3.) There is danger that the Southern whites will, as a rule, misinterpret the meaning of the exodus. Many are inclined to underrate its importance, and those who appreciate its significance are apt to look for temporary and superficial remedies. The vague promises made at the Vicksburg convention, which was controlled by the whites, and called to consider the emigration movement, have had no influence with the negroes, because they have heard such promises before. Had the convention adopted some definite plan of action, such as ex-Governor Foote, of Mississippi, submitted, its session might not have been in vain. This plan was to establish a committee in every county, composed of men who have the confidence of both whites and blacks, that should be auxiliary to the public authorities, listen to complaints, and arbitrate, advise, conciliate, or prosecute, as each case should demand. It is short-sighted for the Southern people to make mere temporary concessions, such as have been made in some cases this year, for that course would establish an annual strike. It is folly for them to suppose they can stem the tide of emigration by influencing the regular lines of steamboats not to carry the refugees, for the people of the North will see that the blacks shall not be detained in the South against their will. It is unwise for them to devise schemes for importing Chinese, or encouraging the immigration of white labor as a substitute for negro labor, when they may much better bestir themselves to make the present effective labor content.

(4.) Education will be the most useful agent to employ in the permanent harmonizing of the two races, and the redemption of both from the faults and follies which constitute their troubles. It is not the education of the negro alone, whose ambition for learning is increasing notably with every new generation, but the education of the mass of the young whites, that is needed to inculcate more tolerance of color and opinion, to give them an aspiration beyond that of riding a horse and hanging a "nigger," and to enable them to set a better example to the imitative blacks in the way of work and frugality. The blacks need the education to protect them from designing white men; the whites need it to teach them that their own interests will be best served by abandoning bulldozing of all kinds.

(5.) Reform in the land tenure, by converting the plantation monopolies into small holdings; abolition of the credit system, by abandoning the laws which sustain it; a diversification of crops; and attention to new manufacturing, maritime, and commercial enterprises, —these are the material changes that are most needed. They can be secured only through the active and earnest efforts of the whites. The blacks will be found responsive.

(6.) The hope of the negro exodus at its present stage, or even if it shall continue another season, is that the actual loss of the valuable labor that has gone, and the prospective loss of more labor that is anxious to go, will induce the intelligent and responsible classes at the South to overcome their own prejudices, and to compel the extremists, irreconcilables, and politicians generally, of all parties, to abandon agitation, and give the South equal peace and equal chance for black and white.

3

The Chinese in San Francisco
(1885)

THE SAN FRANCISCO BOARD OF SUPERVISORS

In 1885, the Supervisors of San Francisco ordered a special committee to investigate the living conditions in China Town. Of course, the Supervisors did not act with the intention of ordering the owners of the slum housing in that district to clean up their facilities. Rather the Supervisors were concerned with the increasing numbers of Chinese immigrants to their city, and sought to blame the Chinese for living in such substandard housing. Just three years earlier, pressure from California's Congressional Delegation had led to the Chinese Exclusion Act, a ten-year suspension of all Chinese immigration.

Questions to Consider

- Why did the committee choose to focus on the living conditions of the Chinese if they were not interested in improving this environment?
- What is the significance of the fact that so many servants in the city were Chinese?
- With immigration already halted, what purpose did the Supervisors hope to accomplish with this published report?

All great cities have their slums and localities where filth, disease, crime and misery abound; but in the very best aspect which "Chinatown" can be made to present, it must stand apart, conspicuous and beyond them all in the extreme degree of all these horrible attributes, the rankest outgrowth of human degradation that can be found upon this continent. Here it may truly be said that human beings exist under conditions (as regards their mode of life and the air they breathe) scarcely one degree above those under which the rats of our water-front and other vermin live, breathe and have their being. And this order of things seems inseparable from the very nature of the race, and probably must be accepted and borne with—must be endured, if it cannot be cured—restricted and looked after, so far as possible, with unceasing vigilance, so that, whatever of benefit, "of degree," even, that may be derived from such modification of the evil of their presence among us, may at least be attained, not daring to hope that there can be any radical remedy for the great overshadowing evil which the Chinese immigration has inflicted upon this people....

Your Committee has found, both from their own and individual observations and from the reports of their surveyors, that it is almost the universal custom among the Chinese to herd together as compactly as possible, both as regards living and sleeping-rooms and sleeping-accommodations. It is almost an invariable rule that every "bunk" in Chinatown (beds being almost unknown in that locality) is occupied by two persons. Not only is this true, but in very many instances these bunks are again occupied by "relays" in the day time, so that there is no hour, night, or day, when there are not thousands of Chinamen sleeping under the effects of opium, or otherwise, in the bunks which we have found there....

There are apparently in Chinatown but few families living as such, with legitimate children. In most instances the wives are kept in a state of seclusion, carefully guarded and watched, as though "eternal vigilance" on the part of the husband "is the price of their virtue." Wherever there are families belonging to the better class of the Chinese, the women are guarded and secluded in the most careful manner. Wherever the sex has been found in the pursuance of this investigation under other conditions, with some few exceptions, the rule seems to be that they are here in a state of concubinage, or else to follow the admitted calling of the prostitute....

The most revolting feature of all, however, is found in the fact that there are so large a number of children growing up as the associates, and perhaps the proteges of the professional prostitutes. In one house, alone, on Sullivan's Alley, your Committee found the inmates to be nineteen prostitutes and sixteen children. In the localities habited largely by prostitutes, women and children, who apparently occupy this intermediate family relationship alluded to, live in adjoining apartments and intermingle freely, leading to the conclusion that prostitution is a recognized and not immoral calling with the race, and that it is impossible to tell by a survey of their domestic customs where the family relationship leaves off and prostitution begins....

The investigations which have been carried on by your Committee have developed another disgusting and surprising feature. It is in reference to white prostitution in that locality. The map accompanying this report shows in what sections and to what extent of area white prostitution exists in Chinatown. The number of degraded women who ply this vocation there is unknown. But the point that will impress itself more strongly upon the ordinary mind is that these women obtain their patronage almost entirely from the Chinese themselves. Their habitations seem to have been taken up in the Chinese quarter solely for this purpose, and their mode of life seems to be modeled after that of the Mongolian, to a larger extent than after the manners and customs of the race to which they belong.

Many, if not most of them, confirmed victims to the opium habit in one form or another, they present pictures of pallid wretchedness hard to parallel in any community where total depravity rules supreme, and their sex sinks to the lowest point of human degrada-

Source: William B. Farwell, *The Chinese at Home and Abroad* (San Francisco, 1885), part 2: pp. 5–6, 8–9, 14–18, 20–21, 23, 25–26, 30–31, 33–34, 37–40, 43, 58–61, 63.

tion. The Chinese drug and opium stores at night usually contain numbers of these wretched beings seeking opium or medicaments for the physical diseases to which they are constantly subjected; and more wan, sad, hopeless and wretched-looking faces the human eye seldom encounters in the streets or slums of the most populous cities of the world.

This is a feature of prostitution in Chinatown with which it is difficult and perhaps impossible to deal. Your Committee can only point out the conditions under which it exists as one of the numerous evils which attach to and grow out of the presence of the Chinese among us. It is one of the many counts in the indictment against the race, and upon which we hold them up for trial before the public opinion of our country, from which we bespeak a just and wise verdict. For the poor, wretched woman who enters this particular walk of life there need be no punishment other than her own miseries; no word of reproach, but all our pity. Let her "who enters here leave hope behind."

White Women Living with Chinamen

Another surprising as well as disgusting feature developed in this investigation is the fact that there are numerous instances of white women living and cohabiting with Chinamen in the relation of wives and mistresses....

There is hardly a phase of life in Chinatown that does not furnish a striking example of constant violation of municipal laws. It may almost be said that the whole Chinese community exists in open defiance of the law, and, as a matter susceptible of clear demonstration, they are at present, and long have been, stronger than the law, (as it is administered), to which we of other races are sternly held amenable....

To assume that our local laws cannot be effectually enforced in the case of the Chinese is to admit that race, which we so heartily despise, is stronger than we are, and to abandon the principles for which we are contending.

Violations of Sanitary Laws in Chinatown

In a sanitary point of view Chinatown presents a singular anomaly. With the habits, manners, customs and whole economy of life violating every accepted rule of hygiene; with open cesspools, exhalations from water-closets, sinks, urinals and sewers tainting the atmosphere with noxious vapors and stifling odors; with people herded and packed in damp cellars, living literally the life of vermin, badly fed and clothed, addicted to the daily use of opium to the extent that many hours

of each day or night are passed in the delirious stupe-faction of its influence, it is not to be denied that, as a whole, the general health of this locality compares more than favorably with other sections of the city which are surrounded by far more favorable conditions.

It seems impossible to account for this condition of things upon any other theory than that of the constant fumigation to which Chinatown is subjected, as has already been suggested in this report. Open wood fired from cellar to attic, cigars, tobacco and opium pipes, all contribute hourly clouds of smoke to the fumigation process, and probably prevent the generation and spread of zymotic diseases that otherwise could scarcely fail to rapidly decimate the Chinese population of San Francisco, and effectually adjust the Chinese immigration question without the aid of treaty or Congressional intervention. These preventive influences can never be a sufficient guard against cholera or any other like visitation, however, and are not and cannot be sufficient to justify the municipal authorities in tolerating the unclean mode of life that prevails in Chinatown. This mode of life must always make this locality a threatening source of pestilential danger to the community at large whenever pestilence comes in any form, borne upon the wings of the wind, or stealing in "like a thief in the night," by any other of the mysterious pathways which it too often [threads] so silently, without warning of its approach, until it is upon us with its deadly influences.

...There is, and can be, no possible excuse for these violations of law. It involves the public health and public safety, and calls for immediate remedial action.

The instances where the water-closets, sinks, etc., discharge into open cesspools, and where there are other violations of the sections quoted, are more than numerous....

In the building on Jackson street, sometimes called "the Palace Hotel," and occupied by about 400 people, there are four water-closets in the center of the court on each of the floors, all running together below in one common cesspool, all open with no trap, and all in a horrible filthy condition....

At 714 Jackson street, in the basement, occupied by seven Chinese prostitutes and two children, there are no water-closets, and the slops and filth generated in this underground slum are flung into the street as an extra generous contribution to the rotting garbage that daily accumulates there, or disposed of in other ways unknown to your Committee....

Someday, when Pestilence shall fold her black wings and alight among us to gorge her lust for death, there will be such other tangible evidences of the dire influences that will grow out of this condition of things as will appeal in unanswerable anguish to our hearts as well as our senses, and lead to vain regrets that we have not long ago enforced the laws and corrected this terrible evil....

Descend into the basement of almost any building in Chinatown at night; pick your way by the aid of the policeman's candle along the dark and narrow passageway, black and grimy with a quarter of a century's accumulation of filth; step with care lest you fall into a cesspool of sewage abominations with which these subterranean depths abound. Now follow your guide through a door, which he forces, into a sleeping-room. The air is thick with smoke and fetid with an indescribable odor of reeking vapors. The atmosphere is tangible. Tangible—if we may be licensed to so use the word in this instance—to four out of the five human senses. Tangible to the sight, tangible to the touch, tangible to the taste, and, oh, how tangible to the smell! You may even hear it as the opium-smoker sucks it through his pipe bowl into his tainted lungs, and you breathe it yourself as if it were of the substance and tenacity of tar. It is a sense of a horror you have never before experienced, revolting to the last degree, sickening and stupefying. Through this semi-opaque atmosphere you discover perhaps eight or ten—never less than two or three—bunks, the greater part or all are occupied by two persons, some in a state of stupefaction from opium, some rapidly smoking themselves into that condition, and all in dirt and filth. Before the door was opened for your entrance every aperture was closed, and here, had they not been thus rudely disturbed, they would have slept in the dense and poisonous atmosphere until morning, proof against the baneful effects of the carbonic acid gas generated by this human defiance of chemical laws, and proof against all the zymotic poisons that would be fatal to a people of any other race in an hour of such surroundings and such conditions.

It is from such pest-holes as these that the Chinese cooks and servants who are employed in our houses come. Cleanly though they may be, in appearance, while acting in the capacity of domestic servants, they are nevertheless born and reared in these habits of life. The facility with which they put on habits of decency when they become cooks and servants simply adds other testimony to their ability to adapt themselves to circumstances when it is their interest to do so. But the instinct of the race remains unchanged; and when the Chinese servant leaves employment in an American household he joyfully hastens back to his slum and his burrow, to the grateful luxury of his normal surroundings, vice, filth, and an atmosphere of horror....

The Chinese Labor Problem

The essentially American policy of a tariff for protection to home industry is not alone on trial as against the opposing doctrine of Free Trade. Protection against the "pauper labor of Europe" as a system of public policy may be advocated, upheld and practiced as we will, but it is clear that the doctrine is absolutely nullified, and the laws that are enacted to support it are successfully and effectually evaded by the importation, not of the *products* of pauper labor, but of pauper labor itself, of a far lower grade than that of Europe, viz., the Asiatic....

The result of such a competition is indisputable. Either the American laborer must come down to a level with the imported "little brown man" in habits of life and desires, or he must become a helpless pauper himself.

This is not the gospel of the "Sand Lot;" it is the gospel of political truth, upon which all parties should agree who have the welfare of society at heart, and to whom humanity itself ought not to plead in vain.

It appears from this Exhibit that there are employed in Chinatown to-day not less than 2,326 Chinese workmen engaged in the manufacture of clothing of various descriptions, boots and shoes, leather, cigars, etc., all of which is produced for consumption here in competition with the American workmen engaged in the same line of manufacture. Most of this labor is carried on through the use of the best modern machinery, in the operation of which the Chinese workman becomes adept in a short space of time....

In the manufacture of clothing, ladies' underwear, shirts, etc., 1,245 sewing machines are kept actively at work, operated by male laborers with a skill that is equal to the best efforts of the American woman, as well as the American man, in this direction, and all run with such quick-handed, untiring energy, that it suggests one of the most curious physiological problems of the day to understand how a people, nurtured and fed as they are, can possess the vitality and physical force necessary to the results which they achieve in this direction.

Most of this labor is carried on by "piece-work" and to fill orders for large "down-town commercial houses" engaged in the sale of the class of goods thus produced. The heavy, strong-stitched jean overalls which find so large a market on this coast, are made by the Chinese workmen at the rate of about fifty-five cents per dozen pairs. The work thus produced—at a price which would reduce the American worker, male or female, to a lower level than the "woman, weary and wan" whose misery Hood depicted so graphically in "The Song of the Shirt"—the Chinaman thrives upon, and is prosperous and happy. But it is a prosperity and a happiness that is based upon a mode of life that a homeless cur upon the streets might not envy, upon which the American laborer could not exist until a succession of generations had so brutalized and blunted his race proclivities that he had degenerated into a condition worse than barbarism and become a curse to civilization, instead of what he is to-day, the vital strength of the nation....

"The Heathen Chinee"

"The little brown man," as he is designated by one of the most prominent members of the United States Senate, and a representative of a State that is commonly assumed to stand in the forefront of human progress, is considered by many Christians as a most fitting subject for Missionary work and conversion to Christianity....

For true missionary work your Committee have the most unbounded respect and sympathy. For efforts in this direction that the stern experience of the past thirty-five years have demonstrated by cold practical results to be more than sterile and barren, and for those who have wasted their labor in the field, your Committee can entertain no other sentiment than that of charitable pity. For those who, in spite of every proof of its utter uselessness, continue to be the advocates of Chinese immigration with this "hope of conversion" doctrine as one of the main reasons and justification of their action, we have nothing but contempt and disgust....

And Senator Hoar, and his followers, who would fain open wide our gates to the "little brown man," that he may be converted to Christianity and share in the blessings of American citizenship, may possibly find food for new reflection by a careful study of some of the naked facts which your Committee have been enabled to present upon this branch of the subject. In this view of the matter, then, your Committee consider it their duty to invite public attention to the following facts:

The proofs, as developed by this investigation and which are so plain as to be beyond question, are these: The Chinese brought here with them and have successfully maintained and perpetuated the grossest habits of bestiality practiced by the human race. The twin vices of gambling in its most defiant form, and the opium habit, they have not only firmly planted here for their own delectation and the gratification of the grosser passions, but they have succeeded in so spreading these vitiating evils as to have added thousands of proselytes to the practice of these vices from our own blood and race. The lowest possible form of prostitution—partaking of both slavery and prostitution—they have planted and fostered to a lusty growth among us, and have innoculated our youth not only with the virus of immorality in its most hideous form but have, through the same sources, physically poisoned the blood of thousands by the innoculation with diseases the most frightful that flesh is heir to, and furnishing posterity with a line of scrofulous and leprous victims that might better never have been born than to curse themselves and mankind at large with their contagious presence. They have suc-

cessfully overridden and defied the laws of morality in every form, and the statutory laws of the State and municipality. They have driven the American laborer to the wall and taken the bread from the mouths of thousands of deserving families, while all that missionary work has done among them, all that contact with Christianity has accomplished in the line of conversion to "the true faith," is as imperceptible and as slow in its results as in the influence of the smallest comet that ever blazed into view in planetary space upon the great orbs that traverse their appointed pathways within the solar system to which they belong. Let us see if this is not the fact.

First, as is shown upon the map accompanying this report, the "Joss House" is, proportioned to population, even more common in Chinatown than are the edifices of the Christian church in other portions of the city. Idols of the most hideous form and feature squat upon their altars, from which license, in the belief of the Chinaman, sufficient to justify crime or vice of any degree may be had for the asking. Idols that typify, not the precepts of morality taught by Confucius, carved and created by the mechanical fancy of the most skillful Mongolian artist into every conceivable distortion of feature and limb, more frequently represent and give license to the practice of a vice, than a virtue to be inculcated and lived up to. Even the "Goddess of Prostitution" sits enthroned upon her altar in more than one Joss House in San Francisco, and licenses her votaries to the practice of nameless indulgences and the most bestial gratification of their sensuous lusts. Let the sceptic who views this statement as an exaggeration or misrepresentation of fact visit the Joss House of San Francisco and he will no longer doubt; for it is the truth....

There never was a more wicked and shameful exhibition of detestable, narrow-minded bigotry than that which seeks to justify Chinese immigration by linking it with a scheme for the salvation of souls. The beasts of the field, the vagrant dogs that the Pound-master gathers upon the streets to put to death by drowning, are vastly better worthy of our commiseration than the whole Mongolian race when they seek to overrun our country and blast American welfare and progress with their miserable, contaminating presence....

The Chinese Children and the Public Schools

We have shown that there are 722 children of Chinese parentage in Chinatown. Most if not all of these were born here, and are to all intents and purposes "native Americans." Though "native" they are not "to the manner born," because in every attribute of juvenile life they are Mongolian, as much so as if born in the province of Canton. The very exclusiveness and clannishness of the Chinese has so far preserved these children from contact with the Caucasian race, and not one word of English, or any other language than Chinese, can they articulate....

The point is, what shall we do with the Chinese children born upon our soil, though partaking in no respect of the proclivities and habits of any other known race except those of their own progenitors? And this opens the question that has often been agitated as to their admission to the public schools, and their right, under the law, to share the benefits to be derived from the public school fund. We have shown that there is no distinct line of demarcation—here at least—between domestic life and prostitution. We have shown that the painted harlots of the slums and alleys, the women who are bought and sold to the slavery of prostitution, are surrounded by children in some instances, and intermingle freely with the border class of family life where other children abound....

What, then, shall be said if the doors of the schoolhouses are to be opened to admit children reared in such an atmosphere?

...Speaking no language but the Chinese, born and nurtured in filth and degradation, it is scarcely probable that any serious attempt could be made to mingle them with the other children of our public schools without kindling a blaze of revolution in our midst. And again, by what right, constitutional or statutory, can we set apart separate schools and a separate fund for their education or maintenance? And yet something must be done with them, some action must be taken to rid them of their race proclivities and habits if we would protect posterity from unlimited evil consequences. Here there may well be a field for true missionary work and a problem that will tax the wisdom and patience of mankind to solve. If the immigration of the race were effectually stopped the riddle would be less intricate to deal with. But "restrictions" which at present exist, how to deal with this constantly increasing number of Mongolian children, born and nurtured in such conditions of immorality and degradation, becomes indeed a more serious problem than any which the American people have ever yet been called upon to solve, not exceeding the abrogation of African slavery and the horrors which attended its achievement.

If those children could be separated from their parents and scattered among our own people, away from the populous centers, the question involved would be perhaps easy of adjustment. The laws of nature and of men prohibit this, while the laws of morality, and the law of self-protection, must compel our own people to sternly prohibit them from mingling with our children in the public schools, or as companions and playmates. What, then, we again ask, is to be done with the Chinese children, born upon our soil, and that are yet to be born, in ratio co-equal in its increase with the increase of immigrations? To this inquiry there seems to be but one answer. Chinese immigration must stop!—absolutely stop!! For it is beyond the ingenuity of men to deal fairly with this phase of the question, except by a reversal of the laws of nature.

...The real remedy is the eventual stoppage of Chinese immigration, by such absolute, autocratic Congressional legislation as shall make it physically impossible for the Chinamen to land upon our shores, except, perhaps, in a commercial capacity alone, or as a student seeking the advantages of our educational institutions. Such legislation, perhaps, cannot be secured until the Eastern mind is educated on the Chinese question as have been the minds of the people upon this coast. And the best way to accomplish that end is to so deal with the Chinese here by local laws, made to be enforced, so as to drive them from our midst to mingle with Eastern communities, and to educate them by contact with their presence, as they have educated us through the same process, up to a realizing sense of the frightfully disastrous results growing out of their presence among them....

Chinatown occupies that portion of San Francisco which, geographically and topographically, is by far the fairest and naturally the most valuable section of the city. It was the section which naturally attracted the attention of the early pioneers, and there they have located their offices and their homes. The advance guard of the Mongolian army saw that the location was good, and they advanced upon and captured it. Its capture was but a work of form, for civilization retreats instinctively from contact with the race with the same feeling of horror that the fair and innocent maiden would exhibit in shrinking from the proffered embrace of an unclean leper....

4

Wounded Knee (1890)

JAMES MOONEY

Originally it was called the Battle of Wounded Knee. The U.S. Army claimed that the soldiers had acted in self-defense and awarded commendations to its men, including the Congressional Medal of Honor to one soldier who continued to shoot fleeing Indians even after burning his hand on his overheated Hotchkiss gun. James Mooney of the Bureau of Ethnology was on hand to interview the survivors. The Bureau had sent Mooney west to observe the Ghost Dance, a religious revival among the Plains Indians that many in Washington saw as a threat. The nativist spiritualism of the Ghost Dance convinced many people, especially among the Sioux, to flee their reservations and seek salvation in the old ways. The efforts of the Army to return the Sioux to their reservation led to the tragedy now known as the Massacre of Wounded Knee.

Questions to Consider

• Did the Army have any alternative to opening fire on the Indians?

• What accounts for the willingness of these soldiers to kill fleeing civilians?

• What recourse did the Indians have after Wounded Knee?

On the morning of December 29, 1890, preparations were made to disarm the Indians preparatory to taking them to the agency and thence to the railroad. In obedience to instructions the Indians had pitched their tipis on the open plain a short distance west of the creek and surrounded on all sides by the soldiers. In the center of the camp the Indians had hoisted a white flag as a sign of peace and a guarantee of safety. Behind them was a dry ravine running into the creek, and on a slight rise in the front was posted the battery of four Hotchkiss machine guns, trained directly on the Indian camp. In front, behind, and on both flanks of the camp were posted the various troops of cavalry, a portion of two troops, together with the Indian scouts, being dismounted and drawn up in front of the Indians at the distance of only a few yards from them. Big Foot[1] himself was ill of pneumonia in his tipi, and Colonel [James W.] Forsyth, who had taken command as senior officer, had provided a tent warmed with a camp stove for his reception.

Shortly after 8 oclock in the morning the warriors were ordered to come out from the tipis and deliver their arms. They came forward and seated themselves on the ground in front of the troops. They were then ordered to go by themselves into their tipis and bring out and surrender their guns. The first twenty went and returned in a short time with only two guns. It seemed evident that they were unwilling to give them up, and after consultation of the officers part of the soldiers were ordered up to within ten yards of the group of

---

Source: James Mooney, *The Ghost-Dance Religion and Wounded Knee* (Washington, D.C., 1896), pp. 868–886.

[1] Leader of this band of Sioux and widely respected as a mediator.—*Ed.*

warriors, while another detachment of troops was ordered to search the tipis. After a thorough hunt these last returned with about forty rifles, most of which, however, were old and of little value. The search had consumed considerable time and created a good deal of excitement among the women and children, as the soldiers found it necessary in the process to overturn the beds and other furniture of the tipis and in some instances drove out the inmates. All this had its effect on their husbands and brothers, already wrought up to a high nervous tension and not knowing what might come next. While the soldiers had been looking for the guns Yellow Bird, a medicine-man, had been walking about among the warriors, blowing on an eagle-bone whistle, and urging them to resistance, telling them that the soldiers would become weak and powerless, and that the bullets would be unavailing against the sacred "ghost shirts," which nearly every one of the Indians wore. As he spoke in the Sioux language, the officers did not at once realize the dangerous drift of his talk, and the climax came too quickly for them to interfere. It is said one of the searchers now attempted to raise the blanket of a warrior. Suddenly Yellow Bird stooped down and threw a handful of dust into the air, when, as if this were the signal, a young Indian, said to have been Black Fox from Cheyenne river, drew a rifle from under his blanket and fired at the soldiers, who instantly replied with a volley directly into the crowd of warriors and so near that their guns were almost touching. From the number of sticks set up by the Indians to mark where the dead fell, as seen by the author a year later, this one volley must have killed nearly half the warriors.... The survivors sprang to their feet, throwing their blankets from their shoulders as they rose, and for a few minutes there was a terrible hand to hand struggle, where every man's thought was to kill. Although many of the warriors had no guns, nearly all had revolvers and knives in their belts under their blankets, together with some of the murderous warclubs still carried by the Sioux. The very lack of guns made the fight more bloody, as it brought the combatants to closer quarters.

At the first volley the Hotchkiss guns trained on the camp opened fire and sent a storm of shells and bullets among the women and children, who had gathered in front of the tipis to watch the unusual spectacle of military display. The guns poured in 2-pound explosive shells at the rate of nearly fifty per minute, mowing down everything alive. The terrible effect may be judged from the fact that one woman survivor, Blue Whirlwind, with whom the author conversed, received fourteen wounds, while each of her two little boys was also wounded by her side. In a few minutes 200 Indian men, women, and children, with 60 soldiers, were lying dead and wounded on the ground,[2] the tipis had been torn down by the shells and some of them were burning above the helpless wounded, and the surviving handful of Indians were flying in wild panic to the shelter of the ravine, pursued by hundreds of maddened soldiers and followed up by a raking fire from the Hotchkiss guns, which had been moved into position to sweep the ravine.

There can be no question that the pursuit was simply a massacre, where fleeing women, with infants in their arms, were shot down after resistance had ceased and when almost every warrior was stretched dead or dying on the ground. On this point such a careful writer as Herbert Welsh says: "From the fact that so many women and children were killed, and that their bodies were found far from the scene of action, and as though they were shot down while flying, it would look as though blind rage had been at work, in striking contrast to the moderation of the Indian police at the Sitting Bull fight when they were assailed by women."... Commissioner Morgan in his official report says that "Most of the men, including Big Foot, were killed around his tent, where he lay sick. The bodies of the women and children were scattered along a distance of two miles from the scene of the encounter."...

This is no reflection on the humanity of the officer in charge. On the contrary, Colonel Forsyth had taken measures to guard against such an occurrence by separating the women and children, as already stated, and had also endeavored to make the sick chief, Big Foot, as comfortable as possible.... Strict orders had also been issued to the troops that women and children were not to be hurt. The butchery was the work of infuriated soldiers whose comrades had just been shot down without cause or warning. In justice to a brave regiment it must be said that a number of the men were new recruits... who had never before been under fire, were not yet imbued with military discipline, and were probably unable in the confusion to distinguish between men and women by their dress.

After examining all the official papers bearing on the subject in the files of the War Department and the Indian Office...; after gathering all that might be obtained from unofficial printed sources and from conversation with survivors and participants in the engagement on both sides, and after going over the battle-ground..., the author arrives at the conclusion that when the sun rose on Wounded Knee on the fatal

---

[2] At least 153 Indians, including 44 women and 18 children, were killed on the spot. It is estimated that another twenty to thirty died of their wounds. Twenty-five soldiers were killed, most by their comrades.—*Ed.*

morning of December 29, 1890, no trouble was anticipated or premeditated by either Indians or troops; that the Indians in good faith desired to surrender and be at peace, and that the officers in the same good faith had made preparations to receive their surrender and escort them quietly to the reservation; that in spite of the pacific intent of Big Foot and his band, the medicine-man, Yellow Bird, at the critical moment urged the warriors to resistance and gave the signal for the attack; that the first shot was fired by an Indian, and that the Indians were responsible for the engagement; that the answering volley and attack by the troops was right and justifiable, but that the wholesale slaughter of women and children was unnecessary and inexcusable....

On New Year's day of 1891, three days after the battle, a detachment of troops was sent out to Wounded Knee to gather up and bury the Indian dead and to bring in the wounded who might be still alive on the field. In the meantime there had been a heavy snowstorm, culminating in a blizzard. The bodies of the slaughtered men, women, and children were found lying about under the snow, frozen stiff and covered with blood.... Almost all the dead warriors were found lying near where the fight began, about Big Foot's tipi, but the bodies of the women and children were found scattered along for 2 miles from the scene of the encounter, showing that they had been killed while trying to escape.... A number of women and children were found still alive, but all badly wounded or frozen, or both, and most of them died after being brought in. Four babies were found alive under the snow, wrapped in shawls and lying beside their dead mothers, whose last thought had been of them. They were all badly frozen and only one lived. The tenacity of life so characteristic of wild people as well as of wild beasts was strikingly illustrated in the case of these wounded and helpless Indian women and children who thus lived three days through a Dakota blizzard, without food, shelter, or attention to their wounds. It is a commentary on our boasted Christian civilization that although there were two or three salaried missionaries at the agency not one went out to say a prayer over the poor mangled bodies of these victims of war....

A long trench was dug and into it were thrown all the bodies, piled one upon another like so much cordwood, until the pit was full.... Many of the bodies were stripped by the whites, who went out in order to get the "ghost shirts," and the frozen bodies were thrown into the trench stiff and naked. They were only dead Indians. As one of the burial party said, "It was a thing to melt the heart of a man, if it was of stone, to see those little children, with their bodies shot to pieces, thrown naked into the pit." The dead soldiers had already been brought in and buried decently at the agency. When the writer visited the spot the following winter, the Indians had put up a wire fence around the trench and smeared the posts with sacred red medicine paint....

A baby girl of only three or four months was found under the snow, carefully wrapped up in a shawl, beside her dead mother, whose body was pierced by two bullets. On her head was a little cap of buckskin, upon which the American flag was embroidered in bright beadwork. She had lived through all the exposure, being only slightly frozen, and soon recovered after being brought in to the agency. Her mother being killed, and, in all probability, her father also, she was adopted by General Colby, commanding the Nebraska state troops. The Indian women in camp gave her the poetic name of Zitkala-noni, "Lost Bird," and by the family of her adoption she was baptized under the name of Marguerite.... She is now (1896) living in the general's family at Washington, a chubby little girl 6 years of ages, as happy with her dolls and playthings as a little girl of that age ought to be....

A little boy of four years, the son of Yellow Bird, the medicine-man, was playing on his pony in front of a tipi when the firing began. As he described it some time ago in lisping English: "My father ran and fell down and the blood came out of his mouth [he was shot through the head], and then a soldier put his gun up to my white pony's nose and shot him, and then I ran and a policeman got me." As his father was thus killed and his mother was already dead, he was adopted by Mrs Lucy Arnold, who had been a teacher among the Sioux and knew his family.... She had already given him his name, Herbert Zitkalazi, the last word being the Sioux form of his father's name, "Yellow Bird." She brought him back with her to Washington, where he soon learned English and became a general favorite of all who knew him for his affectionate disposition and unusual intelligence, with genuine boyish enthusiasm in all he undertook....

When we think of these children and consider that only by the merest accident they escaped the death that overtook a hundred other children at Wounded Knee, who may all have had in themselves the same possibilities of affection, education, and happy usefulness, we can understand the sickening meaning of such affairs as the Chivington massacre in Colorado and the Custer fight on the Washita, where the newspaper reports merely that "the enemy was surprised and the Indian camp destroyed."

[These Sioux accounts of events leading up to and at Wounded Knee are from a meeting with the Commissioner of Indian Affairs in Washington, D.C., in February 1891.]

...*TURNING HAWK*, Pine Ridge[3].... A certain falsehood [the Ghost Dance] came to our agency from the west which had the effect of a fire upon the Indians, and when this certain fire came upon our people those who had farsightedness and could see into the matter made up their minds to stand up against it and fight it. The reason we took this hostile attitude to this fire was because we believed that...the people in authority did not like this thing and we were quietly told that we must give up or have nothing to do with this certain movement. Though this is the advice from our good friends in the east, there were, of course, many silly young men who were longing to become identified with the movement, although they knew that there was nothing absolutely bad, nor did they know there was anything absolutely good, in connection with the movement.

In the course of time we heard that the soldiers were moving toward the scene of trouble. After awhile some of the soldiers finally reached our place and we heard that a number of them also reached our friends at Rosebud.[4] Of course, when a large body of soldiers is moving toward a certain direction they inspire a more or less amount of awe, and it is natural that the women and children who see this large moving mass are made afraid of it and be put in a condition to make them run away.... [W]hile the soldiers were there, there was constantly a great deal of false rumor flying back and forth. The special rumor I have in mind is the threat that the soldiers had come there to disarm the Indians entirely and to take away all their horses from them. That was the oft-repeated story.

So constantly repeated was this story that our friends from Rosebud, instead of going to Pine Ridge, the place of their destination, veered off and went to some other direction toward the "Bad Lands." We did not know definitely how many, but understood there were 300 lodges of them, about 1,700 people....

Well, the people after veering off in this way, many of [us] who believe in peace and order at our agency, were very anxious that some influence should be brought upon these people.... So we sent out peace commissioners [including Turning Hawk] to the people who were thus running away from their agency.

I understood at the time that they were simply going away from fear because of so many soldiers. So constant was the word of these good men from Pine Ridge agency that finally they succeeded in getting away half of the party from Rosebud, from the place where they took refuge, and finally were brought to the agency at Pine Ridge....

The remnant of the party from Rosebud not taken to the agency finally reached the wilds of the Bad Lands. Seeing that we had succeeded so well, once more we sent to the same party in the Bad Lands and succeeded in bringing these very Indians out of the depths of the Bad Lands and were being brought toward the agency. When we were about a day's journey from our agency we heard that a certain party of Indians (Big Foot's band) from the Cheyenne River agency was coming toward Pine Ridge in flight.

CAPTAIN SWORD.[5] ...There were a number of Ogalallas, old men and several school boys, coming back with that very same party, and one of the very seriously wounded boys was a member of the Ogalalla boarding school at Pine Ridge agency. He was not on the warpath, but was simply returning home to his agency and to his school after a summer visit to relatives on the Cheyenne river.

TURNING HAWK. When we heard that these people were coming toward our agency we also heard this. These people were coming toward Pine Ridge agency, and when they were almost on the agency they were met by the soldiers and surrounded and finally taken to the Wounded Knee creek, and there at a given time their guns were demanded. When they had delivered them up, the men were separated from their families, from their tipis, and taken to a certain spot. When the guns were thus taken and the men thus separated, there was a crazy man, a young man of very bad influence and in fact a nobody, among that bunch of Indians fired his gun, and of course the firing of a gun must have been the breaking of a military rule of some sort, because immediately the soldiers returned fire and indiscriminate killing followed.

SPOTTED HORSE. This man shot an officer in the army; the first shot killed this officer. I was a voluntary scout at that encounter and I saw exactly what was done, and that was what I noticed; that the first shot killed an officer. As soon as this shot was fired the Indians immediately began drawing their knives, and they were exhorted from all sides to desist, but this was not obeyed. Consequently the firing began immediately on the part of the soldiers.

TURNING HAWK.[6] All the men who were in a bunch were killed right there, and those who escaped that first fire got into the ravine, and as they went along up the ravine for a long distance they were pursued on

---

[3] Turning Hawk was one of the leaders of the Oglalas (a Sioux tribe) at Pine Ridge, a reservation in South Dakota.—*Ed.*
[4] The major Sioux reservation in South Dakota.—*Ed.*

[5] George Sword, captain of the Pine Ridge Indian Police.—*Ed.*
[6] A Sioux opponent of the Ghost Dance.—*Ed.*

both sides by the soldiers and shot down, as the dead bodies showed afterwards. The women were standing off at a different place from where the men were stationed, and when the firing began, those of the men who escaped the first onslaught went in one direction up the ravine, and then the women, who were bunched together at another place, went entirely in a different direction through an open field, and the women fared the same fate as the men who went up the deep ravine.

AMERICAN HORSE.[7]   The men were separated, as has already been said, from the women, and they were surrounded by the soldiers. Then came next the village of the Indians and that was entirely surrounded by the soldiers also. When the firing began, of course the people who were standing immediately around the young man who fired the first shot were killed right together, and then they turned their guns, Hotchkiss guns, etc., upon the women who were in the lodges standing there under a flag of truce, and of course as soon as they were fired upon they fled, the men fleeing in one direction and the women running in two different directions. So that there were three general directions in which they took flight.

There was a women with an infant in her arms who was killed as she almost touched the flag of truce, and the women and children of course were strewn all along the circular village until they were dispatched. Right near the flag of truce a mother was shot down with her infant; the child not knowing that its mother was dead was still nursing, and that especially was a very sad sight. The women as they were fleeing with their babes were killed together, shot right through, and the women who were very heavy with child were also killed. All the Indians fled in these three directions, and after most all of them had been killed a cry was made that all those who were not killed or wounded should come forth and they would be safe. Little boys who were not wounded came out of their places of refuge, and as soon as they came in sight a number of soldiers surrounded them and butchered them there.

Of course we all feel very sad about this affair. I stood very loyal to the government all through those troublesome days, and believing so much in the government and being so loyal to it, my disappointment was very strong, and I have come to Washington with a very great blame on my heart. Of course it would have been all right if only the men were killed; we would feel almost grateful for it. But the fact of the killing of the women, and more especially the killing of the young boys and girls who are to go to make up the future strength of the Indian people, is the saddest part of the whole affair and we feel it very sorely....

[An old Sioux song contains these lines:

For the fires grow cold and the dances fail,
And the songs in their echoes die;
And what have we left but the graves beneath,
And, above, the waiting sky?]

---

[7] Oglala opponent of the Ghost Dance at Pine Ridge. — *Ed.*

5

Populist Party Platform (1892)

THE POPULIST PARTY

In July 1892, the members of the People's Party of America, generally known as the Populists, assembled in Omaha to organize a national effort at reform. Their platform, largely the work of Igantius Donnelly of Minnesota, set forth their main grievances and hopes for change. The party also nominated General James B. Weaver as their candidate for President. Weaver received over a million votes and carried four Western states.

Questions to Consider

- Why were economic issues at the center of the Populists' platform?
- Why didn't the Populists enjoy greater success in the cities?

Assembled upon the 116th anniversary of the Declaration of Independence, the People's Party of America, in their first national convention, invoking upon their action the blessing of Almighty God, put forth in the name and on behalf of the people of this country, the following preamble and declaration of principles:

The conditions which surround us best justify our co-operation; we meet in the midst of a nation brought to the verge of moral, political, and material ruin. Corruption dominates the ballot box, the Legislatures, the Congress, and touches even the ermine of the bench. The people are demoralized; most of the States have been compelled to isolate the voters at the polling places to prevent universal intimidation and bribery. The newspapers are largely subsidized or muzzled, public opinion silenced, business prostrated, homes covered with mortgages, labor impoverished, and the land concentrating in the hands of capitalists. The urban workmen are denied the right to organize for self-protection, imported pauperized labor beats down their wages, a hireling standing army, unrecognized by our laws, is established to shoot them down, and they are rapidly degenerating into European conditions. The fruits of the toil of millions are boldly stolen to build up colossal fortunes for a few, unprecedented in the history of mankind; and the possessors of those, in turn, despite the Republic and endanger liberty. From the same prolific womb of governmental injustice we breed the two great classes—tramps and millionaires.

The national power to create money is appropriated to enrich bondholders; a vast public debt payable in legal tender currency has been funded into gold-bearing bonds, thereby adding millions to the burdens of the people.

Silver, which has been accepted as coin since the dawn of history, has been demonetized to add to the purchasing power of gold by decreasing the value of all forms of property as well as human labor, and the supply of currency is purposely abridged to fatten usurers, bankrupt enterprise, and enslave industry. A vast conspiracy against mankind has been organized on two continents, and it is rapidly taking possession of the world. If not met and overthrown at once it forebodes terrible social convulsions, the destruction of civilization, or the establishment of an absolute despotism.

We have witnessed for more than a quarter of a century the struggles of the two great political parties for power and plunder, while grievous wrongs have been inflicted upon the suffering people. We charge that the controlling influences dominating both these parties have permitted the existing dreadful conditions to develop without serious effort to prevent or restrain them. Neither do they now promise us any substantial reform. They have agreed together to ignore, in the coming campaign, every issue but one. They propose to drown the outcries of a plundered people with the uproar of a sham battle over the tariff, so that capitalists, corporations, national banks, rings, trusts, watered stock, the demonetization of silver and the oppressions of the usurers may all be lost sight of. They propose to sacrifice our homes, lives, and children on the altar of mammon; to destroy the multitude in order to secure corruption funds from the millionaires.

Assembled on the anniversary of the birthday of the nation, and filled with the spirit of the grand general and chief who established our independence, we seek to restore the government of the Republic to the hands of "the plain people," with which class it originated. We assert our purposes to be identical with the purposes of the National Constitution; to form a more perfect union and establish justice, insure domestic tranquillity, provide for the common defence, promote the general welfare, and secure the blessings of liberty for ourselves and our posterity.

We declare that this Republic can only endure as a free government while built upon the love of the whole people for each other and for the nation; that it cannot be pinned together by bayonets; that the civil war is over, and that every passion and resentment which grew out of it must die with it, and that we must be in fact, as we are in name, one united brotherhood of free [men].

Our country finds itself confronted by conditions for which there is no precedent in the history of the world; our annual agricultural productions amount to billions of dollars in value, which must, within a few weeks or months, be exchanged for billions of dollars' worth of commodities consumed in their production; the existing currency supply is wholly inadequate to make this exchange; the results are falling prices, the formation of combines and rings, the impoverishment of the produc-

Source: Edward McPherson, *A Hand-Book of Politics for 1892* (Washington, D.C., 1892), pp. 269–272.

ing class. We pledge ourselves that if given power we will labor to correct these evils by wise and reasonable legislation, in accordance with the terms of our platform.

We believe that the power of government—in other words, of the people—should be expanded (as in the case of the postal service) as rapidly and as far as the good sense of an intelligent people and the teachings of experience shall justify, to the end that oppression, injustice, and poverty shall eventually cease in the land.

While our sympathies as a party of reform are naturally upon the side of every proposition which will tend to make men intelligent, virtuous, and temperate, we nevertheless regard these questions, important as they are, as secondary to the great issues now pressing for solution, and upon which not only our individual prosperity but the very existence of free institutions depend; and we ask all men to first help us to determine whether we are to have a republic to administer before we differ as to the conditions upon which it is to be administered, believing that the forces of reform this day organized will never cease to move forward until every wrong is remedied and equal rights and equal privileges securely established for all the men and women of this country. We declare, therefore—

First—That the union of the labor forces of the United States this day consummated shall be permanent and perpetual; may its spirit enter into all hearts for the salvation of the Republic and the uplifting of mankind.

Second—Wealth belongs to him who creates it, and every dollar taken from industry without an equivalent is robbery. "If any will not work, neither shall he eat." The interests of rural and civic labor are the same; their enemies are identical.

Third—We believe that the time has come when the railroad corporations will either own the people or the people must own the railroads, and should the government enter upon the work of owning and managing all railroads, we should favor an amendment to the Constitution by which all persons engaged in the government service shall be placed under a civil-service regulation of the most rigid character, so as to prevent the increase of the power of the national administration by the use of such additional government employees.

FINANCE—We demand a national currency, safe, sound, and flexible, issued by the general government only, a full legal tender for all debts, public and private, and that without the use of banking corporations, a just, equitable, and efficient means of distribution direct to the people, at a tax not to exceed 2 per cent. per annum, to be provided as set forth in the sub-treasury plan of the Farmers' Alliance, or a better system; also by pay-

ments in discharge of its obligations for public improvements.

1. We demand free and unlimited coinage of silver and gold at the present legal ratio of 16 to 1.
2. We demand that the amount of circulating medium be speedily increased to not less than $50 per capita.
3. We demand a graduated income tax.
4. We believe that the money of the country should be kept as much as possible in the hands of the people, and hence we demand that all State and national revenues shall be limited to the necessary expenses of the government, economically and honestly administered.
5. We demand that postal savings banks be established by the government for the safe deposit of the earnings of the people and to facilitate exchange.

TRANSPORTATION—Transportation being a means of exchange and a public necessity, the government should own and operate the railroads in the interest of the people. The telegraph, telephone, like the post-office system, being a necessity for the transmission of news, should be owned and operated by the government in the interest of the people.

LAND—The land, including all the natural sources of wealth, is the heritage of the people, and should not be monopolized for speculative purposes, and alien ownership of land should be prohibited. All land now held by railroads and other corporations in excess of their actual needs, and all lands now owned by aliens should be reclaimed by the government and held for actual settlers only.

Supplementary Resolutions from Platform Committee

Whereas, other questions have been presented for our consideration, we hereby submit the following, not as a part of the Platform of the People's Party, but as resolutions expressive of the sentiment of this Convention:

1. RESOLVED, That we demand a free ballot and a fair count in all elections, and pledge ourselves to secure it to every legal voter without Federal intervention, through the adoption by the States of the unperverted Australian or secret ballot system.
2. RESOLVED, That the revenue derived from a graduated income tax should be applied to the reduction of the burden of taxation now levied upon the domestic industries of this country.

3. RESOLVED, That we pledge our support to fair and liberal pensions to ex-Union soldiers and sailors.

4. RESOLVED, That we condemn the fallacy of protecting American labor under the present system, which opens our ports to the pauper and criminal classes of the world and crowds out our wage-earners; and we denounce the present ineffective laws against contract labor, and demand the further restriction of undesirable emigration.

5. RESOLVED, That we cordially sympathize with the efforts of organized workingmen to shorten the hours of labor, and demand a rigid enforcement of the existing eight-hour law on Government work, and ask that a penalty clause be added to the said law.

6. RESOLVED, That we regard the maintenance of a large standing army of mercenaries, known as the Pinkerton system, as a menace to our liberties, and we demand its abolition; and we condemn the recent invasion of the Territory of Wyoming by the hired assassins of plutocracy, assisted by Federal officers.

7. RESOLVED, That we commend to the favorable consideration of the people and the reform press the legislative system known as the initiative and referendum.

8. RESOLVED, That we favor a constitutional provision limiting the office of President and Vice-President to one term, and providing for the election of Senators of the United States by a direct vote of the people.

9. RESOLVED, That we oppose any subsidy or national aid to any private corporation for any purpose.

10. RESOLVED, That this convention sympathizes with the Knights of Labor and their righteous contest with the tyrannical combine of clothing manufacturers of Rochester, and declare it to be the duty of all who hate tyranny and oppression to refuse to purchase the goods made by the said manufacturers, or to patronize any merchants who sell such goods.

6

The Significance of the Frontier in American History (1893)

FREDERICK JACKSON TURNER

No academic paper has ever produced an impact equal to that of Frederick Jackson Turner's "The Significance of the Frontier in American History." Initially delivered at the Chicago Columbian Exposition of 1893 celebrating the 400th anniversary of Columbus's first voyage to the Western Hemisphere, Turner's essay provided the leading paradigm for understanding American history over the next half century, at least. Turner built his thesis on the revelation in the 1890 census that the United States no longer had a clear line of frontier, that the nation had filled up its continental borders. Thus, a long period of American expansion had come to a close, but not without leaving permanent marks on the American character. Turner's insistence that its frontier experience explained the development of democracy in the United States made sense to historians and the general public, generating a popular sense of American exceptionalism and promoting a high cultural valuation of the frontier. Though the recipient of sustained criticism by historians over the last fifty years, the Turner Thesis remains extremely influential among scholars and upon popular culture.

Questions to Consider

- Does the end of the frontier mean the end of democracy as well?
- What role did the cities and industrial development play in Turner's America?
- How is frontier defined?

In a recent bulletin of the Superintendent of the Census for 1890 appear these significant words: "Up to and including 1880 the country had a frontier of settlement, but at present the unsettled area has been so broken into by isolated bodies of settlement that there can hardly be said to be a frontier line. In the discussion of its extent, its westward movement, etc., it can not, therefore, any longer have a place in the census reports." This brief official statement marks the closing of a great historic movement. Up to our own day American history has been in a large degree the history of the colonization of the Great West. The existence of an area of free land, its continuous recession, and the advance of American settlement westward, explain American development.

Behind institutions, behind constitutional forms and modifications, lie the vital forces that call these organs into life and shape them to meet changing conditions. The peculiarity of American institutions is, the fact that they have been compelled to adapt themselves to the changes of an expanding people—to the changes involved in crossing a continent, in winning a wilderness, and in developing at each area of this progress out of the primitive economic and political conditions of the frontier into the complexity of city life. Said Calhoun in 1817, "We are great, and rapidly—I was about to say fearfully—growing!" So saying, he touched the distinguishing feature of American life. All peoples show development; the germ theory of politics has been sufficiently emphasized. In the case of most nations, however, the development has occurred in a limited area, and if the nation has expanded, it has met other growing peoples whom it has conquered. But in the case of the United States we have a different phenomenon. Limiting our attention to the Atlantic coast, we have the familiar phenomenon of the evolution of institutions in a limited area, such as the rise of representative government; the differentiation of simple colonial governments into complex organs; the progress from primitive industrial society, without division of labor, up to manufacturing civilization. But we have in addition to this a recurrence of the process of evolution in each western area reached in the process of expansion. Thus American development has exhibited not merely advance along a single line, but a return to primitive conditions on a continually advancing frontier line, and a new development for that area. American social development has been continually beginning over again on the frontier. This perennial rebirth, this fluidity of American life, this expansion westward with its new opportunities, its continuous touch with the simplicity of primitive society, furnish the forces dominating American character. The true point of view in the history of this nation is not the Atlantic coast, it is the Great West. Even the slavery struggle…occupies its important place in American history because of its relation to westward expansion.

In this advance, the frontier is the outer edge of the wave—the meeting point between savagery and civilization. Much has been written about the frontier from the point of view of border warfare and the chase, but as a field for the serious study of the economist and the historian it has been neglected.

The American frontier is sharply distinguished from the European frontier—a fortified boundary line running through dense populations. The most significant thing about the American frontier is, that it lies at the hither edge of free land. In the census reports it is treated as the margin of that settlement which has a density of two or more to the square mile. The term is an elastic one, and for our purposes does not need sharp definition….

In the settlement of America we have to observe how European life entered the continent, and how America modified and developed that life and reacted on Europe. Our early history is the study of European germs developing in an American environment. Too ex-

Source: Frederick Jackson Turner, *The Frontier in American History* (New York, 1920), pp. 1–38.

clusive attention has been paid by institutional students to the Germanic origins, too little to the American factors. The frontier is the line of most rapid and effective Americanization. The wilderness masters the colonist. It finds him a European in dress, industries, tools, modes of travel, and thought. It takes him from the railroad car and puts him in the birch canoe. It strips off the garments of civilization and arrays him in the hunting shirt and the moccasin. It puts him in the log cabin of the Cherokee and Iroquois and runs an Indian palisade around him. Before long he has gone to planting Indian corn and plowing with a sharp stick; he shouts the war cry and takes the scalp in orthodox Indian fashion. In short, at the frontier the environment is at first too strong for the man. He must accept the conditions which it furnishes, or perish, and so he fits himself into the Indian clearings and follows the Indian trails. Little by little he transforms the wilderness, but the outcome is not the old Europe, not simply the development of Germanic germs, any more than the first phenomenon was a case of reversion to the Germanic mark. The fact is, that here is a new product that is American. At first, the frontier was the Atlantic coast. It was the frontier of Europe in a very real sense. Moving westward, the frontier became more and more American. As successive terminal moraines result from successive glaciations, so each frontier leaves its traces behind it, and when it becomes a settled area the region still partakes of the frontier characteristics. Thus the advance of the frontier has meant a steady movement away from the influence of Europe, a steady growth of independence on American lines. And to study this advance, the men who grew up under these conditions, and the political, economic, and social results of it, is to study the really American part of our history.

In the course of the seventeenth century the frontier was advanced up the Atlantic river courses, just beyond the "fall line," and the tidewater region became the settled area. In the first half of the eighteenth century another advance occurred. Traders followed the Delaware and Shawnese Indians to the Ohio as early as the end of the first quarter of the century.... The end of the first quarter of the century saw the advance of the Scotch-Irish and the Palatine Germans up the Shenandoah Valley into the western part of Virginia, and along the Piedmont region of the Carolinas. The Germans in New York pushed the frontier of settlement up the Mohawk to German Flats.... The King attempted to arrest the advance by his proclamation of 1763, forbidding settlements beyond the sources of the rivers flowing into the Atlantic; but in vain. In the period of the Revolution the frontier crossed the Alleghanies into Kentucky and Tennessee, and the upper waters of the Ohio were settled. When the first census was taken in 1790, the continuous settled area was bounded by a line which ran near the coast of Maine, and included New England ex-

cept a portion of Vermont and New Hampshire, New York along the Hudson and up the Mohawk about Schenectady, eastern and southern Pennsylvania, Virginia well across the Shenandoah Valley, and the Carolinas and eastern Georgia. Beyond this region of continuous settlement were the small settled areas of Kentucky and Tennessee, and the Ohio, with the mountains intervening between them and the Atlantic area, thus giving a new and important character to the frontier. The isolation of the region increased its peculiarly American tendencies, and the need of transportation facilities to connect it with the East called out important schemes of internal improvement, which will be noted farther on. The "West," as a self-conscious section, began to evolve.

From decade to decade distinct advances of the frontier occurred. By the census of 1820 the settled area included Ohio, southern Indiana and Illinois, southeastern Missouri, and about one-half of Louisiana. This settled area had surrounded Indian areas, and the management of these tribes became an object of political concern. The frontier region of the time lay along the Great Lakes, where Astor's American Fur Company operated in the Indian trade, and beyond the Mississippi, where Indian traders extended their activity even to the Rocky Mountains....

The rising steam navigation on western waters, the opening of the Erie Canal, and the westward extension of cotton culture added five frontier states to the Union in this period. [Francis] Grund, writing in 1836, declares: "It appears then that the universal disposition of Americans to emigrate to the western wilderness, in order to enlarge their dominion over inanimate nature, is the actual result of an expansive power which is inherent in them, and which by continually agitating all classes of society is constantly throwing a large portion of the whole population on the extreme confines of the State, in order to gain space for its development. Hardly is a new State or Territory formed before the same principle manifests itself again and gives rise to a further emigration; and so is it destined to go on until a physical barrier must finally obstruct its progress."

In the middle of this century the line indicated by the present eastern boundary of Indian Territory, Nebraska, and Kansas marked the frontier of the Indian country. Minnesota and Wisconsin still exhibited frontier conditions, but the distinctive frontier of the period is found in California, where the gold discoveries had sent a sudden tide of adventurous miners, and in Oregon, and the settlements in Utah. As the frontier had leaped over the Alleghenies, so now it skipped the Great Plains and the Rocky Mountains; and in the same way that the advance of the frontiersmen beyond the Alleghenies had caused the rise of important questions of transportation and internal improvement, so now the settlers beyond the Rocky Mountains needed means of communication with the East, and in the furnishing of these arose the settlement of the Great Plains and the development of still another kind of frontier life. Railroads, fostered by land grants, sent an increasing tide of immigrants into the Far West. The United States Army fought a series of Indian wars in Minnesota, Dakota, and the Indian Territory.

By 1880 the settled area had been pushed into northern Michigan, Wisconsin, and Minnesota, along Dakota rivers, and in the Black Hills region, and was ascending the rivers of Kansas and Nebraska. The development of mines in Colorado had drawn isolated frontier settlements into that region, and Montana and Idaho were receiving settlers. The frontier was found in these mining camps and the ranches of the Great Plains. The superintendent of the census for 1890 reports, as previously stated, that the settlements of the West lie so scattered over the region that there can no longer be said to be a frontier line.

In these successive frontiers we find natural boundary lines which have served to mark and to affect the characteristics of the frontiers.... The fall line marked the frontier of the seventeenth century; the Alleghanies that of the eighteenth; the Mississippi that of the first quarter of the nineteenth; the Missouri that of the middle of this century (omitting the California movement); and the belt of the Rocky Mountains and the arid tract, the present frontier. Each was won by a series of Indian wars.

At the Atlantic frontier one can study the germs of processes repeated at each successive frontier. We have the complex European life sharply precipitated by the wilderness into the simplicity of primitive conditions. The first frontier had to meet its Indian question, its question of the disposition of the public domain, of the means of intercourse with older settlements, of the extension of political organization, of religious and educational activity. And the settlement of these and similar questions for one frontier served as a guide for the next. The American student...may study the origin of our land policies in the colonial land policy; he may see how the system grew by adapting the statutes to the customs of the successive frontiers. He may see how the mining experience in the lead regions of Wisconsin, Illinois, and Iowa was applied to the mining laws of the Sierras, and how our Indian policy has been a series of experimentations on successive frontiers. Each tier of new States has found in the older ones material for its constitutions. Each frontier has made similar contributions to American character....

But with all these similarities there are essential differences, due to the place element and the time element. It is evident that the farming frontier of the Mississippi Valley presents different conditions from the mining frontier of the Rocky Mountains. The frontier reached by the Pacific Railroad, surveyed into rectangles, guarded by the United States Army, and recruited by the daily immigrant ship, moves forward at a swifter pace and in a different way than the frontier reached by the birch canoe or the pack horse. The geologist traces patiently the shores of ancient seas, maps their areas, and compares the older and the newer. It would be a work worth the historian's labors to mark these various frontiers and in detail compare one with another. Not only would there result a more adequate conception of American development and characteristics, but invaluable additions would be made to the history of society.

[Achille] Loria, the Italian economist, has urged the study of colonial life as an aid in understanding the stages of European development, affirming that colonial settlement is for economic science what the mountain is for geology, bringing to light primitive stratifications. "America," he says, "has the key to the historical enigma which Europe has sought for centuries in vain, and the land which has no history reveals luminously the course of universal history." There is much truth in this. The United States lies like a huge page in the history of society. Line by line as we read this continental page from West to East we find the record of social evolution. It begins with the Indian and the hunter; it goes on to tell of the disintegration of savagery by the entrance of the trader, the pathfinder of civilization; we read the annals of the pastoral stage in ranch life; the exploitation of the soil by the raising of unrotated crops of corn and wheat in sparsely settled farming communities; the intensive culture of the denser farm settlement; and finally the manufacturing organization with city and factory system. This page is familiar to the student of census statistics, but how little of it has been used by our historians. Particularly in eastern States this page is a palimpsest. What is now a manufacturing State was in an earlier decade an area of intensive farming. Earlier yet it had been a wheat area, and still earlier the "range" had attracted the cattleherder. Thus Wisconsin, now developing manufacture, is a State with varied agricultural interests. But earlier it was given over to almost exclusive grain-raising, like North Dakota at the present time.

Each of these areas has had an influence in our economic and political history; the evolution of each into a higher stage has worked political transformations. But what constitutional historian has made any adequate attempt to interpret political facts by the light of these social areas and changes?

The Atlantic frontier was compounded of fisherman, fur-trader, miner, cattle-raiser, and farmer. Excepting the fisherman, each type of industry was on the march toward the West, impelled by an irresistible attraction. Each passed in successive waves across the continent. Stand at Cumberland Gap and watch the procession of civilization, marching single file—the buffalo following the trail to the salt springs, the Indian, the fur-trader and hunter, the cattle-raiser, the pioneer farmer—and the frontier has passed by. Stand at South Pass in the Rockies a century later and see the same procession with wider intervals between. The unequal rate of advance compels us to distinguish the frontier into the trader's frontier, the rancher's frontier, or the miner's frontier, and the farmer's frontier. When the mines and the cowpens were still near the fall line the traders' pack trains were tinkling across the Alleghanies, and the French on the Great Lakes were fortifying their posts, alarmed by the British trader's birch canoe. When the trappers scaled the Rockies, the farmer was still near the mouth of the Missouri.

Why was it that the Indian trader passed so rapidly across the continent? What effects followed from the trader's frontier? The trade was coeval with American discovery. The Norsemen, Vespuccius, Verrazani, Hudson, John Smith, all trafficked for furs. The Plymouth pilgrims settled in Indian cornfields, and their first return cargo was of beaver and lumber. The records of the various New England colonies show how steadily exploration was carried into the wilderness by this trade. What is true for New England is, as would be expected, even plainer for the rest of the colonies. All along the coast from Maine to Georgia the Indian trade opened up the river courses. Steadily the trader passed westward, utilizing the older lines of French trade. The Ohio, the Great Lakes, the Mississippi, the Missouri, and the Platte, the lines of western advance, were ascended by traders. They found the passes in the Rocky Mountains and guided Lewis and Clark, Frémont, and Bidwell. The explanation of the rapidity of this advance is connected with the effects of the trader on the Indian. The trading post left the unarmed tribes at the mercy of those that had purchased fire-arms—a truth which the Iroquois Indians wrote in blood, and so the remote and unvisited tribes gave eager welcome to the trader. "The savages," wrote La Salle, "take better care of us French than of their own children; from us only can they get guns and goods." This accounts for the trader's power and the rapidity of his advance. Thus the disintegrating forces of civilization entered the wilderness. Every river valley and Indian trail became a fissure in Indian society, and so that society became honeycombed. Long before the pioneer farmer appeared on the scene, primitive Indian life had passed away. The farmers met Indians armed with guns. The trading frontier, while

steadily undermining Indian power by making the tribes ultimately dependent on the whites, yet, through its sale of guns, gave to the Indian increased power of resistance to the farming frontier. French colonization was dominated by its trading frontier; English colonization by its farming frontier. There was an antagonism between the two frontiers as between the two nations. Said Duquesne to the Iroquois, "Are you ignorant of the difference between the king of England and the king of France? Go see the forts that our king has established and you will see that you can still hunt under their very walls. They have been placed for your advantage in places which you frequent. The English, on the contrary, are no sooner in possession of a place than the game is driven away. The forest falls before them as they advance, and the soil is laid bare so that you can scarce find the wherewithal to erect a shelter for the night."

And yet, in spite of this opposition of the interests of the trader and the farmer, the Indian trade pioneered the way for civilization. The buffalo trail became the Indian trail, and this became the trader's "trace;" the trails widened into roads, and the roads into turnpikes, and these in turn were transformed into railroads.... The trading posts reached by these trails were on the sites of Indian villages which had been placed in positions suggested by nature; and these trading posts, situated so as to command the water systems of the country, have grown into such cities as Albany, Pittsburgh, Detroit, Chicago, St. Louis, Council Bluffs, and Kansas City. Thus civilization in America has followed the arteries made by geology, pouring an ever richer tide through them, until at last the slender paths of aboriginal intercourse have been broadened and interwoven into the complex mazes of modern commercial lines; the wilderness has been interpenetrated by lines of civilization growing ever more numerous. It is like the steady growth of a complex nervous system for the originally simple, inert continent. If one would understand why we are to-day one nation, rather than a collection of isolated states, he must study this economic and social consolidation of the country. In this progress from savage conditions lie topics for the evolutionist.

The effect of the Indian frontier as a consolidating agent in our history is important. From the close of the seventeenth century various intercolonial congresses have been called to treat with Indians and establish common measures of defense. Particularism was strongest in colonies with no Indian frontier. This frontier stretched along the western border like a cord of union. The Indian was a common danger, demanding united action. Most celebrated of these conferences was the Albany congress of 1754, called to treat with the Six Nations, and to consider plans of union. Even a cursory reading of the plan proposed by the congress reveals the importance of the frontier. The powers of the general council and the officers were, chiefly, the determination of peace and war with the Indians, the regulation of Indian trade, the purchase of Indian lands, and the creation and government of new settlements as a security against the Indians. It is evident that the unifying tendencies of the Revolutionary period were facilitated by the previous coöperation in the regulation of the frontier. In this connection may be mentioned the importance of the frontier, from that day to this, as a military training school, keeping alive the power of resistance to aggression, and developing the stalwart and rugged qualities of the frontiersman.

…The ranges of the Great Plains, with ranch and cowboy and nomadic life, are things of yesterday and of to-day. The experience of the Carolina cowpens guided the ranchers of Texas. One element favoring the rapid extension of the rancher's frontier is the fact that in a remote country lacking transportation facilities the product must be in small bulk, or must be able to transport itself, and the cattle raiser could easily drive his product to market. The effect of these great ranches on the subsequent agrarian history of the localities in which they existed should be studied.

The maps of the census reports show an uneven advance of the farmer's frontier, with tongues of settlement pushed forward and with indentations of wilderness. In part this is due to Indian resistance, in part to the location of river valleys and passes, in part to the unequal force of the centers of frontier attraction. Among the important centers of attraction may be mentioned the following: fertile and favorably situated soils, salt springs, mines, and army posts.

The frontier army post, serving to protect the settlers from the Indians, has also acted as a wedge to open the Indian country, and has been a nucleus for settlement. In this connection mention should also be made of the government military and exploring expeditions in determining the lines of settlement. But all the more important expeditions were greatly indebted to the earliest pathmakers, the Indian guides, the traders and trappers, and the French voyageurs, who were inevitable parts of governmental expeditions from the days of Lewis and Clark. Each expedition was an epitome of the previous factors in western advance.

…The early settlers were tied to the coast by the need of salt, without which they could not preserve their meats or live in comfort…. An annual pilgrimage to the coast for salt thus became essential. Taking flocks or furs and ginseng root, the early settlers sent their pack trains after seeding time each year to the coast. This proved to be an important educational influence, since it was almost the only way in which the pioneer learned what was going on in the East. But when discovery was made of the salt springs of the Kanawha, and the Holston, and Kentucky, and central New York, the West began to be freed from dependence on the coast. It was in part the effect of finding these salt springs that enabled settlement to cross the mountains.

From the time the mountains rose between the pioneer and the seaboard, a new order of Americanism arose. The West and the East began to get out of touch of each other. The settlements from the sea to the mountains kept connection with the rear and had a certain solidarity. But the over-mountain men grew more and more independent. The East took a narrow view of American advance, and nearly lost these men. Kentucky and Tennessee history bears abundant witness to the truth of this statement. The East began to try to hedge and limit westward expansion. Though Webster could declare that there were no Alleghanies in his politics, yet in politics in general they were a very solid factor.

The exploitation of the beasts took hunter and trader to the west, the exploitation of the grasses took the rancher west, and the exploitation of the virgin soil of the river valleys and prairies attracted the farmer. Good soils have been the most continuous attraction to the farmer's frontier. The land hunger of the Virginians drew them down the rivers into Carolina, in early colonial days; the search for soils took the Massachusetts men to Pennsylvania and to New York. As the eastern lands were taken up migration flowed across them to the west. Daniel Boone, the great backwoodsman, who combined the occupations of hunter, trader, cattle-raiser, farmer, and surveyor—learning, probably from the traders, of the fertility of the lands of the upper Yadkin,…left his Pennsylvania home with his father, and passed down the Great Valley road to that stream. Learning from a trader of the game and rich pastures of Kentucky, he pioneered the way for the farmers to that region. Thence he passed to the frontier of Missouri, where his settlement was long a landmark on the frontier. Here again he helped to open the way for civilization, finding salt licks, and trails, and land. His son was among the earliest trappers in the passes of the Rocky Mountains, and his party are said to have been the first to camp on the present site of Denver. His grandson, Col. A. J. Boone, of Colorado, was a power among the Indians of the Rocky Mountains, and was appointed an agent by the government. Kit Carson's mother was a Boone. Thus this family epitomizes the backwoodsman's advance across the continent.

The farmer's advance came in a distinct series of waves. In Peck's New Guide to the West, published in Boston in 1837, occurs this suggestive passage:

Generally, in all the western settlements, three classes, like the waves of the ocean, have rolled one after the other. First comes the pioneer, who depends for the subsistence of his family chiefly upon the natural growth of vegetation, called the "range," and the proceeds of hunting. His implements of agriculture are rude, chiefly of his own make, and his efforts directed mainly to a crop of corn…. A log cabin, and…a field of a dozen acres…are enough for his occupancy. It is quite immaterial whether he ever becomes the owner of the soil. He is the occupant for the time being, pays no rent, and feels as independent as the "lord of the manor." With a horse, cow, and one or two breeders of swine, he strikes into the woods with his family, and becomes the founder of a new county, or perhaps state. He builds his cabin, gathers around him a few other families of similar tastes and habits, and occupies till the range is somewhat subdued, and hunting a little precarious, or, which is more frequently the case, till the neighbors crowd around, roads, bridges, and fields annoy him, and he lacks elbow room…. [Then] he "breaks for the high timber,"…or migrates to Arkansas or Texas, to work the same process over.

The next class of emigrants purchase the lands, add field to field, clear out the roads, throw rough bridges over the streams, put up hewn log houses with glass windows and brick or stone chimneys, occasionally plant orchards, build mills, schoolhouses, court-houses, etc., and exhibit the picture and forms of plain, frugal, civilized life.

Another wave rolls on. The men of capital and enterprise come. The settler is ready to sell out and take the advantage of the rise in property, push farther into the interior and become, himself, a man of capital and enterprise in turn. The small village rises to a spacious town or city; substantial edifices of brick, extensive fields, orchards, gardens, colleges, and churches are seen…. Thus wave after wave is rolling westward; the real Eldorado is still farther on….

Omitting those of the pioneer farmers who move from the love of adventure, the advance of the more steady farmer is easy to understand. Obviously the immigrant was attracted by the cheap lands of the frontier, and even the native farmer felt their influence strongly. Year by year the farmers who lived on soil whose returns were diminished by unrotated crops were offered the virgin soil of the frontier at nominal prices. Their growing families demanded more lands, and these were dear. The competition of the unexhausted, cheap, and easily tilled prairie lands compelled the farmer either to go west and continue the exhaustion of the soil on a new frontier, or to adopt intensive culture. Thus the census of 1890 shows, in the Northwest, many counties in which there is an absolute or a relative decrease of population. These States have been sending farmers to advance the frontier on the plains, and have themselves begun to turn to intensive farming and to manufacture. A decade before this, Ohio had shown the same transition stage. Thus the demand for land and the love of wilderness freedom drew the frontier ever onward.

Having now roughly outlined the various kinds of frontiers, and their modes of advance, chiefly from the point of view of the frontier itself, we may next inquire what were the influences on the East and on the Old World….

First, we note that the frontier promoted the formation of a composite nationality for the American people. The coast was preponderantly English, but the later tides of continental immigration flowed across to the free lands. This was the case from the early colonial days. The Scotch-Irish and the Palatine Germans, or "Pennsylvania Dutch," furnished the dominant element in the stock of the colonial frontier. With these peoples were also the freed indented servants, or redemptioners, who at the expiration of their time of service passed to the frontier…. In the crucible of the frontier the immigrants were Americanized, liberated, and fused into a mixed race, English in neither nationality nor characteristics. The process has gone on from the early days to our own. Burke and other writers in the middle of the eighteenth century believed that Pennsylvania was "threatened with the danger of being wholly foreign in language, manners, and perhaps even inclinations."… In the middle of the present century the German element in Wisconsin was already so considerable that leading publicists looked to the creation of a German state out of the commonwealth by concentrating their colonization. Such examples teach us to beware of misinterpreting the fact that there is a common English speech in America into a belief that the stock is also English.

In another way the advance of the frontier decreased our dependence on England. The coast, particularly of the South, lacked diversified industries, and was dependent on England for the bulk of its supplies. In the South there was even a dependence on the Northern colonies for articles of food…. Before long the frontier created a demand for merchants. As it retreated from the coast it became less and less possible for England to bring her supplies directly to the consumer's wharfs, and carry away staple crops, and staple crops began to give way to diversified agriculture for a time. The effect of this phase of the frontier action upon the northern section is perceived when we realize how the advance of the frontier aroused seaboard cities like Boston, New York, and Baltimore, to engage in rivalry for what Washington called "the extensive and valuable trade of a rising empire."

The legislation which most developed the powers of the national government, and played the largest part in its activity, was conditioned on the frontier. Writers have discussed the subjects of tariff, land, and internal improvement, as subsidiary to the slavery question. But when American history comes to be rightly viewed it will be seen that the slavery question is an incident. In the period from the end of the first half of the present century to the close of the Civil War slavery rose to primary, but far from exclusive, importance.... The growth of nationalism and the evolution of American political institutions were dependent on the advance of the frontier....

...The pioneer needed the goods of the coast, and so the grand series of internal improvement and railroad legislation began, with potent nationalizing effects. Over internal improvements occurred great debates, in which grave constitutional questions were discussed. Sectional groupings appear in the votes, profoundly significant for the historian. Loose construction increased as the nation marched westward. But the West was not content with bringing the farm to the factory. Under the lead of Clay—"Harry of the West"—protective tariffs were passed, with the cry of bringing the factory to the farm. The disposition of the public lands was a third important subject of national legislation influenced by the frontier.

The public domain has been a force of profound importance in the nationalization and development of the government. The effects of the struggle of the landed and the landless States, and of the Ordinance of 1787, need no discussion. Administratively the frontier called out some of the highest and most vitalizing activities of the general government. The purchase of Louisiana was perhaps the constitutional turning point in the history of the Republic, inasmuch as it afforded both a new area for national legislation and the occasion of the downfall of the policy of strict construction. But the purchase of Louisiana was called out by frontier needs and demands. As frontier States accrued to the Union the national power grew.... [Lucius Q. C.] Lamar explained: "In 1789 the States were the creators of the Federal Government; in 1861 the Federal Government was the creator of a large majority of the States."

When we consider the public domain from the point of view of the sale and disposal of the public lands we are again brought face to face with the frontier. The policy of the United States in dealing with its lands is in sharp contrast with the European system of scientific administration. Efforts to make this domain a source of revenue, and to withhold it from emigrants in order that settlement might be compact, were in vain. The jealousy and the fears of the East were powerless in the face of the demands of the frontiersmen. John Quincy Adams was obliged to confess: "My own system of administration, which was to make the national domain the inexhaustible fund for progressive and unceasing internal improvement, has failed." The reason is obvious; a system of administration was not what the West demanded: it wanted land. Adams states the situation as follows: "The slaveholders of the South have bought the coöperation of the western country by the bribe of the western lands, abandoning to the new Western States their own proportion of the public property and aiding them in the design of grasping all the lands into their own hands...."

"No subject," said Henry Clay, "which has presented itself to the present, or perhaps any preceding, Congress, is of greater magnitude than that of the public lands." When we consider the far-reaching effects of the government's land policy upon political, economic, and social aspects of American life, we are disposed to agree with him. But this legislation was framed under frontier influences, and under the lead of Western statesmen like [Thomas H.] Benton and [Andrew] Jackson....

It is safe to say that the legislation with regard to land, tariff, and internal improvements—the American system of the nationalizing Whig party—was conditioned on frontier ideas and needs. But it was not merely in legislative action that the frontier worked against the sectionalism of the coast. The economic and social characteristics of the frontier worked against sectionalism. The men of the frontier had closer resemblances to the Middle region than to either of the other sections....

The Middle region, entered by New York harbor, was an open door to all Europe. The tide-water part of the South represented typical Englishmen, modified by a warm climate and servile labor, and living in baronial fashion on great plantations; New England stood for a special English movement—Puritanism. The Middle region was less English than the other sections. It had a wide mixture of nationalities, a varied society, the mixed town and county system of local government, a varied economic life, many religious sects.... It represented that composite nationality which the contemporary United States exhibits, that juxtaposition of non-English groups, occupying a valley or a little settlement, and presenting reflections of the map of Europe in their variety. It was democratic and nonsectional, if not national; "easy, tolerant, and contented;" rooted strongly in material prosperity. It was typical of the modern United States. It was least sectional, not only because it lay between North and South, but also because with no barriers to shut out its frontiers from its settled region, and with a system of connecting waterways, the Middle region mediated between East and West as well as between North and South. Thus it became the typically American region....

It was this nationalizing tendency of the West that transformed the democracy of Jefferson into the national republicanism of Monroe and the democracy of Andrew Jackson. The West of the War of 1812, the West of Clay, and Benton and Harrison, and Andrew Jackson, shut off by the Middle States and the mountains from the coast sections, had a solidarity of its own with national tendencies. On the tide of the Father of Waters, North and South met and mingled into a nation. Interstate migration went steadily on—a process of cross-fertilization of ideas and institutions. The fierce struggle of the sections over slavery on the western frontier does not diminish the truth of this statement; it proves the truth of it. Slavery was a sectional trait that would not down, but in the West it could not remain sectional. It was the greatest of frontiersmen who declared: "I believe this Government can not endure permanently half slave and half free. It will become all of one thing or all of the other." Nothing works for nationalism like intercourse within the nation. Mobility of population is death to localism, and the western frontier worked irresistibly in unsettling population. The effect reached back from the frontier and affected profoundly the Atlantic coast and even the Old World.

But the most important effect of the frontier has been in the promotion of democracy here and in Europe. As has been indicated, the frontier is productive of individualism. Complex society is precipitated by the wilderness into a kind of primitive organization based on the family. The tendency is anti-social. It produces antipathy to control, and particularly to any direct control. The tax-gatherer is viewed as a representative of oppression. Professor [Herbert L.] Osgood...has pointed out that the frontier conditions prevalent in the colonies are important factors in the explanation of the American Revolution, where individual liberty was sometimes confused with absence of all effective government. The same conditions aid in explaining the difficulty of instituting a strong government in the period of the confederacy. The frontier individualism has from the beginning promoted democracy.

The frontier States that came into the Union in the first quarter of a century of its existence came in with democratic suffrage provisions, and had reactive effects of the highest importance upon the older States whose peoples were being attracted there. An extension of the franchise became essential. It was *western* New York that forced an extension of suffrage in the constitutional convention of that State in 1821; and it was *western* Virginia that compelled the tide-water region to put a more liberal suffrage provision in the constitution framed in 1830, and to give to the frontier region a more nearly proportionate representation with the tide-water aristocracy. The rise of democracy as an effective force in the nation came in with western preponderance under Jackson and William Henry Harrison, and it meant the triumph of the frontier—with all of its good and with all of its evil elements....

So long as free land exists, the opportunity for a competency exists, and economic power secures political power. But the democracy born of free land, strong in selfishness and individualism, intolerant of administrative experience and education, and pressing individual liberty beyond its proper bounds, has its dangers as well as its benefits. Individualism in America has allowed a laxity in regard to governmental affairs which has rendered possible the spoils system and all the manifest evils that follow from the lack of a highly developed civic spirit. In this connection may be noted also the influence of frontier conditions in permitting lax business honor, inflated paper currency and wild-cat banking. The colonial and revolutionary frontier was the region whence emanated many of the worst forms of an evil currency. The West in the War of 1812 repeated the phenomenon on the frontier of that day, while the speculation and wild-cat banking of the period of the crisis of 1837 occurred on the new frontier belt of the next tier of States. Thus each one of the periods of lax financial integrity coincides with periods when a new set of frontier communities had arisen, and coincides in area with these successive frontiers, for the most part. The recent Populist agitation is a case in point.... A primitive society can hardly be expected to show the intelligent appreciation of the complexity of business interests in a developed society....

The East has always feared the result of an unregulated advance of the frontier, and has tried to check and guide it. The English authorities would have checked settlement at the headwaters of the Atlantic tributaries and allowed the "savages to enjoy their deserts in quiet lest the peltry trade should decrease."...

But the English Government was not alone in its desire to limit the advance of the frontier and guide its destinies. Tide-water Virginia and South Carolina gerrymandered those colonies to insure the dominance of the coast in their legislatures.... Jefferson would reserve from settlement the territory of his Louisiana Purchase north of the thirty-second parallel, in order to offer it to the Indians in exchange for their settlements east of the Mississippi. "When we shall be full on this side," he writes, "we may lay off a range of States on the western bank from the head to the mouth, and so range after range, advancing compactly as we multiply." Madison went so far as to argue to the French minister that the United States had no interest in seeing population extend itself on the right bank of the Mississippi, but should rather fear it.... Even Thomas Benton, the man of widest views of the destiny of the West, at this stage of his career declared that along the ridge of the Rocky Mountains "the western limits of the Republic should be drawn, and the statue of the fabled god Terminus should be raised upon its highest peak, never to be thrown down." But the attempts to limit the boundaries, to restrict land sales and settlement, and to deprive the West of its share of political power were all in vain. Steadily the frontier of settlement advanced and carried with it individualism, democracy, and nationalism, and powerfully affected the East and the Old World.

The most effective efforts of the East to regulate the frontier came through its educational and religious activity, exerted by interstate migration and by organized societies. Speaking in 1835, Dr. Lyman Beecher declared: "It is equally plain that the religious and political destiny of our nation is to be decided in the West," and he pointed out that the population of the West "is assembled from all the States of the Union and from all the nations of Europe, and is rushing in like the waters of the flood, demanding for its moral preservation the immediate and universal action of those institutions which discipline the mind and arm the conscience and the heart. And so various are the opinions and habits,...and so sparse are the settlements of the West, that no homogeneous public sentiment can be formed to legislate immediately into being the requisite institutions. And yet they are all needed immediately in their utmost perfection and power. A nation is being 'born in a day.'... But what will become of the West if her prosperity rushes up to such a majesty of power, while those great institutions linger which are necessary to form the mind and the conscience and the heart of that vast world? It must not be permitted.... Let no man at the East quiet himself and dream of liberty, whatever may become of the West.... Her destiny is our destiny."

...The New England preacher and school-teacher left their mark on the West. The dread of Western emancipation from New England's political and economic control was paralleled by her fears lest the West cut loose from her religion. Commenting in 1850 on reports that settlement was rapidly extending northward in Wisconsin, the editor of the *Home Missionary* writes: "We scarcely know whether to rejoice or mourn over this extension of our settlements. While we sympathize in whatever tends to increase the physical resources and prosperity of our country, we can not forget that with all these dispersions into remote and still remoter corners of the land the supply of the means of grace is becoming relatively less and less." Acting in accordance

with such ideas, home missions were established and Western colleges were erected. As seaboard cities like Philadelphia, New York, and Baltimore strove for the mastery of Western trade, so the various denominations strove for the possession of the West. Thus an intellectual stream from New England sources fertilized the West. Other sections sent their missionaries; but the real struggle was between sects. The contest for power and the expansive tendency furnished to the various sects by the existence of a moving frontier must have had important results on the character of religious organization in the United States. The multiplication of rival churches in the little frontier towns had deep and lasting social effects....

From the conditions of frontier life came intellectual traits of profound importance. The works of travelers along each frontier from colonial days onward describe certain common traits, and these traits have, while softening down, still persisted as survivals in the place of their origin, even when a higher social organization succeeded. The result is that to the frontier the American intellect owes its striking characteristics. That coarseness and strength combined with acuteness and inquisitiveness; that practical, inventive turn of mind, quick to find expedients; that masterful grasp of material things, lacking in the artistic but powerful to effect great ends; that restless, nervous energy; that dominant individualism, working for good and for evil, and withal that buoyancy and exuberance which comes with freedom—these are traits of the frontier, or traits called out elsewhere because of the existence of the frontier. Since the days when the fleet of Columbus sailed into the waters of the New World, America has been another name for opportunity, and the people of the United States have taken their tone from the incessant expansion which has not only been open but has even been forced upon them. He would be a rash prophet who should assert that the expansive character of American life has now entirely ceased. Movement has been its dominant fact, and, unless this training has no effect upon a people, the American energy will continually demand a wider field for its exercise. But never again will such gifts of free land offer themselves. For a moment, at the frontier, the bonds of custom are broken and unrestraint is triumphant. There is not *tabula rasa*. The stubborn American environment is there with its imperious summons to accept its conditions; the inherited ways of doing things are also there; and yet, in spite of environment, and in spite of custom, each frontier did indeed furnish a new field of opportunity, a gate of escape from the bondage of the past; and freshness, and confidence, and scorn of older society, impatience of its restraints and its ideas, and indifference to its lessons, have accompanied the frontier. What the Mediterranean Sea was to the Greeks, breaking the bond of custom, offering new experiences, calling out new institutions and activities, that, and more, the ever retreating frontier has been to the United States directly, and to the nations of Europe more remotely. And now, four centuries from the discovery of America, at the end of a hundred years of life under the Constitution, the frontier has gone, and with its going has closed the first period of American history.

7

Atlanta Exposition Address (1895)

B O O K E R   T .   W A S H I N G T O N

In 1895, Booker T. Washington was the President of the Tuskegee Normal and Industrial Institute, a school in Alabama dedicated to providing vocational training to African-Americans. In September of that year, Washington spoke before the Cotton States and International Exposition in Atlanta. The fair's organizers hoped to win respectability for the concept of the "New South," a South with racism subsumed in a larger pursuit of economic success. Georgia's former governor, Rufus Bullock, introduced Washington, who had been born a slave, as "a representative of Negro enterprise and Negro civilization." Washington's short speech, with its promise of racial accommodation was an enormous success, immediately elevating Washington to a nationally recognized leader of black Americans.

Questions to Consider

- What did Washington hope that African-Americans would gain by abandoning their long-standing insistence on equal rights?
- Why did his position not provoke anger from other black leaders and inspire relief among white leaders?

Mr. President and Gentlemen of the Board of Directors and Citizens

One-third of the population of the South is of the Negro race. No enterprise seeking the material, civil, or moral welfare of this section can disregard this element of our population and reach the highest success. I but convey to you, Mr. President and Directors, the sentiment of the masses of my race when I say that in no way have the value and manhood of the American Negro been more fittingly and generously recognized than by the managers of this magnificent Exposition at every stage of its progress. It is a recognition that will do more to cement the friendship of the two races than any occurrence since the dawn of our freedom.

Not only this, but the opportunity here afforded will awaken among us a new era of industrial progress. Ignorant and inexperienced, it is not strange that in the first years of our new life we began at the top instead of at the bottom; that a seat in Congress or the state legis-

Source: Booker T. Washington, *Up from Slavery* (New York, 1901), pp. 218–225.

lature was more sought than real estate or industrial skill; that the political convention or stump speaking had more attractions than starting a dairy farm or truck garden.

A ship lost at sea for many days suddenly sighted a friendly vessel. From the mast of the unfortunate vessel was seen a signal, "Water, water; we die of thirst!" The answer from the friendly vessel at once came back, "Cast down your bucket where you are." A second time the signal, "Water, water; send us water!" ran up from the distressed vessel, and was answered, "Cast down your bucket where you are." And a third and fourth signal for water was answered, "Cast down your bucket where you are." The captain of the distressed vessel, at last heeding the injunction, cast down his bucket, and it came up full of fresh, sparkling water from the mouth of the Amazon River. To those of my race who depend on bettering their condition in a foreign land or who underestimate the importance of cultivating friendly relations with the Southern white man, who is their next-door neighbour, I would say: "Cast down your bucket where you are"—cast it down in making friends in every manly way of the people of all races by whom we are surrounded.

Cast it down in agriculture, mechanics, in commerce, in domestic service, and in the professions. And in this connection it is well to bear in mind that whatever other sins the South may be called to bear, when it comes to business, pure and simple, it is in the South that the Negro is given a man's chance in the commercial world, and in nothing is this Exposition more eloquent than in emphasizing this chance. Our greatest danger is that in the great leap from slavery to freedom we may overlook the fact that the masses of us are to live by the productions of our hands, and fail to keep in mind that we shall prosper in proportion as we learn to dignify and glorify common labour and put brains and skill into the common occupations of life; shall prosper in proportion as we learn to draw the line between the superficial and the substantial, the ornamental gewgaws of life and the useful. No race can prosper till it learns that there is as much dignity in tilling a field as in writing a poem. It is at the bottom of life we must begin, and not at the top. Nor should we permit our grievances to overshadow our opportunities.

To those of the white race who look to the incoming of those of foreign birth and strange tongue and habits for the prosperity of the South, were I permitted I would repeat what I say to my own race, "Cast down your bucket where you are." Cast it down among the eight millions of Negroes whose habits you know, whose fidelity and love you have tested in days when to have proved treacherous meant the ruin of your firesides. Cast down your bucket among these people who have, without strikes and labour wars, tilled your fields, cleared your forests, builded your railroads and cities, and brought forth treasures from the bowels of the earth, and helped make possible this magnificent representation of the progress of the South. Casting down your bucket among my people, helping and encouraging them as you are doing on these grounds, and to education of head, hand, and heart, you will find that they will buy your surplus land, make blossom the waste places in your fields, and run your factories. While doing this, you can be sure in the future, as in the past, that you and your families will be surrounded by the most patient, faithful, law-abiding, and unresentful people that the world has seen. As we have proved our loyalty to you in the past, in nursing your children, watching by the sick-bed of your mothers and fathers, and often following them with tear-dimmed eyes to their graves, so in the future, in our humble way, we shall stand by you with a devotion that no foreigner can approach, ready to lay down our lives, if need be, in defence of yours, interlacing our industrial, commercial, civil, and religious life with yours in a way that shall make the interests of both races one. In all things that are purely social we can be as separate as the fingers, yet one as the hand in all things essential to mutual progress.

There is no defence or security for any of us except in the highest intelligence and development of all. If anywhere there are efforts tending to curtail the fullest growth of the Negro, let these efforts be turned into stimulating, encouraging, and making him the most useful and intelligent citizen. Effort or means so invested will pay a thousand per cent interest. These efforts will be twice blessed—"blessing him that gives and him that takes."

There is no escape through law of man or God from the inevitable:—

> The laws of changeless justice bind
>   Oppressor with oppressed;
> And close as sin and suffering joined
>   We march to fate abreast.

Nearly sixteen millions of hands will aid you in pulling the load upward, or they will pull against you the load downward. We shall constitute one-third and more of the ignorance and crime of the South, or one-third its intelligence and progress; we shall contribute one-third to the business and industrial prosperity of the South, or we shall prove a veritable body of death, stagnating, depressing, retarding every effort to advance the body politic.

Gentlemen of the Exposition, as we present to you our humble effort at an exhibition of our progress, you must not expect overmuch. Starting thirty years ago with ownership here and there in a few quilts and pumpkins and chickens (gathered from miscellaneous sources), remember the path that has led from these to the inventions and production of agricultural implements, buggies, steam-engines, newspapers, books, statuary, carving, paintings, the management of drugstores and banks, has not been trodden without contact with thorns and thistles. While we take pride in what we exhibit as a result of our independent efforts, we do not for a moment forget that our part in this exhibition would fall far short of your expectations but for the constant help that has come to our educational life, not only from the Southern states, but especially from Northern philanthropists, who have made their gifts a constant stream of blessing and encouragement.

The wisest among my race understand that the agitation of questions of social equality is the extremest folly, and that progress in the enjoyment of all the privileges that will come to us must be the result of severe and constant struggle rather than of artificial forcing. No race that has anything to contribute to the markets of the world is long in any degree ostracized. It is important and right that all privileges of the law be ours, but it is vastly more important that we be prepared for the exercises of these privileges. The opportunity to earn a dollar in a factory just now is worth infinitely more than the opportunity to spend a dollar in an opera-house.

In conclusion, may I repeat that nothing in thirty years has given us more hope and encouragement, and drawn us so near to you of the white race, as this opportunity offered by the Exposition; and here bending, as it were, over the altar that represents the results of the struggles of your race and mine, both starting practically empty-handed three decades ago, I pledge that in your effort to work out the great and intricate problem which God has laid at the doors of the South, you shall have at all times the patient, sympathetic help of my race; only let this be constantly in mind, that, while from representations in these buildings of the product of field, of forest, of mine, of factory, letters, and art, much good will come, yet far above and beyond material benefits will be that higher good, that, let us pray God, will come, in a blotting out of sectional differences and racial animosities and suspicions, in a determination to administer absolute justice, in a willing obedience among all classes to the mandates of law. This, this, coupled with our material prosperity, will bring into our beloved South a new heaven and a new earth.

8

Plessy v. Ferguson (1896)

U.S. SUPREME COURT

The segregation of the races has a long history in the United States. But in the years after the failure of Reconstruction, Southern state governments passed a series of laws seeking to institutionalize a permanent and precise segregation of the races. Homer Plessy, a citizen of Louisiana, was understood to be one-eighth black and seven-eighths white. In the eyes of the law he was therefore black and not allowed to mingle with white citizens on public transportation. To Plessy and his attorney the case was simple: the Fourteenth Amendment to the Constitution recognized the right of all persons to the equal protection of the law. The Supreme Court, with one exception, failed to appreciate that reasoning. John Marshall Harlan's dissent remains one of the most cogent and meaningful ever registered by a justice. In the aftermath of the Plessy decision, state governments felt justified in extending segregation to nearly every corner of American life.

Questions to Consider

- How does the Court reconcile segregation and the guarantee of equality before the law?
- What does the Court think would be the consequences of segregation?
- What does Justice Harlan mean when he speaks of the Constitution being "color-blind"?

Mr. Justice Brown, after stating the case, delivered the opinion of the court.

This case turns upon the constitutionality of an act of the General Assembly of the State of Louisiana, passed in 1890, providing for separate railway carriages for the white and colored races....

The first section of the statute enacts "that all railway companies carrying passengers in their coaches in this State, shall provide equal but separate accommodations for the white, and colored races, by providing two or more passenger coaches for each passenger train, or by dividing the passenger coaches by a partition so as to secure separate accommodations: *Provided,* That this section shall not be construed to apply to street railroads. No person or persons, shall be admitted to occupy seats in coaches, other than, the ones, assigned, to them on account of the race they belong to."

By the second section it was enacted "that the officers of such passenger trains shall have power and are hereby required to assign each passenger to the coach or compartment used for the race to which such passenger belongs; any passenger insisting on going into a coach or compartment to which by race he does not belong, shall be liable to a fine of twenty-five dollars, or in lieu thereof to imprisonment for a period of not more than twenty days in the parish prison...."

The third section provides...that "nothing in this act shall be construed as applying to nurses attending children of the other race." The fourth section is immaterial.

The information filed in the criminal District Court charged in substance that Plessy, being a passenger between two stations within the State Louisiana, was assigned by officers of the company to the coach used for the race to which he belonged, but he insisted upon going into a coach used by the race to which he did not belong. Neither in the information nor plea was his particular race or color averred.

The petition for the writ of prohibition averred that petitioner was seven eighths Caucasian and one eighth African blood; that the mixture of colored blood was

not discernible in him, and that he was entitled to every right, privilege and immunity secured to citizens of the United States of the white race; and that, upon such theory, he took possession of a vacant seat in a coach where passengers of the white race were accommodated, and was ordered by the conductor to vacate said coach and take a seat in another assigned to persons of the colored race, and having refused to comply with such demand he was forcibly ejected with the aid of a police officer, and imprisoned in the parish jail to answer a charge of having violated the above act.

The constitutionality of this act is attacked upon the ground that it conflicts both with the Thirteenth Amendment of the Constitution, abolishing slavery, and the Fourteenth Amendment, which prohibits certain restrictive legislation on the part of the States.

1. That it does not conflict with the Thirteenth Amendment, which abolished slavery and involuntary servitude, except as a punishment for crime, is too clear for argument. Slavery implies involuntary servitude—a state of bondage; the ownership of mankind as a chattel, or at least the control of the labor and services of one man for the benefit of another, and the absence of a legal right to the disposal of his own person, property and services....

A statute which implies merely a legal distinction between the white and colored races—a distinction which is founded in the color of the two races, and which must always exist so long as white men are distinguished from the other race by color—has no tendency to destroy the legal equality of the two races, or reëstablish a state of involuntary servitude. Indeed, we do not understand that the Thirteenth Amendment is strenuously relied upon by the plaintiff in error in this connection.

2. ...The proper construction of [the Fourteenth] amendment was first called to the attention of this court in the *Slaughter-house cases,* 16 Wall. 36, which involved, however, not a question of race, but one of exclusive privileges. The case did not call for any expression of opinion as to the exact rights it was intended to secure to the colored race, but it was said generally that its main purpose was to establish the citizenship of the negro; to give definitions of citizenship of the United States and of the States, and to protect from the hostile legislation of the States the privileges and immunities of

Source: 163 *U.S. Reports* (Washington, D. C., 1896), pp. 537–564.

citizens of the United States, as distinguished from those of citizens of the States.

The object of the amendment was undoubtedly to enforce the absolute equality of the two races before the law, but in the nature of things it could not have been intended to abolish distinctions based upon color, or to enforce social, as distinguished from political equality, or a commingling of the two races upon terms unsatisfactory to either. Laws permitting, and even requiring, their separation in places where they are liable to be brought into contact do not necessarily imply the inferiority of either race to the other, and have been generally, if not universally, recognized as within the competency of the state legislatures in the exercise of their police power. The most common instance of this is connected with the establishment of separate schools for white and colored children, which has been held to be a valid exercise of the legislative power even by courts of States where the political rights of the colored race have been longest and most earnestly enforced....

Laws forbidding the intermarriage of the two races may be said in a technical sense to interfere with the freedom of contract, and yet have been universally recognized as within the police power of the State....

The distinction between laws interfering with the political equality of the negro and those requiring the separation of the two races in schools, theatres and railway carriages has been frequently drawn by this court. Thus in *Strauder* v. *West Virginia*, 100 U. S. 303, it was held that a law of West Virginia limiting to white male persons, 21 years of age and citizens of the State, the right to sit upon juries, was a discrimination which implied a legal inferiority in civil society, which lessened the security of the right of the colored race, and was a step toward reducing them to a condition of servility....

While we think the enforced separation of the races, as applied to the internal commerce of the State, neither abridges the privileges or immunities of the colored man, deprives him of his property without due process of law, nor denies him the equal protection of the laws, within the meaning of the Fourteenth Amendment, we are not prepared to say that the conductor, in assigning passengers to the coaches according to their race, does not act at his peril, or that the provision of the second section of the act, that denies to the passenger compensation in damages for a refusal to receive him into the coach in which he properly belongs, is a valid exercise of the legislative power. Indeed, we understand it to be conceded by the State's attorney, that such part of the act as exempts from liability the railway company and its officers is unconstitutional. The power to assign to a particular coach obviously implies the power to determine to which race the passenger belongs, as well as the power to determine who, under the laws of the particular State, is to be deemed a white, and who a colored

person. This question, though indicated in the brief of the plaintiff in error, does not properly arise upon the record in this case, since the only issue made is as to the unconstitutionality of the act, so far as it requires the railway to provide separate accommodations, and the conductor to assign passengers according to their race.

It is claimed by the plaintiff in error that, in any mixed community, the reputation of belonging to the dominant race, in this instance the white race, is *property*, in the same sense that a right of action, or of inheritance, is property. Conceding this to be so, for the purposes of this case, we are unable to see how this statute deprives him of, or in any way affects his right to, such property. If he be a white man and assigned to a colored coach, he may have his action for damages against the company for being deprived of his so called property. Upon the other hand, if he be a colored man and be so assigned, he has been deprived of no property, since he is not lawfully entitled to the reputation of being a white man.

In this connection, it is also suggested by the learned counsel for the plaintiff in error that the same argument that will justify the state legislature in requiring railways to provide separate accommodations for the two races will also authorize them to require separate cars to be provided for people whose hair is of a certain color, or who are aliens, or who belong to certain nationalities, or to enact laws requiring colored people to walk upon one side of the street, and white people upon the other, or requiring white men's houses to be painted white, and colored men's black, or their vehicles or business signs to be of different colors, upon the theory that one side of the street is as good as the other, or that a house or vehicle of one color is as good as one of another color. The reply to all this is that every exercise of the police power must be reasonable, and extend only to such laws as are enacted in good faith for the promotion for the public good, and not for the annoyance or oppression of a particular class....

So far, then, as a conflict with the Fourteenth Amendment is concerned, the case reduces itself to the question whether the statute of Louisiana is a reasonable regulation, and with respect to this there must necessarily be a large discretion on the part of the legislature. In determining the question of reasonableness it is at liberty to act with reference to the established usages, customs and traditions of the people, and with a view to the promotion of their comfort, and the preservation of the public peace and good order. Gauged by this standard, we cannot say that a law which authorizes or even requires the separation of the two races in public conveyances is unreasonable, or more obnoxious to the Fourteenth Amendment than the acts of Congress requiring separate schools for colored children in the District of Columbia, the constitutionality of which does not seem to have been questioned, or the corresponding acts of state legislatures.

We consider the underlying fallacy of the plaintiff's argument to consist in the assumption that the enforced separation of the two races stamps the colored race with a badge of inferiority. If this be so, it is not by reason of anything found in the act, but solely because the colored race chooses to put that construction upon it. The argument necessarily assumes that if, as has been more than once the case, and is not unlikely to be so again, the colored race should become the dominant power in the state legislature, and should enact a law in precisely similar terms, it would thereby relegate the white race to an inferior position. We imagine that the white race, at least, would not acquiesce in this assumption. The argument also assumes that social prejudices may be overcome by legislation, and that equal rights cannot be secured to the negro except by an enforced commingling of the two races. We cannot accept this proposition. If the two races are to meet upon terms of social equality, it must be the result of natural affinities, a mutual appreciation of each other's merits and a voluntary consent of individuals. As was said by the Court of Appeals of New York in *People v. Gallagher,* 93 N. Y. 438, 448, "this end can neither be accomplished nor promoted by laws which conflict with the general sentiment of the community upon whom they are designed to operate. When the government, therefore, has secured to each of its citizens equal rights before the law and equal opportunities for improvement and progress, it has accomplished the end for which it was organized and performed all of the functions respecting social advantages with which it is endowed." Legislation is powerless to eradicate racial instincts or to abolish distinctions based upon physical differences, and the attempt to do so can only result in accentuating the difficulties of the present situation. If the civil and political rights of both races be equal one cannot be inferior to the other civilly or politically. If one race be inferior to the other socially, the Constitution of the United States cannot put them upon the same plane.

It is true that the question of the proportion of colored blood necessary to constitute a colored person, as distinguished from a white person, is one upon which there is a difference of opinion in the different States, some holding that any visible admixture of black blood stamps the person as belonging to the colored race,...others that it depends upon the preponderance of blood,...and still others that the predominance of white blood must only be in the proportion of three fourths.... But these are questions to be determined under the laws of each State and are not properly put in issue in this case. Under the allegations of his petition it may undoubtedly become a question of importance

whether, under the laws of Louisiana, the petitioner belongs to the white or colored race.

The judgment of the court below is, therefore,

Affirmed.

Mr. Justice Harlan dissenting.

By the Louisiana statute,...[o]nly "nurses attending children of the other race" are excepted from the operation of the statute. No exception is made of colored attendants travelling with adults.... If a colored maid insists upon riding in the same coach with a white woman whom she has been employed to serve, and who may need her personal attention while travelling, she is subject to be fined or imprisoned for such an exhibition of zeal in the discharge of duty.

...[W]e have before us a state enactment that compels, under penalties, the separation of the two races in railroad passenger coaches, and makes it a crime for a citizen of either race to enter a coach that has been assigned to citizens of the other race.

Thus the State regulates the use of a public highway by citizens of the United States solely upon the basis of race.

However apparent the injustice of such legislation may be, we have only to consider whether it is consistent with the Constitution of the United States.

That a railroad is a public highway, and that the corporation which owns or operates it is in the exercise of public functions, is not, at this day, to be disputed. Mr. Justice Nelson, speaking for this court in *New Jersey Steam Navigation Co.* v. *Merchants' Bank,* 6 How. 344, 382, said that a common carrier was in the exercise "of a sort of public office, and has public duties to perform, from which he should not be permitted to exonerate himself without the assent of the parties concerned."...

In respect of civil rights, common to all citizens, the Constitution of the United States does not, I think, permit any public authority to know the race of those entitled to be protected in the enjoyment of such rights. Every true man has pride of race, and under appropriate circumstances when the rights of others, his equals before the law, are not to be affected, it is his privilege to express such pride and to take such action based upon it as to him seems proper. But I deny that any legislative body or judicial tribunal may have regard to the race of citizens when the civil rights of those citizens are involved. Indeed such legislation, as that here in question, is inconsistent not only with that equality of rights which pertains to citizenship, National and State, but with the personal liberty enjoyed by every one within the United States.

The Thirteenth Amendment does not permit the withholding or the deprivation of any right necessarily inhering in freedom. It not only struck down the institution of slavery as previously existing in the United States, but it prevents the imposition of any burdens or disabilities that constitute badges of slavery or servitude. It decreed universal civil freedom in this country. This court has so adjudged. But that amendment having been found inadequate to the protection of the rights of those who had been in slavery, it was followed by the Fourteenth Amendment, which added greatly to the dignity and glory of American citizenship, and to the security of personal liberty.... These two amendments, if enforced according to their true intent and meaning, will protect all the civil rights that pertain to freedom and citizenship....

These notable additions to the fundamental law were welcomed by the friends of liberty throughout the world. They removed the race line from our governmental systems. They had, as this court has said, a common purpose, namely, to secure "to a race recently emancipated, a race that through many generations have been held in slavery, all the civil rights that the superior race enjoy." They declared, in legal effect, this court has further said, "that the law in the States shall be the same for the black as for the white; that all persons, whether colored or white, shall stand equal before the laws of the States, and, in regard to the colored race, for whose protection the amendment was primarily designed, that no discrimination shall be made against them by law because of their color."...

It was said in argument that the statute of Louisiana does not discriminate against either race, but prescribes a rule applicable alike to white and colored citizens. But this argument does not meet the difficulty. Every one knows that the statute in question had its origin in the purpose, not so much to exclude white persons from railroad cars occupied by blacks, as to exclude colored people from coaches occupied by or assigned to white persons.... The fundamental objection, therefore, to the statute is that it interferes with the personal freedom of citizens.... If a white man and a black man choose to occupy the same public conveyance on a public highway, it is their right to do so, and no government, proceeding alone on grounds of race, can prevent it without infringing the personal liberty of each.

It is one thing for railroad carriers to furnish, or to be required by law to furnish, equal accommodations for all whom they are under a legal duty to carry. It is quite another thing for government to forbid citizens of the white and black races from travelling in the same public conveyance, and to punish officers of railroad companies for permitting persons of the two races to occupy the same passenger coach. If a State can prescribe, as a rule of civil conduct, that whites and blacks shall not travel as passengers in the same railroad coach, why may it not so regulate the use of the streets of its cities and towns as to compel white citizens to keep on one side of a street and black citizens to keep on the other? Why may it not, upon like grounds, punish whites and blacks who ride together in street cars or in open vehicles on a public road or street? Why may it not require sheriffs to assign whites to one side of a court-room and blacks to the other? And why may it not also prohibit the commingling of the two races in the galleries of legislative halls or in public assemblages convened for the consideration of the political questions of the day? Further, if this statute of Louisiana is consistent with the personal liberty of citizens, why may not the State require the separation in railroad coaches of native and naturalized citizens of the United States, or of Protestants and Roman Catholics?

The answer given at the argument to these questions was that regulations of the kind they suggest would be unreasonable, and could not, therefore, stand before the law. Is it meant that the determination of questions of legislative power depends upon the inquiry whether the statute whose validity is questioned is, in the judgment of the courts, a reasonable one, taking all the circumstances into consideration? A statute may be unreasonable merely because a sound public policy forbade its enactment. But I do not understand that the courts have anything to do with the policy or expediency of legislation. A statute may be valid, and yet, upon grounds of public policy, may well be characterized as unreasonable....

The white race deems itself to be the dominant race in this country. And so it is, in prestige, in achievements, in education, in wealth and in power. So, I doubt not, it will continue to be for all time, if it remains true to its great heritage and holds fast to the principles of constitutional liberty. But in view of the Constitution, in the eye of the law, there is in this country no superior, dominant, ruling class of citizens. There is no caste here. Our Constitution is color-blind, and neither knows nor tolerates classes among citizens. In respect of civil rights, all citizens are equal before the law. The humblest is the peer of the most powerful. The land regards man as man, and takes no account of his surroundings or of his color when his civil rights as guaranteed by the supreme law of the land are involved. It is, therefore, to be regretted that this high tribunal, the final expositor of the fundamental law of the land, has reached the conclusion that it is competent for a State to regulate the enjoyment by citizens of their civil rights solely upon the basis of race.

In my opinion, the judgment this day rendered will, in time, prove to be quite as pernicious as the decision made by this tribunal in the *Dred Scott case*.... The recent amendments of the Constitution, it was supposed, had eradicated these principles from our institutions. But it seems that we have yet, in some of the States, a dominant race—a superior class of citizens, which assumes to regulate the enjoyment of civil rights, common to all citizens, upon the basis of race. The present decision, it may well be apprehended, will not only stimulate aggressions, more or less brutal and irritating, upon the admitted rights of colored citizens, but will encourage the belief that it is possible, by means of state enactments, to defeat the beneficent purposes which the people of the United States had in view when they adopted the recent amendments of the Constitution, by one of which the blacks of this country were made citizens of the United States and of the States in which they respectively reside, and whose privileges and immunities, as citizens, the States are forbidden to abridge. Sixty millions of whites are in no danger from the presence here of eight millions of blacks. The destinies of the two races, in this country, are indissolubly linked together, and the interests of both require that the common government of all shall not permit the seeds of race hate to be planted under the sanction of law. What can more certainly arouse race hate, what more certainly create and perpetuate a feeling of distrust between these races, than state enactments, which, in fact, proceed on the ground that colored citizens are so inferior and degraded that they cannot be allowed to sit in public coaches occupied by white citizens? That, as all will admit, is the real meaning of such legislation as was enacted in Louisiana.

The sure guarantee of the peace and security of each race is the clear, distinct, unconditional recognition by our governments, National and State, of every right that inheres in civil freedom, and of the equality before the law of all citizens of the United States without regard to race. State enactments, regulating the enjoyment of civil rights, upon the basis of race, and cunningly devised to defeat legitimate results of the war, under the pretence of recognizing equality of rights, can have no other result than to render permanent peace impossible, and to keep alive a conflict of races, the continuance of which must do harm to all concerned. This question is not met by the suggestion that social equality cannot exist between the white and black races in this country. That argument, if it can be properly regarded as one, is scarcely worthy of consideration....

There is a race so different from our own that we do not permit those belonging to it to become citizens of the United States. Persons belonging to it are, with few exceptions, absolutely excluded from our country. I allude to the Chinese race. But by the statute in question, a Chinaman can ride in the same passenger coach with white citizens of the United States, while citizens of the black race in Louisiana, many of whom, perhaps, risked their lives for the preservation of the Union, who are entitled, by law, to participate in the political control of the State and nation, who are not excluded, by law or by reason of their race, from public stations of any kind, and who have all the legal rights that belong to white citizens, are yet declared to be criminals, liable to imprisonment, if they ride in a public coach occupied by citizens of the white race. It is scarcely just to say that a colored citizen should not object to occupying a public coach assigned to his own race. He does not object, nor, perhaps, would he object to separate coaches for his race, if his rights under the law were recognized. But he objects, and ought never to cease objecting to the proposition, that citizens of the white and black races can be adjudged criminals because they sit, or claim the right to sit, in the same public coach on a public highway.

The arbitrary separation of citizens, on the basis of race, while they are on a public highway, is a badge of servitude wholly inconsistent with the civil freedom and the equality before the law established by the Constitution. It cannot be justified upon any legal grounds.

If evils will result from the commingling of the two races upon public highways established for the benefit of all, they will be infinitely less than those that will surely come from state legislation regulating the enjoyment of civil rights upon the basis of race. We boast of the freedom enjoyed by our people above all other peoples. But it is difficult to reconcile that boast with a state of the law which, practically, puts the brand of servitude and degradation upon a large class of our fellow-citizens, our equals before the law. The thin disguise of "equal" accommodations for passengers in railroad coaches will not mislead any one, nor atone for the wrong this day done....

I do not deem it necessary to review the decisions of state courts to which reference was made in argument. Some, and the most important, of them are wholly inapplicable, because rendered prior to the adoption of the last amendments of the Constitution, when colored people had very few rights which the dominant race felt obliged to respect. Others were made at a time when public opinion, in many localities, was dominated by the institution of slavery; when it would not have been safe to do justice to the black man; and when, so far as the rights of blacks were concerned, race prejudice was, practically, the supreme law of the land. Those decisions cannot be guides in the era introduced by the recent amendments of the supreme law, which established universal civil freedom, gave citizenship to all born or naturalized in the United States and residing here, obliterated the race line from our systems of governments, National and State, and placed our free institutions upon the broad and sure foundation of the equality of all men before the law.

I am of opinion that the statute of Louisiana is inconsistent with the personal liberty of citizens, white and black, in that State, and hostile to both the spirit and letter of the Constitution of the United States. If laws of like character should be enacted in the several States of the Union, the effect would be in the highest degree mischievous. Slavery, as an institution tolerated by law would, it is true, have disappeared from our country, but there would remain a power in the States, by sinister legislation, to interfere with the full enjoyment of the blessings of freedom; to regulate civil rights, common to all citizens, upon the basis of race; and to place in a condition of legal inferiority a large body of American citizens, now constituting a part of the political community called the People of the United States, for whom, and by whom through representatives, our government is administered. Such a system is inconsistent with the guarantee given by the Constitution to each State of a republican form of government, and may be stricken down by Congressional action, or by the courts in the discharge of their solemn duty to maintain the supreme law of the land, anything in the constitution or laws of any State to the contrary notwithstanding.

For the reasons stated, I am constrained to withhold my assent from the opinion and judgment of the majority.

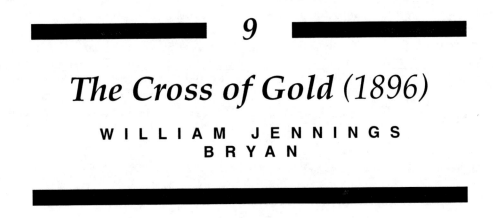

9

The Cross of Gold (1896)

WILLIAM JENNINGS BRYAN

The election of 1896 hinged largely on the question of currency. The Republicans insisted on the gold standard, while the Democrats were leaning toward bimetallism (gold and silver) when they met in Chicago in July. The last speaker on the silver question was a thirty-six-year-old former representative from Nebraska, William Jennings Bryan. His speech electrified the convention, which burst into sustained cheering and shouting for an hour. The following day Bryan was selected as the Democratic nominee for president. He lost the election to Republican William McKinley.

Questions to Consider

- What difference did it make whether the United States had a gold or a silver standard?
- Why was Bryan's speech so remarkably effective?

The Great Speech That Swept the Convention Like a Cyclone

Mr. Chairman and Gentleman of the Convention: I would be presumptuous, indeed, to present myself against the distinguished gentleman to whom you have listened, if this were but a measuring of ability, but this is not a contest among persons. The humblest citizen in all the land when clad in the armor of a righteous cause is stronger than all the whole hosts of error that they can bring. I come to speak to you in defense of a cause as holy as the cause of liberty, the cause of humanity. [Loud applause.]

When this debate is concluded a motion will be made to lay upon the table the resolution offered in commendation of the Administration, and also the res-

Source: C. M. Stevans, ed., *Bryan and Sewall and the Great Issue of 1896* (New York, 1896), pp. 68–78.

olution in condemnation of the Administration. I shall object to bringing this question down to a level of persons. The individual is an atom: he is born, he acts, he dies, but principles are eternal, and this has been a contest of principle.

Never before in the history of this country has there been witnessed such a contest as that through which we have passed. Never before in the history of American politics has a great issue been fought out as this issue has been by the voters themselves. On the 4th of March, 1895, a few Democrats, most of them members of Congress, issued an address to the Democrats of the nation asserting that the money question was the paramount issue of the hour, asserting also the right of a majority of the Democratic party to control the position of the party on this paramount issue, concluding with the request that all believers in free coinage of silver in the Democratic party should organize and take charge of and control the policy of the Democratic party.

Three months later, at Memphis, an organization was perfected, and the silver Democrats went forth openly and boldly and courageously proclaiming their belief, and declaring that if successful they would crystallize in a platform the declaration which they had made; and then began the conflict with a zeal approaching the zeal which inspired the Crusaders who followed Peter the Hermit. Our silver Democrats went forth from victory unto victory until they are assembled now, not to discuss, not to debate, but to enter the judgment rendered by the plain people of this country. [Applause.]

In this contest brother has been arrayed against brother and father against father. The warmest ties of love and acquaintance and association have been disregarded. Old leaders have been cast aside when they refused to give expression to the sentiments of those whom they would lead, and new leaders have sprung up to give direction to this cause of truth. [Cheers.]

Thus has the contest been waged, and we have assembled here under as binding and solemn instructions as were ever fastened upon the representatives of a people. We do not come as individuals. Why, as individuals we might have been glad to compliment the gentleman from New York [Senator Hill]. But we knew that the people for whom we speak would never be willing to put him in a position where he could thwart the will of the Democratic party. [Cheers.] I say it was not a question of persons; it was a question of principle, and it is not with gladness, my friends, that we find ourselves brought into conflict with those who are now arrayed on the other side.

The gentleman who just preceded [Governor Russell] spoke of the old State of Massachusetts. Let me assure him that not one person in all this convention entertains the least hostility to the people of the State of Massachusetts. [Applause.] But we stand here representing people who are the equals before the law of the largest citizens in the State of Massachusetts. [Applause.] When you come before us and tell us that we shall disturb your business interests, we reply that you have disturbed our business interests by your course. [Great applause and cheering.]

We say to you that you have made too limited in its application the definition of the business man. The man who is employed for wages is as much a business man as his employer. The attorney in a country town is as much a business man as the corporation counsel in a great metropolis. The merchant at the cross-roads store is as much a business man as the merchant of New York. The farmer who goes forth in the morning and toils all day, begins in the spring and toils all summer, and by the application of brain and muscle to the natural resources of this country creates wealth, is as much a business man as the man who goes upon the board of trade and bets upon the price of grain. The miners who go a thousand feet into the earth or climb two thousand feet upon the cliffs and bring forth from their hiding-places the precious metals to be poured in the channels of trade are as much business men as the few financial magnates who in a back room corner the money of the world.

We come to speak for this broader class of business men. Ah, my friends, we say not one word against those who live upon the Atlantic coast; but those hardy pioneers who braved all the dangers of the wilderness, who have made the desert to blossom as the rose— those pioneers away out there, rearing their children near to nature's heart, where they can mingle their voices with the voices of the birds; out there where they have erected schoolhouses for the education of their young, and churches where they praise their Creator, and cemeteries where sleep the ashes of their dead, are as deserving of the consideration of this party as any people in this country. [Great applause.]

It is for these that we speak. We do not come as aggressors. Our war is not a war of conquest. We are fighting in the defense of our homes, our families, and posterity. [Loud applause.] We have petitioned, and our petitions have been scorned. We have entreated, and our entreaties have been disregarded. We have begged and they have mocked, and our calamity came. We beg no longer. We entreat no more. We petition no more. We defy them. [Great applause and confusion in the silver delegations.]

The gentleman from Wisconsin has said he fears a Robespierre. My friend, in this land of the free you need fear no tyrant who will spring up from among the people. What we need is an Andrew Jackson to stand as Jackson stood against the encroachments of aggrandized wealth. [Great applause.]

They tell us that this platform was made to catch votes. We reply to them that changing conditions make new issues; that the principles upon which rests Democracy are as everlasting as the hills, but that they must be applied to new conditions as they arise. Conditions have arisen, and we are attempting to meet those conditions. They tell us that the income tax ought not to be brought in here. That is a new idea. They criticise us for our criticism of the Supreme Court of the United States. My friends, we have not criticised, we have simply called attention to what you know. If you want criticisms, read the dissenting opinions of the court. That will give you criticisms. [Applause.] They say we passed an unconstitutional law. I deny it—the income tax was not unconstitutional when it was passed. It was not unconstitutional when it went before the Supreme Court for the first time. It did not become unconstitutional until one judge changed his mind, and we cannot be expected to know when a judge will change his mind. [Applause, and a voice, "Hit 'em again!"]

The income tax is a just law. It simply intends to put the burdens of government justly upon the backs of the people. I am in favor of an income tax. [Applause.] When I find a man who is not willing to pay his share of the burden of the government which protects him, I find a man who is unworthy to enjoy the blessings of a government like ours. [Applause.] He says that we are opposing the national-bank currency. It is true. If you will read what Thomas Benton said, you will find that he said that in searching history he could find but one parallel to Andrew Jackson. That was Cicero, who destroyed the conspiracies of Catiline and saved Rome. He did for Rome what Jackson did when he destroyed the bank conspiracy and saved America. [Applause.]

We say in our platform that we believe that the right to coin money and issue money is a function of government. We believe it. We believe it is a part of sovereignty, and can no more, with safety, be delegated to private individuals than we could afford to delegate to private individuals the power to make penal statutes or to levy laws for taxation. [Applause.] Mr. Jefferson, who was once regarded as good Democratic authority, seems to have a different opinion from the gentleman who has addressed us on the part of the minority. Those who are opposed to this proposition tell us that the issue of paper money is a function of the bank, and that the Government ought to go out of the banking business. I stand with Jefferson, rather than with them, and tell them, as he did, that the issue of money is a function of the Government, and that the banks ought to go out of the government business.

They complain about the plank which declares against the life tenure in office. They have tried to strain it to mean that which it does not mean. What we oppose in that plank is the life tenure that is being built up in Washington which excludes from participation in the

benefits the humbler members of our society. I cannot dwell longer in my limited time. [Cries of "Go on! Go on!"]

Let me call attention to two or three great things. The gentleman from New York says that he will propose an amendment providing that this change in our laws shall not affect contracts already made. Let me remind him that there is no intention of affecting those contracts, which, according to the present laws, are made payable in gold. But if he means to say that we cannot change our monetary system without protecting those who have loaned money before the change was made, I want to ask him where, in law or in morals, he can find authority for not protecting the debtors, when the act of 1873 was passed, but now insists that we must protect the creditor. He says he also wants to amend this law and provide that if we fail to maintain a parity within a year we will then suspend the coinage of silver. We reply that when we advocate a thing which we believe will be successful we are not compelled to raise a doubt as to our own sincerity by trying to show what we will do if we can. I ask him, if he will apply his logic to us, why does he not apply it to himself? He says that he wants this country to try to secure an international agreement. Why doesn't he tell us what he is going to do if they fail to secure an international agreement? There is more reason for him to do that than for us to fail to maintain the parity. They have tried for thirty years—for thirty years—to secure an international agreement, and those are waiting for it most patiently who don't want it at all. [Cheering and laughter, long continued.]

Now, my friends, let me come to the great paramount issue. If they ask us here why it is that we say more on the money question than we say upon the tariff question, I reply that if protection has slain its thousands, the gold standard has slain its tens of thousands. If they ask us why we did not embody all these things in our platform which we believe, we reply to them that when we have restored the money of the Constitution all other necessary reforms will be possible, and that until that is done there is no reform that can be accomplished. [Cheers.] Why is it that within three months such a change has come over the sentiment of this country? Three months ago, when it was confidently asserted that those who believed in the gold standard would frame our platform and nominate our candidate, even the advocates of the gold standard did not think that we could elect a President, but they had good reason for the suspicion, because there is scarcely a State here to-day asking for the gold standard that is not within the absolute control of the Republican party. [Loud cheering.]

But note the change. Mr. McKinley was nominated at St. Louis upon a platform that declared for the maintenance of the gold standard until it should be changed into bimetallism by an international agreement. Mr. McKinley was the most popular man among the Republicans, and everybody three months ago in the Republican party prophesied his election. How is it to-day? Why, that man who used to boast that he looked like Napoleon [laughter and cheering]—that man shudders to-day when he thinks that he was nominated on the anniversary of the battle of Waterloo. Not only that, but as he listens he can hear with ever-increasing distinctness the sound of the waves as they beat upon the lonely shores of St. Helena. [Cheers.]

Why this change? Ah, my friends, is not the change evident to any one who will look at the matter? It is no private character, however pure, no personal popularity, however great, that can protect from the avenging wrath of an indignant people the man who will either declare that he is in favor of fastening the gold standard upon this people, or who is willing to surrender the right of self-government and place the legislative control in the hands of foreign potentates and powers. [Cheers.]

We go forth confident that we shall win. Why? Because upon the paramount issue in this campaign there is not a spot of ground upon which the enemy will dare to challenge battle. Why, if they tell us that the gold standard is a good thing, we point to their platform and tell them that their platform pledges the party to get rid of a gold standard and substitute bimetallism. [Applause.]

If the gold standard is a good thing, why try to get rid of it? [Laughter and continued applause.] If the gold standard—and I might call your attention to the fact that some of the very people who are in this convention to-day and who tell you that we ought to declare in favor of international bimetallism and thereby declare that a gold standard is wrong and that the principle of bimetallism is better—these very people four months ago were open and avowed advocates of the gold standard and telling us that we could not legislate two metals together even with all the world. [Renewed applause and cheers.]

I want to suggest this truth, that if the gold standard is a good thing we ought to declare in favor of its retention and not in favor of abandoning it; and if the gold standard is a bad thing, why should we wait until some other nations are willing to help us to let go? [Applause.] Here is the line of battle. We care not upon which issue they force the fight. We are prepared to meet them on either issue or on both. If they tell us that the gold standard is the standard of civilization, we reply to them that this, the most enlightened of all the nations of the earth, has never declared for a gold standard, and both the parties this year are declaring against it. [Applause.] If the gold standard is the standard of civilization, why, my friends, should we not have it? So if they come to meet us on that, we can present the history of our nation.

More than that, we can tell them this, that they will search the pages of history in vain to find a single instance in which the common people of any land have ever declared themselves in favor of a gold standard. [Applause.] They can find where the holders of fixed investments have. Mr. Carlisle said in 1878 that this was a struggle between the idle holders of idle capital and the struggling masses who produce the wealth and pay the taxes of the country; and, my friends, it is simply a question that we shall decide upon which side shall the Democratic party fight? Upon the side of the idle holders of idle capital or upon the side of the struggling masses? That is the question that the party must answer first, and then it must be answered by each individual hereafter.

The sympathies of the Democratic party, as described by the platform, are on the side of the struggling masses, who have ever been the foundation of the Democratic party. [Applause.] There are two ideas of government. There are those who believe that if you just legislate to make the well-to-do prosperous, their prosperity will leak through on those below. The Democratic idea has been that if you legislate to make the masses prosperous their prosperity will find its way up and through every class and rest upon it. [Applause.]

You come to us and tell us that the great cities are in favor of the gold standard. I tell you that the great cities rest upon these broad and fertile prairies. Burn down your cities and leave our farms, and your cities will spring up again as if by magic. But destroy our farms and the grass will grow in the streets of every city in this country. [Applause.] My friends, we shall declare that this nation is able to legislate for its own people on every question without waiting for the aid or consent of any other nation on earth. [Applause.] Upon that issue we expect to carry every single State in this Union. [Applause.]

I shall not slander the fair State of Massachusetts nor the State of New York by saying that when its citizens are confronted with the proposition, is this nation able to attend to its own business?—I will not slander either one by saying that the people of those States will declare our helpless impotency as a nation to attend to our own business.

It is the issue of 1776 over again. Our ancestors, when but three million, had the courage to declare their political independence of every other nation upon earth. Shall we, their descendants, when we have grown to seventy million, declare that we are less independent than our forefathers? No, my friends, it will never be the judgment of this people.

Therefore we care not upon what lines the battle is fought. If they say bimetallism is good, but we cannot have it till some nation helps us, who reply that, instead of having a gold standard because England has, we shall restore bimetallism and then let England have bimetallism because the United States has. [Applause.] If they dare to come out in the open and defend the gold standard as a good thing, we shall fight them to the uttermost, having behind us the producing masses of this nation and the world. Having behind us the commercial interests, and the laboring interests, and all the toiling masses, we shall answer their demands for a gold standard by saying to them, you shall not press down upon the brow of labor this crown of thorns. You shall not crucify mankind upon a cross of gold.

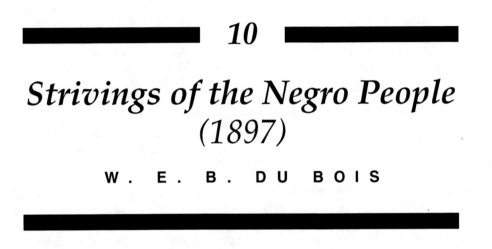

10

Strivings of the Negro People
(1897)

W. E. B. DU BOIS

Unlike his intellectual opponent for leadership of America's black community, Booker T. Washington, W. E. B. Du Bois saw no advantage to accommodation with white racists. He insisted on the racial and social equality of black and white Americans and devoted his life to battling for the rights of his fellow African-Americans. In this piece, published in *The Atlantic Monthly*, Du Bois crafted a sophisticated vision of the anomalous place of blacks in America. A professor of history and economics at Atlanta University, Du Bois helped found the National Association for the Advancement of Colored People in 1909.

Questions to Consider

- What does Du Bois mean when he says that black Americans possess a "double-consciousness"?
- What prevents a man from being "both a Negro and an American"?

Between me and the other world there is ever an unasked question: unasked by some through feelings of delicacy; by others through the difficulty of rightly framing it. All, nevertheless, flutter round it. They approach me in a half-hesitant sort of way, eye me curiously or compassionately, and then, instead of saying directly, How does it feel to be a problem? they say, I know an excellent colored man in my town; or, I fought at Mechanicsville; or, Do not these Southern outrages make your blood boil? At these I smile, or am in-

Source: W. E. B. DuBois, "Strivings of the Negro People," *Atlantic Monthly*, 80 (1897): pp. 194–198.

terested, or reduce the boiling to a simmer, as the occasion may require. To the real question, How does it feel to be a problem? I answer seldom a word.

And yet, being a problem is a strange experience,—peculiar even for one who has never been anything else, save perhaps in babyhood and in Europe. It is in the early days of rollicking boyhood that the revelation first bursts upon one, all in a day, as it were. I remember well when the shadow swept across me. I was a little thing, away up in the hills of New England, where the dark Housatonic winds between Hoosac and Taghanic to the sea. In a wee wooden schoolhouse, something put it into the boys' and girls' heads to buy gorgeous visiting-cards—ten cents a package—and exchange. The exchange was merry, till one girl, a tall newcomer, refused my card,—refused it peremptorily, with a glance. Then it dawned upon me with a certain suddenness that I was different from the others; or like, mayhap, in heart and life and longing, but shut out from their world by a vast veil. I had thereafter no desire to tear down that veil, to creep through; I held all beyond it in common contempt, and lived above it in a region of blue sky and great wandering shadows. That sky was bluest when I could beat my mates at examination-time, or beat them at a foot-race, or even beat their stringy heads. Alas, with the years all this fine contempt began to fade; for the world I longed for, and all its dazzling opportunities, were theirs, not mine. But they should not keep these prizes, I said; some, all, I would wrest from them. Just how I would do it I could never decide: by reading law, by healing the sick, by telling the wonderful tales that swam in my head,—some way. With other black boys the strife was not so fiercely sunny: their youth shrunk into tasteless sycophancy, or into silent hatred of the pale world about them and mocking distrust of everything white; or wasted itself in a bitter cry, Why did God make me an outcast and a stranger in mine own house? The "shades of the prison-house" closed round about us all: walls strait and stubborn to the whitest, but relentlessly narrow, tall, and unscalable to sons of night who must plod darkly on in resignation, or beat unavailing palms against the stone, or steadily, half hopelessly watch the streak of blue above.

After the Egyptian and Indian, the Greek and Roman, the Teuton and Mongolian, the Negro is a sort of seventh son, born with a veil, and gifted with second-sight in this American world,—a world which yields him no self-consciousness, but only lets him see himself through the revelation of the other world. It is a peculiar sensation, this double-consciousness, this sense of always looking at one's self through the eyes of others, of measuring one's soul by the tape of a world that looks on in amused contempt and pity. One ever feels his two-ness,—an American, a Negro; two souls, two thoughts, two unreconciled strivings; two warring

ideals in one dark body, whose dogged strength alone keeps it from being torn asunder. The history of the American Negro is the history of this strife,—this longing to attain self-conscious manhood, to merge his double self into a better and truer self. In this merging he wishes neither of the older selves to be lost. He does not wish to Africanize America, for America has too much to teach the world and Africa; he does not wish to bleach his Negro blood in a flood of white Americanism, for he believes—foolishly, perhaps, but fervently—that Negro blood has yet a message for the world. He simply wishes to make it possible for a man to be both a Negro and an American without being cursed and spit upon by his fellows, without losing the opportunity of self-development.

This is the end of his striving: to be a co-worker in the kingdom of culture, to escape both death and isolation, and to husband and use his best powers. These powers, of body and of mind, have in the past been so wasted and dispersed as to lose all effectiveness, and to seem like absence of all power, like weakness. The double-aimed struggle of the black artisan, on the one hand to escape white contempt for a nation of mere hewers of wood and drawers of water, and on the other hand to plough and nail and dig for a poverty-stricken horde, could only result in making him a poor craftsman, for he had but half a heart in either cause. By the poverty and ignorance of his people the Negro lawyer or doctor was pushed toward quackery and demagogism, and by the criticism of the other world toward an elaborate preparation that overfitted him for his lowly tasks. The would-be black savant was confronted by the paradox that the knowledge his people needed was a twice-told tale to his white neighbors, while the knowledge which would teach the white world was Greek to his own flesh and blood. The innate love of harmony and beauty that set the ruder souls of his people a-dancing, a-singing, and a-laughing raised but confusion and doubt in the soul of the black artist; for the beauty revealed to him was the soul-beauty of a race which his larger audience despised, and he could not articulate the message of another people.

This waste of double aims, this seeking to satisfy two unreconciled ideals, has wrought sad havoc with the courage and faith and deeds of eight thousand thousand people, has sent them often wooing false gods and invoking false means of salvation, and has even at times seemed destined to make them ashamed of themselves. In the days of bondage they thought to see in one divine event the end of all doubt and disappointment; eighteenth-century Rousseauism never worshiped freedom with half the unquestioning faith that the American Negro did for two centuries. To him slavery was, indeed, the sum of all villainies, the cause of all sorrow, the root of all prejudice; emancipation was the key to a promised land of sweeter beauty than ever stretched before the eyes of wearied Israelites. In his songs and exhortations swelled one refrain, liberty; in his tears and curses the god he implored had freedom in his right hand. At last it came,—suddenly, fearfully, like a dream. With one wild carnival of blood and passion came the message in his own plaintive cadences:—

"Shout, O children!
    Shout, you're free!
The Lord has bought your liberty!"

Years have passed away, ten, twenty, thirty. Thirty years of national life, thirty years of renewal and development, and yet the swarthy ghost of Banquo sits in its old place at the national feast. In vain does the nation cry to its vastest problem,—

"Take any shape but that, and my firm nerves
Shall never tremble!"

The freedman has not yet found in freedom his promised land. Whatever of lesser good may have come in these years of change, the shadow of a deep disappointment rests upon the Negro people,—a disappointment all the more bitter because the unattained ideal was unbounded save by the simple ignorance of a lowly folk.

The first decade was merely a prolongation of the vain search for freedom, the boon that seemed ever barely to elude their grasp,—like a tantalizing will-o'-the-wisp, maddening and misleading the headless host. The holocaust of war, the terrors of the Kuklux Klan, the lies of carpet-baggers, the disorganization of industry, and the contradictory advice of friends and foes left the bewildered serf with no new watchword beyond the old cry for freedom. As the decade closed, however, he began to grasp a new idea. The ideal of liberty demanded for its attainment powerful means, and these the Fifteenth Amendment gave him. The ballot, which before he had looked upon as a visible sign of freedom, he now regarded as the chief means of gaining and perfecting the liberty with which war had partially endowed him. And why not? Had not votes made war and emacipated millions? Had not votes enfranchised the freedmen? Was anything impossible to a power that had done all this? A million black men started with renewed zeal to vote themselves into the kingdom. The decade fled away,—a decade containing, to the freedman's mind, nothing but suppressed votes, stuffed ballot-boxes, and election outrages that nullified his vaunted right of suffrage. And yet that decade from 1875 to 1885 held another powerful movement, the rise of another ideal to guide the unguided, another pillar of fire by night after a clouded day. It was the ideal of

"book-learning;" the curiosity, born of compulsory ignorance, to know and test the power of the cabalistic letters of the white man, the longing to know. Mission and night schools began in the smoke of battle, ran the gauntlet of reconstruction, and at last developed into permanent foundations. Here at last seemed to have been discovered the mountain path to Canaan; longer than the highway of emancipation and law, steep and rugged, but straight, leading to heights high enough to overlook life.

Up the new path the advance guard toiled, slowly, heavily, doggedly; only those who have watched and guided the faltering feet, the misty minds, the dull understandings of the dark pupils of these schools know how faithfully, how piteously, this people strove to learn. It was weary work. The cold statistician wrote down the inches of progress here and there, noted also where here and there a foot had slipped or some one had fallen. To the tired climbers, the horizon was ever dark, the mists were often cold, the Canaan was always dim and far away. If, however, the vistas disclosed as yet no goal, no resting-place, little but flattery and criticism, the journey at least gave leisure for reflection and self-examination; it changed the child of emancipation to the youth with dawning self-consciousness, self-realization, self-respect. In those sombre forests of his striving his own soul rose before him, and he saw himself,—darkly as through a veil; and yet he saw in himself some faint revelation of his power, of his mission. He began to have a dim feeling that, to attain his place in the world, he must be himself, and not another. For the first time he sought to analyze the burden he bore upon his back, that dead-weight of social degradation partially masked behind a half-named Negro problem. He felt his poverty; without a cent, without a home, without land, tools, or savings, he had entered into competition with rich, landed, skilled neighbors. To be a poor man is hard, but to be a poor race in a land of dollars is the very bottom of hardships. He felt the weight of his ignorance,—not simply of letters, but of life, of business, of the humanities; the accumulated sloth and shirking and awkwardness of decades and centuries shackled his hands and feet. Nor was his burden all poverty and ignorance. The red stain of bastardy, which two centuries of systematic legal defilement of Negro women had stamped upon his race, meant not only the loss of ancient African chastity, but also the hereditary weight of a mass of filth from white whoremongers and adulterers, threatening almost the obliteration of the Negro home.

A people thus handicapped ought not to be asked to race with the world, but rather allowed to give all its time and thought to its own social problems. But alas! while sociologists gleefully count his bastards and his prostitutes, the very soul of the toiling, sweating black man is darkened by the shadow of a vast despair. Men call the shadow prejudice, and learnedly explain it as the natural defense of culture against barbarism, learning against ignorance, purity against crime, the "higher" against the "lower" races. To which the Negro cries Amen! and swears that to so much of this strange prejudice as is founded on just homage to civilization, culture, righteousness, and progress he humbly bows and meekly does obeisance. But before that nameless prejudice that leaps beyond all this he stands helpless, dismayed, and well-nigh speechless; before that personal disrespect and mockery, the ridicule and systematic humiliation, the distortion of fact and wanton license of fancy, the cynical ignoring of the better and boisterous welcoming of the worse, the all-pervading desire to inculcate disdain for everything black, from Toussaint to the devil,—before this there rises a sickening despair that would disarm and discourage any nation save that black host to whom "discouragement" is an unwritten word.

They still press on, they still nurse the dogged hope,—not a hope of nauseating patronage, not a hope of reception into charmed social circles of stock-jobbers, pork-packers, and earl-hunters, but the hope of a higher synthesis of civilization and humanity, a true progress, with which the chorus "Peace, good will to men,"

"May make one music as before,
But vaster."

Thus the second decade of the American Negro's freedom was a period of conflict, of inspiration and doubt, of faith and vain questionings, of *Sturm und Drang*. The ideals of physical freedom, of political power, of school training, as separate all-sufficient panaceas for social ills, became in the third decade dim and overcast. They were the vain dreams of credulous race childhood; not wrong, but incomplete and oversimple. The training of the schools we need to-day more than ever,—the training of deft hands, quick eyes and ears, and the broader, deeper, higher culture of gifted minds. The power of the ballot we need in sheer self-defense, and as a guarantee of good faith. We may misuse it, but we can scarce do worse in this respect than our whilom [former] masters. Freedom, too, the long-sought, we still seek,—the freedom of life and limb, the freedom to work and think. Work, culture, and liberty,—all these we need, not singly, but together; for to-day these ideals among the Negro people are gradually coalescing, and finding a higher meaning in the unifying ideal of race,—the ideal of fostering the traits and talents of the Negro, not in opposition to, but in conformity with, the greater ideals of the American republic, in order that some day, on American soil, two world races may give each to each those characteristics which both so sadly lack. Already we come not altogether empty-handed: there is to-day no true American music but the sweet wild melodies of the Negro slave; the American fairy tales are Indian and African; we are the sole oasis of simple faith and reverence in a dusty desert of dollars and smartness. Will America be poorer if she replace her brutal, dyspeptic blundering with the light-hearted but determined Negro humility; or her coarse, cruel wit with loving, jovial good humor; or her Annie Rooney with Steal Away?

Merely a stern concrete test of the underlying principles of the great republic is the Negro problem, and the spiritual striving of the freedmen's sons is the travail of souls whose burden is almost beyond the measure of their strength, but who bear it in the name of an historic race, in the name of this the land of their fathers' fathers, and in the name of human opportunity.

11

Under Fire in Cuba (1898)

H O R A C E   W .   B I V I N S

Horace W. Bivins was a sergeant in the famous Tenth U.S. Cavalry, the African-American unit known as the "Buffalo Soldiers." Bivins, an oft-decorated veteran of Indian campaigns, begins his account on the Western frontier, then describes the role of the Tenth Cavalry in the invasion of Cuba and the dramatic Battle of San Juan Hill. Bivins' account was published the following year in *Under Fire with the Tenth U.S. Cavalry*, compiled by Herschel V. Cashin and several other prominent African-Americans. As the preface to this book notes, there is a tendency for "the average historian to either entirely ignore or very grudgingly acknowledge the courage, valor, and patriotism of a so-called *alien race*." After the Battle of San Juan Hill, the glory all seemed to accrue to Teddy Roosevelt and his Rough Riders. The memoirs of Sergeant Bivins and many others like him told a more complete and interesting story.

Questions to Consider

- Why did the Tenth U.S. Cavalry receive little attention in the aftermath of the war, even being denied the right to parade in some victory celebrations?
- Why would African Americans enlist in an army which not only segregated them, but would not allow them to serve as officers?

I entered Hampton School, June 13, 1885, at which place I received my first military training. Having a very great desire for adventure and to see the wild West, I enlisted in the United States army, November 7, 1887, at Washington, D.C. Ten days later I was sent to Jefferson Barracks, Missouri. After receiving a few lessons in mounted and dismounted drill I was assigned to Troop E, Tenth Cavalry. Major Kelley was then captain of the troop. I joined my troop at Fort Grant, Arizona Territory, June 19, 1888. In a few days my troop was ordered to take the field. It was reported that some Indians had left the San Carlos Reservation and were *en route* to Old Mexico.

We scouted along St. Pedro River east and west. For thirty days we were searching for Indian trails, but found none. We then returned to the post. On February 22, 1889, my troop was ordered to San Carlos, Arizona Territory. We arrived there after four days' hard march. Our camp was established on the north side and along the Gila River. I was detailed as lineman. I had to ride and keep the telegraph line in good repair between Camp Carlos and Globe, a mining camp about thirty-five miles from San Carlos.

There were two troops of the Tenth Cavalry, F and E; G Troop of the Fourth Cavalry and companies C and G of the Twenty-fourth Infantry. There were several thousands of Indians on this reservation. I often had to ride the line alone, and had to pass within two miles of a band of hostile Indians who had intrenched themselves on the heights opposite Benson's Camp, within twelve miles of Carlos.

Churchana, an Indian chief, had established his headquarters near Benson's Camp and defied the government to arrest him. We kept a detail of twelve men and one noncommissioned officer at Benson's Camp, two miles from the hostile intrenchment. It was a very unpleasant duty that I had to perform, as often I had to pass this camp in the night.

April 9, 1889, Lieutenant (now Captain) Watson, Lieutenant Dade and Lieutenant Littebrant of the Tenth, with three troops and sixty Indian scouts, surrounded the hostile camp and demanded their surrender, which was accepted on conditions. The Indian chief was to identify and turn over all the murderers and the government was not to prosecute him. When the fact became known among the Indians that the chief was going to surrender they mutinied, and in the fight four were killed, and the chief was stabbed in several places and was admitted in the government hospital. Lieutenant Watson at daybreak planted two Hotchkiss guns, six hundred yards east of their fortified position, and trained the guns on their works, and thus effected the surrender.

These same guns helped to form our battery before Santiago, and of which I was gunner.

After the surrender of the Indians my troop was ordered to change stations with troop I of our regiment. We arrived at Fort Apache, Arizona Territory, October 17, 1889, after a seven days' march over a rough and rocky road. I was detailed as clerk in the regimental adjutant's office, November 10, 1889, and served until made corporal, June 15, 1890. My first target practice with the rifle was at San Carlos. I stood No. 2 in the troop of sixty men although it was the first time that I had ever shot a rifle. I was made sharpshooter in that year, 1889, and have ever since led my troop in marksmanship. I represented my troop in 1892, '93, and '94, winning eight medals and badges at the department competition. I also in 1894 won three gold medals when I represented the Department of the Dakotas at the

---

Source: Herschel V. Cashin et al., *Under Fire with the Tenth U.S. Cavalry* (New York, 1899), pp. 58–62, 68–74, 78–94, 96–106.

army competition at Fort Sheridan and carried off the first gold medal.

Our regiment was ordered to Chickamauga, April 14, 1898. My troop, G, at this time, was in the field. First Lieutenant W. H. Smith and Second Lieutenant Johnson and thirty-eight enlisted men had been ordered to do patrol duty in the Blackfeet Reservation, which the government had announced would be thrown open for settlement on the 15th of April, 1898.

When the order came for us to go South, General Henry sent a telegram for the troop to report at the post as soon as possible. The troop arrived at post at 2:30 P.M. on the 18th, looking very much fatigued, having patrolled the Canadian line, a portion of the Rocky Mountains and St. Mary's Lake, a part of the time wading through mud and water from two to three feet deep and more than half of the time without anything to eat.

We left Fort Assinniboine, Montana, April 19th. We were delayed near a little town in Wisconsin about twenty-two hours on account of the burning of a bridge just before we reached it. It was thought that it was burned on purpose to have us lie over there.

We received great ovations all along the line. Thousands of people were thronged at the places where we would stop and we were treated royally; at Madison, Wisconsin, we were presented with enough flags to decorate our train and were given cigars and many other pleasantries. Our band would play in response to the ovations that were given us from time to time.

After reaching Illinois we received both flags and flowers from the ladies and schoolgirls. I planted one of the flags given me on the crest of San Juan Hill, July 1, 1898. As we neared the South the great demonstrations became less fervent. There were no places that we entered in which we were courteously treated.

The signs over the waiting room doors at the Southern depots were a revelation to us. Some read thus: "White waiting room." On the door of a lunch room we read: "Niggers are not allowed inside." We were traveling in palace cars and the people were much surprised that we did not occupy the "Jim Crow" cars, *the curse of the South.*

At Nashville, Tennessee, we were met by thousands of people, both white and colored. Our band played in response to the cheers that went up from the great multitude. After leaving Nashville we were soon in Chickamauga, and our regiment, notwithstanding the fact that we had just come from the extreme cold of the Northwest began the routine duties of camp life and put in several hours at hard drill. We soon became well-seasoned warriors under the discipline required in war. Not a word of complaint was heard in the lines as our men were marched and countermarched under the hot sun in preparing them for the hardships of the campaign in Cuba. General Wheeler, when first visiting our regiment at Lakeland, Florida, was much impressed by the appearance of our men and said that we looked like fighters. And there were in our lines many Indian fighters who were anxious to get a whack at the Spaniards....

Next morning we arose early. The boys were singing: "The Battleship Maine," "A Hot Time in Cuba," etc. General Miles was there and witnessed the embarkation. We were all in readiness in Port Tampa Bay. Early on the morning of the 14th the officers and enlisted men were keyed up to a very high pitch of excitement at the flinging out of battle flags. At first the little Lyden hoisted a good-sized flag to her masthead, then a huge one at the stern which was quite as large if not larger than herself, which made it appear that she had her hands full. The Wasp then showed her two big flags. Then the Anne with three at her masthead, each of which looked as large as an acre of ground. Last of all the Topeka hoisted three, one at the foremast head, one at the main masthead and one at the stern, which were so large that they made her have the appearance of one huge American flag. It seemed as if no Spaniard, unless he were totally blind, could fail to see that we were Americans with warships.

We left the bay and went as far as quarantine station (twenty-five miles), anchored and remained there until 3 P.M. Ten minutes before 3 P.M. the little revenue cutter came splitting through the water. As it neared us the officer on board, by the aid of a trumpet, said "We will pull out at once.... We will sail in columns of three with the battleship Helena at the head of the columns." She went flitting through the water from transport to transport giving the order. When that final order was given to leave, the information ran through the ships like electricity. In a few minutes every man was on the upper deck. It required the strictest of army discipline to suppress the enthusiastic delight of the men. This was the case on each transport. A few minutes later every transport was in motion.

June 14, 1898, will ever be a memorable day in the history of the American Republic, for on that day the advance guard of the military expedition sailed for Cuba pursuant to the orders of General N. A. Miles, commanding United States army.

June 15th I arose just as the brilliant sun, the king of day, was to all appearance emerging from the bosom of the great ocean, and to my surprise I beheld thirty-six transports in columns of three, the battleship Helena at the head of the columns and several gunboats as rear guard and flankers. No land could be seen as far as the eye could reach, nothing but the beautiful blue waters of the Gulf of Mexico. An escort consisting of several gun and torpedo boats joined us off Dry Tortugas about 11:45 P.M.... We sighted land east of us at 3:45 P.M. June

17th we saw land to the southwest. Several islands could be seen near Point Lookout lighthouse in Bahama Channel. A small sailboat came near us from the lighthouse. From its masthead was flying the American flag and under it the Cuban flag. The crew consisted of three Cubans (two of them very dark and one light). Cheer after cheer went up from our boys. The Cubans seemed to be overwhelmed with joy.

June 18th and 19th we passed several high mountain peaks. We did not know where we were until on the 20th, about 9 A.M. We came in sight of Morro Castle at 11 A.M. and oh, what a beautiful spectacle!

…5 P.M. Sampson's fleet began to shell the hills in the vicinity of the castle. Our bands began to play "A Hot Time in Cuba." (Never heard sweeter music.) June 21st I was up early and as soon as I could use my glasses I was looking in every direction and found that we were near our fleet and not many miles from Morro Castle. At 9 A.M. the order was signaled "We will try to land." At 10 A.M. we received orders to pull near the armored cruiser New York, which we did. A Cuban officer was transferred from the New York to our transport as pilot to go sixteen miles down the bay, west of Santiago, to deliver some rations to the insurgent army, in camp along the shore, and in the mountainous region….

On June 21st plans for landing were made and transmitted to the various commanders. On the morning of the 22d the navy bombarded all the villages along the coast in the vicinity of Daiquiri, and under the cover of this fire an unopposed landing was made by our troops at Daiquiri.

At 5:25 P.M. June 22d a lieutenant ascended a steep hill at Daiquiri and planted our flag on the top of a blockhouse. As Old Glory was being hoisted to the top of the flagpole every boat in the bay whistled with all their might; the bands played 'The Star Spangled Banner,' and thousands of cheers went up from the brave Americans. Indeed, it was a sight never to be forgotten.

As the water in the bay was not deep enough for ships to come alongside of the wharf it was necessary to make the landing in small boats belonging to the transports and the navy. The navy furnished the steam launches to tow these boats back and forth between the shore and the transports. The work was slow and very difficult, as the surf was rough and the breakers very dangerous. Two men were drowned while effecting a landing. Their bodies were found next morning and buried. These were the first of our expedition to be placed under Spanish soil. Several horses died on the voyage.

As soon as our troops landed they formed and marched inland, taking position along the banks of the Daiquiri River, and extending to a distance of about three miles from the village of that name. A number of Cubans who had been landed the night previous at a point east of Daiquiri marched westward and entered Daiquiri from the land side about the same time that our first troops landed.

Our landing was slow. No horses were landed the first day, and less than one division of soldiers succeeded in getting ashore. On June 23d the landing of troops continued and the advance pushed on to Siboney, a coast village about nine miles distant from Daiquiri. Horses and mules were landed by swimming and guiding and towing them by the use of small boats. We used our boats, as all of the steam launches were engaged in carrying the soldiers ashore. It was hard work to land the horses and mules; the surf being rough, we had to land them through breakers. Several of the boats were thrown up against the rocks and rendered useless. In the afternoon of the 22d we began to land troops at Siboney where the beach was smoother than at Daiquiri. There was at first no wharf at Siboney, but later a very small one was built by the engineers from timber found in a saw mill nearby. At Daiquiri we found that the Spaniards had burned a car and a roundhouse and set fire to the wharf; but we reached shore before any damage was done the wharf.

Perhaps a battalion of Spaniards would have been captured at Siboney if a single staff officer could have had a horse to carry the order, but the Spaniards retreated toward Santiago.

Early in the morning of the 24th we reached a point, Las Guasimas, about four miles west of Siboney where a skirmish had occurred the day before between Cubans and Spaniards in which one Cuban was killed and eight wounded. Here we met a portion of the enemy posted behind stone walls on a very high and steep hill, and facing a point in the road which it was necessary for our troops to pass in marching from a sunken road into an open space. The march from Daiquiri to this point was made in such great haste that our men threw away several thousand blankets and clothing of almost every kind—blouses, trousers and underwear. The sun was so very hot that the men found it impossible to carry such a large roll.

Here occurred what has since been called the battle of Las Guasimas. The First and Tenth (colored) regiments of regular cavalry (dismounted) deployed and charged up the hill in front. The First Volunteer Cavalry deployed upon the other ridge road from Siboney, which forks at this point with a valley road and charged in flank on the left, driving the enemy from their position, but not until we had sustained a severe loss in both killed and wounded.

Our forces pushed on and at nightfall occupied a line a mile or more in advance of the position occupied by the enemy in the morning. The conduct of the troops, both white and colored, regular and volunteer, was most gallant and soldierly, and General Young's dispositions, plans and executions were skillful, dashing and successful. Generals Young and Wheeler, and all the other officers, displayed great bravery by walking the skirmish line encouraging the men to keep under cover and take deliberate aim. The fire from the enemy was terrific.

…On the morning of the 26th we marched as far as Savilla-El Pozo on the Santiago road. Our advance continued, the outpost having reached points within three or four miles from the city of Santiago. The light batteries as they came up passed through General Kent's division and went into camp near General Wheeler's division, about the center of the entire army as it stood. The mounted squadron of the Second Cavalry occupied a position near the light batteries. On this date, also, transports containing reinforcements began to arrive (the transports that were considerably out in Santiago Bay).

The 26th was a trying day. Two-thirds of our packing outfit having been left in the boat, we had to pack ammunition on our gun carriages. We had to travel over a rough and rocky road. I carried a box of Hotchkiss shells for a long distance over a rough road, and was sick several days from being strained, but did not go on the sick report. The sun was very hot. We reached Savilla-El Pozo at 11:30 A.M. and camped on the road leading to Santiago. On our arrival we found a large force of insurgents in camp in a mango grove.

On June 27th a Spanish spy was captured about two and a half miles from our camp near El Caney by a Cuban. This spy was up in a mango tree on a high knoll drawing a map of our camp and pickets. He was taken before the commander of the Cuban division. Four Cuban officers and two sentinels took him to General Wheeler's headquarters, only 250 yards away. On being examined, several important papers were found under the sweatband of his hat. This spy was recognized by several Cuban officers as a deserter from the Spanish lines who entered the lines of the Cubans. Soon after he surrendered to the Spanish, giving them much information. He was then taken before General Young. Two Cuban officers, mounted, and two sentinels, dismounted, took the spy and went up the road towards General Shafter's camp. Our gun detachment was in camp at the entrance and to the left of a large gate; as the Cuban officers passed us I brought the men to attention and saluted, they returned with a machete salute. Our spy went the way of all spies in war time.

…Orders were issued for an attack to take place July 1st on El Caney, with a view of making a turning movement, swinging well to our right and passing through the village of El Caney, striking the left flank of the enemy, perhaps ultimately reaching to the northern side of Santiago. In order that the troops should be in posi-

tion to begin this movement early in the morning, we were moved out of camp late in the afternoon of the 30th. Each man was given three days' rations—eighteen hard-tacks and nine slices of raw bacon. We marched the early part of the night, bivouacking near the road ready to take up our position in the battle line at earliest dawn. It is worthy of note that the moon favored us during all the latter part of June and the early part of July, enabling us to use many hours of the night that would not have been possible in darkness.

The Second Brigade was composed of the First and Tenth Regular Cavalry, the First Volunteer Cavalry (Rough Riders) and the little battery, consisting of one officer, First Lieutenant Hughes, and twenty-eight men of the Tenth Cavalry; twelve mules and four Hotchkiss guns. At early dawn of July 1st the troops of General Lawton's division started into the position previously designated for them to occupy. The one battery of artillery was assigned to duty with this division. For the day, they occupied a position overlooking the village of El Caney, 2,400 yards distant. General Chaffee's brigade took up a position east of the village, ready to carry the town as soon as it should be bombarded by the artillery. General Ludlow's brigade took up a position to the west of the village in order to cut off the retreat of the Spaniards when they should be driven out and attempt to retreat to the city of Santiago.

The artillery (Capron's Battery) opened fire with shrapnel at what appeared to be a column of cavalry moving along the road from El Caney toward Santiago, firing a few shots at the blockhouses, then a few at the hedges where the enemy's infantry seemed to be located, and then firing a few shots at the village. All this time a continuous fire of musketry, partly firing at will and partly by volleys, was kept up in all parts of the lines. These lines were drawn closer toward the enemy's works and the brigade in reserve was brought up on the line….

…Between 1 and 2 o'clock the division commander directed the battery of artillery to concentrate its fire upon the stone fort or blockhouse, situated on the highest point in the village, on the northern side. This fort was built of brick, with walls about a foot thick, about 35×45 feet. The practice of the artillery against it was very effective, knocking great holes in the fort. The infantry of Generals Chaffee, Bates and Miles' brigade then made an assault upon the work and carried it….

June 30th while lying under a mango tree drawing a map of our camp…I received orders from detachment commander to march our detachment to regimental headquarters for muster. This was about 8 A.M. The order was obeyed. Our detachment was mustered under a big mango tree. About 11 A.M. I received orders to get our detachment in readiness to move. Each man of our brigade was given three days' rations. General

Garcia's command of about 5,000 insurgents began to pass as early as 7:30 A.M. They were still passing at 1:30 P.M. In this command I saw soldiers of all sizes and complexions, some carrying guns, some machetes, some ammunition, some large sacks of rations (such a load as one of our pack mules could scarcely carry), some large sacks of mangoes and with several so sick that it was difficult for them to walk. At 2 P.M. General Wheeler's division, First Cavalry brigade, composed of Third, Sixth and Ninth Cavalry, General Sumner commanding, the Second Cavalry brigade, consisting of the First, Tenth and First Volunteer Cavalry (Rough Riders), General Young commanding, took up the march for El Pozo. El Pozo is the name of a ruined plantation about three miles from Santiago....

A general movement of all the troops was begun. The road trail and its condition were wretched. The dense thicket confined men and teams to a single trail. Our battery had to stop 143 times in the three miles' march. There were several fords across the Rio Seco and other small streams, which, with the mudholes, caused long delays for the artillery and prohibited a rapid advance of our troops. Night overtook us before we had gone half the distance. The utmost confusion prevailed; bodies of troops in their eagerness to go forward cut others in two repeatedly. It was midnight before the march of three miles was accomplished. (Several did not find their command until next morning, although the moon shone brightly.) After we reached camp the boys made coffee in their tin cups, ate their two hard-tacks and a slice of bacon, after which we were told that we would advance on Santiago early in the morning....

...Soon after dawn we began to hear cannonading and musketry firing in the vicinity of El Caney, which told us that General Lawton's division had attacked the enemy....

Grimes' Battery was ordered into position on El Pozo Hill at it 6:43 A.M. He opened fire on blockhouses out from the city. After we had fired several shots the enemy replied with shrapnel fire at correct range and with accurately adjusted fuse. When the battery opened fire I was so anxious to get the range that I went upon the hill (one hundred yards away). Just as I reached the battery Captain Grimes gave the command: "With shrapnel at 2,800 yards, load!" Several general officers were at the battery in action. At that moment I heard a deep roar near the city, like distant thunder. In a few seconds a shell came over the battery just a few feet above it and went 100 yards beyond and burst among our men, killing two and wounding several. An officer was near me, mounted; the shell passed so near him that his horse shied and the saddle turned, throwing him to the ground. I went to his assistance, then ran down the hill to my battery. Just as I reached it a shell burst about ten feet directly over me, wounding Private

Watson, Troop F, Tenth Cavalry, and a piece of it struck one of our ammunition boxes, exposing the shells. It was lucky that it did not explode, as there were 175 shells in the pile. I reported to our battery commander: "Sir," I asked, "do you wish to bring the battery into action?" He directed that the mules should be taken to shelter and ammunition placed out of range of the Spanish guns.

The third shell landed on Grimes' Battery, killing one officer, two gunners and wounding several. The firing was kept up for some time. At 8:30 A.M. the cavalry division began to march toward Santiago. The dynamite gun in front, with our little Hotchkiss battery (colored) following close behind. General Wheeler's division was in rear of the battery. General Kent's division followed and moved across a stream. A balloon was hoisted in our advance. As we reached the balloon the officer in it asked: "Is there a general officer present?" and dropped a message directing a mounted messenger to carry it to General Wheeler as quickly as possible. Then he said: "Tell General Wheeler to prepare for an attack; the Spaniards have formed a battle line three hundred yards in front of us." The next moment shot and shell began to rain at the balloon and the advancing columns. Lieutenant Hughes' battery with the dynamite gun was hurried to the front and placed in position seventy-five yards beyond the San Juan River (we forded the river). The dynamite gun took position a short distance to our right. We planted our guns near the spot where the Spaniards had formed their battle line. They had retreated only a short distance and concealed themselves in the tall sage brush, but kept up a steady fire.

As we reached the stream I found Lieutenant Ord (afterward killed in this battle) making a reconnaissance from a large tree on the banks of the stream. Mauser bullets were flying through this tree clipping off twigs all around him. He gave valuable information as to the position of the enemy, and the condition of the ground over which we had to pass. He remained up this tree until repeatedly ordered down. After crossing the stream the command was given orders to go to the front and in less than five minutes we were in position training our guns on the blockhouses on San Juan Hill. A delay of one hour and a half was caused by waiting for all troops to get into position then the whole force advanced. The charge was made and carried the enemy's first line of intrenchments. The Tenth Cavalry charged up the steep hill and captured the blockhouse and San Juan Hill.

Our battery kept up the fire on the blockhouse and intrenchments on San Juan Hill until the blockhouse to the right was taken by the Rough Riders and the Tenth Cavalry. When we opened up with artillery (our little battery firing black powder instead of smokeless) we instantly drew all the fire in the vicinity. Ten minutes after we had opened fire two of our gunners were wounded. Sergeant Taylor, Troop E, and Sanders, Troop B, Tenth Cavalry. They landed several shots among the enemy before they fell victims to the Spanish mauser bullet.

While sighting my gun to fire the eighth shot, a bullet passed through the thick iron plated hub of the gun carriage wheel and struck me near the left temple. It stunned me for about two minutes. I recovered, resighted my gun, pulled the lanyard, then watched with my glasses the result of the shot. It dropped in the Spanish trenches. Great confusion occurred. I could see Spanish officers with raised pistols or drawn swords at each end of the trenches. Some were using their swords on the men to keep them from retreating. I fired several shots—loading and firing the gun myself. Every time the gun was fired it would jump back from five to eight feet. I would load, place it in position, sight it, pull the lanyard, then watch the result of my shot....

...We moved down the road, crossed a small stream, turned to the right and took position on a ridge between the two blockhouses. We passed several dead and wounded. I passed my troop commander, First Lieutenant William H. Smith and First Lieutenant William E. Shipp, Tenth Cavalry lying dead, but did not know them. We were then ordered to take position on San Juan Hill.

We reached that point about 1:30 P.M., and then opened fire on the blockhouse and trenches in the basin in which Santiago lies at six hundred yards' range. About fifty sharpshooters were stationed in this house, which had portholes all around it and even holes cut through the roof large enough to sight a gun. Our shots were very effective, knocking great holes in the house, rendering it untenable and killing a large number of men. During our shelling some would attempt to run out of the blockhouse only to be mowed down by Lieutenant Parker's (of the Rough Riders) gatling guns and mausers. We captured several prisoners and about two thousand mauser and brass explosive cartridges. The mauser cartridges were used by Lieutenant Parker in his two mauser guns, against the enemy. Many a Spaniard bit the dust pierced with his own cartridges. At 5:15 we withdrew from the field, having used nearly all of our ammunition in firing from the hill. In the afternoon of the 1st our commander would fire three shots, Corporal Jones, C Troop, would fire three, then I would fire three alternately. It was a hot day and we had no water. Some of us had canteens but they had been pierced by bullets. All of this time we were under a terrific fire. We camped at the dressing station on San Juan River where we first went into action. Just before

dark Major Wint, Tenth Cavalry, was brought in wounded. At the close of the first day's battle our men were occupying the crest all along San Juan Hill, six hundred yards from the enemy's intrenchment, and one and a half-miles from the city of Santiago....

As soon as our troop took San Juan Hill they began to dig intrenchments. The work was pushed day and night. All night our men were digging as they were under constant fire during the day.

July 2d we were up early and ate whatever we could pick up. At dawn the battle began. Our commander received orders to move his detachment near division headquarters. We loaded our ammunition and moved and established our camp ninety yards from General Wheeler's headquarters. On this morning three batteries of the artillery went into action near Fort San Juan. Firing black powder instead of smokeless they of course instantly drew all the fire in the vicinity, and being unable to work the guns we were obliged to withdraw. As I came up I saw one of the gunners digging out a shot that a Spanish gunner had landed in the muzzle of his gun.

During the day there were a great many casualties resulting not entirely from aimed fire, but from bullets clearing the crest of our intrenchments and going far beyond, striking men as they were coming up into position, or as they were going back and forth bringing water and caring for the wounded. Many casualties also resulted from the fire of sharpshooters stationed in trees so thick with foliage that they could not be seen. Just as we were about to break camp a doctor was shot dead within twenty feet of me, while in the act of mounting his horse to go upon the firing line. Notwithstanding the deadly fire of the sharpshooters men were to remain within our lines and continue firing. How very inhuman was it for the enemy to fire upon our Red Cross—shooting doctors and members of the hospital corps while dressing a wound or carrying a wounded man to the rear! This seems incredible. I know of one wounded man being carried to the hospital by three men; when near the hospital one was shot dead, then the second man fell, while the third man dragged his wounded comrade into the bushes and waited until a squad of men came along and assisted in carrying the wounded man to the desired place....

About 9 P.M., everything being quiet, the boys were lying around on the ground when the sentinel said in a very loud voice: "Halt, who comes there?" Then the crack of a gun was heard and several shots followed. We then knew that the Spaniards were making a night attack. A general fire all along the line of pickets began. General Wheeler ordered reinforcements to be brought up, which were only one hundred yards in the rear, under the crest of the hill. Then the crack of thousands of guns was heard. Lieutenant Parker opened up with his machine guns (four gatling guns and two mauser guns). The fire was kept up about one hour. The Spaniards were repulsed with a great loss, so reported.

On the 3d a Spaniard, a deserter from the Spanish lines, came into our lines and said that on the night before they were given rum and were told that they must capture San Juan Hill that night. They charged up near our lines but the fire was so terrific they retreated in disorder and their loss was very heavy. It was the first time that they had ventured out of their intrenchments. Our loss was very small. General Hawkins was wounded....

Soon after 9 A.M. we began to hear a great cannonading in front of Morro Castle, which soon told us that the Spanish fleet had left the harbor and that we were about to witness the greatest naval fight in the history of man. The very earth seemed to tremble while the battle was raging. Firing on either side of the land forces nearly ceased.

Every one was eager to hear the result of the naval battle. Negotiations for surrender began at 1 P.M. General Shafter sent a flag of truce to General Linares, commander of the Spanish forces, asking for his unconditional surrender which was refused. At 2 P.M. Major Hayes brought the good news that the Spanish fleet was destroyed by our navy without the loss of a single ship to us. What joy!...

We worked all night. Colonel Baldwin having received several thousand sacks they were filled with earth and breastworks were made of them. The Spaniards were not idle. Every morning one could see quite readily that a large amount of work had been done by them. They even went so far as to cover their trenches with earth like our bomb proofs to protect them from our shrapnel fire. The city of Santiago by this time was completely invested on the eastern and northern sides.

July 8th the work of planting the mortars was about completed, and we were ready to do some great work, notwithstanding we had been toiling day and night, and had to go a mile for water and get wood wherever we could. Our food was hardtack, bacon, roasted beef and a few tomatoes (we had to buy the most we got). Our men began to get sick. Several were dragged out of the river. They were either wounded in battle and died or were drowned. The doctors gave orders that all drinking water should be boiled. This order was not strictly carried out. It was so hot that the men in many cases paid no attention to it. I found two springs near a mango and cocoanut grove and reported it. It was fixed

up and a guard from the Ninth Cavalry was stationed to guard these springs day and night. All of our drinking water came from them. I have been there when more than a hundred men would be in line waiting for their turn.

July 9th several deserters from the Spanish lines came over to our lines and reported that food was very scarce in the city....

July 12th General Miles arrived at headquarters in the afternoon. A conference was held with the Spanish commander on the 13th. After being present at the capitulation on the 14th, General Miles returned to his ship in the port of Siboney. The articles of surrender were signed under a mango tree between the lines.

On July 15th we moved all along our line out of the mud and water that we had been in since July 1st. Our mattress was the ground and our cover the sky. Every night a heavy dew would fall, such as has never been seen in any part of the United States. The sun was extremely hot. We had to kneel or lie down in the trenches to avoid its rays. It was no uncommon thing to see a man taken out of the trenches overcome by the heat. Our men began to show their exposure, but not half so much as our white comrades did....

July 17th a telegram of congratulation reached us. At 11:45 we were assembled and heard the reading of it. Then we were drawn up in line to witness the surrender. At 12 P.M. the Spanish column began to march toward us. Our band played several pieces.

On July 18th the whole cavalry division moved to Camp Hamilton, about four miles northeast of the city. The day was very hot. Several of the men (mostly white) had to fall out of line, overcome by the heat....

On July 26th, as I rode over the battlefield, I could plainly see in many places the earth drenched in human blood. On my return to camp I was taken sick with the fever and had camp dysentery. I was carried to the hospital on a litter and for twelve days lay at the point of death. The doctors gave me up to die. For six days I did not eat anything. Our hospital was situated on the brow of a hill, our only covering was a fly stretched above us. There were fourteen of us under this one fly. We had to lie with our heads uphill and dig holes in the ground with our heels to keep from slipping down on our comrades. It rained daily and as our tent fly did not shed water very well and both ends of course being open, we kept wet day and night. We had to lie on the wet ground.... A colored surgeon, Dr. A. M. Brown, United States Volunteers, was assigned to our regiment, but before his arrival, our chaplain, William T. Anderson, who is also an M.D. by profession, had arrived and had given relief to many of the sick men of our regiment. He had a large case of medicine with him, and I owe my life to his treatment. He administered to us until he was stricken down himself. Words cannot tell the change of affairs in our regiment after Surgeon Brown's arrival. He moved the hospital to where General Wheeler's headquarters were, put in bunks for all of the sick and members of the corps. It seemed as though he was just in time to save us…. Under Surgeon Brown's supervision our sick list soon began to decrease.

I returned to duty August 10th…but at 9:30 A.M., August 11th, a telegram came ordering our regiment to prepare to return to the United States….

…We had done our duty as United States soldiers and were now sailing for our home. Although leaving a few of our comrades behind us to await the great resurrection morning, we were indeed glad to get away from the direful distress that we were forced to witness each day.

12

The Strenuous Life (1900)

THEODORE ROOSEVELT

To many then and since, Theodore Roosevelt appeared to be the perfect symbol of the United States at the beginning of the twentieth century. Boisterous, self-confident, and aggressively vigorous, Roosevelt bounded onto the national stage during the Spanish-American War of 1898 as the commander of the 1st Volunteer Cavalry, or Rough Riders. In 1900, Roosevelt, the governor of New York, spoke for millions of Americans who felt that the United States had to recover the energy of its frontier heritage. A historian as well as a politician, Roosevelt had already written a multivolume study of the West. The Republican Party selected Roosevelt as William McKinley's running mate in the 1900 election. Following the assassination of McKinley in September 1901, Roosevelt became the youngest president in American history, using that high office as a "bully pulpit" to call upon his country to embrace "the strenuous life." The following address was delivered to a men's club in Chicago.

Questions to Consider

- What is the point of all this strenuous endeavor?
- Is Roosevelt concerned that vigorous activity could produce evil as well as good?

In speaking to you, men of the greatest city of the West, men of the State which gave to the country Lincoln and Grant, men who preëminently and dis-

tinctly embody all that is most American in the American character, I wish to preach, not the doctrine of ignoble ease, but the doctrine of the strenuous life, the life of toil and effort, of labor and strife; to preach that highest form of success which comes, not to the man who desires mere easy peace, but to the man who does not shrink from danger, from hardship, or from bitter

Source: Theodore Roosevelt, *The Strenuous Life* (New York, 1900), pp. 1–21.

toil, and who out of these wins the splendid ultimate triumph.

A life of slothful ease, a life of that peace which springs merely from lack either of desire or of power to strive after great things, is as little worthy of a nation as of an individual. I ask only that what every self-respecting American demands from himself and from his sons shall be demanded of the American nation as a whole. Who among you would teach your boys that ease, that peace, is to be the first consideration in their eyes—to be the ultimate goal after which they strive? You men of Chicago have made this city great, you men of Illinois have done your share, and more than your share, in making America great, because you neither preach nor practise such a doctrine. You work yourselves, and you bring up your sons to work. If you are rich and are worth your salt, you will teach your sons that though they may have leisure, it is not to be spent in idleness; for wisely used leisure merely means that those who possess it, being free from the necessity of working for their livelihood, are all the more bound to carry on some kind of non-remunerative work in science, in letters, in art, in exploration, in historical research—work of the type we most need in this country, the successful carrying out of which reflects most honor upon the nation. We do not admire the man of timid peace. We admire the man who embodies victorious effort; the man who never wrongs his neighbor, who is prompt to help a friend, but who has those virile qualities necessary to win in the stern strife of actual life. It is hard to fail, but it is worse never to have tried to succeed. In this life we get nothing save by effort. Freedom from effort in the present merely means that there has been stored up effort in the past. A man can be freed from the necessity of work only by the fact that he or his fathers before him have worked to good purpose. If the freedom thus purchased is used aright, and the man still does actual work, though of a different kind, whether as a writer or a general, whether in the field of politics or in the field of exploration and adventure, he shows he deserves his good fortune. But if he treats this period of freedom from the need of actual labor as a period, not of preparation, but of mere enjoyment, even though perhaps not of vicious enjoyment, he shows that he is simply a cumberer of the earth's surface, and he surely unfits himself to hold his own with his fellows if the need to do so should again arise. A mere life of ease is not in the end a very satisfactory life, and, above all, it is a life which ultimately unfits those who follow it for serious work in the world.

In the last analysis a healthy state can exist only when the men and women who make it up lead clean, vigorous, healthy lives; when the children are so trained that they shall endeavor, not to shirk difficulties, but to overcome them; not to seek ease, but to know how to wrest triumph from toil and risk. The man must be glad to do a man's work, to dare and endure and to labor; to keep himself, and to keep those dependent upon him. The woman must be the housewife, the helpmeet of the homemaker, the wise and fearless mother of many healthy children. In one of Daudet's powerful and melancholy books he speaks of "the fear of maternity, the haunting terror of the young wife of the present day." When such words can be truthfully written of a nation, that nation is rotten to the heart's core. When men fear work or fear righteous war, when women fear motherhood, they tremble on the brink of doom; and well it is that they should vanish from the earth, where they are fit subjects for the scorn of all men and women who are themselves strong and brave and high-minded.

As it is with the individual, so it is with the nation. It is a base untruth to say that happy is the nation that has no history. Thrice happy is the nation that has a glorious history. Far better it is to dare mighty things, to win glorious triumphs, even though checkered by failure, than to take rank with those poor spirits who neither enjoy much nor suffer much, because they live in the gray twilight that knows not victory nor defeat. If in 1861 the men who loved the Union had believed that peace was the end of all things, and war and strife the worst of all things, and had acted up to their belief, we would have saved hundreds of thousands of lives, we would have saved hundreds of millions of dollars. Moreover, besides saving all the blood and treasure we then lavished, we would have prevented the heartbreak of many women, the dissolution of many homes, and we would have spared the country those months of gloom and shame when it seemed as if our armies marched only to defeat. We could have avoided all this suffering simply by shrinking from strife. And if we had thus avoided it, we would have shown that we were weaklings, and that we were unfit to stand among the great nations of the earth. Thank God for the iron in the blood of our fathers, the men who upheld the wisdom of Lincoln, and bore sword or rifle in the armies of Grant! Let us, the children of the men who proved themselves equal to the mighty days, let us, the children of the men who carried the great Civil War to a triumphant conclusion, praise the God of our fathers that the ignoble counsels of peace were rejected; that the suffering and loss, the blackness of sorrow and despair, were unflinchingly faced, and the years of strife endured; for in the end the slave was freed, the Union restored, and the mighty American republic placed once more as a helmeted queen among nations.

We of this generation do not have to face a task such as that our fathers faced, but we have our tasks, and woe to us if we fail to perform them! We cannot, if we would, play the part of China, and be content to rot by inches in ignoble ease within our borders, taking no interest in what goes on beyond them, sunk in a scrambling commercialism; heedless of the higher life, the life of aspiration, of toil and risk, busying ourselves only with the wants of our bodies for the day, until suddenly we should find, beyond a shadow of question, what China has already found, that in this world the nation that has trained itself to a career of unwarlike and isolated ease is bound, in the end, to go down before other nations which have not lost the manly and adventurous qualities. If we are to be a really great people, we must strive in good faith to play a great part in the world. We cannot avoid meeting great issues. All that we can determine for ourselves is whether we shall meet them well or ill. In 1898 we could not help being brought face to face with the problem of war with Spain. All we could decide was whether we should shrink like cowards from the contest, or enter into it as beseemed a brave and high-spirited people; and, once in, whether failure or success should crown our banners. So it is now. We cannot avoid the responsibilities that confront us in Hawaii, Cuba, Porto Rico, and the Philippines. All we can decide is whether we shall meet them in a way that will redound to the national credit, or whether we shall make of our dealings with these new problems a dark and shameful page in our history. To refuse to deal with them at all merely amounts to dealing with them badly. We have a given problem to solve. If we undertake the solution, there is, of course, always danger that we may not solve it aright; but to refuse to undertake the solution simply renders it certain that we cannot possibly solve it aright. The timid man, the lazy man, the man who distrusts his country, the over-civilized man, who has lost the great fighting, masterful virtues, the ignorant man, and the man of dull mind, whose soul is incapable of feeling the mighty lift that thrills "stern men with empires in their brains"—all these, of course, shrink from seeing the nation undertake its new duties; shrink from seeing us build a navy and an army adequate to our needs; shrink from seeing us do our share of the world's work, by bringing order out of chaos in the great, fair tropic islands from which the valor of our soldiers and sailors has driven the Spanish flag. These are the men who fear the strenuous life, who fear the only national life which is really worth leading. They believe in that cloistered life which saps the hardy virtues in a nation, as it saps them in the individual; or else they are wedded to that base spirit of gain and greed which recognizes in commercialism the be-all and end-all of national life, instead of realizing that, though an indispensable element, it is, after all, but one of the many elements that go to make up true national greatness. No country can long endure if its foundations are not laid deep in the material prosperity which comes from thrift, from business energy and enterprise, from hard, unsparing effort in the fields of industrial activity; but neither was any nation ever yet truly great if it relied upon material prosperity alone. All honor must be paid to the architects of our material prosperity, to the great captains of industry who have built our factories and our railroads, to the strong men who toil for wealth with brain or hand; for great is the debt of the nation to these and their kind. But our debt is yet greater to the men whose highest type is to be found in a statesman like Lincoln, a soldier like Grant. They showed by their lives that they recognized the law of work, the law of strife; they toiled to win a competence for themselves and those dependent upon them; but they recognized that there were yet other and even loftier duties—duties to the nation and duties to the race.

We cannot sit huddled within our own borders and avow ourselves merely an assemblage of well-to-do hucksters who care nothing for what happens beyond. Such a policy would defeat even its own end; for as the nations grow to have ever wider and wider interests, and are brought into closer and closer contact, if we are to hold our own in the struggle for naval and commercial supremacy, we must build up our power without our own borders. We must build the isthmian canal, and we must grasp the points of vantage which will enable us to have our say in deciding the destiny of the oceans of the East and the West.

So much for the commercial side. From the standpoint of international honor the argument is even stronger. The guns that thundered off Manila and Santiago left us echoes of glory, but they also left us a legacy of duty. If we drove out a medieval tyranny only to make room for savage anarchy, we had better not have begun the task at all. It is worse than idle to say that we have no duty to perform, and can leave to their fates the islands we have conquered. Such a course would be the course of infamy. It would be followed at once by utter chaos in the wretched islands themselves. Some stronger, manlier power would have to step in and do the work, and we would have shown ourselves weaklings, unable to carry to successful completion the labors that great and high-spirited nations are eager to undertake.

The work must be done; we cannot escape our responsibility; and if we are worth our salt, we shall be glad of the chance to do the work—glad of the chance to show ourselves equal to one of the great tasks set modern civilization. But let us not deceive ourselves as to the importance of the task. Let us not be misled by vainglory into underestimating the strain it will put on our powers. Above all, let us, as we value our own self-respect, face the responsibilities with proper seriousness, courage, and high resolve. We must demand the highest order of integrity and ability in our public men who are to grapple with these new problems. We must hold to a rigid accountability those public servants who show unfaithfulness to the interests of the nation or inability to rise to the high level of the new demands upon our strength and our resources.

Of course we must remember not to judge any public servant by any one act, and especially should we beware of attacking the men who are merely the occasions and not the causes of disaster. Let me illustrate what I mean by the army and the navy. If twenty years ago we had gone to war, we should have found the navy as absolutely unprepared as the army. At that time our ships could not have encountered with success the fleets of Spain any more than nowadays we can put untrained soldiers, no matter how brave, who are armed with archaic black-powder weapons, against well-drilled regulars armed with the highest type of modern repeating rifle. But in the early eighties the attention of the nation became directed to our naval needs. Congress most wisely made a series of appropriations to build up a new navy, and under a succession of able and patriotic secretaries, of both political parties, the navy was gradually built up, until its material became equal to its splendid personnel, with the result that in the summer of 1898 it leaped to its proper place as one of the most brilliant and formidable fighting navies in the entire world. We rightly pay all honor to the men controlling the navy at the time it won these great deeds, honor to Secretary Long and Admiral Dewey, to the captains who handled the ships in action, to the daring lieutenants who braved death in the smaller craft, and to the heads of bureaus at Washington who saw that the ships were so commanded, so armed, so equipped, so well engined, as to insure the best results. But let us also keep ever in mind that all of this would not have availed if it had not been for the wisdom of the men who during the preceding fifteen years had built up the navy. Keep in mind the secretaries of the navy during those years; keep in mind the senators and congressmen who by their votes gave the money necessary to build and to armor the ships, to construct the great guns, and to train the crews; remember also those who actually did build the ships, the armor, and the guns; and remember the admirals and captains who handled battle-ship, cruiser, and torpedo-boat on the high seas, alone and in squadrons, developing the seamanship, the gunnery, and the power of acting together, which their successors utilized so gloriously at Manila and off Santiago. And, gentlemen, remember the converse, too. Remember that justice has two sides. Be just to those who built up the navy, and, for the sake of the future of the country, keep in mind those who opposed its building up. Read the "Congressional Record." Find out the senators and congressmen who opposed the grants for building the new ships; who opposed the purchase of armor, without which the ships were worthless; who

opposed any adequate maintenance for the Navy Department, and strove to cut down the number of men necessary to man our fleets. The men who did these things were one and all working to bring disaster on the country. They have no share in the glory of Manila, in the honor of Santiago. They have no cause to feel proud of the valor of our sea-captains, of the renown of our flag. Their motives may or may not have been good, but their acts were heavily fraught with evil. They did ill for the national honor, and we won in spite of their sinister opposition.

Now, apply all this to our public men of to-day. Our army has never been built up as it should be built up. I shall not discuss with an audience like this the puerile suggestion that a nation of seventy millions of freemen is in danger of losing its liberties from the existence of an army of one hundred thousand men, three fourths of whom will be employed in certain foreign islands, in certain coast fortresses, and on Indian reservations. No man of good sense and stout heart can take such a proposition seriously. If we are such weaklings as the proposition implies, then we are unworthy of freedom in any event. To no body of men in the United States is the country so much indebted as to the splendid officers and enlisted men of the regular army and navy. There is no body from which the country has less to fear, and none of which it should be prouder, none which it should be more anxious to upbuild.

Our army needs complete reorganization,—not merely enlarging,—and the reorganization can only come as the result of legislation. A proper general staff should be established, and the positions of ordnance, commissary, and quartermaster officers should be filled by detail from the line. Above all, the army must be given the chance to exercise in large bodies. Never again should we see, as we saw in the Spanish war, major-generals in command of divisions who had never before commanded three companies together in the field. Yet, incredible to relate, Congress has shown a queer inability to learn some of the lessons of the war. There were large bodies of men in both branches who opposed the declaration of war, who opposed the ratification of peace, who opposed the upbuilding of the army, and who even opposed the purchase of armor at a reasonable price for the battle-ships and cruisers, thereby putting an absolute stop to the building of any new fighting-ships for the navy. If, during the years to come, any disaster should befall our arms, afloat or ashore, and thereby any shame come to the United States, remember that the blame will lie upon the men whose names appear upon the roll-calls of Congress on the wrong side of these great questions. On them will lie the burden of any loss of our soldiers and sailors, of any dishonor to the flag; and upon you and the people of this country will lie the blame if you do not repudiate, in no unmistakable way, what these men have done. The blame will not rest upon the untrained commander of untried troops, upon the civil officers of a department the organization of which has been left utterly inadequate, or upon the admiral with an insufficient number of ships; but upon the public men who have so lamentably failed in forethought as to refuse to remedy these evils long in advance, and upon the nation that stands behind those public men.

So, at the present hour, no small share of the responsibility for the blood shed in the Philippines, the blood of our brothers, and the blood of their wild and ignorant foes, lies at the thresholds of those who so long delayed the adoption of the treaty of peace, and of those who by their worse than foolish words deliberately invited a savage people to plunge into a war fraught with sure disaster for them—a war, too, in which our own brave men who follow the flag must pay with their blood for the silly, mock humanitarianism of the prattlers who sit at home in peace.

The army and the navy are the sword and the shield which this nation must carry if she is to do her duty among the nations of the earth—if she is not to stand merely as the China of the western hemisphere. Our proper conduct toward the tropic islands we have wrested from Spain is merely the form which our duty has taken at the moment. Of course we are bound to handle the affairs of our own household well. We must see that there is civic honesty, civic cleanliness, civic good sense in our home administration of city, State, and nation. We must strive for honesty in office, for honesty toward the creditors of the nation and of the individual; for the widest freedom of individual initiative where possible, and for the wisest control of individual initiative where it is hostile to the welfare of the many. But because we set our own household in order we are not thereby excused from playing our part in the great affairs of the world. A man's first duty is to his own home, but he is not thereby excused from doing his duty to the State; for if he fails in this second duty it is under the penalty of ceasing to be a freeman. In the same way, while a nation's first duty is within its own borders, it is not thereby absolved from facing its duties in the world as a whole; and if it refuses to do so, it merely forfeits its right to struggle for a place among the peoples that shape the destiny of mankind.

In the West Indies and the Philippines alike we are confronted by most difficult problems. It is cowardly to shrink from solving them in the proper way; for solved they must be, if not by us, then by some stronger and more manful race. If we are too weak, too selfish, or too foolish to solve them, some bolder and abler people must undertake the solution. Personally, I am far too firm a believer in the greatness of my country and the power of my countrymen to admit for one moment that we shall ever be driven to the ignoble alternative.

The problems are different for the different islands. Porto Rico is not large enough to stand alone. We must govern it wisely and well, primarily in the interest of its own people. Cuba is, in my judgment, entitled ultimately to settle for itself whether it shall be an independent state or an integral portion of the mightiest of republics. But until order and stable liberty are secured, we must remain in the island to insure them, and infinite tact, judgment, moderation, and courage must be shown by our military and civil representatives in keeping the island pacified, in relentlessly stamping out brigandage, in protecting all alike, and yet in showing proper recognition to the men who have fought for Cuban liberty. The Philippines offer a yet graver problem. Their population includes half-caste and native Christians, warlike Moslems, and wild pagans. Many of their people are utterly unfit for self-government, and show no signs of becoming fit. Others may in time become fit but at present can only take part in self-government under a wise supervision, at once firm and beneficent. We have driven Spanish tyranny from the islands. If we now let it be replaced by savage anarchy, our work has been for harm and not for good. I have scant patience with those who fear to undertake the task of governing the Philippines, and who openly avow that they do fear to undertake it, or that they shrink from it because of the expense and trouble; but I have even scanter patience with those who make a pretense of humanitarianism to hide and cover their timidity, and who cant about "liberty" and the "consent of the governed," in order to excuse themselves for their unwillingness to play the part of men. Their doctrines, if carried out, would make it incumbent upon us to leave the Apaches of Arizona to work out their own salvation, and to decline to interfere in a single Indian reservation. Their doctrines condemn your forefathers and mine for ever having settled in these United States.

England's rule in India and Egypt has been of great benefit to England, for it has trained up generations of men accustomed to look at the larger and loftier side of public life. It has been of even greater benefit to India and Egypt. And finally, and most of all, it has advanced the cause of civilization. So, if we do our duty aright in the Philippines, we will add to that national renown which is the highest and finest part of national life, will greatly benefit the people of the Philippine Islands, and, above all, we will play our part well in the great work of uplifting mankind. But to do this work, keep ever in mind that we must show in a very high degree the qualities of courage, of honesty, and of good judgment. Resistance must be stamped out. The first and all-important work to be done is to establish the supremacy of our flag. We must put down armed resistance before we can accomplish anything else, and there should be no parleying, no faltering, in dealing with our foe. As for those in our own country who encourage the foe, we can afford contemptuously to disregard them; but it must be remembered that their utterances are not saved from being treasonable merely by the fact that they are despicable.

When once we have put down armed resistance, when once our rule is acknowledged, then an even more difficult task will begin, for then we must see to it that the islands are administered with absolute honesty and with good judgment. If we let the public service of the islands be turned into the prey of the spoils politician, we shall have begun to tread the path which Spain trod to her own destruction. We must send out there only good and able men, chosen for their fitness, and not because of their partizan service, and these men must not only administer impartial justice to the natives and serve their own government with honesty and fidelity, but must show the utmost tact and firmness, remembering that, with such people as those with whom we are to deal, weakness is the greatest of crimes, and that next to weakness comes lack of consideration for their principles and prejudices.

I preach to you, then, my countrymen, that our country calls not for the life of ease but for the life of strenuous endeavor. The twentieth century looms before us big with the fate of many nations. If we stand idly by, if we seek merely swollen, slothful ease and ignoble peace, if we shrink from the hard contests where men must win at hazard of their lives and at the risk of all they hold dear, then the bolder and stronger peoples will pass us by, and will win for themselves the domination of the world. Let us therefore boldly face the life of strife, resolute to do our duty well and manfully; resolute to uphold righteousness by deed and by word; resolute to be both honest and brave, to serve high ideals, yet to use practical methods. Above all, let us shrink from no strife, moral or physical, within or without the nation, provided we are certain that the strife is justified, for it is only through strife, through hard and dangerous endeavor, that we shall ultimately win the goal of true national greatness.

Fifth Annual Message (1905)

THEODORE ROOSEVELT

Twice during Theodore Roosevelt's presidency, European nations made military efforts to force Latin American nations to pay their debts—in Venezuela in 1902 and the Dominican Republic in 1904. In each instance Roosevelt intervened with naval forces and insisted on U.S. mediation. In his annual message to Congress, delivered in December 1905, Roosevelt sought to legitimatize such actions with what would become known as Roosevelt's Corollary to the Monroe Doctrine. In Roosevelt's view, the Monroe Doctrine justified the United States in behaving as a sort of policeman for the entire Western Hemisphere.

Questions to Consider

- What gives the United States the right to police the Western Hemisphere?
- What limitations does Roosevelt place on American power?
- Is Roosevelt suggesting some fundamental change in American foreign policy?

To the Senate and the House of Representatives:

…This renders it proper at this time to say something as to the general attitude of this Government toward peace. More and more war is coming to be looked upon as in itself a lamentable and evil thing. A wanton or useless war, or a war of mere aggression—in short, any war begun or carried on in a conscienceless spirit, is to be condemned as a peculiarly atrocious crime against all humanity. We can, however, do nothing of permanent value for peace unless we keep ever clearly in mind the ethical element which lies at the root of the problem. Our aim is righteousness. Peace is normally the hand-maiden of righteousness; but when peace and righteousness conflict then a great and upright people can never for a moment hesitate to follow the path which leads toward righteousness, even though that path also leads to war. There are persons who advocate peace at any price; there are others who, following a false analogy, think that because it is no longer necessary in civilized countries for individuals to protect their rights with a strong hand, it is therefore unnecessary for nations to be ready to defend their rights. These persons would do irreparable harm to any nation that adopted their principles, and even as it is they seriously hamper the cause which they advocate by tending to render it absurd in the eyes of sensible and patriotic men. There can be no worse foe of mankind in general, and of his own country in particular, than the demagogue of war, the man who in mere folly or to serve his own selfish ends continually rails at and abuses other nations, who seeks to excite his countrymen against foreigners on insufficient pretexts, who excites and inflames a perverse and aggressive national vanity, and who may on occasions wantonly bring on conflict between his nation and some other nation. But there are demagogues of peace just as there are demagogues of war, and in any such movement as this for The Hague conference it is essential not to be misled by one set of extremists any more than by the other. Whenever it is possible for a nation or an individual to work for real peace, assuredly it is failure of duty not so to strive, but if war is necessary and righteous then either the man or the nation shrinking from it forfeits all title to self-respect. We have scant sympathy with the sentimentalist who dreads oppression less than physical suffering, who would prefer a shameful peace to the pain and toil sometimes lamentably necessary in order to secure a righteous peace. As yet there is only a partial and imperfect analogy between international law and internal or municipal law, because there is no sanction of force for executing the former while there is in the case of the latter. The private citizen is protected in his rights by the law, because the law rests in the last resort upon force exercised through the forms of law. A man does not have to defend his rights with his own hand, because he can call upon the police, upon the sheriff's posse, upon the militia, or in certain extreme cases upon the army, to defend him. But there is no such sanction of force for international law. At present there could be no greater calamity than for the free peoples, the enlightened, independent, and peace-loving peoples, to disarm while yet leaving it open to any barbarism or despotism to remain armed. So long as the world is as unorganized as now the armies and navies of those peoples who on the whole stand for justice, offer not only the best, but the only possible, security for a just peace. For instance, if the United States alone, or in company only with the other nations that on the whole tend to act justly, disarmed, we might sometimes avoid bloodshed, but we would cease to be of weight in securing the peace of justice—the real peace for which the most law-abiding and high-minded men must at times be willing to fight. As the world is now, only that nation is equipped for peace that knows how to fight, and that will not shrink from fighting if ever the conditions become such that war is demanded in the name of the highest morality.

So much it is emphatically necessary to say in order both that the position of the United States may not be misunderstood, and that a genuine effort to bring nearer the day of the peace of justice among the nations may not be hampered by a folly which, in striving to achieve the impossible, would render it hopeless to attempt the achievement of the practical. But, while recognizing most clearly all above set forth, it remains our clear duty to strive in every practicable way to bring nearer the time when the sword shall not be the arbiter among nations. At present the practical thing to do is to try to minimize the number of cases in which it must be the arbiter, and to offer, at least to all civilized powers, some substitute for war which will be available in at least a considerable number of instances. Very much can be done through another Hague conference in this direction, and I most earnestly urge that this Nation do all in its power to try to further the movement and to make the result of the decisions of The Hague conference effective. I earnestly hope that the conference may be able to devise some way to make arbitration between nations the customary way of settling international disputes in all save a few classes of cases, which should themselves be as sharply defined and rigidly limited as the present governmental and social development of the world will permit. If possible, there should be a gen-

Source: James D. Richardson, ed., *A Compilation of the Messages and Papers of the Presidents* 16 (New York, 1920): pp. 7353, 7371–7377.

eral arbitration treaty negotiated among all the nations represented at the conference. Neutral rights and property should be protected at sea as they are protected on land. There should be an international agreement to this purpose and a similar agreement defining contraband of war.

During the last century there has been a distinct diminution in the number of wars between the most civilized nations. International relations have become closer and the development of The Hague tribunal is not only a symptom of this growing closeness of relationship, but is a means by which the growth can be furthered. Our aim should be from time to time to take such steps as may be possible toward creating something like an organization of the civilized nations, because as the world becomes more highly organized the need for navies and armies will diminish. It is not possible to secure anything like an immediate disarmament, because it would first be necessary to settle what peoples are on the whole a menace to the rest of mankind, and to provide against the disarmament of the rest being turned into a movement which would really chiefly benefit these obnoxious peoples; but it may be possible to exercise some check upon the tendency to swell indefinitely the budgets for military expenditure. Of course such an effort could succeed only if it did not attempt to do too much; and if it were undertaken in a spirit of sanity as far removed as possible from a merely hysterical pseudo-philanthropy. It is worth while pointing out that since the end of the insurrection in the Philippines this Nation has shown its practical faith in the policy of disarmament by reducing its little army one-third. But disarmament can never be of prime importance; there is more need to get rid of the causes of war than of the implements of war.

I have dwelt much on the dangers to be avoided by steering clear of any mere foolish sentimentality because my wish for peace is so genuine and earnest; because I have a real and great desire that this second Hague conference may mark a long stride forward in the direction of securing the peace of justice throughout the world. No object is better worthy the attention of enlightened statesmanship than the establishment of a surer method than now exists of securing justice as between nations, both for the protection of the little nations and for the prevention of war between the big nations. To this aim we should endeavor not only to avert bloodshed, but, above all, effectively to strengthen the forces of right. The Golden Rule should be, and as the world grows in morality it will be, the guiding rule of conduct among nations as among individuals; though the Golden Rule must not be construed, in fantastic manner, as forbidding the exercise of the police power. This mighty and free Republic should ever deal with all other States, great or small, on a basis of high

honor, respecting their rights as jealously as it safeguards its own.

One of the most effective instruments for peace is the Monroe Doctrine as it has been and is being gradually developed by this Nation and accepted by other nations. No other policy could have been as efficient in promoting peace in the Western Hemisphere and in giving to each nation thereon the chance to develop along its own lines. If we had refused to apply the doctrine to changing conditions it would now be completely outworn, would not meet any of the needs of the present day, and, indeed, would probably by this time have sunk into complete oblivion. It is useful at home, and is meeting with recognition abroad because we have adapted our application of it to meet the growing and changing needs of the hemisphere. When we announce a policy such as the Monroe Doctrine we thereby commit ourselves to the consequences of the policy, and those consequences from time to time alter. It is out of the question to claim a right and yet shirk the responsibility for its exercise. Not only we, but all American republics who are benefited by the existence of the doctrine, must recognize the obligations each nation is under as regards foreign peoples no less than its duty to insist upon its own rights.

That our rights and interests are deeply concerned in the maintenance of the doctrine is so clear as hardly to need argument. This is especially true in view of the construction of the Panama Canal. As a mere matter of self-defense we must exercise a close watch over the approaches to this canal; and this means that we must be thoroughly alive to our interests in the Caribbean Sea.

There are certain essential points which must never be forgotten as regards the Monroe Doctrine. In the first place we must as a Nation make it evident that we do not intend to treat it in any shape or way as an excuse for aggrandizement on our part at the expense of the republics to the south. We must recognize the fact that in some South American countries there has been much suspicion lest we should interpret the Monroe Doctrine as in some way inimical to their interests, and we must try to convince all the other nations of this continent once and for all that no just and orderly Government has anything to fear from us. There are certain republics to the south of us which have already reached such a point of stability, order, and prosperity that they themselves, though as yet hardly consciously, are among the guarantors of this doctrine. These republics we now meet not only on a basis of entire equality, but in a spirit of frank and respectful friendship, which we hope is mutual. If all of the republics to the south of us will only grow as those to which I allude have already grown, all need for us to be the especial champions of the doctrine will disappear, for no stable and growing American Republic wishes to see some great non-American military power acquire territory in its neighborhood. All that this country desires is that the other republics on this continent shall be happy and prosperous; and they cannot be happy and prosperous unless they maintain order within their boundaries and behave with a just regard for their obligations toward outsiders. It must be understood that under no circumstances will the United States use the Monroe Doctrine as a cloak for territorial aggression. We desire peace with all the world, but perhaps most of all with the other peoples of the American Continent. There are, of course, limits to the wrongs which any self-respecting nation can endure. It is always possible that wrong actions toward this Nation, or toward citizens of this Nation, in some State unable to keep order among its own people, unable to secure justice from outsiders, and unwilling to do justice to those outsiders who treat it well, may result in our having to take action to protect our rights; but such action will not be taken with a view to territorial aggression, and it will be taken at all only with extreme reluctance and when it has become evident that every other resource has been exhausted.

Moreover, we must make it evident that we do not intend to permit the Monroe Doctrine to be used by any nation on this Continent as a shield to protect it from the consequences of its own misdeeds against foreign nations. If a republic to the south of us commits a tort [wrongful act] against a foreign nation, such as an outrage against a citizen of that nation, then the Monroe Doctrine does not force us to interfere to prevent punishment of the tort, save to see that the punishment does not assume the form of territorial occupation in any shape. The case is more difficult when it refers to a contractual obligation. Our own Government has always refused to enforce such contractual obligations on behalf of its citizens by an appeal to arms. It is much to be wished that all foreign governments would take the same view. But they do not; and in consequence we are liable at any time to be brought face to face with disagreeable alternatives. On the one hand, this country would certainly decline to go to war to prevent a foreign government from collecting a just debt; on the other hand, it is very inadvisable to permit any foreign power to take possession, even temporarily, of the custom houses of an American Republic in order to enforce the payment of its obligations; for such temporary occupation might turn into a permanent occupation. The only escape from these alternatives may at any time be that we must ourselves undertake to bring about some arrangement by which so much as possible of a just obligation shall be paid. It is far better that this country should put through such an arrangement, rather than allow any foreign country to undertake it. To do so insures the defaulting republic from having to pay debt of an improper character under duress, while it also in-

sures honest creditors of the republic from being passed by in the interest of dishonest or grasping creditors. Moreover, for the United States to take such a position offers the only possible way of insuring us against a clash with some foreign power. The position is, therefore, in the interest of peace as well as in the interest of justice. It is of benefit to our people; it is of benefit to foreign peoples; and most of all it is really of benefit to the people of the country concerned.

This brings me to what should be one of the fundamental objects of the Monroe Doctrine. We must ourselves in good faith try to help upward toward peace and order those of our sister republics which need such help. Just as there has been a gradual growth of the ethical element in the relations of one individual to another, so we are, even though slowly, more and more coming to recognize the duty of bearing one another's burdens, not only as among individuals, but also as among nations.

Santo Domingo, in her turn, has now made an appeal to us to help her, and not only every principle of wisdom but every generous instinct within us bids us respond to the appeal. It is not of the slightest consequence whether we grant the aid needed by Santo Domingo as an incident to the wise development of the Monroe Doctrine or because we regard the case of Santo Domingo as standing wholly by itself, and to be treated as such, and not on general principles or with any reference to the Monroe Doctrine. The important point is to give the needed aid, and the case is certainly sufficiently peculiar to deserve to be judged purely on its own merits. The conditions in Santo Domingo have for a number of years grown from bad to worse until a year ago all society was on the verge of dissolution. Fortunately, just at this time a ruler sprang up in Santo Domingo, who, with his colleagues, saw the dangers threatening their country and appealed to the friendship of the only great and powerful neighbor who possessed the power, and as they hoped also the will to help them. There was imminent danger of foreign intervention. The previous rulers of Santo Domingo had recklessly incurred debts, and owing to her internal disorders she had ceased to be able to provide means of paying the debts. The patience of her foreign creditors had become exhausted, and at least two foreign nations were on the point of intervention, and were only prevented from intervening by the unofficial assurance of this Government that it would itself strive to help Santo Domingo in her hour of need. In the case of one of these nations, only the actual opening of negotiations to this end by our Government prevented the seizure of territory in Santo Domingo by a European power. Of the debts incurred some were just, while some were not of a character which really renders it obligatory on or proper for Santo Domingo to pay them in full. But she could not pay any of them unless some stability was assured her Government and people.

Accordingly, the Executive Department of our Government negotiated a treaty under which we are to try to help the Dominican people to straighten out their finances. This treaty is pending before the Senate. In the meantime a temporary arrangement has been made which will last until the Senate has had time to take action upon the treaty. Under this arrangement the Dominican Government has appointed Americans to all the important positions in the customs service, and they are seeing to the honest collection of the revenues, turning over 45 per cent. to the Government for running expenses and putting the other 55 per cent. into a safe depository for equitable division in case the treaty shall be ratified, among the various creditors, whether European or American.

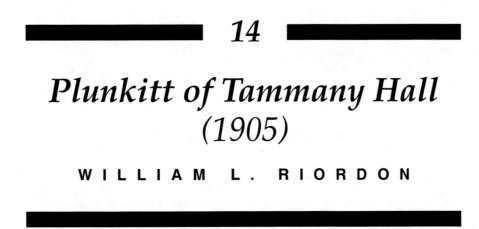

14

Plunkitt of Tammany Hall (1905)

W I L L I A M   L .   R I O R D O N

George Washington Plunkitt is an American success story. The son of Irish immigrants, born into the poorest neighborhood in New York City, Plunkitt quit school at the age of eleven to work in a butcher shop. He then worked his way up to shop owner, contractor, and millionaire. Of course, the fact that he was one of Tammany Hall's most valuable ward bosses helps to explain that success. Starting in 1854, the Democratic organization of Tammany Hall essentially ran New York City until 1934. Tammany offered the poor of New York some return on their vote. In 1905 the reporter William L. Riordon sought to get inside the workings of this political machine by interviewing Plunkitt; Riordon heard more than he expected. The subtitle of Riordon's popular book sums it up well: "A series of very plain talks on very practical politics, delivered by ex-Senator George Washington Plunkitt, the Tammany Philosopher, from his rostrum—the New York County Court House bootblack stand."

Questions to Consider

- According to Plunkitt, what is the difference between honest and dishonest graft?
- Was there any way in which Plunkitt was not adhering to basic American values by maximizing his profit?
- How can anyone, such as Plunkitt, object to civil service reform?
- What role do ideas play in politics?

Honest Graft and Dishonest Graft

Everybody is talkin' these days about Tammany men growin' rich on graft, but nobody thinks of drawin' the distinction between honest graft and dishonest graft. There's all the difference in the world between the two. Yes, many of our men have grown rich in politics. I have myself. I've made a big fortune out of the game, and I'm gettin' richer every day, but I've not gone in for dishonest graft—blackmailin' gamblers, saloonkeepers, disorderly people, etc.—and neither has any of the men who have made big fortunes in politics.

There's an honest graft, and I'm an example of how it works. I might sum up the whole thing by sayin': "I seen my opportunities and I took 'em."

Just let me explain by examples. My party's in power in the city, and it's goin' to undertake a lot of public improvements. Well, I'm tipped off, say, that they're going to lay out a new park at a certain place.

I see my opportunity and I take it. I go to that place and I buy up all the land I can in the neighborhood. Then the board of this or that makes its plan public, and there is a rush to get my land, which nobody cared particular for before.

Ain't it perfectly honest to charge a good price and make a profit on my investment and foresight? Of course, it is. Well, that's honest graft.

Or supposin' it's a new bridge they're goin' to build. I get tipped off and I buy as much property as I can that has to be taken for approaches. I sell at my own price later on and drop some more money in the bank.

Wouldn't you? It's just like lookin' ahead in Wall Street or in the coffee or cotton market. It's honest graft, and I'm lookin' for it every day in the year. I will tell you frankly that I've got a good lot of it, too.

I'll tell you of one case. They were goin' to fix up a big park, no matter where. I got on to it, and went lookin' about for land in that neighborhood.

I could get nothin' at a bargain but a big piece of swamp, but I took it fast enough and held on to it. What turned out was just what I counted on. They couldn't make the park complete without Plunkitt's swamp, and they had to pay a good price for it. Anything dishonest in that?

Up in the watershed I made some money, too. I bought up several bits of land there some years ago and made a pretty good guess that they would be bought up for water purposes later by the city.

Somehow, I always guessed about right, and shouldn't I enjoy the profit of my foresight? It was rather amusin' when the condemnation commissioners came along and found piece after piece of the land in the name of George Plunkitt of the Fifteenth Assembly District, New York City. They wondered how I knew just what to buy. The answer is—I seen my opportunity and I took it. I haven't confined myself to land; anything that pays is in my line.

For instance, the city is repavin' a street and has several hundred thousand old granite blocks to sell. I am on hand to buy, and I know just what they are worth.

How? Never mind that. I had a sort of monopoly of this business for a while, but once a newspaper tried to do me. It got some outside men to come over from Brooklyn and New Jersey to bid against me.

Was I done? Not much. I went to each of the men and said: "How many of these 250,000 stones do you want?" One said 20,000, and another wanted 15,000, and other wanted 10,000. I said: "All right, let me bid for the lot, and I'll give each of you all you want for nothin'."

They agreed, of course. Then the auctioneer yelled: "How much am I bid for these 250,000 fine pavin' stones?"

"Two dollars and fifty cents," says I.

"Two dollars and fifty cents!" screamed the auctioneer. "Oh, that's a joke! Give me a real bid."

He found the bid was real enough. My rivals stood silent. I got the lot for $2.50 and gave them their share. That's how the attempt to do Plunkitt ended, and that's how all such attempts end.

I've told you how I got rich by honest graft. Now, let me tell you that most politicians who are accused of robbin' the city get rich the same way.

They didn't steal a dollar from the city treasury. They just seen their opportunities and took them. That is why, when a reform administration comes in and spends a half million dollars in tryin' to find the public robberies they talked about in the campaign, they don't find them.

The books are always all right. The money in the city treasury is all right. Everything is all right. All they can show is that the Tammany heads of departments looked after their friends, within the law, and gave them what opportunities they could to make honest graft. Now, let me tell you that's never goin' to hurt Tammany with the people. Every good man looks after his friends, and any man who doesn't isn't likely to be popular. If I have a good thing to hand out in private life, I give it to a friend. Why shouldn't I do the same in public life?

Another kind of honest graft. Tammany has raised a good many salaries. There was an awful howl by the reformers, but don't you know that Tammany gains ten votes for every one it lost by salary raisin'?

The Wall Street banker thinks it shameful to raise a department clerk's salary from $1500 to $1800 a year, but every man who draws a salary himself says: "That's all right. I wish it was me." And he feels very much like votin' the Tammany ticket on election day, just out of sympathy.

Source: William L. Riordon, *Plunkitt of Tamany Hall* (New York, 1905), pp. 3–6, 11–20, 25–28, 81–83.

Tammany was beat in 1901 because the people were deceived into believin' that it worked dishonest graft. They didn't draw a distinction between dishonest and honest graft, but they saw that some Tammany men grew rich, and supposed they had been robbin' the city treasury or levyin' blackmail on disorderly houses, or workin' in with the gamblers and lawbreakers.

As a matter of policy, if nothing else, why should the Tammany leaders go into such dirty business, when there is so much honest graft lyin' around when they are in power? Did you ever consider that?

Now, in conclusion, I want to say that I don't own a dishonest dollar. If my worst enemy was given the job of writin' my epitaph when I'm gone, he couldn't do more than write:

"George W. Plunkitt. He Seen His Opportunities, and He Took 'Em."…

The Curse of Civil Service Reform

This civil service law is the biggest fraud of the age. It is the curse of the nation. There can't be no real patriotism while it lasts. How are you goin' to interest our young men in their country if you have no offices to give them when they work for their party? Just look at things in this city today. There are ten thousand good offices, but we can't get at more than a few hundred of them. How are we goin' to provide for the thousands of men who worked for the Tammany ticket? It can't be done. These men were full of patriotism a short time ago. They expected to be servin' their city, but when we tell them that we can't place them, do you think their patriotism is goin' to last? Not much. They say: "What's the use of workin' for your country anyhow? There's nothin' in the game." And what can they do? I don't know, but I'll tell you what I do know. I know more than one young man in past years who worked for the ticket and was just overflowin' with patriotism, but when he was knocked out by the civil service humbug he got to hate his country and became an Anarchist.

This ain't no exaggeration. I have good reason for sayin' that most of the Anarchists in this city today are men who ran up against civil service examinations. Isn't it enough to make a man sour on his country when he wants to serve it and won't be allowed unless he answers a lot of fool questions about the number of cubic inches of water in the Atlantic and the quality of sand in the Sahara desert? There was once a bright young man in my district who tackled one of these examinations. The next I heard of him he had settled down in Herr Most's saloon smokin' and drinkin' beer and talkin' socialism all day. Before that time he had never drank anything but whisky. I knew what was comin' when a young Irishman drops whisky and takes to beer and long pipes in a German saloon. That young man is today one of the wildest Anarchists in town. And just to

think! He might be a patriot but for that cussed civil service.

…What did the people mean when they voted for Tammany? What is representative government, anyhow? Is it all a fake that this is a government of the people, by the people and for the people? If it isn't a fake, then why isn't the people's voice obeyed and Tammany men put in all the offices?

When the people elected Tammany, they knew just what they were doin'. We didn't put up any false pretenses. We didn't go in for humbug civil service and all that rot. We stood as we have always stood, for rewardin' the men that won the victory. They call that the spoils system. All right; Tammany is for the spoils system, and when we go in we fire every anti-Tammany man from office that can be fired under the law. It's an elastic sort of law and you can bet it will be stretched to the limit. Of course the Republican State Civil Service Board will stand in the way of our local Civil Service Commission all it can; but say!—suppose we carry the State sometime, won't we fire the upstate Board all right? Or we'll make it work in harmony with the local board, and that means that Tammany will get everything in sight. I know that the civil service humbug is stuck into the constitution, too, but, as Tim Campbell said: "What's the constitution among friends?"

Say, the people's voice is smothered by the cursed civil service law; it is the root of all evil in our government. You hear of this thing or that thing goin' wrong in the nation, the State or the city. Look down beneath the surface and you can trace everything wrong to civil service. I have studied the subject and I know. The civil service humbug is underminin' our institutions and if a halt ain't called soon this great republic will tumble down like a Park Avenue house when they were buildin' the subway, and on its ruins will rise another Russian government.

This is an awful serious proposition. Free silver and the tariff and imperialism and the Panama Canal are triflin' issues when compared to it. We could worry along without any of these things, but civil service is sappin' the foundation of the whole shootin' match. Let me argue it out for you. I ain't up on sillygisms, but I can give you some arguments that nobody can answer.

First, this great and glorious country was built up by political parties; second, parties can't hold together if their workers don't get the offices when they win; third, if the parties go to pieces, the government they built up must go to pieces, too; fourth, then there'll be h———to pay.

Could anything be clearer than that? Say, honest now; can you answer that argument? Of course you won't deny that the government was built up by the great parties. That's history, and you can't go back of the returns. As to my second proposition, you can't deny that either. When parties can't get offices, they'll bust.... How are you goin' to keep up patriotism if this thing goes on? You can't do it. Let me tell you that patriotism has been dying out fast for the last twenty years. Before then when a party won, its workers got everything in sight. That was somethin' to make a man patriotic. Now, when a party wins and its men come forward and ask for their rewards, the reply is, "Nothin' doin', unless you can answer a list of questions about Egyptian mummies and how many years it will take for a bird to wear out a mass of iron as big as the earth by steppin' on it once in a century?"

I have studied politics and men for forty-five years, and I see how things are driftin'. Sad indeed is the change that has come over the young men, even in my district, where I try to keep up the fire of patriotism by gettin' a lot of jobs for my constituents, whether Tammany is in or out. The boys and men don't get excited any more when they see a United States flag or hear "The Star-Spangled Banner." They don't care no more for firecrackers on the Fourth of July. And why should they? What is there in it for them? They know that no matter how hard they work for their country in a campaign, the jobs will go to fellows who can tell about the mummies and the bird steppin' on the iron. Are you surprised then that the young men of the country are beginnin' to look coldly on the flag and don't care to put up a nickel for firecrackers?

Say, let me tell of one case. After the battle of San Juan Hill, the Americans found a dead man with a light complexion, red hair and blue eyes. They could see he wasn't a Spaniard, although he had on a Spanish uniform. Several officers looked him over, and then a private of the Seventy-first Regiment saw him and yelled, "Good Lord, that's Flaherty." That man grew up in my district, and he was once the most patriotic American boy on the West Side. He couldn't see a flag without yellin' himself hoarse.

Now, how did he come to be lying dead with a Spanish uniform on? I found out all about it, and I'll vouch for the story. Well, in the municipal campaign of 1897, that young man, chockful of patriotism, worked day and night for the Tammany ticket. Tammany won, and the young man determined to devote his life to the service of the city. He picked out a place that would suit him, and sent in his application to the head of department. He got a reply that he must take a civil service examination to get the place. He didn't know what these examinations were, so he went, all lighthearted, to the Civil Service Board. He read the questions about the mummies, the bird on the iron, and all the other fool questions—and he left that office an enemy of the country that he had loved so well. The mummies and the bird blasted his patriotism. He went to Cuba, enlisted in the Spanish army at the breakin' out of the war, and died fightin' his country.

That is but one victim of the infamous civil service....

Now, what is goin' to happen when civil service crushes out patriotism? Only one thing can happen: the republic will go to pieces. Then a czar or a sultan will turn up, which brings me to the fourthly of my argument—that is, there will be h——— to pay. And that ain't no lie.

Reformers Only Mornin' Glories

College professors and philosophers who go up in a balloon to think are always discussin' the question: "Why Reform Administrations Never Succeed Themselves!" The reason is plain to anybody who has learned the a, b, c of politics.

I can't tell just how many of these movements I've seen started in New York during my forty years in politics, but I can tell you how many have lasted more than a few years—none. There have been reform committees of fifty, of sixty, of seventy, of one hundred and all sorts of numbers that started out to do up the regular political organizations. They were mornin' glories—looked lovely in the mornin' and withered up in a short time, while the regular machines went on flourishin' forever, like fine old oaks. Say, that's the first poetry I ever worked off. Ain't it great?

Just look back a few years. You remember the People's Municipal League that nominated Frank Scott for mayor in 1890? Do you remember the reformers that got up that league? Have you ever heard of them since? I haven't. Scott himself survived because he had always been a first-rate politician, but you'd have to look in the newspaper almanacs of 1891 to find out who made up the People's Municipal League. Oh, yes! I remember one name: Ollie Teall; dear, pretty Ollie and his big dog. They're about all that's left of the League.

Now take the reform movement of 1894. A lot of good politicians joined in that—the Republicans, the State Democrats, the Stecklerites and the O'Brienites, and they gave us a lickin', but the real reform part of the affair, the Committee of Seventy that started the thing goin', what's become of those reformers? What's become of Charles Stewart Smith? Where's Bangs? Do you ever hear of Cornell, the iron man, in politics now? Could a search party find R. W. G. Welling? Have you seen the name of Fulton McMahon or McMahon Fulton—I ain't sure which—in the papers lately? Or Preble Tucker? Or—but it's no use to go through the list of the reformers who said they sounded in the death knell of Tammany in 1894. They're gone for good, and Tammany's pretty well, thank you. They did the talkin' and posin', and the politicians in the movement got all the plums. It's always the case.

The Citizens' Union has lasted a little bit longer than the reform crowd that went before them, but that's because they learned a thing or two from us. They learned how to put up a pretty good bluff—and bluff counts a lot in politics. With only a few thousand members, they had the nerve to run the whole Fusion movement, make the Republicans and other organizations come to their headquarters to select a ticket and dictate what every candidate must do or not do. I love nerve, and I've had a sort of respect for the Citizens' Union lately, but the Union can't last. Its people haven't been trained to politics, and whenever Tammany calls their bluff they lay right down. You'll never hear of the Union again after a year or two.

And, by the way, what's become of the good government clubs, the political nurseries of a few years ago?… What's become of the infants who were to grow up and show us how to govern the city? I know what's become of the nursery that was started in my district. You can find pretty much the whole outfit over in my headquarters, Washington Hall.

The fact is that a reformer can't last in politics. He can make a show for a while, but he always comes down like a rocket. Politics is as much a regular business as the grocery or the dry-goods or the drug business. You've got to be trained up to it or you're sure to fail. Suppose a man who knew nothing about the grocery trade suddenly went into the business and tried to conduct it according to his own ideas. Wouldn't he make a mess of it? He might make a splurge for a while, as long as his money lasted, but his store would soon be empty. It's just the same with a reformer. He hasn't been brought up in the difficult business of politics and he makes a mess of it every time.

I've been studyin' the political game for forty-five years, and I don't know it all yet. I'm learnin' somethin' all the time. How, then, can you expect what they call "business men" to turn into politics all at once and make a success of it? It is just as if I went up to Columbia University and started to teach Greek. They usually last about as long in politics as I would last at Columbia.

You can't begin too early in politics if you want to succeed at the game. I began several years before I could vote, and so did every successful leader in Tammany Hall. When I was twelve years old I made myself useful around the district headquarters and did work at all the polls on election day. Later on, I hustled about gettin' out voters who had jags on or who were too lazy to come to the polls. There's a hundred ways that boys can help, and they get an experience that's the first real step in statesmanship. Show me a boy that hustles for the organization on election day, and I'll show you a comin' statesman.

…Of course, you may have some business or occupation on the side, but the great business of your life must be politics if you want to succeed in it.…

To Hold Your District: Study Human Nature and Act Accordin'

There's only one way to hold a district: you must study human nature and act accordin'. You can't study human nature in books. Books is a hindrance more than anything else. If you have been to college, so much the worse for you. You'll have to unlearn all you learned before you can get right down to human nature, and unlearnin' takes a lot of time. Some men can never forget what they learned at college. Such men may get to be district leaders by a fluke, but they never last.

To learn real human nature you have to go among the people, see them and be seen. I know every man, woman, and child in the Fifteenth District, except them that's been born this summer—and I know some of them, too. I know what they like and what they don't like, what they are strong at and what they are weak in, and I reach them by approachin' at the right side.

For instance, here's how I gather in the young men. I hear of a young feller that's proud of his voice, thinks that he can sing fine. I ask him to come around to Washington Hall and join our Glee Club. He comes and sings, and he's a follower of Plunkitt for life. Another young feller gains a reputation as a baseball player in a vacant lot. I bring him into our baseball club. That fixes him. You'll find him workin' for my ticket at the polls next election day. Then there's the feller that likes rowin' on the river, the young feller that makes a name as a waltzer on his block, the young feller that's handy with his dukes—I rope them all in by givin' them opportunities to show themselves off. I don't trouble them with political arguments. I just study human nature and act accordin'.

But you may say this game won't work with the high-toned fellers, the fellers that go through college and then join the Citizens' Union. Of course it wouldn't work. I have a special treatment for them. I ain't like the patent medicine man that gives the same medicine for all diseases. The Citizens' Union kind of a young man! I love him! He's the daintiest morsel of the lot, and he don't often escape me.

Before telling you how I catch him, let me mention that before the election last year, the Citizens' Union said they had four hundred or five hundred enrolled voters in my district. They had a lovely headquarters, too, beautiful roll-top desks and the cutest rugs in the world. If I was accused of havin' contributed to fix up the nest for them, I wouldn't deny it under oath. What do I mean by that? Never mind. You can guess from the sequel, if you're sharp.

Well, election day came. The Citizens' Union's candidate for Senator, who ran against me, just polled five votes in the district, while I polled something more than 14,000 votes. What became of the 400 or 500 Citizens'

Union enrolled voters in my district? Some people guessed that many of them were good Plunkitt men all along and worked with the Cits just to bring them into the Plunkitt camp by election day. You can guess that way, too, if you want to. I never contradict stories about me, especially in hot weather. I just call your attention to the fact that on last election day 395 Citizens' Union enrolled voters in my district were missin' and unaccounted for....

As to the older voters, I reach them, too. No, I don't send them campaign literature. That's rot. People can get all the political stuff they want to read—and a good deal more, too—in the papers. Who reads speeches, nowadays, anyhow? It's bad enough to listen to them. You ain't goin' to gain any votes by stuffin' the letter boxes with campaign documents. Like as not you'll lose votes, for there's nothin' a man hates more than to hear the letter carrier ring his bell and go to the letter box expectin' to find a letter he was lookin' for, and find only a lot of printed politics. I met a man this very mornin' who told me he voted the Democratic State ticket last year just because the Republicans kept crammin' his letter box with campaign documents.

What tells in holdin' your grip on your district is to go right down among the poor families and help them in the different ways they need help. I've got a regular system for this. If there's a fire in Ninth, Tenth, or Eleventh Avenue, for example, any hour of the day or night, I'm usually there with some of my election district captains as soon as the fire engines. If a family is burned out I don't ask whether they are Republicans or Democrats, and I don't refer them to the Charity Organization Society, which would investigate their case in a month or two and decide they were worthy of help about the time they are dead from starvation. I just get quarters for them, buy clothes for them if their clothes were burned up, and fix them up till they get things runnin' again. It's philanthropy, but it's politics, too—mighty good politics. Who can tell how many votes one of these fires bring me? The poor are the most grateful people in the world, and, let me tell you, they have more friends in their neighborhoods than the rich have in theirs....

Another thing, I can always get a job for a deservin' man. I make it a point to keep on the track of jobs, and it seldom happens that I don't have a few up my sleeve ready for use. I know every big employer in the district and in the whole city, for that matter, and they ain't in the habit of sayin' no to me when I ask them for a job.

And the children—the little roses of the district! Do I forget them? Oh, no! They know me, every one of them, and they know that a sight of Uncle George and candy means the same thing. Some of them are the best kind of vote-getters. I'll tell you a case. Last year a little Eleventh Avenue rosebud, whose father is a Repub-

lican, caught hold of his whiskers on election day and said she wouldn't let go till he'd promise to vote for me. And she didn't....

Bosses Preserve the Nation

When I retired from the Senate, I thought I would take a good, long rest, such a rest as a man needs who has held office for about forty years, and has held four different offices in one year [State Senator, County Supervisor, Alderman, and Magistrate] and drawn salaries from three of them at the same time. Drawin' so many salaries is rather fatiguin', you know, and, as I said, I started out for a rest; but when I seen how things were goin' in New York State, and how a great big black shadow hung over us, I said to myself: "No rest for you, George. Your work ain't done. Your country still needs you and you mustn't lay down yet."

What was the great big black shadow? It was the primary election law, amended so as to knock out what are called the party bosses by lettin' in everybody at the primaries and givin' control over them to state officials. Oh, yes, that is a good way to do up the so-called bosses, but have you ever thought what would become of the country if the bosses were put out of business, and their places were taken by a lot of cart-tail orators and college graduates? It would mean chaos. It would be just like takin' a lot of dry-goods clerks and settin' them to run express trains on the New York Central Railroad. It makes my heart bleed to think of it. Ignorant people are always talkin' against party bosses, but just wait till the bosses are gone! Then, and not until then, will they get the right sort of epitaphs, as Patrick Henry or Robert Emmet said.

Look at the bosses of Tammany Hall in the last twenty years. What magnificent men! To them New York City owes pretty much all it is today. John Kelly, Richard Croker, and Charles F. Murphy—what names in American history compares with them, except Washington and Lincoln? They built up the grand Tammany organization, and the organization built up New York. Suppose the city had to depend for the last twenty years on irresponsible concerns like the Citizens' Union, where would it be now? You can make a pretty good guess if you recall the Strong and Low administrations when there was no boss, and the heads of departments were at odds all the time with each other, and the Mayor was at odds with the lot of them. They spent so much time in arguin' and makin' grandstand play, that the interests of the city were forgotten. Another administration of that kind would put New York back a quarter of a century.

Then see how beautiful a Tammany city government runs, with a so-called boss directin' the whole shootin' match! The machinery moves so noiseless that you wouldn't think there was any. If there's any differences of opinion, the Tammany leader settles them quietly, and his orders go every time. How nice it is for the people to feel that they can get up in the mornin' without bein' afraid of seein' in the papers that the Commissioner of Water Supply has sandbagged the Dock Commissioner, and that the Mayor and heads of the departments have been taken to the police court as witnesses! That's no joke. I remember that, under Strong, some commissioners came very near sandbaggin' one another.

Of course, the newspapers like the reform administration. Why? Because these administrations, with their daily rows, furnish as racy news as prizefights or divorce cases. Tammany don't care to get in the papers. It goes right along attendin' to business quietly and only wants to be let alone. That's one reason why the papers are against us.

Some papers complain that the bosses get rich while devotin' their lives to the interests of the city. What of it? If opportunities for turnin' an honest dollar comes their way, why shouldn't they take advantage of them, just as I have done? As I said, in another talk, there is honest graft and dishonest graft. The bosses go in for the former. There is so much of it in this big town that they would be fools to go in for dishonest graft.

Now, the primary election law threatens to do away with the boss and make the city government a menagerie. That's why I can't take the rest I counted on. I'm goin' to propose a bill for the next session of the legislature repealin' this dangerous law, and leavin' the primaries entirely to the organizations themselves, as they used to be. Then will return the good old times, when our district leaders could have nice comfortable primary elections at some place selected by themselves and let in only men that they approved of as good Democrats. Who is a better judge of the Democracy of a man who offers his vote than the leader of the district? Who is better equipped to keep out undesirable voters?

The men who put through the primary law are the same crowd that stand for the civil service blight and they have the same objects in view—the destruction of governments by party, the downfall of the constitution and hell generally.

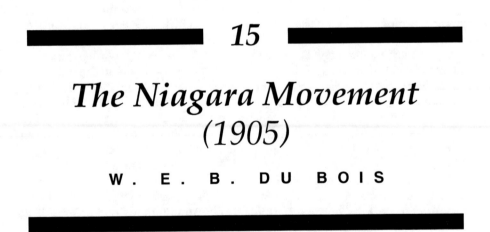

15

The Niagara Movement (1905)

W. E. B. DU BOIS

In his "Atlanta Compromise" of 1895, Booker T. Washington proposed that black Americans would not question their political and social subjugation as long as they were allowed to develop economically. Many other African-Americans objected to Washington's willingness to accept racism as a fact of life. Meeting secretly in 1905 on the Canadian side of the border at Niagara Falls (not Buffalo, as Du Bois writes), a group of prominent black intellectuals, led by W. E. B. Du Bois, formed the Niagara Movement to fight for full human rights. The organization enjoyed some small successes and garnered a great deal of attention, but suffered from a serious lack of funds. In 1910, at Du Bois's urging, the Niagara Movement disbanded and reformed in an alliance with white liberals as the National Association for the Advancement of Colored People (NAACP).

Questions to Consider

- What were the attractions of the Niagara Movement for black Americans?
- Why was it dominated by intellectuals?

What is the Niagara Movement? The Niagara Movement is an organization composed at present of fifty-four men resident in eighteen states of the United States. These men having common aspirations have banded themselves together into an organization. This organization was perfected at a meeting held at Buffalo, N. Y., July 11, 12 and 13, 1905, and was called "The Niagara Movement." The present membership, which of course we hope to enlarge as we find others of like thought and ideal, consists of ministers, lawyers, editors, business men and teachers. The honor of founding the organization belongs to F. L. McGhee, who first suggested it; C. C. Bentley, who planned the method of organization and W. M. Trotter, who put the backbone into the platform.

The organization is extremely simple and is designed for effective work. Its officers are a general secretary and treasurer, a series of state secretaries and a number of secretaries of specific committees. Its membership in each State constitutes the State organization under the State secretary.

Why this organization is needed. The first exclamation of any one hearing of this new movement will naturally be: "Another!" Why, we may legitimately be asked, should men attempt another organization after the failures of the past? We answer soberly but earnestly, "For that very reason." Failure to organize Negro-Americans for specific objects in the past makes it all the more imperative that we should keep trying until we succeed. Today we have no organization devoted to the general interests of the African race in America. The Afro-American Council, while still in existence, has done practically nothing for three years, and is today, so far as effective membership and work is concerned, little more than a name. For specific objects we have two organizations, the New England Suffrage League and the Negro Business League. There is, therefore, without the slightest doubt room for a larger national organization. What now is needed for the success of such an organization? If the lessons of the past are read aright there is demanded:

1. Simplicity of organization.
2. Definiteness of aim.

The country is too large, the race too scattered and the rank and file too unused to organized effort to attempt to impose a vast machine-like organization upon a wavering, uncertain constituency. This has been the mistakes of several efforts at united work among us. Effective organization must be simple—a banding together of men on lines essentially as simple as those of a village debating club. What is the essential thing in such organization. Manifestly it is like-mindedness. Agreement in the object to be worked for, or in other words, *definiteness of aim.*

Among ten million people enduring the stress under which we are striving there must of necessity be great and far-reaching differences of opinions. It is idle, even nonsensical, to suppose that a people just beginning self-mastery and self-guidance should be able from the start to be in perfect accord as to the wisdom or expediency of certain policies. And some universal agreement is impossible. The best step is for those who agree to unite for the realization of those things on which they have reached agreement. This is what the Niagara movement has done. It has simply organized and its members agree as to certain great ideals and lines of policy. Such people as are in agreement with them it invites to co-operation and membership. Other persons it seeks to convert to its way of thinking; it respects their opinion, but believes thoroughly in its own. This the world teaches us is the way of progress.

What the Niagara Movement proposes to do. What now are the principles upon which the membership of the Niagara Movement are agreed? As set forth briefly in the constitution, they are as follows:

(a) Freedom of speech and criticism.

(b) An unfettered and unsubsidized press.

(c) Manhood suffrage.

(d) The abolition of all caste distinctions based simply on race and color.

(e) The recognition of the principle of human brotherhood as a practical present creed.

(f) The recognition of the highest and best training as the monopoly of no class or race.

(g) A belief in the dignity of labor.

(h) United effort to realize these ideals under wise and courageous leadership.

All these things we believe are of great and instant importance; there has been a determined effort in this country to stop the free expression of opinion among black men; money has been and is being distributed in

Source: W. E. B. Du Bois, "The Niagara Movement," *The Voice of the Negro* vol. 2, no. 9 (September 1905), pp. 619–622.

considerable sums to influence the attitude of certain Negro papers; the principles of democratic government *are* losing ground, and caste distinctions are growing in all directions. Human brotherhood is spoken of today with a smile and a sneer; effort is being made to curtail the educational opportunities of the colored children; and while much is said about money-making, not enough is said about efficient, self-sacrificing toil of head and hand. Are not all these things worth striving for? *The Niagara Movement* proposes to gain these ends. All this is very well, answers the objector, but the ideals are impossible of realization. We can never gain our freedom in this land. To which we reply: We certainly cannot unless we try. If we expect to gain our rights by nerveless acquiescence in wrong, then we expect to do what no other nation ever did. What must we do then? We must complain. Yes, plain, blunt complaint, ceaseless agitation, unfailing exposure of dishonesty and wrong—this is the ancient, unerring way to liberty, and we must follow it. I know the ears of the American people have become very sensitive to Negro complaints of late and profess to dislike whining. Let that worry none. No nation on earth ever complained and whined so much as this nation has, and we propose to follow the example. Next we propose to work. These are the things that we as black men must try to do:

To press the matter of stopping the curtailment of our political rights.

To urge Negroes to vote intelligently and effectively.

To push the matter of civil rights.

To organize business co-operation.

To build school houses and increase the interest in education.

To open up new avenues of employment and strengthen our hold on the old.

To distribute tracts and information in regard to the laws of health.

To bring Negroes and labor unions into mutual understanding.

To study Negro history.

To increase the circulation of honest, unsubsidized newspapers and periodicals.

To attack crime among us by all civilized agencies. In fact to do all in our power by word or deed to increase the efficiency of our race, the enjoyment of its manhood, rights and the performance of its just duties.

This is a large program. It cannot be realized in a short time. But something can be done and we are going to do something. It is interesting to see how the platform and program has been received by the country. In not a single instance has the justice of our demands been denied. The *Law Register* of Chicago acknowledges openly that "the student of legal and political history is aware that every right secured by men either individually or as a nation has been won only after asserting the right and sometimes fighting for it. And when a people begin to voice their demand for a right and keep it up, they ultimately obtain the right as a rule." The *Mail and Express* says that this idea is "that upon which the American white man has founded his success."—all this *but*—and then have come the excuses: The *Outlook* thinks that "A child should use other language." It is all right for the white men says the *Mail and Express,* but black men—well they had better "work." Complaint has a horrible and almost a treasonable sound to the *Tribune* while the *Chicago Record-Herald* of course makes the inevitable discovery of "Social Equality." Is not this significant? Is justice in the world to be finally and definitely labelled white and that with your apathetic consent? Are we not men enough to protest, or shall the sneer of the *Outlook* and its kind be proven true that out of ten millions there are only a baker's dozen who will follow these fifty Negro-Americans and dare to stand up and be counted as demanding every single right that belongs to free American citizens? This is the critical time, Black men of America; the staggering days of Emancipation, of childhood are gone.

"God give us men! A time like this demands
Strong minds, great hearts, true faith, and ready
    hands;
Men whom lust of office does not kill;
Men whom the spoils of office cannot buy;
Men who possess opinions and a will;
Men who have honor, men who will not lie;
Men who can stand before a demagogue,
And damn his treacherous flatterers without
    winking.
Tall men, sun-crowned, who live above the fog
In public duty and private thinking.
For when the rabble, with their thumb worn creeds,
Their large professions and their little deeds,
Mingle in selfish strife—lo, Freedom weeps,
Wrong rules the land, and waiting Justice sleeps.["]

16

Lynch Law (1907)

BENJAMIN TILLMAN

In Brownsville, Texas, on August 13, 1906, a company of black soldiers got in a gunfight with the local police after a series of racist provocations. That incident became a national issue, leading many Southern members of Congress to argue that no blacks should be allowed to serve in the military. One of those endorsing that position was South Carolina's Senator Benjamin "Pitchfork Ben" Tillman. In the following speech, delivered on the floor of the United States Senate on January 21, 1907, Tillman constructed an imagined history of the South since the Civil War as a justification for the denial of rights to, and the lynching of, black Americans.

Questions to Consider

- How does Tillman justify stealing elections through such methods as "stuffed ballot boxes"?
- Why does Tillman refer to African-Americans as "creatures"?
- Is lynching a form of law?

Mr. Tillman. ...In speaking about my own attitude, I knew as well as anybody else that the South would tumble over itself in this Chamber and out of it in approval of the President's action in the Brownsville case. My own constituents approve it. All the southern people approve it. Why? Because they do not believe there ought to be any negroes in the Army at all, and they are glad to get rid of them, however unjustly that riddance is obtained. And recollecting the actions of the negro soldiers who were quartered in the South in 1866 and 1867, the outrages, the infamies, the cruelties that were perpetrated upon our people by them, there is no wonder that we hate the very idea of a negro soldier wearing the uniform of the United States and representing authority....

During my twelve years of service here I have borne malice toward no man, and I am sorry to find that without provocation, that I am aware of, I have excited it in a man whom until now I thought to be my friend.

It is but my nature to be blunt and outspoken, and I have never taught my tongue the art of double dealing; and if there is any vice in men I abhor more than any other it is hypocrisy, and I am too old to begin to practice it now.

A brief statement of facts which are fresh in the minds of all who heard the Senator's speech will explain my meaning. He began that speech with a sneering comment on my lynching record, or my ideas on lynching. In the course of his argument the Senator from Wisconsin was discussing the inability of the President to find out who the guilty soldiers were who had shot up Brownsville, and, having asserted with great positiveness that there were no grounds for criticism, I presumed, in an orderly and respectful way, to ask a question, and this was what was said on both sides....

Mr. Tillman. I said it is the fundamental principle of English and American liberty that every man shall be considered innocent until he is proved guilty—

Source: *The Congressional Record—Senate*, 59th Congress, 2d Session, vol. 41, pt. 2 (January, 1907), pp. 1437–1443.

Mr. Spooner.   Proved guilty where?

Mr. Tillman.   In a court, of course. And that ten guilty had better escape than one innocent suffer. Does the Senator object to that?

Mr. Spooner.   Mr. President, the statement is accurate, generally speaking, but with what grace can the Senator, using that as a foundation, charge usurpation in this case and a violation of fundamental principles of liberty upon the President of the United States? Is not that principle applicable to a black man in the South as well as to the white man in the South or the white man in the North? The Senator, who says, "We shot them, we killed them, and we will do it again,"…

Mr. Tillman.   …At this stage of the debate it dawned on me for the first time that the Senator from Wisconsin had intentionally and in cold blood brought things to this pass in order to give him the opportunity to carry out his preconceived plan, and I recalled that in a preceding part of his speech he had used language which caused me at the time to feel aggrieved, but I let it pass, because I had no desire to get into an altercation with the Senator or to indulge in any of those running discussions which have marked our debates in the past, when it was a case of cut and thrust with no blows below the belt.…

…I will repeat the statement of fact and circumstances. It was in 1876, thirty years ago, and the people of South Carolina had been living under negro rule for eight years. There was a condition bordering upon anarchy. Misrule, robbery, and murder were holding high carnival. The people's substance was being stolen, and there was no incentive to labor. Our legislature was composed of a majority of negroes, most of whom could neither read nor write. They were the easy dupes and tools of as dirty a band of vampires and robbers as ever preyed upon a prostrate people. There was riotous living in the statehouse and sessions of the legislature lasting from year to year.

Our lawmakers never adjourned. They were getting a per diem. They felt that they could increase their income by remaining in session all the while. They were taxing us to death and confiscating our property. We felt the very foundations of our civilization crumbling beneath our feet, that we were sure to be engulfed by the black flood of barbarians who were surrounding us and had been put over us by the Army under the reconstruction acts. The sun of hope had disappeared behind a cloud of gloom and despair, and a condition had arisen such as has never been the lot of white men at any time in the history of the world to endure. Life ceased to be worth having on the terms under which we were living, and in desperation we determined to take the government away from the negroes.

We reorganized the Democratic party with one plank, and only one plank, namely, that "this is a white man's country and white men must govern it." Under that banner we went to battle. We had 8,000 negro militia organized by carpetbaggers. The carpetbag governor had come to Washington and had persuaded General Grant to transcend his authority by issuing to the State its quota of arms under the militia appropriation for twenty years in advance, in order to get enough to equip these negro soldiers. They used to drum up and down the roads with their fifes and their gleaming bayonets, equipped with new Springfield rifles and dressed in the regulation uniform. It was lawful, I suppose, but these negro soldiers or this negro militia—for they were never soldiers—growing more and more bold, let drop talk among themselves where the white children might hear their purpose, and it came to our ears. This is what they said:

> The President is our friend. The North is with us. We intend to kill all the white men, take the land, marry the white women, and then these white children will wait on us.

Those fellows forgot that there were in South Carolina some forty-odd thousand ex-Confederate soldiers, men who had worn the gray on a hundred battlefields; men who had charged breastworks defended by men in blue; men who had held lines of battle charged by men in blue; men who had seen real battles, where heroes fought. They forgot that putting in uniform a negro man with not sense enough to get out of a shower of rain did not make him a soldier. So when this condition of desperation had reached the unbearable point; when, as I say, despair had come upon us, we set to work to take the government away from them.

We knew—who knew better?—that the North then was a unit in its opposition to southern ideas, and that it was their purpose to perpetuate negro governments in those States where it could be done by reason of there being a negro majority. Having made up our minds, we set about it as practical men.

I do not say it in a boastful spirit, although I am proud to say it, that the people of South Carolina are the purest-blooded Americans in America. They are the descendants of the men who fought with Marion, with Sumter, with Pickens, and our other heroes in the Revolution. We have had no admixture of outsiders, except a small trickling in from the North and from other Southern States.

Clashes came. The negro militia grew unbearable and more and more insolent. I am not speaking of what I have read; I am speaking of what I know, of what I saw. There were two militia companies in my township and a regiment in my county. We had clashes with these negro militiamen. The Hamburg riot was one clash, in which seven negroes and one white man were killed. A month later we had the Ellenton riot, in which no one ever knew how many negroes were killed, but there were forty or fifty or a hundred. It was a fight between barbarism and civilization, between the African and the Caucasian, for mastery.

It was then that "we shot them;" it was then that "we killed them;" it was then that "we stuffed ballot boxes." After the troops came and told us, "You must stop this rioting," we had decided to take the government away from men so debased as were the negroes—I will not say baboons; I never have called them baboons; I believe they are men, but some of them are so near akin to the monkey that scientists are yet looking for the missing link. We saw the evil of giving the ballot to creatures of this kind, and saying that one vote shall count regardless of the man behind the vote and whether that vote would kill mine. So we thought we would let you see that it took something else besides having the shape of a man to make a man.

Grant sent troops to maintain the carpetbag government in power and to protect the negroes in the right to vote. He merely obeyed the law. I have no fault to find with him. It was his policy, as he announced, to enforce the law, because if it were bad then it would be repealed. Then it was that we stuffed ballot boxes, because desperate diseases require desperate remedies, and having resolved to take the State away, we hesitated at nothing.

It is undoubted that the Republicans will assume all responsibility for the condition in the South at that time. They have never shirked it. The Senator from Wisconsin acknowledged his participation in it the other day. He has no apology to make for it. I do not ask anybody to apologize for it; I am only justifying our own action. I want to say now that we have not shot any negroes in South Carolina on account of politics since 1876. We have not found it necessary. [Laughter.] Eighteen hundred and seventy-six happened to be the hundredth anniversary of the Declaration of Independence, and the action of the white men of South Carolina in taking the State away from the negroes we regard as a second declaration of independence by the Caucasian from African barbarism.

The other day the Senator from Wisconsin defined liberty. "Liberty is that," I believe he said, "which is permitted by law to be done." The Senator has the right to give whatever idea of liberty he may have, and I have no objection to that. In a general way it is a very good definition. But I here declare that if the white men of South Carolina had been content to obey the laws which had been forced down our throats at the point of the bayonet and submit to the reconstruction acts which had thrust the ballot into the hands of ignorant and debased negroes, slaves five years before, and only two or three generations removed from the barbarians of

Africa, the state of South Carolina to-day would be a howling wilderness, a second Santo Domingo. It took the State fifteen years to recover and begin to move forward again along the paths of development and progress; and in consequence of the white men interpreting the word "liberty" to mean the liberty of white people and not the license of black ones, the State is to-day in the very vanguard of southern progress, and can point to the result as the absolute justification for every act which we performed in '76, however lawless our acts may be in the eyes of the Senator from Wisconsin.

South Carolina and Louisiana were the two last States to throw off the blood-sucking vampires which had been set over them by the reconstruction acts....

Have I ever advocated lynch law at any time or at any place? I answer on my honor, "Never!" I have justified it for one crime, and one only, and I have consistently and persistently maintained that attitude for the last fourteen years. As governor of South Carolina I proclaimed that, although I had taken the oath of office to support the law and enforce it, I would lead a mob to lynch any man, black or white, who had ravished a woman, black or white. This is my attitude calmly and deliberately taken, and justified by my conscience in the sight of God.

Mr. President, the Senator from Wisconsin speaks of "lynching bees." As far as lynching for rape is concerned, the word is a misnomer. When stern and sad-faced white men put to death a creature in human form who has deflowered a white woman, there is nothing of the "bee" about it. There is more of the feeling of participating as mourner at a funeral. They have avenged the greatest wrong, the blackest crime in all the category of crimes, and they have done it, not so much as an act of retribution in behalf of the victim as a duty and as a warning as to what any man may expect who shall repeat the offense. They are looking to the protection of their own loved ones.

The Senator from Wisconsin prates about the law. He erects the law into a deity which must be worshiped regardless of justice. He has studied law books until his mind has become saturated with the bigotry which ignores the fundamental principle in this Government: "Law is nothing more than the will of the people." There are written laws and unwritten laws, and the unwritten laws are always the very embodiment of savage justice. The Senator from Wisconsin is incapable of understanding conditions in the South or else he has lost those natural impulses which for centuries have been the characteristics of the race to which we belong.

Tacitus tells us that the "Germanic people were ever jealous of the virtue of their women." Germans, Saxons, Englishmen, they are practically one, springing from the same great root. That trinity of words, the noblest and holiest in our language, womanhood, wifehood, motherhood, have Saxon origin. I believe with Wordsworth—it is my religion—

A mother is a mother still, the noblest thing alive.

And a man who speaks with lightness or flippancy or discusses cold-bloodedly a matter so vital as the purity and chastity of womanhood is a disgrace to his own mother and unworthy the love of a good wife.

Look at our environment in the South, surrounded, and in a very large number of counties and in two States outnumbered, by the negroes—engulfed, as it were, in a black flood of semi-barbarians. Our farmers, living in segregated farmhouses, more or less thinly scattered through the country, have negroes on every hand. For forty years these have been taught the damnable heresy of equality with the white man, made the puppet of scheming politicians, the instrument for the furtherance of political ambitions. Some of them have just enough education to be able to read, but not always to understand what they read. Their minds are those of children, while they have the passions and strength of men. Taught that they are oppressed, and with breasts pulsating with hatred of the whites, the younger generation of negro men are roaming over the land, passing back and forth without hindrance, and with no possibility of adequate police protection to the communities in which they are residing.

Now let me suppose a case. Let us take any Senator on this floor—I will not particularize—take him from some great and well-ordered State in the North, where there are possibly twenty thousand negroes, as there are in Wisconsin, with over two million whites. Let us carry this Senator to the backwoods in South Carolina, put him on a farm miles from a town or railroad, and environed with negroes. We will suppose he has a fair young daughter just budding into womanhood: and recollect this, the white women of the South are in a state of siege; the greatest care is exercised that they shall at all times where it is possible not be left alone or unprotected, but that can not always and in every instance be the case. That Senator's daughter undertakes to visit a neighbor or is left home alone for a brief while. Some lurking demon who has watched for the opportunity seizes her: she is choked or beaten into insensibility and ravished, her body prostituted, her purity destroyed, her chastity taken from her, and a memory branded on her brain as with a red-hot iron to haunt her night and day as long as she lives. Moore has drawn us the picture in most graphic language:

One fatal remembrance, one sorrow that throws
Its bleak shade alike o'er our joys and our woes,

To which life nothing darker or brighter can bring,
For which joy hath no balm and affliction no sting.

In other words, a death in life. This young girl thus blighted and brutalized drags herself to her father and tells him what has happened. Is there a man here with red blood in his veins who doubts what impulses the father would feel? Is it any wonder that the whole countryside rises as one man and with set, stern faces seek the brute who has wrought this infamy? Brute, did I say? Why, Mr. President, this crime is a slander on the brutes. No beast of the field forces his female. He waits invitation. It has been left for something in the shape of a man to do this terrible thing. And shall such a creature, because he has the semblance of a man, appeal to the law? Shall men coldbloodedly stand up and demand for him the right to have a fair trial and be punished in the regular course of justice? So far as I am concerned he has put himself outside the pale of the law, human and divine. He has sinned against the Holy Ghost. He has invaded the holy of holies. He has struck civilization a blow, the most deadly and cruel that the imagination can conceive. It is idle to reason about it; it is idle to preach about it. Our brains reel under the staggering blow and hot blood surges to the heart. Civilization peels off us, any and all of us who are men, and we revert to the original savage type whose impulses under any and all such circumstances has always been to "kill! kill! kill!"

I do not know what the Senator from Wisconsin would do under these circumstances; neither do I care. I have three daughters, but, so help me God, I had rather find either one of them killed by a tiger or a bear and gather up her bones and bury them, conscious that she had died in the purity of her maidenhood, than have her crawl to me and tell me the horrid story that she had been robbed of the jewel of her womanhood by a black fiend. The wild beast would only obey the instinct of nature, and we would hunt him down and kill him just as soon as possible. What shall we do with a man who has outbruted the brute and committed an act which is more cruel than death? Try him? Drag the victim into court, for she alone can furnish legal evidence, and make her testify to the fearful ordeal through which she has passed, undergoing a second crucifixion?…

…Our rule is to make the woman witness, prosecutor, judge, and jury. I have known Judge Lynch's court to sit for a week while suspect after suspect has been run down and arrested, and in every instance they were brought into the presence of the victim, and when she said, "That is not the man," he was set free; but when she said, "That is the man," civilization asserted itself, and death, speedy and fearful, let me say—certainly speedy—was meted out. I have never advocated, I have deprecated and denounced, burning for this or any other crime. I believe it brutalizes any man who participates in a cruel punishment like that. I am satisfied to get out of the world such creatures.

As far as the people of the South are concerned, it is said I do not represent them here. Somehow or other I seem to represent one State, and I do not hesitate to assert that it is my religious belief that on this subject of rape I voice the feeling and the purpose of 95 per cent of the true white men of the Southern States. Whether I do or not, I voice my own. I am not ashamed of them. I have no apologies to make for them.

The Senators from Wisconsin and Colorado may rave, the newspapers may howl, but men who were reared by virtuous mothers and who revere womanly purity as the most priceless jewel of their civilization will do as we of the South have done. On this question I take back nothing and apologize for nothing. I spurn and scorn the charlatanry and cant, the hypocrisy and cowardice, the insolence and effrontery of any and all men who call my motives in question....

...You can not pick up a paper any day but that you will find an appeal from some negro in the North, some convention, some resolution of some kind somewhere denouncing the wrongs done the negroes in the South and demanding justice for them. Those papers circulate in the South. They go everywhere. Our schools, supported by the taxes paid by the white people, are educating these negroes to read such appeals....

The Republican party itself has forsaken its old war cry of "the fatherhood of God and the brotherhood of man." It has denied the Filipinos any participation in the Government, proclaiming that they are not fit. The southern people know they are unfit. We do not dispute it; but in the name of common sense and honest dealing, if the Filipinos are unfit, why are the negroes fit? Everybody knows that the Caucasian stands first, the Mongolian second, the Malay third, the Indian fourth, and the negro fifth in the scale of civilization as fixed by ethnologists. We have had to deal with the other four races besides our own. We have excluded the Chinese. Why? In order to satisfy the selfish desire of white men who are interested. We have butchered the Indian and taken his land. We have settled him. We have denied that the Malay is fit. Yet here we stand proclaiming that the African is fit.

The disfranchisement of the negro in the South for the time being has been acquiesced in by the people of the North without protest, but the fourteenth and the fifteenth amendments are the law of the land. Of course there is great doubt as to whether they were ever adopted in a constitutional way. I should like to hear the Senators from Wisconsin and Ohio, after studying the question a little, argue the point as a purely legal one, without reference to political conditions.

As a discussion of the race question in general goes on throughout the country and the future status of the negro in the United States and how to ameliorate conditions which are well-nigh intolerable now will more and more attract attention to the fundamental question as to whether or not the races are equal, must come to the front. It will be settled finally on that basis, yes or no. If the majority of the white people make up their minds that the negroes are not their equals, they will sooner or later put it in the law that they shall not have a part of the inheritance of the white race.

There was an irrepressible conflict in 1860 between slavery and freedom: between the idea of a confederation of States and a perpetual Union. Is there any man bold enough to deny that there is an irrepressible conflict now between civilization and barbarism and that the living together upon an absolute plane of equality of the two races in the South—one the highest, the other the lowest in the scale—is an impossibility without strife or bloodshed?

Let the newspapers of the country answer. Take up on any day you please a paper published anywhere and read of these conflicts and murders and ravishings, and all that sort of thing. Is it too much for me to say that the American people want this question investigated and discussed calmly and without passion or partisan bias, and have their lawmakers here set about trying to do something? That is all I am trying to accomplish. I do not expect to live to see any change in the Constitution of the United States one way or another. I doubt if there is a man in this Chamber who will ever see it changed by amendment.

But I do not plead for the white people of the South alone. In the ultimate conclusion of this issue we will take care of ourselves, and if we can not do it without help we will get in the North all the recruits who believe in white supremacy and white civilization that we want or need. Thank God, "blood is thicker than water." But we do not want to have to go through the fearful ordeal and crime of butchering the negro.

I realize that there are millions of good negroes, if they are let alone and not taught heresies and criminal thoughts and feelings and actions. I should like to see this good, easy, good-for-nothing people given a chance to live. Give them justice; give them equal rights before the law; enable them to get property and keep it, and be protected in its enjoyment; give them life, liberty, and the pursuit of happiness, provided their happiness does not destroy mine....

..."Old Black Joe"...is a full-blooded negro, about 60 years old. He has been living with me thirty-five years. He now has the keys to my home in South Carolina. He has full charge and control over my stock, my plantation. He is in every way a shining example of what the negro can be and how he can get along with the white man peacefully and pleasantly and honorably, enjoying all of his liberties and rights....

...There were in the South at that time [1861] 4,000,000 negroes, 800,000 males of adult age. The women and children of the white men who were in the Confederate army were left there, entirely helpless for support and protection, with these negroes. With 800,000 negro men, there is not of record a solitary instance of one white woman having been wronged until near the close of the war, when some of the negro soldiers who had been poisoned by contact with northern ideas come along and perpetrated some outrages....

Talk to me about hating these people! I do not do it. We took them as barbarians, fresh from Africa, the first generation we will say, or some of them twice removed, some of them once removed, some of them thrice removed, some of them a fourth removed from barbarism, but the bulk of them only twice. We taught them that there was a God. We gave them what little knowledge of civilization they have to-day. We taught them to tell the truth. We taught them not to steal. We gave them those characteristics which differentiate the barbarian and savage from the civilized man.

Slavery died, and it ought to have died. The South was not responsible for it. It had been recognized in the Constitution. It had been guaranteed. The slaves had not been brought from Africa in southern ships. The barbarian was civilized by us. You struck the shackles off of him. What have you made of him? With all the Confederate soldiers gone to war, no woman was harmed. With all the white men in the South at home, every week some woman is offered up as a sacrifice to this African Minotaur. Senators will all recall the myth of the Minotaur, the monster which came from the sea and ravaged the lands of the Athenians. In order that the Athenians might get relief he made an agreement that if they would pay a tribute of ten young men and young maidens every year he would relieve them from this depredation. The Minotaur was killed by Theseus, but, before this happened, once a year ten maidens were sent to him to be devoured. The South to-day is offering up anywhere from 40 to 100 maidens and matrons to this modern beast that has been bred by fanaticism and political greed....

...These negroes move where they please. They have a little smattering of education. Some of them have white blood in their veins and taught that they are as good as the white man, they ask, Why not as good as a white woman? And when caste feeling and race pride and every instinct that influences and controls the white women makes them spurn the thought, rape follows. Murder and rape become a monomania. The negro becomes a fiend in human form.

We can not police those people to-day under the fourteenth amendment without taking from the whites their own liberties. In my desperation to seek some remedy to prevent rape and not have the necessity of avenging rape, I have gone so far as to plead with the people of the South to inaugurate a passport system, by which we should keep in control and under supervision all of the wandering classes, white and black.

Race hatred grows day by day....

17

Wealth and Its Uses (1907)

A N D R E W   C A R N E G I E

The living symbol of America's rag-to-riches mythology, Andrew Carnegie emigrated from Scotland with his family in 1848, and by 1900 was one of the richest men in the world. In 1901 Carnegie's companies formed the core of the new United States Steel Corporation. After the formation of this giant industry, Carnegie retired from business, devoting himself to philanthropy and spreading his personal philosophy, "The Gospel of Wealth," arguing that the rich should hold their wealth in trust for the public good. Carnegie lived up to his ideal of giving, donating $350,000,000 to build libraries, promote higher education, and establish the Carnegie Endowment for International Peace.

Questions to Consider

- Why does Carnegie think the rich should give away much of their wealth?
- What are the advantages of poverty?
- How does inherited wealth fit into Carnegie's philosophy?

"Wealth," as Mr. Gladstone has recently said, "is the business of the world." That the acquisition of money is the business of the world arises from the fact that, with few unfortunate exceptions, young men are born to poverty, and therefore under the salutary operation of that remarkably wise law which makes for their good: "Thou shalt earn thy bread by the sweat of thy brow."

It is the fashion nowadays to bewail poverty as an evil, to pity the young man who is not born with a silver spoon in his mouth; but I heartily subscribe to President Garfield's doctrine, that "The richest heritage a young man can be born to is poverty." I make no idle prediction when I say that it is from that class from whom the good and the great will spring. It is not from the sons of the millionnaire or the noble that the world receives its teachers, its martyrs, its inventors, its statesmen, its poets, or even its men of affairs. It is from the cottage of the poor that all these spring. We can scarcely read one among the few "immortal names that were not born to die," or who has rendered exceptional service to our race, who had not the advantage of being cradled, nursed, and reared in the stimulating school of poverty. There is nothing so enervating, nothing so deadly in its effects upon the qualities which lead to the highest achievement, moral or intellectual, as hereditary wealth. And if there be among you a young man who feels that he is not compelled to exert himself in order to earn and live from his own efforts, I tender him my profound sympathy....

One gets a great many good things from the New York *Sun*.... I beg to read this to you as one of its numerous rays of light:

Our Boys

Every moralist hard up for a theme asks at intervals: What is the matter with the sons of our rich and great men? The question is followed by statistics on the wickedness and bad endings of such sons.

The trouble with the moralists is that they put the question wrong end first. There is nothing wrong with those foolish sons, except that they are unlucky; but there is something wrong with their fathers....

Source: Andrew Carnegie, *Empire of Business* (Buffalo, 1907), pp. 125–136, 138–144.

He ruins his children, and then, when he gets old, profusely and sadly observes that he has done everything for them, and yet they have disappointed him. He who gives to his son an office which he has not deserved and enables him to disgrace his father and friends, deserves no more sympathy than any Mr. Fagin deliberately educating a boy to be dishonest.

The fat, useless pug-dogs which young women drag wheezing about at the end of strings are not to blame for their condition, and the same thing is true of rich men's sons. The young women who overfeed the dogs and the fathers who ruin their sons have themselves to thank.

No man would advocate the thing, perhaps; but who can doubt that if there could be a law making it impossible for a man to inherit anything but a good education and a good constitution, it would supply us in short order with a better lot of men?...

It is not the poor young man who goes forth to his work in the morning and labours until evening that we should pity. It is the son of the rich man to whom Providence has not been so kind as to trust with this honourable task. It is not the busy man, but the man of idleness, who should arouse our sympathy and cause us sorrow. "Happy is the man who has found his work," says Carlyle. I say, "Happy is the man who has to work and to work hard, and work long." A great poet has said: "He prayeth best who loveth best." Some day this may be parodied into: "He prayeth best who worketh best." An honest day's work well performed is not a bad sort of prayer. The cry goes forth often nowadays, "Abolish poverty!" but fortunately this cannot be done; and the poor we are always to have with us. Abolish poverty, and what would become of the race? Progress, development, would cease. Consider its future if dependent upon the rich. The supply of the good and the great would cease, and human society retrograde into barbarism. Abolish luxury, if you please, but leave us the soil, upon which alone the virtues and all that is precious in human character grow; poverty—honest poverty.

I will assume for the moment, gentlemen, that you were all fortunate enough to be born poor. Then the first question that presses upon you is this: What shall I learn to do for the community which will bring me in exchange enough wealth to feed, clothe, lodge, and keep me independent of charitable aid from others?...

The young man, therefore, who resolves to make himself useful to his kind, and therefore entitled to receive in return from a grateful community which he benefits the sum necessary for his support, sees clearly one of the highest duties of a young man. He meets the vital question immediately pressing upon him for decision, and decides it rightly.

So far, then, there is no difference about the acquisition of wealth. Every one is agreed that it is the first duty of a young man to so train himself as to be self-supporting. Nor is there difficulty about the next step, for the young man cannot be said to have performed the whole of his duty if he leaves out of account the contingencies of life, liability to accident, illness, and trade depressions like the present. Wisdom calls upon him to have regard for these things; and it is a part of his duty that he begin to save a portion of his earnings and invest them, not in speculation, but in securities or in property, or in a legitimate business in such form as will, perhaps, slowly but yet surely grow into the reserve upon which he can fall back in emergencies or in old age, and live upon his own savings. I think we are all agreed as to the advisability—nay, the duty—of laying up a competence, and hence to retain our self-respect.

Besides this, I take it that some of you have already decided, just as soon as possible to ask "a certain young lady" to share his lot, or perhaps his lots, and, of course, he should have a lot or two to share. Marriage is a very serious business indeed, and gives rise to many weighty considerations. "Be sure to marry a woman with good common-sense," was the advice given me by my mentor, and I just hand it down to you. Common sense is the most uncommon and most valuable quality in man or woman. But before you have occasion to provide yourself with a helpmate, there comes the subject upon which I am to address you—"Wealth"—not wealth in millions, but simply revenue sufficient for modest, independent living. This opens up the entire subject of wealth in a greater or less degree.

Now, what is wealth? How is it created and distributed? There are not far from us immense beds of coal which have lain for millions of years useless, and therefore valueless. Through some experiment, or perhaps accident, it was discovered that black stone would burn and give forth heat. Men sank shafts, erected machinery, mined and brought forth coal, and sold it to the community. It displaced the use of wood as fuel, say at one-half the cost. Immediately every bed of coal became valuable because useful, or capable of being made so; and here a new article worth hundreds, yes, thousands of millions was added to the wealth of the community. A Scotch mechanic one day, as the story goes, gazing into the fire upon which water was boiling in a kettle, saw the steam raise the lid, as hundreds of thousands had seen before him; but none saw in that sight what he did—the steam engine, which does the work of the world at a cost so infinitely trifling compared with what the plans known before involved, that the wealth of the world has been increased one dares not estimate how much. The saving that the community makes is the root of wealth in any branch of material development. Now, a young man's labour or service to the community creates wealth just in proportion as his service is useful to the community, as it either saves or improves upon existing methods. Commodore Vanderbilt saw, I think, thirteen different short railway lines between New York and Buffalo, involving thirteen different managements, and a disjointed and tedious service. Albany, Schenectady, Utica, Syracuse, Auburn, Rochester, etc., were heads of some of these companies. He consolidated them all, making one direct line, over which your Empire State Express flies fifty-one miles an hour, the fastest time in the world; and a hundred passengers patronize the lines where one did in olden days. He rendered the community a special service, which, being followed by others, reduces the cost of bringing food from the prairies of the West to your doors to a trifling sum per ton. He produced, and is every day producing, untold wealth to the community by so doing, and the profit he reaped for himself was but a drop in the bucket compared with that which he showered upon the State and the nation....

...It is a great mistake for young men to say to themselves, "Oh! we cannot enter into business." If any of you have saved as much as $50 or $100, I do not know any branch of business into which you cannot plunge at once. You can get your certificate of stock and attend the meeting of stockholders, make your speeches and suggestions, quarrel with the president, and instruct the management of the affairs of the company, and have all the rights and influence of an owner....

The principal complaint against our industrial conditions of to-day is that they cause great wealth to flow into the hands of the few. Well, of the very few, indeed, is this true. It was formerly so, as I have explained, immediately after the new inventions had changed the conditions of the world. To-day it is not true. Wealth is being more and more distributed among the many. The amount of the combined profits of labour and capital which goes to labour was never so great as to-day, the amount going to capital never so small. While the earnings of capital have fallen more than one-half, in many cases have been entirely obliterated, statistics prove that the earnings of labour were never so high as they were previous to the recent unprecedented depression in business, while the cost of living,—the necessaries of life,—have fallen in some cases nearly one-half. Great Britain has an income tax, and our country is to be subject to this imposition for a time. The British returns show that during the eleven years from 1876 to 1887 the number of men receiving from $750 to $2,500 per year, increased more than 21 per cent., while the number receiving from $5,000 to $25,000 actually decreased 2 1/2 per cent.

You may be sure, gentlemen, that the question of the distribution of wealth is settling itself rapidly under present conditions, and settling itself in the right direc-

tion. The few rich are getting poorer, and the toiling masses are getting richer. Nevertheless, a few exceptional men may yet make fortunes, but these will be more moderate than in the past. This may not be quite as fortunate for the masses of the people as is now believed, because great accumulations of wealth in the hands of one enterprising man who still toils on are sometimes most productive of all the forms of wealth....

The bees of a hive do not destroy the honey-making bees, but the drones. It will be a great mistake for the community to shoot the millionaires, for they are the bees that make the most honey, and contribute most to the hive even after they have gorged themselves full. It is a remarkable fact that any country is prosperous and comfortable in proportion to the number of its millionnaires. Take Russia, with its population little better than serfs, and living at the point of starvation upon the meanest fare—such fare as none of our people could or would eat, and you find comparatively few millionnaires, excepting the Emperor and a few nobles who own the land.... In the old home of our race, in Britain, which is the richest country in the world save one—our own—there are more millionnaires in pounds sterling (which may be considered the European standard) than in the whole of the rest of Europe, and its people are better off than in any other. You come to our own land: we probably have more millionnaires and multimillionnaires, both in pounds and dollars, than all the rest of the world put together....

The inventions of to-day lead to concentrating industrial and commercial affairs into huge concerns. You cannot work the Bessemer process successfully without employing thousands of men upon one spot. You could not make the armour for ships without first expending seven millions of dollars, as the Bethlehem Company has spent. You cannot make a yard of cotton goods in competition with the world without having an immense factory and thousands of men and women aiding in the process. The great electric establishment here in your town succeeds because it has spent millions and is prepared to do its work upon a great scale. Under such conditions it is impossible but that wealth will flow into the hands of a few men in prosperous times beyond their needs....

But assuming that surplus wealth flows into the hands of a few men, what is their duty? How is the struggle for dollars to be lifted from the sordid atmosphere surrounding business and made a noble career? Now, wealth has hitherto been distributed in three ways: The first and chief one is by willing it at death to the family. Now, beyond bequeathing to those dependent upon one the revenue needful for modest and independent living, is such a use of wealth either right or wise? I ask you to think over the result, as a rule, of millions given over to young men and women, the sons and daughters of the millionnaire. You will find that, as a rule, it is not good for the daughters; and this is seen in the character and conduct of the men who marry them. As for the sons, you have their condition as described in the extract which I read you from *The Sun*. Nothing is truer than this, that as a rule the "almighty dollar" bequeathed to sons or daughters by millions proves an almighty curse. It is not the good of the child which the millionnaire parent considers when he makes these bequests, it is his own vanity; it is not affection for the child, it is self-glorification for the parent which is at the root of this injurious disposition of wealth. There is only one thing to be said for this mode, it furnishes one of the most efficacious means of rapid distribution of wealth ever known.

There is a second use of wealth, less common than the first, which is not so injurious to the community, but which should bring no credit to the testator. Money is left by millionnaires to public institutions when they must relax their grasp upon it. There is no grace, and can be no blessing, in giving what cannot be withheld. It is no gift, because it is not cheerfully given, but only granted at the stern summons of death. The miscarriage of these bequests, the litigation connected with them, and the manner in which they are frittered away seem to prove that the Fates do not regard them with a kindly eye. We are never without a lesson that the only mode of producing lasting good by giving large sums of money is for the millionnaire to give as close attention to its distribution during his life as he did to its acquisition....

The third use, and the only noble use of surplus wealth, is this: That it be regarded as a sacred trust, to be administered by its possessor, into whose hands it flows, for the highest good of the people. Man does not live by bread alone, and five or ten cents a day more revenue scattered over thousands would produce little or no good. Accumulated into a great fund and expended as Mr. Cooper expended it for the Cooper Institute, it establishes something that will last for generations. It will educate the brain, the spiritual part of man. It furnishes a ladder upon which the aspiring poor may climb; and there is no use whatever, gentlemen, trying to help people who do not help themselves. You cannot push any one up a ladder unless he be willing to climb a little himself. When you stop boosting, he falls, to his injury. Therefore, I have often said, and I now repeat, that the day is coming, and already we see its dawn, in which the man who dies possessed of millions of available wealth which was free and in his hands ready to be distributed will die disgraced.... By administering surplus wealth during life great wealth may become a blessing to the community, and the occupation of the business man accumulating wealth may be elevated so as to rank with any profession. In this way he may take rank even with the physician, one of the highest of our professions, because he too, in a sense, will be a physician, looking after and trying not to cure, but to prevent, the ills of humanity. To those of you who are compelled or who desire to follow a business life and to accumulate wealth, I commend this idea. The epitaph which every rich man should wish himself justly entitled to is that seen upon the monument to Pitt:

> He lived without ostentation,
>   And he died poor.

18

Social Ethics (1911)

JANE ADDAMS

A social reformer of enormous energy and influence, Jane Addams began her long career by opening Hull House in 1889 to help poor immigrant families in Chicago. Over the years she launched a number of reform groups, including the Women's International League for Peace and Freedom; worked to change working conditions, housing regulations, and the juvenile courts; and was actively involved in politics, playing a leading role in Theodore Roosevelt's 1912 campaign for the presidency. Addams was often out of step with her times, a champion of both racial and gender equality and a pacifist who opposed U.S. entry into World War I. At a time of triumphant *laissez-faire* ideology, Addams insisted on the duty of the individual to help those less fortunate. In 1931 Addams was awarded the Nobel prize for peace. Addams wrote a number of books and articles encouraging people to join her progressive causes, as well as analyzing the motivations and methods of reformers. In the process she essentially created the modern job of social worker.

Questions to Consider

- Why should people devote energy to helping others?
- How can the charity worker overcome cultural differences?

Charitable Effort

All those hints and glimpses of a larger and more satisfying democracy, which literature and our own hopes supply, have a tendency to slip away from us and to leave us sadly unguided and perplexed when we attempt to act upon them.

Our conceptions of morality, as all our other ideas, pass through a course of development; the difficulty comes in adjusting our conduct, which has become hardened into customs and habits, to these changing moral conceptions. When this adjustment is not made, we suffer from the strain and indecision of believing one hypothesis and acting upon another.

Probably there is no relation in life which our democracy is changing more rapidly than the charitable relation—that relation which obtains between benefactor and beneficiary; at the same time there is no point of contact in our modern experience which reveals so clearly the lack of that equality which democracy implies. We have reached the moment when democracy has made such inroads upon this relationship, that the complacency of the old-fashioned charitable man is gone forever; while, at the same time, the very need and existence of charity, denies us the consolation and freedom which democracy will at last give.

It is quite obvious that the ethics of none of us are clearly defined, and we are continually obliged to act in circles of habit, based upon convictions which we no longer hold. Thus our estimate of the effect of environment and social conditions has doubtless shifted faster than our methods of administrating charity have changed. Formerly when it was believed that poverty was synonymous with vice and laziness, and that the prosperous man was the righteous man, charity was administered harshly with a good conscience; for the charitable agent really blamed the individual for his poverty, and the very fact of his own superior prosperity gave him a certain consciousness of superior morality. We have learned since that time to measure by other standards, and have ceased to accord to the money-earning capacity exclusive respect; while it is still rewarded out of all proportion to any other, its possession is by no means assumed to imply the possession of the highest moral qualities. We have learned to judge men by their social virtues as well as by their business capacity, by their devotion to intellectual and disinterested aims, and by their public spirit, and we naturally resent being obliged to judge poor people so solely upon the industrial side. Our democratic instinct instantly takes alarm. It is largely in this modern tendency to judge all men by one democratic standard, while the old charitable attitude commonly allowed the use of two standards, that much of the difficulty adheres. We know that unceasing bodily toil becomes wearing and brutalizing, and our position is totally untenable if we judge large numbers of our fellows solely upon their success in maintaining it.

The daintily clad charitable visitor who steps into the little house made untidy by the vigorous efforts of her hostess, the washerwoman, is no longer sure of her superiority to the latter; she recognizes that her hostess after all represents social value and industrial use, as over against her own parasitic cleanliness and a social standing attained only through status.

The only families who apply for aid to the charitable agencies are those who have come to grief on the industrial side; it may be through sickness, through loss of work, or for other guiltless and inevitable reasons; but the fact remains that they are industrially ailing, and must be bolstered and helped into industrial health. The charity visitor, let us assume, is a young college woman, well-bred and open-minded; when she visits the family assigned to her, she is often embarrassed to find herself obliged to lay all the stress of her teaching and advice upon the industrial virtues, and to treat the members of the family almost exclusively as factors in the industrial system. She insists that they

Source: Jane Addams, *Democracy and Social Ethics* (New York, 1911), pp. 13–20, 22–32, 44–45, 58–59, 63–64, 66–70.

must work and be self-supporting, that the most dangerous of all situations is idleness, that seeking one's own pleasure, while ignoring claims and responsibilities, is the most ignoble of actions. The members of her assigned family may have other charms and virtues—they may possibly be kind and considerate of each other, generous to their friends, but it is her business to stick to the industrial side. As she daily holds up these standards, it often occurs to the mind of the sensitive visitor, whose conscience has been made tender by much talk of brotherhood and equality, that she has no right to say these things; that her untrained hands are no more fitted to cope with actual conditions than those of her broken-down family.

The grandmother of the charity visitor could have done the industrial preaching very well, because she did have the industrial virtues and housewifely training. In a generation our experiences have changed, and our views with them; but we still keep on in the old methods, which could be applied when our consciences were in line with them, but which are daily becoming more difficult as we divide up into people who work with their hands and those who do not. The charity visitor belonging to the latter class is perplexed by recognitions and suggestions which the situation forces upon her. Our democracy has taught us to apply our moral teaching all around, and the moralist is rapidly becoming so sensitive that when his life does not exemplify his ethical convictions, he finds it difficult to preach.

Added to this is a consciousness, in the mind of the visitor, of a genuine misunderstanding of her motives by the recipients of her charity, and by their neighbors. Let us take a neighborhood of poor people, and test their ethical standards by those of the charity visitor, who comes with the best desire in the world to help them out of their distress. A most striking incongruity, at once apparent, is the difference between the emotional kindness with which relief is given by one poor neighbor to another poor neighbor, and the guarded care with which relief is given by a charity visitor to a charity recipient. The neighborhood mind is at once confronted not only by the difference of method, but by an absolute clashing of two ethical standards.

A very little familiarity with the poor districts of any city is sufficient to show how primitive and genuine are the neighborly relations. There is the greatest willingness to lend or borrow anything, and all the residents of the given tenement know the most intimate family affairs of all the others. The fact that the economic condition of all alike is on a most precarious level makes the ready outflow of sympathy and material assistance the most natural thing in the world. There are numberless instances of self-sacrifice quite unknown in the circles where greater economic advantages make that kind of intimate knowledge of one's neighbors impossible. An Irish family in which the man has lost his place, and the

woman is struggling to eke out the scanty savings by day's work, will take in the widow and her five children who have been turned into the street, without a moment's reflection upon the physical discomforts involved....

The evolutionists tell us that the instinct to pity, the impulse to aid his fellows, served man at a very early period, as a rude rule of right and wrong. There is no doubt that this rude rule still holds among many people with whom charitable agencies are brought into contact, and that their ideas of right and wrong are quite honestly outraged by the methods of these agencies. When they see the delay and caution with which relief is given, it does not appear to them a conscientious scruple, but as the cold and calculating action of a selfish man. It is not the aid that they are accustomed to receive from their neighbors, and they do not understand why the impulse which drives people to "be good to the poor" should be so severely supervised. They feel, remotely, that the charity visitor is moved by motives that are alien and unreal. They may be superior motives, but they are different, and they are "agin nature." They cannot comprehend why a person whose intellectual perceptions are stronger than his natural impulses, should go into charity work at all. The only man they are accustomed to see whose intellectual perceptions are stronger than his tenderness of heart, is the selfish and avaricious man who is frankly "on the make." If the charity visitor is such a person, why does she pretend to like the poor? Why does she not go into business at once?

We may say, of course, that it is a primitive view of life, which thus confuses intellectuality and business ability; but it is a view quite honestly held by many poor people who are obliged to receive charity from time to time. In moments of indignation the poor have been known to say: "What do you want, anyway? If you have nothing to give us, why not let us alone and stop your questionings and investigations?" "They investigated me for three weeks, and in the end gave me nothing but a black character," a little woman has been heard to assert. This indignation, which is for the most part taciturn, and a certain kindly contempt for her abilities, often puzzles the charity visitor. The latter may be explained by the standard of worldly success which the visited families hold. Success does not ordinarily go, in the minds of the poor, with charity and kindheartedness, but rather with the opposite qualities. The rich landlord is he who collects with sternness, who accepts no excuse, and will have his own. There are moments of irritation and of real bitterness against him, but there is still admiration, because he is rich and successful. The good-natured landlord, he who pities and spares his poverty-pressed tenants, is seldom rich. He often lives in the back of his house, which he has owned for a long time, perhaps has inherited; but he has been able to accumulate little. He commands the genuine love and devotion of many a poor soul, but he is treated with a certain lack of respect. In one sense he is a failure. The charity visitor, just because she is a person who concerns herself with the poor, receives a certain amount of this good-natured and kindly contempt, sometimes real affection, but little genuine respect. The poor are accustomed to help each other and to respond according to their kindliness; but when it comes to worldly judgment, they use industrial success as the sole standard. In the case of the charity visitor who has neither natural kindness nor dazzling riches, they are deprived of both standards, and they find it of course utterly impossible to judge of the motive of organized charity.

Even those of us who feel most sorely the need of more order in altruistic effort and see the end to be desired, find something distasteful in the juxtaposition of the words "organized" and "charity." We say in defence that we are striving to turn this emotion into a motive, that pity is capricious, and not to be depended on; that we mean to give it the dignity of conscious duty. But at bottom we distrust a little a scheme which substitutes a theory of social conduct for the natural promptings of the heart, even although we appreciate the complexity of the situation. The poor man who has fallen into distress, when he first asks aid, instinctively expects tenderness, consideration, and forgiveness. If it is the first time, it has taken him long to make up his mind to take the step. He comes somewhat bruised and battered, and instead of being met with warmth of heart and sympathy, he is at once chilled by an investigation and an intimation that he ought to work. He does not recognize the disciplinary aspect of the situation....

When the agent or visitor appears among the poor, and they discover that under certain conditions food and rent and medical aid are dispensed from some unknown source, every man, woman, and child is quick to learn what the conditions may be, and to follow them. Though in their eyes a glass of beer is quite right and proper when taken as any self-respecting man should take it; though they know that cleanliness is an expensive virtue which can be required of few; though they realize that saving is well-nigh impossible when but a few cents can be laid by at a time; though their feeling for the church may be something quite elusive of definition and quite apart from daily living: to the visitor they gravely laud temperance and cleanliness and thrift and religious observance. The deception in the first instances arises from a wondering inability to understand the ethical ideals which can require such impossible virtues, and from an innocent desire to please. It is easy to trace the development of the mental suggestions thus received. When A discovers that B, who is very little worse off than he, receives good things from an inexhaustible supply intended for the poor at large, he feels that he too has a claim for his share, and step by step there is developed the competitive spirit which so horrifies charity visitors when it shows itself in a tendency to "work" the relief-giving agencies....

If a poor woman knows that her neighbor next door has no shoes, she is quite willing to lend her own, that her neighbor may go decently to mass, or to work; for she knows the smallest item about the scanty wardrobe, and cheerfully helps out. When the charity visitor comes in, all the neighbors are baffled as to what her circumstances may be. They know she does not need a new pair of shoes, and rather suspect that she has a dozen pairs at home; which, indeed, she sometimes has. They imagine untold stores which they may call upon, and her most generous gift is considered niggardly, compared with what she might do. She ought to get new shoes for the family all round, "she sees well enough that they need them." It is no more than the neighbor herself would do, has practically done, when she lent her own shoes. The charity visitor has broken through the natural rule of giving, which, in a primitive society, is bounded only by the need of the recipient and the resources of the giver; and she gets herself into untold trouble when she is judged by the ethics of that primitive society.

The neighborhood understands the selfish rich people who stay in their own part of town, where all their associates have shoes and other things. Such people don't bother themselves about the poor; they are like the rich landlords of the neighborhood experience. But this lady visitor, who pretends to be good to the poor, and certainly does talk as though she were kindhearted, what does she come for, if she does not intend to give them things which are so plainly needed?

The visitor says, sometimes, that in holding her poor family so hard to a standard of thrift she is really breaking down a rule of higher living which they formerly possessed; that saving, which seems quite commendable in a comfortable part of town, appears almost criminal in a poorer quarter where the next-door neighbor needs food, even if the children of the family do not.

She feels the sordidness of constantly being obliged to urge the industrial view of life. The benevolent individual of fifty years ago honestly believed that industry and self-denial in youth would result in comfortable possessions for old age. It was, indeed, the method he had practised in his own youth, and by which he had probably obtained whatever fortune he possessed. He therefore reproved the poor family for indulging their children, urged them to work long hours, and was utterly untouched by many scruples which afflict the contemporary charity visitor. She says sometimes, "Why must I talk always of getting work and saving money, the things I know nothing about? If it were anything else I had to urge, I could do it; anything like Latin prose, which I had worried through myself, it would not be so hard." But she finds it difficult to connect the experiences of her youth with the experiences of the visited family.

Because of this diversity in experience, the visitor is continually surprised to find that the safest platitude may be challenged. She refers quite naturally to the "horrors of the saloon," and discovers that the head of her visited family does not connect them with "horrors" at all. He remembers all the kindnesses he has received there, the free lunch and treating which goes on, even when a man is out of work and not able to pay up; the loan of five dollars he got there when the charity visitor was miles away and he was threatened with eviction. He may listen politely to her reference to "horrors," but considers it only "temperance talk."...

The struggle for existence, which is so much harsher among people near the edge of pauperism, sometimes leaves ugly marks on character, and the charity visitor finds these indirect results most mystifying. Parents who work hard and anticipate an old age when they can no longer earn, take care that their children shall expect to divide their wages with them from the very first. Such a parent, when successful, impresses the immature nervous system of the child thus tyrannically establishing habits of obedience, so that the nerves and will may not depart from this control when the child is older. The charity visitor, whose family relation is lifted quite out of this, does not in the least understand the industrial foundation for this family tyranny....

The greatest difficulty is experienced when the two standards come sharply together, and when both sides make an attempt at understanding and explanation. The difficulty of making clear one's own ethical standpoint is at times insurmountable. A woman who had bought and sold school books stolen from the school fund,—books which are all plainly marked with a red stamp,—came to Hull House one morning in great distress because she had been arrested, and begged a resident "to speak to the judge." She gave as a reason the fact that the House had known her for six years, and had once been very good to her when her little girl was buried. The resident more than suspected that her visitor knew the school books were stolen when buying them, and any attempt to talk upon that subject was evidently considered very rude. The visitor wished to get out of her trial, and evidently saw no reason why the House should not help her. The alderman was out of town, so she could not go to him. After a long conversation the visitor entirely failed to get another point of view and went away grieved and disappointed at a refusal, thinking the resident simply disobliging; wondering, no doubt, why such a mean woman had once been good to her; leaving the resident, on the other hand, utterly baffled and in the state of mind she would have

been in, had she brutally insisted that a little child should lift weights too heavy for its undeveloped muscles.

Such a situation brings out the impossibility of substituting a higher ethical standard for a lower one without similarity of experience....

Of what use is all this striving and perplexity? Has the experience any value? It is certainly genuine, for it induces an occasional charity visitor to live in a tenement house as simply as the other tenants do. It drives others to give up visiting the poor altogether, because, they claim, it is quite impossible unless the individual becomes a member of a sisterhood, which requires, as some of the Roman Catholic sisterhoods do, that the member first take the vows of obedience and poverty, so that she can have nothing to give save as it is first given to her, and thus she is not harassed by a constant attempt at adjustment.

Both the tenement-house resident and the sister assume to have put themselves upon the industrial level of their neighbors, although they have left out the most awful element of poverty, that of imminent fear of starvation and a neglected old age.

The young charity visitor who goes from a family living upon a most precarious industrial level to her own home in a prosperous part of the city, if she is sensitive at all, is never free from perplexities which our growing democracy forces upon her.

We sometimes say that our charity is too scientific, but we would doubtless be much more correct in our estimate if we said that it is not scientific enough....

Let us take the example of a timid child, who cries when he is put to bed because he is afraid of the dark. The "soft-hearted" parent stays with him, simply because he is sorry for him and wants to comfort him. The scientifically trained parent stays with him, because he realizes that the child is in a stage of development in which his imagination has the best of him, and in which it is impossible to reason him out of a belief in ghosts. These two parents, wide apart in point of view, after all act much alike, and both very differently from the pseudo-scientific parent, who acts from dogmatic conviction and is sure he is right. He talks of developing his child's self-respect and good sense, and leaves him to cry himself to sleep, demanding powers of self-control and development which the child does not possess. There is no doubt that our development of charity methods has reached this pseudo-scientific and stilted stage. We have learned to condemn unthinking, ill-regulated kind-heartedness, and we take great pride in mere repression much as the stern parent tells the visitor below how admirably he is rearing the child, who is hysterically crying upstairs and laying the foundation for future nervous disorders. The pseudo-scientific spirit, or rather, the undeveloped stage of our philanthropy, is perhaps most clearly revealed in our tendency to lay constant stress on negative action. "Don't give;" "don't break down self-respect," we are constantly told. We distrust the human impulse as well as the teachings of our own experience, and in their stead substitute dogmatic rules for conduct. We forget that the accumulation of knowledge and the holding of convictions must finally result in the application of that knowledge and those convictions to life itself....

The Hebrew prophet made three requirements from those who would join the great forward-moving procession led by Jehovah. "To love mercy" and at the same time "to do justly" is the difficult task; to fulfil the first requirement alone is to fall into the error of indis-

criminate giving with all its disastrous results; to fulfil the second solely is to obtain the stern policy of withholding, and it results in such a dreary lack of sympathy and understanding that the establishment of justice is impossible. It may be that the combination of the two can never be attained save as we fulfil still the third requirement—"to walk humbly with God," which may mean to walk for many dreary miles beside the lowliest of His creatures, not even in that peace of mind which the company of the humble is popularly supposed to afford, but rather with the pangs and throes to which the poor human understanding is subjected whenever it attempts to comprehend the meaning of life.

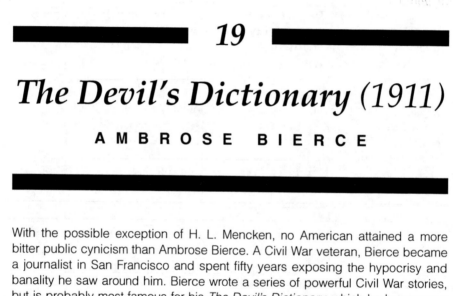

19

The Devil's Dictionary (1911)

AMBROSE BIERCE

With the possible exception of H. L. Mencken, no American attained a more bitter public cynicism than Ambrose Bierce. A Civil War veteran, Bierce became a journalist in San Francisco and spent fifty years exposing the hypocrisy and banality he saw around him. Bierce wrote a series of powerful Civil War stories, but is probably most famous for his *The Devil's Dictionary*, which he began as a column in 1881. Bierce, who may have been the most unpopular man in the United States, vanished mysteriously in northern Mexico in 1913, at the age of seventy-one. No one has ever determined why he went to Mexico or what became of him there.

Questions to Consider

- Why did the American public react so negatively to Bierce's sarcasm?
- Do you find any validity to some of Bierce's definitions?

A

ABASEMENT, *n.*   A decent and customary mental attitude in the presence of wealth or power. Peculiarly ap-

propriate in an employee when addressing an employer....

ABSTAINER, *n.*   A weak person who yields to the temptation of denying himself a pleasure. A total abstainer is one who abstains from everything but abstention, and especially from inactivity in the affairs of others....

ADMINISTRATION, *n.*   An ingenious abstraction in politics, designed to receive the kicks and cuffs due to

Source: Ambrose Bierce, *The Devil's Dictionary,* vol. 7 of *The Collected Works of Ambrose Bierce* (New York, 1911).

the premier or president. A man of straw, proof against bad-egging and dead-catting....

ADMIRATION, *n.*   Our polite recognition of another's resemblance to ourselves....

AIR, *n.*   A nutritious substance supplied by a bountiful Providence for the fattening of the poor....

ALLIANCE, *n.*   In international politics, the union of two thieves who have their hands so deeply inserted in each other's pocket that they cannot separately plunder a third....

AMBITION, *n.*   An overmastering desire to be vilified by enemies while living and made ridiculous by friends when dead....

ARMOR, *n.*   The kind of clothing worn by a man whose tailor is a blacksmith....

ASPERSE, *v.t.*   Maliciously to ascribe to another vicious actions which one has not had the temptation and opportunity to commit....

B

...BABE or BABY, *n.*   A misshapen creature of no particular age, sex, or condition, chiefly remarkable for the violence of the sympathies and antipathies it excites in others, itself without sentiment or emotion. There have been famous babes; for example, little Moses, from whose adventure in the bulrushes the Egyptian hierophants of seven centuries before doubtless derived their idle tale of the child Osiris being preserved on a floating lotus leaf....

BACCHUS, *n.*   A convenient deity invented by the ancients as an excuse for getting drunk....

BACKBITE, *v.t.*   To speak of a man as you find him when he can't find you....

BAPTISM, *n.*   A sacred rite of such efficacy that he who finds himself in heaven without having undergone it will be unhappy forever....

BAROMETER, *n.*   An ingenious instrument which indicates what kind of weather we are having....

BATTLE, *n.*   A method of untying with the teeth a political knot that would not yield to the tongue....

BEFRIEND, *v.t.*   To make an ingrate....

BEGGAR, *n.*   One who has relied on the assistance of his friends....

BIRTH, *n.*   The first and direst of all disasters....

BORE, *n.*   A person who talks when you wish him to listen....

BOUNDARY, *n.*   In political geography, an imaginary line between two nations, separating the imaginary rights of one from the imaginary rights of the other....

BRAIN, *n.*   An apparatus with which we think that we think. That which distinguishes the man who is content to *be* something from the man who wishes to *do* something. A man of great wealth, or one who has been pitchforked into high station, has commonly such a headful of brain that his neighbors cannot keep their hats on. In our civilization, and under our republican form of government, brain is so highly honored that it is rewarded by exemption from the cares of office....

BRIDE, *n.*   A woman with a fine prospect of happiness behind her.

BRUTE, *n.*   See HUSBAND.

C

...CALAMITY, *n.*   A more than commonly plain and unmistakable reminder that the affairs of this life are not of our own ordering. Calamities are of two kinds: misfortune to ourselves, and good fortune to others....

CAT, *n.*   A soft, indestructible automaton provided by nature to be kicked when things go wrong in the domestic circle....

CHRISTIAN, *n.*   One who believes that the New Testament is a divinely inspired book admirably suited to the spiritual needs of his neighbor. One who follows the teachings of Christ in so far as they are not inconsistent with a life of sin....

CLERGYMAN, *n.*   A man who undertakes the management of our spiritual affairs as a method of bettering his temporal ones....

COMMERCE, *n.*   A kind of transaction in which A plunders from B the goods of C, and for compensation B picks the pocket of D of money belonging to E....

CONSERVATIVE, *n.*   A statesman who is enamored of existing evils, as distinguished from the Liberal, who wishes to replace them with others....

CONSUL, *n.*   In American politics, a person who having failed to secure an office from the people is given one by the Administration on condition that he leave the country.

CONSULT, *v.t.*   To seek another's approval of a course already decided on.

CONTEMPT, *n.*   The feeling of a prudent man for an enemy who is too formidable safely to be opposed....

CONVENT, *n.*   A place of retirement for women who wish for leisure to meditate upon the vice of idleness.

CONVERSATION, *n.*   A fair for the display of the minor mental commodities, each exhibitor being too intent upon the arrangement of his own wares to observe those of his neighbor....

CORPORATION, *n.*   An ingenious device for obtaining individual profit without individual responsibility....

CYNIC, *n.*   A blackguard whose faulty vision sees things as they are, not as they ought to be. Hence the custom among the Scythians of plucking out a cynic's eyes to improve his vision.

D

...DAY, *n.*   A period of twenty-four hours, mostly misspent. This period is divided into two parts, the day proper and the night, or day improper—the former devoted to sins of business, the latter consecrated to the other sort. These two kinds of social activity overlap....

DEBT, *n.*   An ingenious substitute for the chain and whip of the slave-driver....

DESTINY, *n.*   A tyrant's authority for crime and fool's excuse for failure....

DICTIONARY, *n.*   A malevolent literary device for cramping the growth of a language and making it hard and inelastic. This dictionary, however, is a most useful work....

DIPLOMACY, *n.*   The patriotic art of lying for one's country....

DISCUSSION, *n.*   A method of confirming others in their errors....

DISTANCE, *n.*   The only thing that the rich are willing for the poor to call theirs and keep.

DISTRESS, *n.*   A disease incurred by exposure to the prosperity of a friend....

DOG, *n.*   A kind of additional or subsidiary Deity designed to catch the overflow and surplus of the world's worship. This Divine Being in some of his smaller and silkier incarnations takes, in the affection of Woman, the place to which there is no human male aspirant. The Dog is a survival—an anachronism. He toils not, neither does he spin, yet Solomon in all his glory never lay upon a door-mat all day long, sun-soaked and fly-fed and fat, while his master worked for the means wherewith to purchase an idle wag of the Solomonic tail, seasoned with a look of tolerant recognition....

DUTY, *n.*   That which sternly impels us in the direction of profit, along the line of desire....

E

...EDUCATION, *n.*   That which discloses to the wise and disguises from the foolish their lack of understanding....

EGOTIST, *n.*   A person of low taste, more interested in himself than in me....

ELECTRICITY, *n.*   The power that causes all natural phenomena not known to be caused by something else....

ELOQUENCE, *n.*   The art of orally persuading fools that white is the color that it appears to be. It includes the gift of making any color appear white.

ELYSIUM, *n.*   An imaginary delightful country which the ancients foolishly believed to be inhabited by the spirits of the good. This ridiculous and mischievous fable was swept off the face of the earth by the early Christians—may their souls be happy in Heaven!

EMANCIPATION, *n.*   A bondman's change from the tyranny of another to the despotism of himself....

EULOGY, *n.*   Praise of a person who has either the advantages of wealth and power, or the consideration to be dead.

EVANGELIST, *n.*   A bearer of good tidings, particularly (in a religious sense) such as assure us of our own salvation and the damnation of our neighbors....

F

...FAITH, *n.*   Belief without evidence in what is told by one who speaks without knowledge, of things without parallel.

FAMOUS, *adj.*   Conspicuously miserable....

FEAST, *n.*   A festival. A religious celebration usually signalized by gluttony and drunkenness, frequently in honor of some holy person distinguished for abstemiousness....

FIDELITY, *n.*   A virtue peculiar to those who are about to be betrayed....

FLAG, *n.*   A colored rag borne above troops and hoisted on forts and ships. It appears to serve the same purpose as certain signs that one sees on vacant lots in London—"Rubbish may be shot here."...

FORGETFULNESS, *n.*   A gift of God bestowed upon debtors in compensation for their destitution of conscience....

FRIENDLESS, *adj.*   Having no favors to bestow. Destitute of fortune. Addicted to utterance of truth and common sense....

FUTURE, *n.*   That period of time in which our affairs prosper, our friends are true and our happiness is assured.

G

GALLOWS, *n.*   A stage for the performance of miracle plays, in which the leading actor is translated to heaven. In this country the gallows is chiefly remarkable for the number of persons who escape it....

GHOST, *n.*   The outward and visible sign of an inward fear....

GRAVE, *n.*   A place in which the dead are laid to await the coming of the medical student....

GUNPOWDER, *n.*   An agency employed by civilized nations for the settlement of disputes which might become troublesome if left unadjusted....

H

HABEAS CORPUS. A writ by which a man may be taken out of jail when confined for the wrong crime.

HABIT, *n.*   A shackle for the free....

HAND, *n.* A singular instrument worn at the end of the human arm and commonly thrust into somebody's pocket....

HANGMAN, *n.* An officer of the law charged with duties of the highest dignity and utmost gravity, and held in hereditary disesteem by a populace having a criminal ancestry. In some of the American States his functions are now performed by an electrician, as in New Jersey, where executions by electricity have recently been ordered—the first instance known to this lexicographer of anybody questioning the expediency of hanging Jerseymen.

HAPPINESS, *n.* An agreeable sensation arising from contemplating the misery of another.

HARANGUE, *n.* A speech by an opponent, who is known as an harangue-outang....

HASH, *x.* There is no definition for this word—nobody knows what hash is....

HEARSE, *n.* Death's baby-carriage....

HEATHEN, *n.* A benighted creature who has the folly to worship something that he can see and feel....

HEBREW, *n.* A male Jew, as distinguished from the Shebrew, an altogether superior creation.

HELPMATE, *n.* A wife, or bitter half....

HIPPOGRIFF, *n.* An animal (now extinct) which was half horse and half griffin. The griffin was itself a compound creature, half lion and half eagle. The hippogriff was actually, therefore, only one-quarter eagle, which is two dollars and fifty cents in gold. The study of zoology is full of surprises.

HISTORIAN, *n.* A broad-gauge gossip.

HISTORY, *n.* An account mostly false, of events mostly unimportant, which are brought about by rulers mostly knaves, and soldiers mostly fools....

HOMICIDE, *n.* The slaying of one human being by another. There are four kinds of homicide: felonious, excusable, justifiable, and praiseworthy, but it makes no great difference to the person slain whether he fell by one kind or another—the classification is for advantage of the lawyers....

I

...IDIOT, *n.* A member of a large and powerful tribe whose influence in human affairs has always been dominant and controlling....

IGNORAMUS, *n.* A person unacquainted with certain kinds of knowledge familiar to yourself, and having certain other kinds that you know nothing about....

IMBECILITY, *n.* A kind of divine inspiration, or sacred fire affecting censorious critics of this dictionary....

IMMORAL, *adj.* Inexpedient....

IMPARTIAL, *adj.* Unable to perceive any promise of personal advantage from espousing either side of a controversy or adopting either of two conflicting opinions....

IMPUNITY, *n.* Wealth....

INEXPEDIENT, *adj.* Not calculated to advance one's interests....

INFIDEL, *n.* In New York, one who does not believe in the Christian religion; in Constantinople, one who does....

J

J is a consonant in English, but some nations use it as a vowel—than which nothing could be more absurd. Its original form, which has been but slightly modified, was that of the tail of a subdued dog, and it was not a letter but a character, standing for a Latin verb, *jacere,* "to throw," because when a stone is thrown at a dog the dog's tail assumes that shape. This is the origin of the letter, as expounded by the renowned Dr. Jocolpus Bumer, of the University of Belgrade, who established his conclusions on the subject in a work of three quarto volumes and committed suicide on being reminded that the j in the Roman alphabet had originally no curl.

K

...KILL, *v.t.* To create a vacancy without nominating a successor.

KILT, *n.* A costume sometimes worn by Scotchmen in America and Americans in Scotland....

KLEPTOMANIAC, *n.* A rich thief....

KORAN, *n.* A book which the Mohammedans foolishly believe to have been written by divine inspiration, but which Christians know to be a wicked imposture, contradictory to the Holy Scriptures.

L

LABOR, *n.* One of the processes by which A acquires property for B.

LAND, *n.* A part of the earth's surface, considered as property. The theory that land is property subject to private ownership and control is the foundation of modern society, and is eminently worthy of the superstructure. Carried to its logical conclusion, it means that some have the right to prevent others from living; for the right to own implies the right exclusively to occupy; and in fact laws of trespass are enacted wherever property in land is recognized. It follows that if the whole area of *terra firma* is owned by A, B and C, there will be no place for D, E, F and G to be born, or, born as trespassers, to exist....

LAWFUL, *adj.* Compatible with the will of a judge having jurisdiction.

LAWYER, *n.* One skilled in circumvention of the law....

LIAR, *n.* A lawyer with a roving commission.

LIBERTY, *n.* One of Imagination's most precious possessions....

LICKSPITTLE, *n.* A useful functionary, not infrequently found editing a newspaper....

LOGIC, *n.* The art of thinking and reasoning in strict accordance with the limitations and incapacities of the human misunderstanding. The basic of logic is the syllogism, consisting of a major and a minor premise and a conclusion—thus:

Major Premise: Sixty men can do a piece of work sixty times as quickly as one man.

Minor Premise: One man can dig a post-hole in sixty seconds; therefore—

Conclusion: Sixty men can dig a post-hole in one second.

This may be called the syllogism arithmetical, in which, by combining logic and mathematics, we obtain a double certainty and are twice blessed....

LOVE, *n.* A temporary insanity curable by marriage or by removal of the patient from the influences under which he incurred the disorder....

M

...MALEFACTOR, *n.* The chief factor in the progress of the human race....

MAMMALIA, *n. pl.* A family of vertebrate animals whose females in a state of nature suckle their young, but when civilized and enlightened put them out to nurse, or use the bottle.

MAMMON, *n.* The god of the world's leading religion. The chief temple is in the holy city of New York....

MAN, *n.* An animal so lost in rapturous contemplation of what he thinks he is as to overlook what he indubitably ought to be. His chief occupation is extermination of other animals and his own species, which, however, multiplies with such insistent rapidity as to infest the whole habitable earth and Canada....

MARTYR, *n.* One who moves along the line of least reluctance to a desired death....

MAYONNAISE, *n.* One of the sauces which serve the French in place of a state religion....

MERCHANT, *n.* One engaged in a commercial pursuit. A commercial pursuit is one in which the thing pursued is a dollar.

MERCY, *n.* An attribute beloved of detected offenders....

MISDEMEANOR, *n.* An infraction of the law having less dignity than a felony and constituting no claim to admittance into the best criminal society....

MISS, *n.* A title with which we brand unmarried women to indicate that they are in the market....

MORAL, *adj.* Conforming to a local and mutable standard of right. Having the quality of general expediency....

MYTHOLOGY, *n.* The body of a primitive people's beliefs concerning its origin, early history, heroes, deities and so forth, as distinguished from the true accounts which it invents later.

N

...NEIGHBOR, *n.* One whom we are commanded to love as ourselves, and who does all he knows how to make us disobedient....

NIRVANA, *n.* In the Buddhist religion, a state of pleasurable annihilation awarded to the wise, particularly to those wise enough to understand it....

NOVEL, *n.* A short story padded....

O

...OBSTINATE, *adj.* Inaccessible to the truth as it is manifest in the splendor and stress of our advocacy....

OCCIDENT, *n.* The part of the world lying west (or east) of the Orient. It is largely inhabited by Christians, a powerful sub-tribe of the Hypocrites, whose principal industries are murder and cheating, which they are pleased to call "war" and "commerce." These, also, are the principal industries of the Orient.

OCEAN, *n.* A body of water occupying about two-thirds of a world made for man—who has no gills....

OLD, *adj.* In that stage of usefulness which is not inconsistent with general inefficiency, as an *old man.* Discredited by lapse of time and offensive to the popular taste, as an *old* book....

ONCE, *adv.* Enough....

OPIATE, *n.* An unlocked door in the prison of Identity. It leads into the jail yard....

OPPOSITION, *n.* In politics the party that prevents the Government from running amuck by hamstringing it....

OVEREAT, *v.* To dine....

OYSTER, *n.* A slimy, gobby shellfish which civilization gives men the hardihood to eat without removing its entrails! The shells are sometimes given to the poor.

P

PAIN, *n.* An uncomfortable frame of mind that may have a physical basis in something that is being done to the body, or may be purely mental, caused by the good fortune of another....

PATIENCE, *n.* A minor form of despair, disguised as a virtue....

PATRIOTISM, *n.* Combustible rubbish ready to the torch of any one ambitious to illuminate his name.

In Dr. Johnson's famous dictionary patriotism is defined as the last resort of a scoundrel. With all due respect to an enlightened but inferior lexicographer I beg to submit that it is the first.

PEACE, *n.* In international affairs, a period of cheating between two periods of fighting....

PEDIGREE, *n.* The known part of the route from an arboreal ancestor with a swim bladder to an urban descendant with a cigarette....

PERSEVERANCE, *n.* A lowly virtue whereby mediocrity achieves an inglorious success....

PHILANTHROPIST, *n.* A rich (and usually bald) old gentleman who has trained himself to grin while his conscience is picking his pocket....

PHILOSOPHY, *n.* A route of many roads leading from nowhere to nothing....

PHYSICIAN, *n.* One upon whom we set our hopes when ill and our dogs when well....

PIETY, *n.* Reverence for the Supreme Being, based upon His supposed resemblance to man....

POCKET, *n.* The cradle of motive and the grave of conscience. In woman this organ is lacking; so she acts without motive, and her conscience, denied burial, remains ever alive, confessing the sins of others....

POLITENESS, *n.* The most acceptable hypocrisy.

POLITICS, *n.* A strife of interests masquerading as a contest of principles. The conduct of public affairs for private advantage.

POLITICIAN, *n.* An eel in the fundamental mud upon which the superstructure of organized society is reared. When he wriggles he mistakes the agitation of his tail for the trembling of the edifice. As compared with the statesman, he suffers the disadvantage of being alive....

POSITIVE, *adj.* Mistaken at the top of one's voice....

PRAY, *v.* To ask that the laws of the universe be annulled in behalf of a single petitioner confessedly unworthy....

PRECEDENT, *n.* In Law, a previous decision, rule or practice which, in the absence of a definite statute, has whatever force and authority a Judge may choose to give it, thereby greatly simplifying his task of doing as he pleases....

PREJUDICE, *n.* A vagrant opinion without visible means of support....

PRESIDENCY, *n.* The greased pig in the field game of American politics....

Q

...QUILL, *n.* An implement of torture yielded by a goose and commonly wielded by an ass....

QUORUM, *n.* A sufficient number of members of a deliberative body to have their own way and their own way of having it. In the United States Senate a quorum consists of the chairman of the Committee on Finance and a messenger from the White House; in the House of Representatives, of the Speaker and the devil....

R

RABBLE, *n.* In a republic, those who exercise a supreme authority tempered by fraudulent elections. The rabble is like the sacred Simurgh, of Arabian fable—omnipotent on condition that it do nothing. (The word is Aristocratese, and has no exact equivalent in our tongue, but means, as nearly as may be, "soaring swine.")

RACK, *n.* An argumentative implement formerly much used in persuading devotees of a false faith to embrace the living truth. As a call to the unconverted the rack never had any particular efficacy, and is now held in light popular esteem.

RADICALISM, *n.* The conservatism of to-morrow injected into the affairs of to-day....

RASCAL, *n.* A fool considered under another aspect.

RASCALITY, *n.* Stupidity militant....

RASH, *adj.* Insensible to the value of our advice....

REALLY, *adv.* Apparently....

REASONABLE, *adj.* Accessible to the infection of our own opinions. Hospitable to persuasion, dissuasion and evasion.

REBEL, *n.* A proponent of a new misrule who has failed to establish it.

RECOLLECT, *v.* To recall with additions something not previously known....

REDEMPTION, *n.* Deliverance of sinners from the penalty of their sin, through their murder of the deity against whom they sinned. The doctrine of Redemption is the fundamental mystery of our holy religion, and whoso believeth in it shall not perish, but have everlasting life in which to try to understand it....

RED-SKIN, *n.* A North American Indian, whose skin is not red—at least not on the outside....

RELIGION, *n.* A daughter of Hope and Fear, explaining to Ignorance the nature of the Unknowable....

RESIDENT, *adj.* Unable to leave....

RESOLUTE, *adj.* Obstinate in a course that we approve....

RESPONSIBILITY, *n.* A detachable burden easily shifted to the shoulders of God, Fate, Fortune, Luck or one's neighbor. In the days of astrology it was customary to unload it upon a star....

RETALIATION, *n.* The natural rock upon which is reared the Temple of Law.

RETRIBUTION, *n.* A rain of fire-and-brimstone that falls alike upon the just and such of the unjust as have not procured shelter by evicting them....

REVELATION, *n.* A famous book in which St. John the Divine concealed all that he knew. The revealing is done by the commentators, who know nothing....

REVOLUTION, *n.* In politics, an abrupt change in the form of misgovernment.... Revolutions are usually accompanied by a considerable effusion of blood, but are accounted worth it—this appraisement being made by beneficiaries whose blood had not the mischance to be shed....

RIOT, *n.* A popular entertainment given to the military by innocent bystanders....

S

SABBATH, *n.* A weekly festival having its origin in the fact that God made the world in six days and was arrested on the seventh....

SAINT, *n.* A dead sinner revised and edited....

SCRIPTURES, *n.* The sacred books of our holy religion, as distinguished from the false and profane writings on which all other faiths are based....

SELF-ESTEEM, *n.* An erroneous appraisement.

SELF-EVIDENT, *adj.* Evident to one's self and to nobody else....

SENATE, *n.* A body of elderly gentlemen charged with high duties and misdemeanors....

SLANG, *n.* The grunt of the human hog (*Pignoramus intolerabilis*) with an audible memory. The speech of one who utters with his tongue what he thinks with his ear, and feels the pride of a creator in accomplishing the feat of a parrot....

T

...TEETOTALER, *n.* One who abstains from strong drink, sometimes totally, sometimes tolerably totally.

TELEPHONE, *n.* An invention of the devil which abrogates some of the advantages of making a disagreeable person keep his distance....

TOMB, *n.* The House of Indifference. Tombs are now by common consent invested with a certain sanctity, but when they have been long tenanted it is considered no sin to break them open and rifle them, the famous Egyptologist, Dr. Huggyns, explaining that a tomb may be innocently "glened" as soon as its occupant is done "smellynge," the soul being then all exhaled. This reasonable view is now generally accepted by archaeologists, whereby the noble science of Curiosity has been greatly dignified....

TRIAL, *n.* A formal inquiry designed to prove and put upon record the blameless characters of judges, advocates and jurors. In order to effect this purpose it is necessary to supply a contrast in the person of one who is called the defendant.... If the contrast is made sufficiently clear this person is made to undergo such an affliction as will give the virtuous gentlemen a comfortable sense of their immunity, added to that of their worth. In our day the accused is usually a human being, or a socialist, but in mediaeval times, animals, fishes, reptiles and insects were brought to trial. A beast that had taken human life, or practiced sorcery, was duly arrested, tried and, if condemned, put to death by the public executioner.... D'Addosio relates from the court records many trials of pigs, bulls, horses, cocks, dogs, goats, etc., greatly, it is believed, to the betterment of their conduct and morals....

TRICHINOSIS, *n.* The pig's reply to proponents of porcophagy....

TRUTHFUL, *adj.* Dumb and illiterate.

U

...ULTIMATUM, *n.* In diplomacy, a last demand before resorting to concessions....

UN-AMERICAN, *adj.* Wicked, intolerable, heathenish....

UNIVERSALIST, *n.* One who foregoes the advantage of a Hell for persons of another faith....

URBANITY, *n.* The kind of civility that urban observers ascribe to dwellers in all cities but New York....

V

...VANITY, *n.* The tribute of a fool to the worth of the nearest ass....

VOTE, *n.* The instrument and symbol of a freeman's power to make a fool of himself and a wreck of his country.

W

...WALL STREET, *n.* A symbol of sin for every devil to rebuke. That Wall Street is a den of thieves is a belief that serves every unsuccessful thief in place of a hope in Heaven....

WAR, *n.* A by-product of the arts of peace. The most menacing political condition is a period of international amity.... War loves to come like a thief in the night; professions of eternal amity provide the night....

WHEAT, *n.* A cereal from which a tolerably good whiskey can with some difficulty be made, and which is used also for bread....

WHITE, *adj. and n.* Black....

X

X in our alphabet being a needless letter has an added invincibility to the attacks of the spelling reformers, and like them, will doubtless last as long as the language. X is the sacred symbol of ten dollars....

Y

YANKEE, *n.* In Europe, an American. In the Northern States of our Union, a New Englander. In the Southern States the word is unknown. (See DAMYANK.)...

YEAR, *n.* A period of three hundred and sixty-five disappointments....

Z

...ZEAL, *n.* A certain nervous disorder afflicting the young and inexperienced. A passion that goeth before a sprawl....

ZIGZAG, *v.t.* To move forward uncertainly, from side to side, as one carrying the white man's burden....

ZOÖLOGY, *n.* The science and history of the animal kingdom, including its king, the House Fly....

20

Monopoly, or Opportunity?
(1912)

W O O D R O W   W I L S O N

The right to create monopolies was the essential issue of the 1912 election. Theodore Roosevelt, the Progressive candidate, held that monopolies were an unavoidable part of the modern economy, but that they could be regulated for the benefit of society. The Democratic candidate, Woodrow Wilson, hoped to prevent the creation of monopolies through a federal regulation that would foster competition. Wilson maintained faith in the ability of small businesses to fuel economic growth. In his campaign speeches, such as the following, Wilson promised a "New Freedom" based on a renewal of competition.

Questions to Consider

- Is there a nostalgic component to Wilson's views?
- Can big business be restrained from dominating government?

I admit the popularity of the theory that the trusts have come about through the natural development of business conditions in the United States, and that

Source: Woodrow Wilson, *The New Freedom* (New York, 1913), pp. 164–170, 172–180.

it is a mistake to try to oppose the processes by which they have been built up, because those processes belong to the very nature of business in our time, and that therefore the only thing we can do, and the only thing we ought to attempt to do, is to accept them as inevitable arrangements and make the best out of it that we can by regulation.

I answer, nevertheless, that this attitude rests upon a confusion of thought. Big business is no doubt to a large extent necessary and natural. The development of business upon a great scale, upon a great scale of cooperation, is inevitable, and, let me add, is probably desirable. But that is a very different matter from the development of trusts, because the trusts have not grown. They have been artificially created; they have been put together, not by natural processes, but by the will, the deliberate planning will, of men who were more powerful than their neighbors in the business world, and who wished to make their power secure against competition.

The trusts do not belong to the period of infant industries. They are not the products of the time, that old laborious time, when the great continent we live on was undeveloped, the young nation struggling to find itself and get upon its feet amidst older and more experienced competitors. They belong to a very recent and very sophisticated age, when men knew what they wanted and knew how to get it by the favor of the government.

Did you ever look into the way a trust was made? It is very natural, in one sense, in the same sense in which human greed is natural. If I haven't efficiency enough to beat my rivals, then the thing I am inclined to do is to get together with my rivals and say: "Don't let's cut each other's throats; let's combine and determine prices for ourselves; determine the output, and thereby determine the prices: and dominate and control the market." That is very natural. That has been done ever since freebooting was established. That has been done ever since power was used to establish control. The reason that the masters of combination have sought to shut out competition is that the basis of control under competition is brains and efficiency. I admit that any large corporation built up by the legitimate processes of business, by economy, by efficiency, is natural; and I am not afraid of it, no matter how big it grows. It can stay big only by doing its work more thoroughly than anybody else. And there is a point of bigness,—as every business man in this country knows, though some of them will not admit it,—where you pass the limit of efficiency and get into the region of clumsiness and unwieldiness. You can make your combine so extensive that you can't digest it into a single system; you can get so many parts that you can't assemble them as you would an effective piece of machinery. The point of efficiency is overstepped in the natural process of development oftentimes, and it has been overstepped many times in the artificial and deliberate formation of trusts.

A trust is formed in this way: a few gentlemen "promote" it—that is to say, they get it up, being given enormous fees for their kindness, which fees are loaded on to the undertaking in the form of securities of one kind or another. The argument of the promoters is, not that every one who comes into the combination can carry on his business more efficiently than he did before; the argument is: we will assign to you as your share in the pool twice, three times, four times, or five times what you could have sold your business for to an individual competitor who would have to run it on an economic and competitive basis. We can afford to buy it at such a figure because we are shutting out competition. We can afford to make the stock of the combination half a dozen times what it naturally would be and pay dividends on it, because there will be nobody to dispute the prices we shall fix.

Talk of that as sound business? Talk of that as inevitable? It is based upon nothing except power. It is not based upon efficiency. It is no wonder that the big trusts are not prospering in proportion to such competitors as they still have in such parts of their business as competitors have access to; they are prospering freely only in those fields to which competition has no access..... The United States Steel Corporation is gaining in its supremacy in the American market only with regard to the cruder manufactures of iron and steel, but wherever, as in the field of more advanced manufactures of iron and steel, it has important competitors, its portion of the product is not increasing, but is decreasing, and its competitors, where they have a foothold, are often more efficient than it is.

Why? Why, with unlimited capital and innumerable mines and plants everywhere in the United States, can't they beat the other fellows in the market? Partly because they are carrying too much. Partly because they are unwieldy. Their organization is imperfect. They bought up inefficient plants along with efficient, and they have got to carry what they have paid for, even if they have to shut some of the plants up in order to make any interest on their investments; or, rather, not interest on their investments, because that is an incorrect word,—on their alleged capitalization. Here we have a lot of giants staggering along under an almost intolerable weight of artificial burdens, which they have put on their own backs, and constantly looking about lest some little pigmy with a round stone in a sling may come out and slay them.

For my part, I want the pigmy to have a chance to come out. And I foresee a time when the pigmies will be so much more athletic, so much more astute, so much more active, than the giants, that it will be a case of Jack the giant-killer. Just let some of the youngsters I know have a chance and they'll give these gentlemen points. Lend them a little money. They can't get any now. See to it that when they have got a local market they can't be squeezed out of it. Give them a chance to capture that market and then see them capture another one and another one, until these men who are carrying an intolerable load of artificial securities find that they have got to get down to hard pan to keep their foothold at all....

I take my stand absolutely, where every progressive ought to take his stand, on the proposition that private monopoly is indefensible and intolerable. And there I will fight my battle. And I know how to fight it. Everybody who has even read the newspapers knows the means by which these men built up their power and created these monopolies. Any decently equipped lawyer can suggest to you statutes by which the whole business can be stopped. What these gentlemen do not want is this: they do not want to be compelled to meet all comers on equal terms. I am perfectly willing that they should beat any competitor by fair means; but I know the foul means they have adopted, and I know that they can be stopped by law. If they think that coming into the market upon the basis of mere efficiency, upon the mere basis of knowing how to manufacture goods better than anybody else and to sell them cheaper than anybody else, they can carry the immense amount of water that they have put into their enterprises in order to buy up rivals, then they are perfectly welcome to try it. But there must be no squeezing out of the beginner, no crippling his credit; no discrimination against retailers who buy from a rival; no threats against concerns who sell supplies to a rival; no holding back of raw material from him; no secret arrangements against him. All the fair competition you choose, but no unfair competition of any kind....

...If you want to know how brains count, originate some invention which will improve the kind of machinery they are using, and then see if you can borrow enough money to manufacture it. You may be offered something for your patent by the corporation,—which will perhaps lock it up in a safe and go on using the old machinery; but you will not be allowed to manufacture. I know men who have tried it, and they could not get the money, because the great money lenders of this country are in the arrangement with the great manufacturers of this country, and they do not propose to see their control of the market interfered with by outsiders. And who are outsiders? Why, all the rest of the people of the United States are outsiders.

They are rapidly making us outsiders with respect even of the things that come from the bosom of the earth, and which belong to us in a peculiar sense. Certain monopolies in this country have gained almost complete control of the raw material, chiefly in the mines, out of which the great body of manufactures are carried on, and they now discriminate, when they will, in the sale of that raw material between those who are rivals of the monopoly and those who submit to the monopoly. We must soon come to the point where we shall say to the men who own these essentials of industry that they have got to part with these essentials by sale to all citizens of the United States with the same readiness and upon the same terms. Or else we shall tie up the resources of this country under private control in such fashion as will make our independent development absolutely impossible....

...And when you reflect that the twenty-four men who control the United States Steel Corporation, for example, are either presidents or vice-presidents or directors in 55 per cent. of the railways of the United States, reckoning by the valuation of those railroads and the amount of their stock and bonds, you know just how close the whole thing is knitted together in our industrial system, and how great the temptation is. These twenty-four gentlemen administer that corporation as if it belonged to them. The amazing thing to me is that the people of the United States have not seen that the administration of a great business like that is not a private affair; it is a public affair.

I have been told by a great many men that the idea I have, that by restoring competition you can restore industrial freedom, is based upon a failure to observe the actual happenings of the last decades in this country; because, they say, it is just free competition that has made it possible for the big to crush the little.

I reply, it is not free competition that has done that; it is illicit competition. It is competition of the kind that the law ought to stop, and can stop,—this crushing of the little man.

You know, of course, how the little man is crushed by the trusts. He gets a local market. The big concerns come in and undersell him in his local market, and that is the only market he has; if he cannot make a profit there, he is killed. They can make a profit all through the rest of the Union, while they are underselling him in his locality, and recouping themselves by what they can earn elsewhere. Thus their competitors can be put out of business, one by one, wherever they dare to show a head. Inasmuch as they rise up only one by one, these big concerns can see to it that new competitors never come into the larger field.... If ever a competitor who by good luck has plenty of money does break into the wider market, then the trust has to buy him out, paying three or four times what the business is worth. Following such a purchase it has got to pay the interest on the price it has paid for the business, and it has got to tax the whole people of the United States, in order to pay the interest on what it borrowed to do that, or on the stocks and bonds it issued to do it with. Therefore the big trusts, the big combinations, are the most wasteful, the most uneconomical, and, after they pass a certain size, the most inefficient, way of conducting the industries of this country.

A notable example is the way in which Mr. Carnegie was bought out of the steel business. Mr. Carnegie could build better mills and make better steel rails and make them cheaper than anybody else connected with what afterward became the United States Steel Corporation. They didn't dare leave him outside. He had so much more brains in finding out the best processes; he had so much more shrewdness in surrounding himself with the most successful assistants; he knew so well when a young man who came into his employ was fit for promotion and was ripe to put at the head of some branch of his business and was sure to make good, that he could undersell every mother's son of them in the market for steel rails. And they bought him out at a price that amounted to three or four times,—I believe actually five times,—the estimated value of his properties and of his business, because they couldn't beat him in competition. And then in what they charged afterward for their product,—the product of his mills included,—they made us pay the interest on the four or five times the difference.

That is the difference between a big business and a trust. A trust is an arrangement to get rid of competition, and a big business is a business that has survived competition by conquering in the field of intelligence and economy. A trust does not bring efficiency to the aid of business; it *buys efficiency out of business*. I am for big business, and I am against the trusts.

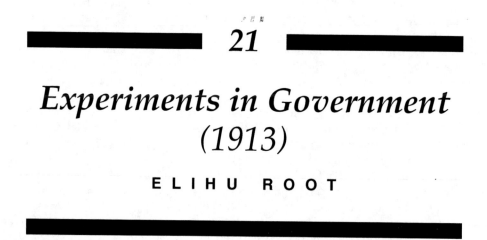

21

Experiments in Government
(1913)

E L I H U   R O O T

Winner of the Nobel Peace Prize in 1912, Elihu Root was one of the most respected men in America. Though essentially conservative, Root favored the cautious progressive reforms fostered by Theodore Roosevelt, for whom he had served as secretary of war and secretary of state. Elected to the U.S. Senate from New York, Root worked for change, carefully and slowly effected. The following speech was delivered as one of the Stafford Little Lectures at Princeton University.

Questions to Consider

- In what way was Root's attitude toward participatory democracy different from that of more liberal progressives?
- How does one determine what change is appropriate?

There are two separate processes going on among the civilized nations at the present time. One is an assault by socialism against the individualism which underlies the social system of western civilization. The other is an assault against existing institutions upon the ground that they do not adequately protect and develop the existing social order. It is of this latter process in our own country that I wish to speak, and I assume an agreement, that the right of individual liberty and the inseparable right of private property which

Source: Elihu Root, *Addresses on Government and Citizenship* (Cambridge, Mass., 1916), pp. 79–89, 91–97.

lie at the foundation of our modern civilization ought to be maintained.

…Production and commerce pay no attention to state lines. The life of the country is no longer grouped about state capitals, but about the great centers of continental production and trade. The organic growth which must ultimately determine the form of institutions has been away from the mere union of states towards the union of individuals in the relation of national citizenship.

The same causes have greatly reduced the independence of personal and family life. In the eighteenth century life was simple. The producer and consumer were near together and could find each other. Every one who had an equivalent to give in property or service could readily secure the support of himself and his family without asking anything from government except the preservation of order. Today almost all Americans are dependent upon the action of a great number of other persons mostly unknown. About half of our people are crowded into the cities and large towns. Their food, clothes, fuel, light, water—all come from distant sources, of which they are in the main ignorant, through a vast, complicated machinery of production and distribution with which they have little direct relation. If anything occurs to interfere with the working of the machinery, the consumer is individually helpless. To be certain that he and his family may continue to live he must seek the power of combination with others, and in the end he inevitably calls upon that great combination of all citizens which we call government to do something more than merely keep the peace—to regulate the machinery of production and distribution and safeguard it from interference so that it shall continue to work.

A similar change has taken place in the conditions under which a great part of our people engage in the industries by which they get their living. Under comparatively simple industrial conditions the relation between employer and employee was mainly a relation of individual to individual with individual freedom of contract and freedom of opportunity essential to equality in the commerce of life. Now, in the great manufacturing, mining and transportation industries of the country, instead of the free give and take of individual contract there is substituted a vast system of collective bargaining between great masses of men organized and acting through their representatives, or the individual on the one side accepts what he can get from superior power on the other. In the movement of these mighty forces of organization the individual laborer, the individual stockholder, the individual consumer, is helpless.

There has been another change of conditions through the development of political organization. The theory of political activity which had its origin approximately in the administration of President Jackson, and which is characterized by Marcy's declaration that "to the victors belong the spoils," tended to make the possession of office the primary and all-absorbing purpose of political conflict. A complicated system of party organization and representation grew up under which a disciplined body of party workers in each state supported each other, controlled the machinery of nomination, and thus controlled nominations. The members of state legislatures and other officers, when elected, felt a more acute responsibility to the organization which could control their renomination than to the electors, and therefore became accustomed to shape their conduct according to the wishes of the nominating organization. Accordingly the real power of government came to be vested to a high degree in these unofficial political organizations, and where there was a strong man at the head of an organization his control came to be something very closely approaching dictatorship. Another feature of this system aggravated its evils. As population grew, political campaigns became more expensive. At the same time, as wealth grew, corporations for production and transportation increased in capital and extent of operations and became more dependent upon the protection or toleration of government. They found a ready means to secure this by contributing heavily to the campaign funds of political organizations, and therefore their influence played a large part in determining who should be nominated and elected to office. So that in many states political organizations controlled the operations of government, in accordance with the wishes of the managers of the great corporations. Under these circumstances our governmental institutions were not working as they were intended to work, and a desire to break up and get away from this extra constitutional method of controlling our constitutional government has caused a great part of the new political methods of the last few years.

It is manifest that the laws which were entirely adequate, under the conditions of a century ago, to secure individual and public welfare must be in many respects inadequate to accomplish the same results under all these new conditions; and our people are now engaged in the difficult but imperative duty of adapting their laws to the life of today. The changes in conditions have come very rapidly and a good deal of experiment will be necessary to find out just what government can do and ought to do to meet them.

The process of devising and trying new laws to meet new conditions naturally leads to the question whether we need not merely to make new laws but also to modify the principles upon which our government is based and the institutions of government designed for the application of those principles to the affairs of life. Upon this question it is of the utmost importance that we proceed with considerate wisdom….

When proposals are made to change these institutions there are certain general considerations which should be observed.

The first consideration is that free government is impossible except through prescribed and established governmental institutions, which work out the ends of government through many separate human agents, each doing his part in obedience to law. Popular will cannot execute itself directly except through a mob. Popular will cannot get itself executed through an irresponsible executive, for that is simple autocracy. An executive limited only by the direct expression of popular will cannot be held to responsibility against his will, because, having possession of all the powers of government, he can prevent any true, free, and general expression adverse to himself, and unless he yields voluntarily he can be overturned only by a revolution.... A system with a plebiscite at one end and Louis Napoleon at the other could not give France free government; and it was only after the humiliation of defeat in a great war and the horrors of the Commune that the French people were able to establish a government which would really execute their will through carefully devised institutions in which they gave their chief executive very little power indeed.

We should, therefore, reject every proposal which involves the idea that the people can rule merely by voting, or merely by voting and having one man or group of men to execute their will.

A second consideration is that in estimating the value of any system of governmental institutions due regard must be had to the true functions of government and to the limitations imposed by nature upon what it is possible for government to accomplish. We all know of course that we cannot abolish all the evils in this world by statute or by the enforcement of statutes, nor can we prevent the inexorable law of nature which decrees that suffering shall follow vice, and all the evil passions and folly of mankind. Law cannot give to depravity the rewards of virtue, to indolence the rewards of industry, to indifference the rewards of ambition, or to ignorance the rewards of learning. The utmost that government can do is measurably to protect men, not against the wrong they do themselves but against wrong done by others, and to promote the long, slow process of educating mind and character to a better knowledge and nobler standards of life and conduct. We know all this, but when we see how much misery there is in the world and instinctively cry out against it, and when we see some things that government may do to mitigate it, we are apt to forget how little after all it is possible for any government to do, and to hold the particular government of the time and place to a standard of responsibility which no government can possibly meet. The chief motive power which has moved

mankind along the course of development which we call the progress of civilization has been the sum total of intelligent selfishness in a vast number of individuals, each working for his own support, his own gain, his own betterment. It is that which has cleared the forests and cultivated the fields and built the ships and railroads, made the discoveries and inventions, covered the earth with commerce, softened by intercourse the enmities of nations and races, and made possible the wonders of literature and of art. Gradually, during the long process, selfishness has grown more intelligent, with a broader view of individual benefit from the common good, and gradually the influences of nobler standards of altruism, of justice, and human sympathy have impressed themselves upon the conception of right conduct among civilized men. But the complete control of such motives will be the millennium....

A third consideration is that it is not merely useless but injurious for government to attempt too much. It is manifest that to enable it to deal with the new conditions I have described we must invest government with authority to interfere with the individual conduct of the citizen to a degree hitherto unknown in this country. When government undertakes to give the individual citizen protection by regulating the conduct of others towards him in the field where formerly he protected himself by his freedom of contract, it is limiting the liberty of the citizen whose conduct is regulated and taking a step in the direction of paternal government. While the new conditions of industrial life make it plainly necessary that many such steps shall be taken, they should be taken only so far as they are necessary and are effective. Interference with individual liberty by government should be jealously watched and restrained, because the habit of undue interference destroys that independence of character without which in its citizens no free government can endure.

We should not forget that while institutions receive their form from national character they have a powerful reflex influence upon that character. Just so far as a nation allows its institutions to be moulded by its weaknesses of character rather than by its strength it creates an influence to increase weakness at the expense of strength.

The habit of undue interference by government in private affairs breeds the habit of undue reliance upon government in private affairs at the expense of individual initiative, energy, enterprise, courage, independent manhood.

The strength of self-government and the motive power of progress must be found in the characters of the individual citizens who make up a nation. Weaken individual character among a people by comfortable reliance upon paternal government and a nation soon becomes incapable of free self-government and fit only to be governed: the higher and nobler qualities of national life that make for ideals and effort and achievement become atrophied and the nation is decadent.

A fourth consideration is that in the nature of things all government must be imperfect because men are imperfect....

It is not unusual to see governmental methods reformed and after a time, long enough to forget the evils that caused the change, to have a new movement for a reform which consists in changing back to substantially the same old methods that were cast out by the first reform.

The recognition of shortcomings or inconveniences in government is not by itself sufficient to warrant a change of system. There should be also an effort to estimate and compare the short-comings and inconveniences of the system to be substituted, for although they may be different they will certainly exist.

A fifth consideration is that whatever changes in government ought to be made, we should follow the method which undertakes as one of its cardinal points to hold fast that which is good.... Human nature does not change very much. The forces of evil are hard to control now as they always have been. It is easy to fail and hard to succeed in reconciling liberty and order. In dealing with this most successful body of governmental institutions the question should not be what sort of government do you or I think we should have. What you and I think on such a subject is of very little value indeed. The question should be: How can we adapt our laws and the workings of our government to the new conditions which confront us without sacrificing any essential element of this system of government which has so nobly stood the test of time and without abandoning the political principles which have inspired the growth of its institutions? For there are political principles, and nothing can be more fatal to self-government than to lose sight of them under the influence of apparent expediency.

In attempting to answer this question we need not trouble ourselves very much about the multitude of excited controversies which have arisen over new methods of extra constitutional-political organization and procedure. Direct nominations, party enrollments, instructions to delegates, presidential preference primaries, independent nominations, all relate to forms of voluntary action outside the proper field of governmental institutions. All these new political methods are the result of efforts of the rank and file of voluntary parties to avoid being controlled by the agents of their own party organization, and to get away from real evils in the form of undue control by organized minorities with the support of organized capital. None of these expedients is an end in itself. They are tentative, experimental. They are movements not towards something definite

but away from something definite. They may be inconvenient or distasteful to some of us, but no one need be seriously disturbed by the idea that they threaten our system of government. If they work well they will be an advantage. If they work badly they will be abandoned and some other expedient will be tried, and the ultimate outcome will doubtless be an improvement upon the old methods....

The Constitution of the United States deals in the main with essentials. There are some non-essential directions such as those relating to the methods of election and of legislation, but in the main it sets forth the foundations of government in clear, simple, concise terms. It is for this reason that it has stood the test of more than a century with but slight amendment, while the modern state constitutions, into which a multitude of ordinary statutory provisions are crowded, have to be changed from year to year. The peculiar and essential qualities of the government established by the Constitution are:

First, it is representative.

Second, it recognizes the liberty of the individual citizen as distinguished from the total mass of citizens, and it protects that liberty by specific limitations upon the power of government.

Third, it distributes the legislative, executive and judicial powers, which make up the sum total of all government, into three separate departments, and specifically limits the powers of the officers in each department.

Fourth, it superimposes upon a federation of state governments, a national government with sovereignty acting directly not merely upon the states, but upon the citizens of each state, within a line of limitation drawn between the powers of the national government and the powers of the state governments.

Fifth, it makes observance of its limitations requisite to the validity of laws, whether passed by the nation or by the states, to be judged by the courts of law in each concrete case as it arises.

Every one of these five characteristics of the government established by the Constitution was a distinct advance beyond the ancient attempts at popular government, and the elimination of any one of them would be a retrograde movement and a reversion to a former and discarded type of government. In each case it would be the abandonment of a distinctive feature of government which has succeeded, in order to go back and try again the methods of government which have failed. Of course we ought not to take such a backward step except under the pressure of inevitable necessity.

The first two of the characteristics which I have enumerated, those which embrace the conception of representative government and the conception of individual liberty, were the products of the long process of development of freedom in England and America. They were not invented by the makers of the Constitution. They have been called inventions of the Anglo-Saxon race. They are the chief contributions of that race to the political development of civilization....

The initiative and compulsory referendum are attempts to cure the evils which have developed in our practice of representative government by means of a return to the old, unsuccessful, and discarded method of direct legislation and by rehabilitating one of the most impracticable of Rousseau's theories. Every candid student of our governmental affairs must agree that the evils to be cured have been real and that the motive which has prompted the proposal of the initiative and referendum is commendable. I do not think that these expedients will prove wise or successful ways of curing these evils for reasons which I will presently indicate; but it is not necessary to assume that their trial will be destructive of our system of government. They do not aim to destroy representative government, but to modify and control it, and were it not that the effect of these particular methods is likely to go beyond the intention of their advocates they would not interfere seriously with representative government except in so far as they might ultimately prove to be successful expedients. If they did not work satisfactorily they would be abandoned, leaving representative government still in full force and effectiveness.

There is now a limited use of the referendum upon certain comparatively simple questions. No one has ever successfully controverted the view expressed by Burke in his letter to the electors of Bristol, that his constituents were entitled not merely to his vote but to his judgment, even though they might not agree with it....

In this field the weakness, both of the initiative and of the compulsory referendum, is that they are based upon a radical error as to what constitutes the true difficulty of wise legislation. The difficulty is not to determine what ought to be accomplished but to determine how to accomplish it. The affairs with which statutes have to deal as a rule involve the working of a great number and variety of motives incident to human nature, and the working of those motives depends upon complicated and often obscure facts of production, trade, social life, with which men generally are not familiar and which require study and investigation to understand. Thrusting a rigid prohibition or command into the operation of these forces is apt to produce quite unexpected and unintended results. Moreover, we already have a great body of laws, both statutory and customary, and a great body of judicial decisions as to the meaning and effect of existing laws. The result of adding a new law to this existing body of laws is that we get, not the simple consequence which the words,

taken by themselves, would seem to require, but a resultant of forces from the new law taken in connection with all existing laws. A very large part of the litigation, injustice, dissatisfaction, and contempt for law which we deplore, results from ignorant and inconsiderate legislation with perfectly good intentions. The only safeguard against such evils and the only method by which intelligent legislation can be reached is the method of full discussion, comparison of views, modification and amendment of proposed legislation in the light of discussion and the contribution and conflict of many minds. This process can be had only through the procedure of representative legislative bodies. Representative government is something more than a device to enable the people to have their say when they are too numerous to get together and say it. It is something more than the employment of experts in legislation. Through legislative procedure a different kind of treatment for legislative questions is secured by concentration of responsibility, by discussion, and by opportunity to meet objection with amendment. For this reason the attempt to legislate by calling upon the people by popular vote to say yes or no to complicated statutes must prove unsatisfactory and on the whole injurious. In ordinary cases the voters will not and cannot possibly bring to the consideration of proposed statutes the time, attention, and knowledge required to determine whether such statutes will accomplish what they are intended to accomplish; and the vote usually will turn upon the avowed intention of such proposals rather than upon their adequacy to give effect to the intention....

The measures submitted at one time in some of the western states now fill considerable volumes.

With each proposal the voter's task becomes more complicated and difficult.

Yet our ballots are already too complicated. The great blanket sheets with scores of officers and hundreds of names to be marked are quite beyond the intelligent action in detail of nine men out of ten.

The most thoughtful reformers are already urging that the voter's task be made more simple by giving him fewer things to consider and act upon at the same time.

This is the substance of what is called the Short Ballot reform; and it is right, for the more questions divide public attention the fewer questions the voters really decide for themselves on their own judgment and the greater the power of the professional politician.

There is moreover a serious danger to be apprehended from the attempt at legislation by the initiative and compulsory referendum, arising from its probable effect on the character of representative bodies. These expedients result from distrust of legislatures. They are based on the assertion that the people are not faithfully represented in their legislative bodies, but are misrepresented. The same distrust has led to the encumbering of modern state constitutions by a great variety of minute limitations upon legislative power. Many of these constitutions, instead of being simple framework of government, are bulky and detailed statutes legislating upon subjects which the people are unwilling to trust the legislature to deal with. So between the new constitutions, which exclude the legislatures from power, and the referendum, by which the people overrule what they do, and the initiative, by which the people legislate in their place, the legislative representatives who were formerly honored, are hampered, shorn of power, relieved of responsibility, discredited, and treated as unworthy of confidence. The unfortunate effect of such treatment upon the character of legislatures and the kind of men who will be willing to serve in them can well be imagined. It is the influence of such treatment that threatens representative institutions in our country.

Granting that there have been evils in our legislative system which ought to be cured, I cannot think that this is the right way to cure them. It would seem that the true way is for the people of the country to address themselves to the better performance of their own duty in selecting their legislative representatives and in holding those representatives to strict responsibility for their action. The system of direct nominations, which is easy of application in the simple proceeding of selecting members of a legislature, and the short ballot reform aim at accomplishing that result. I think that along these lines the true remedy is to be found. No system of self-government will continue successful unless the voters have sufficient public spirit to perform their own duty at the polls, and the attempt to reform government by escaping from the duty of selecting honest and capable representatives, under the idea that the same voters who fail to perform that duty will faithfully perform the far more onerous and difficult duty of legislation, seems an exhibition of weakness rather than of progress.

22

The Achievements and Aspirations of Labor (1914)

S A M U E L   G O M P E R S

In the early twentieth century the labor movement in the United States was sharply divided between radical socialist groups such as the I.W.W. and the more moderate American Federation of Labor. Arrayed against both was the power of corporate America, which often found active support in the police power of the state. The corporations, organized into the National Association of Manufacturers, also found a powerful ally in America's traditional individualism; industrial leaders often argued that unions interfered with the individual worker's right to negotiate a private contract with the employer. Samuel Gompers, the founding president of the A. F. of L., an office he held nearly every year until his death in 1924, appeared before the Commission on Industrial Relations in May 1914, to appeal for the rights of labor to organize. For the first time, workers had a U.S. president, Woodrow Wilson, who demonstrated some sympathy for their position. Gompers compiled his testimony, edited and rewritten, into a pamphlet that was issued by the A. F. of L.

Questions to Consider

- What, according to Gompers, do America's workers want?
- Why does the A. F. of L. oppose socialism?

The American Federation of Labor was formed in 1881 in Pittsburgh. I was elected its first vice-president. With the exception of three terms I have been President of the A. F. of L. since that time.

The Federation covers practically the whole field of industry. There are no limitations as to membership. The only requirement, so far as the A. F. of L. is concerned, is that the organization desiring affiliation shall be composed of wage-earners.

The A. F. of L., as its name implies, is a federation, and not, as it is often mistakenly called, an organization. It is a federation of organizations, each of which has its own government, determined by its own needs and requirements, the result of the experiences of the members of the organization. This right to self-government was recognized in the beginning and has been reaffirmed and adhered to as consistently as possible. The Federation has no powers except those which are authorized and conceded by the organizations which compose it. These powers are enumerated in its written constitution and the definite direction of conventions....

The affiliated organizations are held together by moral obligation, a spirit of camaraderie, a spirit of group patriotism, a spirit of mutual assistance.

There are no coercive methods used by the A. F. of L. to prevent the withdrawal or secession of any affiliated organization. The Western Federation of Miners, for instance, withdrew from the A. F. of L. about 1896. There were many efforts and many suggestions made to induce individual unions belonging to the Western Federation of Miners to join the A. F. of L. as local unions. Not only were these efforts discouraged but the proposal was repudiated.

Similarly, no coercion is used in regard to national organizations which are not affiliated to the A. F. of L. We feel that it is the duty of every wage-worker to belong to the union of his trade or calling; that it is the duty of the local union of a trade or calling to belong to the national or international union of that trade or calling; and that it is equally the moral duty of every national or international organization of bona fide workingmen to belong to the A. F. of L. But coercive methods are never employed.

...There was a constant continual growth until September 30, 1913, the date for which the chart was made, at which time the membership upon which per capita tax was paid to the A. F. of L. was 2,054,526. There has been an increase in membership since then.

...The five departments were created for the mutual protection, the advancement of the individual trades or callings of the industries interested in the departments. On this map are represented the 42 state federations of labor, the 639 local trade and federal labor unions, the 621 city central bodies, the 317 local councils—that is, of the trades primarily represented in the departments—and the 20,046 local trade unions. The chart as made up illustrates the ligaments, the heartstrings, we might say, of the Federation. The membership of the organizations affiliated to the A. F. of L. is composed of adults, chiefly men, but there are some women. If you allow five to a family it is only fair to assume that associated and identified with the A. F. of L. we have about 11,000,000.

Recognizing the fact that associated effort is of greater influence and power to secure a given object than is individual effort the first purpose toward which the A. F. of L. directs its efforts is the encouragement of trade and labor unions and the closer federation of such unions. These efforts are concerned with local, state, national, and international bodies, the establishment of departments and central bodies in order that the organizations may aid and assist each other in industrial struggles. They aim at the protection of the rights and the interests of the members and of all working people, the promotion and the advancement of their economic, political, and social rights. They aim to make life better worth living in our day, so that the workers may be in a better position to meet any problem that may confront future generations. In a word, the organizations leave no effort untried by which the working people may find betterment in any field of human activity.

There is no limit to the courses which may be pursued by the A. F. of L. that are calculated to be of aid to the people of our country, primarily the working people. Of course I could go into detail, but the omission of any one factor could and would be interpreted as a delimitation of the Federation's activities. So I include the sum total of human activities regardless of what fields they may be, anything which can aid, promote, ad-

---

Source: Samuel Gompers, *The American Labor Movement: Its Makeup, Achievements and Aspirations* (Washington, D.C., 1914), pp. 7–8, 10–24, 27–35.

vance, or protect the rights and interests of the working people, to establish better conditions and to work for the greatest sum total of human happiness. At no place in their scheme or rules, or in their order of development, is there a limit placed upon the work and the activities of the A. F. of L.....

The A. F. of L. has expressed itself in favor of shortening the workday in keeping with the increased productiveness of machinery. The demand and the movement for a shorter workday had been going on for nearly fifteen or twenty years prior to the organization of the A. F. of L., but it has had a more concrete form and expression since the A. F. of L. was organized in 1881.

The A. F. of L. declared that concerted effort should be made by the working people of the United States to secure the eight-hour workday. On May 1, 1886, the Federation offered its services to be helpful to the organizations in the establishment of the eight-hour workday by conferences between workmen and employers, by correspondence, by publications, agitation and education....

The A. F. of L. is in favor of a shorter workday, and a progressive decrease of working hours in keeping with the development of machinery and the use of productive forces. The Federation has recognized the need for greater opportunities and more time for rest, leisure and cultivation among the workers. It favors a rest of not less than a day and a half in each week. We insist upon one entire day of rest in each week....

The Federation favors securing more effective inspection of workshops, factories, and mines, and has worked for the accomplishment of that purpose.

The Federation does not favor the employment of children under 16 years of age and has endeavored to forbid such employment.

It favors forbidding interstate transportation of the products of convict labor and the products of all uninspected factories and mines.

The A. F. of L. favors direct employment of workers by the United States government, state governments, and municipal governments without intervention of contractors, and has accomplished this to a large degree.

The A. F. of L. is not in favor of fixing, by legal enactment, certain minimum wages. The attempts of the government to establish wages at which workmen may work, according to the teachings of history, will result in a long era of industrial slavery....

There is now a current movement to increase wages by a proposal to determine a minimum wage by political authorities. It is a maxim in law that once a court is given jurisdiction over an individual it has the power, the field, and authority to exercise that jurisdiction. "I fear the Greeks even when they bear gifts." An attempt to entrap the American workmen into a species of slavery, under guise of an offer of this character is resented by the men and women of the American trade union movement.

When the question of fixing, by legal enactment, minimum wages for women was before the Executive Council of the A. F. of L. for investigation and discussion, and subsequently before the convention of the A. F. of L., there was a great diversion of views. I am betraying no confidence when I say that. The official decision of the convention was that the subject was worthy of further discussion and consideration. In my judgment the proposal to establish by law a minimum wage for women, though well meant, is a curb upon the rights, the natural development, and the opportunity for development of the women employed in the industries of our country.

If the legislature should once fix a minimum wage it would have the opportunity to use the machinery of the state to enforce work at that rate whether the workers desired to render services or not. I am very suspicious of the activities of governmental agencies. I apprehend that once the state is allowed to fix a minimum rate, the state would also take the right to compel men or women to work at that rate. I have some apprehension that if the legislature were allowed to establish a maximum workday it might also compel workmen to work up to the maximum allowed. I ought to say, however, that I am in favor of the legal enactment fixing the maximum hours of labor for all workmen in direct government employment and for those who work for contractors substituted for governmental authority.

The A. F. of L. is in favor of fixing the maximum number of hours of work for children, minors, and women. It does not favor a legal limitation of the workday for adult men workers. The unions have very largely established the shorter workday by their own initiative, power and influence; they have done it for themselves. The A. F. of L. is opposed to limiting, by legal statutory authority, the hours of work for men in private industries. The A. F. of L. has apprehensions as to the wisdom of placing in the hands of the government additional powers which may be used to the detriment of the working people. It particularly opposes this policy when the things can be done by the workmen themselves....

The A. F. of L. encourages the practice of its various affiliated organizations in endeavoring to secure a shorter workday by means of collective agreements with employers in the various industries, but it opposes reaching the same result by means of a law binding upon all employers in a given state, or throughout the union. If there were a movement and a possibility of establishing an eight-hour workday and a minimum wage by legal enactment throughout the land, the

Federation would oppose such policies, because it has in a large measure accomplished the same purposes and will accomplish them by the initiative of the associations or the organizations and by the grit and courage of the manhood and womanhood of the men and women of the A. F. of L. That these results have been accomplished through the initiative and voluntary association of the workers precludes the question of having legal enactment for the same purpose. In addition, the giving of jurisdiction to government and to governmental agencies is always dangerous when it comes to governing the working people.

The A. F. of L. favors a system of non-contributing old-age pensions for workers who have reached a certain age to be established by legal enactment and maintained by governmental machinery. The Federation favors a general system of state insurance against sickness, disability, and accidents. It has not endorsed state insurance of unemployment. In regard to the problem of unemployment the Federation proposes to shorten the workday of the employes, that they may share with the unemployed the work that is to be performed, and thereby tend constantly toward the elimination of unemployment. The American workman refuses to regard unemployment as a permanent evil attending the industrial and economic forces of our country. The American workmen propose to share work with those who are unemployed and thereby to help to find work for the unemployed.

The A. F. of L. encourages and stimulates the workmen in their efforts to secure a constantly increasing share in the products of labor, an increasing share in the consumption and use of things produced, thereby giving employment to the unemployed, the only effective way by which that can be done....

The existence of the organized labor movement in 1907, as well as its existence today, has been and is the most potent force in our country to prevent the establishment of conditions that would or will re-act to the great detriment of the working people of our country. During the financial panic of 1907, the determination of the labor movement to prevent, to resist at all hazards any attempt to reduce wages was a clarion call to the workers and a warning to the employers that they must not apply in our time the old methods of meeting the defects or the faults of their own planning.

The A. F. of L. and the bona fide organized labor movement are more concerned in doing the actual work of alleviating the present bad conditions than in promulgating programs. It is the easiest thing in the world to promulgate programs which are but simple, idle, elusive words and mean nothing substantial to the people....

The A. F. of L. favors unrestricted and equal suffrage for men and women, and has done much to advance that cause.

It favors the initiative, referendum, and recall....

It favors restriction of the powers of judges to nullify laws and to set them aside as unconstitutional.

The Federation favors making the Constitution of the United States amendable by an easier method than provided at present. The present method of amendment is very cumbersome and slow. A written constitution is a chart which ought not to be subject to changes at every ebb and flow of the tide, but ought to be more easily changed than is now possible. The Federation favors curbing the powers of courts to punish for alleged contempts committed in connection with labor disputes.

It favors the enactment of further measures for general education and particularly for vocational education in useful pursuits....

The A. F. of L. is in favor of the free administration of justice. The measures advocated by the A. F. of L. include those things which are essential for the development and the betterment of the working people of America. As a matter of fact, the Socialist party has purloined the demands and the vocabulary of the American labor movement and has adopted them as its own. These demands have been promulgated, declared for, and fought for, and in many instances accomplished by the A. F. of L. and the organized labor movement of the country. They have been put into the Socialist party platform simply as vote catchers. Some of them have been adopted by the Republican party and by the Democratic party....

The workers of the United States do not receive the full product of their labor. It is impossible for any one to say definitely what proportion the workers receive in payment for their labor, but due to the organized labor movement they have received and are receiving a larger share of the product of their labor than ever before in the history of modern industry. One of the functions of organized labor is to increase the share of the workers in the product of their labor. Organized labor makes constantly increasing demands upon society for rewards for the services which the workers give to society and without which civilized life would be impossible. The process of increasing the share is not always gradual, but it is continual. The organized labor movement has generally succeeded in forcing an increase in the proportion the workers receive of the general product.

The working people—and I prefer to say working people and to speak of them as really human beings—are prompted by the same desires, the same hopes of a better life as are all other people. They are not willing to wait for a better life until after they have shuffled off this mortal coil but they want improvements here and now. They want to make conditions better for their children so that they may be prepared to meet other and new problems of their time. The working people are pressing forward, making their demands and presenting their claims with whatever power they can exercise in a natural, normal manner to secure a larger and constantly increasing share of what they produce. They are working toward the highest and the best ideals of social justice.

The intelligent, common-sense workingmen prefer to deal with the problems of today, with which they must contend if they want to make advancements, rather than to deal with a picture and a dream which have never had, and, I am sure, will never have, any reality in the affairs of humanity, and which threaten, if they could be introduced, the most pernicious system for circumscribing effort and activity that has ever been invented....

In improving conditions from day to day the organized labor movement has no "fixed program" for human progress. If you start out with a program everything must conform to it. With theorists, if facts do not conform to their theories, then so much the worse for the facts. Their declarations of theories and actions refuse to be hampered by facts. We do not set any particular standard, but work for the best possible conditions immediately obtainable for the workers. When they are obtained then we strive for better.

It does not require any elaborate social philosophy or great discernment to know that a wage of $3 a day and a workday of eight hours in sanitary workshops are better than $2.50 a day and a workday of twelve hours under perilous conditions. The working people will not stop when any particular point is reached; they will never stop in their efforts to obtain a better life for themselves, for their wives, for their children, and for all humanity. The object is to attain complete social justice.

The Socialist party has for its purpose the abolition of the present system of wages. Many employers agree with that purpose—the abolition of wages. But the A. F. of L. goes beyond the system which those dreamers have conceived.

The movement of the working people, whether under the A. F. of L. or not, will simply follow the human impulse for improvement in conditions wherever that may lead, and wherever that may lead they will go without aiming at any theoretical goal. Human impulse for self-betterment will lead constantly to the material, physical, social, and moral betterment of the people. We decline to commit our labor movement to any species of speculative philosophy.

The full value of production does not go to the actual working men today. A portion goes to investment, superintendence, agencies for the creation of wants among people, and many other things. Some of these are legitimate factors in industry entitled to reward, but many of them should be eliminated. The legitimate factors are superintendency, the creation of wants, administration, returns for investment in so far as it is honest investment and does not include watered stock or inflated holdings.

Whether or not dividends should be paid as an incident to stock ownership regardless of the personal services performed, the activity or inactivity of the owner of the stock, depends altogether upon whether the investment is an honest one. An honest investment is an honest actual physical investment. I am out of harmony with and opposed to the manipulation of stocks and of the stock market and all manner of speculation. I will do whatever I can to eliminate speculation involved in stocks and the fundamentals of stock jobbery and stock sales. The vast sums of money paid annually in dividends on stocks and interest on bonds by corporations managing and operating important industries constitute a very large proportion of the incomes from these industries. This is an unfair distribution of the incomes from industries. The owners, stockholders or bondholders of modern corporations receive from this distribution an unearned income which is taken from the product of the labor of those who produce it.

The efforts of the American labor movement to secure a larger share of the income are directed against all who illegitimately stand between the workers and the attainment of a better life. This class includes all who have not made honest investment in honest enterprise. Employers, capitalists, stockholders, bondholders—the capitalist class generally—oppose the efforts of the workers in the A. F. of L. and in other organizations to obtain a larger share of the product. Very much of the opposition to the efforts of the working people to secure improved conditions has come from those who obtain what may be called an unearned share in the distribution. The beneficiaries of the present system of distribution desire to retain as much as possible of their present share or to increase that proportion. But an additional reason that leads to opposition is that there are employers who live in the twentieth century, yet who have the mental outlook of the sixteenth century in their attitude toward the working people, and who still imagine that they are "masters of all they survey." These employers think that any attempt upon the part of the working people to secure improvements in their condition is a spirit of rebellion that must be frowned down. But we organized workers have found that after we have had some contests with employers, whether we have won the battle or lost it, if we but maintain our organization there is less difficulty thereafter in reaching a joint agreement or a collective bargain involving improved conditions of the workers.

The stronger the organization of the workers the greater the likelihood of their securing concessions. These concessions are not altogether because of the strength shown by the employes, but result in part from the changed attitude of the employer....

Because employers as a class are interested in maintaining or increasing their share of the general product and because workers are determined to demand a greater and ever greater share of this same general product the economic interests between these two are not harmonious. Upon this point I have been repeatedly misrepresented by socialist writers and orators whose frequent repetitions of that misrepresentation have finally convinced them of the truth of their assertion. No amount of emphatic repudiation of that statement, no matter how often that repudiation and denial have been expressed, has secured a change in the assertion that my position was contrary to the one I have just stated.

From my earliest understanding of the conditions that prevail in the industrial world I have been convinced and I have asserted that the economic interests of the employing class and those of the working class are not harmonious. That has been my position ever since—never changed in the slightest. There are times when, for temporary purposes, interests are reconcilable; but they are temporary only.

When a fair and reasonable opportunity presents itself for continued improvement in the conditions of the workers, the movement of the workers must necessarily go on and will go on. It will not be dominated by the so-called intellectuals or butters in. The working class movement to be most effective must be conducted by the workers themselves. It is conducted by the working people in the interests of the working people....

...The number of employers who refuse to accede to Labor's demands is growing smaller and smaller. As a matter of fact, there are more employers today who live under collective bargains with their organized employes than at any other time in the history of the industrial world.

In the initial stages of the altered relations between workers and employers improvements are forced upon employers by collective bargains, strikes, and boycotts. Later there is a realization upon the part of the employers that it is more costly to enter into long strikes and lockouts than to concede conditions without interrupting the industry. As the vision and the understanding of the employer change, his attitude toward his workmen and the relation between employer and workers also change, so that the sentiments and views of employers

are often in entire accord with those of the organizations of working people.

However the gains made by the organized labor movement in this country have generally been wrung from the employing classes. What workingmen of America have obtained in improved conditions, higher wages, shorter hours of labor, was not handed to them on a silver platter. They have had to organize, they have had to show their teeth, they have had to strike, they have had to go hungry, and to make sacrifices in order to impress upon the employers their determination to be larger sharers in the products of labor....

...It is most difficult for any one to determine motives. I can judge only people's acts, and I know that the acts of these men in the Civic Federation have never been hostile to the interests of the working people. There is no such thing as co-operation between the leaders of the labor movement and the leaders of the N. C. F. What I have done in that organization is to endeavor to impress upon all the interests and the welfare of the workers. So far as I am concerned I can go anywhere where men are assembled and where they consider the questions affecting working people. I can meet with them and bring the message of Labor to them. I argue and contend for the rights of the working people, and if I can influence men to any act of helpfulness toward any one thing in which the working people are interested I have accomplished something. I have never felt that I have come away with my skirts besmirched, my character impaired, or my determination to toil and to struggle decreased or impeded in any degree. I would appeal to the devil and his mother-in-law to help Labor if Labor could be aided in that way....

In regard to minimum wage legislation I think it is generally regarded that children, women minors anyway, and perhaps women, are the wards of the nation. They are not enfranchised, they have no political rights, and they have not yet attained any of the economic rights that workingmen have. They have not thus far protected themselves industrially as the men have. They have not as yet to any large extent shown a capacity to protect themselves. They have sometimes shown this capacity, and have made magnificent fighting and self-sacrificing trade unionists....

The labor movement in this country has already become political as well as economic. I am not prepared to say what the next or the future generations may develop; but to the A. F. of L., and I suppose to the American working people, it is of less consequence what instrumentality is employed in the accomplishment of the purpose than the accomplishment of the purpose itself. We have in the United States secured legislation of the most substantial character without the use or the necessity of a so-called independent labor party. It must be borne in mind that England, Belgium, and Germany are practically industrial countries. The United States, despite the fact that it is becoming an industrial country, is still largely an agricultural country. The agricultural workers are almost wholly unorganized and widely separated from each other.

There is no application of the conditions prevailing in many other countries to the United States. Bear in mind, too, this fact: some may say it is simply form, but in truth we have a republic. We have no established church; we have no established monarchy. The elements and essentials to political freedom obtain in the United States. Compulsory military service does not exist. All these elements of opposition which exist in many European countries do not obtain here. European workers are justified in establishing a political party and in seeking to remedy these conditions first. There is no necessity, in the United States at least, for dealing with these problems. Our problems are primarily industrial. I have my day dreams, and build my castles in the air, and sometimes allow my mind to run riot; but when I want to be of some service to my fellow workers now and hereafter I am going to get down to terra firma and help them in their present struggle.

The A. F. of L. through its organizations has accomplished much. I know that the American trade union movement has done much not only for the working people but also for the American nation, because there is not anything that the organized labor movement can do for its members that will not have its reflex in the conditions of all other workers. The shorter workday, increased wages, better shop conditions, the character of the treatment of the men and women who work as compared to the general treatment of the workers in other countries are incomparable....

It has frequently been charged that the A. F. of L. and its affiliated organizations make no attempt to organize unskilled men in industries; but there are local unions of unskilled men whose membership reaches several thousands, even ten or fifteen thousand in one local union, as in the case of the local union of building laborers in Chicago. One of the leaflets published by the A. F. of L. issued for over twenty years and distributed in the millions, contains this statement: "To maintain high wages all of the trades and callings must be organized; the lack of organization among the unskilled vitally affects the skilled; general organization of skilled and unskilled can only be accomplished by united action."...

Although the I. W. W. claims to be the champion of the unskilled workers, its total membership (as stated by its own officers), in good standing, amounts to 14,300. There are affiliated to the A. F. of L. either directly as local unions or indirectly through affiliated organizations, single locals whose membership equals or exceeds that of the entire membership of the I. W. W.;

for instance, the Chicago locals of the hodcarriers and building laborers, and of the street-car men.

The A. F. of L. employs a large number of salaried organizers whose services are directed toward the organization of unskilled laborers. It disburses at least two-thirds of the money derived from per capita tax for the purpose of organizing the unskilled. In addition the affiliated nationals and internationals assist in the organization of the unskilled assistants and laborers of all kinds connected with their trades and callings. The statement that the A. F. of L. does not organize the unskilled workers of the country is an untruth. It is an unfounded statement made by the opponents of the A. F. of L. who have repeated it so often that many people are induced to repeat and believe it....

The A. F. of L. holds that whatever a man may be so long as he works honestly and seeks to wrong no other man or to advantage himself at the cost to another, and seeks to maintain this standard regardless of how any toilers may happen to be employed, he is a man. Though the A. F. of L. does not advocate strikes, yet it encourages them when all other means to obtain justice for the toilers have failed. It urges that the workers when struck, strike back as best they can. Though strikes do not always win, even those alleged to be lost at least induce employers to forbear in the future and teach them a lesson they do not readily forget; namely, that Labor is the most important factor in production and entitled to a voice in the question of wages, hours, and conditions under which work shall be performed.

The A. F. of L. stands as the most potent factor in all our country in defense of the right of free assemblage, free speech, and free press. It endeavors to unite all classes of wage-earners under one head through their several organizations with the purpose in view that class, race, creed, political, and trade prejudices may be abolished and that moral and financial support may be given to all. It aims to allow in the light of experience the utmost liberty of each organization in the conduct of its own affairs consistent with the generally understood practice of the identity and solidarity of Labor....

The A. F. of L. endorses as basic these economic principles: That no trade or calling can long maintain wages, hours, and conditions above the common level; that to maintain high wages all trades and callings must be organized; that lack of organization among the unskilled vitally affects the skilled whether organized or unorganized; that generally organization of skilled and unskilled workers can be accomplished only by united action—federation; that the history of the labor movement demonstrates the necessity for the union of individuals and that logic implies a union of unions—federation.

The A. F. of L. urges the concentration of efforts to organize all the workers within the ranks of the organized, fair and open contest for the different views which may be entertained upon measures proposed to move the grand army of labor onward and forward. In no organization on earth is there such toleration, so great a scope, and so free a forum as within the ranks of the A. F. of L., and nowhere is there such a fair opportunity afforded for the advocacy of a new or brighter thought. The A. F. of L. affirms as one of the cardinal principles of the trade union movement that the working people must organize, unite, and federate, irrespective of creed, color, sex, nationality or politics.

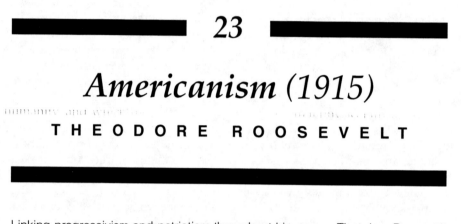

23

Americanism (1915)

THEODORE ROOSEVELT

Linking progressivism and patriotism throughout his career, Theodore Roosevelt sought to define Americanism as a distinct culture marked by social equality. At the same time, he maintained that the United States must be strong and activistic, and involved in the affairs of the world. As the Great War in Europe entered its second year, Roosevelt worried that many Americans would be guided by their cultural heritage rather than patriotism. The latter, he felt, demanded "preparedness," the enhancement of America's military resources. Roosevelt delivered the following speech before the Knights of Columbus, an Italian fraternal order, in Carnegie Hall, New York, on October 12, 1915.

Questions to Consider

- What is "hyphenated Americanism" and why does Roosevelt condemn it?
- What must Americans be prepared to confront?
- Is anyone left out of Roosevelt's inclusive citizenship?

Four centuries and a quarter have gone by since Columbus by discovering America opened the greatest era in world history. Four centuries have passed since the Spaniards began that colonization on the main land which has resulted in the growth of the nations of Latin-America. Three centuries have passed since, with the settlements on the coasts of Virginia and Massachusetts, the real history of what is now the United States began. All this we ultimately owe to the action of an Italian seaman in the service of a Spanish King and a Spanish Queen. It is eminently fitting that one of the largest and most influential social organizations of this great Republic,—a Republic in which the tongue is English, and the blood derived from many sources—should, in its name, commemorate the great Italian. It is eminently fitting to make an address on Americanism before this society.

We of the United States need above all things to remember that, while we are by blood and culture kin to each of the nations of Europe, we are also separate from each of them. We are a new and distinct nationality. We are developing our own distinctive culture and civilization, and the worth of this civilization will largely depend upon our determination to keep it distinctively

Source: Theodore Roosevelt, *Fear God and Take Your Own Part* (New York, 1916), pp. 357–376.

our own. Our sons and daughters should be educated here and not abroad. We should freely take from every other nation whatever we can make of use, but we should adopt and develop to our own peculiar needs what we thus take, and never be content merely to copy.

Our nation was founded to perpetuate democratic principles. These principles are that each man is to be treated on his worth as a man without regard to the land from which his forefathers came and without regard to the creed which he professes. If the United States proves false to these principles of civil and religious liberty, it will have inflicted the greatest blow on the system of free popular government that has ever been inflicted. Here we have had a virgin continent on which to try the experiment of making out of divers race stocks a new nation and of treating all the citizens of that nation in such a fashion as to preserve them equality of opportunity in industrial, civil and political life. Our duty is to secure each man against any injustice by his fellows.

One of the most important things to secure for him is the right to hold and to express the religious views that best meet his own soul needs. Any political movement directed against any body of our fellow citizens because of their religious creed is a grave offense against American principles and American institutions. It is a wicked thing either to support or to oppose a man because of the creed he professes. This applies to Jew and Gentile, to Catholic and Protestant, and to the man who would be regarded as unorthodox by all of them alike. Political movements directed against certain men because of their religious belief, and intended to prevent men of that creed from holding office, have never accomplished anything but harm. This was true in the days of the "Know-Nothing" and Native-American parties in the middle of the last century; and it is just as true to-day. Such a movement directly contravenes the spirit of the Constitution itself. Washington and his associates believed that it was essential to the existence of this Republic that there should never be any union of Church and State; and such union is partially accomplished wherever a given creed is aided by the State or when any public servant is elected or defeated because of his creed. The Constitution explicitly forbids the requiring of any religious test as a qualification for holding office. To impose such a test by popular vote is as bad as to impose it by law. To vote either for or against a man because of his creed is to impose upon him a religious test and is a clear violation of the spirit of the Constitution.

Moreover, it is well to remember that these movements never achieve the end they nominally have in view. They do nothing whatsoever except to increase among the men of the various churches the spirit of sectarian intolerance which is base and unlovely in any civilization but which is utterly revolting among a free people that profess the principles we profess. No such movement can ever permanently succeed here. All that it does is for a decade or so greatly to increase the spirit of theological animosity, both among the people to whom it appeals and among the people whom it assails. Furthermore, it has in the past invariably resulted, in so far as it was successful at all, in putting unworthy men into office; for there is nothing that a man of loose principles and of evil practices in public life so desires as the chance to distract attention from his own shortcomings and misdeeds by exciting and inflaming theological and sectarian prejudice.

We must recognize that it is a cardinal sin against democracy to support a man for public office because he belongs to a given creed or to oppose him because he belongs to a given creed. It is just as evil as to draw the line between class and class, between occupation and occupation in political life. No man who tries to draw either line is a good American. True Americanism demands that we judge each man on his conduct, that we so judge him in private life and that we so judge him in public life. The line of cleavage drawn on principle and conduct in public affairs is never in any healthy community identical with the line of cleavage between creed and creed or between class and class. On the contrary, where the community life is healthy, these lines of cleavage almost always run nearly at right angles to one another. It is eminently necessary to all of us that we should have able and honest public officials in the nation, in the city, in the state. If we make a serious and resolute effort to get such officials of the right kind, men who shall not only be honest but shall be able and shall take the right view of public questions, we will find as a matter of fact that the men we thus choose will be drawn from the professors of every creed and from among men who do not adhere to any creed.

For thirty-five years I have been more or less actively engaged in public life, in the performance of my political duties, now in a public position, now in a private position. I have fought with all the fervor I possessed for the various causes in which with all my heart I believed; and in every fight I thus made I have had with me and against me Catholics, Protestants and Jews. There have been times when I have had to make the fight for or against some man of each creed on grounds of plain public morality, unconnected with questions of public policy. There were other times when I have made such a fight for or against a given man, not on grounds of public morality, for he may have been morally a good man, but on account of his attitude on questions of public policy, of governmental principle. In both cases, I have always found myself fighting beside, and fighting against, men of every creed. The one sure way to have secured the defeat of every good principle worth fighting for would have been to have permitted the fight to be changed into one along sectarian lines and inspired by the spirit of sectarian bitterness, either for the purpose of putting into public life or of keeping out of public life the believers in any given creed. Such conduct represents an assault upon Americanism. The man guilty of it is not a good American.

I hold that in this country there must be complete severance of Church and State; that public moneys shall not be used for the purpose of advancing any particular creed; and therefore that the public schools shall be non-sectarian and no public moneys appropriated for sectarian schools. As a necessary corollary to this, not only the pupils but the members of the teaching force and the school officials of all kinds must be treated exactly on a par, no matter what their creed; and there must be no more discrimination against Jew or Catholic or Protestant than discrimination in favor of Jew, Catholic or Protestant. Whoever makes such discrimination is an enemy of the public schools.

What is true of creed is no less true of nationality. There is no room in this country for hyphenated Americanism. When I refer to hyphenated Americans, I do not refer to naturalized Americans. Some of the very best Americans I have ever known were naturalized Americans, Americans born abroad. But a hyphenated American is not an American at all. This is just as true of the man who puts "native" before the hyphen as of the man who puts German or Irish or English or French before the hyphen. Americanism is a matter of the spirit and of the soul. Our allegiance must be purely to the United States. We must unsparingly condemn any man who holds any other allegiance. But if he is heartily and singly loyal to this Republic, then no matter where he was born, he is just as good an American as any one else.

The one absolutely certain way of bringing this nation to ruin, of preventing all possibility of its continuing to be a nation at all, would be to permit it to become a tangle of squabbling nationalities, an intricate knot of German-Americans, Irish-Americans, English-Americans, French-Americans, Scandinavian-Americans or Italian-Americans, each preserving its separate nationality, each at heart feeling more sympathy with Europeans of that nationality than with the other citizens of the American Republic. The men who do not become Americans and nothing else are hyphenated Americans; and there ought to be no room for them in this country. The man who calls himself an American citizen and who yet shows by his actions that he is primarily the citizen of a foreign land, plays a thoroughly mischievous part in the life of our body politic. He has no place here; and the sooner he returns to the land to which he feels his real heart-allegiance, the bet-

ter it will be for every good American. There is no such thing as a hyphenated American who is a good American. The only man who is a good American is the man who is an American and nothing else.

I appeal to history. Among the generals of Washington in the Revolutionary War were Greene, Putnam and Lee, who were of English descent; Wayne and Sullivan, who were of Irish descent; Marion, who was of French descent; Schuyler, who was of Dutch descent, and Muhlenberg and Herkimer, who were of German descent. But they were all of them Americans and nothing else, just as much as Washington. Carroll of Carrollton was a Catholic; Hancock a Protestant; Jefferson was heterodox from the standpoint of any orthodox creed; but these and all the other signers of the Declaration of Independence stood on an equality of duty and right and liberty, as Americans and nothing else.

So it was in the Civil War. Farragut's father was born in Spain and Sheridan's father in Ireland; Sherman and Thomas were of English and Custer of German descent; and Grant came of a long line of American ancestors whose original home had been Scotland. But the Admiral was not a Spanish-American; and the Generals were not Scotch-Americans or Irish-Americans or English-Americans or German-Americans. They were all Americans and nothing else. This was just as true of Lee and of Stonewall Jackson and of Beauregard.

When in 1909 our battlefleet returned from its voyage around the world, Admirals Wainwright and Schroeder represented the best traditions and the most efficient action in our navy; one was of old American blood and of English descent; the other was the son of German immigrants. But one was not a native-American and the other a German-American. Each was an American pure and simple. Each bore allegiance only to the flag of the United States. Each would have been incapable of considering the interests of Germany or of England or of any other country except the United States.

To take charge of the most important work under my administration, the building of the Panama Canal, I chose General Goethals. Both of his parents were born in Holland. But he was just plain United States....

In my Cabinet at the time there were men of English and French, German, Irish and Dutch blood, men born on this side and men born in Germany and Scotland; but they were all Americans and nothing else; and every one of them was incapable of thinking of himself or of his fellow-countrymen, excepting in terms of American citizenship. If any one of them had anything in the nature of a dual or divided allegiance in his soul, he never would have been appointed to serve under me, and he would have been instantly removed when the discovery was made. There wasn't one of them who was capable of desiring that the policy of the United States should be shaped with reference to the interests of any foreign country or with consideration for anything, outside of the general welfare of humanity, save the honor and interest of the United States, and each was incapable of making any discrimination whatsoever among the citizens of the country he served, of our common country, save discrimination based on conduct and on conduct alone.

For an American citizen to vote as a German-American, an Irish-American or an English-American is to be a traitor to American institutions; and those hyphenated Americans who terrorize American politicians by threats of the foreign vote are engaged in treason to the American Republic.

Now this is a declaration of principles. How are we in practical fashion to secure the making of these principles part of the very fiber of our national life? First and foremost let us all resolve that in this country hereafter we shall place far less emphasis upon the question of right and much greater emphasis upon the matter of duty. A republic can't succeed and won't succeed in the tremendous international stress of the modern world unless its citizens possess that form of high-minded patriotism which consists in putting devotion to duty before the question of individual rights. This must be done in our family relations or the family will go to pieces; and no better tract for family life in this country can be imagined than the little story called "Mother," written by an American woman, Kathleen Norris, who happens to be a member of your own church.

What is true of the family, the foundation stone of our national life, is not less true of the entire superstructure. I am, as you know, a most ardent believer in national preparedness against war as a means of securing that honorable and self-respecting peace which is the only peace desired by all high-spirited people. But it is an absolute impossibility to secure such preparedness in full and proper form if it is an isolated feature of our policy. The lamentable fate of Belgium has shown that no justice in legislation or success in business will be of the slightest avail if the nation has not prepared in advance the strength to protect its rights. But it is equally true that there cannot be this preparation in advance for military strength unless there is a solid basis of civil and social life behind it. There must be social, economic and military preparedness all alike, all harmoniously developed; and above all there must be spiritual and mental preparedness.

There must be not merely preparedness in things material; there must be preparedness in soul and mind. To prepare a great army and navy without preparing a proper national spirit would avail nothing. And if there is not only a proper national spirit but proper national intelligence, we shall realize that even from the standpoint of the army and navy some civil preparedness is indispensable. For example, a plan for national defence which does not include the most far-reaching use and co-operation of our railroads must prove largely futile. These railroads are organized in time of peace. But we must have the most carefully thought out organization from the national and centralized standpoint in order to use them in time of war. This means first that those in charge of them from the highest to the lowest must understand their duty in time of war, must be permeated with the spirit of genuine patriotism; and second, that they and we shall understand that efficiency is as essential as patriotism; one is useless without the other.

Again: every citizen should be trained sedulously by every activity at our command to realize his duty to the nation. In France at this moment the workingmen who are not at the front are spending all their energies with the single thought of helping their brethren at the front by what they do in the munition plants, on the railroads, in the factories. It is a shocking, a lamentable thing that many of the trade unions of England have taken a directly opposite view. It is doubtless true that many of their employers have made excessive profits out of war conditions; and the Government should have drastically controlled and minimized such profit-making. Such wealthy men should be dealt with in radical fashion; but their misconduct doesn't excuse the misconduct of those labor men who are trying to make gains at the cost of their brethren who fight in the trenches. The thing for us Americans to realize is that we must do our best to prevent similar conditions from growing up here. Business men, professional men, and wage workers alike must understand that there should be no question of their enjoying any rights whatsoever unless in the fullest way they recognize and live up to the duties that go with those rights. This is just as true of the corporation as of the trade union, and if either corporation or trade union fails heartily to acknowledge this truth, then its activities are necessarily anti-social and detrimental to the welfare of the body politic as a whole. In war time, when the welfare of the nation is at stake, it should be accepted as axiomatic that the employer is to make no profit out of the war save that which is necessary to the efficient running of the business and to the living expenses of himself and family, and that the wage worker is to treat his wage from exactly the same standpoint and is to see to it that the labor organization to which he belongs is, in all its activities, subordinated to the service of the nation.

Now there must be some application of this spirit in times of peace or we cannot suddenly develop it in time of war. The strike situation in the United States at this time is a scandal to the country as a whole and discreditable alike to employer and employee. Any employer who fails to recognize that human rights come first and that the friendly relationship between himself and those working for him should be one of partnership and comradeship in mutual help no less than self-help is recreant to his duty as an American citizen and it is to his interest, having in view the enormous destruction of life in the present war, to conserve, and to train to higher efficiency alike for his benefit and for its, the labor supply. In return any employee who acts along the lines publicly advocated by the men who profess to speak for the I. W. W. is not merely an open enemy of business but of this entire country and is out of place in our government.

You, Knights of Columbus, are particularly fitted to play a great part in the movement for national solidarity, without which there can be no real efficiency in either peace or war. During the last year and a quarter it has been brought home to us in startling fashion that many of the elements of our nation are not yet properly fused. It ought to be a literally appalling fact that members of two of the foreign embassies in this country have been discovered to be implicated in inciting their fellow-countrymen, whether naturalized American citizens or not, to the destruction of property and the crippling of American industries that are operating in accordance with internal law and international agreement. The malign activity of one of these embassies, the Austrian, has been brought home directly to the ambassador in such shape that his recall has been forced. The activities of the other, the German, have been set forth in detail by the publication in the press of its letters in such fashion as to make it perfectly clear that they were of the same general character. Of course, the two embassies were merely carrying out the instructions of their home governments.

Nor is it only the Germans and Austrians who take the view that as a matter of right they can treat their countrymen resident in America, even if naturalized citizens of the United States, as their allies and subjects to be used in keeping alive separate national groups profoundly anti-American in sentiment if the contest comes between American interests and those of foreign lands in question. It has recently been announced that the Russian government is to rent a house in New York as a national center to be Russian in faith and patriotism, to foster the Russian language and keep alive the national feeling in immigrants who come hither. All of this is utterly antagonistic to proper American sentiment, whether perpetrated in the name of Germany, of Austria, of Russia, of England, or France or any other country.

We should meet this situation by on the one hand seeing that these immigrants get all their rights as American citizens, and on the other hand insisting that they live up to their duties as American citizens. Any discrimination against aliens is a wrong, for it tends to put the immigrant at a disadvantage and to cause him to feel bitterness and resentment during the very years when he should be preparing himself for American citizenship. If an immigrant is not fit to become a citizen, he should not be allowed to come here. If he is fit, he should be given all the rights to earn his own livelihood, and to better himself, that any man can have. Take such a matter as the illiteracy test; I entirely agree with those who feel that many very excellent possible citizens would be barred improperly by an illiteracy test. But why do you not admit aliens under a bond to learn to read and write English within a certain time? It would then be a duty to see that they were given ample opportunity to learn to read and write and that they were deported if they failed to take advantage of the opportunity. No man can be a good citizen if he is not at least in process of learning to speak the language of his fellow-citizens. And an alien who remains here without learning to speak English for more than a certain number of years should at the end of that time be treated as having refused to take the preliminary steps necessary to complete Americanization and should be deported. But there should be no denial or limitation of the alien's opportunity to work, to own property and to take advantage of civic opportunities. Special legislation should deal with the aliens who do not come here to be made citizens. But the alien who comes here intending to become a citizen should be helped in every way to advance himself, should be removed from every possible disadvantage and in return should be required under penalty of being sent back to the country from which he came, to prove that he is in good faith fitting himself to be an American citizen. We should set a high standard, and insist on men reaching it; but if they do reach it we should treat them as on a full equality with ourselves.

Therefore, we should devote ourselves as a preparative to preparedness, alike in peace and war, to secure the three elemental things; one, a common language, the English language; two, the increase in our social loyalty—citizenship absolutely undivided, a citizenship which acknowledges no flag except the flag of the United States and which emphatically repudiates all duality of national loyalty; and third, an intelligent and resolute effort for the removal of industrial and social unrest, an effort which shall aim equally to secure every man his rights and to make every man understand that unless he in good faith performs his duties he is not entitled to any rights at all.

The American people should itself do these things for the immigrants. If we leave the immigrant to be helped by representatives of foreign governments, by foreign societies, by a press and institutions conducted in a foreign language and in the interest of foreign governments, and if we permit the immigrants to exist as alien groups, each group sundered from the rest of the citizens of the country, we shall store up for ourselves bitter trouble in the future.

I am certain that the only permanently safe attitude for this country as regards national preparedness for self-defense is along the lines of obligatory universal service on the Swiss model. Switzerland is the most democratic of nations. Its army is the most democratic army in the world. There isn't a touch of militarism or aggressiveness about Switzerland. It has been found as a matter of actual practical experience in Switzerland that the universal military training has made a very marked increase in social efficiency and in the ability of the man thus trained to do well for himself in industry. The man who has received the training is a better citizen, is more self-respecting, more orderly, better able to hold his own, and more willing to respect the rights of others, and at the same time he is a more valuable and better paid man in his business. We need that the navy and the army should be greatly increased and that their efficiency as units and in the aggregate should be increased to an even greater degree than their numbers. An adequate regular reserve should be established. Economy should be insisted on, and first of all in the abolition of useless army posts and navy yards. The National Guard should be supervised and controlled by the Federal War Department. Training camps such as at Plattsburg should be provided on a nation-wide basis and the government should pay the expenses. Foreign-born as well as native-born citizens should be brought together in those camps; and each man at the camp should take the oath of allegiance as unreservedly and unqualifiedly as the men of the regular army and navy now take it. Not only should battleships, battle cruisers, submarines, aircraft, ample coast and field artillery be provided and a greater ammunition supply system, but there should be a utilization of those engaged in such professions as the ownership and management of motor cars, aviation, and the profession of engineering…. Moreover, the government should deal with conservation of all necessary war supplies such as mine products, potash, oil lands and the like. Furthermore, all munition plants should be carefully surveyed with special reference to their geographic distribution. Provision should be made for munition and supply factories west of the Alleghenies. Finally, remember that the men must be sedulously trained in peace to use this material or we shall merely prepare our ships, guns and products as gifts to the enemy. All of these things should be done in any event. But let us never forget that the most important of all things is to introduce universal military service.

Let me repeat that this preparedness against war must be based upon efficiency and justice in the handling of ourselves in time of peace. If belligerent governments, while we are not hostile to them but merely neutral, strive nevertheless to make of this nation many nations, each hostile to the others and none of them loyal to the central government, then it may be accepted as certain that they would do far worse to us in time of war. If Germany and Austria encourage strikes and sabotage in our munition plants while we are neutral it may be accepted as axiomatic that they would do far worse to us if we were hostile. It is our duty from the standpoint of self-defence to secure the complete Americanization of our people; to make of the many peoples of this country a united nation, one in speech and feeling and all, so far as possible, sharers in the best that each has brought to our shores.

The foreign-born population of this country must be an Americanized population—no other kind can fight the battles of America either in war or peace. It must talk the language of its native-born fellow citizens, it must possess American citizenship and American ideals—and therefore we native born citizens must ourselves practice a high and fine idealism, and shun as we would the plague the sordid materialism which treats pecuniary profit and gross bodily comfort as the only evidences of success. It must stand firm by its oath of allegiance in word and deed and must show that in very fact it has renounced allegiance to every prince, potentate or foreign government. It must be maintained on an American standard of living so as to prevent labor disturbances in important plants and at critical times. None of these objects can be secured as long as we have immigrant colonies, ghettos, and immigrant sections, and above all they cannot be assured so long as we consider the immigrant only as an industrial asset. The immigrant must not be allowed to drift or to be put at the mercy of the exploiter. Our object is not to imitate one of the older racial types, but to maintain a new American type and then to secure loyalty to this type. We cannot secure such loyalty unless we make this a country where men shall feel that they have justice and also where they shall feel that they are required to perform the duties imposed upon them. The policy of "Let alone" which we have hitherto pursued is thoroughly vicious from two standpoints. By this policy we have permitted the immigrants, and too often the native-born laborers as well, to suffer injustice. Moreover, by this policy we have failed to impress upon the immigrant and upon the native-born as well that they are expected to do justice as well as to receive justice, that they are expected to be heartily and actively and single-mindedly loyal to the flag no less than to benefit by living under it.

We cannot afford to continue to use hundreds of thousands of immigrants merely as industrial assets while they remain social outcasts and menaces any more than fifty years ago we could afford to keep the black man merely as an industrial asset and not as a human being. We cannot afford to build a big industrial plant and herd men and women about it without care for their welfare. We cannot afford to permit squalid overcrowding or the kind of living system which makes impossible the decencies and necessities of life. We cannot afford the low wage rates and the merely seasonal industries which mean the sacrifice of both individual and family life and morals to the industrial machinery. We cannot afford to leave American mines, munitions plants and general resources in the hands of alien workmen, alien to America and even likely to be made hostile to America by machinations such as have recently been provided in the case of the above-named foreign embassies in Washington. We cannot afford to run the risk of having in time of war men working on our railways or working in our munition plants who would in the name of duty to their own foreign countries bring destruction to us. Recent events have shown us that incitements to sabotage and strikes are in the view of at least two of the great foreign powers of Europe within their definition of neutral practices. What would be done to us in the name of war if these things are done to us in the name of neutrality?…

Even in the matter of national defence there is such a labyrinth of committees and counsels and advisers that there is a tendency on the part of the average citizen to become confused and do nothing. I ask you to help strike the note that shall unite our people. As a people we must be united. If we are not united we shall slip into the gulf of measureless disaster. We must be strong in purpose for our own defence and bent on securing justice within our borders. If as a nation we are split into warring camps, if we teach our citizens not to look upon one another as brothers but as enemies divided by the hatred of creed for creed or of those of one race against those of another race, surely we shall fail and

our great democratic experiment on this continent will go down in crushing overthrow. I ask you here to-night and those like you to take a foremost part in the movement—a young men's movement—for a greater and better America in the future.

All of us, no matter from what land our parents came, no matter in what way we may severally worship our Creator, must stand shoulder to shoulder in a united America for the elimination of race and religious prejudice. We must stand for a reign of equal justice to both big and small. We must insist on the maintenance of the American standard of living. We must stand for an adequate national control which shall secure a better training of our young men in time of peace, both for the work of peace and for the work of war. We must direct every national resource, material and spiritual, to the task not of shirking difficulties, but of training our people to overcome difficulties. Our aim must be, not to make life easy and soft, not to soften soul and body, but to fit us in virile fashion to do a great work for all mankind. This great work can only be done by a mighty democracy, with those qualities of soul, guided by those qualities of mind, which will both make it refuse to do injustice to any other nation, and also enable it to hold its own against aggression by any other nation. In our relations with the outside world, we must abhor wrongdoing, and disdain to commit it, and we must no less disdain the baseness of spirit which tamely submits to wrongdoing. Finally and most important of all, we must strive for the establishment within our own borders of that stern and lofty standard of personal and public morality which shall guarantee to each man his rights, and which shall insist in return upon the full performance by each man of his duties both to his neighbor and to the great nation whose flag must symbolize in the future as it has symbolized in the past the highest hopes of all mankind.

24

War Message (1917)

W O O D R O W   W I L S O N

Woodrow Wilson had been reelected President in 1916 in part because, as his slogan said, "He kept us out of war." But early in 1917 Germany resumed unrestricted submarine warfare. Wilson, frustrated with what he took to be a series of aggressive actions by the German government, delivered the following address to a joint session of Congress on April 2, 1917. Listing America's grievances, he called on Congress to declare war against Germany. Wilson acknowledged in his speech the dangers inherent in entering the war and had predicted the day before that a declaration of war would lead to a termination of America's basic freedoms. Nonetheless, the country responded with enthusiasm, and Congress declared war with little dissent.

Questions to Consider

- Why does Wilson think the United States should join this European conflict?
- What, according to Wilson, are America's goals in entering the war?
- What does Wilson mean when he states that he would treat dissent "with a firm hand of stern repression"?

Gentlemen of the Congress: I have called the Congress into extraordinary session because there are serious, very serious, choices of policy to be made, and made immediately which it was neither right nor constitutionally permissible that I should assume the responsibility of making.

On the third of February last, I officially laid before you the extraordinary announcement of the Imperial German Government that on and after the first day of February it was its purpose to put aside all restraints of law or of humanity and use its submarines to sink every vessel that sought to approach either the ports of Great Britain and Ireland or the western coast of Europe or any of the ports controlled by the enemies of Germany within the Mediterranean. That had seemed to be the object of the German submarine warfare earlier in the war; but since April of last year the Imperial Government had somewhat restrained the commanders of its undersea craft, in conformity with its promise then given to us that passenger boats should not be sunk, and that due warning would be given to all other vessels which its submarines might seek to destroy, when no resistance was offered or escape attempted, and care taken that their crews were given at least a fair chance to save their lives in their open boats. The precautions taken were meager and haphazard enough, as was proved in distressing instance after instance in the progress of the cruel and unmanly business, but a certain degree of restraint was observed.

The new policy has swept every restriction aside. Vessels of every kind, whatever their flag, their charac-

ter, their cargo, their destination, their errand, have been ruthlessly sent to the bottom without warning and without thought of help or mercy for those on board— the vessels of friendly neutrals along with those of belligerents. Even hospital ships and ships carrying relief to the sorely bereaved and stricken people of Belgium, though the latter were provided with safe conduct through the proscribed areas by the German Government itself, and were distinguished by unmistakable marks of identity, have been sunk with the same reckless lack of compassion or of principle.

I was for a little while unable to believe that such things would in fact be done by any government that had hitherto subscribed to the humane practices of civilized nations. International law had its origin in the attempt to set up some law which would be respected and observed upon the seas, where no nation had right of dominion and where lay the free highways of the world. By painful stage after stage has that law been built up, with meager enough results, indeed, after all was accomplished that could be accomplished, but always with a clear view, at least, of what the heart and conscience of mankind demanded.

This minimum of right the German Government has swept aside under the plea of retaliation and necessity, and because it had no weapons which it could use at sea except these which it is impossible to employ as it is employing them without throwing to the winds all scruples of humanity or of respect for the understandings that were supposed to underlie the intercourse of the world.

I am not now thinking of the loss of property involved, immense and serious as that is, but only of the wanton and wholesale destruction of the lives of noncombatants, men, women and children, engaged in pursuits which have always, even in the darkest period of

Source: *Supplement to the Messages and Papers of the Presidents, Covering the Second Term of Woodrow Wilson, March 4, 1917, to March 4, 1921* (Washington, D.C., 1921), pp. 8226–8233.

modern history, been deemed innocent and legitimate. Property can be paid for; the lives of peaceful and innocent people cannot be.

The present German submarine warfare against commerce is a warfare against mankind. It is a war against all nations. American ships have been sunk, American lives taken in ways which it has stirred us very deeply to learn of, but the ships and people of other neutral and friendly nations have been sunk and overwhelmed in the waters in the same way. There has been no discrimination. The challenge is to all mankind. Each nation must decide for itself how it will meet it. The choice we make for ourselves must be made with a moderation of counsel and a temperateness of judgment befitting our character and our motives as a nation.

We must put excited feeling away. Our motive will not be revenge or the victorious assertion of the physical might of the nation, but only the vindication of right, of human right, of which we are only a single champion.

When I addressed the Congress on the 26th of February last, I thought that it would suffice to assert our neutral right with arms; our right to use the sea against unlawful interference; our right to keep our people safe against unlawful violence. But armed neutrality, it now appears, is impracticable. Because submarines are in effect outlaws when used as the German submarines have been used against merchant shipping, it is impossible to defend ships against their attacks as the law of nations has assumed that merchantmen would defend themselves against privateers or cruisers, visible craft giving chase upon the open sea. It is common prudence in such circumstances, grim necessity indeed, to endeavor to destroy them before they have shown their own intention. They must be dealt with upon sight, if dealt with at all.

The German Government denies the right of neutrals to use arms at all within the areas of the sea which it has prescribed, even in the defense of rights which no modern publicist has ever before questioned their right to defend. The intimation is conveyed that the armed guards which we have placed on our merchant ships will be treated as beyond the pale of law and subject to be dealt with as pirates would be. Armed neutrality is ineffectual enough at best; in such circumstances and in the face of such pretensions, it is worse than ineffectual; it is likely only to produce what it was meant to prevent; it is practically certain to draw us into the war without either the rights or the effectiveness of belligerents.

There is one choice we cannot make, we are incapable of making—we will not choose the path of submission and suffer the most sacred rights of our nation and our people to be ignored or violated. The wrongs against which we now array ourselves are no common wrongs; they cut to the very roots of human life.

With a profound sense of the solemn and even tragical character of the step I am taking and of the grave responsibilities which it involves, but in unhesitating obedience to what I deem my constitutional duty, I advise that the Congress declare the recent course of the Imperial German Government to be, in fact, nothing less than war against the Government and people of the United States; that it formally accept the status of belligerent which has thus been thrust upon it; and that it take immediate steps not only to put the country in a more thorough state of defense, but also to exert all its power and employ all its resources to bring the Government of the German Empire to terms and end the war.

What this will involve is clear. It will involve the utmost practicable co-operation in counsel and action with the governments now at war with Germany; and, as incident to that, the extension to those governments of the most liberal financial credits, in order that our resources may, so far as possible, be added to theirs. It will involve the organization and mobilization of all the material resources of the country to supply the materials of war and serve the incidental needs of the nation in the most abundant and yet the most economical and efficient way possible. It will involve the immediate full equipment of the navy in all respects, but particularly in supplying it with the best means of dealing with the enemy's submarines. It will involve the immediate addition to the armed forces of the United States already provided for by law in case of war at least 500,000 men, who should, in my opinion, be chosen upon the principle of universal liability to service, and also the authorization of subsequent additional increments of equal force so soon as they may be needed and can be handled in training.

It will involve also, of course, the granting of adequate credits to the Government, sustained, I hope, so far as they can equitably be sustained, by the present generation, by well-conceived taxation. I say sustained so far as may be equitable by taxation because it seems to me that it would be most unwise to base the credits which will now be necessary entirely on money borrowed. It is our duty, I most respectfully urge, to protect our people so far as we may against the very serious hardships and evils which would be likely to arise out of the inflation which would be produced by vast loans.

In carrying out the measures by which these things are to be accomplished, we should keep constantly in mind the wisdom of interfering as little as possible in our own preparation and in the equipment of our own military forces with the duty—for it will be a very practical duty—of supplying the nations already at war with Germany with the materials which they can obtain only from us or by our assistance. They are in the field, and we should help them in every way to be effective there.

I shall take the liberty of suggesting, through the several executive departments of the Government, for the consideration of your committees, measures for the accomplishment of the several objects I have mentioned. I hope that it will be your pleasure to deal with them as having been framed after very careful thought by the branch of the Government upon which the responsibility of conducting the war and safeguarding the nation will most directly fall.

While we do these things, these deeply momentous things, let us be very clear, and make very clear to all the world what our motives and our objects are. My own thought has not been driven from its habitual and normal course by the unhappy events of the last two months, and I do not believe that the thought of the nation has been altered or clouded by them.

I have exactly the same things in mind now that I had in mind when I addressed the Senate on the 22d of January last; the same that I had in mind when I addressed the Congress on the 3d of February and on the 26th of February. Our object now, as then, is to vindicate the principles of peace and justice in the life of the world as against selfish and autocratic power and to set up among the really free and self-governed peoples of the world such a concert of purpose and of action as will henceforth insure the observance of those principles.

Neutrality is no longer feasible or desirable where the peace of the world is involved and the freedom of its peoples, and the menace to that peace and freedom lies in the existence of autocratic governments backed by organized force which is controlled wholly by their will, not by the will of their people. We have seen the last of neutrality in such circumstances.

We are at the beginning of an age where it will be insisted that the same standards of conduct and of responsibility for wrong done shall be observed among nations and their governments that are observed among the individual citizens of civilized states.

We have no quarrel with the German people. We have no feeling toward them but one of sympathy and friendship. It was not upon their impulse that their Government acted in entering this war. It was not with their previous knowledge or approval.

It was a war determined upon as wars used to be determined upon in the old, unhappy days when peoples were nowhere consulted by their rulers and wars were provoked and waged in the interest of dynasties or of little groups of ambitious men who were accustomed to use their fellow-men as pawns and tools.

Self-governed nations do not fill their neighbor states with spies or set the course of intrigue to bring about some critical posture of affairs which will give them an opportunity to strike and make conquest. Such designs can be successfully worked out only under cover and where no one has the right to ask questions.

Cunningly contrived plans of deception or aggression, carried, it may be, from generation to generation, can be worked out and kept from the light only within the privacy of courts or behind the carefully guarded confidences of a narrow and privileged class. They are happily impossible where public opinion commands and insists upon full information concerning all the nation's affairs.

A steadfast concert for peace can never be maintained except by a partnership of democratic nations. No autocratic government could be trusted to keep faith within it or observe its covenants. It must be a league of honor, a partnership of opinion. Intrigue would eat its vitals away; the plottings of inner circles who could plan what they would and render account to no one would be a corruption seated at its very heart. Only free peoples can hold their purpose and their honor steady to a common end and prefer the interests of mankind to any narrow interest of their own.

Does not every American feel that assurance has been added to our hope for the future peace of the world by the wonderful and heartening things that have been happening within the last few weeks in Russia?

Russia was known by those who knew her best to have been always in fact democratic at heart, in all the vital habits of her thought, in all the intimate relationships of her people that spoke their natural instinct, their habitual attitude toward life.

The autocracy that crowned the summit of her political structure, long as it had stood and terrible as was the reality of its power, was not in fact Russian in origin, character or purpose; and now it has been shaken off and the great generous Russian people have been added in all their native majesty and might to the forces that are fighting for a freedom in the world, for justice and for peace. Here is a fit partner for a league of honor.

One of the things that has served to convince us that the Prussian autocracy was not and could never be our friend is that from the very outset of the present war it has filled our unsuspecting communities and even our offices of government with spies and set criminal intrigues everywhere afoot against our national unity of council, our peace within and without, our industries and our commerce.

Indeed, it is now evident that its spies were here even before the war began; and it unhappily is not a matter of conjecture, but a fact proved in our courts of justice, that the intrigues which have more than once come perilously near to disturbing the peace and dislocating the industries of the country have been carried on at the instigation, with the support, and even under the personal direction of official agents of the Imperial Government accredited to the Government of the United States.

Even in checking these things and trying to extirpate them, we have sought to put the most generous interpretation possible upon them because we knew that their source lay, not in any hostile feeling or purpose of the German people toward us (who were, no doubt, as ignorant of them as we ourselves were), but only in the selfish designs of a government that did what it pleased and told its people nothing. But they have played their part in serving to convince us at last that that government entertains no real friendship for us and means to act against our peace and security at its convenience. That it means to stir up enemies against us at our very doors, the intercepted note to the German Minister at Mexico City is eloquent evidence.

We are accepting this challenge of hostile purpose because we know that in such a government, following such methods, we can never have a friend; and that in the presence of its organized power always lying in wait to accomplish we know not what purpose, there can be no assured security for the democratic governments of the world.

We are now about to accept gauge of battle with this natural foe to liberty and shall, if necessary, spend the whole force of the nation to check and nullify its pretensions and end its power. We are glad, now that we see the facts with no veil of false pretense about them, to fight thus for the ultimate peace of the world and for the liberation of its peoples, the German peoples included; for the rights of nations great and small and the privilege of men everywhere to choose their way of life and of obedience. The world must be made safe for democracy. Its peace must be planted upon the tested foundations of political liberty.

We have no selfish ends to serve. We desire no conquest, no dominion. We seek no indemnities for ourselves, no material compensation for the sacrifices we shall freely make. We are but one of the champions of the rights of mankind. We shall be satisfied when those rights have been made as secure as the faith and the freedom of the nations can make them.

Just because we fight without rancor and without selfish object, seeking nothing for ourselves but what we shall wish to share with all free peoples, we shall, I feel confident, conduct our operations as belligerents without passion and ourselves observe with proud punctilio the principles of right and of fair play we profess to be fighting for.

I have said nothing of the Governments allied with the Imperial Government of Germany because they have not made war upon us or challenged us to defend our right and our honor. The Austro-Hungarian Government has, indeed, avowed its unqualified indorsement and acceptance of the reckless and lawless submarine warfare adopted now without disguise by the Imperial German Government, and it has therefore not been possible for this Government to receive Count Tarnowski, the Ambassador recently accredited to this Government by the Imperial and Royal Government of Austria-Hungary; but that Government has not actually engaged in warfare against citizens of the United States on the seas, and I take the liberty, for the present at least, of postponing a discussion of our relations with the authorities at Vienna. We enter this war only where we are clearly forced into it because there are no other means of defending our rights.

It will be all the easier for us to conduct ourselves as belligerents in a high spirit of right and fairness because we act without animus, not in enmity toward a people nor with the desire to bring any injury or disadvantage upon them, but only in armed opposition to an irresponsible Government which has thrown aside all considerations of humanity and of right and is running amuck.

We are, let me say again, the sincere friends of the German people, and shall desire nothing so much as the early re-establishment of intimate relations of mutual advantage between us—however hard it may be for them, for the time being, to believe that this is spoken from our hearts. We have borne with their present Government through all these bitter months because of that friendship—exercising a patience and forbearance which would otherwise have been impossible. We shall, happily, still have an opportunity to prove that friendship in our daily attitude and actions toward the millions of men and women of German birth and native sympathy who live among us and share our life, and we shall be proud to prove it toward all who are in fact loyal to their neighbors and to the Government in the hour of test. They are, most of them, as true and loyal Americans as if they had never known any other fealty or allegiance. They will be prompt to stand with us in rebuking and restraining the few who may be of a different mind and purpose.

If there should be disloyalty, it will be dealt with with a firm hand of stern repression; but if it lifts its head at all, it will lift it only here and there and without countenance, except from a lawless and malignant few.

It is a distressing and oppressive duty, gentlemen of the Congress, which I have performed in thus addressing you. There are, it may be, many months of fiery trial and sacrifice ahead of us. It is a fearful thing to lead this great peaceful people into war, into the most terrible and disastrous of all wars, civilization itself seeming to be in the balance. But the right is more precious than peace, and we shall fight for the things which we have always carried nearest our hearts—for democracy, for the right of those who submit to authority to have a voice in their own governments, for the rights and liberties of small nations, for a universal domination of right by such a concert of free peoples as shall bring peace and safety to all nations and make the world itself at last free. To such a task we can dedicate our lives and our fortunes, everything that we are and everything that we have, with the pride of those who know that the day has come when America is privileged to spend her blood and her might for the principles that gave her birth and happiness and the peace which she has treasured. God helping her, she can do no other.

WOODROW WILSON

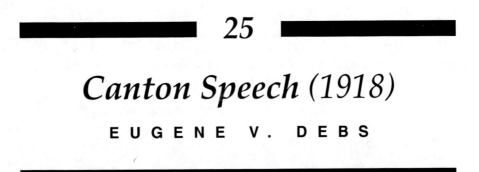

25

Canton Speech (1918)

E U G E N E   V .   D E B S

Eugene V. Debs, national secretary of the Brotherhood of Locomotive Firemen, became famous (or notorious) for his leadership in the 1894 Pullman Strike. In 1898 Debs helped found the Social Democratic Party, serving as its candidate five times and winning nearly a million votes in 1912. Debs opposed America's participation in World War I, encouraging young Americans to avoid service in the military. For one such speech, delivered in Canton, Ohio, on June 16, 1918, Debs was arrested and convicted of sedition. A unanimous Supreme Court refused to overturn Debs's conviction (the second time the Court chose to leave Debs in jail), and it took the personal pardon of Republican President Warren Harding to free Debs from jail on Christmas day, 1921. [Audience responses, mostly applause, have been eliminated.]

Questions to Consider

- How is it possible for an American to commit sedition against his government?
- What does Debs find wrong with the government of the United States?

Comrades, friends and fellow-workers....
To speak for labor; to plead the cause of the men and women and children who toil; to serve the working class, has always been to me a high privilege.

I have just returned from a visit over yonder (pointing to the workhouse), where three of our most loyal comrades [Ruthenberg, Baker, and Wagenknecht] are paying the penalty for their devotion to the cause of the working class. They have come to realize, as many of us have, that it is extremely dangerous to exercise the constitutional right of free speech in a country fighting to make Democracy safe in the world.

I realize that, in speaking to you this afternoon, that there are certain limitations placed upon the right of free speech. I must be exceedingly careful, prudent, as to what I say, and even more careful and more prudent as to how I say it. I may not be able to say all I think; but I am not going to say anything that I do not think. But, I would rather a thousand times be a free soul in jail than to be a sycophant and coward on the streets. They

Source: *The Debs White Book: Full Text of Important Documents in Famous Debs Case* (Girard, Kansas, 1919), pp. 3–16, 20–36.

may put those boys in jail—and some of the rest of us in jail—but they cannot put the Socialist movement in jail. Those prison bars separate their bodies from ours, but their souls are here this afternoon. They are simply paying the penalty that all men have paid in all of the ages of history for standing erect, and for seeking to pave the way to better conditions for mankind.

If it had not been for the men and women, who, in the past have had the moral courage to go to jail, we would still be in the jungles....

There is but one thing that you have to be concerned about, and that is that you keep four-square with the principles of the international Socialist movement. It is only when you begin to compromise that trouble begins. So far as I am concerned, it does not matter what others may say, or think, or do, as long as I am sure that I am right with myself and the cause. There are so many who seek refuge in the popular side of a great question. On account of that, I hope, as a Socialist, I have long since learned how to stand alone.

For the last month I have been traveling over the Hoosier State; and, let me say to you, that, in all my connection with the Socialist movement, I have never seen such meetings, such enthusiasm, such unity of purpose; never have I seen such a promising outlook as there is today, notwithstanding the statement they have published repeatedly that our leaders had deserted us. Well, for myself, I never had much faith in leaders, anyway. I am willing to be charged with almost anything, rather than to be charged with being a leader. I am suspicious of leaders, myself, and especially of the intellectual variety. Give me the rank and file every day in the week. If you go to the City of Washington, and you examine the pages of the Congressional Directory, you will find that almost all of those corporation lawyers and cowardly politicians, members of Congress, and misrepresentatives of the masses—you will find that almost all of them claim, in glowing terms, that they have risen from the ranks to places of eminence and distinction. I am so glad that I cannot make that claim for myself. I would be ashamed to admit that I had risen from the ranks. When I rise it will be with the ranks, and not from the ranks....

The Socialists of Ohio, it appears, are very much alive this year. The party has been killed recently which, no doubt, accounts for its extraordinary activity. There is nothing that helps the Socialist party so much as receiving an occasional death blow. The oftener it is killed the more boundless, the more active, the more energetic, the more powerful it becomes.

They who have been reading the capitalist newspapers realize what a capacity they have for lying. We have been reading them lately. They know all about the...Socialist party movement, except what is true. Only the other day they took an article that I had written...and they made it appear that I had undergone a marvelous transformation. I had suddenly become changed—suddenly come to my senses; I had ceased to be a wicked Socialist, and had become a respectable Socialist, a patriotic Socialist—as if I had ever been anything else.

What was the purpose of this deliberate misrepresentation? It is so self-evident that it suggests itself. The purpose was to sow the seed of dissension in our ranks; to have it appear that we were divided among ourselves; that we were pitted against each other, to our mutual undoing. But Socialists were not born yesterday. They know how to read capitalist newspapers; and to believe exactly opposite what they read.

Why should a Socialist be discouraged on the eve of the greatest triumph in all the history of the Socialist movement? It is true that these are anxious, trying days for us all—testing days for the women and men who are upholding the banner of the working class in the struggle of the working class of all the world against the exploiters of all the world; a time in which the weak and cowardly will falter and fail and desert. They lack the fiber to endure the revolutionary test; they fall away; they disappear as if they had never been. On the other hand, they who are animated with the unconquerable spirit of the Social revolution, they who have the moral courage to stand erect and assert their convictions; stand by them; fight for them; go to jail or to hell for them, if need be—they are writing their...names in fadeless letters in the history of mankind....

Are we opposed to Prussian militarism? Why we have been fighting it since the day the Socialist movement was born; and we are going to continue to fight it, day and night, until it is wiped from the face of the earth. Between us there is no truce—no compromise.

But, before I proceed along this line, let me recall a little history, in which, I think, we are all interested.

In 1869 that grand old warrior of the Socialist revolution, the elder Liebknecht, was arrested and sentenced to prison for three months, because of his war, as a Socialist, on the Kaiser and on the Junkers that rule Germany. In the meantime the Franco-Prussian war broke out. Liebknecht and Bebel were the Socialist members in the Reichstag. They were the only two who had the courage to protest against taking Alsace-Lorraine from France and annexing it to Germany. And for this they were sent two years to a prison fortress charged with high treason; because, even in that early day, almost fifty years ago, the leaders, these forerunners of the international Socialist movement, were fighting the Kaiser and fighting the junkers of Germany.

They have continued to fight them from that day to this. Multiplied thousands of them have languished in the jails of Germany because of their heroic warfare upon the ruling class of that country.

Let us come down the line a little further. You remember that, at the close of Theodore Roosevelt's second term as President, he went over to Africa to make war on some of his ancestors. You remember that, at the close of his expedition, he visited all of the capitals of Europe; and he was wined and dined, dignified and glorified by all of the Kaisers and Czars and Emperors of the old world. He visited Potsdam while the Kaiser was there; and, according to the accounts published in the American newspapers, he and the Kaiser were soon on the most familiar terms. They were hilariously intimate with each other, and slapped each other on the back.... He knew the Kaiser then just as well as he knows him now. He knew that he was the Kaiser, the Beast of Berlin. And yet, he permitted himself to be entertained by the Beast of Berlin.... And while Roosevelt was being entertained royally by the German Kaiser, that same Kaiser was putting the leaders of the Socialist party in jail for fighting the Kaiser and the junkers of Germany.... Who was fighting for Democracy? Roosevelt? Roosevelt, who was honored by the Kaiser, or the Socialists who were in jail by the order of the Kaiser?...

...Now, after being the guest of Emperor William, the Beast of Berlin, he came back to this country, and he wants you to send ten million men over there to kill the Kaiser; to murder his former friend and pal. Rather queer, isn't it? And yet, he is the patriot, and we are the traitors. And I challenge you to find a Socialist anywhere on the face of the earth who was ever the guest of the Beast of Berlin, except as an inmate of his prison....

A little more history along the same line. In 1902 Prince Henry paid a visit to this country.... Prince Henry is the brother of King William. Prince Henry is another Beast of Berlin, an autocrat, an aristocrat, a junker of junkers—very much despised by our American patriots. He...was received by Congress, by several state legislatures—among others, by the state legislature of Massachusetts, then in session. He was invited there by the capitalist captains of that so-called commonwealth. And when Prince Henry came there, there was one member of that body who kept his self-respect, put on his hat, and, as Henry, the Prince, walked in, that member of the body walked out. And that was James F. Carey, the Socialist member of that body. All of the rest—all of the rest of the representatives in the Massachusetts legislature...joined in doing honor, in the most servile spirit, to the high representative of the autocracy of Europe. And the only man who

left that body was a Socialist. And yet, and yet they have the hardihood to claim that they are fighting autocracy and we are in the service of the German government....

I hate, I loathe, I despise junkerdom. I have no earthly use for the junkers of Germany, and not one particle more use for the junkers in the United States.

They tell us we live in a great Republic; our institutions are Democratic; we are a free people. This is too much, even as a joke. It is not a subject for levity; it is an exceedingly serious matter.

To whom do the Wall Street junkers in our country...marry their daughters? After they have wrung the countless hundreds of millions from your sweat, your agony, your life-blood, in a time of war as well as in a time of peace, they invest these billions and millions in the purchase of titles of broken-down aristocrats, and to buy counts of no-account. Are they satisfied to wed their daughters to honest working men? to real democrats? Oh, no. They scour the markets of Europe for fellows who have titles and nothing else. And they swap their millions for the titles; so that matrimony, with them, becomes entirely a matter of money, literally so.

These very gentry, who are today wrapped up in the American flag,...claim that they are only patriots, who have their magnifying glasses in hand...scanning the country for some evidence of disloyalty,...ready to apply the brand to the men who dare to even whisper opposition to junker rule in the United States. No wonder Johnson said that "Patriotism is the last refuge of scoundrels." He had the Wall Street gentry in mind, or their prototypes, at least; for in every age it has been the tyrant who has wrapped himself in the cloak of patriotism, or religion, or both.

They would have you believe that the Socialist party consists, in the main, of disloyalists, and traitors. It is true, in a certain sense. We are disloyalists and traitors to the real traitors of this nation; to the gang that, on the Pacific coast, are trying to hang Tom Mooney, in spite of the protest of the whole civilized world.[1]...

Let us review another bit of history....The United Railways, consisting of a lot of plutocrats...organized in the Chamber of Commerce, absolutely own and control the City of San Francisco. It is their private reservation. Their will is the supreme law. Take your stand against them, you are doomed. They do not hesitate to plot murder to perpetuate their murderous regime. Tom Mooney was the only representative of the working

---

[1] Tom Mooney was imprisoned for throwing a bomb in San Francisco despite very compelling evidence placing him at a distant location.—*Ed.*

class they could not control. They owned the railways; they controlled the great industries;...they were the political rulers; from their decision there was no appeal— the real autocrats of the Pacific coast—as infamous as any that ever ruled in Germany or any other country. And when their rule became so corrupt that, at last, a grand jury was found that indicted them, and they were placed on trial, and Francis J. Heney...had been selected by the national administration to assist in the prosecution, this same gang, represented by the Chamber of Commerce..., hire[d] a murderer to shoot Francis J. Heney down in the court room, and he did. Francis J. Heney happened to live through it. But that wasn't their fault. The identically same gang...are also for the execution of Tom Mooney. Every...one of them claims to be an arch-patriot; every one insists through his newspapers that he is fighting to make Democracy safe in the world. What humbug! What rot! What false pretense! These autocrats, these tyrants, these red-handed robbers and murderers, the patriots, while the men who have the courage to stand up face to face with them and fight them in the interest of their exploited victims—they are the disloyalists and traitors. If this be true, I want to take my place side by side with the traitors in this fight.

Why, the other day they sent Kate Richards O'Hare[2] to the penitentiary for ten years. Oh, just think of sentencing a woman to the penitentiary for talking. The United States, under the rule of the plutocracy, is the only country that would send a woman to the penitentiary for ten years for exercising her constitutional right of free speech. If this be treason let them make the most of it.

...The only testimony against [O'Hare] was that of a hired witness. And when thirty farmers, men and women, who were in the audience she addressed— heard the speech, when they went to Bismarck to testify in her favor, to swear that she had never used the language she was charged with having used, the judge refused to allow them to go upon the stand. This would seem incredible to me, if I had not had some experience of my own with a Federal court.

Who appoints the Federal judges? The people? In all of the history of the country, the working class have never named a Federal judge. There are 121, and every solitary one of them holds his position, his tenure, through the influence and power of corporate capital. The corporation and trusts dictate their appointment. And when they go to the bench, they go, not to serve the people, but to serve the interests that placed them where they are.

Why, the other day, by a vote of five to four—a kind of craps game—...they declared the child labor law unconstitutional, a law secured after twenty years of education and agitation on the part of all kinds of people. And yet, by a majority of one, the Supreme Court, a body of corporation lawyers...wiped it from the statute books, and this in a Democracy, so that we may still continue to grind the flesh and blood and bones of puny little children into profits for the junkers of Wall Street. And this in a country that is fighting to make Democracy safe in the world. The history of this country is being written in the blood of the childhood they have murdered.

These are not very palatable truths to them. They do not like to hear them; and they do not want you to hear them. And that is why they brand us as undesirable citizens, and as disloyalists, and as traitors. If we were...traitors to the people, we would be eminently respectable citizens of the republic; we could hold high office, and we could ride in limousines; and could be pointed out as people who had succeeded in life, in honorable pursuits. It is precisely because we are disloyal to the traitors that we are loyal to the people of this country....

...What a wonderful compliment they paid us. They are afraid that we might contaminate you. You are their wards; they are your guardians. They must see to it that our vicious doctrines don't reach your ears. And so, in our Democracy, under our free institutions, they flatter our press, and they imagine that they have silenced revolutionary propaganda. What a mistake they made. We ought to pass a resolution of thanks and gratitude to them. Thousands of people, who have never heard of our paper before, are now inquiring for it, wanting to see it....

Rose Pastor Stokes[3].... Here is another heroic and inspiring comrade. She had her millions of dollars. Did it restrain her an instant?... She went out to render her service to the cause in this day of crises, and they sent her to the penitentiary for ten years. Think of it! Ten years! What had she said? Not any more than I have said here this afternoon. I want to admit...without argument, that if Rose Pastor Stokes is guilty, so am I.... And if she ought to be sent to the penitentiary for ten years, so ought I.

What did she say? Why, she said that a government—a government could not serve both the profit-

---

[2] A prominent Socialist sent to prison for opposing U.S. participation in the war. She was released in 1920 and ran as Debs's vice presidential running mate.—*Ed.*

[3] A cigar maker and prominent Socialist who married the Socialist millionaire James G. P. Stokes.—*Ed.*

eers and the victims of the profiteers. Isn't that true? Certainly.

Roosevelt said a thousand times more in the same paper, The Kansas City Star. Roosevelt said, the other day, that he would be heard if he went to jail. He knows very well that he will not go to jail. He is laying his wires for the Republican nomination in 1920. And he would do everything possible to discredit Wilson.... That is your wonderful rivalry between the two patriotic parties—the Republican party and the Democratic party, the twins. They are not going to have any agitation between them this fall. They are all patriots this time, and they are going to combine to prevent the election of any disloyal Socialists. I haven't heard anybody anywhere tell me of any difference between them. Do you know of any? Not the slightest. One is in, the other is out. This is all the difference there is between them....

They just want to silence [Stoke's] voice during the war. The cases will be appealed, and they will remain pending in court many a month, perhaps years. What a compliment it is to the Socialist movement for telling the truth. The truth will make the people free. And the truth must not be permitted to reach the people. The truth has always been dangerous to the rule of the rogue, the exploiter, the robber. So the truth must be suppressed. That is why they are trying to drive out the Socialist movement; and every time they make the attempt, they add ten thousand voices proclaiming that Socialism has come to stay....

I went to Warren some years ago. It happened to be at the time that President McKinley was assassinated. In common with all others, I deplored that tragic event. There is not a Socialist, who would have been guilty of that crime. We do not attack individuals. We don't wreak our vengeance upon any individual opposed to our faith. We have no fight with individuals. We are capable of teaching those who hate us. We do not hate them; we know better.... There is not any room in our heart for hate, except for a system—a system in which it is possible for one man to achieve a tremendous fortune doing nothing, while millions upon millions suffer and struggle and agonize and die for the bare necessities of life.

McKinley had been assassinated. I was booked to speak at Portsmouth. All of the ministers of Portsmouth met in a special session, and they passed a resolution that Debs, more than any other person, was responsible for the assassination of our beloved President.... And so all of these pious gentry, the followers of the meek and lowly, as they believed, met and said I must not be permitted to enter the city. And they had the mayor to issue an order not permitting me to speak.... Soon after I was booked to speak at Warren...I was...ordered to leave the hotel. I was exceedingly undesirable that day. I was served with notice that the hall would not be open, and that I would not be permitted to speak.... I sent word to the mayor that I would speak in Warren that night, according to the schedule, or I would leave Warren in a box.

I went to the hall, and the Grand Army of the Republic had a special meeting, and in full uniform they all went to the hall and occupied the front seats, in order to pounce upon me and take good care of me if my speech did not suit them. I went to the hall and made my speech. I told them who was responsible for the assassination. I said: "As long as there is misery caused by robbery at the bottom, there will be assassination at the top." I showed them that it was their capitalist system that was responsible; that impoverished and brutalized the ancestors of the poor, witless boy who murdered the President. Yes, I made the speech that night. When I left there I was still very undesirable.

I returned some years thereafter. It seems that the whole population of Warren was out. I was received with open arms. I was no longer a demagogue; I was no longer a fanatic; I was no longer an undesirable. I had become exceedingly honorable simply because the Socialists had increased in numbers and in power....

Oh, it is the minorities who have made the histories of this world! They who have had the courage to take their places at the front; they who have been true enough to themselves to speak the truth that is in them; they who have opposed the established order of things; who have espoused the cause of the suffering, struggling poor;...who have upheld the cause of righteousness; they have paved the way to civilization. Oh, there are so many who remain upon the popular side. They lack the courage to join a despised minority; they lack the fiber that endures. They are to be pitied, and not treated with contempt; they cannot help it. But, thank God, in every age and every nation there have been that few, and they have been sufficient; and...they suffered, they sacrificed, they went to jail; they had their bones broken upon the wheel; they were burned at the stake, and had their ashes scattered to the four winds by the hands of hate. We are under obligation to them, because of what they suffered for us; and the only way we can cancel that obligation is by doing or seeking to do in the interest of those who are to come after us.

And this is the high purpose of every Socialist on the face of the earth. Everywhere they are animated by the same lofty principle; everywhere they have the same noble ideal; everywhere they are clasping hands across the boundary lines; everywhere they are calling one another comrades, the blessed word that springs from the heart and soul of unity;...and they are waging the war...of the working class of the world against the ruling class.... They never take a backward step; the heart of the international Socialist never beats retreat; they are pushing forward. They are pressing forward, here, there, everywhere, in all of the zones that girdle this globe; everywhere these awakening workers, these class-conscious proletarians, these horny-fisted children of honest toil, everywhere wiping out the boundary lines;…everywhere having their hearts attuned to the most sacred cause that ever challenged men and women to action in all the history of the world. Everywhere moving toward Democracy; everywhere marching toward the sunrise, their faces all aglow with the light of the coming day. These are the Socialists; these are the most zealous, the most enthusiastic crusaders the world has ever known. They are making history that will light the horizon in the coming generations; they are bound upon emancipating the human race….

Do you wish to hasten it? Join the Socialist party. Don't wait for the morrow. Come now. Enroll your name; take your place where you belong. You cannot do your duty by proxy. You have got to do something yourself, and do it squarely, and look yourself in the face while you are doing it; and you will have no occasion to blush; you will know what it is to be a man or woman…. You need to know that you are fit for something better than slavery and cannon fodder. You need to know that you were not created to work and to produce to impoverish yourself and to enrich an idle exploiter. You need to know that you have a soul to develop, a manhood to sustain. You need to know that it is your duty to rise above the animal plane. You need to know that it is for you to know something about literature, and about science, and about art. You need to know that you are on the edge of a great new world. You need to get in touch with your comrades; you need to become conscious of your interest and your power as a class…. You need to know as long as you are ignorant, as long as you are indifferent, as long as you are content, as long as you are unorganized, you will remain exactly where you are. You will be exploited; you will have to beg for a job; you will get just enough to keep you in working order; and you will be looked down upon with contempt by the very parasite that lives out of your sweat and unpaid labor. If you would be respected, you have got to begin by respecting yourself. Stand up, and look yourself in the face, and see a man for the first time….

To turn your back on that corrupt Republican party, and that still more corrupt Democratic party—the gold-dust boys of the ruling class, yes, it counts for something. To step out of those great, popular, subsidized capitalist parties, and get into a minority party that stands for a principle, and fights for a cause. Make that change; it will be the most important change you have ever made in your life; and you will thank me to your

dying day—or living day—a Socialist never dies—you will thank me for having made the suggestion. It was a day of days for me. I remember it so well. I passed from darkness to light. It came like a flash, just as great, seething, throbbing Russia, in a flash, was transformed from the land of supreme darkness to a land of living light. There is something splendid in the prompting of the heart to be true to yourself, especially so in a crisis.

You are in the crucible today, Mr. Socialist. You are going to be tried, to what extent no one knows. If you are weak-fibred, that weakness will be sought out, and located. And if, through that weakness, you are conquered, you may be driven out of the Socialist movement. We will have to bid good-bye to you. You are not the stuff of which Revolutionists are made. We are sorry for you, unless you happen to be an intellectual. The intellectuals, a good many of them, are already gone. No—no loss on our side, nor any gain on theirs.

But, when discussing the intellectual phase of this question, I am always amused by it…. What would become of the men that are sheep unless they had shepherds to lead them out of the wilderness into the land flowing with milk and honey? Oh, yes, "Ye are my sheep." In other words, "Ye are my mutton." And, if you had no intellectuals you could have no movement. They rule through their intellectuals in the capitalistic party. They have their so-called leaders. In the Republican and Democratic party you are not called upon to think…. You simply do the voting…. The capitalist system affects to have great regard for intellect. They give themselves credit for having superior brains. We used to tell them sometime ago that the time would come when the working class would rule. They said: "Never in the world will they rule. It requires brains to rule." Implying that the workers have none.

We used to say that the people ought to own the railroads and operate them for the benefit of the people. We advocated that twenty years ago. They said: "You have got to have brains to run the trains." And the other day McAdoo[4] fired all the brains. So, haven't all the trains been coming and going exactly on time? Have you noticed any change since the brains are gone? It is a brainless system now. It is operated by hand. But a good deal more efficiently than it was operated by brains before. And this determines infallibly the quality of capitalist brains. It is the kind of brains you can get at a very reasonable figure at the market houses…. Give me a hundred capitalists,…and let me ask them a dozen simple questions about the history of their country, and I will show you that they are as ignorant as unlettered school-

---

[4] William McAdoo, Woodrow Wilson's son-in-law, was responsible for bringing the railroads under national control during the war.—*Ed.*

boys. They know nothing of history; they are ignorant of sociology; they are strangers to science; but they know how to gouge; how to rob, and do it legally....

They are talking about your patriotic duty. Among other things, they are advising you to cultivate war gardens.... While they are doing this, a government war report shows that practically 52 per cent of the arable tillable soil is held out of use by the profiteers, by the land manipulators—held out of use. They, themselves, do not cultivate it.... They...keep it idle to enrich themselves; to pocket the hundreds of dollars of unearned increment. Who is it that makes their land valuable while it is fenced in and kept out of use? It is the people. Who pockets this tremendous value? The landlords.... Who is the patriot? And while we are upon the subject, I want you to think upon the term "land-lord." Landlord. Lord of the land? This lord of the land is a great patriot. This lord, who professionally owns the earth, tells you that he is fighting to make the world safe for Democracy—he, who shuts all humanity out—and he who profiteers at the expense of the people who have been slain by multiplied thousands, under the pretense of being the great patriot...; he it is that you need to wipe from power. It is he...that is a menace to your loyalty and your liberty far more than the Prussian junker on the other side of the Atlantic ocean....

Again, they tell you there is a coal famine now.... The State of Indiana, where I live, is largely underlaid with coal. There is an inexhaustible supply of it. The coal is beneath our feet. It is within touch—all that we can possibly use. And here are the miners; they are ready to enter the mines. There is the machinery ready to be put into operation to increase the output to any desired capacity. And yet,...six hundred thousand coal miners in this country are not permitted to work more than half time.... They tell you that you ought to buy your coal right away. You may freeze to death next winter if you do not.... Oh, yes, I think you ought to do this if you vote the Republican or Democratic ticket. Now we have private ownership of the coal mines. And this is the result of private ownership of this great social utility. The coal mines are privately owned, and the operators want a scarcity of coal. Why? So they can boost the prices indefinitely.... They make more money out of the scarcity of coal. So there is collusion between the operators and the railroads. The operators say there are no cars, and the railroad men say no coal. And between them they simply humbug, delude, defraud the people.

...We Socialists say: Take possession of the mines in the name of the people. Set the miners at work; give every miner that works all the coal he produces.... Then he can build himself a comfortable home; live in it; enjoy it; he can provide himself and his wife and children with clothes...wholesome food in abundance, and the people will get coal at just what it costs to mine it.

Oh, that is Socialism as far as it goes. But you are not in favor of that program. It is too visionary. So continue to pay three prices for coal, and get your coal when winter comes, because you prefer to vote the capitalist ticket. You are still in the capitalist state of mind.... A change is needed. Yes, yes. Not of party, but change of system; a change from despotism to Democracy, wide as the world.... A change from brutehood to brotherhood; and to accomplish this you have got to organize; and you have got to organize industrially. Not along the zig-zag, craft lines laid down by Sam Gompers,[5] who, through all of his career, has been on the side of the master class. You never hear the capitalist press speak of him except in praise and adulation. He has become a great patriot. Oh, yes. Gompers, who was never on the unpopular side of any question or of any proposition; always conservative, satisfied to leave the labor problem to be settled at the banquet board with Elihu Root, Andy Carnegie and the rest of the plutocrats. When they drank wine together and smoked scab cigars, then the labor question was settled....

What you need is to organize, not along craft lines, but along revolutionary industrial lines. You will never vote in the Socialist republic. You are needed to organize it; and you have got to organize it in the industries—unite in the industries. The industrial union is the forerunner of industrial Democracy.... United, very often your power becomes invincible.... And when you organize industrially, you will soon learn that you can manage industry as well as operate industry. You can soon find that you don't need the idle for your masters. They are simply parasites. They don't give you work. You give them jobs taking what you produce, and that is all. Their function is to take what you produce. You can dispose of them.... You ought to own your own tools; you ought to control your own jobs; you ought to be industrial free men instead of industrial slaves.... Then unite in the Socialist party.... Vote as you strive.... See that your party embraces the working class. It is the only working class party, the party that expresses the interest, the hope, the aspirations of the toilers of the world.... Take your place in the ranks. Help to inspire the weak and to strengthen the faltering; and do your share to speed the coming of that brighter and better day for us all. Then, when we vote together and act together on the industrial plane, we will develop the supreme power of the one class that can bring permanent peace to the world.... We will conquer the public power. We will transfer the title deeds of the railroads, the telegraph lines, the mills, the great industries—we

---

[5] President of the American Federation of Labor who worked to help mobilize workers during World War I.—*Ed.*

will transfer them to the people.... We will have industrial Democracy.... We will be the first free nation whose government belongs to the people. Oh, this change will be universal; it will be permanent; it looks towards the light; it paves the way to emancipation....

Yes, we are going to sweep into power in this nation, and in every other nation on earth. We are going to destroy the capitalist institutions; we are going to re-create them as legally free institutions. Before our very eyes the world is being destroyed. The world of capitalism is collapsing; the world of Socialism is rising.

...We Socialists are the builders of the world that is to be.... We are inviting—aye, challenging you this afternoon, in the name of your own manhood, to join us. Help do your part. In due course of time the hour will strike, and this great cause—the greatest in history—will proclaim the emancipation of the working class and the brotherhood of all mankind.

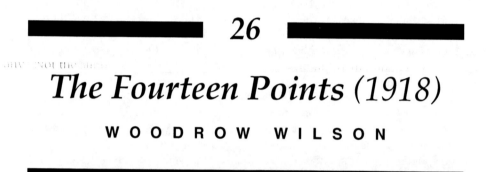

26

The Fourteen Points (1918)

WOODROW WILSON

As American troops finally entered combat in Europe, Woodrow Wilson attempted to give shape to the nation's war aims, while suggesting the terms under which peace could be attained short of total victory. Delivered before Congress on January 8, 1918, this "program of the world's peace," which became known as "the Fourteen Points," transformed Wilson into an international leader of great moral authority. Clearly a great many common people in America and Europe shared Wilson's vision for the postwar world. When Germany finally sued for peace, its government did so with the expectation that the Fourteen Points would serve as the basis for all future negotiations.

Questions to Consider

- Why would America's enemies come to find hope in the Fourteen Points?
- How did Wilson think that his program would produce world peace?

Gentlemen of the Congress: Once more, as repeatedly before, the spokesmen of the Central Empires have indicated their desire to discuss the objects of the war and the possible basis of a general peace. Parleys have been in progress at Brest-Litovsk between Russian representatives and representatives of the Central Powers, to which the attention of all the belligerents has been invited for the purpose of ascertaining whether it may be possible to extend these parleys into a general conference with regard to terms of peace and settlement.... The representatives of the Central Powers...presented an outline of settlement which... proposed no concessions at all, either to the sovereignty of Russia or to the preferences of the population with whose fortunes it dealt, but meant, in a word, that the Central Empires were to keep every foot of territory their armed forces had occupied—every province, every city, every point of vantage—as a permanent addition to their territories and their power. It is a reasonable conjecture that the general principles of settlement

Source: *Supplement to the Messages and Papers of the Presidents, Covering the Second Term of Woodrow Wilson, March 4, 1917, to March 4, 1921* (Washington, D.C., 1921), pp. 8421–8426.

which they at first suggested originated with the more liberal statesmen of Germany and Austria, the men who have begun to feel the force of their own peoples' thought and purpose, while the concrete terms of actual settlement came from the military leaders who have no thought but to keep what they have got. The negotiations have been broken off. The Russian representatives were sincere and in earnest. They cannot entertain such proposals of conquest and domination.

The whole incident is full of significance. It is also full of perplexity. With whom are the Russian representatives dealing? For whom are the representatives of the Central Empires speaking? Are they speaking for the majorities of their respective Parliaments or for the minority parties, that military and imperialistic minority which has so far dominated their whole policy and controlled the affairs of Turkey and of the Balkan States which have felt obliged to become their associates in this war? The Russian representatives have insisted, very justly, very wisely, and in the true spirit of modern democracy, that the conferences they have been holding with the Teutonic and Turkish statesmen should be held with open, not closed, doors, and all the world has been audience, as was desired....

...Not once, but again and again, we have laid our whole thought and purpose before the world, not in general terms only, but each time with sufficient definition to make it clear what sort of definite terms of settlement must necessarily spring out of them.... There is no confusion of counsel among the adversaries of the Central Powers, no uncertainty of principle, no vagueness of detail. The only secrecy of counsel, the only lack of fearless frankness, the only failure to make definite statement of the objects of the war, lie with Germany and her allies. The issues of life and death hang upon these definitions. No statesman who has the least conception of his responsibility ought for a moment to permit himself to continue this tragical and appalling outpouring of blood and treasure unless he is sure beyond a peradventure that the objects of the vital sacrifice are part and parcel of the very life of society and that the people for whom he speaks think them right and imperative as he does.

There is, moreover, a voice calling for these definitions of principle and of purpose which is, it seems to me, more thrilling and more compelling than any of the many moving voices with which the troubled air of the world is filled. It is the voice of the Russian people. They are prostrate and all but helpless, it would seem, before the grim power of Germany, which has hitherto known no relenting and no pity. Their power apparently is shattered. And yet their soul is not subservient.... They call to us to say what it is that we desire, in what, if in anything, our purpose and our spirit differ from theirs; and I believe that the people of the United States would wish me to respond with utter

simplicity and frankness. Whether their present leaders believe it or not, it is our heartfelt desire and hope that some way may be opened whereby we may be privileged to assist the people of Russia to attain their utmost hope of liberty and ordered peace.

It will be our wish and purpose that the processes of peace, when they are begun, shall be absolutely open, and that they shall involve and permit henceforth no secret understandings of any kind. The day of conquest and aggrandizement is gone by; so is also the day of secret covenants entered into in the interest of particular governments and likely at some unlooked-for moment to upset the peace of the world....

We entered this war because violations of right had occurred which touched us to the quick and made the life of our own people impossible unless they were corrected and the world secured once for all against their recurrence. What we demand in this war, therefore, is nothing peculiar to ourselves. It is that the world be made fit and safe to live in; and particularly that it be made safe for every peace-loving nation which, like our own, wishes to live its own life, determine its own institutions, be assured of justice and fair dealings by the other peoples of the world, as against force and selfish aggression. All the peoples of the world are in effect partners in this interest, and for our own part we see very clearly that unless justice be done to others it will not be done to us.

The program of the world's peace, therefore, is our program, and that program, the only possible program, as we see it, is this:

I.—Open covenants of peace, openly arrived at, after which there shall be no private international understandings of any kind, but diplomacy shall proceed always frankly and in the public view.

II.—Absolute freedom of navigation upon the seas, outside territorial waters, alike in peace and in war, except as the seas may be closed in whole or in part by international action for the enforcement of international covenants.

III.—The removal, so far as possible, of all economic barriers and the establishment of an equality of trade conditions among all the nations consenting to the peace and associating themselves for its maintenance.

IV.—Adequate guarantees given and taken that national armaments will be reduced to the lowest point consistent with domestic safety.

V.—Free, open-minded, and absolutely impartial adjustment of all colonial claims, based upon a strict observance of the principle that in determining all such questions of sovereignty the interests of the population concerned must have equal weight with the equitable claims of the Government whose title is to be determined.

VI.—The evacuation of all Russian territory and such a settlement of all questions affecting Russia as will secure the best and freest cooperation of the other nations of the world in obtaining for her an unhampered and unembarrassed opportunity for the independent determination of her own political development and national policy, and assure her of a sincere welcome into the society of free nations under institutions of her own choosing; and, more than a welcome, assistance also of every kind that she may need and may herself desire....

VII.—Belgium, the whole world will agree, must be evacuated and restored, without any attempt to limit the sovereignty which she enjoys in common with all other free nations. No other single act will serve as this will serve to restore confidence among the nations in the laws which they have themselves set and determined for the government of their relations with one another. Without this healing act the whole structure and validity of international law is forever impaired.

VIII.—All French territory should be freed and the invaded portions restored, and the wrong done to France by Prussia in 1871 in the matter of Alsace-Lorraine, which has unsettled the peace of the world for nearly fifty years, should be righted, in order that peace may once more be made secure in the interest of all.

IX.—A readjustment of the frontiers of Italy should be effected along clearly recognizable lines of nationality.

X.—The peoples of Austria-Hungary, whose place among the nations we wish to see safeguarded and assured, should be accorded the freest opportunity of autonomous development.

XI.—Rumania, Serbia, and Montenegro should be evacuated; occupied territories restored; Serbia accorded free and secure access to the sea; and the relations of the several Balkan States to one another determined by friendly counsel along historically established lines of allegiance and nationality; and international guarantees of the political and economic independence and territorial integrity of the several Balkan States should be entered into.

XII.—The Turkish portions of the present Ottoman Empire should be assured a secure sovereignty, but the other nationalities which are now under Turkish rule should be assured an undoubted security of life and an absolutely unmolested opportunity of autonomous development, and the Dardanelles should be permanently opened as a free passage to the ships and commerce of all nations under international guarantees.

XIII.—An independent Polish State should be erected which should include the territories inhabited by indisputably Polish populations, which should be assured a free and secure access to the sea, and whose political and economic independence and territorial integrity should be guaranteed by international covenant.

XIV.—A general association of nations must be formed under specific covenants for the purpose of affording mutual guarantees of political independence and territorial integrity to great and small states alike.

In regard to these essential rectifications of wrong and assertions of right, we feel ourselves to be intimate partners of all the governments and peoples associated together against the imperialists. We cannot be separated in interest or divided in purpose. We stand together until the end.

For such arrangements and covenants we are willing to fight and to continue to fight until they are achieved; but only because we wish the right to prevail and desire a just and stable peace, such as can be secured only by removing the chief provocations to war, which this program does remove. We have no jealousy of German greatness, and there is nothing in this program that impairs it. We grudge her no achievement or distinction of learning or of pacific enterprise such as have made her record very bright and very enviable. We do not wish to injure her or to block in any way her legitimate influence or power. We do not wish to fight her either with arms or with hostile arrangements of trade, if she is willing to associate herself with us and the other peace-loving nations of the world in covenants of justice and law and fair dealing. We wish her only to accept a place of equality among the peoples of the world—the new world in which we now live—instead of a place of mastery.

Neither do we presume to suggest to her any alteration or modification of her institutions. But it is necessary, we must frankly say, and necessary as a preliminary to any intelligent dealings with her on our part, that we should know whom her spokesmen speak for when they speak to us, whether for the Reichstag majority or for the military party and the men whose creed is imperial domination.

We have spoken, now, surely, in terms too concrete to admit of any further doubt or question. An evident principle runs through the whole program I have outlined. It is the principle of justice to all peoples and nationalities, and their right to live on equal terms of liberty and safety with one another, whether they be strong or weak. Unless this principle be made its foundation, no part of the structure of international justice can stand. The people of the United States could act upon no other principle, and to the vindication of this principle they are ready to devote their lives, their honor, and everything that they possess. The moral climax of this, the culminating and final war for human liberty, has come, and they are ready to put their own strength, their own highest purpose, their own integrity and devotion to the test.

27

The Great Steel Strike (1919)

W I L L I A M   Z .   F O S T E R

The return of American troops from World War I and the cuts in production resulting from the termination of government contracts led to increasing unemployment in American industry. Steel workers were especially affected. Owners and
management absolutely refused to negotiate with labor unions, provoking worker
frustration. Symbolizing this intransigence was Judge Elbert Gary of United
States Steel, who would not even speak to representatives from the unions. In
September 1919, a quarter of a million U.S. Steel workers walked off the job.
Throughout western Pennsylvania, U.S. Steel become a law unto itself, imposing
martial law and importing thousands of "special deputies" to guard the mills and
break up union meetings. With union workers attacking scabs, the state sent in
the militia to attack the workers. In the midst of this chaos, Judge Gary warned
the federal government that the nation was on the verge of a Bolshevik revolution.
The federal government, like much of the public, accepted this explanation and
sent in the army to restore order, end the strike, and destroy the union. All of
these goals were attained. After the strike had been broken with force, William Z.
Foster collected the following documents.

Questions to Consider

- Were the union's demands socialist, as Judge Gary charged?
- Why did Judge Gary refuse to speak with union representatives?

The Great Steel Strike and Its Lessons

…[T]he following general demands, based on accurate
surveys of the situation, and subject to revision over the
conference table, were formulated:

1. Right of collective bargaining
2. Reinstatement of all men discharged for union
   activities with pay for time lost

Source: William Z. Foster, *The Great Steel Strike and Its Lessons*
(New York, 1920), pp. 77–83, 106–108, 110–112, 125–132,
138–139.

3. Eight-hour day
4. One day's rest in seven
5. Abolition of 24-hour shift
6. Increases in wages sufficient to guarantee
   American standard of living
7. Standard scales of wages in all trades and classi-
   fications of workers
8. Double rates of pay for all overtime after
   8 hours, holiday and Sunday work
9. Check-off system of collecting union dues and
   assessments
10. Principles of seniority to apply in the mainte-
    nance, reduction and increase of working forces
11. Abolition of company unions

12. Abolition of physical examination of applicants for employment

So plain, fair and equitable are these demands that to reasonable people they require no defence. The only explanation they might need relates to #9 and #12. The check-off was to apply only to the mining end of the steel industry, and the abolition of the physical examination was to put a stop to the rank discrimination practiced by the companies through their medical departments.

A month was allowed in which to take the vote. Each trade looked after its own members, with the National Committee voting those men who were enrolled but not yet turned over to their respective unions, and in some cases the unorganized also. Enthusiasm was intense. The steel workers saw a glimmer of hope and welcomed with open arms the opportunity to right their crying wrongs. When the vote was tabulated in Youngstown, Ohio, on August 20, it was found that every trade had voted overwhelmingly for a strike in case no settlement could be reached. Whole districts voted to a man in the affirmative. Of all the thousands of ballots cast in Homestead, Braddock, Rankin, McKeesport, Vandergrift, Pittsburgh and Monessen not one was in the negative. Donora produced one "no" vote, with the great Youngstown, Chicago and Cleveland districts about the same. Everywhere the sentiment was practically unanimous to make a stand. The vote was calculated conservatively at 98 per cent. for a strike. The Conference Committee was accordingly instructed to request a conference with the heads of the United States Steel Corporation and the big independent companies, and if at the end of ten days no such meeting had been arranged, to set the strike date.

Taking no further chances on unanswered letters, the Committee bearded Mr. Gary in his lair at 71 Broadway. He was in but refused to meet the Committee, requesting that its proposition be submitted in writing. The Committee thereupon sent him the following request for a conference:

New York, August 26, 1919

Hon. Elbert H. Gary, Chairman Finance Committee,
United States Steel Corporation,
71 Broadway, New York City
Dear Sir:

During a general campaign of organization and education conducted under the auspices of the American Federation of Labor, many thousands of men employed in the iron and steel industry made application and were enrolled as members of the various organizations to which they were assigned.

This work has been carried on to a point where we feel justified in stating to you that we represent the sentiment of the vast majority of the employees in this industry, and, acting in behalf of them, we solicit of you that a hearing be given to the undersigned Committee, who have been selected by the duly accredited representatives of the employees, to place before you matters that are of vital concern to them, and concerning hours of labor, wages, working conditions and the right of collective bargaining.

The committee called at your office at 3 P.M., Tuesday, August 26, and requested a conference. We were advised by your messenger that you wished to be excused from a personal interview at this time and requested us to have our business in writing and whatever matters we wished to submit would be taken up by yourself and your colleagues and given consideration.

Therefore we are submitting in brief the principal subjects that we desired to have a conference on. The committee has an important meeting in another city on Thursday next and will leave New York at 5 o'clock on August 27, 1919. May we respectfully request that your answer be sent before that time to Mr. John Fitzpatrick, Continental Hotel, Broadway and Forty-first Street, New York City.

Very truly yours,

JOHN FITZPATRICK
D. J. DAVIS
WM. HANNON
EDW. J. EVANS
WM. Z. FOSTER
Committee

To this letter Mr. Gary replied as follows:

UNITED STATES STEEL CORPORATION
Office of the Chairman,
New York, August 27, 1919

Messrs. John Fitzpatrick, David J. Davis, William Hannon, Wm. Z. Foster, Edw. J. Evans, Committee
Gentlemen:

Receipt of your communication of August 26 instant is acknowledged.

We do not think you are authorized to represent the sentiment of a majority of the employees of the United States Steel Corporation and its subsidiaries. We express no opinion concerning any other members of the iron and steel industry.

As heretofore publicly stated and repeated, our Corporation and subsidiaries, although they do not combat labor unions as such, decline to discuss business with them. The Corporation and subsidiaries are opposed to the "closed shop." They stand for the "open shop," which permits one to engage in any line of employment whether one does or does not belong to a labor union. This best promotes the welfare of both employees and employers. In view of the well-known attitude as above expressed, the officers of the Corporation respectfully decline to discuss with you, as representatives of a labor union, any matter relating to employees. In doing so no personal discourtesy is intended.

In all decisions and acts of the Corporation and subsidiaries pertaining to employees and employment their interests are of highest importance. In wage rates, living and working conditions, conservation of life and health, care and comfort in times of sickness or old age, and providing facilities for the general welfare and happiness of employees and their families, the Corporation and subsidiaries have endeavored to occupy a leading and advanced position among employers.

It will be the object of the Corporation and subsidiaries to give such consideration to employees as to show them their loyal and efficient service in the past is appreciated, and that they may expect in the future fair treatment.

Respectfully yours,

E. H. GARY, CHAIRMAN

In a last effort to prevail upon Mr. Gary to yield his tyrannical position, the committee addressed him this further communication:

New York City, Aug. 27, 1919.
Hon. Elbert H. Gary, Chairman
Finance Committee, United States Steel Corporation, 71 Broadway, New York, N. Y.
Dear Sir:

We have received your answer to our request for a conference on behalf of the employees of your Corporation, and we understand the first paragraph of your answer to be an absolute refusal on the part of your corporation to concede to your employees the right of collective bargaining.

You question the authority of our committee to represent the majority of your employees. The only way by which we can prove our authority is to put the strike vote into effect and we sincerely hope that you will not force a strike to prove this point.

We asked for a conference for the purpose of arranging a meeting where the questions of wages, hours, conditions of employment, and collective bargaining might be discussed. Your answer is a flat refusal for such conference, which raises the question, if the accredited representatives of your employees and the international

unions affiliated with the American Federation of Labor and the Federation itself are denied a conference, what chance have the employees as such to secure any consideration of the views they entertain or the complaints they are justified in making.

We noted particularly your definition of the attitude of your Corporation on the question of the open and closed shop, and the positive declaration in refusing to meet representatives of union labor. These subjects are matters that might well be discussed in conference. There has not anything arisen between your Corporation and the employees whom we represent in which the question of "the closed shop" has been even mooted.

We read with great care your statement as to the interest the Corporation takes in the lives and welfare of the employees and their families, and if that were true even in a minor degree, we would not be pressing consideration, through a conference, of the terrible conditions that exist. The conditions of employment, the home life, the misery in the hovels of the steel workers is beyond description. You may not be aware that the standard of life of the average steel worker is below the pauper line, which means that charitable institutions furnish to the pauper a better home, more food, clothing, light and heat than many steel workers can bring into their lives upon the compensation received for putting forth their very best efforts in the steel industry. Surely this is a matter which might well be discussed in conference.

You also made reference to the attitude of your Corporation in not opposing or preventing your employees from joining labor organizations. It is a matter of common knowledge that the tactics employed by your Corporation and subsidiaries have for years most effectively prevented any attempt at organization by your employees. We feel that a conference would be valuable to your Corporation for the purpose of getting facts of which, judging from your letter, you seem to be misinformed.

Some few days are still at the disposal of our committee before the time limit will have expired when there will be no discretion left to the committee but to enforce the decree of your employees whom we have the honor to represent.

We submit that reason and fairness should obtain rather than that the alternative shall be compulsory upon us.

Surely reasonable men can find a common ground upon which we can all stand and prosper.

If you will communicate with us further upon this entire matter, please address your communication to the National Hotel, Washington, D. C., where we will be Thursday and Friday, August 28 and 29.

Very truly yours,

JOHN FITZPATRICK
D. J. DAVIS
WM. HANNON
EDW. J. EVANS
WM. Z. FOSTER
Committee

...Although the United States Steel Corporation was recognized as the arch enemy of the unions, the strike was not directed against it alone. Every iron and steel mill and furnace in the country not working under union agreements was included. This meant at least 95 per cent. of the industry, because the only agreements of any consequence were between some of the smaller companies and the Amalgamated Association. A number of these concerns were affected also, their agreements relating only to skilled workers, and the plants having to close when the laborers struck. This occurred quite extensively in the Cleveland, Youngstown and Pittsburgh districts.

Considering the large number of them involved and their traditions of isolated action, the unions displayed reasonably good solidarity in going "over the top" against the Steel Trust. The battle line was far from perfect, however. Much harm was done the morale of the strikers by local unions here and there that were under the sway of ignorant blockheads or designing tools of the bosses, refusing to recognize the National Committee's strike call and insisting upon getting instructions from their own headquarters, meanwhile scabbing it in the mills. And the worst of it was that sometimes it was difficult, or even impossible to have the necessary instructions issued....

But in spite of opposition, blundering and treachery, the steel workers had spoken. Mr. Gary was answered. Previous to the strike, he declared that the unions represented only an insignificant minority of his men, the great bulk of his working force being satisfied. He compelled the Committee to show its credentials. Result: 365,600 steel workers laid down their tools. This estimated total has never been disputed by the steel companies....

It was the misfortune of the steel strike to occur in the midst of the post-war reaction, which still persists unabated, and which constitutes the most shameful page in American history. Ours are days when the organized employers, inspired by a horrible fear of the onward sweep of revolution in Europe and the irresistible advance of the labor movement in this country, are robbing the people over-night of their most precious rights, the fruits of a thousand years of struggle. And the people, not yet recovered from war hysteria and misled by a corrupt press, cannot perceive the outrage. They even glory in their degradation. Free speech, free press, free assembly, as we once knew these rights, are now things of the past. What poor rudiments of them remain depend upon the whims of a Burleson, or the rowdy element of the American Legion. Hundreds of idealists, guilty of nothing more than a temperate expression of their honest views, languish in prison serving sentences so atrocious as to shock the world— although Europe has long since released its war and political prisoners. Working class newspapers are raided, denied the use of the mails and suppressed. Meetings are broken up by Chamber of Commerce mobs or thugs in public office. The right of asylum is gone—the infamous Palmer is deporting hundreds who dare to hold views different from his. The right of the workers to organize is being systematically curtailed; and crowning shame of all, workingmen can no longer have legislative representatives of their own choosing. In a word, America, from being the most forward-looking, liberty-loving country in the world, has in two short years become one of the most reactionary. We in this country are patiently enduring tyranny that would not be tolerated in England, France, Italy, Russia or Germany. Our great war leaders promised us the New Freedom; they have given us the White Terror.

Realizing full well the reactionary spirit of the times, the steel companies proceeded safely to extremes to crush the steel strike, dubbed by them an attempt at violent revolution. To accomplish their end they stuck at nothing. One of their most persistent and determined efforts was to deprive the steel workers of their supposedly inalienable right to meet and talk together. Throughout the strike, whenever and wherever they could find municipal or court officials willing to do their bidding, the steel barons abolished the rights of free speech and free assembly, so precious to strikers. Few districts escaped this evil, but as usual, Pennsylvania felt the blow earliest and heaviest. Hardly had the strike started when the oily Schwab prohibited meetings in Bethlehem; the Allegheny and West Penn Steel Companies did the same at Natrona, jailing organizer J. McCaig for "inciting to riot"; in the Sharon-Farrell district the steel workers, denied their constitutional rights in their home towns, had to march several miles over into Ohio (America they called it) in order to hold their meetings.

Along the Monongahela river the shut-down was complete. Following Sheriff Haddock's proclamation and the "riots" at Clairton and Glassport, it was only a few days until the city and borough officials had completely banned strike meetings in all the territory from Charleroi to Pittsburgh. The unions' free-speech, free-assembly victory of the past summer was instantly cancelled. For forty-one miles through the heart of America's steel industry, including the important centers of Monessen, Donora, Clairton, Wilson, Glassport, McKeesport, Duquesne, Homestead, Braddock, Rankin, etc., not a meeting of the steel workers could be held. Even in Pittsburgh itself meetings were prohibited everywhere except in Labor Temple. The steel-collared city officials never could quite muster the gall to close Labor's own building—or perhaps because it is so far from the mills and so poorly situated for meetings they felt it to be of no use to the strikers. Thus the Steel Trust gave its workers a practical demonstration of what is meant by the phrase, "making the world safe for democracy."...

When on a mission of terrorism the first thing the State Troopers do is to get their horses onto the sidewalks, the better to ride down the pedestrians. Unbelievable though it may seem, they actually ride into stores and inner rooms. Picture the horror of a foreign worker and his family, already badly frightened, at seeing a mounted policeman crashing into their kitchen. The horses are highly trained. Said an N. E. A. news dispatch, Sept. 26th, 1919:

> Horses of the Pennsylvania State Constabulary are trained not to turn aside, as a horse naturally will do, when a person stands in its way, but to ride straight over any one against whom they are directed. Lizzie, a splendid black mare ridden by Trooper John A. Thorp, on duty at Homestead, uses her teeth as well as her heels when in action. Her master will sometimes dismount, leaving Lizzie to hold a striker with her strong jaws, while he takes up the pursuit of others on foot.

If this is thought to be an overdrawn statement, read the following affidavit:

Butler, Pa., October 3, 1919

I, Jacob Sazuta,
21 Bessemer Ave.,
Lyndora, Pa.

Commenced work for the Standard Steel Car Company in September, 1913, as laborer. About October 1916 was promoted to car fitter....

On August 25, [1919] after receiving my pay, I was standing looking in a store window, when State Trooper No. 52 rode his horse upon me, THE HORSE STEPPING ON MY LEFT FOOT. Trooper No. 52 ordered me to move on, BUT AS THE HORSE WAS STANDING ON MY FOOT I COULD NOT MOVE. He then struck me across the head with his club, cutting a gash in the left side of my head that took the doctor three stitches to close up the wound. After hitting me with his club, he kept chasing me with his horse.

JACOB SAZUTA

Sworn and subscribed before me this third day of October, 1919.

E. L. CEFFERI, NOTARY PUBLIC.

A few affidavits, and extracts from affidavits, taken at random from among the hundreds in possession of the National Committee, will indicate the general conditions prevailing in the several districts:

Clairton, Pa.

John Doban, Andy Niski and Mike Hudak were walking home along the street when the State Police came and arrested the three, making ten holes in Mike Hudak's head. Were under arrest three days. Union bailed them out, $1,000.00 each.

*****

Butler, Pa., Oct. 3, 1919.

I, James Torok,
Storekeeper,
103 Standard Ave.,
Lyndora, Pa.,

On about August 15, 1919, I saw State Troopers chase a crippled man who could not run as fast as his horse, and run him down, the horse bumping him in the back with his head, knocked him down. Later three men were coming to my store to buy some things; the State Troopers ran their horses right on them and chased them home. One of the men stopped and said: "I have to go to the store," and the Trooper said: "Get to hell out of here, you sons —— ————, or I will kill you," and started after them again, and the people ran home and stayed away from the store.

JAMES TOROK

Sworn to and subscribed before me this 3rd day of October, 1919.

E. L. PEFFER, NOTARY PUBLIC.

*****

Homestead, Pa.

...two State Policemen made a forcible entry into the home of deponent, Trachn Yenchenke, at 327 Third Ave., Homestead, Pa., and came to the place where deponent was asleep, kicked him and punched him, and handled him with extreme violence and took deponent without any explanation, without permitting deponent to dress, dragged him half naked from his home to waiting automobile and conveyed him against his will to the Homestead Police Station.... Fined $15.10.

TRACHN YENCHENKE

*****

Monessen, Pa.

...Concetta Cocchiara, 8 months advanced in a state of pregnancy, was out shopping with her sister. Two State Policemen brusquely ordered them home and when they did not move fast enough to suit, followed them home, forced himself into the house and struck affiant with a stick on the head and grabbed her by the hair and pulled her from the kitchen and forced her into a patrol wagon and took her to the borough jail....
Sworn to before Henry Fusarini, Notary Public, October 11, 1919.

*****

Newcastle, Pa.

John Simpel,
1711 Morris Ave.,
Newcastle.

On Sept. 22, about 5:30 P.M. he was walking along towards his home on Moravia Street. Hearing shots fired he stopped in the middle of the street and was instantly struck by bullets three times, one bullet going through his leg, one through his finger, while the third entered his back and went through his body, coming out through his abdomen. The shots were fired from inside the gates of the Carnegie Steel Company's plant. Mr. Simpel believes the shots were fired from a machine gun, because of their rapid succession. He fell on the ground and lay there for about ten minutes, until he was picked up by a young boy.... He is now totally disabled. He has a wife and a child and is 48 years of age....

JAS. A. NORRINGTON, SECRETARY

******

Farrell, Pa.

...There were four men killed here, one in a quarrel in a boarding house and three by the Cossacks. Half a dozen were wounded, one of them a woman. She was shot in the back by a Cossack, while on her way to the butcher shop....

S. COATES, SECRETARY

Many hundreds of similar cases could be cited. In the steel strike a score were killed, almost all on the workers' side; hundreds were seriously injured, and thousands unjustly jailed. To the State Constabulary attaches the blame for a large share of this tyranny. The effect of their activities was to create a condition in Western Pennsylvania, bordering on a reign of terror. Yet it is extremely difficult to definitely fasten their crimes upon them. No matter how dastardly the outrage, when the Steel Trust cracks its whip the local authorities and leading citizens come forth with a mass of affidavits, "white-washing" the thuggery in question, and usually sufficing to cast serious doubts on the statements of the few worker witnesses courageous enough to raise their voices. What is to be thought of the following incident?

Testifying before the Senate Committee investigating the strike, Mr. Gompers related how, in an organizing campaign in Monessen, Pa. several years ago, A. F. of L. organizer Jefferson D. Pierce was bludgeoned by Steel Trust thugs, receiving injuries that resulted in his death. Mr. Gompers had his facts straight. Yet the very next day, Mr. Gary, testifying before the same Committee, produced a sworn statement from the son of Mr. Pierce containing the following assertions:

I was with my father the night he received his injuries in Monessen, Pa., and wish to state very emphatically that his injury was not caused by any one connected with the United States Steel Corporation. On the contrary, it was caused by a member of the I. W. W. organization from out of town, who was sent there at the time to create trouble, as the I. W. W. organization was then trying to gain control of the organizing situation. I wish again most emphatically to refute Mr. Gompers' statement that this injury was caused by some one connected with the United States Steel Corporation.

Upon being questioned, Mr. Gary "thought" that Mr. Pierce is employed at Worcester, Mass. by the American Steel and Wire Company, a subsidiary of the U. S. Steel Corporation.

Fortunately, however, in the steel strike the photographer secured a proof of State Police brutality which the most skilled Steel Trust apologists cannot explain away—a picture of the typically vicious assault upon Mr. R. Dressel, a hotel keeper of 532 Dickson St. (foreign quarter), Homestead, Pa. I quote from the latter's statement in connection therewith:

I, Rudolph Dressel, of the aforesaid address, do hereby make this statement of my own volition and without solicitation from any one. That on the 23rd day of September I was standing in front of my place of business at the aforesaid address and a friend of mine, namely, Adolph Kuehnemund, came to visit and consult me regarding personal matters. As I stood as shown in the picture above mentioned with my friend, the State Constabulary on duty in Homestead came down Dickson St. They had occasion to ride up and down the street several times and finally stopped directly in front of me and demanded that I move on. Before I had time to comply I was struck by the State Policeman. (The attitude of said Policeman is plainly shown in the aforesaid picture, and his threatening club is plainly seen descending towards me.)

My friend and I then entered my place of business and my friend a few minutes afterwards looked out on the street over the summer doors. The policeman immediately charged him and being unable to enter my place of business on horseback, dismounted and entered into my place of business on foot.

My friend being frightened at what had happened to me retired to a room in the rear of my place of business. The Policeman entered this room, accompanied by another State Police, and without cause, reason or excuse, struck my friend and immediately thereafter arrested him. I was personally present at his hearing before Burgess P. H. McGuire of the above city, at which none of the aforesaid policemen were heard or even present. Burgess asked my friend what he was arrested for, and my friend referred to me inasmuch as he himself did not know. The Burgess immediately replied, "We have no time to hear your witnesses," and thereupon levied a fine of $10.00 and costs upon him. My friend having posted a forfeit of $25.00, the sum of $15.45 was deducted therefrom.

The State Constabulary were sent, unasked for, into the quiet steel towns for the sole purpose of intimidating the strikers. The following took place at the meeting of the Braddock Borough Council, October 6:

Mr. Verosky. (County detective and council member) "Mr. Chairman, the citizens of the borough wish to know by whose authority the State Constabulary was called into Braddock to take up their quarters here and to practically relieve the police of their duties, by patrolling the streets on foot, mounted, and always under arms."

Mr. Holtzman. (President of Council) "I surely do not know who called them into town, but were I the Burgess, I would make it my business to find out, in view of the fact that the Constabulary is neither wanted nor needed here."

Mr. Verosky. "Well, in that case, the Burgess may throw some light on the subject."

Mr. Callahan. (Burgess) "The question comes to me as a surprise and I am sure that I don't know by whose authority the Constabulary was called in."

Everything was calm in Braddock until the State Police came in. Then the trouble began. It was the same nearly everywhere. The arrival of these men was always the signal for so-called riots, and wholesale clubbing, shooting and jailing of strikers....

Suppression of the rights of free speech and free assembly; gigantic organized campaigns of outlawry by the State Police and armies of selected plug-uglies; subornation and intimidation of city, county, state and federal officials and police; prostitution of the courts— these are some of the means used to crush the strike of the steel workers, and to force these over-worked, under-paid toilers still deeper into the mire of slavery. And the whole monstrous crime was hypocritically committed in the name of a militant, 100 per cent. Americanism.

28

The Case Against the "Reds" *(1920)*

A. MITCHELL PALMER

America's involvement in World War I brought with it a concerted effort to decimate all radical movements in the United States. Federal, state, and local governments imprisoned labor organizers, pacifists, anarchists, and socialists, including presidential candidate Eugene V. Debs. The Bolshevik Revolution in

Russia in November 1917, gave a particular urgency to these efforts, as many Americans feared the export of radical European ideas. Even after the war ended, the government did not relent in its antileftist prosecutions. Beginning in November 1919, Attorney General A. Mitchell Palmer launched a nationwide campaign against foreign-born radicals. In January 1920, federal agents arrested four thousand of these "subversives," deporting nearly three thousand of them to the Soviet Union. Palmer hoped that his public war against radicalism would earn him the Democratic nomination for the presidency, an ambition he did not realize.

Questions to Consider

- Do leftists and the foreign-born enjoy Constitutional protections?
- What is Palmer afraid of?

In this brief review of the work which the Department of Justice has undertaken, to tear out the radical seeds that have entangled American ideas in their poisonous theories, I desire not merely to explain what the real menace of communism is, but also to tell how we have been compelled to clean up the country almost unaided by any virile legislation. Though I have not been embarrassed by political opposition, I have been materially delayed because the present sweeping processes of arrests and deportation of seditious aliens should have been vigorously pushed by Congress last spring. The failure of this is a matter of record in the Congressional files....

Like a prairie-fire, the blaze of revolution was sweeping over every American institution of law and order a year ago. It was eating its way into the homes of the American workman, its sharp tongues of revolutionary heat were licking the altars of the churches, leaping into the belfry of the school bell, crawling into the sacred corners of American homes, seeking to replace marriage vows with libertine laws, burning up the foundations of society.

Robbery, not war, is the ideal of communism. This has been demonstrated in Russia, Germany, and in America. As a foe, the anarchist is fearless of his own life, for his creed is a fanaticism that admits no respect of any other creed. Obviously it is the creed of any criminal mind, which reasons always from motives impossible to clean thought. Crime is the degenerate factor in society.

Upon these two basic certainties, first that the "Reds" were criminal aliens, and secondly that the American Government must prevent crime, it was decided that there could be no nice distinctions drawn between the

theoretical ideals of the radicals and their actual violations of our national laws. An assassin may have brilliant intellectuality, he may be able to excuse his murder or robbery with fine oratory, but any theory which excuses crime is not wanted in America. This is no place for the criminal to flourish, nor will he do so, so long as the rights of common citizenship can be exerted to prevent him.

Our Government in Jeopardy

It has always been plain to me that when American citizens unite upon any national issue, they are generally right, but it is sometimes difficult to make the issue clear to them. If the Department of Justice could succeed in attracting the attention of our optimistic citizens to the issue of internal revolution in this country, we felt sure there would be no revolution. The Government was in jeopardy. My private information of what was being done by the organization known as the Communist Party of America, with headquarters in Chicago, of what was being done by the Communist Internationale under their manifesto planned at Moscow last March by Trotzky, Lenine and others, addressed "To the Proletariats of All Countries," of what strides the Communist Labor Party was making, removed all doubt. In this conclusion we did not ignore the definite standards of personal liberty, of free speech, which is the very temperament and heart of the people. The evidence was examined with the utmost care, with a personal leaning toward freedom of thought and word on all questions.

The whole mass of evidence, accumulated from all parts of the country, was scrupulously scanned, not merely for the written or spoken differences of viewpoint as to the Government of the United States, but, in spite of these things, to see if the hostile declarations might not be sincere in their announced motive to im

Source: A. Mitchell Palmer, "The Case Against the 'Reds,'" *The Forum* (Feb. 1920), pp. 173–185.

prove our social order. There was no hope of such a thing.

By stealing, murder and lies, Bolshevism has looted Russia not only of its material strength, but of its moral force. A small clique of outcasts from the East Side of New York has attempted this, with what success we all know. Because a disreputable alien—Leon Bronstein, the man who now calls himself Trotzky—can inaugurate a reign of terror from his throne room in the Kremlin; because this lowest of all types known to New York can sleep in the Czar's bed, while hundreds of thousands in Russia are without food or shelter, should Americans be swayed by such doctrines?

Such a question, it would seem, should receive but one answer from America.

My information showed that communism in this country was an organization of thousands of aliens, who were direct allies of Trotzky. Aliens of the same misshapen caste of mind and indecencies of character, and it showed that they were making the same glittering promises of lawlessness, of criminal autocracy to Americans, that they had made to the Russian peasants. How the Department of Justice discovered upwards of 60,000 of these organized agitators of the Trotzky doctrine in the United States, is the confidential information upon which the Government is now sweeping the nation clean of such alien filth....

...[T]he Espionage Act, approved June 15, 1917, and amended May 16, 1918, was invoked to be used against seditious utterances and acts, although I felt that it was limited to acts and utterances only which tended to weaken the waging of actual hostilities.... Nevertheless, I caused to be brought several test prosecutions in order to obtain a court ruling on the Espionage Law and its application to seditions committed since the cessation of the armed activity of our forces.

I did this because our general statutes as to treason and rebellion do not apply to the present radical activities, with the exception of Section 6 of the Federal Penal Code of 1910, which says:

> If two or more persons in any State or Territory or in any place subject to the jurisdiction of the United States conspire to overthrow, put down or to destroy by force, the Government of the United States, or to levy war against them, or to oppose by force the authority thereof, or by force to prevent, hinder or delay, the execution of any law of the United States, or by force to seize, take or possess any property of the United States, contrary to the authority thereof, they shall each be fined, not more than $5,000 or imprisonment not more than six years, or both.

Although this Act by no means covered individual activities, under this law I prosecuted the El Arieto Society, an anarchistic organization in operation in Buffalo, N. Y., indicting three of its members for circulating a manifesto which was an appeal to the proletariat to arise and destroy the Government of the United States by force, and substitute Bolshevism or anarchy in place thereof. It was printed in Spanish. Phrases such as, "the proletariat of all countries to invite to participate the revolution," "for all others who suffer the evils of servitude must join in the conflict," "to attach the State directly and assail it without hesitation or compunction," were uncompromisingly seditious advice....

On motion to dismiss the indictment, this case came before Judge Hazel of the Western District Court of New York, July 24, 1919, who, after hearing counsel, dismissed the case and discharged the defendants. In his opinion the Court, after citing Section 6, said:

> I do not believe that the acts and deeds set forth in the indictment and the evidence given in support of it establish an offense such as this Section which I have just read contemplates.

However, the language of this Spanish document was so violent and desperate in its declarations of defiance to the existing Government of the United States, that I, at once, placed the entire record of this case before the Commissioner of Immigration, with a recommendation that the defendants involved be deported as undesirable aliens.

All deportation activities conducted since by the Department of Justice against the "Reds" have been with the co-operation of the Department of Labor, which issued the warrants of arrest and deportation recommended by evidence that meets the conditions of the Federal Penal Code of 1910. I pointed out to the Senate certain classes of radical activities that might come under certain sections of this Penal Code:

1. Those who have "attempted to bring about the forcible overthrow of the Government of the United States have committed no crime unless their acts amount to treason, rebellion or seditious conspiracy." This is defined in Section 1, 4 and 6 of the Criminal Code above quoted.

No Laws Against Some "Red" Crimes

There were other activities of the Reds, however, for which there was no legislation. These were:

2. The preaching of anarchy and sedition is not a crime under the general criminal statutes of the United States.
3. Advising the defiance of law is not a crime under the general criminal laws whether the same be done by printing and circulating literature or by the spoken word.

4. Nor is the advising and openly advocating the unlawful obstruction of industry and the unlawful and violent destruction of property a crime under the United States general statutes.

These conclusions were reached after wide consultation with the best criminal lawyers in the country. In my testimony before the sub-committee of the Judiciary Committee of the Senate on July 14, 1919, at its request, I had fully outlined the conditions threatening internal revolution in the nation that confronted us. Legislation which I then recommended to meet this great menace has not been enacted. This is not my fault, for I knew that Congress was fully aware of the "Reds'" activities in this country.

Many States passed certain acts which embodied the basis of my request to Congress for national legislation bearing upon radicalism. California, Indiana, Michigan, New York, Ohio, Pennsylvania, Washington and West Virginia have passed State laws governing the rebellious acts of the "Reds" in their separate territories. These States have infinitely greater legal force at their command against the revolutionary element than the United States Government, for detecting and punishing seditious acts. In their equipment of men to carry out their laws, they far surpass the facilities of the Department of Justice. New York City alone has 12,000 policemen charged with the duty of investigation, and the District Attorney of New York County has a force of over fifty prosecuting attorneys.

Under the appropriations granted by Congress to the Department of Justice, the maximum number of men engaged in the preparation of the violation of all United States laws is limited to about 500 for the entire country. Startling as this fact may seem to the reader who discovers it for the first time, it is the highest testimony to the services of these men, that the Department of Justice of the United States, is today, a human net that no outlaw can escape. It has been netted together in spite of Congressional indifference, intensified by the individual patriotism of its personnel aroused to the menace of revolution, inspired to superlative action above and beyond private interests.

One of the chief incentives for the present activity of the Department of Justice against the "Reds" has been the hope that American citizens will, themselves, become voluntary agents for us, in a vast organization for mutual defense against the sinister agitation of men and women aliens, who appear to be either in the pay or under the criminal spell of Trotzky and Lenine.

Deportations Under Immigration Laws

Temporary failure to seize the alien criminals in this country who are directly responsible for spreading the unclean doctrines of Bolshevism here only increased the

determination to get rid of them. Obviously, their offenses were related to our immigration laws, and it was finally decided to act upon that principle....

By the administration of this law deportations have been made, the law being as follows:

Be it enacted by the Senate and House of Representatives of the United States of America in Congress assembled:

Sec. 1. That aliens who are anarchists; aliens who believe in or advocate the overthrow by force or violence of the Government of the United States or of all forms of law; aliens who disbelieve in or who are opposed to all organized government; aliens who advocate or teach the assassination of public officials; aliens who advocate or teach the unlawful destruction of property; aliens who are members of or affiliated with any organization that entertains a belief in, teaches, or advocates the overthrow by force or by violence of the Government of the United States or of all forms of law, or that entertains or teaches disbelief in or opposition to all organized Government, or that advocates the duty, necessity or propriety of the unlawful assaulting or killing of any officer or officers, either of specific individuals or of officers generally, of the Government of the United States, or of any other organized Government, because of his or their official character, or that advocates or teaches the unlawful destruction of property, shall be excluded from admission into the United States....

Although this law is entirely under the jurisdiction of the Department of Labor, it seemed to be the only means at my disposal of attacking the radical movement. To further this plan, as Congress had seen fit to refuse appropriations to the Department of Labor which might have enabled it to act vigorously against the "Reds," I offered to co-operate with the immigration officials to the fullest extent. My appropriation became available July 19, 1919. I then organized what is known as the Radical Division....

Will Deportations Check Bolshevism?

Behind, and underneath, my own determination to drive from our midst the agents of Bolshevism with increasing vigor and with greater speed, until there are no more of them left among us, so long as I have the responsible duty of that task, I have discovered the hysterical methods of these revolutionary humans with increasing amazement and suspicion. In the confused information that sometimes reaches the people, they are compelled to ask questions which involve the reasons for my acts against the "Reds." I have been asked, for instance, to what extent deportation will check radicalism in this country. Why not ask what will become of the United States Government if these alien radicals are permitted to carry out the principles of the Communist Party as embodied in its so-called laws, aims and regulations?

There wouldn't be any such thing left. In place of the United States Government we should have the horror and terrorism of bolsheviki tyranny such as is destroying Russia now. Every scrap of radical literature demands the overthrow of our existing government. All of it demands obedience to the instincts of criminal minds, that is, to the lower appetites, material and moral. The whole purpose of communism appears to be a mass formation of the criminals of the world to overthrow the decencies of private life, to usurp property that they have not earned, to disrupt the present order of life regardless of health, sex or religious rights. By a literature that promises the wildest dreams of such low aspirations, that can occur to only the criminal minds, communism distorts our social law.

The chief appeal communism makes is to "The Worker." If they can lure the wage-earner to join their own gang of thieves, if they can show him that he will be rich if he steals, so far they have succeeded in betraying him to their own criminal course.

Read this manifesto issued in Chicago:

THE COMMUNIST PARTY MANIFESTO

The world is on the verge of a new era. Europe is in revolt. The masses of Asia are stirring uneasily. Capitalism is in collapse. The workers of the world are seeing a new light and securing new courage. Out of the night of war is coming a new day.

The spectre of communism haunts the world of capitalism. Communism, the hope of the workers to end misery and oppression.

The workers of Russia smashed the front of international Capitalism and Imperialism. They broke the chains of the terrible war; and in the midst of agony, starvation and the attacks of the Capitalists of the world, they are creating a new social order....

The Communist Party of America is the party of the working class. The Communist Party proposes to end Capitalism and organize a workers' industrial republic. The workers must control industry and dispose of the product of industry. The Communist Party is a party realizing the limitation of all existing workers' organizations and proposes to develop the revolutionary movement necessary to free the workers from the oppression of Capitalism. The Communist Party insists that the problems of the American worker are identical with the problems of the workers of the world.

These are the revolutionary tenets of Trotzky and the Communist Internationale. Their manifesto further embraces the various organizations in this country of men and women obsessed with discontent, having disorganized relations to American society. These include the I. W. W.'s, the most radical socialists, the misguided anarchists, the agitators who oppose the limitations of unionism, the moral perverts and the hysterical neurasthenic women who abound in communism. The phraseology of their manifesto is practically the same wording as was used by the Bolsheviks for their International Communist Congress.

The Communist Absorbs the Socialist Party

Naturally the Communist Party has bored its revolutionary points into the Socialist Party. They managed to split the Socialists, for the so-called Left Wing of the Socialist Party is now the Communist Party, which specifically states that it does not intend to capture the bourgeosie [*sic*] parliamentary state, but to conquer and destroy, and that the final objective, mass action, is the medium intended to be used in the conquest and destruction of the bourgeosie state to annihilate the parliamentary state, and introduce a revolutionary dictatorship of the Proletariat.

The Left Wing Socialists declared themselves when they issued a call for a convention held in Chicago, September 1, 1919, to organize a Communist Party. An effort was made at a convention of the Socialist Party of America in Chicago, August 30, 1919, to harmonize differences. Their first plan in harmonious endeavor was to refuse admission to their convention to members of the Left Wing, on the ground that the latter intended to capture it. At the Communist Convention of Left Wing Socialists on September 1, 1919, 129 delegates, representing 55,000 members, attended. Extensive Communist propaganda followed, including the establishment of a paper, "The Communist."

There is no legislation at present which can reach an American citizen who is discontented with our system of American Government, nor is it necessary. The dangerous fact to us is that the Communist Party of America is actually affiliated and adheres to the teaching program and tactics of the 3d Internationale. Consider what this means.

The first congress of the Communist Nationale held March 6, 1919, in Moscow, subscribed to by Trotzky and Lenine, adopted the following:

This makes necessary the disarming of the bourgeosie at the proper time, the arming of the laborer, and the formation of a communist army as the protectors of the rules of the proletariat and the inviolability of the social structure.

When we realize that each member of the Communist Party of America pledges himself to the principles above, set forth, deportation of men and women bound to such a theory is a very mild reformatory sentence.

Have the "Reds" Betrayed Labor?

If I were asked whether the American Federation of Labor had been betrayed by the "Reds," I should refer the inquiry to the manifesto and constitution of the Communist Party of America, in which, under the heading, "Revolutionary Construction," the following paragraph appears:

> But the American Federation of Labor, as a whole, is hopelessly reactionary. At its recent convention the A. F. of L. approved the Versailles Peace Treaty and the League of Nations, and refused to declare its solidarity with Soviet Russia. It did not even protest the blockade of Russia and Hungary! This convention, moreover, did all in its power to break radical unions. The A. F. of L. is united with the Government, securing a privileged status in the governing system of State Capitalism. A Labor Party is being organized—much more conservative than the British Labor Party.

It has been inferred by the "Reds" that the United States Government, by arresting and deporting them, is returning to the autocracy of Czardom, adopting the system that created the severity of Siberian banishment.

My reply to such charges is, that in our determination to maintain our government we are treating our alien enemies with extreme consideration. To deny them the privilege of remaining in a country which they have openly deplored as an unenlightened community, unfit for those who prefer the privileges of Bolshevism, should be no hardship. It strikes me as an odd form of reasoning that these Russian Bolsheviks who extol the Bolshevik rule, should be so unwilling to return to Russia. The nationality of most of the alien "Reds" is Russian and German. There is almost no other nationality represented among them.

It has been impossible in so short a space to review the entire menace of the internal revolution in this country as I know it, but this may serve to arouse the American citizen to its reality, its danger, and the great need of united effort to stamp it out, under our feet, if needs be. It is being done. The Department of Justice will pursue the attack of these "Reds" upon the Government of the United States with vigilance, and no alien, advocating the overthrow of existing law and order in this country, shall escape arrest and prompt deportation.

It is my belief that while they have stirred discontent in our midst, while they have caused irritating strikes, and while they have infected our social ideas with the disease of their own minds and their unclean morals, we can get rid of them! and not until we have done so shall we have removed the menace of Bolshevism for good.

29

Last Statements (1927)

NICOLA SACCO and BARTOLOMEO VANZETTI

The 1920s, famous as a time of wild parties and fads, was also a decade of notable intolerance. The special targets of law enforcement and popular culture were radicals and immigrants. Two Italian radicals, Nicola Sacco and Bartolomeo Vanzetti, became symbols of the oppressive hand of the state. Sacco, a shoemaker, and Vanzetti, a fishmonger, were accused of killing a paymaster and his guard on April 15, 1920, during a robbery of a South Braintree, Massachusetts, shoe factory. Their trial before Judge Webster Thayer involved a great number of irregularities, not the least of which were the close connection between the state-appointed defense attorney and the prosecutor and the oft-stated conviction of the judge that the two defendants were guilty. The fate of Sacco and Vanzetti became an international cause, with thousands of liberals and radicals, from Felix Frankfurter to Eugene V. Debs, joining in the effort to free the two men. In 1927 Judge Thayer oversaw the hearing that reconsidered and confirmed his verdict in the first trial. In broken English, Sacco and Vanzetti condemned the court for its corruption of justice. The pair were executed in the electric chair on August 23, 1927.

Questions to Consider

- Was there any reason to believe that Sacco and Vanzetti were not guilty?
- What about this case captured the attention of an international audience?

Dedham, Massachusetts,
Saturday, April 9, 1927.

Clerk Worthington. Nicola Sacco, have you anything to say why sentence of death should not be passed upon you?

Statement by Nicola Sacco

Yes, sir. I am not an orator. It is not very familiar with me the English language, and as I know, as my friend has told me, my comrade Vanzetti will speak more long, so I thought to give him the chance.

I never know, never heard, even read in history anything so cruel as this Court. After seven years prosecuting they still consider us guilty. And these gentle people here are arrayed with us in this court today.

I know the sentence will be between two class, the oppressed class and the rich class, and there will be always collision between one and the other. We fraternize the people with the books, with the literature. You persecute the people, tyrannize over them and kill them. We try the education of people always. You try to put a path between us and some other nationality that hates each other. That is why I am here today on this bench, for having been the oppressed class. Well, you are the oppressor.

You know it, Judge Thayer,—you know all my life, you know why I have been here, and after seven years that you have been persecuting me and my poor wife, and you still today sentence us to death. I would like to tell all my life, but what is the use?…You forget all the population that has been with us for seven years, to sympathize and give us all their energy and all their kindness. You do not care for them. Among that peoples and the comrades and the working class there is a big

legion of intellectual people which have been with us for seven years, but to not commit the iniquitous sentence, but still the Court goes ahead. And I think I thank you all, you peoples, my comrades who have been with me for seven years, with the Sacco-Vanzetti case, and I will give my friend a chance.

I forget one thing which my comrade remember me. As I said before, Judge Thayer know all my life, and he know that I am never been guilty, never,—not yesterday nor today nor forever.

Clerk Worthington. Bartolomeo Vanzetti, have you anything to say why sentence of death should not be passed upon you?

Statement by Bartolomeo Vanzetti

Yes. What I say is that I am innocent…. That I am not only innocent…but in all my life I have never stole and I have never killed and I have never spilled blood. That is what I want to say. And it is not all. Not only am I innocent of these…crimes, not only in all my life I have never stole, never killed, never spilled blood, but I have struggled all my life, since I began to reason, to eliminate crime from the earth.

Everybody that knows these two arms knows very well that I did not need to go in between the street and kill a man to take the money. I can live with my two arms and live well. But besides that, I can live even without work with my arm for other people. I have had plenty of chance to live independently and to live what the world conceives to be a higher life than not to gain our bread with the sweat of our brow….

…I have refused myself the commodity or glory of life, the pride of life of a good position, because in my consideration it is not right to exploit man. I have refused to go in business because I understand that business is a speculation on profit upon certain people that must depend upon the business man, and I do not consider that that is right and therefore I refuse to do that….

Source: *Commonwealth v. Nicola Sacco and Bartolomeo Vanzetti* (1927), pp. 4895–4902, 4904–4905.

…There is the more good man I ever cast my eyes upon since I lived, a man that will last and will grow always more near and more dear to the people, as far as into the heart of the people, so long as admiration for goodness and for sacrifice will last. I mean Eugene Debs….

…Just because he want the world a little better he was persecuted and slandered from his boyhood to his old age, and indeed he was murdered by the prison. He know, and not only he but every man of understanding in the world, not only in this country but also in the other countries, men that we have provided a certain amount of a record of the times, they all still stick with us, the flower of mankind of Europe, the better writers, the greatest thinkers of Europe, have pleaded in our favor. The scientists, the greatest scientists, the greatest statesmen of Europe, have pleaded in our favor. The people of foreign nations have pleaded in our favor.

Is it possible that only a few on the jury, only two or three men, who would condemn their mother for worldly honor and for earthly fortune; is it possible that they are right against what the world, the whole world has say it is wrong and that I know that it is wrong? If there is one that I should know it, if it is right or if it is wrong, it is I and this man. You see it is seven years that we are in jail. What we have suffered during these seven years no human tongue can say, and yet you see me before you, not trembling, you see me looking you in your eyes straight, not blushing, not changing color, not ashamed or in fear….

…We have proved that there could not have been another Judge on the face of the earth more prejudiced and more cruel than you have been against us. We have proven that. Still they refuse the new trial. We know, and you know in your heart, that you have been against us from the very beginning, before you see us. Before you see us you already know that we were radicals, that we were underdogs, that we were the enemy of the institution that you can believe in good faith in their goodness—I don't want to condemn that—and that it was easy on the time of the first trial to get a verdict of guiltiness.

We know that you have spoke yourself and have spoke your hostility against us, and your despisement against us with friends of yours on the train, at the University Club of Boston, on the Golf Club of Worcester, Massachusetts. I am sure that if the people who know all what you say against us would have the civil courage to take the stand, maybe your Honor—I am sorry to say this because you are an old man, and I have an old father—but maybe you would be beside us in good justice at this time….

I am willing that everybody that does believe me that they can make commission, they can go over there, and

I am very willing that the people should go over there and see whether it is true or not. There are people in Charlestown who are professional robbers, who have been in half the prisons of the United States, that they are steal, or hurt the man, shoot him. By chance he got better, he did not die. Well, the most of them guilty without trial, by self-confession, and by asking the aid of their own partner, and they got 8 to 10, 8 to 12, 10 to 15. None of them has 12 to 15, as you gave me for an attempt at robbery. And besides that, you know that I was not guilty. You know that my life, my private and public life in Plymouth, and wherever I have been, was so exemplary that one of the worst fears of our prosecutor [Frederick Gunn] Katzmann was to introduce proof of our life and of our conduct. He has taken it off with all his might and he has succeeded.

You know if we would have Mr. Thompson, or even the brother McAnarney, in the first trial in Plymouth, you know that no jury would have found me guilty. My first lawyer has been a partner of Mr. Katzmann, as he is still now. My first lawyer of the defense, Mr. [John P.] Vahey, has not defended me, has sold me for thirty golden money like Judas sold Jesus Christ. If that man has not told to you or to Mr. Katzmann that he know that I was guilty, it is because he know that I was not guilty. That man has done everything indirectly to hurt us. He has made long speech with the jury about things that do matter nothing, and on the point of essence to the trial he has passed over with few words or with complete silence. This was a premeditation in order to give to the jury the impression that my own defender has nothing good to say, has nothing good to urge in defense of myself, and therefore go around the bush on little things that amount to nothing and let pass the essential points either in silence or with a very weakly resistance.

We were tried during a time that has now passed into history. I mean by that, a time when there was a hysteria of resentment and hate against the people of our principles, against the foreigner, against slackers, and it seems to me—rather, I am positive of it, that both you and Mr. Katzmann has done all what it were in your power in order to work out, in order to agitate still more the passion of the juror, the prejudice of the juror, against us….

…That a certain witness that was the water boy of the gang of the laborers testified that he take a pail and go to a certain spring, a water spring, to take water for the gang—it was not true that he go to that spring, and therefore it was not true that he see the bandit, and therefore it was not true that he can tell that neither I nor Sacco were the men. But it was introduced to show that it was not true that that man go to that spring, because they know that the Germans has poisoned the water in that spring. That is what he say on that stand over there. Now, in the world chronicle of the time there is not a single happening of that nature. Nobody in America—we have read plenty things bad that the Germans have done in Europe during the war, but nobody can prove and nobody will say that the Germans are bad enough to poison the spring water in this country during the war.

Now, this, it seems, has nothing to do with us directly. It seems to be a thing by incident on the stand between the other thing that is the essence here. But the jury were hating us because we were against the war, and the jury don't know that it makes any difference between a man that is against the war because he believes that the war is unjust, because he hate no country, because he is a cosmopolitan, and a man that is against the war because he is in favor of the other country that fights against the country in which he is, and therefore a spy, and he commits any crime in the country in which he is in behalf of the other country in order to serve the other country. We are not men of that kind. Katzmann know very well that. Katzmann know that we were against the war because we did not believe in the purpose for which they say that the war was done. We believe it that the war is wrong, and we believe this more now after ten years that we understood it day by day,—the consequences and the result of the after war. We believe more now than ever that the war was wrong, and we are against war more now than ever, and I am glad to be on the doomed scaffold if I can say to mankind, "Look out; you are in a catacomb of the flower of mankind. For what? All that they say to you, all that they have promised to you—it was a lie, it was an illusion, it was a cheat, it was a fraud, it was a crime. They promised you liberty. Where is liberty? They promised you prosperity. Where is prosperity? They have promised you elevation. Where is the elevation?…

…Where is the moral good that the War has given to the world? Where is the spiritual progress that we have achieved from the War? Where are the security of life, the security of the things that we possess for our necessity? Where are the respect for human life? Where are the respect and the admiration for the good characteristics and the good of the human nature? Never as now before the war there have been so many crimes, so many corruptions, so many degeneration as there is now.

In the best of my recollection and of my good faith, during the trial Katzmann has told to the jury that a certain Coacci has brought in Italy the money that, according to the State theory, I and Sacco have stole in Braintree. We never steal that money. But Katzmann, when he told that to the jury, he know already that that was not true. He know already that that man was de-

ported in Italy with the Federal policeman after our arrest. I remember well that the Federal policeman with him in their possession—that the Federal policeman has taken away the trunks from the very boarding where he was, and bring the trunks over here and look them over and found not a single money.

Now, I call that murder, to tell to the jury that a friend or comrade or a relative or acquaintance of the charged man, of the indicted man, has carried the money to Italy, when he knows it is not true. I can call that nothing else but a murder, a plain murder….

…In fact, even the telephone poles knew at the time of this trial at Dedham that I was tried and convicted in Plymouth; the jurymen knew that even when they slept…. The jury don't know nothing about us. They have never seen us. The only thing that they know is the bad things that the newspaper have say when we were arrested and the bad story that the newspaper have say on the Plymouth trial….

This is what I say: I would not wish to a dog or to a snake, to the most low and misfortunate creature of the earth—I would not wish to any of them what I have had to suffer for things that I am not guilty of. But my conviction is that I have suffered for things that I am guilty of. I am suffering because I am a radical and indeed I am a radical; I have suffered because I was an Italian, and indeed I am an Italian; I have suffered more for my family and for my beloved than for myself; but I am so convinced to be right that if you could execute me two times, and if I could be reborn two other times, I would live again to do what I have done already.

I have finished. Thank you.

The Court

Under the law of Massachusetts the jury says whether a defendant is guilty or innocent. The Court has absolutely nothing to do with that question. The law of Massachusetts provides that a Judge cannot deal in any way with the facts. As far as he can go under our law is to state the evidence.

During the trial many exceptions were taken. Those exceptions were taken to the Supreme Judicial Court. That Court, after examining the entire record, after examining all the exceptions,—that Court in its final words said, "The verdicts of the jury should stand; exceptions overruled." That being true, there is only one thing that this Court can do. It is not a matter of discretion. It is a matter of statutory requirement, and that being true there is only one duty that now devolves upon this Court, and that is to pronounce the sentences.

First the Court pronounces sentence upon Nicola Sacco. It is considered and ordered by the Court that you, Nicola Sacco, suffer the punishment of death by the passage of a current of electricity through your body within the week beginning on Sunday, the tenth day of July, in the year of our Lord, one thousand, nine hundred and twenty-seven. This is the sentence of the law.

It is considered and ordered by the Court that you, Bartolomeo Vanzetti—

Mr. Vanzetti. Wait a minute, please, your Honor. May I speak for a minute with my lawyer, Mr. Thompson?

Mr. Thompson. I do not know what he wants to say.

The Court. I think I should pronounce the sentence.—Bartolomeo Vanzetti, suffer the punishment of death—

Mr. Sacco. You know I am innocent.... You condemn two innocent men.

The Court. —by the passage of a current of electricity through your body within the week beginning on Sunday, the tenth day of July, in the year of our Lord, one thousand nine hundred and twenty-seven. This is the sentence of the law.

We will now take a recess.

30

Socialist Party Platform (1932)

SOCIALIST PARTY

Opponents of Franklin Roosevelt called him a Socialist. Actual Socialists condemned him as a defender of the capitalist order. In the 1932 election the Socialist Party offered a platform that, if enacted, would have changed American society in several fundamental ways. Roosevelt won an overwhelming victory, but the Socialist candidate, Norman Thomas, received 885,000 votes—an impressive showing for a minor party.

Questions to Consider

- What, according to the Socialists, is wrong with the United States?
- Is there any similarity between the Socialist platform and Roosevelt's New Deal?

We are facing a breakdown of the capitalist system. This situation the Socialist Party has long predicted. In the last campaign it warned the people of the increasing insecurity in American life and urged a program of action which, if adopted, would have saved millions from their present tragic plight.

To-day in every city of the United States jobless men and women by the thousands are fighting the grim battle against want and starvation while factories stand idle and food rots on the ground. Millions of wage earners and salaried workers are hunting in vain for jobs while other millions are only partly employed.

Unemployment and poverty are inevitable products of the present system. Under capitalism the few own our industries. The many do the work. The wage earners and farmers are compelled to give a large part of the product of their labor to the few. The many in the facto-

Source: *The Congressional Record,* July 6, 1932, 72nd Congress, 1st Session, vol. 75, pt. 13, pp. 14702–14703.

ries, mines, shops, offices, and on the farms obtain but a scanty income and are able to buy back only a part of the goods that can be produced in such abundance by our mass industries.

Goods pile up. Factories close. Men and women are discharged. The Nation is thrown into a panic. In a country with natural resources, machinery, and trained labor sufficient to provide security and plenty for all, masses of people are destitute.

Capitalism spells not only widespread economic disaster but class strife. It likewise carries with it an ever-present threat of international war. The struggle of the capitalist class to find world markets and investment areas for their surplus goods and capital was a prime cause of the World War. It is to-day fostering those policies of militarism and imperialism which, if unchecked, [will] lead to another world conflict.

From the poverty, insecurity, unemployment, the economic collapse, the wastes, and the wars of our present capitalistic order only the united efforts of workers and farmers, organized in unions and cooperatives and, above all, in a political party of their own, can save the Nation.

The Republican and Democratic Parties, both controlled by the great industrialists and financiers, have no plan or program to rescue us from the present collapse. In this crisis their chief purpose and desire has been to help the railroads, banks, insurance companies, and other capitalist interests.

The Socialist Party is to-day the one democratic party of the workers whose program would remove the causes of class struggles, class antagonisms, and social evils inherent in the capitalist system.

It proposes to transfer the principal industries of the country from private ownership and autocratic, cruelly inefficient management to social ownership and democratic control. Only by these means will it be possible to organize our industrial life on a basis of planned and steady operation, without periodic breakdowns and disastrous crises.

It proposes the following measures:

Unemployment and Labor Legislation

1. A Federal appropriation of $5,000,000,000 for immediate relief for those in need, to supplement State and local appropriations.

2. A Federal appropriation of $5,000,000,000 for public works and roads, reforestation, slum clearance, and decent homes for the workers, by Federal Government, States, and cities.

3. Legislation providing for the acquisition of land, buildings, and equipment necessary to put the unem-

ployed to work producing food, fuel, and clothing and for the erection of houses for their own use.

4. The 6-hour day and the 5-day week without a reduction of wages.

5. A comprehensive and efficient system of free public employment agencies.

6. A compulsory system of unemployment compensation with adequate benefits, based on contributions by the Government and by employers.

7. Old-age pensions for men and women 60 years of age and over.

8. Health and maternity insurance.

9. Improved systems of workmen's compensation and accident insurance.

10. The abolition of child labor.

11. Government aid to farmers and small-home owners to protect them against mortgage foreclosures and a moratorium on sales for nonpayment of taxes by destitute farmers and unemployed workers.

12. Adequate minimum wage laws.

Social Ownership

1. Public ownership and democratic control of mines, forests, oil, and power resources; public utilities dealing with light and power, transportation and communication, and of all other basic industries.

2. The operation of these publicly owned industries by boards of administration on which the wageworker, the consumer, and the technician are adequately represented; the recognition in each industry of the principles of collective bargaining and civil service.

Banking

Socialization of our credit and currency system and the establishment of a unified banking system, beginning with the complete governmental acquisition of the Federal reserve banks and the extension of the services of the postal savings banks to cover all departments of the banking business and the transference of this department of the post office to a Government-owned banking corporation.

Taxation

1. Steeply increased inheritance taxes and income taxes on the higher incomes and estates of both corporations and individuals.

2. A constitutional amendment authorizing the taxation of all Government securities.

Agriculture

Many of the foregoing measures for socializing the power, banking, and other industries, for raising living standards among the city workers, etc., would greatly benefit the farming population.

As special measures for agricultural upbuilding we propose:

1. The reduction of tax burdens by a shift from taxes on farm property to taxes on incomes, inheritances, excess profits, and other similar forms of taxation.

2. Increased Federal and State subsidies to road building and educational and social services for rural communities.

3. The creation of a Federal marketing agency for the purchase and marketing of agricultural products.

4. The acquisition by bona fide cooperative societies and by governmental agencies of grain elevators, stockyards, packing houses, and warehouses and the conduct of these services on a nonprofit basis. The encouragement of farmers' cooperative societies and of consumers' cooperatives in the cities, with a view of eliminating the middleman.

5. The socialization of Federal land banks and the extension by these banks of long-term credit to farmers at low rates of interest.

6. Social insurance against losses due to adverse weather conditions.

7. The creation of national, regional, and State land utilization boards for the purpose of discovering the best uses of the farming land of the country, in view of the joint needs of agriculture, industry, recreation, water supply, reforestation, etc., and to prepare the way for agricultural planning on a national and, ultimately, on a world scale.

Constitutional Changes

1. Proportional representation.
2. Direct election of the President and Vice President.
3. The initiative and referendum.
4. An amendment to the Constitution to make constitutional amendments less cumbersome.
5. Abolition of the power of the Supreme Court to pass upon the constitutionality of legislation enacted by Congress.
6. The passage of the Socialist party's proposed workers' rights amendment to the Constitution empowering Congress to establish national systems of unemployment, health and accident insurance and old age pensions, to abolish child labor, establish and take over enterprises in manufacture, commerce, transportation,

banking, public utilities, and other business and industries to be owned and operated by the Government and, generally, for the social and economic welfare of the workers of the United States.

(The plank dealing with prohibition has been submitted to a referendum of the party membership.)

Civil Liberties

1. Federal legislation to enforce the first amendment to the Constitution so as to guarantee freedom of speech, press, and assembly, and to penalize officials who interfere with the civil rights of citizens.

2. The abolition of injunctions in labor disputes, the outlawing of "yellow-dog" contracts and the passing of laws enforcing the rights of workers to organize into unions.

3. The immediate repeal of the espionage law and other repressive legislation, and the restoration of civil and political rights to those unjustly convicted under wartime laws.

4. Legislation protecting aliens from being excluded from this country or from citizenship or from being deported on account of their political, social, or economic beliefs, or on account of activities engaged in by them which are not illegal for citizens.

5. Modification of the immigration laws to permit the reuniting of families and to offer a refuge to those fleeing from political or religious persecution.

The Negro

The enforcement of constitutional guarantees of economic, political, and legal equality for the Negro.

The enactment and enforcement of drastic antilynching laws.

International Relations

While the Socialist Party is opposed to all war, it believes that there can be no permanent peace until socialism is established internationally. In the meanwhile, we will support all measures that promise to promote good will and friendship among the nations of the world, including:

1. The reduction of armaments, leading to the goal of total disarmament by international agreement, if possible; but, if that is not possible, by setting an example ourselves. Soldiers, sailors, and workers unemployed

by reason of disarmament to be absorbed, where desired, in a program of public works, to be financed in part by the savings due to disarmament. The abolition of conscription, of military training camps, and the Reserve Officers' Training Corps.

2. The recognition of the Soviet Union and the encouragement of trade and industrial relations with that country.

3. The cancellation of war debts due from the allied governments as part of a program for wiping out war debts and reparations, provided that such cancellation does not release money for armaments but promotes disarmament.

4. The entrance of the United States into the World Court.

5. The entrance of the United States into the League of Nations under conditions which will make it an effective instrument for world peace and renewed cooperation with the working-class parties abroad to the end that the league may be transformed from a league of imperialist powers to a democratic assemblage representative of the aspirations of the common people of the world.

6. The creation of international economic organizations on which labor is adequately represented, to deal with problems of raw material, investments, money, credit, tariffs, and living standards from the viewpoint of the welfare of the masses throughout the world.

7. The abandonment of every degree of military intervention by the United States in the affairs of other countries. The immediate withdrawal of military forces from Haiti and Nicaragua.

8. The withdrawal of United States military and naval forces from China and the relinquishment of American extraterritorial privileges.

9. The complete independence of the Philippines and the negotiation of treaties with other nations safeguarding the sovereignty of these islands.

10. Prohibition of the sales of munitions to foreign powers.

Committed to this constructive program, the Socialist Party calls upon the Nation's workers and upon all fair-minded and progressive citizens to unite with it in a mighty movement against the present drift into social disaster and in behalf of sanity, justice, peace, and freedom.

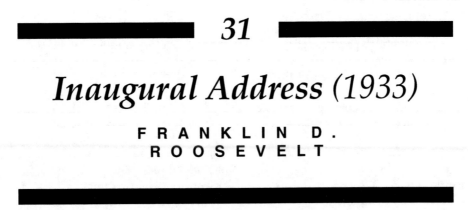

31

Inaugural Address (1933)

FRANKLIN D. ROOSEVELT

On March 4, 1933, at the depths of the worst economic depression in American history, Franklin D. Roosevelt was inaugurated as president. He had soundly defeated his predecessor, Herbert Hoover, in the 1932 election. Clearly, most of the nation held Hoover and the Republican Party's laissez-faire policies responsible for the Great Depression, which saw unemployment rates rise above 30%. In the election, Roosevelt had not offered much in the way of specific proposals for dealing with the crisis other than a promise to balance the federal budget. His inaugural address presented few new details beyond a commitment to vigorous action by the federal government itself. But with that very promise Roosevelt gave the American public hope, an assurance that their government would do something, and that, as the title of Roosevelt's campaign song proclaimed, "happy days are here again."

Questions to Consider

- Why does Roosevelt use military allusions in his address?
- Does Roosevelt suggest any radical alterations in American politics or society?

I am certain that my fellow Americans expect that on my induction into the Presidency I will address them with a candor and a decision which the present situation of our Nation impels. This is preeminently the time to speak the truth, the whole truth, frankly and boldly. Nor need we shrink from honestly facing conditions in our country to-day. This great Nation will endure as it has endured, will revive and will prosper. So, first of all, let me assert my firm belief that the only thing we have to fear is fear itself—nameless, unreasoning, unjustified terror which paralyzes needed efforts to convert retreat into advance. In every dark hour of our national life a leadership of frankness and vigor has met with that understanding and support of the people themselves which is essential to victory. I am convinced that you will again give that support to leadership in these critical days.

In such a spirit on my part and on yours we face our common difficulties. They concern, thank God, only material things. Values have shrunken to fantastic levels; taxes have risen; our ability to pay has fallen; government of all kinds is faced by serious curtailment of income; the means of exchange are frozen in the currents of trade; the withered leaves of industrial enterprise lie on every side; farmers find no markets for their produce; the savings of many years in thousands of families are gone.

More important, a host of unemployed citizens face the grim problem of existence, and an equally great number toil with little return. Only a foolish optimist can deny the dark realities of the moment.

Yet our distress comes from no failure of substance. We are stricken by no plague of locusts. Compared with the perils which our forefathers conquered because they believed and were not afraid, we have still much to be thankful for. Nature still offers her bounty and human efforts have multiplied it. Plenty is at our doorstep, but a generous use of it languishes in the very sight of the supply. Primarily this is because the rulers of the exchange of mankind's goods have failed, through their own stubbornness and their own incompetence, have admitted their failure, and abdicated. Practices of the unscrupulous money changers stand indicted in the court of public opinion, rejected by the hearts and minds of men.

True they have tried, but their efforts have been cast in the pattern of an outworn tradition. Faced by failure of credit they have proposed only the lending of more money. Stripped of the lure of profit by which to induce our people to follow their false leadership, they have resorted to exhortations, pleading tearfully for restored confidence. They know only the rules of a generation of self-seekers. They have no vision, and when there is no vision the people perish.

The money changers have fled from their high seats in the temple of our civilization. We may now restore that temple to the ancient truths. The measure of the restoration lies in the extent to which we apply social values more noble than mere monetary profit.

Happiness lies not in the mere possession of money; it lies in the joy of achievement, in the thrill of creative effort. The joy and moral stimulation of work no longer must be forgotten in the mad chase of evanescent profits. These dark days will be worth all they cost us if they teach us that our true destiny is not to be ministered unto but to minister to ourselves and to our fellow men.

Recognition of the falsity of material wealth as the standard of success goes hand in hand with the abandonment of the false belief that public office and high political position are to be valued only by the standards of pride of place and personal profit; and there must be an end to a conduct in banking and in business which too often has given to a sacred trust the likeness of callous and selfish wrongdoing. Small wonder that confidence languishes, for it thrives only on honesty, on honor, on the sacredness of obligations, on faithful protection, on unselfish performance; without them it can not live.

Restoration calls, however, not for changes in ethics alone. This Nation asks for action, and action now.

Our greatest primary task is to put people to work. This is no unsolvable problem if we face it wisely and courageously. It can be accomplished in part by direct recruiting by the Government itself, treating the task as we would treat the emergency of a war, but at the same time, through this employment, accomplishing greatly needed projects to stimulate and reorganize the use of our natural resources.

Source: *Inaugural Addresses of the Presidents of the United States* (Washington, D.C., 1961), pp. 235–239.

Hand in hand with this we must frankly recognize the overbalance of population in our industrial centers and, by engaging on a national scale in a redistribution, endeavor to provide a better use of the land for those best fitted for the land. The task can be helped by definite efforts to raise the values of agricultural products and with this the power to purchase the output of our cities. It can be helped by preventing realistically the tragedy of the growing loss through foreclosure of our small homes and our farms. It can be helped by insistence that the Federal, State, and local governments act forthwith on the demand that their cost be drastically reduced. It can be helped by the unifying of relief activities which to-day are often scattered, uneconomical, and unequal. It can be helped by national planning for and supervision of all forms of transportation and of communications and other utilities which have a definitely public character. There are many ways in which it can be helped, but it can never be helped merely by talking about it. We must act and act quickly.

Finally, in our progress toward a resumption of work we require two safeguards against a return of the evils of the old order; there must be a strict supervision of all banking and credits and investments; there must be an end to speculation with other people's money, and there must be provision for an adequate but sound currency.

These are the lines of attack. I shall presently urge upon a new Congress in special session detailed measures for their fulfillment, and I shall seek the immediate assistance of the several States.

Through this program of action we address ourselves to putting our own national house in order and making income balance outgo. Our international trade relations, though vastly important, are in point of time and necessity secondary to the establishment of a sound national economy. I favor as a practical policy the putting of first things first. I shall spare no effort to restore world trade by international economic readjustment, but the emergency at home can not wait on that accomplishment.

The basic thought that guides these specific means of national recovery is not narrowly nationalistic. It is the insistence, as a first consideration, upon the interdependence of the various elements in all parts of the United States—a recognition of the old and permanently important manifestation of the American spirit of the pioneer. It is the way to recovery. It is the immediate way. It is the strongest assurance that the recovery will endure.

In the field of world policy I would dedicate this Nation to the policy of the good neighbor—the neighbor who resolutely respects himself and, because he does so, respects the rights of others—the neighbor who respects his obligations and respects the sanctity of his agreements in and with a world of neighbors.

If I read the temper of our people correctly, we now realize as we have never realized before our interdependence on each other; that we can not merely take but we must give as well; that if we are to go forward, we must move as a trained and loyal army willing to sacrifice for the good of a common discipline, because without such discipline no progress is made, no leadership becomes effective. We are, I know, ready and willing to submit our lives and property to such discipline, because it makes possible a leadership which aims at a larger good. This I propose to offer, pledging that the larger purposes will bind upon us all as a sacred obligation with a unity of duty hitherto evoked only in time of armed strife.

With this pledge taken, I assume unhesitatingly the leadership of this great army of our people dedicated to a disciplined attack upon our common problems.

Action in this image and to this end is feasible under the form of government which we have inherited from our ancestors. Our Constitution is so simple and practical that it is possible always to meet extraordinary needs by changes in emphasis and arrangement without loss of essential form. That is why our constitutional system has proved itself the most superbly enduring political mechanism the modern world has produced. It has met every stress of vast expansion of territory, of foreign wars, of bitter internal strife, of world relations.

It is to be hoped that the normal balance of executive and legislative authority may be wholly adequate to meet the unprecedented task before us. But it may be that an unprecedented demand and need for undelayed action may call for temporary departure from that normal balance of public procedure.

I am prepared under my constitutional duty to recommend the measures that a stricken nation in the midst of a stricken world may require. These measures, or such other measures as the Congress may build out of its experience and wisdom, I shall seek, within my constitutional authority, to bring to speedy adoption.

But in the event that the Congress shall fail to take one of these two courses, and in the event that the national emergency is still critical, I shall not evade the clear course of duty that will then confront me. I shall ask the Congress for the one remaining instrument to meet the crisis—broad Executive power to wage a war against the emergency, as great as the power that would be given to me if we were in fact invaded by a foreign foe.

For the trust reposed in me I will return the courage and the devotion that befit the time. I can do no less.

We face the arduous days that lie before us in the warm courage of the national unity; with the clear consciousness of seeking old and precious moral values; with the clean satisfaction that comes from the stern performance of duty by old and young alike. We aim at the assurance of a rounded and permanent national life.

We do not distrust the future of essential democracy. The people of the United States have not failed. In their need they have registered a mandate that they want di-

rect, vigorous action. They have asked for discipline and direction under leadership. They have made me the present instrument of their wishes. In the spirit of the gift I take it.

In this dedication of a Nation we humbly ask the blessing of God. May He protect each and every one of us. May He guide me in the days to come.

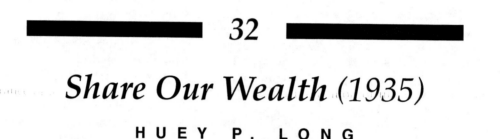

Share Our Wealth (1935)

HUEY P. LONG

No member of Congress in the 1930s was as controversial as Senator Huey P. Long of Louisiana. To his many enemies, he was a potential American dictator. To his supporters, Long alone defended the common man against an avaricious business elite. Elected governor of Louisiana in 1928, Long dominated that state in a way rarely seen in the United States. Despite his ruthless tactics and absolute control of Louisiana's politics, he won the affection of the poor through a series of public works projects which improved the lives of thousands of people. In 1932 Long was elected to the Senate, where he quickly became a national figure by attacking both parties for their failure to deal with the Depression. Organizing the Share Our Wealth Society with the slogan "every man a king," Long planned an independent run for the presidency in 1936. But the "Kingfish," as he liked to be called, was gunned down in the Louisiana capitol by a political opponent in 1935.

Questions to Consider

- What exactly does Long want to do?
- Would it have been possible or legal?
- How does Long's program differ from Roosevelt's New Deal?

The Share Our Wealth Principles

(The Share Our Wealth Society proposes to enforce the traditions on which this country was founded, rather

than to have them harmed; we aim to carry out the guaranties of our immortal Declaration of Independence and our Constitution of the United States, as interpreted by our forefathers who wrote them and who gave them to us; we will make the works and compacts of the pilgrim fathers, taken from the laws of God, from which we were warned never to depart, breathe into our Government again that spirit of liberty, justice, and

Source: *Congressional Record,* May 23, 1935, 1st Session, vol. 74, pt. 7, pp. 8040–8043.

mercy which they inspired in our founders in the days when they gave life and hope to our country. God has beckoned fullness and peace to our land; our fore-fathers have set the guide stakes so that none need fail to share in this abundance. Will we now have our gen-eration, and the generations which are to come, cheated of such heritage because of the greed and control of wealth and opportunity by 600 families?)

To members and well-wishers of the Share Our Wealth Society:

For 20 years I have been in the battle to provide that, so long as America has, or can produce, an abundance of things which make life comfortable and happy, that none should own so much of the things which he does not need and cannot use as to deprive the balance of the people of a reasonable proportion of the necessities and conveniences of life. The whole line of my political thought has always been that America must face the time when the whole country would shoulder the oblig-ation which it owes to every child born on earth—that is, a fair chance to life, liberty, and happiness.

I had been in the United States Senate only a few days when I began my effort to make the battle for a distribution of wealth among all the people a national issue for the coming elections. On July 2, 1932, pursuant to a promise made, I heard Franklin Delano Roosevelt, accepting the nomination of the Democratic Party at the Chicago convention for President of the United States, use the following words:

> Throughout the Nation, men and women, forgotten in the political philosophy of the Government for the last years, look to us here for guidance and for a more equitable opportunity to share in the distribu-tion of the national wealth.

It therefore seemed that all we had to do was to elect our candidate and that then my object in public life would be accomplished....

It is not out of place for me to say that the support which I brought to Mr. Roosevelt to secure his nomina-tion and election as President—and without which it was hardly probable he would ever have been nomi-nated—was on the assurances which I had that he would take the proper stand for the redistribution of wealth in the campaign. He did that much in the cam-paign; but after his election, what then? I need not tell you the story. We have not time to cry over our disap-pointments, over promises which others did not keep, and over pledges which were broken.

We have not a moment to lose.

It was after my disappointment over the Roosevelt policy, after he became President, that I saw the light. I soon began to understand that, regardless of what we had been promised, our only chance of securing the ful-fillment of such pledges was to organize the men and the women of the United States so that they were a force capable of action, and capable of requiring such a policy from the lawmakers and from the President after they took office. That was the beginning of the Share Our Wealth Society movement.

Let me say to the members and well-wishers that in this movement, the principles of which have received the endorsement of every leader of this time, and of other times, I am not concerned over my personal posi-tion or political fortune; I am only interested in the suc-cess of the cause; and on any day or at any time when, by our going for any person or for any party, we can better, or more surely or more quickly secure home, comfort, education, and happiness for our people, that there is no ambition of mine which will stand in the way. But there can be no minimum of success until every child in this land is fed, clothed, and housed com-fortably and made happy with opportunity for educa-tion and a chance in life.

Even after the present President of the United States had thrown down the pledge which he had made time after time, and rather indicated the desire, instead, to have all the common people of America fed from a half-starvation dole, while the plutocrats of the United States were allowed to wax richer and richer, even after that, I made the public proposition that if he would re-turn to his promise and carry out the pledge given to the people and to me that, regardless of all that had passed, I would again support his administration to the limit of my ability.

Of course, however, I was not blind; I had long since come to the understanding that he was chained to other purposes and to other interests which made impossible his keeping the words which he uttered to the people.

I delayed using this form of call to the members and well-wishers of the Share Our Wealth Society until we had progressed so far as to convince me that we could succeed either before or in the next national election of November 1936. Until I became certain that the spirit of the people could be aroused throughout the United States, and that, without any money—because I have none, except such little as I am given—the people could be persuaded to perfect organizations throughout the counties and communities of the country, I did not want to give false hopes to any of those engaged with me in this noble work. But I have seen and checked back enough, based upon the experiences which I have had in my public career, to know that we can, with much more ease, win the present fight, either between now and the next national campaign, or else in the next na-tional campaign—I say with much more ease than many other battles which I have won in the past but which did not mean near so much.

We now have enough societies and enough mem-bers, to say nothing of the well-wishers, who—if they will put their shoulders to the wheel and give us one-half of the time which they do not need for anything else—can force the principles of the Share Our Wealth Society to the forefront, to where no person participating in national affairs can ignore them further.

Now, here is what I ask the officers and members and well-wishers of all the Share Our Wealth Societies to do—two things, to wit:

First. If you have a Share Our Wealth Society in your neighborhood—or, if you have not one, organize one—meet regularly, and let all members, men and women, go to work as quickly and as hard as they can to get every person in the neighborhood to become a member and to go out with them to get more members for the society. If members do not want to go into the society already organized in their community, let them organize another society. We must have them as members in the movement, so that, by having their cooperation, on short notice we can all act as one person for the one object and purpose of providing that in the land of plenty there shall be comfort for all. The organized 600 families who control the wealth of America have been able to keep the 125,000,000 people in bondage because they have never once known how to effectually strike for their fair demands.

Second. Get a number of members of the Share Our Wealth Society to immediately go into all other neighborhoods of your county and into the neighborhoods of the adjoining counties, so as to get the people in the other communities and in the other counties to organize more Share Our Wealth Societies there; that will mean we can soon get about the work of perfecting a complete, unified organization that will not only hear promises but will compel the fulfillment of pledges made to the people.

It is impossible for the United States to preserve itself as a republic or as a democracy when 600 families own more of this Nation's wealth—in fact, twice as much—as all the balance of the people put together. Ninety-six percent of our people live below the poverty line, while 4 percent own 87 percent of the wealth. America can have enough for all to live in comfort and still permit millionaires to own more than they can ever spend and to have more than they can ever use; but America cannot allow the multimillionaires and the billionaires, a mere handful of them, to own everything unless we are willing to inflict starvation upon 125,000,000 people.

We looked upon the year 1929 as the year when too much was produced for the people to consume. We were told, and we believed, that the farmers raised too much cotton and wool for the people to wear and too much food for the people to eat. Therefore, much of it went to waste, some rotted, and much of it was burned

or thrown into the river or into the ocean. But, when we picked up the bulletin of the Department of Agriculture for that year 1929, we found that, according to the diet which they said everyone should eat in order to be healthy, multiplying it by 120,000,000, the number of people we had in 1929, had all of our people had the things which the Government said they should eat in order to live well, we did not have enough even in 1929 to feed the people. In fact, these statistics show that in some instances we had from one-third to one-half less than the people needed, particularly of milk, eggs, butter, and dried fruits.

But why in the year 1929 did it appear we had too much? Because the people could not buy the things they wanted to eat, and needed to eat. That showed the need for and duty of the Government then and there, to have forced a sharing of our wealth, and a redistribution, and Roosevelt was elected on the pledge to do that very thing.

But what was done? Cotton was plowed under the ground. Hogs and cattle were burned by the millions. The same was done to wheat and corn, and farmers were paid starvation money not to raise and not to plant because of the fact that we did not want so much because of people having no money with which to buy. Less and less was produced, when already there was less produced than the people needed if they ate what the Government said they needed to sustain life. God forgive those rulers who burned hogs, threw milk in the river, and plowed under cotton while little children cried for meat and milk and something to put on their naked backs!

But the good God who placed this race on earth did not leave us without an understanding of how to meet such problems; nor did the Pilgrim fathers who landed at Plymouth in 1620 fail to set an example as to how a country and a nation of people should act under such circumstances.... God's law commanded that the wealth of the country should be redistributed ever so often, so that none should become too rich and none should become too poor; it commanded that debts should be canceled and released ever so often, so that the human race would not be loaded with a burden which it could never pay. When the Pilgrims landed at Plymouth in 1620, they established their law by compact, signed by everyone who was on board the *Mayflower,* and it provided that at the end of every 7 years the finances of their newly founded country would be readjusted and that all debts would be released and property redistributed, so that none should starve in the land of plenty, and none should have an abundance of more than he needed. These principles were preserved in the Declaration of Independence, signed in 1776, and in our Constitution. Our great statesmen, such men as James Madison, who wrote the Constitution of the United States, and Daniel Webster, its greatest exponent, admonished the generations of America to come that they must never forget to require the redistribution of wealth if they desired that their Republic should live.

And, now, what of America? Will we allow the political sports, the high heelers, the wiseacres, and those who ridicule us in our misery and poverty to keep us from organizing these societies in every hamlet so that they may bring back to life this law and custom of God and of this country? Is there a man or woman with a child born on the earth, or who expects ever to have a child born on earth, who is willing to have it raised under the present-day practices of piracy, where it comes into life burdened with debt, condemned to a system of slavery by which the sweat of its brow throughout its existence must go to satisfy the vanity and the luxury of a leisurely few, who can never be made to see that they are destroying the root and branch of the greatest country ever to have risen? Our country is calling; the laws of the Lord are calling; the graves of our forefathers would open today if their occupants could see the bloom and flower of their creation withering and dying because the greed of the financial masters of this country has starved and withheld from mankind those things produced by his own labor. To hell with the ridicule of the wise street-corner politician. Pay no attention to any newspaper or magazine that has sold its columns to perpetuate this crime against the people of America. Save this country. Save mankind. Who can be wrong in such a work, and who cares what consequences may come following the mandates of the Lord, of the Pilgrims, of Jefferson, Webster, and Lincoln? He who falls in this fight falls in the radiance of the future. Better to make this fight and lose than to be a party to a system that strangles humanity.

It took the genius of labor and the lives of all Americans to produce the wealth of this land. If any man, or 100 men, wind up with all that has been produced by 120,000,000 people, that does not mean that those 100 men produced the wealth of the country; it means that those 100 men stole, directly or indirectly, what 125,000,000 people produced. Let no one tell you that the money masters made this country. They did no such thing. Very few of them ever hewed the forest; very few ever hacked a crosstie; very few ever nailed a board; fewer of them ever laid a brick. Their fortunes came from manipulated finance, control of government, rigging of markets, the spider webs that have grabbed all businesses; they grab the fruits of the land, the conveniences and the luxuries that are intended for 125,000,000 people, and run their heelers to our meetings to set up the cry, "We earned it honestly." The Lord says they did no such thing. The voices of our forefathers say they did no such thing. In this land of abundance, they have no right to impose starvation, misery, and pestilence for the purpose of vaunting their own pride and greed.

Whenever any newspaper or person, whether he be a private individual or an officer of the Government, says that our effort to limit the size of fortunes is contrary to the principles of our Government, he is too ignorant to deserve attention. Either he knows that what he says is untrue or else he is too ignorant to know what the truth is.

We can go further than that: Whenever any person says that he is following any Christian religion; or, if he be a Jew, if he says he is following the religion of the Jews; or even if he be a Chinaman, if he is following the teachings of Confucius, he cannot say that he thinks his own religion is sound unless he is willing to follow the principles to share the wealth of the land. Such is taught and required in the lines of the Bible, both in the New Testament and in the Old Testament, and the divine warning of those pages, repeated time and again, is that unless there is a comfortable living guaranteed to the man at the bottom, and unless the size of the big man's fortune is so limited as to allow the common run of people a fair share of the earth's fruits and blessings, that a race of people cannot survive.

If a man declare himself to be an American, and a believer in the American principles, then from the day that this country was founded until the present time, whether it be by the French or by the English, he must profess the share-our-wealth principles, or else he is not following the American doctrine. When the Pilgrims landed at Plymouth, here was a part of their compact and law:…

…Lincoln freed the black man, but today the white and the black are shackled far worse than any colored person in 1860.

The debt structure alone has condemned the American people to bondage worse than the Egyptians ever forged upon the Israelites. Right now America's debts, public and private, are $262,000,000,000, and nearly all of it has been laid on the shoulders of those who have nothing. It is a debt of more than $2,000 to every man, woman, or child. They can never pay it. They never have paid such debts. No one expects them to pay it. But such is the new form of slavery imposed upon the civilization of America; and the street-corner sports and hired political tricksters, with the newspapers whom they have perverted, undertake to laugh to scorn the efforts of the people to throw off this yoke and bondage; but we were told to do so by the Lord, we were told to do so by the Pilgrim Fathers, we were guaranteed such should be done by our Declaration of Independence and by the Constitution of the United States.

Here is the whole sum and substance of the share-our-wealth movement:

1. Every family to be furnished by the Government a homestead allowance, free of debt, of not less than one-third the average family wealth of the country, which means, at the lowest, that every family shall have the reasonable comforts of life up to a value of from $5,000 to $6,000. No person to have a fortune of more than 100 to 300 times the average family fortune, which means that the limit to fortunes is between $1,500,000 and $5,000,000, with annual capital levy taxes imposed on all above $1,000,000.

2. The yearly income of every family shall be not less than one-third of the average family income, which means that, according to the estimates of the statisticians of the United States Government and Wall Street, no family's annual income would be less than from $2,000 to $2,500. No yearly income shall be allowed to any person larger than from 100 to 300 times the size of the average family income, which means that no person would be allowed to earn in any year more than from $600,000 to $1,800,000, all to be subject to present income-tax laws.

3. To limit or regulate the hours of work to such an extent as to prevent overproduction; the most modern and efficient machinery would be encouraged, so that as much would be produced as possible so as to satisfy all demands of the people, but to also allow the maximum time to the workers for recreation, convenience, education, and luxuries of life.

4. An old-age pension to the persons over 60.

5. To balance agricultural production with what can be consumed according to the laws of God, which includes the preserving and storage of surplus commodities to be paid for and held by the Government for the emergencies when such are needed. Please bear in mind, however, that when the people of America have had money to buy things they needed, we have never had a surplus of any commodity. This plan of God does not call for destroying any of the things raised to eat or wear, nor does it countenance wholesale destruction of hogs, cattle, or milk.

6. To pay the veterans of our wars what we owe them and to care for their disabled.

7. Education and training for all children to be equal in opportunity in all schools, colleges, universities, and other institutions for training in the professions and vocations of life; to be regulated on the capacity of children to learn, and not on the ability of parents to pay the costs. Training for life's work to be as much universal and thorough for all walks in life as has been the training in the arts of killing.

8. The raising of revenue and taxes for the support of this program to come from the reduction of swollen fortunes from the top, as well as for the support of public works to give employment whenever there may be any slackening necessary in private enterprise.

I now ask those who read this circular to help us at once in this work of giving life and happiness to our people—not a starvation dole upon which someone may live in misery from week to week. Before this miserable system of wreckage has destroyed the life germ of respect and culture in our American people let us save what was here, merely by having none too poor and none too rich. The theory of the Share Our Wealth Society is to have enough for all, but not to have one with so much that less than enough remains for the balance of the people....

Let everyone who feels he wishes to help in our work start right out and go ahead. One man or woman is as important as any other. Take up the fight! Do not wait for someone else to tell you what to do. There are no high lights in this effort. We have no State managers and no city managers. Everyone can take up the work, and as many societies can be organized as there are people to organize them. One is the same as another. The reward and compensation is the salvation of humanity. Fear no opposition. "He who falls in this fight falls in the radiance of the future!"

Yours sincerely,

HUEY P. LONG,

United States Senator, Washington, D. C.

33

Day of Infamy (1941)

FRANKLIN D. ROOSEVELT

At noon on December 8, 1941, the day after the Japanese attack on Pearl Harbor, President Franklin D. Roosevelt appeared before both Houses of Congress, the Supreme Court, and his cabinet. In a short but powerful speech, Roosevelt called on Congress to declare war on Japan. With only a lone dissent, Congress approved such a declaration. The following day, Germany and Italy declared war on the United States.

Questions to Consider

- Does Roosevelt offer any explanation for the Japanese attack?
- Did the United States have any alternative to a declaration of war?

Yesterday, December 7, 1941—a date which will live in infamy—the United States of America was suddenly and deliberately attacked by naval and air forces of the Empire of Japan.

The United States was at peace with that nation and, at the solicitation of Japan, was still in conversation with its Government and its Emperor looking toward the maintenance of peace in the Pacific. Indeed, 1 hour after Japanese air squadrons had commenced bombing in Oahu, the Japanese Ambassador to the United States and his colleague delivered to the Secretary of State a formal reply to a recent American message. While this reply stated that it seemed useless to continue the existing diplomatic negotiations, it contained no threat or hint of war or armed attack.

It will be recorded that the distance of Hawaii from Japan makes it obvious that the attack was deliberately planned many days or even weeks ago. During the intervening time the Japanese Government has deliberately sought to deceive the United States by false statements and expressions of hope for continued peace.

The attack yesterday on the Hawaiian Islands has caused severe damage to American naval and military forces. Very many American lives have been lost. In addition American ships have been reported torpedoed on the high seas between San Francisco and Honolulu.

Yesterday the Japanese Government also launched an attack against Malaya.

Last night Japanese forces attacked Hong Kong.

Last night Japanese forces attacked Guam.

Last night Japanese forces attacked the Philippine Islands.

Last night the Japanese attacked Wake Island.

This morning the Japanese attacked Midway Island.

Japan has, therefore, undertaken a surprise offensive extending throughout the Pacific area. The facts of yesterday speak for themselves. The people of the United States have already formed their opinions and well understand the implications to the very life and safety of our Nation.

As Commander in Chief of the Army and Navy I have directed that all measures be taken for our defense.

Always will we remember the character of the onslaught against us.

No matter how long it may take us to overcome this premeditated invasion, the American people, in their righteous might, will win through to absolute victory.

Source: *Congressional Record,* 77th Congress, 1st session (1941), vol. 87, pt. 9, pp. 9519–9520.

I believe I interpret the will of the Congress and of the people when I assert that we will not only defend ourselves to the uttermost but will make very certain that this form of treachery shall never endanger us again.

Hostilities exist. There is no blinking at the fact that our people, our territory, and our interests are in grave danger.

With confidence in our armed forces—with the unbounded determination of our people—we will gain the inevitable triumph—so help us God.

I ask that the Congress declare that since the unprovoked and dastardly attack by Japan on Sunday, December 7, a state of war has existed between the United States and the Japanese Empire.

34

Four Freedoms (1941)

FRANKLIN D. ROOSEVELT

When President Franklin D. Roosevelt delivered his annual State of the Union speech to Congress on January 6, 1941, the war in Europe was entering its second year. Over the previous few months Roosevelt and Prime Minister Winston Churchill had worked out the details of "lend-lease," a program intended to supply Britain with munitions and ships. In the following speech Roosevelt hoped to increase public support for his pro-British policies by clarifying what was at stake for America in the European conflict. Though U.S. entry to the war was nearly a year away, Roosevelt's "Four Freedoms" can be taken as a public expression of future war aims.

Questions to Consider

- Were Roosevelt's critics fair in charging him with sneaking the United States into World War II?

- Why should the United States be "the arsenal of democracy," as Roosevelt called it in an earlier speech?

Address of the President of the United States

...I address you, the Members of the Seventy-seventh Congress, at a moment unprecedented in the history of

Source: *Congressional Record,* 77th Congress, 1st session (1941), vol. 87, pt. 1, pp. 44–47.

the Union. I use the word "unprecedented," because at no previous time has American security been as seriously threatened from without as it is today.

Since the permanent formation of our Government under the Constitution, in 1789, most of the periods of crises in our history have related to our domestic affairs. Fortunately, only one of these—the 4-year War between the States—ever threatened our national unity. Today, thank God, 130,000,000 Americans, in 48 States, have forgotten points of the compass in our national unity.

It is true that prior to 1914 the United States often had been disturbed by events in other continents. We had even engaged in two wars with European nations and in a number of undeclared wars in the West Indies, in the Mediterranean, and in the Pacific for the maintenance of American rights and for the principles of peaceful commerce. In no case, however, had a serious threat been raised against our national safety or our independence.

What I seek to convey is the historic truth that the United States, as a nation, has at all times maintained opposition to any attempt to lock us in behind an ancient Chinese wall while the procession of civilization went past. Today, thinking of our children and their children, we oppose enforced isolation for ourselves or for any part of the Americas....

Even when the World War broke out in 1914 it seemed to contain only small threat of danger to our own American future. But as time went on the American people began to visualize what the downfall of democratic nations might mean to our own democracy.

We need not overemphasize imperfections in the peace of Versailles. We need not harp on failure of the democracies to deal with problems of world reconstruction. We should remember that the peace of 1919 was far less unjust than the kind of "pacification" which began even before Munich and which is being carried on under the new order of tyranny that seeks to spread over every continent today. The American people have unalterably set their faces against that tyranny.

Every realist knows that the democratic way of life is at this moment being directly assailed in every part of the world—assailed either by arms or by secret spreading of poisonous propaganda by those who seek to destroy unity and promote discord in nations still at peace.

During 16 months this assault has blotted out the whole pattern of democratic life in an appalling number of independent nations, great and small. The assailants are still on the march, threatening other nations, great and small.

Therefore, as your President, performing my constitutional duty to "give to the Congress information of the state of the Union," I find it necessary to report that the future and the safety of our country and of our democracy are overwhelmingly involved in events far beyond our borders.

Armed defense of democratic existence is now being gallantly waged in four continents. If that defense fails, all the population and all the resources of Europe, Asia, Africa, and Australasia will be dominated by the conquerors. The total of those populations and their resources greatly exceeds the sum total of the population and resources of the whole of the Western Hemisphere—many times over.

In times like these it is immature—and incidentally untrue—for anybody to brag that an unprepared America, single-handed, and with one hand tied behind its back, can hold off the whole world.

No realistic American can expect from a dictator's peace international generosity, or return of true independence, or world disarmament, or freedom of expression, or freedom of religion—or even good business.

Such a peace would bring no security for us or for our neighbors. "Those who would give up essential liberty to purchase a little temporary safety deserve neither liberty nor safety."[1]

As a Nation we may take pride in the fact that we are soft-hearted; but we cannot afford to be soft-headed.

We must always be wary of those who, with sounding brass and a tinkling cymbal, preach the "ism" of appeasement.

We must especially beware of that small group of selfish men who would clip the wings of the American eagle in order to feather their own nests.

I have recently pointed out how quickly the tempo of modern warfare could bring into our very midst the physical attack which we must expect if the dictator nations win this war.

There is much loose talk of our immunity from immediate and direct invasion from across the seas. Obviously, as long as the British Navy retains its power, no such danger exists. Even if there were no British Navy, it is not probable that any enemy would be stupid enough to attack us by landing troops in the United States from across thousands of miles of ocean, until it had acquired strategic bases from which to operate.

But we learn much from the lessons of the past years in Europe—particularly the lesson of Norway, whose essential seaports were captured by treachery and surprise built up over a series of years.

The first phase of the invasion of this Hemisphere would not be the landing of regular troops. The necessary strategic points would be occupied by secret agents and their dupes, and great numbers of them are already here, and in Latin America.

As long as the aggressor nations maintain the offensive, they, not we, will choose the time and the place and the method of their attack.

That is why the future of all American republics is today in serious danger.

That is why this annual message to the Congress is unique in our history.

That is why every member of the executive branch of the Government and every Member of the Congress face great responsibility—and great accountability.

---

[1] Benjamin Franklin.—*Ed.*

The need of the moment is that our actions and our policy should be devoted primarily—almost exclusively—to meeting this foreign peril. For all our domestic problems are now a part of the great emergency.

Just as our national policy in internal affairs has been based upon a decent respect for the rights and dignity of all our fellow-men within our gates, so our national policy in foreign affairs has been based on a decent respect for the rights and dignity of all nations, large and small. And the justice of morality must and will win in the end.

Our national policy is this:

First, by an impressive expression of the public will and without regard to partisanship, we are committed to all-inclusive national defense.

Second, by an impressive expression of the public will and without regard to partisanship, we are committed to full support of all those resolute peoples, everywhere, who are resisting aggression and are thereby keeping war away from our hemisphere. By this support, we express our determination that the democratic cause shall prevail, and we strengthen the defense and security of our own Nation.

Third, by an impressive expression of the public will and without regard to partisanship, we are committed to the proposition that principles of morality and considerations for our own security will never permit us to acquiesce in a peace dictated by aggressors and sponsored by appeasers. We know that enduring peace cannot be bought at the cost of other people's freedom.

In the recent national election there was no substantial difference between the two great parties in respect to that national policy. No issue was fought out on this line before the American electorate. Today it is abundantly evident that American citizens everywhere are demanding and supporting speedy and complete action in recognition of obvious danger.

Therefore, the immediate need is a swift and driving increase in our armament production.

Leaders of industry and labor have responded to our summons. Goals of speed have been set. In some cases these goals are being reached ahead of time; in some cases we are on schedule;...and in some cases—and I am sorry to say very important cases—we are all concerned by the slowness of the accomplishment of our plans.

The Army and Navy, however, have made substantial progress during the past year. Actual experience is improving and speeding up our methods of production with every passing day. And today's best is not good enough for tomorrow.

I am not satisfied with the progress thus far made.... None of us will be satisfied until the job is done....

To give two illustrations:

We are behind schedule in turning out finished airplanes; we are working day and night to solve the innumerable problems and to catch up.

We are ahead of schedule in building warships; but we are working to get even further ahead of schedule.

To change a whole nation from a basis of peacetime production of implements of peace to a basis of wartime production of implements of war is no small task. And the greatest difficulty comes at the beginning of the program, when new tools and plant facilities and new assembly lines and shipways must first be constructed....

The Congress, of course, must rightly keep itself informed at all times of the progress of the program. However, there is certain information, as the Congress itself will readily recognize, which, in the interests of our own security and those of the nations we are supporting must of needs be kept in confidence.

New circumstances are constantly begetting new needs for our safety. I shall ask this Congress for greatly increased new appropriations and authorizations to carry on what we have begun.

I also ask this Congress for authority and for funds sufficient to manufacture additional munitions and war supplies of many kinds, to be turned over to those nations which are now in actual war with aggressor nations.

Our most useful and immediate role is to act as an arsenal for them as well as for ourselves. They do not need manpower. They do need billions of dollars' worth of the weapons of defense.

The time is near when they will not be able to pay for them in ready cash. We cannot, and will not, tell them they must surrender merely because of present inability to pay for the weapons which we know they must have.

I do not recommend that we make them a loan of dollars with which to pay for these weapons....

I recommend that we make it possible for those nations to continue to obtain war materials in the United States, fitting their orders into our own program. Nearly all of their matériel would, if the time ever came, be useful for our own defense.

Taking counsel of expert military and naval authorities, considering what is best for our own security, we are free to decide how much should be kept here and how much should be sent abroad to our friends who, by their determined and heroic resistance, are giving us time in which to make ready our own defense.

For what we send abroad we shall be repaid, within a reasonable time following the close of hostilities, in similar materials or, at our option, in other goods of many kinds which they can produce and which we need.

Let us say to the democracies, "We Americans are vitally concerned in your defense of freedom. We are putting forth our energies, our resources, and our organizing powers to give you the strength to regain and maintain a free world. We shall send you, in ever-increasing numbers, ships, planes, tanks, guns. This is our purpose and our pledge."

In fulfillment of this purpose we will not be intimidated by the threats of dictators that they will regard as a breach of international law and as an act of war our aid to the democracies which dare to resist their aggression. Such aid is not an act of war, even if a dictator should unilaterally proclaim it so to be.

When the dictators are ready to make war upon us, they will not wait for an act of war on our part. They did not wait for Norway or Belgium or the Netherlands to commit an act of war.

Their only interest is in a new one-way international law, which lacks mutuality in its observance and, therefore, becomes an instrument of oppression.

The happiness of future generations of Americans may well depend upon how effective and how immediate we can make our aid felt. No one can tell the exact character of the emergency situations that we may be called upon to meet. The Nation's hands must not be tied when the Nation's life is in danger.

We must all prepare to make the sacrifices that the emergency—as serious as war itself—demands. Whatever stands in the way of speed and efficiency in defense preparations must give way to the national need.

A free nation has the right to expect full cooperation from all groups. A free nation has the right to look to the leaders of business, of labor, and of agriculture to take the lead in stimulating effort, not among other groups but within their own groups.

The best way of dealing with the few slackers or trouble makers in our midst is, first, to shame them by patriotic example; and if that fails, to use the sovereignty of government to save government.

As men do not live by bread alone, they do not fight by armaments alone. Those who man our defenses, and those behind them who build our defenses, must have the stamina and courage which come from an unshakable belief in the manner of life which they are defending. The mighty action which we are calling for cannot be based on a disregard of all things worth fighting for.

The Nation takes great satisfaction and much strength from the things which have been done to make its people conscious of their individual stake in the preservation of democratic life in America. Those things have toughened the fiber of our people, have renewed their faith and strengthened their devotion to the institutions we make ready to protect.

Certainly this is no time to stop thinking about the social and economic problems which are the root cause of the social revolution which is today a supreme factor in the world.

There is nothing mysterious about the foundations of a healthy and strong democracy. The basic things expected by our people of their political and economic systems are simple. They are:

Equality of opportunity for youth and for others.

Jobs for those who can work.

Security for those who need it.

The ending of special privilege for the few.

The preservation of civil liberties for all.

The enjoyment of the fruits of scientific progress in a wider and constantly rising standard of living.

These are the simple and basic things that must never be lost sight of in the turmoil and unbelievable complexity of our modern world. The inner and abiding strength of our economic and political systems is dependent upon the degree to which they fulfill these expectations.

Many subjects connected with our social economy call for immediate improvement.

As examples:

We should bring more citizens under the coverage of old-age pensions and unemployment insurance.

We should widen the opportunities for adequate medical care.

We should plan a better system by which persons deserving or needing gainful employment may obtain it.

I have called for personal sacrifice. I am assured of the willingness of almost all Americans to respond to that call.

A part of the sacrifice means the payment of more money in taxes. In my Budget message I recommend that a greater portion of this great defense program be paid for from taxation than we are paying today. No person should try, or be allowed, to get rich out of this program; and the principle of tax payments in accordance with ability to pay should be constantly before our eyes to guide our legislation.

If the Congress maintains these principles, the voters, putting patriotism ahead of pocketbooks, will give you their applause.

In the future days, which we seek to make secure, we look forward to a world founded upon four essential human freedoms.

The first is freedom of speech and expression everywhere in the world.

The second is freedom of every person to worship God in his own way everywhere in the world.

The third is freedom from want, which, translated into world terms, means economic understandings which will secure to every nation a healthy peacetime life for its inhabitants everywhere in the world.

The fourth is freedom from fear—which, translated into world terms, means a world-wide reduction of armaments to such a point and in such a thorough fashion that no nation will be in a position to commit an act of physical aggression against any neighbor—anywhere in the world.

That is no vision of a distant millennium. It is a definite basis for a kind of world attainable in our own time and generation. That kind of world is the very antithesis of the so-called new order of tyranny which the dictators seek to create with the crash of a bomb.

To that new order we oppose the greater conception—the moral order. A good society is able to face schemes of world domination and foreign revolutions alike without fear.

Since the beginning of our American history we have been engaged in change—in a perpetual peaceful revolution—a revolution which goes on steadily, quietly adjusting itself to changing conditions—without the concentration camp or the quicklime in the ditch. The world order which we seek is the cooperation of free countries, working together in a friendly, civilized society.

This Nation has placed its destiny in the hands and heads and hearts of its millions of free men and women; and its faith in freedom under the guidance of God. Freedom means the supremacy of human rights everywhere. Our support goes to those who struggle to gain those rights or keep them. Our strength is in our unity of purpose.

To that high concept there can be no end save victory.

35

Effects of the Atomic Bombs (1945)

THE UNITED STATES STRATEGIC BOMBING SURVEY

Few actions of the United States government remain as controversial as those that terminated World War II. On August 6, 1945, a single atomic bomb was dropped on the Japanese city of Hiroshima. Three days later a second bomb was detonated at Nagasaki. No one at the time knew exactly what this new form of weaponry would accomplish, which was reason enough for several prominent American scientists to oppose its use. Within days it was obvious to the world that the United States possessed the most awesome and destructive technology imaginable. In 1944 a joint Army-Navy group, the United States Strategic Bombing Survey, had been organized to study the effect of the air war on the military, economic, and political structures of Germany and Japan. Their report on Hiroshima and Nagasaki enormously influenced both government policy and popular perceptions of the power of atomic bombs.

Questions to Consider

- What lessons were learned from these atomic attacks?
- Was the United States justified in its use of these bombs?

The Attacks and Damage

1. *The attacks.*—A single atomic bomb, the first weapon of its type ever used against a target, exploded over the city of Hiroshima at 0815 on the morning of 6 August 1945. Most of the industrial workers had already reported to work, but many workers were enroute and nearly all the school children and some industrial employees were at work in the open on the program of building removal to provide firebreaks and disperse valuables to the country. The attack came 45 minutes after the "all clear" had been sounded from a previous alert. Because of the lack of warning and the populace's indifference to small groups of planes, the explosion came as an almost complete surprise, and the people had not taken shelter. Many were caught in the open, and most of the rest in flimsily constructed homes or commercial establishments.

The bomb exploded slightly northwest of the center of the city. Because of this accuracy and the flat terrain and circular shape of the city, Hiroshima was uniformly and extensively devastated. Practically the entire densely or moderately built-up portion of the city was leveled by blast and swept by fire. A "fire-storm," a phenomenon which has occurred infrequently in other conflagrations, developed in Hiroshima: fires springing up almost simultaneously over the wide flat area around the center of the city drew in air from all directions. The inrush of air easily overcame the natural ground wind, which had a velocity of only about 5 miles per hour. The "fire-wind" attained a maximum velocity of 30 to 40 miles per hour 2 to 3 hours after the explosion. The "fire-wind" and the symmetry of the built-up center of the city gave a roughly circular shape to the 4.4 square miles which were almost completely burned out.

The surprise, the collapse of many buildings, and the conflagration contributed to an unprecedented casualty rate. Seventy to eighty thousand people were killed, or missing and presumed dead, and an equal number were injured. The magnitude of casualties is set in relief by a comparison with the Tokyo fire raid of 9–10 March 1945, in which, though nearly 16 square miles were destroyed, the number killed was no larger, and fewer people were injured.

At Nagasaki, 3 days later, the city was scarcely more prepared, though vague references to the Hiroshima disaster had appeared in the newspaper of 8 August. From the Nagasaki Prefectural Report on the bombing, something of the shock of the explosion can be inferred:

The day was clear with not very much wind—an ordinary midsummer's day. The strain of continuous air attack on the city's population and the severity of the summer had vitiated enthusiastic air raid precautions....

The city remained on the warning alert, but when two B-29's were again sighted coming in the raid signal was not given immediately; the bomb was dropped at 1102 and the raid signal was given a few minutes later, at 1109. Thus only about 400 people were in the city's tunnel shelters, which were adequate for about 30 percent of the population.

When the atomic bomb exploded, an intense flash was observed first, as though a large amount of magnesium had been ignited, and the scene grew hazy with white smoke. At the same time at the center of the explosion, and a short while later in other areas, a tremendous roaring sound was heard and a crushing blast wave and intense heat were felt. The people of Nagasaki, even those who lived on the outer edge of the blast, all felt as though they had sustained a direct hit, and the whole city suffered damage such as would have resulted from direct hits everywhere by ordinary bombs.

The zero area, where the damage was most severe, was almost completely wiped out and for a short while after the explosion no reports came out of that area. People who were in comparatively damaged areas reported their condition under the impression that they had received a direct hit. If such a great amount of damage could be wreaked by a near miss, then the power of the atomic bomb is unbelievably great.

In Nagasaki, no fire storm arose, and the uneven terrain of the city confined the maximum intensity of damage to the valley over which the bomb exploded. The area of nearly complete devastation was thus much smaller; only about 1.8 square miles. Casualties were lower also; between 35,000 and 40,000 were killed, and about the same number injured. People in the tunnel shelters escaped injury, unless exposed in the entrance shaft.

The difference in the totals of destruction to lives and property at the two cities suggests the importance of the special circumstances of layout and construction of the cities, which affect the results of the bombings and must be considered in evaluating the effectiveness of the atomic bombs....

Hiroshima before the war was the seventh largest city in Japan, with a population of over 340,000, and was the principal administrative and commercial center of the southwestern part of the country. As the headquarters of the Second Army and of the Chugoku Regional Army, it was one of the most important military command stations in Japan, the site of one of the

---

Source: The United States Strategic Bombing Survey, *The Effects of the Atomic Bombs on Hiroshima and Nagasaki* (Washington, D.C., 1946), pp. 3–20, 22–23.

largest military supply depots, and the foremost military shipping point for both troops and supplies. Its shipping activities had virtually ceased by the time of the attack, however, because of sinkings and the mining of the Inland Sea. It had been relatively unimportant industrially before the war, ranking only twelfth, but during the war new plants were built that increased its significance. These factories were not concentrated, but spread over the outskirts of the city; this location, we shall see, accounts for the slight industrial damage.

The impact of the atomic bomb shattered the normal fabric of community life and disrupted the organizations for handling the disaster. In the 30 percent of the population killed and the additional 30 percent seriously injured were included corresponding proportions of the civic authorities and rescue groups. A mass flight from the city took place, as persons sought safety from the conflagration and a place for shelter and food. Within 24 hours, however, people were streaming back by the thousands in search of relatives and friends and to determine the extent of their property loss. Road blocks had to be set up along all routes leading into the city, to keep curious and unauthorized people out. The bulk of the dehoused population found refuge in the surrounding countryside; within the city the food supply was short and shelter virtually nonexistent....

The status of medical facilities and personnel dramatically illustrates the difficulties facing authorities. Of more than 200 doctors in Hiroshima before the attack, over 90 percent were casualties and only about 30 physicians were able to perform their normal duties a month after the raid. Out of 1,780 nurses, 1,654 were killed or injured. Though some stocks of supplies had been dispersed, many were destroyed. Only three out of 45 civilian hospitals could be used, and two large Army hospitals were rendered unusable. Those within 3,000 feet of ground zero were totally destroyed, and the mortality rate of the occupants was practically 100 percent....

Fire-fighting and rescue units were equally stripped of men and equipment. Father Siemes[1] reports that 30 hours elapsed before organized rescue parties were observed. In Hiroshima, only 16 pieces of fire-fighting equipment were available for fighting the conflagration, three of them borrowed. However, it is unlikely that any public fire department in the world, even without damage to equipment or casualties to personnel, could have prevented development of a conflagration in Hiroshima, or combatted it with success at more than a few locations along its perimeter. The total fire damage would not have been much different.

---

[1] A German-born Jesuit who taught at Jochi University in Tokyo, who happened to be in the Hiroshima area when the bomb detonated.—*Ed.*

All utilities and transportation services were disrupted over varying lengths of time. In most cases, however, the demand fell off even more precipitously than the available supply, and where the service was needed it could be restored at a minimal level....

By 1 November, the population of Hiroshima was back to 137,000. The city required complete rebuilding. The entire heart, the main administrative and commercial as well as residential section, was gone. In this area only about 50 buildings, all of reinforced concrete, remained standing. All of these suffered blast damage and all save about a dozen were almost completely gutted by fire; only 5 could be used without major repairs....

...The official Japanese figures summed up the building destruction at 62,000 out of a total of 90,000 buildings in the urban area, or 69 percent. An additional 6,000 or 6.6 percent were severely damaged, and most of the others showed glass breakage or disturbance of roof tile. These figures show the magnitude of the problem facing the survivors.

Despite the absence of sanitation measures, no epidemics are reported to have broken out. In view of the lack of medical facilities, supplies, and personnel, and the disruption of the sanitary system, the escape from epidemics may seem surprising. The experience of other bombed cities in Germany and Japan shows that this is not an isolated case. A possible explanation may lie in the disinfecting action of the extensive fires. In later weeks, disease rates rose, but not sharply....

At Nagasaki, the scale of destruction was greater than at Hiroshima, though the actual area destroyed was smaller because of the terrain and the point of fall of the bomb. The Nagasaki Prefectural Report describes vividly the impress of the bomb on the city and its inhabitants:

> Within a radius of 1 kilometer from ground zero, men and animals died almost instantaneously from the tremendous blast pressure and heat; houses and other structures were smashed, crushed and scattered; and fires broke out. The strong complex steel members of the structures of the Mitsubishi Steel Works were bent and twisted like jelly and the roofs of the reinforced concrete National Schools were crumpled and collapsed, indicating a force beyond imagination. Trees of all sizes lost their branches or were uprooted or broken off at the trunk....

General Effects

1. *Casualties.*—The most striking result of the atomic bombs was the great number of casualties. The exact number of dead and injured will never be known because of the confusion after the explosions. Persons un-

accounted for might have been burned beyond recognition in the falling buildings, disposed of in one of the mass cremations of the first week of recovery, or driven out of the city to die or recover without any record remaining. No sure count of even the preraid populations existed. Because of the decline in activity in the two port cities, the constant threat of incendiary raids, and the formal evacuation programs of the Government, an unknown number of the inhabitants had either drifted away from the cities or been removed according to plan. In this uncertain situation, estimates of casualties have generally ranged between 100,000 and 180,000 for Hiroshima, and between 50,000 and 100,000 for Nagasaki. The Survey believes the dead at Hiroshima to have been between 70,000 and 80,000, with an equal number injured; at Nagasaki over 35,000 dead and somewhat more than that injured seems the most plausible estimate.

Most of the immediate casualties did not differ from those caused by incendiary or high-explosive raids. The outstanding difference was the presence of radiation effects, which became unmistakable about a week after the bombing. At the time of impact, however, the causes of death and injury were flash burns, secondary effects of blast and falling debris, and burns from blazing buildings....

The seriousness of these radiation effects may be measured by the fact that 95 percent of the traced survivors of the immediate explosion who were within 3,000 feet suffered from radiation disease....

A plausible estimate of the importance of the various causes of death would range as follows:

Flash burns, 20 to 30 percent.
Other injuries, 50 to 60 percent.
Radiation sickness, 15 to 20 percent....

Flash burns.—The flash of the explosion, which was extremely brief, emitted radiant heat travelling at the speed of light. Flash burns thus followed the explosion instantaneously. The fact that relatively few victims suffered burns of the eyeballs should not be interpreted as an indication that the radiant heat followed the flash, or that time was required to build up to maximum heat intensity. The explanation is simply that the structure of the eye is more resistant to heat than is average human skin, and near ground zero the recessed position of the eyeball offered protection from the overhead explosion. Peak temperatures lasted only momentarily.

Survivors in the two cities stated that people who were in the open directly under the explosion of the bomb were so severely burned that the skin was charred dark brown or black and that they died within a few minutes or hours....

Because of the brief duration of the flash wave and the shielding effects of almost any objects—leaves and clothing as well as buildings—there were many interesting cases of protection. The radiant heat came in a direct line like light, so that the area burned corresponded to this directed exposure. Persons whose sides were toward the explosion often showed definite burns of both sides of the back while the hollow of the back escaped. People in buildings or houses were apparently burned only if directly exposed through the windows. The most striking instance was that of a man writing before a window. His hands were seriously burned but his exposed face and neck suffered only slight burns due to the angle of entry of the radiant heat through the window.

Flash burns were largely confined to exposed areas of the body, but on occasion would occur through varying thicknesses of clothing. Generally speaking, the thicker the clothing the more likely it was to give complete protection against flash burns. One woman was burned over the shoulder except for a T-shaped area about one-fourth inch in breadth; the T-shaped area corresponded to an increased thickness of the clothing from the seam of the garment. Other people were burned through a single thickness of kimono but were unscathed or only slightly affected underneath the lapel. In other instances, skin was burned beneath tightly fitting clothing but was unburned beneath loosely fitting portions. Finally, white or light colors reflected heat and afforded some protection; people wearing black or dark-colored clothing were more likely to be burned.

...Comparatively few instances were reported of arms or legs being torn from the body by flying debris. Another indication of the rarity of over-pressure is the scarcity of ruptured eardrums. Among 106 victims examined by the Japanese in Hiroshima on 11 and 12 August, only three showed ruptured eardrums....

Injuries produced by falling and flying debris were much more numerous, and naturally increased in number and seriousness nearer the center of the affected area. The collapse of the buildings was sudden, so that thousands of people were pinned beneath the debris. Many were able to extricate themselves or received aid in escaping, but large numbers succumbed either to their injuries or to fire before they could be extricated. The flimsiness of Japanese residential construction should not be allowed to obscure the dangers of collapse; though the walls and partitions were light, the houses had heavy roof timbers and heavy roof tiles. Flying glass from panels also caused a large number of casualties, even up to 15,000 feet from ground zero.

The number of burns from secondary fires was slight among survivors, but it was probable that a large number of the deaths in both cities came from the burning of people caught in buildings. Eyewitness accounts agree that many fatalities occurred in this way, either immediately or as a result of the lack of care for those who did extricate themselves with serious burns. There are no references, however, to people in the streets succumbing either to heat or to carbon monoxide as they did in Tokyo or in Hamburg, Germany. A few burns resulted from clothing set afire by the flash wave, but in most cases people were able to beat out such fires without serious injury to the skin.

Radiation disease.—The radiation effects upon survivors resulted from the gamma rays liberated by the fission process rather than from induced radio-activity or the lingering radio-activity of deposits of primary fission products. Both at Nagasaki and at Hiroshima, pockets of radio-activity have been detected where fission products were directly deposited, but the degree of activity in these areas was insufficient to produce casualties. Similarly, induced radio-activity from the interaction of neutrons with matter caused no authenticated fatalities. But the effects of gamma rays—here used in a general sense to include all penetrating high-frequency radiations and neutrons that caused injury—are well established, even though the Allies had no observers in the affected areas for several weeks after the explosions.

Our understanding of radiation casualties is not complete. In part the deficiency is in our basic knowledge of how radiation affects animal tissue. In the words of Dr. Robert Stone of the Manhattan Project, "The fundamental mechanism of the action of radiation on living tissues has not been understood...."

According to the Japanese, those individuals very near the center of the explosion but not affected by flash burns or secondary injuries became ill within 2 or 3 days. Bloody diarrhea followed, and the victims expired, some within 2 to 3 days after the onset and the majority within a week. Autopsies showed remarkable changes in the blood picture—almost complete absence of white blood cells, and deterioration of bone marrow. Mucous membranes of the throat, lungs, stomach, and the intestines showed acute inflammation.

The majority of the radiation cases, who were at greater distances, did not show severe symptoms until 1 to 4 weeks after the explosion, though many felt weak and listless on the following day. After a day or two of mild nausea and vomiting, the appetite improved and the person felt quite well until symptoms reappeared at a later date.... Within 12 to 48 hours, fever became evident. In many instances it reached only 100° Fahrenheit and remained for only a few days. In other cases, the temperature went as high as 104° or 106° Fahrenheit. The degree of fever apparently had a direct relation to the degree of exposure to radiation. Once developed, the fever was usually well sustained, and in those cases terminating fatally it continued high until the end. If the fever subsided, the patient usually showed a rapid disappearance of other symptoms and soon regained his feeling of good health. The other symptoms commonly seen were shortage of white corpuscles, loss of hair, in-

flammation and gangrene of the gums, inflammation of the mouth and pharynx, ulceration of the lower gastrointestinal tract, small livid spots (petechiae) resulting from escape of blood into the tissues of the skin or mucous membrane, and larger hemorrhages of gums, nose and skin....

A decrease in the number of white blood corpuscles in the circulating blood appears to have been a constant accompaniment of radiation disease, even existing in some milder cases without other radiation effects. The degree of leukopenia was probably the most accurate index of the amount of radiation a person received. The normal white blood count averages 5,000 to 7,000: leukopenia is indicated by a count of 4,000 or less. The white blood count in the more severe cases ranged from 1,500 to 0, with almost entire disappearance of the bone marrow. The moderately severe cases showed evidence of degeneration of bone marrow and total white blood counts of 1,500 to 3,000. The milder cases showed white blood counts of 3,000 to 4,000 with more minor degeneration changes in the bone marrow. The changes in the system for forming red blood corpuscles developed later, but were equally severe.

Radiation clearly affected reproduction, though the extent has not been determined. Sterility has been a common finding throughout Japan, especially under the conditions of the last 2 years, but there are signs of an increase in the Hiroshima and Nagasaki areas to be attributed to the radiation. Sperm counts done in Hiroshima under American supervision revealed low sperm counts or complete aspermia for as long as 3 months afterward in males who were within 5,000 feet of the center of the explosion. Cases dying of radiation disease showed clear effects on spermatogenesis. Study of sections of ovaries from autopsied radiation victims has not yet been completed. The effects of the bomb on pregnant women are marked, however. Of women in various stages of pregnancy who were within 3,000 feet of ground zero, all known cases have had miscarriages. Even up to 6,500 feet they have had miscarriages or premature infants who died shortly after birth. In the group between 6,500 and 10,000 feet, about one-third have given birth to apparently normal children. Two months after the explosion, the city's total incidence of miscarriages, abortions, and premature births was 27 percent as compared with a normal rate of 6 percent. Since other factors than radiation contributed to this increased rate, a period of years will be required to learn the ultimate effects of mass radiation upon reproduction....

Unfortunately, no exact definition of the killing power of radiation can yet be given, nor a satisfactory account of the sort and thickness of concrete or earth that will shield people.... In the meanwhile the awesome lethal effects of the atomic bomb and the insidious additional peril of the gamma rays speak for themselves.

There is reason to believe that if the effects of blast and fire had been entirely absent from the bombing, the number of deaths among people within a radius of one-half mile from ground zero would have been almost as great as the actual figures and the deaths among those within 1 mile would have been only slightly less. The principal difference would have been in the time of the deaths. Instead of being killed outright as were most of these victims, they would have survived for a few days or even 3 or 4 weeks, only to die eventually of radiation disease....

2. *Morale.*—As might be expected, the primary reaction to the bomb was fear—uncontrolled terror, strengthened by the sheer horror of the destruction and suffering witnessed and experienced by the survivors....

The behavior of the living immediately after the bombings, as described earlier, clearly shows the state of shock that hindered rescue efforts. A Nagasaki survivor illustrates succinctly the mood of survivors:

> ...I was working at the office. I was talking to a friend at the window. I saw the whole city in a red flame, then I ducked. The pieces of the glass hit my back and face. My dress was torn off by the glass. Then I got up and ran to the mountain where the good shelter was.

The two typical impulses were those: Aimless, even hysterical activity or flight from the city to shelter and food.

The accentuated effect of these bombs came not only from the surprise and their crushing power, but also from the feeling of security among the inhabitants of the two cities before the attacks. Though Nagasaki had undergone five raids in the previous year, they had not been heavy, and Hiroshima had gone almost untouched until the morning of 6 August 1945. In both cities many people felt that they would be spared, and the various rumors in circulation supporting such feeling covered a wide range of wishful thoughts. There were so many Christians there, many Japanese-Americans came from Hiroshima, the city was a famous beauty spot—these and other even more fantastic reasons encouraged hopes. Other people felt vaguely that their city was being saved for "something big," however....

3. *The Japanese decision to surrender.*—The further question of the effects of the bombs on the morale of the Japanese leaders and their decision to abandon the war is tied up with other factors. The atomic bomb had more effect on the thinking of Government leaders than on the morale of the rank and file of civilians outside of the target areas. It cannot be said, however, that the atomic bomb convinced the leaders who effected the

peace of the necessity of surrender. The decision to seek ways and means to terminate the war, influenced in part by knowledge of the low state of popular morale, had been taken in May 1945 by the Supreme War Guidance Council.

As early as the spring of 1944, a group of former prime ministers and others close to the Emperor had been making efforts toward bringing the war to an end....

Thus the problem facing the peace leaders in the Government was to bring about a surrender despite the hesitation of the War Minister and the opposition of the Army and Navy chiefs of staff. This had to be done, moreover, without precipitating counter measures by the Army which would eliminate the entire peace group. This was done ultimately by bringing the Emperor actively into the decision to accept the Potsdam terms. So long as the Emperor openly supported such a policy and could be presented to the country as doing so, the military, which had fostered and lived on the idea of complete obedience to the Emperor, could not effectively rebel.

A preliminary step in this direction had been taken at the Imperial Conference on 26 June. At this meeting, the Emperor, taking an active part despite his custom to the contrary, stated that he desired the development of a plan to end the war as well as one to defend the home islands. This was followed by a renewal of earlier efforts to get the Soviet Union to intercede with the United States, which were effectively answered by the Potsdam Declaration on 26 July and the Russian declaration of war on 9 August.

The atomic bombings considerably speeded up these political maneuverings within the government. This in itself was partly a morale effect, since there is ample evidence that members of the Cabinet were worried by the prospect of further atomic bombings, especially on the remains of Tokyo. The bombs did not convince the military that defense of the home islands was impossible, if their behavior in Government councils is adequate testimony. It did permit the Government to say, however, that no army without the weapon could possibly resist an enemy who had it, thus saving "face" for the Army leaders and not reflecting on the competence of Japanese industrialists or the valor of the Japanese soldier. In the Supreme War Guidance Council voting remained divided, with the war minister and the two chiefs of staff unwilling to accept unconditional surrender. There seems little doubt, however, that the bombing of Hiroshima and Nagasaki weakened their inclination to oppose the peace group.

The peace effort culminated in an Imperial conference held on the night of 9 August and continued into the early hours of 10 August, for which the stage was set by the atomic bomb and the Russian war declaration. At this meeting the Emperor, again breaking his customary silence, stated specifically that he wanted acceptance of the Potsdam terms.

A quip was current in high Government circles at this time that the atomic bomb was the real Kamikaze, since it saved Japan from further useless slaughter and destruction. It is apparent that in the atomic bomb the Japanese found the opportunity which they had been seeking, to break the existing deadlock within the Government over acceptance of the Potsdam terms.

The Nuremberg Trials (1946)

INTERNATIONAL MILITARY TRIBUNAL

The crimes of Nazi Germany are incalculable. The forty-two volumes of the first Nuremberg war crime trials, held in 1945 and 1946, from which the following documents are selected, are but a beginning to any such effort. Even the prosecutors had no idea beforehand just how completely horrific Nazi atrocities were. Repeatedly, the observers and participants were reduced to stunned silence as the former leaders of Nazi Germany detailed their heinous crimes against humanity. Words seemed incapable of expressing what Hannah Arendt would later call "the banality of evil"—the daily routine of mass murder expressed in the rationalizing language of bureaucrats. Those on trial seemed capable of offering only two defenses: that they were just following orders and that it was Adolf Hitler's fault. Ultimately, the Nuremberg trials were not just about punishing a select group of Nazi criminals—they also addressed the nature of evil and human responsibility.

Questions to Consider

- Were these trials, as has often been charged, a case of victors punishing losers?
- Was following orders an adequate defense?
- Did the German people bear any responsibility for the Holocaust unleashed by the Nazis?
- Can the results of the Nuremberg trials be applied to other situations, from Vietnam to Bosnia?

Marie Claude Vaillant-Couturier

[Marie Claude Vaillant-Couturier was only thirty-three years old when she appeared before the International Military Tribunal. She was a hero of the French Resistance, a Knight of the Legion of Honor, a deputy in the French Constituent Assembly, and the survivor of three years in German concentration camps. The story she presented to the court caught most people by surprise, for the full horrors of the concentration camps were just becoming public. She is questioned here by Charles Dubost, one of the French prosecutors.]

Source: *Trial of the Major War Criminals Before the International Military Tribunal* (Nuremberg, Germany, 1947), 6: pp. 203–216, 11: pp. 397–401.

MME. VAILLANT-COUTURIER. I was arrested on 9 February 1942 by Petain's French police, who handed me over to the German authorities after 6 weeks. I arrived on 20 March at Santé prison in the German quarter. I was questioned on 9 June 1942. At the end of my interrogation they wanted me to sign a statement which was not consistent with what I had said. I refused to sign it. The officer who had questioned me threatened me; and when I told him that I was not afraid of death nor of being shot, he said, "But we have at our disposal means for killing that are far worse than merely shooting." And the interpreter said to me, "You do not know what you have just done. You are going to leave for a concentration camp in Germany. One never comes back from there."

M. DUBOST. You were then taken to prison?

MME. VAILLANT-COUTURIER. I was taken back to the Santé prison where I was placed in solitary confinement....

M. DUBOST. When did you leave for Auschwitz?

MME. VAILLANT-COUTURIER. I left for Auschwitz on 23 January 1943, and arrived there on the 27th.... It was a terrible journey. We were 60 in a car and we were given no food or drink during the journey. At the various stopping places we asked the Lorraine soldiers of the Wehrmacht who were guarding us whether we would arrive soon; and they replied, "If you knew where you are going you would not be in a hurry to get there."

We arrived at Auschwitz at dawn. The seals on our cars were broken, and we were driven out by blows with the butt end of a rifle, and taken to the Birkenau Camp, a section of the Auschwitz Camp. It is situated in the middle of a great plain, which was frozen in the month of January. During this part of the journey we had to drag our luggage. As we passed through the door we knew only too well how slender our chances were that we would come out again, for we had already met columns of living skeletons going to work; and as we entered we sang "The Marseillaise" to keep up our courage.

We were led to a large shed, then to the disinfecting station. There our heads were shaved and our registration numbers were tattooed on the left forearm. Then we were taken into a large room for a steam bath and a cold shower. In spite of the fact that we were naked, all this took place in the presence of SS men and women. We were then given clothing which was soiled and torn, a cotton dress and jacket of the same material.

...[T]oward the evening an orchestra came in. It was snowing and we wondered why they were playing music. We then saw that the camp foremen were returning to the camp. Each foreman was followed by men who were carrying the dead. As they could hardly drag themselves along, every time they stumbled they were put on their feet again by being kicked or by blows with the butt end of a rifle.

After that we were taken to the block where we were to live. There were no beds but only bunks, measuring 2 by 2 meters, and there nine of us had to sleep the first night without any mattress or blanket. We remained in blocks of this kind for several months. We could not sleep all night, because every time one of the nine moved—this happened unceasingly because we were all ill—she disturbed the whole row.

At 3:30 in the morning the shouting of the guards woke us up, and with cudgel blows we were driven from our bunks to go to roll call. Nothing in the world could release us from going to the roll call; even those who were dying had to be dragged there. We had to stand there in rows of five until dawn, that is, 7 or 8 o'clock in the morning in winter;...until the Aufseherinnen, the German women guards in uniform, came to count us. They had cudgels and they beat us more or less at random.

We had a comrade, Germaine Renaud, a school teacher..., who had her skull broken before my eyes from a blow with a cudgel during the roll call.

The work at Auschwitz consisted of clearing demolished houses, road building, and especially the draining of marsh land. This was by far the hardest work, for all day long we had our feet in the water and there was the danger of being sucked down. It frequently happened that we had to pull out a comrade who had sunk in up to the waist.

During the work the SS men and women who stood guard over us would beat us with cudgels and set their dogs on us. Many of our friends had their legs torn by the dogs. I even saw a woman torn to pieces and die under my very eyes when Tauber, a member of the SS, encouraged his dog to attack her and grinned at the sight.

The causes of death were extremely numerous. First of all, there was the complete lack of washing facilities. When we arrived at Auschwitz, for 12,000 internees there was only one tap of water, unfit for drinking, and it was not always flowing. As this tap was in the German wash house we could reach it only by passing through the guards, who were German common-law women prisoners, and they beat us horribly as we went by. It was therefore almost impossible to wash ourselves or our clothes. For more than 3 months we remained without changing our clothes. When there was snow, we melted some to wash in. Later, in the spring, when we went to work we would drink from a puddle by the road-side and then wash our underclothes in it. We took turns washing our hands in this dirty water. Our companions were dying of thirst, because we got only half a cup of some herbal tea twice a day.

M. DUBOST. Please describe in detail one of the roll calls at the beginning of February.

MME. VAILLANT-COUTURIER. On 5 February [1943] there was what is called a general roll call…. In the morning at 3:30 the whole camp was awakened and sent out on the plain…. We remained out in front of the camp until 5 in the afternoon, in the snow, without any food. Then when the signal was given we had to go through the door one by one, and we were struck in the back with a cudgel, each one of us, in order to make us run. Those who could not run, either because they were too old or too ill were caught by a hook and taken to Block 25, "waiting block" for the gas chamber. On that day 10 of the French women of our convoy were thus caught and taken to Block 25.

When all the internees were back in the camp, a party to which I belonged was organized to go and pick up the bodies of the dead which were scattered over the plain as on a battlefield. We carried to the yard of Block 25 the dead and the dying without distinction, and they remained there stacked up in a pile.

This Block 25, which was the anteroom of the gas chamber, if one may express it so, is well known to me because at that time we had been transferred to Block 26 and our windows opened on the yard of Number 25. One saw stacks of corpses piled up in the courtyard, and from time to time a hand or a head would stir among the bodies, trying to free itself. It was a dying woman attempting to get free and live. The rate of mortality in that block was even more terrible than elsewhere because, having been condemned to death, they received food or drink only if there was something left in the cans in the kitchen; which means that very often they went for several days without a drop of water….

M. DUBOST. What did they do to the internees who came to roll call without shoes?

MME. VAILLANT-COUTURIER. The Jewish internees who came without shoes were immediately taken to Block 25.

M. DUBOST. They were gassed then?

MME. VAILLANT-COUTURIER. They were gassed for any reason whatsoever. Their conditions were moreover absolutely appalling. Although we were crowded 800 in a block and could scarcely move, they were 1,500 to a block of similar dimensions, so that many of them could not sleep or even lie down during the whole night.

M. DUBOST. Can you talk about the Revier?

MME. VAILLANT-COUTURIER. …The Revier was the blocks where the sick were put. This place could not be given the name of hospital, because it did not correspond in any way to our idea of a hospital.

To go there one had first to obtain authorization from the block chief who seldom gave it. When it was finally granted we were led in columns to the infirmary where, no matter what weather, whether it snowed or rained, even if one had a temperature of 40° (centigrade) one had to wait for several hours standing in a queue to be admitted. It frequently happened that patients died outside before the door of the infirmary, before they could get in. Moreover, lining up in front of the infirmary was dangerous because if the queue was too long the SS came along, picked up all the women who were waiting, and took them straight to Block Number 25.

M. DUBOST. That is to say, to the gas chamber?

MME. VAILLANT-COUTURIER. That is to say to the gas chamber. That is why very often the women preferred not to go to the Revier and they died at their work or at roll call. Every day, after the evening roll call in winter time, dead were picked up who had fallen into the ditches….

M. DUBOST. How were you fed?

MME. VAILLANT-COUTURIER. We had 200 grams of bread, three-quarters or half a liter—it varied—of soup made from swedes [rutabaga], and a few grams of margarine or a slice of sausage in the evening, this daily…. Regardless of the work that was exacted from the internee….

M. DUBOST. Will you tell us about experiments, if you witnessed any?

MME. VAILLANT-COUTURIER. …I have seen in the Revier, because I was employed at the Revier, the queue of young Jewesses from Salonika who stood waiting in front of the X-ray room for sterilization. I also know that they performed castration operations in the men's camp. Concerning the experiments performed on women I am well informed, because my friend, Doctor Hadé Hautval of Montbéliard, who has returned to France, worked for several months in that block nursing the patients; but she always refused to participate in those experiments. They sterilized women either by injections or by operation or with rays. I saw and knew several women who had been sterilized. There was a very high mortality rate among those operated upon….

M. DUBOST. What was the aim of the SS?

MME. VAILLANT-COUTURIER. Sterilization—they did not conceal it. They said that they were trying to find the best method for sterilizing so as to replace the native population in the occupied countries by Germans after one generation, once they had made use of the inhabitants as slaves to work for them.

M. DUBOST. In the Revier did you see any pregnant women?

MME. VAILLANT-COUTURIER. Yes. The Jewish women, when they arrived in the first months of pregnancy, were subjected to abortion. When their pregnancy was near the end, after confinement, the babies were drowned in a bucket of water. I know that because I worked in the Revier and the woman who was in charge of that task was a German midwife, who was imprisoned for having performed illegal operations. After a while another doctor arrived and for 2 months they did not kill the Jewish babies. But one day an order came from Berlin saying that again they had to be done away with. Then the mothers and their babies were called to the infirmary. They were put in a lorry and taken away to the gas chamber….

M. DUBOST. Who meted out punishments?

MME. VAILLANT-COUTURIER. The SS leaders, men and women.

M. DUBOST. What was the nature of the punishments?

MME. VAILLANT-COUTURIER. Bodily ill-treatment in particular. One of the most usual punishments was 50 blows with a stick on the loins. They were administered with a machine which I saw, a swinging apparatus manipulated by an SS. There were also endless roll calls day and night, or gymnastics; flat on the belly, get up, lie down, up, down, for hours, and anyone who fell was beaten unmercifully and taken to Block 25.

M. DUBOST. How did the SS behave towards the women? And the women SS?

MME. VAILLANT-COUTURIER. At Auschwitz there was a brothel for the SS and also one for the male internees of the staff, who were called "Kapo." Moreover, when the SS needed servants, they came accompanied by the Oberaufseherin, that is, the woman commandant of the camp, to make a choice during the process of disinfection. They would point to a young girl, whom the Oberaufseherin would take out of the ranks. They would look her over and make jokes about her physique; and if she was pretty and they liked her, they would hire her as a maid with the consent of the Oberaufseherin, who would tell her that she was to obey them absolutely no matter what they asked of her.

M. DUBOST. Why did they go during disinfection?

MME. VAILLANT-COUTURIER. Because during the disinfection the women were naked….

M. DUBOST. Then, according to you, everything was done to degrade those women in their own sight?

MME. VAILLANT-COUTURIER. Yes.

M. DUBOST. What do you know about the convoy of Jews which arrived from Romainville about the same time as yourself?

MME. VAILLANT-COUTURIER. When we left Romainville the Jewesses who were there at the same time as ourselves were left behind. They were sent to Drancy and subsequently arrived at Auschwitz, where we found them again 3 weeks later…. Of the original 1,200 only 125 actually came to the camp; the others were immediately sent to the gas chambers. Of these 125 not one was left alive at the end of 1 month.

The transports operated as follows:

When we first arrived, whenever a convoy of Jews came, a selection was made; first the old men and women, then the mothers and the children were put into trucks together with the sick or those whose constitution appeared to be delicate. They took in only the young women and girls as well as the young men who were sent to the men's camp.

Generally speaking, of a convoy of about 1,000 to 1,500, seldom more than 250—and this figure really was the maximum—actually reached the camp. The rest were immediately sent to the gas chamber.

At this selection also, they picked out women in good health between the ages of 20 and 30, who were sent to the experimental block; and young girls and slightly older women, or those who had not been selected for that purpose, were sent to the camp where, like ourselves, they were tattooed and shaved.

There was also, in the spring of 1944, a special block for twins. It was during the time when large convoys of Hungarian Jews—about 700,000—arrived. Dr. Mengele, who was carrying out the experiments, kept back from each convoy twin children and twins in general, regardless of their age, so long as both were present. So we had both babies and adults on the floor at that block. Apart from blood tests and measuring I do not know what was done to them.

M. DUBOST. Were you an eye witness of the selections on the arrival of the convoys?

MME. VAILLANT-COUTURIER. Yes, because when we worked at the sewing block in 1944, the block where we lived directly faced the stopping place of the trains. The system had been improved. Instead of making the selection at the place where they arrived, a side line now took the train practically right up to the gas chamber; and the stopping place, about 100 meters from the gas chamber, was right opposite our block though, of course, separated from us by two rows of barbed wire. Consequently, we saw the unsealing of the cars and the soldiers letting men, women, and children out of them. We then witnessed heart-rending scenes; old couples forced to part from each other, mothers made to abandon their young daughters, since the latter were sent to the camp, whereas mothers and children were sent to the gas chambers. All these people were unaware of the fate awaiting them. They were merely upset at being separated, but they did not know that they were going to their death. To render their welcome more pleasant at this time—June–July 1944—an orchestra composed of internees, all young and pretty girls dressed in little white blouses and navy blue skirts, played during the selection…gay tunes such as "The Merry Widow," the "Barcarolle" from "The Tales of Hoffman," and so forth. They were then informed that this was a labor camp and since they were not brought into the camp they saw only the small platform surrounded by flowering plants. Naturally, they could not realize what was in store for them. Those selected for the gas chamber, that is, the old people, mothers, and children, were escorted to a red-brick building.

M. DUBOST. …They were not tattooed?

MME. VAILLANT-COUTURIER. No. They were not even counted.

M. DUBOST. You were tattooed?

MME. VAILLANT-COUTURIER. Yes, look. [*The witness showed her arm.*] They were taken to a red brick building, which bore the letters "Baden," that is to say "Baths." There, to begin with, they were made to undress and given a towel before they went into the so-called shower room. Later on, at the time of the large convoys from Hungary, they had no more time left to play-act or to pretend; they were brutally undressed....

...Once the people were undressed they took them into a room which was somewhat like a shower room, and gas capsules were thrown through an opening in the ceiling. An SS man would watch the effect produced through a porthole. At the end of 5 or 7 minutes, when the gas had completed its work, he gave the signal to open the doors; and men with gas masks—they too were internees—went into the room and removed the corpses. They told us that the internees must have suffered before dying, because they were closely clinging to one another and it was very difficult to separate them.

After that a special squad would come to pull out gold teeth and dentures; and again, when the bodies had been reduced to ashes, they would sift them in an attempt to recover the gold.

At Auschwitz there were eight crematories but, as from 1944, these proved insufficient. The SS had large pits dug by the internees, where they put branches, sprinkled with gasoline, which they set on fire. Then they threw the corpses into the pits. From our block we could see after about three-quarters of an hour or an hour after the arrival of a convoy, large flames coming from the crematory, and the sky was lighted up by the burning pits.

One night we were awakened by terrifying cries. And we discovered, on the following day, from the men working in the Sonderkommando—the "Gas Kommando"—that on the preceding day, the gas supply having run out, they had thrown the children into the furnaces alive....

Rudolf Hoess

[Incredibly, Rudolf Hoess, commandant of Auschwitz, appeared before the International Military Tribunal not as a defendant, but as a witness for the defense. Kurt Kauffmann, attorney for SS commander Ernst Kaltenbrunner, called Hoess to the stand in an effort to show that the SS was not directly responsible for the extermination camp.]

DR. KAUFFMANN. From 1940 to 1943, you were the Commander of the camp at Auschwitz. Is that true?

HOESS. Yes.

DR. KAUFFMANN. And during that time, hundreds of thousands of human beings were sent to their death there. Is that correct?

HOESS. Yes.

DR. KAUFFMANN. Is it true that you, yourself, have made no exact notes regarding the figures of the number of those victims because you were forbidden to make them?

HOESS. Yes, that is correct.

DR. KAUFFMANN. Is it furthermore correct that exclusively one man by the name of Eichmann had notes about this, the man who had the task of organizing and assembling these people?

HOESS. Yes.

DR. KAUFFMANN. Is it furthermore true that Eichmann stated to you that in Auschwitz a total sum of more than 2 million Jews had been destroyed?

HOESS. Yes.

DR. KAUFFMANN. Men, women, and children?

HOESS. Yes....

DR. KAUFFMANN. What was the highest number of human beings, prisoners, ever held at one time at Auschwitz?

HOESS. The highest number of internees held at one time at Auschwitz, was about 140,000 men and women.

DR. KAUFFMANN. Is it true that in 1941 you were ordered to Berlin to see Himmler? Please state briefly what was discussed.

HOESS. Yes. In the summer of 1941 I was summoned to Berlin to Reichsführer SS Himmler to receive personal orders. He told me something to the effect...that the Fuhrer had given the order for a final solution of the Jewish question. We, the SS, must carry out that order. If it is not carried out now then the Jews will later on destroy the German people....

DR. KAUFFMANN. And after the arrival of the transports were the victims stripped of everything they had? Did they have to undress completely; did they have to surrender their valuables? Is that true?

HOESS. Yes.

DR. KAUFFMANN. And then they immediately went to their death?

HOESS. Yes.

DR. KAUFFMANN. I ask you, according to your knowledge, did these people know what was in store for them?

HOESS. The majority of them did not, for steps were taken to keep them in doubt about it and suspicion would not arise that they were to go to their death. For instance, all doors and all walls bore inscriptions to the effect that they were going to undergo a delousing operation or take a shower. This was made known in several languages to the internees by other internees who had come in with earlier transports and who were being used as auxiliary crews during the whole action.

DR. KAUFFMANN. And then, you told me the other day, that death by gassing set in within a period of 3 to 15 minutes. Is that correct?

HOESS. Yes.

DR. KAUFFMANN. You also told me that even before death finally set in, the victims fell into a state of unconsciousness?

HOESS. Yes. From what I was able to find out myself or from what was told me by medical officers, the time necessary for reaching unconsciousness or death varied according to the temperature and the number of people present in the chambers. Loss of consciousness took place within a few seconds or a few minutes.

DR. KAUFFMANN. Did you yourself ever feel pity with the victims, thinking of your own family and children?

HOESS. Yes.

DR. KAUFFMANN. How was it possible for you to carry out these actions in spite of this?

HOESS. In view of all these doubts which I had, the only one and decisive argument was the strict order and the reason given for it by the Reichsführer Himmler....

37

The Marshall Plan (1947)

GEORGE C. MARSHALL

Europe had been devastated by World War II. The economies of even the victorious nations were in shambles. In the context of the emerging Cold War with the Soviet Union, most of Europe seemed ripe for conquest in the eyes of President Harry Truman and his aides. Secretary of State George Marshall, chief of staff during the war, felt that the most efficient way to save Europe from the Communists was to aid the economic recovery of the whole continent. Despite the staggering cost, estimated at some twenty billion dollars, Truman felt that the long-term investment in an economically healthy Western Europe was well worth the risk. In the commencement address on June 5, 1947 at Harvard University, Marshall presented a plan for European recovery, promising American aid even to the Soviets and their subject nations.

Questions to Consider

- Why did the Soviet Union refuse to participate in the Marshall Plan?
- What did the United States have to gain by spending so much money to rebuild its economic competitors?

I need not tell you gentlemen that the world situation is very serious. That must be apparent to all intelligent people. I think one difficulty is that the problem is one of such enormous complexity that the very mass of facts presented to the public by press and radio make it exceedingly difficult for the man in the street to reach a clear appraisement of the situation. Furthermore, the people of this country are distant from the troubled areas of the earth and it is hard for them to comprehend the plight and consequent reactions of the long-suffering peoples, and the effect of those reactions on their governments in connection with our efforts to promote peace in the world.

In considering the requirements for the rehabilitation of Europe, the physical loss of life, the visible destruction of cities, factories, mines, and railroads was correctly estimated, but it has become obvious during

Source: *Department of State Bulletin* 17 (June 15, 1947), pp. 1159–1160.

recent months that this visible destruction was probably less serious than the dislocation of the entire fabric of European economy. For the past 10 years conditions have been highly abnormal. The feverish preparation for war and the more feverish maintenance of the war effort engulfed all aspects of national economies. Machinery has fallen into disrepair or is entirely obsolete. Under the arbitrary and destructive Nazi rule, virtually every possible enterprise was geared into the German war machine. Long-standing commercial ties, private institutions, banks, insurance companies, and shipping companies disappeared, through loss of capital, absorption through nationalization, or by simple destruction. In many countries, confidence in the local currency has been severely shaken. The breakdown of the business structure of Europe during the war was complete. Recovery has been seriously retarded by the fact that two years after the close of hostilities a peace settlement with Germany and Austria has not been agreed upon. But even given a more prompt solution of these difficult problems, the rehabilitation of the economic structure of Europe quite evidently will require a much longer time and greater effort than had been foreseen.

There is a phase of this matter which is both interesting and serious. The farmer has always produced the foodstuffs to exchange with the city dweller for the other necessities of life. This division of labor is the basis of modern civilization. At the present time it is threatened with breakdown. The town and city industries are not producing adequate goods to exchange with the food-producing farmer. Raw materials and fuel are in short supply. Machinery is lacking or worn out. The farmer or the peasant cannot find the goods for sale which he desires to purchase. So the sale of his farm produce for money which he cannot use seems to him an unprofitable transaction. He, therefore, has withdrawn many fields from crop cultivation and is using them for grazing. He feeds more grain to stock and finds for himself and his family an ample supply of food, however short he may be on clothing and the other ordinary gadgets of civilization. Meanwhile people in the cities are short of food and fuel. So the governments are forced to use their foreign money and credits to procure these necessities abroad. This process exhausts funds which are urgently needed for reconstruction. Thus a very serious situation is rapidly developing which bodes no good for the world. The modern system of the division of labor upon which the exchange of products is based is in danger of breaking down.

The truth of the matter is that Europe's requirements for the next three or four years of foreign food and other essential products—principally from America—are so much greater than her present ability to pay that she must have substantial additional help or face economic, social, and political deterioration of a very grave character.

The remedy lies in breaking the vicious circle and restoring the confidence of the European people in the economic future of their own countries and of Europe as a whole. The manufacturer and the farmer throughout wide areas must be able and willing to exchange their products for currencies the continuing value of which is not open to question.

Aside from the demoralizing effect on the world at large and the possibilities of disturbances arising as a result of the desperation of the people concerned, the consequences to the economy of the United States should be apparent to all. It is logical that the United States should do whatever it is able to do to assist in the return of normal economic health in the world, without which there can be no political stability and no assured peace. Our policy is directed not against any country or doctrine but against hunger, poverty, desperation, and chaos. Its purpose should be the revival of a working economy in the world so as to permit the emergence of political and social conditions in which free institutions can exist. Such assistance, I am convinced, must not be on a piecemeal basis as various crises develop. Any assistance that this Government may render in the future should provide a cure rather than a mere palliative. Any government that is willing to assist in the task of recovery will find full cooperation, I am sure, on the part of the United States Government. Any government which maneuvers to block the recovery of other countries cannot expect help from us. Furthermore, governments, political parties, or groups which seek to perpetuate human misery in order to profit therefrom politically or otherwise will encounter the opposition of the United States.

It is already evident that, before the United States Government can proceed much further in its efforts to alleviate the situation and help start the European world on its way to recovery, there must be some agreement among the countries of Europe as to the requirements of the situation and the part those countries themselves will take in order to give proper effect to whatever action might be undertaken by this Government. It would be neither fitting nor efficacious for this Government to undertake to draw up unilaterally a program designed to place Europe on its feet economically. This is the business of the Europeans. The initiative, I think, must come from Europe. The role of this country should consist of friendly aid in the drafting of a European program and of later support of such a program so far as it may be practical for us to do so. The program should be a joint one, agreed to by a number, if not all European nations.

An essential part of any successful action on the part of the United States is an understanding on the part of the people of America of the character of the problem and the remedies to be applied. Political passion and prejudice should have no part. With foresight, and a willingness on the part of our people to face up to the vast responsibility which history has clearly placed upon our country, the difficulties I have outlined can and will be overcome.

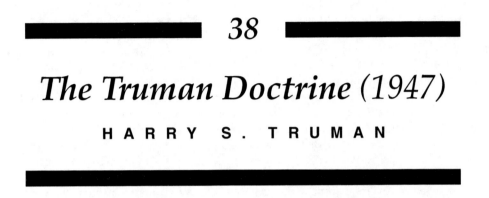

38

The Truman Doctrine (1947)

H A R R Y   S .   T R U M A N

In the aftermath of World War II, Communists attempted to seize power in Greece and Turkey. Those governments, backed by the British, resisted with military force. But in 1947 Great Britain informed the U.S. government that it could no longer maintain the expense of continuing aid to those nations. President Harry Truman personally appeared before a joint session of Congress on March 12, 1947, to request that the United States abandon its historic commitment to nonintervention in Europe during peacetime and extend full aid to Greece and Turkey. Congress approved what has since become known as the "Truman Doctrine" by huge majorities.

Questions to Consider

- Why does Truman frame his request in the context of an international conflict?
- What American interests were involved in the political fate of Greece and Turkey?

Special Message to the Congress on Greece and Turkey

Mr. President, Mr. Speaker, Members of the Congress of the United States:

The gravity of the situation which confronts the world today necessitates my appearance before a joint session of the Congress.

The foreign policy and the national security of this country are involved.

One aspect of the present situation, which I present to you at this time for your consideration and decision, concerns Greece and Turkey.

The United States has received from the Greek Government an urgent appeal for financial and economic assistance. Preliminary reports from the American Economic Mission now in Greece and reports from the American Ambassador in Greece corroborate the statement of the Greek Government that assistance is imperative if Greece is to survive as a free nation.

I do not believe that the American people and the Congress wish to turn a deaf ear to the appeal of the Greek Government.

Greece is not a rich country. Lack of sufficient natural resources has always forced the Greek people to work hard to make both ends meet. Since 1940, this industrious, peace loving country has suffered invasion, four years of cruel enemy occupation, and bitter internal strife.

When forces of liberation entered Greece they found that the retreating Germans had destroyed virtually all

Source: *Public Papers of the Presidents of the United States, Harry S. Truman, 1947* (Washington, D.C., 1948), pp. 176–180.

the railways, roads, port facilities, communications, and merchant marine. More than a thousand villages had been burned. Eighty-five percent of the children were tubercular. Livestock, poultry, and draft animals had almost disappeared. Inflation had wiped out practically all savings.

As a result of these tragic conditions, a militant minority, exploiting human want and misery, was able to create political chaos which, until now, has made economic recovery impossible.

Greece is today without funds to finance the importation of those goods which are essential to bare subsistence. Under these circumstances the people of Greece cannot make progress in solving their problems of reconstruction. Greece is in desperate need of financial and economic assistance to enable it to resume purchases of food, clothing, fuel and seeds. These are indispensable for the subsistence of its people and are obtainable only from abroad. Greece must have help to import the goods necessary to restore internal order and security so essential for economic and political recovery.

The Greek Government has also asked for the assistance of experienced American administrators, economists and technicians to insure that the financial and other aid given to Greece shall be used effectively in creating a stable and self-sustaining economy and in improving its public administration.

The very existence of the Greek state is today threatened by the terrorist activities of several thousand armed men, led by Communists, who defy the government's authority at a number of points, particularly along the northern boundaries. A Commission appointed by the United Nations Security Council is at present investigating disturbed conditions in northern Greece and alleged border violations along the frontier between Greece on the one hand and Albania, Bulgaria, and Yugoslavia on the other.

Meanwhile, the Greek Government is unable to cope with the situation. The Greek army is small and poorly equipped. It needs supplies and equipment if it is to restore authority to the government throughout Greek territory.

Greece must have assistance if it is to become a self-supporting and self-respecting democracy.

The United States must supply this assistance. We have already extended to Greece certain types of relief and economic aid but these are inadequate.

There is no other country to which democratic Greece can turn.

No other nation is willing and able to provide the necessary support for a democratic Greek government.

The British Government, which has been helping Greece, can give no further financial or economic aid after March 31. Great Britain finds itself under the necessity of reducing or liquidating its commitments in several parts of the world, including Greece.

We have considered how the United Nations might assist in this crisis. But the situation is an urgent one requiring immediate action, and the United Nations and its related organizations are not in a position to extend help of the kind that is required.

It is important to note that the Greek Government has asked for our aid in utilizing effectively the financial and other assistance we may give to Greece, and in improving its public administration. It is of the utmost importance that we supervise the use of any funds made available to Greece, in such a manner that each dollar spent will count toward making Greece self-supporting, and will help to build an economy in which a healthy democracy can flourish.

No government is perfect. One of the chief virtues of a democracy, however, is that its defects are always visible and under democratic processes can be pointed out and corrected. The government of Greece is not perfect. Nevertheless it represents 85 percent of the members of the Greek Parliament who were chosen in an election last year. Foreign observers, including 692 Americans, considered this election to be a fair expression of the views of the Greek people.

The Greek Government has been operating in an atmosphere of chaos and extremism. It has made mistakes. The extension of aid by this country does not mean that the United States condones everything that the Greek Government has done or will do. We have condemned in the past, and we condemn now, extremist measures of the right or the left. We have in the past advised tolerance, and we advise tolerance now.

Greece's neighbor, Turkey, also deserves our attention.

The future of Turkey as an independent and economically sound state is clearly no less important to the freedom-loving peoples of the world than the future of Greece. The circumstances in which Turkey finds itself today are considerably different from those of Greece. Turkey has been spared the disasters that have beset Greece. And during the war, the United States and Great Britain furnished Turkey with material aid.

Nevertheless, Turkey now needs our support.

Since the war Turkey has sought additional financial assistance from Great Britain and the United States for the purpose of effecting that modernization necessary for the maintenance of its national integrity.

That integrity is essential to the preservation of order in the Middle East.

The British Government has informed us that, owing to its own difficulties, it can no longer extend financial or economic aid to Turkey.

As in the case of Greece, if Turkey is to have the assistance it needs, the United States must supply it. We are the only country able to provide that help.

I am fully aware of the broad implications involved if the United States extends assistance to Greece and Turkey, and I shall discuss these implications with you at this time.

One of the primary objectives of the foreign policy of the United States is the creation of conditions in which we and other nations will be able to work out a way of life free from coercion. This was a fundamental issue in the war with Germany and Japan. Our victory was won over countries which sought to impose their will, and their way of life, upon other nations.

To ensure the peaceful development of nations, free from coercion, the United States has taken a leading part in establishing the United Nations. The United Nations is designed to make possible lasting freedom and independence for all its members. We shall not realize our objectives, however, unless we are willing to help free peoples to maintain their free institutions and their national integrity against aggressive movements that seek to impose upon them totalitarian regimes. This is no more than a frank recognition that totalitarian regimes imposed upon free peoples, by direct or indirect aggression, undermine the foundations of international peace and hence the security of the United States.

The peoples of a number of countries of the world have recently had totalitarian regimes forced upon them against their will. The Government of the United States has made frequent protests against coercion and intimidation, in violation of the Yalta agreement, in Poland, Rumania, and Bulgaria. I must also state that in a number of other countries there have been similar developments.

At the present moment in world history nearly every nation must choose between alternative ways of life. The choice is too often not a free one.

One way of life is based upon the will of the majority, and is distinguished by free institutions, representative government, free elections, guarantees of individual liberty, freedom of speech and religion, and freedom from political oppression.

The second way of life is based upon the will of a minority forcibly imposed upon the majority. It relies upon terror and oppression, a controlled press and radio, fixed elections, and the suppression of personal freedoms.

I believe that it must be the policy of the United States to support free peoples who are resisting attempted subjugation by armed minorities or by outside pressures.

I believe that we must assist free peoples to work out their own destinies in their own way.

I believe that our help should be primarily through economic and financial aid which is essential to economic stability and orderly political processes.

The world is not static, and the *status quo* is not sacred. But we cannot allow changes in the *status quo* in violation of the Charter of the United Nations by such methods as coercion, or by such subterfuges as political infiltration. In helping free and independent nations to maintain their freedom, the United States will be giving effect to the principles of the Charter of the United Nations.

It is necessary only to glance at a map to realize that the survival and integrity of the Greek nation are of grave importance in a much wider situation. If Greece should fall under the control of an armed minority, the effect upon its neighbor, Turkey, would be immediate and serious. Confusion and disorder might well spread throughout the entire Middle East.

Moreover, the disappearance of Greece as an independent state would have a profound effect upon those countries in Europe whose peoples are struggling against great difficulties to maintain their freedoms and their independence while they repair the damages of war.

It would be an unspeakable tragedy if these countries, which have struggled so long against overwhelming odds, should lose that victory for which they sacrificed so much. Collapse of free institutions and loss of independence would be disastrous not only for them but for the world. Discouragement and possibly failure would quickly be the lot of neighboring peoples striving to maintain their freedom and independence.

Should we fail to aid Greece and Turkey in this fateful hour, the effect will be far reaching to the West as well as to the East.

We must take immediate and resolute action.

I therefore ask the Congress to provide authority for assistance to Greece and Turkey in the amount of $400,000,000 for the period ending June 30, 1948. In requesting these funds, I have taken into consideration the maximum amount of relief assistance which would be furnished to Greece out of the $350,000,000 which I recently requested that the Congress authorize for the prevention of starvation and suffering in countries devastated by the war.

In addition to funds, I ask the Congress to authorize the detail of American civilian and military personnel to Greece and Turkey, at the request of those countries, to assist in the tasks of reconstruction, and for the purpose of supervising the use of such financial and material assistance as may be furnished. I recommend that authority also be provided for the instruction and training of selected Greek and Turkish personnel.

Finally, I ask that the Congress provide authority which will permit the speediest and most effective use, in terms of needed commodities, supplies, and equipment, of such funds as may be authorized.

If further funds, or further authority, should be needed for the purposes indicated in this message, I shall not hesitate to bring the situation before the Congress. On this subject the Executive and Legislative branches of the Government must work together.

This is a serious course upon which we embark.

I would not recommend it except that the alternative is much more serious.

The United States contributed $341,000,000,000 toward winning World War II. This is an investment in world freedom and world peace.

The assistance that I am recommending for Greece and Turkey amounts to little more than 1/10 of 1 percent of this investment. It is only common sense that we should safeguard this investment and make sure that it was not in vain.

The seeds of totalitarian regimes are nurtured by misery and want. They spread and grow in the evil soil of poverty and strife. They reach their full growth when the hope of a people for a better life has died.

We must keep that hope alive.

The free peoples of the world look to us for support in maintaining their freedoms.

If we falter in our leadership, we may endanger the peace of the world—and we shall surely endanger the welfare of this Nation.

Great responsibilities have been placed upon us by the swift movement of events.

I am confident that the Congress will face these responsibilities squarely.

39

Address to Congress (1951)

D O U G L A S   M A C A R T H U R

General Douglas MacArthur, commander of U.S. forces in the Pacific during World War II and of the American occupation of Japan, had taken command in South Korea in 1950 when it looked as though the Communists would triumph. In the brilliant Inchon campaign, MacArthur reversed the direction of the war, leading his troops north toward the Chinese border. It was at that point that China intervened, and the Korean War turned into a ceaseless battle of attrition. MacArthur tried to persuade the U.S. government to authorize air attacks on Chinese targets and a complete blockade of China. President Truman, fearing a wider war, rejected these suggestions. MacArthur went public with his disagreement with Truman, talking freely to reporters and congressmen of the president's errors in judgment. To Truman, such actions were rank insubordination, endangering civilian control of the military, and he removed MacArthur from command on April 11, 1951. Republicans responded by inviting MacArthur to address both houses of Congress a week later. His speech encapsulated distinct views of how to proceed within a broad consensus on hostility to the Communist menace.

Questions to Consider

- Why does MacArthur feel it necessary to confront the Communist threat in Asia as well as Europe?

- Why does MacArthur not fear an expansion of the war in Korea?

Mr. President, Mr. Speaker, and distinguished Members of the Congress, I stand on this rostrum with a sense of deep humility and great pride—humility in the wake of those great American architects of our history who have stood here before me, pride in the reflection that this forum of legislative debate represents human liberty in the purest form yet devised. [Applause.] Here are centered the hopes, and aspirations, and faith of the entire human race.

I do not stand here as advocate for any partisan cause, for the issues are fundamental and reach quite beyond the realm of partisan consideration. They must be resolved on the highest plane of national interest if our course is to prove sound and our future protected. I trust, therefore, that you will do me the justice of receiving that which I have to say as solely expressing the considered viewpoint of a fellow American. I address you with neither rancor nor bitterness in the fading twilight of life with but one purpose in mind—to serve my country. [Applause.]

The issues are global and so interlocked that to consider the problems of one sector, oblivious to those of another, is but to court disaster for the whole.

While Asia is commonly referred to as the gateway to Europe, it is no less true that Europe is the gateway to Asia, and the broad influence of the one cannot fail to have its impact upon the other.

There are those who claim our strength is inadequate to protect on both fronts—that we cannot divide our effort. I can think of no greater expression of defeatism. [Applause.] If a potential enemy can divide his strength on two fronts, it is for us to counter his effort.

The Communist threat is a global one. Its successful advance in one sector threatens the destruction of every other sector. You cannot appease or otherwise surrender to communism in Asia without simultaneously undermining our efforts to halt its advance in Europe. [Applause.]

Beyond pointing out these general truisms, I shall confine my discussion to the general areas of Asia. Before one may objectively assess the situation now existing there, he must comprehend something of Asia's past and the revolutionary changes which have marked her course up to the present. Long exploited by the so-called colonial powers, with little opportunity to achieve any degree of social justice, individual dignity, or a higher standard of life such as guided our own noble administration of the Philippines, the peoples of Asia found their opportunity in the war just past to throw off the shackles of colonialism, and now see the dawn of new opportunity, a heretofore unfelt dignity and the self-respect of political freedom.

Mustering half of the earth's population and 60 percent of its natural resources, these peoples are rapidly consolidating a new force, both moral and material, with which to raise the living standard and erect adaptations of the design of modern progress to their own distinct cultural environments. Whether one adheres to the concept of colonization or not, this is the direction of Asian progress and it may not be stopped. It is a corollary to the shift of the world economic frontiers, as the whole epicenter of world affairs rotates back toward the area whence it started. In this situation it becomes vital that our own country orient its policies in consonance with this basic evolutionary condition rather than pursue a course blind to the reality that the colonial era is now past and the Asian peoples covet the right to shape their own free destiny. What they seek now is friendly guidance, understanding, and support, not imperious direction [applause]; the dignity of equality, not the shame of subjugation. Their prewar standards of life, pitifully low, is infinitely lower now in the devastation left in war's wake. World ideologies play little part in Asian thinking and are little understood. What the peoples strive for is the opportunity for a little more food in their stomachs, a little better clothing on their backs, a little firmer roof over their heads, and the realization of the normal nationalist urge for political freedom. These political-social conditions have but an indirect bearing upon our own national security, but do form a backdrop to contemporary planning which must be thoughtfully considered if we are to avoid the pitfalls of unrealism.

Of more direct and immediate bearing upon our national security are the changes wrought in the strategic potential of the Pacific Ocean in the course of the past war. Prior thereto, the western strategic frontier of the United States lay on the littoral line of the Americas with an exposed island salient extending out through Hawaii, Midway, and Guam to the Philippines. That salient proved not an outpost of strength but an avenue of weakness along which the enemy could and did attack. The Pacific was a potential area of advance for any predatory force intent upon striking at the bordering land areas.

All this was changed by our Pacific victory. Our strategic frontier then shifted to embrace the entire Pacific Ocean which became a vast moat to protect us as long as we hold it. Indeed, it acts as a protective shield for all of the Americas and all free lands of the Pacific Ocean area. We control it to the shores of Asia by a chain of islands extending in an arc from the Aleutians to the Mariannas held by us and our free allies.

From this island chain we can dominate with sea and air power every Asiatic port from Vladivostok to Singapore and prevent any hostile movement into the Pacific. Any predatory attack from Asia must be an amphibious effort. No amphibious force can be successful

Source: *Congressional Record,* 82d Congress, 1st session (April 19, 1951), pp. 4123–4125.

without control of the sea lanes and the air over those lanes in its avenue of advance. With naval and air supremacy and modest ground elements to defend bases, any major attack from continental Asia toward us or our friends of the Pacific would be doomed to failure. Under such conditions the Pacific no longer represents menacing avenues of approach for a prospective invader—it assumes instead the friendly aspect of a peaceful lake. Our line of defense is a natural one and can be maintained with a minimum of military effort and expense. It envisions no attack against anyone nor does it provide the bastions essential for offensive operations, but properly maintained would be an invincible defense against aggression.

The holding of this littoral defense line in the western Pacific is entirely dependent upon holding all segments thereof, for any major breach of that line by an unfriendly power would render vulnerable to determined attack every other major segment. This is a military estimate as to which I have yet to find a military leader who will take exception. [Applause.]

For that reason I have strongly recommended in the past as a matter of military urgency that under no circumstances must Formosa fall under Communist control. [Applause.] Such an eventuality would at once threaten the freedom of the Philippines and the loss of Japan, and might well force our western frontier back to the coasts of California, Oregon, and Washington.

To understand the changes which now appear upon the Chinese mainland, one must understand the changes in Chinese character and culture over the past 50 years. China up to 50 years ago was completely nonhomogeneous, being compartmented into groups divided against each other. The war-making tendency was almost nonexistent, as they still followed the tenets of the Confucian ideal of pacifist culture. At the turn of the century, under the regime of Chan So Lin, efforts toward greater homogeneity produced the start of a nationalist urge. This was further and more successfully developed under the leadership of Chiang Kai-shek, but has been brought to its greatest fruition under the present regime, to the point that it has now taken on the character of a united nationalism of increasingly dominant aggressive tendencies. Through these past 50 years, the Chinese people have thus become militarized in their concepts and in their ideals. They now constitute excellent soldiers with competent staffs and commanders. This has produced a new and dominant power in Asia which for its own purposes is allied with Soviet Russia, but which in its own concepts and methods has become aggressively imperialistic with a lust for expansion and increased power normal to this type of imperialism. There is little of the ideological concept either one way or another in the Chinese make-up. The standard of living is so low and the capital accumula-

tion has been so thoroughly dissipated by war that the masses are desperate and avid to follow any leadership which seems to promise the alleviation of local stringencies. I have from the beginning believed that the Chinese Communists' support of the North Koreans was the dominant one. Their interests are at present parallel to those of the Soviet, but I believe that the aggressiveness recently displayed not only in Korea, but also in Indochina and Tibet and pointing potentially toward the south, reflects predominantly the same lust for the expansion of power which has animated every would-be conqueror since the beginning of time. [Applause.]

The Japanese people since the war have undergone the greatest reformation recorded in modern history. With a commendable will, eagerness to learn, and marked capacity to understand, they have, from the ashes left in war's wake, erected in Japan an edifice dedicated to the primacy of individual liberty and personal dignity, and in the ensuing process there has been created a truly representative government committed to the advance of political morality, freedom of economic enterprise and social justice. [Applause.] Politically, economically and socially Japan is now abreast of many free nations of the earth and will not again fail the universal trust. That it may be counted upon to wield a profoundly beneficial influence over the course of events in Asia is attested by the magnificent manner in which the Japanese people have met the recent challenge of war, unrest, and confusion surrounding them from the outside, and checked communism within their own frontiers without the slightest slackening in their forward progress. I sent all four of our occupation divisions to the Korean battle front without the slightest qualms as to the effect of the resulting power vacuum upon Japan. The results fully justified my faith. [Applause.] I know of no nation more serene, orderly, and industrious—nor in which higher hopes can be entertained for future constructive service in the advance of the human race. [Applause.]

Of our former wards, the Philippines, we can look forward in confidence that the existing unrest will be corrected and a strong and healthy nation will grow in the longer aftermath of war's terrible destructiveness. We must be patient and understanding and never fail them, as in our hour of need they did not fail us. [Applause.] A Christian nation, the Philippines stand as a mighty bulwark of Christianity in the Far East, and its capacity for high moral leadership in Asia is unlimited.

On Formosa, the Government of the Republic of China has had the opportunity to refute by action much of the malicious gossip which so undermined the strength of its leadership on the Chinese mainland. [Applause.] The Formosan people are receiving a just and enlightened administration with majority representation on the organs of government; and politically, economically and socially they appear to be advancing along sound and constructive lines.

With this brief insight into the surrounding areas I now turn to the Korean conflict. While I was not consulted prior to the President's decision to intervene in support of the Republic of Korea, that decision, from a military standpoint, proved a sound one [applause] as we hurled back the invaders and decimated his forces. Our victory was complete and our objectives within reach when Red China intervened with numerically superior ground forces. This created a new war and an entirely new situation—a situation not contemplated when our forces were committed against the North Korean invaders—a situation which called for new decisions in the diplomatic sphere to permit the realistic adjustment of military strategy. Such decisions have not been forthcoming. [Applause.]

While no man in his right mind would advocate sending our ground forces into continental China and such was never given a thought, the new situation did urgently demand a drastic revision of strategic planning if our political aim was to defeat this new enemy as we had defeated the old. [Applause.]

Apart from the military need as I saw it to neutralize the sanctuary protection given the enemy north of the Yalu, I felt that military necessity in the conduct of the war made mandatory:

1. The intensification of our economic blockade against China;

2. The imposition of a naval blockade against the China coast;

3. Removal of restrictions on air reconnaissance of China's coast areas and of Manchuria [applause];

4. Removal of restrictions on the forces of the Republic of China on Formosa with logistical support to contribute to their effective operations against the common enemy. [Applause.]

For entertaining these views, all professionally designed to support our forces committed to Korea and bring hostilities to an end with the least possible delay and at a saving of countless American and Allied lives, I have been severely criticized in lay circles, principally abroad, despite my understanding that from a military standpoint the above views have been fully shared in the past by practically every military leader concerned with the Korean campaign, including our own Joint Chiefs of Staff. [Applause, the Members rising.]

I called for reinforcements, but was informed that reinforcements were not available. I made clear that if not permitted to destroy the built-up bases north of the Yalu; if not permitted to utilize the friendly Chinese force of some 600,000 men on Formosa; if not permitted to blockade the China coast to prevent the Chinese Reds from getting succor from without; and if there were to

be no hope of major reinforcements, the position of the command from the military standpoint forbade victory. We could hold in Korea by constant maneuver and at an approximate area where our supply line advantages were in balance with the supply line disadvantages of the enemy, but we could hope at best for only an indecisive campaign, with its terrible and constant attrition upon our forces if the enemy utilized his full military potential. I have constantly called for the new political decisions essential to a solution. Efforts have been made to distort my position. It has been said, in effect, that I am a warmonger. Nothing could be further from the truth. I know war as few other men now living know it, and nothing to me is more revolting. I have long advocated its complete abolition as its very destructiveness on both friend and foe has rendered it useless as a means of settling international disputes. Indeed, on the 2d of September 1945, just following the surrender of the Japanese Nation on the battleship *Missouri*, I formally cautioned as follows:

"Men since the beginning of time have sought peace. Various methods through the ages have been attempted to devise an international process to prevent or settle disputes between nations. From the very start, workable methods were found insofar as individual citizens were concerned, but the mechanics of an instrumentality of larger international scope have never been successful. Military alliances, balances of power, leagues of nations, all in turn failed, leaving the only path to be by way of the crucible of war. The utter destructiveness of war now blots out this alternative. We have had our last chance. If we will not devise some greater and more equitable system, Armageddon will be at our door. The problem basically is theological and involves a spiritual recrudescence and improvement of human character that will synchronize with our almost matchless advances in science, art, literature, and all material and cultural developments of the past 2,000 years. It must be of the spirit if we are to save the flesh." [Applause.]

But once war is forced upon us, there is no other alternative than to apply every available means to bring it to a swift end. War's very object is victory—not prolonged indecision. [Applause.] In war, indeed, there can be no substitute for victory. [Applause.]

There are some who for varying reasons would appease Red China. They are blind to history's clear lesson. For history teaches with unmistakable emphasis that appeasement but begets new and bloodier war. It points to no single instance where the end has justified that means—where appeasement has led to more than a sham peace. Like blackmail, it lays the basis for new and successively greater demands, until, as in blackmail, violence becomes the only other alternative. Why, my soldiers asked of me, surrender military advantages to an enemy in the field? I could not answer.

[Applause.] Some may say to avoid spread of the conflict into an all-out war with China; others, to avoid Soviet intervention. Neither explanation seems valid. For China is already engaging with the maximum power it can commit and the Soviet will not necessarily mesh its actions with our moves. Like a cobra, any new enemy will more likely strike whenever it feels that the relativity in military or other potential is in its favor on a world-wide basis.

The tragedy of Korea is further heightened by the fact that as military action is confined to its territorial limits, it condemns that nation, which it is our purpose to save, to suffer the devastating impact of full naval and air bombardment, while the enemy's sanctuaries are fully protected from such attack and devastation. Of the nations of the world, Korea alone, up to now, is the sole one which has risked its all against communism. The magnificence of the courage and fortitude of the Korean people defies description. [Applause.] They have chosen to risk death rather than slavery. Their last words to me were "Don't scuttle the Pacific." [Applause.]

I have just left your fighting sons in Korea. They have met all tests there and I can report to you without reservation they are splendid in every way. [Applause.] It was my constant effort to preserve them and end this savage conflict honorably and with the least loss of time and a minimum sacrifice of life. Its growing bloodshed has caused me the deepest anguish and anxiety. Those gallant men will remain often in my thoughts and in my prayers always. [Applause.]

I am closing my 52 years of military service. [Applause.] When I joined the Army even before the turn of the century, it was the fulfillment of all my boyish hopes and dreams. The world has turned over many times since I took the oath on the plain at West Point, and the hopes and dreams have long since vanished. But I still remember the refrain of one of the most popular barrack ballads of that day which proclaimed most proudly that—

"Old soldiers never die; they just fade away."

And like the old soldier of that ballad, I now close my military career and just fade away—an old soldier who tried to do his duty as God gave him the light to see that duty.

Good-by.

40

Beyond Containment (1953)

JOHN FOSTER DULLES

On January 15, 1953, Dwight Eisenhower's nominee for Secretary of State, John Foster Dulles, appeared before the Senate Committee on Foreign Relations. Eisenhower had just been elected, in part, out of a popular sense that the United States was losing the Cold War to the Soviet Union. With Senator Joseph McCarthy charging that Communist conspirators had infiltrated the State Department itself, Congress was particularly sensitive to any sign of weakness in America's foreign relations. Dulles, a serious, deeply pious, and often self-righteous individual, was just the man to reassure Congress that no ground would be given to the Communists. Dulles felt that the policy of containment—keeping the Communists from further expansion—was insufficient, that perhaps it was time to "roll back" the Soviet empire.

Questions to Consider

- What was the "Communist threat"?
- What did Dulles suggest that the United States do about it?
- Could Dulles's policy have led to war?

Anticipated Changes in State Department

The Chairman. [Senator Alexander Wiley of Wisconsin] To implement the policy which you have now stated, have you in mind any specific changes you want to bring about in the State Department?

Mr. Dulles. Well, I think the most change that is needed, is a change of heart. You have got the machinery, but the spirit is the thing which counts. It is the spirit and not the letter, as you know, which, according to the Bible, is a very important thing.

The Chairman. You know your Scriptures, sir....

Communist Enslavement of Free Peoples

The Chairman. I am particularly interested in something I read recently, to the effect that you stated you were not in favor of the policy of containment. I think you advocated a more dynamic or positive policy.

Can you tell us more specifically what you have in mind? This, of course, is subject always to your own objections, if you think the question goes beyond a matter of qualifications.

Mr. Dulles. There are a number of policy matters which I would prefer to discuss with the committee in executive session, but I have no objection to saying in open session what I have said before: namely, that we shall never have a secure peace or a happy world so long as Soviet communism dominates one-third of all of the peoples that there are, and is in the process of trying at least to extend its rule to many others.

These people who are enslaved are people who deserve to be free, and who, from our own selfish standpoint, ought to be free because if they are the servile instruments of aggressive despotism, they will eventually be welded into a force which will be highly dangerous to ourselves and to all of the free world....

Therefore, we must always have in mind the liberation of these captive peoples. Now, liberation does not

Source: *Nomination of John Foster Dulles, Secretary of State-Designate: Hearing Before the Committee on Foreign Relations, United States Senate,* 83d Congress, 1st session (1953), pp. 4–6, 10–12.

mean a war of liberation. Liberation can be accomplished by processes short of war. We have, as one example, not an ideal example, but it illustrates my point, the defection of Yugoslavia, under Tito from the domination of Soviet communism.

Well, that rule of Tito is not one which we admire, and it has many aspects of despotism, itself; but at least it illustrates that it is possible to disintegrate this present monolithic structure which, as I say, represents approximately one-third of all the people that there are in the world....

The present tie between China and Moscow is an unholy arrangement which is contrary to the traditions, the hopes, the aspirations of the Chinese people. Certainly we cannot tolerate a continuance of that, or a welding of the 450 million people of China into the servile instruments of Soviet aggression....

Therefore, a policy which only aims at containing Russia where it now is, is, in itself, an unsound policy; but it is a policy which is bound to fail because a purely defensive policy never wins against an aggressive policy. If our only policy is to stay where we are, we will be driven back. It is only by keeping alive the hope of liberation, by taking advantage of that wherever opportunity arises, that we will end this terrible peril which dominates the world, which imposes upon us such terrible sacrifices and so great fears for the future. But all of this can be done and must be done in ways which will not provoke a general war, or in ways which will not provoke an insurrection which would be crushed with bloody violence, such as was the case, for example, when the Russians instigated the Polish revolt, under General Bor, and merely sat by and watched them when the Germans exterminated those who were revolting.

Peaceful Liberation

It must be and can be a peaceful process, but those who do not believe that results can be accomplished by moral pressures, by the weight of propaganda, just do not know what they are talking about.

I ask you to recall the fact that Soviet communism, itself, has spread from controlling 200 million people some 7 years ago to controlling 800 million people today, and it has done that by methods of political warfare, psychological warfare and propaganda, and it has not actually used the Red Army as an open aggressive force in accomplishing that.

Surely what they can accomplish, we can accomplish.

Surely if they can use moral and psychological force, we can use it; and, to take a negative defeatist attitude is not an approach which is conducive to our own welfare, or in conformity with our own historical ideas....

I always recall President Lincoln's remark, when he was on the way to Washington to be inaugurated. He spoke of the Declaration of Independence, and said:

> To me, this Declaration means liberty, not alone to the people of this country, but hope for the world, for all future time.

And, he added:

> I would rather be assassinated on the spot than surrender that principle of the Declaration of Independence.

I think that is a good thing to remember.

Senator [Charles] *Tobey* [of New Hampshire]. Mr. Chairman.

The Chairman.   Let me pursue this further—

Senator Tobey.   I was going to make a comment to Mr. Dulles that would be helpful to him.

The Chairman.   Go ahead.

Scriptural Quotation

Senator Tobey.   Mr. Dulles, you are a man who knows your Bible and your Scripture. You will perhaps remember that passage in the Holy Bible where it was said:

> Have no fellowship with the unfruitful work of darkness, but rather reprove them, for it is a shame even to speak of those things which are done of them in secret. (Ephesians 5: 11–12)

I think that applies to the Soviets....

Senator [H. Alexander] *Smith* of New Jersey. ...In reading some of your addresses, Mr. Dulles, especially the recent address you made, I believe, before a church group in December, I gained the impression that you realize that the big conflict in the world is between the spiritual forces based on faith in a divine power, and the atheism and materialism of the Communists. An ideological struggle is before us, I believe, which concern[s] all our policies and everything that we do.

Is that a fair statement of your position, or do you wish to develop it further?

Communist Threat

Mr. Dulles.   The threat of Soviet communism, in my opinion, is not only the gravest threat that ever faced the United States, but the gravest threat that has ever faced what we call western civilization, or, indeed, any civilization which was dominated by a spiritual faith.

Soviet communism is atheistic in its philosophy and materialistic. It believes that human beings are nothing more than somewhat superior animals, that they have no soul, no spirit, no right to personal dignity, and that the best kind of a world is that world which is organized as a well-managed farm is organized, where certain animals are taken out to pasture, and they are fed and brought back and milked, and they are given a barn as shelter over their heads, and that is a form of society which is most conducive to the material welfare of mankind, that is their opinion. That can be made into a persuasive doctrine, if one does not believe in the spiritual nature of man.

If you do believe in the spiritual nature of man, it is a doctrine which is utterly unacceptable and wholly irreconcilable....

I do not see how, as long as Soviet communism holds those views, and holds also the belief that its destiny is to spread those views throughout the world, and to organize the whole world on that basis, there can be any permanent reconciliation.

That does not exclude the possibility of coming to working agreements of a limited character, but basically, between the doctrine of Soviet communism, and the doctrine of a Christian or Jewish or, indeed, any religion, this is an irreconcilable conflict.

Senator Smith of New Jersey.   I am glad to get your statement of that, because it seemed, from my reading of your speech, that you felt that way. Since I feel very much the same way, I am interested in your views....

Now, Mr. Dulles, the question has been raised in some quarters as to whether you are more interested in one part of the world than in others. On the other hand, I have understood you to take the position of the global nature of present world affairs, rather than particular emphasis on any one area.

Will you give us your thought on that?

Mr. Dulles.   In my opinion, under the modern conditions, both of open warfare and, you might call it, political warfare, there is no geographical area which is effectively defensible without regard to the other. In other words, a condition of interdependence has been forced upon us by modern conditions, and the use to which modern facilities are put by the Soviet Communists.

There are those in Europe, for example, who believe or seem to believe that Europe alone could be made defensible; just as there are people who believe that the United States alone can be made defensible.

We call those people a name, I never liked the use of such names, because they lend themselves to misinterpretation and unfair use, but such people have been called isolationists.

I say, the people in Europe who believe that Europe alone can be defensible, without regard to what happens in Asia and Africa, they are even more blind than those who believe that our own country can be made defensible without regard to what goes on anywhere else.

Global Strategy

Now, the Soviet Communist strategy is global, and to the extent that we give priority to any area, it can only be because the strategy of a global conspiracy requires us to do so.

I think we have been neglectful in failing to take account of the fact that Soviet Communist policy has, from the first time it was laid out fully, I think it was by Stalin in 1924, in a lecture he gave called the Foundations of Leninism, and the charter on strategy and tactics is one of the most fruitful things to study that I know of, and there he makes perfectly clear that in the first instance, the program is to dominate what he calls the colonial and dependent areas, China, India, the Middle East, and that if he can get control of what he calls these reserves of the west, then the west will be weakened and so encircled, itself, that it will fall almost without a struggle to the Communists.

I think there has been a tendency to ignore the fact that Soviet Russia has what you might call an Asia-first policy. That does not mean, of course, that I have any feeling that Asia is more important than Europe. Europe is extremely important, although not just because of its great material power. If you added the industrial power and resources of Western Europe to the Soviet Union, it would very sharply change the balance of material power in the world's steel productive capacity, and things of that sort. That is something that must not happen; but, also it must not happen that that area is so surrounded that it is unable to defend itself. Therefore, we must have a global strategy which takes into account the global strategy of our enemies....

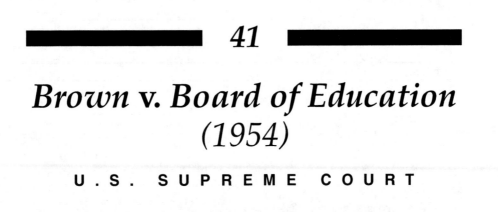

41

Brown v. Board of Education (1954)

U.S. SUPREME COURT

Charles Houston, head of the National Association for the Advancement of Colored People's Legal Defense Fund from 1933 until his death in 1950, devoted his life to fighting the Supreme Court's "separate but equal" decision in *Plessy* v. *Ferguson.* Houston developed the strategy of slowly whittling away at *Plessy* by demonstrating that separate could never be equal. Appreciating the centrality of education in American life, Houston concentrated his efforts there, traveling through the South with his brilliant student, Thurgood Marshall, filming dilapidated black schools and gathering information for his appeals. Marshall took over from Houston in 1950, building on Houston's initial successes. Marshall first argued the case against the Board of Education of Topeka, Kansas, in 1952. With the Court divided over whether to overturn *Plessy,* the justices asked both sides to reargue the case again in the October 1953 term, paying special attention to the intention of the Fourteenth Amendment. The sudden death of Chief Justice Fred Vinson, who had opposed overturning *Plessy,* led to the appointment of a new Chief Justice, the governor of California, Earl Warren. Warren crafted a unanimous decision in favor of putting an end to segregated education by focusing on the question of the harm done to black children, relying on sociological evidence and placing much of the argument in his footnotes. Probably no decision since *Plessy* has had such a long-range impact on the United States.

Questions to Consider

- Why could separate not be equal?
- Is the Court effectively overturning *Plessy* v. *Ferguson* or simply limiting its reach?
- How does the Court propose to desegregate the nation's schools?

Mr. Chief Justice Warren delivered the opinion of the Court.

These cases come to us from the States of Kansas, South Carolina, Virginia, and Delaware. They are premised on different facts and different local conditions, but a common legal question justifies their consideration together in this consolidated opinion.[1]

In each of the cases, minors of the Negro race, through their legal representatives, seek the aid of the courts in obtaining admission to the public schools of their community on a nonsegregated basis. In each instance, they had been denied admission to schools attended by white children under laws requiring or permitting segregation according to race. This segrega-

---

Source: 347 *U.S. Reports* (Washington, D.C., 1954), pp. 483–496.

[1] In the Kansas case, *Brown* v. *Board of Education,* the plaintiffs are Negro children of elementary school age residing in Topeka. They brought this action in the United States District Court for the District of Kansas to enjoin enforcement of a Kansas statute which permits, but does not require, cities of more than 15,000 population to maintain separate school facilities for Negro and white students. Kan. Gen. Stat. § 72–1724 (1949). Pursuant to that authority, the Topeka Board of Education elected to establish segregated elementary schools. Other public schools in the community, however, are operated on a nonsegregated basis. The three-judge District Court, convened under 28 U. S. C. §§ 2281 and 2284, found that segregation in public education has a detrimental effect upon Negro children, but denied relief on the ground that the Negro and white schools were substantially equal with respect to buildings, transportation, curricula, and educational qualifications of teachers. 98 F. Supp. 797. The case is here on direct appeal under 28 U. S. C. § 1253.... [There were three additional cases being considered on appeal, *Briggs* v. *Elliott* (South Carolina), *Davis* v. *County School Board* (Virginia), and *Gebhart* v. *Belton* (Delaware).—Ed.]

tion was alleged to deprive the plaintiffs of the equal protection of the laws under the Fourteenth Amendment. In each of the cases other than the Delaware case, a three-judge federal district court denied relief to the plaintiffs on the so-called "separate but equal" doctrine announced by this Court in *Plessy* v. *Ferguson,* 163 U. S. 537. Under that doctrine, equality of treatment is accorded when the races are provided substantially equal facilities, even though these facilities be separate. In the Delaware case, the Supreme Court of Delaware adhered to that doctrine, but ordered that the plaintiffs be admitted to the white schools because of their superiority to the Negro schools.

The plaintiffs contend that segregated public schools are not "equal" and cannot be made "equal," and that hence they are deprived of the equal protection of the laws. Because of the obvious importance of the question presented, the Court took jurisdiction. Argument was heard in the 1952 Term, and reargument was heard this Term on certain questions propounded by the Court.

Reargument was largely devoted to the circumstances surrounding the adoption of the Fourteenth Amendment in 1868. It covered exhaustively consideration of the Amendment in Congress, ratification by the states, then existing practices in racial segregation, and the views of proponents and opponents of the Amendment. This discussion and our own investigation convince us that, although these sources cast some light, it is not enough to resolve the problem with which we are faced. At best, they are inconclusive. The most avid proponents of the post-War Amendments undoubtedly intended them to remove all legal distinctions among "all persons born or naturalized in the United States." Their opponents, just as certainly, were antagonistic to both the letter and the spirit of the Amendments and wished them to have the most limited effect. What others in Congress and the state legislatures had in mind cannot be determined with any degree of certainty.

An additional reason for the inconclusive nature of the Amendment's history, with respect to segregated schools, is the status of public education at that time.[2] In the South, the movement toward free common schools, supported by general taxation, had not yet taken hold. Education of white children was largely in the hands of private groups. Education of Negroes was almost nonexistent, and practically all of the race were illiterate. In fact, any education of Negroes was forbidden by law in some states. Today, in contrast, many Negroes have achieved outstanding success in the arts and sciences as well as in the business and professional world. It is true that public school education at the time of the Amendment had advanced further in the North, but the effect of the Amendment on Northern States was generally ignored in the congressional debates. Even in the North, the conditions of public education did not approximate those existing today. The curriculum was usually rudimentary; ungraded schools were common in rural areas; the school term was but three months a year in many states; and compulsory school attendance was virtually unknown. As a consequence, it is not surprising that there should be so little in the history of the Fourteenth Amendment relating to its intended effect on public education.

In the first cases in this Court construing the Fourteenth Amendment, decided shortly after its adoption, the Court interpreted it as proscribing all state-imposed discriminations against the Negro race.[3] The doctrine of "separate but equal" did not make its appearance in this Court until 1896 in the case of *Plessy* v. *Ferguson, supra,* involving not education but transporta-

tion.[4] American courts have since labored with the doctrine for over half a century. In this Court, there have been six cases involving the "separate but equal" doctrine in the field of public education. In *Cumming* v. *County Board of Education,* 175 U. S. 528, and *Gong Lum* v. *Rice,* 275 U. S. 78, the validity of the doctrine itself was not challenged.[5] In more recent cases, all on the graduate school level, inequality was found in that specific benefits enjoyed by white students were denied to Negro students of the same educational qualifications. *Missouri ex rel. Gaines* v. *Canada,* 305 U. S. 337; *Sipuel* v. *Oklahoma,* 332 U. S. 631; *Sweatt* v. *Painter,* 339 U. S. 629; *McLaurin* v. *Oklahoma State Regents,* 339 U. S. 637. In none of these cases was it necessary to re-examine the doctrine to grant relief to the Negro plaintiff. And in *Sweatt* v. *Painter, supra,* the Court expressly reserved decision on the question whether *Plessy* v. *Ferguson* should be held inapplicable to public education.

In the instant cases, that question is directly presented. Here, unlike *Sweatt* v. *Painter,* there are findings below that the Negro and white schools involved have been equalized, or are being equalized, with respect to buildings, curricula, qualifications and salaries of teachers, and other "tangible" factors. Our decision, therefore, cannot turn on merely a comparison of these tangible factors in the Negro and white schools involved in each of the cases. We must look instead to the effect of segregation itself on public education.

In approaching this problem, we cannot turn the clock back to 1868 when the Amendment was adopted, or even to 1896 when *Plessy* v. *Ferguson* was written. We must consider public education in the light of its full development and its present place in American life throughout the Nation. Only in this way can it be determined if segregation in public schools deprives these plaintiffs of the equal protection of the laws.

---

[2] For a general study of the development of public education prior to the Amendment, see Butts and Cremin, A History of Education in American Culture (1953), Pts. I, II; Cubberley, Public Education in the United States (1934 ed.), cc. II–XII. School practices current at the time of the adoption of the Fourteenth Amendment are described in Butts and Cremin, *supra,* at 269–275; Cubberley, *supra,* at 288–339, 408–431.... Although the demand for free public schools followed substantially the same pattern in both the North and the South, the development in the South did not begin to gain momentum until about 1850, some twenty years after that in the North.... The low status of Negro education in all sections of the country, both before and immediately after the War, is described in Beale, A History of Freedom of Teaching in American Schools (1941), 112–132, 175–195. Compulsory school attendance laws were not generally adopted until after the ratification of the Fourteenth Amendment, and it was not until 1918 that such laws were in force in all the states. Cubberley, *supra,* at 563–565.

[3] *Slaughter-House Cases,* 16 Wall. 36, 67–72 (1873); *Strauder* v. *West Virginia,* 100 U. S. 303, 307–308 (1880)...

---

[4] The doctrine apparently originated in *Roberts* v. *City of Boston,* 59 Mass. 198, 206 (1850), upholding school segregation against attack as being violative of a state constitutional guarantee of equality. Segregation in Boston public schools was eliminated in 1855. Mass. Acts 1855, c. 256. But elsewhere in the North segregation in public education has persisted in some communities until recent years. It is apparent that such segregation has long been a nationwide problem, not merely one of sectional concern.

[5] In the *Cumming* case, Negro taxpayers sought an injunction requiring the defendant school board to discontinue the operation of a high school for white children until the board resumed operation of a high school for Negro children. Similarly, in the *Gong Lum* case, the plaintiff, a child of Chinese descent, contended only that state authorities had misapplied the doctrine by classifying him with Negro children and requiring him to attend a Negro school.

Today, education is perhaps the most important function of state and local governments. Compulsory school attendance laws and the great expenditures for education both demonstrate our recognition of the importance of education to our democratic society. It is required in the performance of our most basic public responsibilities, even service in the armed forces. It is the very foundation of good citizenship. Today it is a principal instrument in awakening the child to cultural values, in preparing him for later professional training, and in helping him to adjust normally to his environment. In these days, it is doubtful that any child may reasonably be expected to succeed in life if he is denied the opportunity of an education. Such an opportunity, where the state has undertaken to provide it, is a right which must be made available to all on equal terms.

We come then to the question presented: Does segregation of children in public schools solely on the basis of race, even though the physical facilities and other "tangible" factors may be equal, deprive the children of the minority group of equal educational opportunities? We believe that it does.

In *Sweatt* v. *Painter, supra,* in finding that a segregated law school for Negroes could not provide them equal educational opportunities, this Court relied in large part on "those qualities which are incapable of objective measurement but which make for greatness in a law school." In *McLaurin* v. *Oklahoma State Regents, supra,* the Court, in requiring that a Negro admitted to a white graduate school be treated like all other students, again resorted to intangible considerations: "...his ability to study, to engage in discussions and exchange views with other students, and, in general, to learn his profession." Such considerations apply with added force to children in grade and high schools. To separate them from others of similar age and qualifications solely because of their race generates a feeling of inferiority as to their status in the community that may affect their hearts and minds in a way unlikely ever to be undone. The effect of this separation on their educational opportunities was well stated by a finding in the Kansas case by a court which nevertheless felt compelled to rule against the Negro plaintiffs:

> Segregation of white and colored children in public schools has a detrimental effect upon the colored children. The impact is greater when it has the sanction of the law; for the policy of separating the races is usually interpreted as denoting the inferiority of the negro group. A sense of inferiority affects the motivation of a child to learn. Segregation with the sanction of law, therefore, has a tendency to [retard] the educational and mental development of negro children and to deprive them of some of the benefits

they would receive in a racial[ly] integrated school system.

Whatever may have been the extent of psychological knowledge at the time of *Plessy* v. *Ferguson,* this finding is amply supported by modern authority.[6] Any language in *Plessy* v. *Ferguson* contrary to this finding is rejected.

We conclude that in the field of public education the doctrine of "separate but equal" has no place. Separate educational facilities are inherently unequal. Therefore, we hold that the plaintiffs and others similarly situated for whom the actions have been brought are, by reason of the segregation complained of, deprived of the equal protection of the laws guaranteed by the Fourteenth Amendment. This disposition makes unnecessary any discussion whether such segregation also violates the Due Process Clause of the Fourteenth Amendment.

Because these are class actions, because of the wide applicability of this decision, and because of the great variety of local conditions, the formulation of decrees in these cases presents problems of considerable complexity. On reargument, the consideration of appropriate relief was necessarily subordinated to the primary question—the constitutionality of segregation in public education. We have now announced that such segregation is a denial of the equal protection of the laws. In order that we may have the full assistance of the parties in formulating decrees, the cases will be restored to the docket, and the parties are requested to present further argument on Questions 4 and 5 previously propounded by the Court for the reargument this Term.[7] The Attorney General of the United States is again invited to participate. The Attorneys General of the states requiring or permitting segregation in public education will also be permitted to appear as *amici curiae* upon request to do so by September 15, 1954, and submission of briefs by October 1, 1954.

It is so ordered.

---

[6] K. B. Clark, Effect of Prejudice and Discrimination on Personality Development (Midcentury White House Conference on Children and Youth, 1950); Witmer and Kotinsky, Personality in the Making (1952), c. VI; Deutscher and Chein, The Psychological Effects of Enforced Segregation: A Survey of Social Science Opinion, 26 J. Psychol. 259 (1948); Chein, What are the Psychological Effects of Segregation Under Conditions of Equal Facilities?, 3 Int. J. Opinion and Attitude Res. 229 (1949); Brameld, Educational Costs, in Discrimination and National Welfare (MacIver, ed., 1949), 44–48; Frazier, The Negro in the United States (1949), 674–681. And see generally Myrdal, An American Dilemma (1944).

[7] "4. Assuming it is decided that segregation in public schools violates the Fourteenth Amendment...."

42

The Southern Manifesto (1956)

S A M   J .   E R V I N   a n d   O T H E R S

In 1954 the United States Supreme Court ordered an end to segregation. The *Brown v. Board of Education* decision triggered a storm of protest from white Southerners. Though the court did not specify how America's schools should desegregate, white Southern leaders were in no mood for discussion. In March 1956, a group of one hundred Southern members of Congress presented "The Southern Manifesto" to their colleagues, promising to oppose any efforts to integrate their schools. Though introduced by Representative Howard W. Smith of Virginia and Senator Walter F. George of Georgia, the Manifesto seems to have been largely the work of Senator Sam Ervin of South Carolina.

Questions to Consider

- What do the representatives mean by their stated willingness "to resist forced integration by any lawful means"?
- How did *Brown* endanger the Southern way of life?

Deviation from Fundamentals of the Constitution

Mr. [Howard W.] Smith of Virginia. ...Mr. Speaker, in the life of a nation there come times when it behooves her people to pause and consider how far she may have drifted from her moorings, and in prayerful contemplation review the consequences that may ensue from a continued deviation from the course charted by the founders of that nation.

The framework of this Nation, designed in the inspired genius of our forefathers, was set forth in a Constitution, born of tyranny and oppression in a background of bitter strife and anguish and resting upon two fundamental principles:

Source: *The Congressional Record*, 84th Congress, 2nd Session, vol. 102, pt. 4, pp. 4515–4516, 4461–4462.

First, that this was a Government of three separate and independent departments, legislative, executive, and judicial, each supreme in, but limited to, the functions ascribed to it.

Second, that the component parts should consist of independent sovereign States enjoying every attribute and power of autonomous sovereignty save only those specific powers enumerated in the Constitution and surrendered to the Central Government for the better government and security of all.

When repeated deviation from these fundamentals by one of the three departments threatens the liberties of the people and the destruction of the reserved powers of the respective States, in contravention of the principles of that Constitution which all officials of all the three departments are sworn to uphold, it is meet, and the sacred obligation of those devoted to the preservation of the basic limitations on the power of the Central Government to apprise their associates of their alarm and the specific deviations that threaten to change our form of government, without the consent of the governed, in the manner provided by the Constitution.

Assumed power exercised in one field today becomes a precedent and an invitation to indulge in further assumption of powers in other fields tomorrow.

Therefore, when the temporary occupants of high office in the judicial branch deviate from the limitations imposed by the Constitution, some members of the legislative branch feel impelled to call the attention of their colleagues and the country to the dangers inherent in interpretations of the Constitution reversing long established and accepted law and based on expediency at the sacrifice of consistency.

The sentiments here expressed are solely my own, but there is being presented at this hour in the other body by Senator George on behalf of 19 Members of that body, and in this body by myself on behalf of 81 Members of this body, a joint declaration of constitutional principles, which, on behalf of the signatory Members of the House, I ask to be inserted in the Record at the conclusion of my remarks....

Declaration of Constitutional Principles

The unwarranted decision of the Supreme Court in the public school cases is now bearing the fruit always produced when men substitute naked power for established law.

The Founding Fathers gave us a Constitution of checks and balances because they realized the inescapable lesson of history that no man or group of men can be safely entrusted with unlimited power. They framed this Constitution with its provisions for change by amendment in order to secure the fundamentals of government against the dangers of temporary popular passion or the personal predilections of public office-holders.

We regard the decision of the Supreme Court in the school cases as a clear abuse of judicial power. It climaxes a trend in the Federal judiciary undertaking to legislate, in derogation of the authority of Congress, and to encroach upon the reserved rights of the States and the people.

The original Constitution does not mention education. Neither does the 14th amendment nor any other amendment. The debates preceding the submission of the 14th amendment clearly show that there was no intent that it should affect the systems of education maintained by the States.

The very Congress which proposed the amendment subsequently provided for segregated schools in the District of Columbia.

When the amendment was adopted, in 1868, there were 37 States of the Union. Every one of the 26 States that had any substantial racial differences among its people either approved the operation of segregated schools already in existence or subsequently established such schools by action of the same lawmaking body which considered the 14th amendment.

As admitted by the Supreme Court in the public school case (*Brown* v. *Board of Education*), the doctrine of separate but equal schools "apparently originated in *Roberts* v. *City of Boston*…(1849), upholding school segregation against attack as being violative of a State constitutional guarantee of equality." This constitutional doctrine began in the North—not in the South, and it was followed not only in Massachusetts, but in Connecticut, New York, Illinois, Indiana, Michigan, Minnesota, New Jersey, Ohio, Pennsylvania, and other northern States until they, exercising their rights as States through the constitutional processes of local self-government, changed their school systems.

In the case of *Plessy* v. *Ferguson*, in 1896, the Supreme Court expressly declared that under the 14th amendment no person was denied any of his rights if the States provided separate but equal public facilities. This decision has been followed in many other cases. It is notable that the Supreme Court, speaking through Chief Justice Taft, a former President of the United States, unanimously declared, in 1927, in *Lum* v. *Rice*, that the "separate but equal" principle is "within the discretion of the State in regulating its public schools and does not conflict with the 14th amendment."

This interpretation, restated time and again, became a part of the life of the people of many of the States and confirmed their habits, customs, traditions, and way of life. It is founded on elemental humanity and common-sense, for parents should not be deprived by Government of the right to direct the lives and education of their own children.

Though there has been no constitutional amendment or act of Congress changing this established legal principle almost a century old, the Supreme Court of the United States, with no legal basis for such action, undertook to exercise their naked judicial power and substituted their personal political and social ideas for the established law of the land.

This unwarranted exercise of power by the Court, contrary to the Constitution, is creating chaos and confusion in the States principally affected. It is destroying the amicable relations between the white and Negro races that have been created through 90 years of patient effort by the good people of both races. It has planted hatred and suspicion where there has been heretofore friendship and understanding.

Without regard to the consent of the governed, outside agitators are threatening immediate and revolutionary changes in our public-school systems. If done, this is certain to destroy the system of public education in some of the States.

With the gravest concern for the explosive and dangerous condition created by this decision and inflamed by outside meddlers:

We reaffirm our reliance on the Constitution as the fundamental law of the land.

We decry the Supreme Court's encroachments on rights reserved to the States and to the people, contrary to established law and to the Constitution.

We commend the motives of those States which have declared the intention to resist forced integration by any lawful means.

We appeal to the States and people who are not directly affected by these decisions to consider the constitutional principles involved against the time when they, too, on issues vital to them, may be the victims of judicial encroachment.

Even though we constitute a minority in the present Congress, we have full faith that a majority of the American people believe in the dual system of Government which has enabled us to achieve our greatness and will in time demand that the reserved rights of the State and of the people be made secure against judicial usurpation.

We pledge ourselves to use all lawful means to bring about a reversal of this decision which is contrary to the Constitution and to prevent the use of force in its implementation.

In this trying period, as we all seek to right this wrong, we appeal to our people not to be provoked by the agitators and troublemakers invading our States and to scrupulously refrain from disorders and lawless acts.

Signed by:

[NINETEEN] MEMBERS OF THE
UNITED STATES SENATE
[EIGHTY-ONE] MEMBERS OF THE UNITED STATES
HOUSE OF REPRESENTATIVES

Debate in the Senate

Mr. [Strom] Thurmond [of South Carolina].   Mr. President, I am constrained to make a few remarks at this time because I believe a historic event has taken place today in the Senate.

The action of this group of Senators in signing and issuing a Declaration of Constitutional Principles with regard to the Supreme Court decision of May 17, 1954, is most significant. The signers of this declaration represent a large area of this Nation and a great segment of its population. Solemnly and simply we have stated our position on a grave matter so as to make clear there are facts that opposing propagandists have neglected in their zeal to persuade the world there is but one side to this matter.

In suggesting that a meeting of like-minded Senators be held, it was my thought that we should formulate a statement of unity to present our views and the views of our constituents on this subject. My hope also was that the statement issued should be of such nature as to gain the support of all people who love the Constitution; that they would see in this instance the danger of other future encroachments by the Federal Government into fields reserved to the States and the people.

My people in South Carolina sought to avoid any disruption of the harmony which has existed for generations between the white and the Negro races. The effort by outside agitators to end segregation in the public schools has made it difficult to sustain the long-time harmony.

These agitators employed professional racist lawyers with funds contributed by persons who were permitted to deduct the contributions from their taxes. The organization established to receive the funds also enjoys the status of freedom from taxation.

Except for these troublemakers, I believe our people of both races in South Carolina would have continued to progress harmoniously together. Educational progress in South Carolina has been marked by $200 million worth of fine school buildings in the past 4 years, providing true equality, not only for white and Negro pupils, but also for urban and rural communities.

In the South Carolina school district where one of the segregation cases was instigated, the Negro schools are better than the schools for white children. Yet the Negroes continue to seek admission to schools for the white race.

This is sufficient proof that, while South Carolinians of both races are interested in the education of their children, the agitators who traveled a thousand miles to foment trouble are interested in something else. The "something else" they are interested in is the mixing of the races.

They may as well recognize that they cannot accomplish by judicial legislation what they could never succeed in doing by constitutional amendment.

Historical evidence positively refutes the decision of the Supreme Court in the school-segregation cases.

The 39th Congress, which in 1866 framed the 14th amendment to the Constitution—the amendment which contains the equal protection clause—also provided for the operation of segregated schools in the District of Columbia. This is positive evidence that the Congress did not intend to prohibit segregation by the 14th amendment.

The Supreme Court admitted in its opinion in the school cases that "education is perhaps the most important function of State and local governments." But the Court failed to observe the consti[tu]tional guaranties, including the 10th amendment, which reserve control of such matters to the States.

If the Supreme Court could disregard the provisions of the Constitution which were specifically designed to safeguard the rights of the States, we might as well not have a written Constitution. Not only did the Court disregard the Constitution and the historical evidence supporting that revered document; it also disregarded previous decisions of the Court itself.

Between the decision in Plessy against Ferguson in 1896 and the reversal of that opinion on May 17, 1954, 157 cases were decided on the basis of the separate-but-equal doctrine. The United States Supreme Court rendered 11 opinions on that basis; the United States court of appeals 13; United States district courts 27; and State supreme courts, including the District of Columbia, 106.

Such disregard for established doctrine could be justified only if additional evidence were presented which was not available when the earlier decisions were rendered.

No additional evidence was presented to the Court to show the earlier decisions to be wrong. Therefore, the decision handed down on May 17, 1954, was contrary to the Constitution and to legal precedent.

If the Court can say that certain children shall go to certain schools, the Court might also soon attempt to direct the courses to be taught in these schools. It might undertake to establish qualifications for teachers.

I reject the philosophy of the sociologists that the Supreme Court has any authority over local public schools, supported in part by State funds.

The Court's segregation decision has set a dangerous precedent. If, in the school cases, the Court can by decree create a new constitutional provision, not in the written document, it might also disregard the Constitution in other matters. Other constitutional guaranties could be destroyed by new decrees.

I respect the Court as an institution and as an instrument of Government created by the Constitution. I do not and cannot have regard for the nine Justices who rendered a decision so clearly contrary to the Constitution.

The propagandists have tried to convince the world that the States and the people should bow meekly to the decree of the Supreme Court. I say it would be the submission of cowardice if we failed to use every lawful means to protect the rights of the people.

For more than a half a century the propagandists and the agitators applied every pressure of which they were capable to bring about a reversal of the separate-but-equal doctrine. They were successful, but they now contend that the very methods they used are unfair. They want the South to accept the dictation of the Court without seeking recourse. We shall not do so.

I hope all the people of this Nation who believe in the Constitution—North, South, East, and West—will support every lawful effort to have the decision reversed. The Court followed textbooks instead of the Constitution in arriving at the decision.

We are free, morally and legally, to fight the decision. We must oppose to the end every attempt to encroach on the rights of the people.

Legislation by judicial decree, if permitted to go unchallenged, could destroy the rights of the Congress, the rights of the States, and the rights of the people themselves.

When the Court handed down its decision in the school-segregation cases, it attempted to wipe out constitutional or statutory provisions in 17 States and the District of Columbia. Thus, the Court attempted to legislate in a field which even the Congress had no right to invade. A majority of the States affected would never enact such legislation through their legislatures. A vast majority of the people in these States would staunchly oppose such legislation.

The people and the States must find ways and means of preserving segregation in the schools. Each attempt to break down segregation must be fought with every legal weapon at our disposal.

At the same time, equal school facilities for the races must be maintained. The States are not seeking to avoid responsibility. They want to meet all due responsibility, but not under Court decrees which are not based on law.

I hope a greater understanding of the problem which has been thrust upon the South and the Nation will be sought by our colleagues who do not face the segregation problem at home. Other problems of other areas require consideration and understanding. I shall try to give full consideration to them.

All of us have heard a great deal of talk about the persecution of minority groups. The white people of the South are the greatest minority in this Nation. They deserve consideration and understanding instead of the persecution of twisted propaganda.

The people of the South love this country. In all the wars in which this Nation has engaged, no truer American patriots have been found than the people from the South.

I, for one, shall seek to present the views of my people on the floor of the Senate. I shall fight for them in whatever lawful way I can. My hope is that consideration of our views will lead to understanding and that understanding will lead to a rejection of practices contrary to the Constitution.

...*Mr. [Wayne] Morse* [of Oregon].   The hour is indeed historic. It has some of the characteristics of previous historic hours in the Senate, when there was before this body the great constitutional question as to whether or not there was to be equality of justice for all Americans, irrespective of race, color, or creed.

…A unanimous Supreme Court has handed down a decision that makes it perfectly clear that under the Constitution of the United States there cannot be discrimination between white men and black men, so far as the Constitution is concerned.

I say again today that the doctrine of interposition means nothing but nullification, and it means really a determination on the part of certain forces in this country to put themselves above the Supreme Court and above the Constitution. If the gentlemen from the South really want to take such action, let them propose a constitutional amendment that will deny to the colored people of the country equality of rights under the Constitution and see how far they will get with the American people.

Mr. President, I recognize the problems of the South. Unfortunately, I respectfully say, I think too many of our southern colleagues want to take the position that because some of us may live in the North, we have no appreciation of the problems of the South. That is contrary to the fact. But we have reached a point in our history when the great South once again will have to determine whether we are to be governed by law or whether we are to be governed or subverted by the interposition doctrine, which is the doctrine of nullification.

Mr. President, on the basis of the arguments of the proponents of the declaration of principles just submitted by a group of southern Senators you would think today Calhoun was walking and speaking on the floor of the Senate.

I think that, as patriots all, those of us representing areas outside the South, need to sit down with our brethren representing the South, and see what we can do to solve, by reasoned discussion, the great problem which the Supreme Court decision has created. But I first want to say I think it is a correct decision, a sound decision, and a decision that was long overdue.

I say, respectfully, the South has had all the time since the War Between the States to make this adjustment. That is why I am not greatly moved by these last-hour pleas of the South, "We need more time, more time, more time." How much more time is needed in order that equality of justice may be applied to the blacks as well as to the whites in America?

Mr. President, I regret that this declaration has been filed, because I respectfully say such a declaration will not bring about the unanimity of action we will need in order to help solve the school problem in the South.

I close by saying a unanimous Supreme Court, which includes in its membership men with the tradition of the South in their veins, has at long last declared that all Americans are equal, and that the flame of justice in America must burn as brightly in the homes of the blacks as in the homes of the whites.

A historic debate must take place on the floor of the Senate in the not too distant future, because in the weeks immediately ahead the Congress will have to determine whether or not we and the people of the United States shall follow the Supreme Court decision, and recognize, as was laid down in Marbury against Madison, the supremacy of the Court in protecting the American people in their constitutional rights.

Mr. [Hubert] Humphrey [of Minnesota]. Mr. President, this is a truly sad, bewildering, and difficult day in the Senate of the United States. This great body is sworn to uphold the Constitution of the United States. To be sure, on every piece of legislation we make our own individual judgments, as to whether or not we believe it is within the spirit and the letter of our great document, the Constitution.

I do feel, Mr. President, once the Supreme Court of the United States has spoken, not merely upon statutory law, but upon constitutional law, that the presumption is, and should be, that the order of the Court and the rule of the Court is the law of the land—to be obeyed and upheld.

While I do not profess to be an expert in constitutional law, I am familiar with the development of the doctrine of the power and the right of the Supreme Court of the United States to encompass within its jurisdiction the responsibility for ruling upon the constitutionality of State statutes which may or may not be in conflict with the Constitution, the power and the responsibility and the right to rule upon Federal statutes which may or may not be in conflict with the Constitution, and finally the power of the Supreme Court to interpret and to apply the language of the Constitution itself.

Mr. President, the 14th amendment is a part of the Constitution of the United States. The fact that the 14th amendment has not been applied in some specific instances throughout the past decades does not in any way weaken or vitiate this power of law.…

Mr. President, this amendment is all important in our constitutional structure. For years it has been interpreted and primarily applied to the economic interests of our country, under the doctrine of what we call reasonableness, "due process of law" being interpreted as a reasonable rule of law. It was applied that way to economic matters and to large corporate interests.

The Supreme Court, in the case involving school segregation, applied the principle to citizens of the United States, to human beings rather than corporate beings, to people rather than property.

So, Mr. President, I must say with all due respect—and I certainly respect the knowledge and experience of my colleagues—that the Supreme Court did not write the law; it merely applied existing constitutional law. It applied the principle of human equality—equal treatment under the law—Mr. President, which, since July 4, 1776, has been declared as the fundamental tenet of our Republic....

43

Inaugural Address (1961)

JOHN F. KENNEDY

John F. Kennedy was the youngest man ever elected to the presidency. For many Americans, Kennedy's narrow victory symbolized the dawning of a new era in the history of the United States. Kennedy spoke to that image in his inaugural address, stating that "a new generation" had taken responsibility for America's future. Kennedy's speech promised hope for the world, backed by the awesome power of the United States. Both the hope and power would seem meaningless within a few short years.

Questions to Consider

- What does Kennedy mean by insisting that people should "ask what you can do for your country"?

- Is this speech an idealistic call for peace or another example of Cold War militarism?

Mr. Chief Justice, President Eisenhower, Vice President Nixon, President Truman, reverend clergy, fellow citizens, we observe today not a victory of party, but a celebration of freedom—symbolizing an end, as well as a beginning—signifying renewal, as well as change. For I have sworn before you and Almighty God the same solemn oath our forebears prescribed nearly a century and three quarters ago.

The world is very different now. For man holds in his mortal hands the power to abolish all forms of human poverty and all forms of human life. And yet the same revolutionary beliefs for which our forebears fought are still at issue around the globe—the belief that the rights of man come not from the generosity of the state, but from the hand of God.

We dare not forget today that we are the heirs of that first revolution. Let the word go forth from this time and place, to friend and foe alike, that the torch has been passed to a new generation of Americans—born in this century, tempered by war, disciplined by a hard and bitter peace, proud of our ancient heritage—and unwilling to witness or permit the slow undoing of those human rights to which this Nation has always been committed, and to which we are committed today at home and around the world.

Let every nation know, whether it wishes us well or ill, that we shall pay any price, bear any burden, meet any hardship, support any friend, oppose any foe, in order to assure the survival and the success of liberty.

Source: *Inaugural Addresses of the Presidents of the United States* (Washington, D.C., 1961), pp. 267–270.

This much we pledge—and more.

To those old allies whose cultural and spiritual origins we share, we pledge the loyalty of faithful friends. United, there is little we cannot do in a host of cooperative ventures. Divided, there is little we can do—for we dare not meet a powerful challenge at odds and split asunder.

To those new States whom we welcome to the ranks of the free, we pledge our words that one form of colonial control shall not have passed away merely to be replaced by a far greater iron tyranny. We shall not always expect to find them supporting our view. But we shall always hope to find them strongly supporting their own freedom—and to remember that, in the past, those who foolishly sought power by riding the back of the tiger ended up inside.

To those peoples in the huts and villages across the globe struggling to break the bonds of mass misery, we pledge our best efforts to help them help themselves, for whatever period is required—not because the Communists may be doing it, not because we seek their votes, but because it is right. If a free society cannot help the many who are poor, it cannot save the few who are rich.

To our sister republics south of our border, we offer a special pledge—to convert our good words into good deeds, in a new alliance for progress, to assist free men and free governments in casting off the chains of poverty. But this peaceful revolution of hope cannot become the prey of hostile powers. Let all our neighbors know that we shall join with them to oppose aggression or subversion anywhere in the Americas. And let every other power know that this hemisphere intends to remain the master of its own house.

To that world assembly of sovereign states, the United Nations, our last best hope in an age where the instruments of war have far outpaced the instruments of peace, we renew our pledge of support—to prevent it from becoming merely a forum for invective—to strengthen its shield of the new and the weak—and to enlarge the area in which its writ may run.

Finally, to those nations who would make themselves our adversary, we offer not a pledge but a request: that both sides begin anew the quest for peace, before the dark powers of destruction unleashed by science engulf all humanity in planned or accidental self-destruction.

We dare not tempt them with weakness. For only when our arms are sufficient beyond doubt can we be certain beyond doubt that they will never be employed.

But neither can two great and powerful groups of nations take comfort from our present course—both sides overburdened by the cost of modern weapons, both sides rightly alarmed by the steady spread of the deadly atom, yet both racing to alter that uncertain balance of terror that stays the hand of mankind's final war.

So let us begin anew—remembering on both sides that civility is not a sign of weakness, and sincerity is always subject to proof. *Let us never negotiate out of fear. But let us never fear to negotiate.*

Let both sides explore what problems unite us instead of laboring those problems which divide us.

Let both sides, for the first time, formulate serious and precise proposals for the inspection and control of arms—and bring the absolute power to destroy other nations under the absolute control of all nations.

Let both sides seek to invoke the wonders of science instead of its terrors. Together let us explore the stars, conquer the deserts, eradicate disease, tap the ocean depths, and encourage the arts and commerce.

Let both sides unite to heed in all corners of the earth the command of Isaiah—to "undo the heavy burdens and to let the oppressed go free."

And if a beachhead of cooperation may push back the jungle of suspicion, let both sides join in creating a new endeavor, not a new balance of power, but a new world of law, where the strong are just and the weak secure and the peace preserved.

All this will not be finished in the first 100 days. Nor will it be finished in the first 1,000 days, nor in the life of this administration, nor even perhaps in our lifetime on this planet. But let us begin.

In your hands, my fellow citizens, more than in mine, will rest the final success or failure of our course. Since this country was founded, each generation of Americans has been summoned to give testimony to its national loyalty. The graves of young Americans who answered the call to service are found around the globe.

Now the trumpet summons us again—not as a call to bear arms, though arms we need; not as a call to battle, though embattled we are; but a call to bear the burden of a long twilight struggle, year in, and year out, "rejoicing in hope, patient in tribulation"—a struggle against the common enemies of man: tyranny, poverty, disease, and war itself.

Can we forge against these enemies a grand and global alliance, North and South, East and West, that can assure a more fruitful life for all mankind? Will you join in that historic effort?

In the long history of the world, only a few generations have been granted the role of defending freedom in its hour of maximum danger. I do not shrink from this responsibility—I welcome it. I do not believe that any of us would exchange places with any other people or any other generation. The energy, the faith, the devotion which we bring to this endeavor will light our country and all who serve it—and the glow from that fire can truly light the world.

And so, my fellow Americans, ask not what your country can do for you: Ask what you can do for your country.

My fellow citizens of the world: Ask not what America will do for you, but what together we can do for the freedom of man.

Finally, whether you are citizens of America or citizens of the world, ask of us the same high standards of strength and sacrifice which we ask of you. With a good conscience our only sure reward, with history the final judge of our deeds, let us go forth to lead the land we love, asking His blessing and His help, but knowing that here on earth God's work must truly be our own.

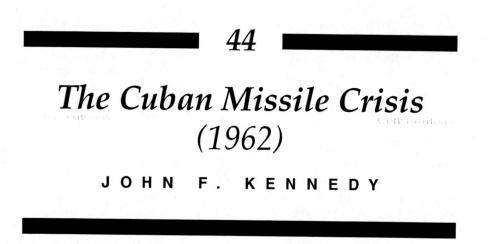

44

The Cuban Missile Crisis (1962)

JOHN F. KENNEDY

In 1962 relations between the two nuclear superpowers, the United States and the Soviet Union, steadily worsened. Both nations resumed atmospheric nuclear tests, dangerously raising levels of radiation in the air. As the Cold War rhetoric intensified, the Soviets secretly began building missile sites in Cuba. When American spy planes discovered this activity, President John F. Kennedy decided to publicly confront the Soviet leader, Nikita Khrushchev. In his nationally broadcast message, delivered on October 22, Kennedy announced a complete blockade of Cuba until the Soviets withdrew the missiles. Years later it would become clear just how close the United States came to war, as many within the White House urged preemptive strikes against the Cuban bases. For five days Americans practiced air-raid drills, and much of the world watched in horror as the two powers approached the brink. Finally, on October 27, Khrushchev indicated a willingness to back down, promising to withdraw the Cuban missiles in return for a promise from Kennedy that the United States would not invade Cuba.

Questions to Consider

- What options other than blockade were available to Kennedy?
- Did Khrushchev have a valid point when he insisted that Soviet missiles in Cuba were no different from U.S. missiles in Turkey?

Good evening, my fellow citizens:

This Government, as promised, has maintained the closest surveillance of the Soviet military buildup on the island of Cuba. Within the past week, unmistakable evidence has established the fact that a series of offensive missile sites is now in preparation on that imprisoned island. The purpose of these bases can be none other than to provide a nuclear strike capability against the Western Hemisphere.

Upon receiving the first preliminary hard information of this nature last Tuesday morning at 9 A.M., I directed that our surveillance be stepped up. And having

Source: *Public Papers of the Presidents: John F. Kennedy, 1962* (Washington, D.C., 1963), pp. 806–809.

now confirmed and completed our evaluation of the evidence and our decision on a course of action, this Government feels obliged to report this new crisis to you in fullest detail.

The characteristics of these new missile sites indicate two distinct types of installations. Several of them include medium range ballistic missiles, capable of carrying a nuclear warhead for a distance of more than 1,000 nautical miles. Each of these missiles, in short, is capable of striking Washington, D.C., the Panama Canal, Cape Canaveral, Mexico City, or any other city in the southeastern part of the United States, in Central America, or in the Caribbean area.

Additional sites not yet completed appear to be designed for intermediate range ballistic missiles—capable of traveling more than twice as far—and thus capable of striking most of the major cities in the Western Hemisphere, ranging as far north as Hudson Bay, Canada, and as far south as Lima, Peru. In addition, jet bombers, capable of carrying nuclear weapons, are now being uncrated and assembled in Cuba, while the necessary air bases are being prepared.

This urgent transformation of Cuba into an important strategic base—by the presence of these large, long-range, and clearly offensive weapons of sudden mass destruction—constitutes an explicit threat to the peace and security of all the Americas, in flagrant and deliberate defiance of the Rio Pact of 1947, the traditions of this Nation and hemisphere, the joint resolution of the 87th Congress, the Charter of the United Nations, and my own public warnings to the Soviets on September 4 and 13. This action also contradicts the repeated assurances of Soviet spokesmen, both publicly and privately delivered, that the arms buildup in Cuba would retain its original defensive character, and that the Soviet Union had no need or desire to station strategic missiles on the territory of any other nation.

The size of this undertaking makes clear that it has been planned for some months. Yet only last month, after I had made clear the distinction between any introduction of ground-to-ground missiles and the existence of defensive antiaircraft missiles, the Soviet Government publicly stated on September 11 that, and I quote, "the armaments and military equipment sent to Cuba are designed exclusively for defensive purposes," that, and I quote the Soviet Government, "there is no need for the Soviet Government to shift its weapons…for a retaliatory blow to any other country, for instance Cuba," and that, and I quote their government, "the Soviet Union has so powerful rockets to carry these nuclear warheads that there is no need to search for sites for them beyond the boundaries of the Soviet Union." That statement was false.

Only last Thursday, as evidence of this rapid offensive buildup was already in my hand, Soviet Foreign Minister Gromyko told me in my office that he was instructed to make it clear once again, as he said his government had already done, that Soviet assistance to Cuba, and I quote, "pursued solely the purpose of contributing to the defense capabilities of Cuba," that, and I quote him, "training by Soviet specialists of Cuban nationals in handling defensive armaments was by no means offensive, and if it were otherwise," Mr. Gromyko went on, "the Soviet Government would never become involved in rendering such assistance." That statement also was false.

Neither the United States of America nor the world community of nations can tolerate deliberate deception and offensive threats on the part of any nation, large or small. We no longer live in a world where only the actual firing of weapons represents a sufficient challenge to a nation's security to constitute maximum peril. Nuclear weapons are so destructive and ballistic missiles are so swift, that any substantially increased possibility of their use or any sudden change in their deployment may well be regarded as a definite threat to peace.

For many years, both the Soviet Union and the United States, recognizing this fact, have deployed strategic nuclear weapons with great care, never upsetting the precarious status quo which insured that these weapons would not be used in the absence of some vital challenge. Our own strategic missiles have never been transferred to the territory of any other nation under a cloak of secrecy and deception; and our history—unlike that of the Soviets since the end of World War II—demonstrates that we have no desire to dominate or conquer any other nation or impose our system upon its people. Nevertheless, American citizens have become adjusted to living daily on the bull's-eye of Soviet missiles located inside the U.S.S.R. or in submarines.

In that sense, missiles in Cuba add to an already clear and present danger—although it should be noted the nations of Latin America have never previously been subjected to a potential nuclear threat.

But this secret, swift, and extraordinary buildup of Communist missiles—in an area well known to have a special and historical relationship to the United States and the nations of the Western Hemisphere, in violation of Soviet assurances, and in defiance of American and hemispheric policy—this sudden, clandestine decision to station strategic weapons for the first time outside of Soviet soil—is a deliberately provocative and unjustified change in the status quo which cannot be accepted by this country, if our courage and our commitments are ever to be trusted again by either friend or foe.

The 1930's taught us a clear lesson: aggressive conduct, if allowed to go unchecked and unchallenged, ultimately leads to war. This nation is opposed to war. We are also true to our word. Our unswerving objective, therefore, must be to prevent the use of these missiles against this or any other country, and to secure their withdrawal or elimination from the Western Hemisphere.

Our policy has been one of patience and restraint, as befits a peaceful and powerful nation, which leads a worldwide alliance. We have been determined not to be diverted from our central concerns by mere irritants and fanatics. But now further action is required—and it is under way; and these actions may only be the beginning. We will not prematurely or unnecessarily risk the costs of worldwide nuclear war in which even the fruits of victory would be ashes in our mouth—but neither will we shrink from that risk at any time it must be faced.

Acting, therefore, in the defense of our own security and of the entire Western Hemisphere, and under the authority entrusted to me by the Constitution as endorsed by the resolution of the Congress, I have directed that the following *initial* steps be taken immediately:

First: To halt this offensive buildup, a strict quarantine on all offensive military equipment under shipment to Cuba is being initiated. All ships of any kind bound for Cuba from whatever nation or port will, if found to contain cargoes of offensive weapons, be turned back. This quarantine will be extended, if needed, to other types of cargo and carriers. We are not at this time, however, denying the necessities of life as the Soviets attempted to do in their Berlin blockade of 1948.

Second: I have directed the continued and increased close surveillance of Cuba and its military buildup. The foreign ministers of the OAS, in their communique of October 6, rejected secrecy on such matters in this hemisphere. Should these offensive military preparations continue, thus increasing the threat to the hemisphere, further action will be justified. I have directed the Armed Forces to prepare for any eventualities; and I trust that in the interest of both the Cuban people and the Soviet technicians at the sites, the hazards to all concerned of continuing this threat will be recognized.

Third: It shall be the policy of this Nation to regard any nuclear missile launched from Cuba against any nation in the Western Hemisphere as an attack by the Soviet Union on the United States, requiring a full retaliatory response upon the Soviet Union.

Fourth: As a necessary military precaution, I have reinforced our base at Guantanamo, evacuated today the dependents of our personnel there, and ordered additional military units to be on a standby alert basis.

Fifth: We are calling tonight for an immediate meeting of the Organ of Consultation under the Organization of American States, to consider this threat to hemispheric security and to invoke articles 6 and 8 of the Rio Treaty in support of all necessary action. The United Nations Charter allows for regional security arrangements—and the nations of this hemisphere decided long ago against the military presence of outside powers. Our other allies around the world have also been alerted.

Sixth: Under the Charter of the United Nations, we are asking tonight that an emergency meeting of the Security Council be convoked without delay to take action against this latest Soviet threat to world peace. Our resolution will call for the prompt dismantling and withdrawal of all offensive weapons in Cuba, under the supervision of U.N. observers, before the quarantine can be lifted.

Seventh and finally: I call upon Chairman Khrushchev to halt and eliminate this clandestine, reckless, and provocative threat to world peace and to stable relations between our two nations. I call upon him further to abandon this course of world domination, and to join in an historic effort to end the perilous arms race and to transform the history of man. He has an opportunity now to move the world back from the abyss of destruction—by returning to his government's own words that it had no need to station missiles outside its own territory, and withdrawing these weapons from Cuba—by refraining from any action which will widen or deepen the present crisis—and then by participating in a search for peaceful and permanent solutions.

This Nation is prepared to present its case against the Soviet threat to peace, and our own proposals for a peaceful world, at any time and in any forum—in the OAS, in the United Nations, or in any other meeting that could be useful—without limiting our freedom of action. We have in the past made strenuous efforts to limit the spread of nuclear weapons. We have proposed the elimination of all arms and military bases in a fair and effective disarmament treaty. We are prepared to discuss new proposals for the removal of tensions on both sides—including the possibilities of a genuinely independent Cuba, free to determine its own destiny. We have no wish to war with the Soviet Union—for we are a peaceful people who desire to live in peace with all other peoples.

But it is difficult to settle or even discuss these problems in an atmosphere of intimidation. That is why this latest Soviet threat—or any other threat which is made either independently or in response to our actions this week—must and will be met with determination. Any hostile move anywhere in the world against the safety and freedom of peoples to whom we are committed—including in particular the brave people of West Berlin—will be met by whatever action is needed.

Finally, I want to say a few words to the captive people of Cuba, to whom this speech is being directly carried by special radio facilities. I speak to you as a friend, as one who knows of your deep attachment to your fatherland, as one who shares your aspirations for liberty and justice for all. And I have watched and the American people have watched with deep sorrow how your nationalist revolution was betrayed—and how your fatherland fell under foreign domination. Now your leaders are no longer Cuban leaders inspired by Cuban ideals. They are puppets and agents of an international conspiracy which has turned Cuba against your friends and neighbors in the Americas—and turned it into the first Latin American country to become a target for nuclear war—the first Latin American country to have these weapons on its soil.

These new weapons are not in your interest. They contribute nothing to your peace and well-being. They can only undermine it. But this country has no wish to cause you to suffer or to impose any system upon you. We know that your lives and land are being used as pawns by those who deny your freedom.

Many times in the past, the Cuban people have risen to throw out tyrants who destroyed their liberty. And I have no doubt that most Cubans today look forward to the time when they will be truly free—free from foreign domination, free to choose their own leaders, free to select their own system, free to own their own land, free to speak and write and worship without fear or degra-

dation. And then shall Cuba be welcomed back to the society of free nations and to the associations of this hemisphere.

My fellow citizens: let no one doubt that this is a difficult and dangerous effort on which we have set out. No one can foresee precisely what course it will take or what costs or casualties will be incurred. Many months of sacrifice and self-discipline lie ahead—months in which both our patience and our will will be tested—months in which many threats and denunciations will keep us aware of our dangers. But the greatest danger of all would be to do nothing.

The path we have chosen for the present is full of hazards, as all paths are—but it is the one most consistent with our character and courage as a nation and our commitments around the world. The cost of freedom is always high—but Americans have always paid it. And one path we shall never choose, and that is the path of surrender or submission.

Our goal is not the victory of might, but the vindication of right—not peace at the expense of freedom, but both peace *and* freedom, here in this hemisphere, and, we hope, around the world. God willing, that goal will be achieved.

Thank you and good night.

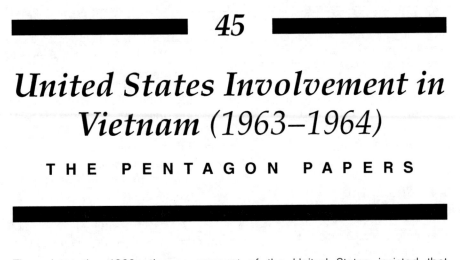

45

United States Involvement in Vietnam (1963–1964)

THE PENTAGON PAPERS

Throughout the 1960s the government of the United States insisted that American troops were in South Vietnam at the request of the democratic government of that country. In 1971 a former Pentagon employee, Daniel Ellsburg, gave to the *New York Times* secret government documents which demonstrated a much less flattering version of the origins of U.S. involvement in Vietnam. Most dramatic was the encouragement John F. Kennedy's administration gave to a group of South Vietnamese generals plotting to overthrow the government of President Ngo Dinh Diem. Key Americans—such as Ambassador Henry Cabot Lodge, Chairman of the Joint Chiefs of Staff Maxwell Taylor, and Secretary of Defense Robert McNamara—were confident that the only hindrance to military success in Vietnam was the corruption and inefficiency of Diem and his bizarre brother, Ngo Dinh Nhu. The coup of November 1, 1963, was successful and culminated in the assassination of Diem and Nhu. But, as McNamara reported to President Lyndon Johnson in December 1963, the situation in Vietnam had actually deteriorated. The only alternative, it seemed to McNamara, was increased American participation in the war. The appointment of General Taylor as ambassador in 1964 put the United States in control of military and political operations in South Vietnam.

Questions to Consider

- Why was the United States so concerned with the fate of South Vietnam?
- What benefits did the United States expect to receive from a change of government in Saigon?
- Who was in charge in South Vietnam?

October 5, 1963, the White House to Ambassador Lodge

In conjunction with decisions and recommendations in separate DEPTEL [State Department telegram], President today approved recommendation that no initiative should now be taken to give any active covert encouragement to a coup. There should, however, be urgent covert effort with closest security under broad guidance of Ambassador to identify and build contacts with possible alternative leadership as and when it appears. Essential that this effort be totally secure and fully deniable and separated entirely from normal political analysis and reporting and other activities of country team. We repeat that this effort is not repeat not to be aimed at active promotion of coup but only at surveillance and readiness. In order to provide plausibility to denial suggest you and no one else in Embassy issue these instructions orally to Acting Station Chief and hold him responsible to you alone for making appropriate contacts and reporting to you alone....

October 5, 1963, Lodge to the State Department

1. Lt. Col. Conein met with Gen. Duong Van Minh at Gen. Minh's Headquarters...for one hour and ten minutes [this] morning.... This meeting was at the initiative of Gen. Minh and has been specifically cleared in advance by Ambassador Lodge. No other persons were present. The conversation was conducted in French.

2. Gen. Minh stated that he must know American Government's position with respect to a change in the Government of Vietnam within the very near future. Gen. Minh added the Generals were aware of the situation...deteriorating rapidly and that action to change the Government must be taken or the war will be lost to the Viet Cong because the Government no longer has the support of the people. Gen. Minh identified among the other Generals participating with him in this plan:

Maj. Gen. Tran Van Don
Brig. Gen. Tran Thien Khiem
Maj. Gen. Tran Van Kim

3. Gen. Minh made it clear that he did not expect any specific American support for an effort on the part of himself and his colleagues to change the Government but he stated he does need American assurances that the USG [U.S. Government] will not [repeat] not attempt to thwart this plan.

4. Gen. Minh also stated that he himself has no political ambitions nor do any of the other General Officers except perhaps, he said laughingly, Gen. Ton That Dinh. Gen. Minh insisted that his only purpose is to win the war. He added emphatically that to do this continuation of American Military and Economic Aid at the present level (He said one and one half million dollars per day) is necessary.

5. Gen. Minh outlined three possible plans for the accomplishment of the change of Government:

a. Assassination of Ngo Dinh Nhu and Ngo Dinh Can keeping President Diem in Office. Gen. Minh said this was the easiest plan to accomplish.

b. The encirclement of Saigon by various military units....

c. Direct confrontation between military units involved in the coup and loyalist military units in Saigon. In effect, dividing the city of Saigon into sectors and cleaning it out pocket by pocket. Gen. Minh claims under the circumstances Diem and Nhu could count on the loyalty of 5,500 troops within the city of Saigon.

6. Conein replied to Gen. Minh that he could not answer specific questions as to USG non-interference nor

Source: U.S. Senate Subcommittee on Public Buildings and Grounds, *The Pentagon Papers*, 92nd Congress, 1st Session, 2 (Washington, DC, 1971), pp. 268, 346–348, 766–768, 780–782, 784–785, 789–793; 3: pp. 494–499.

could he give any advice with respect to tactical planning. He added that he could not advise concerning the best of the three plans....

9. Minh further stated that one of the reasons they are having to act quickly was the fact that many regimental, battalion and company commanders are working on coup plans of their own which could be abortive and a "catastrophe"....

EYES ONLY FOR SECRETARY RUSK FROM LODGE
...While neither General Harkins nor I have great faith in Big Minh, we need instructions on his approach. My recommendation, in which General Harkins concurs, is that Conein when next approached by Minh should:

1. Assure him that US will not attempt to thwart his plans.

2. Offer to review his plans, other than assassination plans.

3. Assure Minh that US aid will be continued to Vietnam under Government which gives promise of gaining support of people and winning the war against the Communists. Point out that it is our view that this is most likely to be the case if Government includes good proportion of well qualified civilian leaders in key positions. (Conein should press Minh for details his thinking Re composition future Government). I suggest the above be discussed with Secretary McNamara and General Taylor who contacted Minh in recent visit.

October 25, 1963, Lodge to McGeorge Bundy [National Security Advisor to President Kennedy]

...6. We should not thwart a *coup* for two reasons. First, it seems at least an even bet that the next government would not bungle and stumble as much as the present one has. Secondly, it is extremely unwise in the long range for us to pour cold water on attempts at a coup, particularly when they are just in their beginning stages. We should remember that this is the only way in which the people in Vietnam can possibly get a change of government. Whenever we thwart attempts at a coup, as we have done in the past, we are incurring very long lasting resentments, we are assuming an undue responsibility for keeping the incumbents in office, and in general are setting ourselves in judgment over the affairs of Vietnam. Merely to keep in touch with this situation and a policy merely limited to "not thwarting" are courses both of which entail some risks but these are lesser risks than either thwarting all coups while they are stillborn or our not being informed of what is happening. All the above is totally distinct from not wanting U.S. military advisors to be distracted by matters which are not in their domain, with which I heartily agree. But obviously this does not conflict with a policy of not thwarting. In judging proposed coups,

we must consider the effect on the war effort. Certainly a succession of fights for control of the Government of Vietnam would interfere with the war effort. It must also be said that the war effort has been interfered with already by the incompetence of the present government and the uproar which this has caused.

7. Gen. Don's intention to have no religious discrimination in a future government is commendable and I applaud his desire not to be "a vassal" of the U.S. But I do not think his promise of a democratic election is realistic. This country simply is not ready for that procedure. I would add two other requirements. First, that there be no wholesale purges of personnel in the government. Individuals who were particularly reprehensible could be dealt with later by the regular legal process. Then I would be impractical, but I am thinking of a government which might include Tri Quang and which certainly should include men of the stature of Mr. Buu, the labor leader....

October 25, 1963, McGeorge Bundy to Lodge

Your [telegram] most helpful.

We will continue to be grateful for all additional information giving increased clarity to prospects of action by Don or others, and we look forward to discussing with you the whole question of control and cutout on your return, always assuming that one of these D-Days does not turn out to be real. We are particularly concerned about hazard that an unsuccessful coup, however carefully we avoid direct engagement, will be laid at our door by public opinion almost everywhere. Therefore, while sharing your view that we should not be in position of thwarting coup, we would like to have option of judging and warning on any plan with poor prospects of success. We recognize that this is a large order, but President wants you to know of our concern....

October 30, 1963, General Paul Harkins [U.S. Commander in Vietnam] to General Maxwell Taylor

...I share your concern.... I am unaware of any change in local situation which indicates necessity for actions directed....

One thing I have found out, Don is either lying or playing both ends against the middle. What he told me is diametrically opposed to what he told Col. Conein. He told Conein the coup will be before November 2nd. He told me he was not planning a coup. I sat with Don and Big Minh for 2 hours during the parade last Saturday. No one mentioned coups....

The Ambassador and I are certainly in touch with each other but whether the communications between us are effective is something else. I will say Cabot's methods of operations are entirely different from Amb Noltings as far as reporting in the military is concerned....

I will have to report you are correct in believing that the Ambassador is forwarding military reports and evaluations without consulting me....

I'm not opposed to a change in government, no indeed, but I'm inclined to feel that at this time the change should be in methods of governing rather than complete change of personnel. I have seen no batting order proposed by any of the coup groups. I think we should take a hard look at any proposed list before we make any decisions. In my contacts here I have seen no one with the strength of character of Diem, at least in fighting communists. Clearly there are no Generals qualified to take over in my opinion.

I am not a Diem man per se. I certainly see the faults in his character. I am here to back 140 million SVN people in their fight against communism and it just happens that Diem is their leader at this time. Most of the Generals I have talked to agree they can go along with Diem, all say its the Nhu family they are opposed to.

Perhaps the pressures we have begun to apply will cause Diem and Nhu to change their ways. This is apparently not evident as yet. I'm sure the pressures we have begun to apply if continued will affect the war effort. To date they have not. I am watching this closely and will report when I think they have.

I do not agree with the Ambassadors assessment... that we are just holding our own....

I would suggest we not try to change horses too quickly. That we continue to take persuasive actions that will make the horses change their course and methods of action. That we win the military effort as quickly as possible, then let them make any and all the changes they want.

After all, rightly or wrongly, we have backed Diem for eight long hard years. To me it seems incongruous now to get him down, kick him around, and get rid of him. The US has been his mother superior and father confessor since he's been in office and he has leaned on us heavily.

Leaders of other under-developed countries will take a dim view of our assistance if they too were led to believe the same fate lies in store for them.

October 30, 1963, Lodge to State Department

1. We must, of course, get best possible estimate of chance of coup's success and this estimate must color our thinking, but do not think we have the power to delay or discourage a coup. Don has made it clear many times that this is a Vietnamese affair. It is theoretically possible for us to turn over the information which has been given to us in confidence to Diem and this would undoubtedly stop the coup and would make traitors out of us. For practical purposes therefore I would say that we have very little influence on what is essentially a Vietnamese affair.... After our efforts not to discourage a coup and this change of heart, we would foreclose any possibility of change of the GVN [Government of South Vietnam] for the better. Diem/Nhu have displayed no intentions to date of a desire to change the traditional methods of control through police action or take any repeat any actions which would undermine the power position or solidarity of the Ngo family.... If our attempt to thwart this coup were successful, which we doubt, it is our firm estimate that younger officers, small groups of military, would then engage in an abortive action creating chaos ideally suited to VC [Viet Cong] objectives.

2. While we will attempt a combined assessment in a following message, time has not permitted substantive examination of this matter with General Harkins. My general view is that the U.S. is trying to bring this medieval country into the 20th Century and that we have made considerable progress in military and economic ways but to gain victory we must also bring them into the 20th Century politically and that can only be done by either a thoroughgoing change in the behavior of the present government or by another government. The Viet Cong problem is partly military but it is also partly psychological and political.

3. ...I believe that we should continue our present position of keeping hands off but continue to monitor and press for more detailed information.... [T]he Generals have probably figured their chances pretty closely and probably also expect that once they begin to move, not only planned units, but other units will join them. We believe that Vietnam's best Generals are involved in directing this effort. If they can't pull it off, it is doubtful other military leadership could do so successfully. It is understandable that the Generals would be reticent to reveal full details of their plan for fear of leaks to the GVN....

We do not believe, however, that we should show any signs of attempting to direct this affair ourselves or of giving the impression of second thoughts on this Vietnamese initiation....

6. We do not believe it wise to ask that "Big Minh" pass his plans to Gen. Stilwell. The Vietnamese believe that there are members of the U.S. military who leak to the Government of Vietnam. I do not doubt that this is an unjust suspicion but it is a fact that this suspicion exists and there is no use in pretending that it does not....

8. ...It does not seem sensible to have the military in charge of a matter which is so profoundly political as a change of government. In fact, I would say to do this would probably be the end of any hope for a change of government here. This is said impersonally as a general proposition, since Gen. Harkins is a splendid General and an old friend of mine to whom I would gladly entrust anything I have....

10. We anticipate that at the outset of the coup, unless it moves with lightning swiftness, the GVN will request me or Gen. Harkins to use our influence to call it off. I believe our responsibilities should be that our influence certainly could not be superior to that of the President who is Commander-in-Chief and that if he is unable to call it off, we would certainly be unable to do so and would merely be risking American lives attempting to interfere in this Vietnamese problem.... If senior Vietnamese personalities and their families requested asylum in the Embassy or other American installations, we would probably have to grant it in light of our previous action with respect to Tri Quang. This will undoubtedly present later problems but hopefully the new government might feel disposed to help us solve this problem. Naturally, asylum would be granted on the same basis as the Buddhists, i.e., physical presence at the Embassy or other location.

11. As to requests from the Generals, they may well have need of funds at the last moment with which to buy off potential opposition. To the extent that these funds can be passed discreetly, I believe we should furnish them, provided we are convinced that the proposed coup is sufficiently well organized to have a good chance of success. If they are successful, they will undoubtedly ask for prompt recognition and some assurance that military and economic aid will continue at normal level. We should be prepared to make these statements if the issue is clear-cut predicating our position on the President's stated desire to continue the war against the VC to final victory.... Should the coup fail, we will have to pick up the pieces as best we can at that time.... American complicity will undoubtedly be charged.... Should the coup prove indecisive and a protracted struggle is in progress, we should probably offer our good offices to help resolve the issue in the interest of the war against the VC. This might hold some benefit in terms of concessions by GVN. We will naturally incur some opprobrium from both sides in our role as mediator. However, this opprobrium would probably be less distasteful than a deadlock which would open the door to the VC. We consider such a deadlock as the least likely possibility of the three....

Heartily agree that a miscalculation could jeopardize position in Southeast Asia. We also run tremendous risks by doing nothing.

If we were convinced that the coup was going to fail, we would, of course, do everything we could to stop it.

13. Gen. Harkins has read this and does not concur.

October 30, 1963, Bundy to Lodge

1. Our reading your thoughtful [telegram] leads us to believe a significant difference of shading may exist on one crucial point (see next para.) and on one or two lesser matters easily clarified.

2. We do not accept as a basis for U.S. policy that we have no power to delay or discourage a coup.... [Y]ou say that if you were convinced that the coup was going to fail you would of course do everything you could to stop it. We believe that on this same basis you should take action to persuade coup leaders to stop or delay any operation which, in your best judgment, does not clearly give high prospect of success....

3. Therefore, if you should conclude that there is not clearly a high prospect of success, you should communicate this doubt to generals in a way calculated to persuade them to desist at least until chances are better. In such a communication you should use the weight of U.S. best advice and explicitly reject any implication that we oppose the effort of the generals because of preference for present regime. We recognize need to bear in mind generals' interpretation of U.S. role in 1960 coup attempt, and your agent should maintain clear distinction between strong and honest advice given as a friend and any opposition to their objectives....

6. This paragraph contains our present standing instructions for U.S. posture in the event of a coup.

a. U.S. authorities will reject appeals for direct intervention from either side, and U.S.-controlled aircraft and other resources will not be committed between the battle lines or in support of either side, without authorization from Washington.

b. In event of indecisive contest, U.S. authorities may in their discretion agree to perform any acts agreeable to both sides, such as removal of key personalities or relay of information. In such actions, however, U.S. authorities will strenuously avoid appearance of pressure on either side. It is not in the interest of USG to be or appear to be either instrument of existing government or instrument of coup.

c. In the event of imminent or actual failure of coup, U.S. authorities may afford asylum in their discretion to those to whom there is any express or implied obligation of this sort. We believe however that in such a case it would be in our interest and probably in interest of those seeking asylum that they seek protection of other Embassies in addition to our own. This point should be made strongly if need arises.

d. But once a coup under responsible leadership has begun, and within these restrictions, it is in the interest of the U.S. Government that it should succeed....

November 1, 1963, Lodge and President Diem

...At 4:30 p.m., Diem called Lodge to ask where he stood and the following conversation ensued:

Diem. Some units have made a rebellion and I want to know what is the attitude of the US?

Lodge. I do not feel well enough informed to be able to tell you. I have heard the shooting, but am not acquainted with all the facts. Also it is 4:30 a.m. in Washington and the US Government cannot possibly have a view.

Diem. But you must have some general ideas. After all, I am a Chief of State. I have tried to do my duty. I want to do now what duty and good sense require. I believe in duty above all.

Lodge. You have certainly done your duty. As I told you only this morning, I admire your courage and your great contributions to your country. No one can take away from you the credit for all you have done. Now I am worried about your physical safety. I have a report that those in charge of the current activity offer you and your brother safe conduct out of the country if you resign. Had you heard this?

Diem. No. (And then after a pause) You have my telephone number.

Lodge. Yes. If I can do anything for your physical safety, please call me.

Diem. I am trying to re-establish order.

December 21, 1963, McNamara to President Johnson

In accordance with your request this morning, this is a summary of my conclusions after my visit to Vietnam on December 19–20.

1. *Summary.* The situation is very disturbing. Current trends, unless reversed in the next 2–3 months, will lead to neutralization at best and more likely to a Communist-controlled state.

2. *The new government* is the greatest source of concern. It is indecisive and drifting. Although Minh states that he, rather than the Committee of Generals, is making decisions, it is not clear that this is actually so. In any event, neither he nor the Committee are experienced in political administration and so far they show little talent for it. There is no clear concept on how to reshape or conduct the strategic hamlet program; the

Province Chiefs, most of whom are new and inexperienced, are receiving little or no direction; military operations, too, are not being effectively directed because the generals are so preoccupied with essentially political affairs. A specific example of the present situation is that General Dinh is spending little or no time commanding III Corps, which is in the vital zone around Saigon and needs full-time direction. I made these points as strongly as possible to Minh, Don, Kim, and Tho.

3. *The Country Team* [i.e., U.S. command in Vietnam] is the second major weakness. It lacks leadership, has been poorly informed, and is not working to a common plan.... Lodge has virtually no official contact with Harkins. Lodge sends in reports with major military implications without showing them to Harkins, and does not show Harkins important incoming traffic. My impression is that Lodge simply does not know how to conduct a coordinated administration. This has of course been stressed to him both by Dean Rusk and myself...and I do not think he is consciously rejecting our advice; he has just operated as a loner all his life and cannot readily change now....

4. *Viet Cong progress* has been great during the period since the coup, with my best guess being that the situation has in fact been deteriorating in the countryside since July to a far greater extent than we realized because of our undue dependence on distorted Vietnamese reporting. The Viet Cong now control very high proportions of the people in certain key provinces, particularly those directly south and west of Saigon. The Strategic Hamlet Program was seriously overextended in these provinces, and the Viet Cong has been able to destroy many hamlets, while others have been abandoned or in some cases betrayed or pillaged by the government's own Self Defense Corps. In these key provinces, the Viet Cong have destroyed almost all major roads, and are collecting taxes at will....

5. *Infiltration* of men and equipment from North Vietnam continues using (a) land corridors through Laos and Cambodia; (b) the Mekong River waterways from Cambodia; (c) some possible entry from the sea and the tip of the Delta. The best guess is that 1000–1500 Viet Cong cadres entered South Vietnam from Laos in the first nine months of 1963....

To counter this infiltration, we reviewed in Saigon various plans providing for cross-border operations into Laos. On the scale proposed, I am quite clear that these would not be politically acceptable or even militarily effective....

6. *Plans for Covert Action into North Vietnam* were prepared as we had requested and were an excellent job. They present a wide variety of sabotage and psychological operations against North Vietnam from which I

believe we should aim to select those that provide maximum pressure with minimum risk....

January 22, 1964, Joint Chiefs of Staff to McNamara

1. National Security Action Memorandum No. 273 makes clear the resolve of the President to ensure victory over the externally directed and supported communist insurgency in South Vietnam. In order to achieve that victory, the Joint Chiefs of Staff are of the opinion that the United States must be prepared to put aside many of the self-imposed restrictions which now limit our efforts, and to undertake bolder actions which may embody greater risks.

2. The Joint Chiefs of Staff are increasingly mindful that our fortunes in South Vietnam are an accurate barometer of our fortunes in all of Southeast Asia. It is our view that if the US program succeeds in South Vietnam it will go far toward stabilizing the total Southeast Asia situation. Conversely, a loss of South Vietnam to the communists will presage an early erosion of the remainder of our position in that subcontinent.

3. Laos, existing on a most fragile foundation now, would not be able to endure the establishment of a communist—or pseudo neutralist—state on its eastern flank. Thailand...would probably be unable to withstand the pressures of infiltration from the north should Laos collapse to the communists in its turn. Cambodia apparently has estimated that our prospects in South Vietnam are not promising and, encouraged by the actions of the French, appears already to be seeking an accommodation with the communists. Should we actually suffer defeat in South Vietnam, there is little reason to believe that Cambodia would maintain even a pretense of neutrality.

4. In a broader sense, the failure of our programs in South Vietnam would have heavy influence on the judgments of Burma, India, Indonesia, Malaysia, Japan, Taiwan, the Republic of Korea, and the Republic of the Philippines with respect to US durability, resolution, and trustworthiness. Finally, this being the first real test of our determination to defeat the communist wars of national liberation formula, it is not unreasonable to conclude that there would be a corresponding unfavorable effect upon our image in Africa and in Latin America.

5. All of this underscores the pivotal position now occupied by South Vietnam in our world-wide confrontation with the communists and the essentiality that the conflict there be brought to a favorable end as soon as possible. However, it would be unrealistic to believe that a complete suppression of the insurgency can take place in one or even two years. The British effort in Malaya is a recent example of a counterinsurgency effort which required approximately ten years before the bulk of the rural population was brought completely under control of the government, the police were able to maintain order, and the armed forces were able to eliminate the guerrilla strongholds.

6. The Joint Chiefs of Staff are convinced that...the United States must make plain to the enemy our determination to see the Vietnam campaign through to a favorable conclusion....

7. Our considerations, furthermore, cannot be confined entirely to South Vietnam. Our experience in the war thus far leads us to conclude that, in this respect, we are not now giving sufficient attention to the broader area problems of Southeast Asia....

8. Currently we and the South Vietnamese are fighting the war on the enemy's terms. He has determined the locale, the timing, and the tactics of the battle while our actions are essentially reactive. One reason for this is the fact that we have obliged ourselves to labor under self-imposed restrictions with respect to impeding external aid to the Viet Cong. These restrictions include keeping the war within the boundaries of South Vietnam, avoiding the direct use of US combat forces, and limiting US direction...to rendering advice to the Government of Vietnam. These restrictions, while they may make our international position more readily defensible, all tend to make the task in Vietnam more complex, time consuming, and in the end, more costly. In addition to complicating our own problem, these self-imposed restrictions may well now be conveying signals of irresolution to our enemies—encouraging them to higher levels of vigor and greater risks. A reversal of attitude and the adoption of a more aggressive program would enhance greatly our ability to control the degree to which escalation will occur. It appears probable that the economic and agricultural disappointments suffered by Communist China, plus the current rift with the Soviets, could cause the communists to think twice about undertaking a large-scale military adventure in Southeast Asia....

9. ...It is our conviction that if support of the insurgency from outside South Vietnam in terms of operational direction, personnel, and material were stopped completely, the character of the war in South Vietnam would be substantially and favorably altered. Because of this conviction, we are wholly in favor of executing the covert actions against North Vietnam which you have recently proposed to the President. We believe, however, that it would be idle to conclude that these efforts will have a decisive effect on the communist determination to support the insurgency; and it is our view

that we must therefore be prepared fully to undertake a much higher level of activity, not only for its beneficial tactical effect, but to make plain our resolution, both to our friends and to our enemies.

10. Accordingly, the Joint Chiefs of Staff consider that the United States must make ready to conduct increasingly bolder actions…:

a. Assign to the US military commander responsibilities for the total US program in Vietnam.

b. Induce the Government of Vietnam to turn over to the United States military commander, temporarily, the actual tactical direction of the war.

c. Charge the United States military commander with complete responsibility for conduct of the program against North Vietnam.

d. Overfly Laos and Cambodia to whatever extent is necessary for acquisition of operational intelligence.

e. Induce the Government of Vietnam to conduct overt ground operations in Laos of sufficient scope to impede the flow of personnel and material southward.

f. Arm, equip, advise, and support the Government of Vietnam in its conduct of aerial bombing of critical targets in North Vietnam and in mining the sea approaches to that country.

g. Advise and support the Government of Vietnam in its conduct of large-scale commando raids against critical targets in North Vietnam.

h. Conduct aerial bombing of key North Vietnam targets, using US resources under Vietnamese cover, and with the Vietnamese openly assuming responsibility for the actions.

i. Commit additional US forces, as necessary, in support of the combat action within South Vietnam.

j. Commit US forces as necessary in direct actions against North Vietnam….

December 20, 1964, Taylor and the Leaders of South Vietnam

Ambassador Taylor. Do all of you understand English? (Vietnamese officers indicated they did, although the understanding of General Thi was known to be weak.) I told you all clearly at General Westmoreland's dinner we Americans were tired of coups. Apparently I wasted my words. Maybe this is because something is wrong with my French because you evidently didn't understand. I made it clear that all the military plans which I know you would like to carry out are dependent on governmental stability. Now you have made a real mess. We cannot carry you forever if you do things like this. Who speaks for this group? Do you have a spokesman?

General Ky. I am not the spokesman for the group but I do speak English. I will explain why the Armed Forces took this action last night [a military coup].

We understand English very well. We are aware of our responsibilities, we are aware of the sacrifices of our people over twenty years. We know you want stability, but you cannot have stability until you have unity….

Recently the Prime Minister showed us a letter he had received from the Chairman of the HNC [High National Council]. This letter told the Prime Minister to beware of the military, and said that maybe the military would want to come back to power. Also the HNC illegally sought to block the retirement of the generals that the Armed Forces Council unanimously recommended be retired in order to improve unity in the Armed Forces.

General Thieu. The HNC cannot be bosses because of the Constitution. Its members must prove that they want to fight.

General Ky. It looks as though the HNC does not want unity. It does not want to fight the Communists.

It has been rumored that our action of last night was an intrigue of Khanh against Minh, who must be retired. Why do we seek to retire these generals? Because they had their chance and did badly…

Yesterday we met, twenty of us, from 1430 to 2030. We reached agreement that we must take some action. We decided to arrest the bad members of the HNC, bad politicians, bad student leaders, and the leaders of the Committee of National Salvation, which is a Communist organization. We must put the trouble-making organizations out of action….

After we explain to the people why we did this at a press conference, we would like to return to our fighting units. We have no political ambitions. We seek strong, unified, and stable Armed Forces to support the struggle and a stable government….

We did what we thought was good for this country; we tried to have a civilian government clean house. If we have achieved it, fine. We are now ready to go back to our units.

Ambassador Taylor. I respect the sincerity of you gentlemen. Now I would like to talk to you about the consequences of what you have done. But first, would any of the other officers wish to speak?

Admiral Cang. It seems that we are being treated as though we were guilty. What we did was good and we did it only for the good of the country.

Ambassador Taylor. Now let me tell you how I feel about it, what I think the consequences are: first of all, this is a military coup that has destroyed the government-making process that, to the admiration of the whole world, was set up last fall largely through the statesman-like acts of the Armed Forces.

You cannot go back to your units, General Ky. You military are now back in power. You are up to your necks in politics.

Your statement makes it clear that you have constituted yourselves again substantially as a Military

Revolutionary Committee. The dissolution of the HNC was totally illegal....

Who commands the Armed Forces? General Khanh?

General Ky. Yes, sir...

General Thieu. ...We do not want to force General Khanh; we advise him. We will do what he orders....

Ambassador Taylor. ...I have been impressed by the high quality of many Vietnamese officers. I am sure that many of the most able men in this country are in uniform. Last fall when the HNC and Huong Government was being formed, I suggested to General Khanh there should be some military participation, but my suggestions were not accepted. It would therefore be natural for some of them now to be called upon to serve in the government. Would you be willing to do so?...

General Ky. Nonetheless, I would object to the idea of the military going back into the government right away. People will say it is a military coup.

Ambassador Taylor and *Ambassador Johnson.* (Together) People will say it anyway....

General Ky. Perhaps it is better if we now let General Khanh and Prime Minister Huong talk.

General Thieu. After all, we did not arrest all the members of the HNC. Of nine members we detained only five. These people are not under arrest. They are simply under controlled residence....

Ambassador Taylor. Our problem now, gentlemen, is to organize our work for the rest of the day. For one thing, the government will have to issue a communique.

General Thieu. We will still have a press conference this afternoon but only to say why we acted as we did.

Ambassador Taylor. I have real troubles on the U.S. side. I don't know whether we will continue to support you after this. Why don't you tell your friends before you act? I regret the need for my blunt talk today but we have lots at stake....

In taking a friendly leave, Ambassador Taylor said: You people have broken a lot of dishes and now we have to see how we can straighten out this mess....

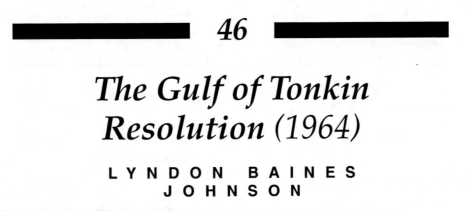

46

The Gulf of Tonkin Resolution (1964)

LYNDON BAINES JOHNSON

On August 4, 1964, two American destroyers, the *Maddox* and *Turner Joy,* were cruising off the coast of North Vietnam as part of a secret U.S.-South Vietnamese sabotage mission. Sonar operators on the *Maddox* became convinced that their ship was under attack, so the ships took evasive action and fired upon an unseen enemy. Later investigations revealed there had been no attack, and President Johnson said that "those dumb stupid sailors were probably shooting at flying fish." Nonetheless, the president seized the opportunity to launch a series of punitive strikes against North Vietnam, and to submit to Congress a resolution prepared by his staff back in May. The Gulf of Tonkin Resolution, approved by the Senate with only two dissenting votes, granted the president the power to make war anywhere he pleased.

Questions to Consider

- Why was Congress willing to give the president such sweeping military authority?
- Why was the United States involved in Southeast Asia?

Special Message from President Lyndon Johnson to the Congress on U.S. Policy in Southeast Asia, August 5, 1964

To the Congress of the United States:

Last night I announced to the American people that the North Vietnamese regime had conducted further deliberate attacks against US naval vessels operating in international waters, and that I had therefore directed air action against gun boats and supporting facilities used in these hostile operations. This air action has now been carried out with substantial damage to the boats and facilities. Two US aircraft were lost in the action.

After consultation with the leaders of both parties in the Congress, I further announced a decision to ask the Congress for a Resolution expressing the unity and determination of the United States in supporting freedom and in protecting peace in Southeast Asia.

These latest actions of the North Vietnamese regime have given a new and grave turn to the already serious situation in Southeast Asia. Our commitments in that area are well known to the Congress. They were first made in 1954 by President Eisenhower. They were further defined in the Southeast Asia Collective Defense Treaty approved by the Senate in February 1955.

This Treaty with its accompanying protocol obligates the United States and other members to act in accordance with their Constitutional processes to meet Communist aggression against any of the parties or protocol states.

Our policy in Southeast Asia has been consistent and unchanged since 1954. I summarized it on June 2 in four simple propositions:

1. *America keeps her word.* Here as elsewhere, we must and shall honor our commitments.

2. *The issue is the future of Southeast Asia as a whole.* A threat to any nation in that region is a threat to all, and a threat to us.

3. *Our purpose is peace.* We have no military, political or territorial ambitions in the area.

4. *This is not just a jungle war, but a struggle for freedom on every front of human activity.* Our military and economic assistance to South Vietnam and Laos in particular has the purpose of helping these countries to repel aggression and strengthen their independence.

The threat to the free nations of Southeast Asia has long been clear. The North Vietnamese regime has constantly sought to take over South Vietnam and Laos. This Communist regime has violated the Geneva Accords for Vietnam. It has systematically conducted a campaign of subversion, which includes the direction, training, and supply of personnel and arms for the conduct of guerrilla warfare in South Vietnamese territory. In Laos, the North Vietnamese regime has maintained military forces, used Laotian territory for infiltration into South Vietnam, and most recently carried out combat operations—all in direct violation of the Geneva Agreements of 1962.

In recent months, the actions of the North Vietnamese regime have become steadily more threatening. In May, following new acts of Communist aggression in Laos, the United States undertook reconnaissance flights over Laotian territory, at the request of the Government of Laos. These flights had the essential mission of determining the situation in territory where Communist forces were preventing inspection by the International Control Commission. When the Communists attacked these aircraft, I responded by furnishing escort fighters with instructions to fire when fired upon. Thus, these latest North Vietnamese attacks on our naval vessels are not the first direct attack on armed forces of the United States.

As President of the United States I have concluded that I should now ask the Congress, on its part, to join in affirming the national determination that all such attacks will be met, and that the U.S. will continue in its basic policy of assisting the free nations of the area to defend their freedom.

As I have repeatedly made clear, the United States intends no rashness, and seeks no wider war. We must make it clear to all that the United States is united in its determination to bring about the end of Communist subversion and aggression in the area. We seek the full and effective restoration of the international agreements signed in Geneva in 1954, with respect to South Vietnam, and again in Geneva in 1962, with respect to Laos.

I recommend a Resolution expressing the support of the Congress for all necessary action to protect our armed forces and to assist nations covered by the SEATO Treaty. At the same time, I assure the Congress that we shall continue readily to explore any avenues of political solution that will effectively guarantee the removal of Communist subversion and the preservation of the independence of the nations of the area.

The Resolution could well be based upon similar resolutions enacted by the Congress in the past—to meet the threat to Formosa in 1955, to meet the threat to the Middle East in 1957, and to meet the threat in Cuba in 1962. It could state in the simplest terms the resolve and support of the Congress for action to deal appropriately with attacks against our armed forces and to defend freedom and preserve peace in Southeast Asia in accordance with the obligations of the United States under the Southeast Asia Treaty. I urge the Congress to enact

Source: *Public Papers of the Presidents of the United States: Lyndon Baines Johnson, 1963–1964* (Washington, D.C., 1966), 2: pp. 930–932; Public Law 88-408, 785 Statutes 384 pp. 310–311.

such a Resolution promptly and thus to give convincing evidence to the aggressive Communist nations, and to the world as a whole, that our policy in Southeast Asia will be carried forward—and that the peace and security of the area will be preserved.

The events of this week would in any event have made the passage of a Congressional Resolution essential. But there is an additional reason for doing so at a time when we are entering on three months of political campaigning. Hostile nations must understand that in such a period the United States will continue to protect its national interests, and that in these matters there is no division among us.

LYNDON B. JOHNSON

Joint Resolution of Congress, August 10, 1964

Joint Resolution to Promote the Maintenance of International Peace and Security in Southeast Asia

Whereas naval units of the Communist regime in Vietnam, in violation of the principles of the Charter of the United Nations and of international law, have deliberately and repeatedly attacked United States naval vessels lawfully present in international waters, and have thereby created a serious threat to international peace; and

Whereas these attacks are part of a deliberate and systematic campaign of aggression that the Communist regime in North Vietnam has been waging against its

neighbors and the nations joined with them in the collective defense of their freedom; and

Whereas the United States is assisting the peoples of Southeast Asia to protect their freedom and has no territorial, military or political ambitions in that area, but desires only that these peoples should be left in peace to work out their own destinies in their own way: Now, therefore be it

Resolved by the Senate and House of Representatives of the United States of America in Congress assembled, That the Congress approves and supports the determination of the President, as Commander in Chief, to take all necessary measures to repel any armed attack against the forces of the United States and to prevent further aggression.

Sec. 2. The United States regards as vital to its national interest and to world peace the maintenance of international peace and security in Southeast Asia. Consonant with the Constitution of the United States and the Charter of the United Nations and in accordance with its obligations under the Southeast Asia Collective Defense Treaty, the United States is, therefore, prepared, as the President determines, to take all necessary steps, including the use of armed force, to assist any member or protocol state of the Southeast Asia Collective Defense Treaty requesting assistance in defense of its freedom.

Sec. 3. This resolution shall expire when the President shall determine that the peace and security of the area is reasonably assured by international conditions created by action of the United Nations or otherwise, except that it may be terminated earlier by concurrent resolution of the Congress.

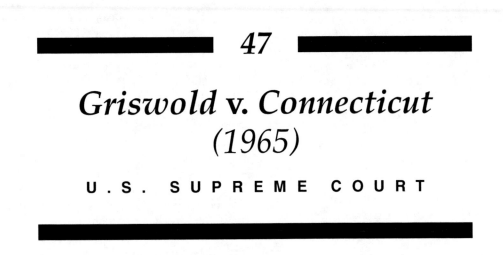

47

Griswold v. Connecticut (1965)

U. S. S U P R E M E C O U R T

Contrary to popular opinion, there is no right to privacy enumerated in the Constitution. States had therefore often interfered in such seemingly private activities as sexual relations, outlawing certain kinds and specifying limitations on others. In 1879 Connecticut not only prohibited the use of any device or drug intended to prevent contraception, but also forbade the supply and even recommendation of such articles. The Supreme Court twice refused to hear challenges to this law, in 1943 and 1961, but granted a hearing in 1965 in response to the prosecution of the Planned Parenthood League of Connecticut and its director. The Court voted seven to two in favor of overturning the law, with Justice William O. Douglas writing the majority decision. Douglas declared a right to privacy inherent in the Constitution, setting the ground for the extension of individual and reproductive rights over the next decade, drawing the ire of many for the Court's "judicial activism," and the praise of others for its support of personal liberty. The impact of *Griswold* was confused by the fact that there were three concurrences and two dissents. Most scholars rate it one of the most significant and controversial decisions by the Warren Court.

Questions to Consider

- What did Douglas mean when he said that privacy is protected as a "penumbra" of the Constitution?

- Is it legitimate for the Court to interpret the Constitution in light of changing social realities and needs?

- How could Justices Black and Stewart deny that the Connecticut law violated a Constitutional right?

Mr. Justice Douglas delivered the opinion of the Court.

Appellant Griswold is Executive Director of the Planned Parenthood League of Connecticut. Appellant Buxton is a licensed physician and a professor at the Yale Medical School who served as Medical Director for the League at its Center in New Haven—a center open and operating from November 1 to November 10, 1961, when appellants were arrested.

They gave information, instruction, and medical advice to *married persons* as to the means of preventing conception. They examined the wife and prescribed the best contraceptive device or material for her use. Fees were usually charged, although some couples were serviced free.

The statues whose constitutionality is involved in this appeal are §§ 53–32 and 54–196 of the General Statutes of Connecticut (1958 rev.). The former provides:

Any person who uses any drug, medicinal article or instrument for the purpose of preventing conception shall be fined not less than fifty dollars or imprisoned not less than sixty days nor more than one year or be both fined and imprisoned.

Section 54–196 provides:

Source: *United States Reports* (Washington, D.C., 1965), 381: pp. 479–531.

Any person who assists, abets, counsels, causes, hires or commands another to commit any offense may be prosecuted and punished as if he were the principal offender.

The appellants were found guilty as accessories and fined $100 each against the claim that the accessory statute as so applied violated the Fourteenth Amendment....

Coming to the merits, we are met with a wide range of questions that implicate the Due Process Clause of the Fourteenth Amendment. Overtones of some arguments suggest that *Lochner* v. *New York*...should be our guide. But we decline that invitation as we did in *West Coast Hotel Co.* v. *Parrish*.... We do not sit as a super-legislature to determine the wisdom, need, and propriety of laws that touch economic problems, business affairs, or social conditions. This law, however, operates directly on an intimate relation of husband and wife and their physician's role in one aspect of that relation.

The association of people is not mentioned in the Constitution nor in the Bill of Rights. The right to educate a child in a school of the parents' choice—whether public or private or parochial—is also not mentioned. Nor is the right to study any particular subject or any foreign language. Yet the First Amendment has been construed to include certain of those rights.

By *Pierce* v. *Society of Sisters*...the right to educate one's children as one chooses is made applicable to the States by the force of the First and Fourteenth Amendments. By *Meyer* v. *Nebraska*...the same dignity is given the right to study the German language in a private school. In other words, the State may not, consistently with the spirit of the First Amendment, contract the spectrum of available knowledge. The right of freedom of speech and press includes not only the right to utter or to print, but the right to distribute, the right to receive, the right to read (*Martin* v. *Struthers*...) and freedom of inquiry, freedom of thought, and freedom to teach (see *Wieman* v. *Updegraff*...)—indeed the freedom of the entire university community. *Sweezy* v. *New Hampshire*...; *Barenblatt* v. *United States*...; *Baggett* v. *Bullitt*.... Without those peripheral rights the specific rights would be less secure. And so we reaffirm the principle of the *Pierce* and the *Meyer* cases.

In *NAACP* v. *Alabama*...we protected the "freedom to associate and privacy in one's associations," noting that freedom of association was a peripheral First Amendment right. Disclosure of membership lists of a constitutionally valid association, we held, was invalid "as entailing the likelihood of a substantial restraint upon the exercise by petitioner's members of their right to freedom of association." *Ibid.* In other words, the First Amendment has a penumbra where privacy is protected from governmental intrusion. In like context, we have protected forms of "association" that are not political in the customary sense but pertain to the social, legal, and economic benefit of the members. *NAACP* v. *Button*.... In *Schware* v. *Board of Bar Examiners*...we held it not permissible to bar a lawyer from practice, because he had once been a member of the Communist Party. The man's "association with that Party" was not shown to be "anything more than a political faith in a political party"...and was not action of a kind proving bad moral character....

Those cases involved more than the "right of assembly"—a right that extends to all irrespective of their race or ideology. *De Jonge* v. *Oregon*.... The right of "association," like the right of belief (*Board of Education* v. *Barnette*...), is more than the right to attend a meeting; it includes the right to express one's attitudes or philosophies by membership in a group or by affiliation with it or by other lawful means. Association in that context is a form of expression of opinion; and while it is not expressly included in the First Amendment its existence is necessary in making the express guarantees fully meaningful.

The foregoing cases suggest that specific guarantees in the Bill of Rights have penumbras, formed by emanations from those guarantees that help give them life and substance. See *Poe* v. *Ullman*...(dissenting opinion). Various guarantees create zones of privacy. The right of association contained in the penumbra of the First Amendment is one, as we have seen. The Third Amendment in its prohibition against the quartering of soldiers "in any house" in time of peace without the consent of the owner is another facet of that privacy.

The Fourth Amendment explicitly affirms the "right of the people to be secure in their persons, houses, papers, and effects, against unreasonable searches and seizures." The Fifth Amendment in its Self-Incrimination Clause enables the citizen to create a zone of privacy which government may not force him to surrender to his detriment. The Ninth Amendment provides: "The enumeration in the Constitution, of certain rights, shall not be construed to deny or disparage others retained by the people."

The Fourth and Fifth Amendments were described in *Boyd* v. *United States*...as protection against all governmental invasions "of the sanctity of a man's home and the privacies of life." We recently referred in *Mapp* v. *Ohio*...to the Fourth Amendment as creating a "right to privacy, no less important than any other right carefully and particularly reserved to the people."...

The present case, then, concerns a relationship lying within the zone of privacy created by several fundamental constitutional guarantees. And it concerns a law which, in forbidding the *use* of contraceptives rather than regulating their manufacture or sale, seeks to achieve its goals by means having a maximum destructive impact upon that relationship. Such a law cannot stand in light of the familiar principle, so often applied by this Court, that a "governmental purpose to control or prevent activities constitutionally subject to state regulation may not be achieved by means which sweep unnecessarily broadly and thereby invade the area of protected freedoms." *NAACP* v. *Alabama*.... Would we allow the police to search the sacred precincts of marital bedrooms for telltale signs of the use of contraceptives? The very idea is repulsive to the notions of privacy surrounding the marriage relationship.

We deal with a right of privacy older than the Bill of Rights—older than our political parties, older than our school system. Marriage is a coming together for better or for worse, hopefully enduring, and intimate to the degree of being sacred. It is an association that promotes a way of life, not causes; a harmony in living, not political faiths; a bilateral loyalty, not commercial or social projects. Yet it is an association for as noble a purpose as any involved in our prior decisions.

Reversed.

Mr. Justice Goldberg, whom The Chief Justice [Earl Warren] and Mr. Justice Brennan join, concurring.

I agree with the Court that Connecticut's birth-control law unconstitutionally intrudes upon the right of marital privacy, and I join in its opinion and judgment. Although I have not accepted the view that "due process" as used in the Fourteenth Amendment incorporates all of the first eight Amendments (see my concurring opinion in *Pointer* v. *Texas*...and the dissenting opinion of MR. JUSTICE BRENNAN in *Cohen* v. *Hurley*...), I do agree that the concept of liberty protects those personal rights that are fundamental, and is not confined to the specific terms of the Bill of Rights. My conclusion that the concept of liberty is not so restricted and that it embraces the right of marital privacy though that right is not mentioned explicitly in the Constitution[1] is supported both by numerous decisions of this Court, referred to in the Court's opinion, and by the language and history of the Ninth Amendment. In reaching the conclusion that the right of marital privacy is protected, as being within the protected penumbra of specific guarantees of the Bill of Rights, the Court refers to the Ninth Amendment.... I add these words to emphasize the relevance of that Amendment to the Court's holding.

The Court stated many years ago that the Due Process Clause protects those liberties that are "so rooted in the traditions and conscience of our people as to be ranked as fundamental."...

This Court, in a series of decisions, has held that the Fourteenth Amendment absorbs and applies to the States those specifics of the first eight amendments which express fundamental personal rights. The language and history of the Ninth Amendment reveal that the Framers of the Constitution believed that there are additional fundamental rights, protected from governmental infringements which exist alongside those fundamental rights specifically mentioned in the first eight constitutional amendments.

The Ninth Amendment reads, "The enumeration in the Constitution, of certain rights, shall not be construed to deny or disparage others retained by the people."...

...The Ninth Amendment to the Constitution may be regarded by some as a recent discovery and may be forgotten by others, but since 1791 it has been a basic part of the Constitution which we are sworn to uphold. To hold that a right so basic and fundamental and so deep-rooted in our society as the right of privacy in marriage may be infringed because that right is not guaranteed in so many words by the first eight amendments to the Constitution is to ignore the Ninth Amendment and to give it no effect whatsoever....

---

[1] My Brother Stewart dissents on the ground that he "can find no... general right of privacy in the Bill of Rights, in any other part of the Constitution, or in any case ever before decided by this Court." *Post*, at 530. He would require a more explicit guarantee than the one which the Court derives from several constitutional amendments. This Court, however, has never held that the Bill of Rights or the Fourteenth Amendment protects only those rights that the Constitution specifically mentions by name....

The logic of the dissents would sanction federal or state legislation that seems to me even more plainly unconstitutional than the statute before us. Surely the Government, absent a showing of a compelling subordinating state interest, could not decree that all husbands and wives must be sterilized after two children have been born to them. Yet by their reasoning such an invasion of marital privacy would not be subject to constitutional challenge because, while it might be "silly," no provision of the Constitution specifically prevents the Government from curtailing the marital right to bear children and raise a family. While it may shock some of my Brethren that the Court today holds that the Constitution protects the right of marital privacy, in my view it is far more shocking to believe that the personal liberty guaranteed by the Constitution does not include protection against such totalitarian limitation of family size, which is at complete variance with our constitutional concepts. Yet, if upon a showing of a slender basis of rationality, a law outlawing voluntary birth control by married persons is valid, then, by the same reasoning, a law requiring compulsory birth control also would seem to be valid. In my view, however, both types of law would unjustifiably intrude upon rights of marital privacy which are constitutionally protected....

Finally, it should be said of the Court's holding today that it in no way interferes with a State's proper regulation of sexual promiscuity or misconduct....

Mr. Justice Harlan, concurring in the judgment.

I fully agree with the judgment of reversal, but find myself unable to join the Court's opinion. The reason is that it seems to me to evince an approach to this case very much like that taken by my Brothers BLACK and STEWART in dissent, namely: the Due Process Clause of the Fourteenth Amendment does not touch this Connecticut statute unless the enactment is found to violate some right assured by the letter or penumbra of the Bill of Rights....

In my view, the proper constitutional inquiry in this case is whether this Connecticut statute infringes the Due Process Clause of the Fourteenth Amendment because the enactment violates basic values "implicit in the concept of ordered liberty," *Palko* v. *Connecticut*....

Mr. Justice Black, with whom Mr. Justice Stewart joins, dissenting.

I agree with my Brother STEWART's dissenting opinion. And like him I do not to any extent whatever base my view that this Connecticut law is constitutional on a belief that the law is wise or that its policy is a good one.

In order that there may be no room at all to doubt why I vote as I do, I feel constrained to add that the law is every bit as offensive to me as it is to my Brethren of the majority and my Brothers HARLAN, WHITE and GOLDBERG who, reciting reasons why it is offensive to them, hold it unconstitutional. There is no single one of the graphic and eloquent strictures and criticisms fired at the policy of this Connecticut law either by the Court's opinion or by those of my concurring Brethren to which I cannot subscribe—except their conclusion that the evil qualities they see in the law make it unconstitutional....

One of the most effective ways of diluting or expanding a constitutionally guaranteed right is to substitute for the crucial word or words of a constitutional guarantee another word or words, more or less flexible and more or less restricted in meaning. This fact is well illustrated by the use of the term "right of privacy" as a comprehensive substitute for the Fourth Amendment's guarantee against "unreasonable searches and seizures." "Privacy" is a broad, abstract and ambiguous concept which can easily be shrunken in meaning but which can also, on the other hand, easily be interpreted as a constitutional ban against many things other than searches and seizures.... I like my privacy as well as the next one, but I am nevertheless compelled to admit that government has a right to invade it unless prohibited by some specific constitutional provision. For these reasons I cannot agree with the Court's judgment and the reasons it gives for holding this Connecticut law unconstitutional....

The due process argument which my Brothers HARLAN and WHITE adopt here is based, as their opinions indicate, on the premise that this Court is vested with power to invalidate all state laws that it considers to be arbitrary, capricious, unreasonable, or oppressive, or on this Court's belief that a particular state law under scrutiny has no "rational or justifying" purpose, or is offensive to a "sense of fairness and justice." If these formulas based on "natural justice," or others which mean the same thing, are to prevail, they require judges to determine what is or is not constitutional on the basis of their own appraisal of what laws are unwise or unnecessary. The power to make such decisions is of course that of a legislative body. Surely it has to be admitted that no provision of the Constitution specifically gives such blanket power to courts to exercise such a supervisory veto over the wisdom and value of legislative policies and to hold unconstitutional those laws which they believe unwise or dangerous. I readily admit that no legislative body, state or national, should pass laws that can justly be given any of the invidious labels invoked as constitutional excuses to strike down state laws. But perhaps it is not too much to say that no legislative body ever does pass laws without believing that they will accomplish a sane, rational, wise and justifiable purpose. While I completely subscribe to the holding of *Marbury* v. *Madison*...and subsequent cases, that our Court has constitutional power to strike down statutes, state or federal, that violate commands of the Federal Constitution. I do not believe that we are granted power by the Due Process Clause or any other constitutional provision or provisions to measure constitutionality by our belief that legislation is arbitrary, capricious or unreasonable, or accomplishes no justifiable purpose, or is offensive to our own notions of "civilized standards of conduct." Such an appraisal of the wisdom of legislation is an attribute of the power to make laws, not of the power to interpret them. The use by federal courts of such a formula or doctrine or whatnot to veto federal or state laws simply takes away from Congress and States the power to make laws based on their own judgment of fairness and wisdom and transfers that power to this Court for ultimate determination—a power which was specifically denied to federal courts by the convention that framed the Constitution....

I repeat so as not to be misunderstood that this Court does have power, which it should exercise, to hold laws unconstitutional where they are forbidden by the Federal Constitution. My point is that there is no provision of the Constitution which either expressly or impliedly vests power in this Court to sit as a supervisory agency over acts of duly constituted legislative bodies and set aside their laws because of the Court's belief that the legislative policies adopted are unreasonable, unwise, arbitrary, capricious or irrational. The adoption of such a loose, flexible, uncontrolled standard for holding laws unconstitutional, if ever it is finally achieved, will amount to a great unconstitutional shift of power to the courts which I believe and am constrained to say will be bad for the courts and worse for the country. Subjecting federal and state laws to such an unrestrained and unrestrainable judicial control as to the wisdom of legislative enactments would, I fear, jeopardize the separation of governmental powers that the Framers set up and at the same time threaten to take away much of the power of States to govern themselves which the Constitution plainly intended them to have....

So far as I am concerned, Connecticut's law as applied here is not forbidden by any provision of the Federal Constitution as that Constitution was written, and I would therefore affirm.

Mr. Justice Stewart, whom Mr. Justice Black joins, dissenting.

Since 1879 Connecticut has had on its books a law which forbids the use of contraceptives by anyone. I think this is an uncommonly silly law. As a practical matter, the law is obviously unenforceable, except in the oblique context of the present case. As a philosophical matter, I believe the use of contraceptives in the relationship of marriage should be left to personal and private choice, based upon each individual's moral, ethical, and religious beliefs. As a matter of social policy, I think professional counsel about methods of birth control should be available to all, so that each individual's choice can be meaningfully made. But we are not asked in this case to say whether we think this law is unwise, or even asinine. We are asked to hold that it violates the United States Constitution. And that I cannot do.

In the course of its opinion the Court refers to no less than six Amendments to the Constitution: the First, the Third, the Fourth, the Fifth, the Ninth, and the Fourteenth. But the Court does not say which of these Amendments, if any, it thinks is infringed by this Connecticut law....

As to the First, Third, Fourth, and Fifth Amendments, I can find nothing in any of them to invalidate this Connecticut law, even assuming that all those Amendments are fully applicable against the States. It has not even been argued that this is a law "respecting an establishment of religion, or prohibiting the free exercise thereof." And surely, unless the solemn process of constitutional adjudication is to descend to the level of a play on words, there is not involved here any abridgment of "the freedom of speech, or of the press; or the right of the people peaceably to assemble, and to petition the Government for a redress of grievances." No soldier has been quartered in any house. There has been no search, and no seizure. Nobody has been compelled to be a witness against himself.

The Court also quotes the Ninth Amendment, and my Brother GOLDBERG's concurring opinion relies heavily upon it. But to say that the Ninth Amendment has anything to do with this case is to turn somersaults with history. The Ninth Amendment, like its companion the Tenth, which this court held "states but a truism that all is retained which has not been surrendered," *United States v. Darby*...was framed by James Madison and adopted by the States simply to make clear that the adoption of the Bill of Rights did not alter the plan that the *Federal* Government was to be a government of express and limited powers, and that all rights and powers not delegated to it were retained by the people and the individual States. Until today no member of this Court has ever suggested that the Ninth Amendment meant anything else, and the idea that a federal court could ever use the Ninth Amendment to annul a law passed by the elected representatives of the people of the State of Connecticut would have caused James Madison no little wonder.

What provision of the Constitution, then, does make this state law invalid? The Court says it is the right of privacy "created by several fundamental constitutional guarantees." With all deference, I can find no such general right of privacy in the Bill of Rights, in any other part of the Constitution, or in any case ever before decided by this Court.

At the oral argument in this case we were told that the Connecticut law does not "conform to current community standards." But it is not the function of this Court to decide cases on the basis of community standards. We are here to decide cases "agreeably to the Constitution and laws of the United States." It is the essence of judicial duty to subordinate our own personal views, our own ideas of what legislation is wise and what is not. If, as I should surely hope, the law before us does not reflect the standards of the people of Connecticut, the people of Connecticut can freely exercise their true Ninth and Tenth Amendment rights to persuade their elected representatives to repeal it. That is the constitutional way to take this law off the books.

48

The Negro Family (1965)

P A T R I C K   M O Y N I H A N

Generally called the Moynihan Report, *The Negro Family* sparked a decade of debate over the nature of domestic relations in America's black community.

Patrick Moynihan, a Harvard sociologist, was an assistant to the Secretary of Labor when he prepared this report in 1965. Moynihan found women serving as heads of households in the majority of African-American families. He went on to suggest that such a "matriarchal dominated" family structure explained more about the poverty of blacks than did discrimination in jobs, education, or housing. The absence of male role models produced a culture of crime, drugs, and illegitimacy, further weakening families. Moynihan demanded action by the federal government to help correct these problems.

Questions to Consider

- What is wrong with having female heads of households?
- What are the origins of "the tangle of pathology" in the black community?
- How can the government alter familial relations?

The Demand for Equality

With these events [segregation] behind us, the nation now faces a different set of challenges, which may prove more difficult to meet, if only because they cannot be cast as concrete propositions of right and wrong.

The fundamental problem here is that the Negro revolution, like the industrial upheaval of the 1930's, is a movement for equality as well as for liberty.

Liberty and Equality are the twin ideals of American democracy. But they are not the same thing. Nor, most importantly, are they equally attractive to all groups at any given time; nor yet are they always compatible, one with the other…. Much of the political history of the American nation can be seen as a competition between these two ideals, as for example, the unending troubles between capital and labor.

By and large, liberty has been the ideal with the higher social prestige in America. It has been the middle class aspiration, par excellence. (Note the assertions of the conservative right that ours is a republic, not a democracy.) Equality, on the other hand, has enjoyed tolerance more than acceptance….

American democracy has not always been successful in maintaining a balance between these two ideals, and notably so where the Negro American is concerned. "Lincoln freed the slaves," but they were given liberty, not equality. It was therefore possible in the century that followed to deprive their descendants of much of their liberty as well….

…The demand for Equality of Opportunity has been generally perceived by white Americans as a demand for liberty, a demand not to be excluded from the competitions of life—at the polling place, in the scholarship examinations, at the personnel office, on the housing market. Liberty does, of course, demand that everyone be free to try his luck, or test his skill in such matters. But these opportunities do not necessarily produce equality: on the contrary, to the extent that winners imply losers, equality of opportunity almost insures inequality of results….

The principal challenge of the next phase of the Negro revolution is to make certain that equality of results will now follow. If we do not, there will be no social peace in the United States for generations.

The Prospect for Equality

The time, therefore, is at hand for an unflinching look at the present potential of Negro Americans to move from where they now are to where they want, and ought to be.

There is no very satisfactory way, at present, to measure social health or social pathology within an ethnic, or religious, or geographical community. Data are few and uncertain, and conclusions drawn from them, including the conclusions that follow, are subject to the grossest error. Nonetheless, the opportunities, no less than the dangers, of the present moment, demand that an assessment be made.

That being the case, it has to be said that there is a considerable body of evidence to support the conclusion that Negro social structure, in particular the Negro family, battered and harassed by discrimination, injustice, and uprooting, is in the deepest trouble. While many young Negroes are moving ahead to unprecedented levels of achievement, many more are falling further and further behind.

After an intensive study of the life of central Harlem, the board of directors of Harlem Youth Opportunities Unlimited, Inc. summed up their findings in one state-

---

Source: Office of Policy Planning and Research, U.S. Department of Labor, *The Negro Family: The Case for National Action* (Washington, D.C., 1965), pp. 2–48.

ment: "Massive deterioration of the fabric of society and its institutions…"

It is the conclusion of this survey of the available national data, that what is true of central Harlem, can be said to be true of the Negro American world in general.

If this is so, it is the single most important social fact of the United States today.

The Negro American Family

At the heart of the deterioration of the fabric of Negro society is the deterioration of the Negro family.

It is the fundamental source of the weakness of the Negro community at the present time.

There is probably no single fact of Negro American life so little understood by whites. The Negro situation is commonly perceived by whites in terms of the visible manifestations of discrimination and poverty, in part because Negro protest is directed against such obstacles, and in part, no doubt, because these are facts which involve the actions and attitudes of the white community as well. It is more difficult, however, for whites to perceive the effect that three centuries of exploitation have had on the fabric of Negro society itself. Here the consequences of the historic injustices done to Negro Americans are silent and hidden from view. But here is where the true injury has occurred: unless this damage is repaired, all the effort to end discrimination and poverty and injustice will come to little.

The role of the family in shaping character and ability is so pervasive as to be easily overlooked. The family is the basic social unit of American life; it is the basic socializing unit….

It may be hazarded that the reason family structure does not loom larger in public discussion of social issues is that people tend to assume that the nature of family life is about the same throughout American society. The mass media and the development of suburbia have created an image of the American family as a highly standardized phenomenon. It is therefore easy to assume that whatever it is that makes for differences among individuals or groups of individuals, it is not a different family structure.

There is much truth to this; as with any other nation, Americans are producing a recognizable family system. But that process is not completed by any means. There are still, for example, important differences in family patterns surviving from the age of the great European migration to the United States, and these variations account for notable differences in the progress and assimilation of various ethnic and religious groups. A number of immigrant groups were characterized by unusually strong family bonds; these groups have characteristically progressed more rapidly than others.

But there is one truly great discontinuity in family structure in the United States at the present time: that between the white world in general and that of the Negro American.

The white family has achieved a high degree of stability and is maintaining that stability.

By contrast, the family structure of lower class Negroes is highly unstable, and in many urban centers is approaching complete breakdown.

…There is considerable evidence that the Negro community is in fact dividing between a stable middle-class group that is steadily growing stronger and more successful, and an increasingly disorganized and disadvantaged lower-class group. There are indications, for example, that the middle-class Negro family puts a higher premium on family stability and the conserving of family resources than does the white middle-class family. The discussion of this paper is not, obviously, directed to the first group excepting as it is affected by the experiences of the second—an important exception….

There are two points to be noted in this context.

First, the emergence and increasing visibility of a Negro middle-class may beguile the nation into supposing that the circumstances of the remainder of the Negro community are equally prosperous, whereas just the opposite is true at present, and is likely to continue so.

Second, the lumping of all Negroes together in one statistical measurement very probably conceals the extent of the disorganization among the lower-class group. If conditions are improving for one and deteriorating for the other, the resultant statistical averages might show no change. Further, the statistics on the Negro family and most other subjects treated in this paper refer only to a specific point in time. They are a vertical measure of the situation at a given moment. They do not measure the experience of individuals over time. Thus the average monthly unemployment rate for Negro males for 1964 is recorded as 9 percent. But *during* 1964, some 29 percent of Negro males were unemployed at one time or another. Similarly, for example, if 36 percent of Negro children are living in broken homes *at any specific moment*, it is likely that a far higher proportion of Negro children find themselves in that situation *at one time or another* in their lives.

Nearly a Quarter of Urban Negro Marriages Are Dissolved.

Nearly a quarter of Negro women living in cities who have ever married are divorced, separated, or are living apart from their husbands….

On the urban frontier, the nonwhite illegitimacy rates are usually higher than the national average, and the increase of late has been drastic.

In the District of Columbia, the illegitimacy rate for nonwhites grew from 21.8 percent in 1950, to 29.5 percent in 1964.

A similar picture of disintegrating Negro marriages emerges from the divorce statistics. Divorces have increased of late for both whites and nonwhites, but at a much greater rate for the latter. In 1940 both groups had a divorce rate of 2.2 percent. By 1964 the white rate had risen to 3.6 percent, but the nonwhite rate had reached 5.1 percent—40 percent greater than the formerly equal white rate.

Almost One-Fourth of Negro Families Are Headed by Females.

As a direct result of this high rate of divorce, separation, and desertion, a very large percent of Negro families are headed by females. While the percentage of such families among whites has been dropping since 1940, it has been rising among Negroes.

The percent of nonwhite families headed by a female is more than double the percent for whites. Fatherless nonwhite families increased by a sixth between 1950 and 1960, but held constant for white families.

It has been estimated that only a minority of Negro children reach the age of 18 having lived all their lives with both their parents.

Once again, this measure of family disorganization is found to be diminishing among white families and increasing among Negro families.

The Breakdown of the Negro Family Has Led to a Startling Increase in Welfare Dependency.

The majority of Negro children receive public assistance under the AFDC program at one point or another in their childhood.

At present, 14 percent of Negro children are receiving AFDC assistance, as against 2 percent of white children. Eight percent of white children receive such assistance at some time, as against 56 percent of nonwhites, according to an extrapolation based on HEW data. (Let it be noted, however, that out of a total of 1.8 million nonwhite illegitimate children in the nation in 1961, 1.3 million were *not* receiving aid under the AFDC program, although a substantial number have, or will, receive aid at some time in their lives.)…

In the beginning, the number of AFDC families in which the father was absent because of desertion was less than a third of the total. Today it is two-thirds. HEW estimates "that between two-thirds and three-fourths of the 50 percent increase from 1948 to 1955 in the number of absent-father families receiving ADC may be explained by an increase in broken homes in the population."…

The steady expansion of this welfare program, as of public assistance programs in general, can be taken as a measure of the steady disintegration of the Negro family structure over the past generation in the United States.

The Roots of the Problem

Slavery

…American slavery was profoundly different from, and in its lasting effects on individuals and their children, indescribably worse than, any recorded servitude, ancient or modern. The peculiar nature of American slavery was noted by Alexis de Tocqueville and others, but it was not until 1948 that Frank Tannenbaum, a South American specialist, pointed to the striking differences between Brazilian and American slavery. The feudal, Catholic society of Brazil had a legal and religious tradition which accorded the slave a place as a human being in the hierarchy of society—a luckless, miserable place, to be sure, but a place withal. In contrast, there was nothing in the tradition of English law or Protestant theology which could accommodate to the fact of human bondage—the slaves were therefore reduced to the status of chattels—often, no doubt, well cared for, even privileged chattels, but chattels nevertheless.…

The Reconstruction

With the emancipation of the slaves, the Negro American family began to form in the United States on a widespread scale. But it did so in an atmosphere markedly different from that which has produced the white American family.

The Negro was given liberty, but not equality. Life remained hazardous and marginal. Of the greatest importance, the Negro male, particularly in the South, became an object of intense hostility, an attitude unquestionably based in some measure on fear.

When Jim Crow made its appearance towards the end of the 19th century, it may be speculated that it was the Negro male who was most humiliated thereby; the male was more likely to use public facilities, which rapidly became segregated once the process began, and just as important, segregation, and the submissiveness it exacts, is surely more destructive to the male than to the female personality. Keeping the Negro "in his place" can be translated as keeping the Negro male in his place: the female was not a threat to anyone.

Unquestionably, these events worked against the emergence of a strong father figure. The very essence of the male animal, from the bantam rooster to the four-star general, is to strut. Indeed, in 19th century America, a particular type of exaggerated male boastfulness became almost a national style. Not for the Negro male. The "sassy nigger" was lynched.

In this situation, the Negro family made but little progress toward the middle-class pattern of the present time. Margaret Mead has pointed out that... "In every known human society, everywhere in the world, the young male learns that when he grows up one of the things which he must do in order to be a full member of society is to provide food for some female and her young." This pattern is not immutable, however: it can be broken, even though it has always eventually reasserted itself.

> Within the family, each new generation of young males learn the appropriate nurturing behavior and superimpose upon their biologically given maleness this learned parental role. When the family breaks down—as it does under slavery,...in periods of extreme social unrest during wars, revolutions, famines, and epidemics...—this delicate line of transmission is broken. Men may flounder badly in these periods, during which the primary unit may again become mother and child, the biologically given, and the special conditions under which man has held his social traditions in trust are violated and distorted.

E. Franklin Frazier makes clear that at the time of emancipation Negro women were already "accustomed to playing the dominant role in family and marriage relations" and that this role persisted in the decades of rural life that followed.

Urbanization

Country life and city life are profoundly different. The gradual shift of American society from a rural to an urban basis over the past century and a half has caused abundant strains, many of which are still much in evidence. When this shift occurs suddenly, drastically, in one or two generations, the effect is immensely disruptive of traditional social patterns.

It was this abrupt transition that produced the wild Irish slums of the 19th Century Northeast. Drunkenness, crime, corruption, discrimination, family disorganization, juvenile delinquency were the routine of that era. In our own time, the same sudden transition has produced the Negro slum—different from, but hardly better than its predecessors, and fundamentally the result of the same process....

Unemployment and Poverty

The impact of unemployment on the Negro family, and particularly on the Negro male, is the least understood of all the developments that have contributed to the present crisis. There is little analysis because there has been almost no inquiry. Unemployment, for whites and nonwhites alike, has on the whole been treated as an economic phenomenon, with almost no attention paid for at least a quarter-century to social and personal consequences....

Work is precisely the one thing the Negro family head in such circumstances has not received over the past generation.

The fundamental, overwhelming fact is that *Negro unemployment,* with the exception of a few years during World War II and the Korean War, *has continued at disaster levels for 35 years....*

Since 1929, the Negro worker has been tremendously affected by the movements of the business cycle and of employment. He has been hit worse by declines than whites, and proportionately helped more by recoveries....

The conclusion from these and similar data is difficult to avoid: During times when jobs were reasonably plentiful...the Negro family became stronger and more stable. As jobs became more and more difficult to find, the stability of the family became more and more difficult to maintain....

In 1963, a prosperous year, 29.2 percent of all Negro men in the labor force were unemployed at some time during the year. Almost half of these men were out of work 15 weeks or more.

The impact of poverty on Negro family structure is no less obvious, although again it may not be widely acknowledged. There would seem to be an American tradition, agrarian in its origins but reinforced by attitudes of urban immigrant groups, to the effect that family morality and stability decline as income and social position rise. Over the years this may have provided some consolation to the poor, but there is little evidence that it is true. On the contrary, higher family incomes are unmistakably associated with greater family stability—which comes first may be a matter for conjecture, but the conjunction of the two characteristics is unmistakable.

The Negro family is no exception. In the District of Columbia, for example, census tracts with median incomes over $8,000 had an illegitimacy rate one-third that of tracts in the category under $4,000.

The Wage System

The American wage system is conspicuous in the degree to which it provides high incomes for individuals, but is rarely adjusted to insure that family, as well as individual needs are met. Almost without exception, the social welfare and social insurance systems of other industrial democracies provide for some adjustment or supplement of a worker's income to provide for the extra expenses of those with families. American arrangements do not, save for income tax deductions.

The Federal minimum wage of $1.25 per hour provides a basic income for an individual, but an income well below the poverty line for a couple, much less a family with children.

The 1965 Economic Report of the President revised the data on the number of persons living in poverty in the United States to take account of the varying needs of families of different sizes, rather than using a flat cut off at the $3,000 income level. The resulting revision illustrates the significance of family size. Using these criteria, the number of poor families is smaller, but the number of large families who are poor increases, and the number of children in poverty rises by more than one-third—from 11 million to 15 million. This means that one-fourth of the Nation's children live in families that are poor.

A third of these children belong to families in which the father was not only present, but was employed the year round. In overall terms, median family income is lower for large families than for small families. Families of six or more children have median incomes 24 percent below families with three. (It may be added that 47 percent of young men who fail the Selective Service education test come from families of six or more.)…

Because in general terms Negro families have the largest number of children and the lowest incomes, many Negro fathers literally cannot support their families. Because the father is either not present, is unemployed, or makes such a low wage, the Negro woman goes to work. Fifty-six percent of Negro women, age 25 to 64, are in the work force, against 42 percent of white women. This dependence on the mother's income undermines the position of the father and deprives the children of the kind of attention, particularly in school matters, which is now a standard feature of middle-class upbringing.…

As with the population as a whole, there is much evidence that children are being born most rapidly in those Negro families with the least financial resources. This is an ancient pattern, but because the needs of children are greater today it is very possible that the education and opportunity gap between the offspring of these families and those of stable middle-class unions is not closing, but is growing wider.…

The Tangle of Pathology

That the Negro American has survived at all is extraordinary—a lesser people might simply have died out, as indeed others have. That the Negro community has not only survived, but in this political generation has entered national affairs as a moderate, humane, and constructive national force is the highest testament to the healing powers of the democratic ideal and the creative vitality of the Negro people.

But it may not be supposed that the Negro American community has not paid a fearful price for the incredible mistreatment to which it has been subjected over the past three centuries.

In essence, the Negro community has been forced into a matriarchal structure which, because it is so out of line with the rest of the American society, seriously retards the progress of the group as a whole, and imposes a crushing burden on the Negro male and, in consequence, on a great many Negro women as well.

There is, presumably, no special reason why a society in which males are dominant in family relationships is to be preferred to a matriarchal arrangement. However, it is clearly a disadvantage for a minority group to be operating on one principle, while the great majority of the population, and the one with the most advantages to begin with, is operating on another. This is the present situation of the Negro. Ours is a society which presumes male leadership in private and public affairs. The arrangements of society facilitate such leadership and reward it. A subculture, such as that of the Negro American, in which this is not the pattern, is placed at a distinct disadvantage.

Here an earlier word of caution should be repeated. There is much evidence that a considerable number of Negro families have managed to break out of the tangle of pathology and to establish themselves as stable, effective units, living according to patterns of American society in general. E. Franklin Frazier has suggested that the middle-class Negro American family is, if anything, more patriarchal and protective of its children than the general run of such families. Given equal opportunities, the children of these families will perform as well or better than their white peers. They need no help from anyone, and ask none.

While this phenomenon is not easily measured, one index is that middle-class Negroes have even fewer children than middle-class whites, indicating a desire to conserve the advances they have made and to insure that their children do as well or better. Negro women who marry early to uneducated laborers have more children than white women in the same situation; Negro women who marry at the common age for the middle class to educated men doing technical or professional work have only four-fifths as many children as their white counterparts.

It might be estimated that as much as half of the Negro community falls into the middle class. However, the remaining half is in desperate and deteriorating circumstances. Moreover, because of housing segregation it is immensely difficult for the stable half to escape from the cultural influences of the unstable one. The children of middle-class Negroes often as not must grow up in, or next to the slums, an experience almost unknown to white middle-class children. They are therefore constantly exposed to the pathology of the disturbed group and constantly in danger of being drawn into it....

Obviously, not every instance of social pathology afflicting the Negro community can be traced to the weakness of family structure. If, for example, organized crime in the Negro community were not largely controlled by whites, there would be more capital accumulation among Negroes, and therefore probably more Negro business enterprises. If it were not for the hostility and fear many whites exhibit towards Negroes, they in turn would be less afflicted by hostility and fear and so on. There is no one Negro community. There is no one Negro problem. There is no one solution. Nonetheless, at the center of the tangle of pathology is the weakness of the family structure. Once or twice removed, it will be found to be the principal source of most of the aberrant, inadequate, or antisocial behavior that did not establish, but now serves to perpetuate the cycle of poverty and deprivation.

It was by destroying the Negro family under slavery that white America broke the will of the Negro people. Although that will has reasserted itself in our time, it is a resurgence doomed to frustration unless the viability of the Negro family is restored.

Matriarchy

A fundamental fact of Negro American family life is the often reversed roles of husband and wife.

Robert O. Blood, Jr. and Donald M. Wolfe, in a study of Detroit families, note that "Negro husbands have unusually low power," and while this is characteristic of all low income families, the pattern pervades the Negro social structure.... In 44 percent of the Negro families studied, the wife was dominant, as against 20 percent of white wives. "Whereas the majority of white families are equalitarian [sic], the largest percentage of Negro families are dominated by the wife."

The matriarchal pattern of so many Negro families reinforces itself over the generations. This process begins with education. Although the gap appears to be closing at the moment, for a long while, Negro females were better educated than Negro males, and this remains true today for the Negro population as a whole....

There is much evidence that Negro females are better students than their male counterparts.

Daniel Thompson of Dillard University...writes:

As low as is the aspirational level among lower class Negro girls, it is considerably higher than among the boys. For example, I have examined the honor rolls in Negro high schools for about 10 years. As a rule,

from 75 to 90 percent of all Negro honor students are girls.

Dr. Thompson reports that 70 percent of all applications for the National Achievement Scholarship Program financed by the Ford Foundation for outstanding Negro high school graduates are girls, despite special efforts by high school principals to submit the names of boys.

The finalists for this new program for outstanding Negro students were recently announced. Based on an inspection of the names, only about 43 percent of all the 639 finalists were male. (However, in the regular National Merit Scholarship program, males received 67 percent of the 1964 scholarship awards.)

Inevitably, these disparities have carried over to the area of employment and income.

In 1 out of 4 Negro families where the husband is present, is an earner, and someone else in the family works, the husband is not the principal earner. The comparable figure for whites is 18 percent.

More important, it is clear that Negro females have established a strong position for themselves in white collar and professional employment, precisely the areas of the economy which are growing most rapidly, and to which the highest prestige is accorded....

The testimony to the effects of these patterns in Negro family structure is widespread, and hardly to be doubted.

Whitney Young: ...The effect on family functioning and role performance of this historical experience [economic deprivation] is what you might predict. Both as a husband and as a father the Negro male is made to feel inadequate, not because he is unlovable or unaffectionate, lacks intelligence or even a gray flannel suit. But in a society that measures a man by the size of his pay check, he doesn't stand very tall in a comparison with his white counterpart. To this situation he may react with withdrawal, bitterness toward society, aggression both within the family and racial group, self-hatred, or crime. Or he may escape through a number of avenues that help him to lose himself in fantasy or to compensate for his low status through a variety of exploits.

Thomas Pettigrew: The Negro wife in this situation can easily become disgusted with her financially dependent husband, and her rejection of him further alienates the male from family life. Embittered by their experiences with men, many Negro mothers often act to perpetuate the mother-centered pattern by taking a greater interest in their daughters than in their sons....

Robin M. Williams, Jr. in a study of Elmira, New York: Only 57 percent of Negro adults reported themselves as married—spouse present, as compared with 78 percent of native white American gentiles, 91 percent of Italian-

American, and 96 percent of Jewish informants. Of the 93 unmarried Negro youths interviewed, 22 percent did not have their mother living in the home with them, and 42 percent reported that their father was not living in their home. One-third of the youths did not know their father's present occupation, and two-thirds of a sample of 150 Negro adults did not know what the occupation of their father's father had been. Forty percent of the youths said that they had brothers and sisters living in other communities; another 40 percent reported relatives living in their home who were not parents, siblings, or grandparent[s].

The Failure of Youth

Williams' account of Negro youth growing up with little knowledge of their fathers, less of their fathers' occupations, still less of family occupational traditions, is in sharp contrast to the experience of the white child. The white family, despite many variants, remains a powerful agency not only for transmitting property from one generation to the next, but also for transmitting no less valuable contracts with the world of education and work.... Children today still learn the patterns of work from their fathers even though they may no longer go into the same jobs.

White children without fathers at least perceive all about them the pattern of men working.

Negro children without fathers flounder—and fail....

A prime index of the disadvantage of Negro youth in the United States is their consistently poor performance on the mental tests that are a standard means of measuring ability and performance in the present generation.

There is absolutely no question of any genetic differential: Intelligence potential is distributed among Negro infants in the same proportion and pattern as among Icelanders or Chinese or any other group. American society, however, impairs the Negro potential....

Martin Deutch and Bert Brown, investigating intelligence test differences between Negro and white 1st and 5th graders of different social classes, found that there is a direct relationship between social class and IQ. As the one rises so does the other: but more for whites than Negroes. This is surely a result of housing segregation, referred to earlier, which makes it difficult for middle-class Negro families to escape the slums....

...[T]he authors look for background variables other than social class which might explain the difference: "One of the most striking differences between the Negro and white groups is the consistently higher frequency of broken homes and resulting family disorganization in the Negro group."...

The scores of fifth graders with fathers absent were lower than the scores of first graders with fathers absent, and while the authors point out that it is cross sectional data and does not reveal the duration of the fathers' absence, "What we might be tapping is the cumulative effect of fatherless years."...

Delinquency and Crime

The combined impact of poverty, failure, and isolation among Negro youth has had the predictable outcome in a disastrous delinquency and crime rate.

In a typical pattern of discrimination, Negro children in all public and private orphanages are a smaller proportion of all children than their proportion of the population although their needs are clearly greater.

On the other hand Negroes represent a third of all youth in training schools for juvenile delinquents.

It is probable that at present, a majority of the crimes against the person, such as rape, murder, and aggravated assault are committed by Negroes. There is, of course, no absolute evidence; inference can only be made from arrest and prison population statistics. The data that follow unquestionably are biased against Negroes, who are arraigned much more casually than are whites, but it may be doubted that the bias is great enough to affect the general proportions....

In Chicago in 1963, three-quarters of the persons arrested for [violent] crimes were Negro; in Detroit, the same proportions held.

In 1960, 37 percent of all persons in Federal and State prisons were Negro. In that year, 56 percent of the homicide and 57 percent of the assault offenders committed to State institutions were Negro.

The overwhelming number of offenses committed by Negroes are directed toward other Negroes: the cost of crime to the Negro community is a combination of that to the criminal and to the victim....

Mary Diggs found that three-fourths—twice the expected ratio—of Philadelphia's Negro delinquents who came before the law during 1948 did not live with both their natural parents.

In predicting juvenile crime, Eleanor and Sheldon Glueck also found that a higher proportion of delinquent than nondelinquent boys came from broken homes. They identified five critical factors in the home environment that made a difference in whether boys would become delinquents: discipline of boy by father, supervision of boy by mother, affection of father for boy, affection of mother for boy, and cohesiveness of family....

Recent psychological research demonstrates the personality effects of being reared in a disorganized home without a father. One study showed that children from fatherless homes seek immediate gratification of their desires far more than children with fathers present. Others revealed that children who hunger for immediate gratification are more prone to delinquency, along with other less social behavior....

The Armed Forces

The ultimate mark of inadequate preparation for life is the failure rate on the Armed Forces mental test. The Armed Forces Qualification Test is not quite a mental test, nor yet an education test. It is a test of ability to perform at an acceptable level of competence. It roughly measures ability that ought to be found in an average 7th or 8th grade student. A grown young man who cannot pass this test is in trouble.

Fifty-six percent of Negroes fail it.

This is a rate almost four times that of the whites....

There is, however, an even more important issue involved in military service for Negroes. Service in the United States Armed Forces is the *only* experience open to the Negro American in which he is truly treated as an equal: not as a Negro equal to a white, but as one man equal to any other man in a world where the category "Negro" and "white" do not exist. If this is a statement of the ideal rather than reality, it is an ideal that is close to realization. In food, dress, housing, pay, work—the Negro in the Armed Forces *is* equal and is treated that way.

There is another special quality about military service for Negro men: it is an utterly masculine world. Given the strains of the disorganized and matrifocal family life in which so many Negro youth come of age, the Armed Forces are a dramatic and desperately needed change: a world away from women, a world run by strong men of unquestioned authority, where discipline, if harsh, is nonetheless orderly and predictable, and where rewards, if limited, are granted on the basis of performance.

The theme of a current Army recruiting message states it as clearly as can be: "In the U.S. Army you get to know what it means to feel like a man."...

Alienation

The term alienation may...serve to sum up the...numerous ways in which large numbers of Negro youth appear to be withdrawing from American society....

Understated or not, the official unemployment rates for Negroes are almost unbelievable.

The unemployment statistics for Negro teenagers— 29 percent in January 1965—reflect lack of training and opportunity in the greatest measure, but it may not be doubted that they also reflect a certain failure of nerve.

"Are you looking for a job?" Secretary of Labor Wirtz asked a young man on a Harlem street corner. "Why?" was the reply.

Richard A. Cloward and Robert Ontell have commented on this withdrawal in a discussion of the Mobilization for Youth project on the lower East Side of New York.

> What contemporary slum and minority youth probably lack that similar children in earlier periods possessed is not motivation but some minimal sense of competence.
>
> We are plagued, in work with these youth, by what appears to be a low tolerance for frustration. They are not able to absorb setbacks. Minor irritants and rebuffs are magnified out of all proportion to reality. Perhaps they react as they do because they are not equal to the world that confronts them, and they know it. And it is the knowing that is devastating....

Narcotic addiction is a characteristic form of withdrawal. In 1963, Negroes made up 54 percent of the addict population of the United States....

There is a larger fact about the alienation of Negro youth than the tangle of pathology described by these statistics. It is a fact particularly difficult to grasp by white persons who have in recent years shown increasing awareness of Negro problems.

The present generation of Negro youth growing up in the urban ghettos has probably less personal contact with the white world than any generation in the history of the Negro American.

Until World War II it could be said that in general the Negro and white worlds lived, if not together, at least side by side. Certainly they did, and do, in the South.

Since World War II, however, the two worlds have drawn physically apart. The symbol of this development was the construction in the 1940's and 1950's of the vast white, middle- and lower-middle class suburbs around all of the Nation's cities. Increasingly the inner cities have been left to Negroes—who now share almost no community life with whites.

In turn, because of this new housing pattern—most of which has been financially assisted by the Federal government—it is probable that the American school system has become *more*, rather than less segregated in the past two decades....

The only religious movement that appears to have enlisted a considerable number of lower class Negro males in Northern cities of late is that of the Black Muslims: a movement based on total rejection of white society, even though it emulates whites more.

In a word: the tangle of pathology is tightening.

The Case for National Action

The object of this study has been to define a problem, rather than propose solutions to it. We have kept within these confines for three reasons.

First, there are many persons, within and without the Government, who do not feel the problem exists, at least in any serious degree. These persons feel that, with the legal obstacles to assimilation out of the way, matters will take care of themselves in the normal course of events....

Second, it is our view that the problem is so interrelated, one thing with another, that any list of program proposals would necessarily be incomplete, and would distract attention from the main point of interrelatedness. We have shown a clear relation between male employment, for example, and the number of welfare dependent children. Employment in turn reflects educational achievement, which depends in large part on family stability, which reflects employment. Where we should break into this cycle, and how, are the most difficult domestic questions facing the United States. We must first reach agreement on what the problem is, then we will know what questions must be answered.

Third, it is necessary to acknowledge the view, held by a number of responsible persons, that this problem may in fact be out of control. This is a view with which we emphatically and totally disagree, but the view must be acknowledged....

However, the argument of this paper does lead to one central conclusion: Whatever the specific elements of a national effort designed to resolve this problem, those elements must be coordinated in terms of one general strategy.

What then is that problem? We feel the answer is clear enough. Three centuries of injustice have brought about deep-seated structural distortions in the life of the Negro American. At this point, the present tangle of pathology is capable of perpetuating itself without assistance from the white world. The cycle can be broken only if these distortions are set right.

In a word, a national effort towards the problems of Negro Americans must be directed towards the question of family structure. The object should be to strengthen the Negro family so as to enable it to raise and support its members as do other families. After that, how this group of Americans chooses to run its affairs, take advantage of its opportunities, or fail to do so, is none of the nation's business....

Such a national effort could be stated thus:

The policy of the United States is to bring the Negro American to full and equal sharing in the responsibilities and rewards of citizenship. To this end, the programs of the Federal government bearing on this objective shall be designed to have the effect, directly or indirectly, of enhancing the stability and resources of the Negro American family.

49

The Watts Riots (1965)

THE CALIFORNIA GOVERNOR'S COMMISSION ON THE LOS ANGELES RIOTS

On August 12, 1965, the complacency of white Americans was shattered by a violent outburst of frustration and anger in Los Angeles. Many whites thought that the recent successes in the Civil Rights Movement, exemplified by the passage of the Civil Rights Act, would lead to a lessening of racial animosity. Most leaders were therefore completely unprepared for the riots that broke out, not in the South, but in the West, in liberal California. What had been largely ignored was the long simmering anger of urban African-Americans over their poverty, mistreatment by largely white police forces, and confinement to ghettos. In August 12, 1965, amidst repeated tales of police brutality, some of them accurate, a crowd began stoning police cars and passing whites. There followed six days of burning, looting, and shooting, culminating in thirty-four deaths, more than a thousand injuries, the destruction of hundreds of buildings, and nearly four thousand arrests. The following account is drawn from the records of the Los Angeles police and was compiled by the California Governor's Commission on the Los Angeles Riots, chaired by John McCone. Though the Commission felt that a small number of criminals bore responsibility for the riots, they estimated that at least seven thousand people took part in the uprising.

Questions to Consider

• Why would angry crowds destroy property in their own communities?

• Was the police response appropriate? What could officials have done to avoid the riot?

August 12, 1965

By 12:20 A.M. approximately 50 to 75 youths were on either side of Avalon Blvd. at Imperial Highway, throwing missiles at passing cars and the police used vehicles with red lights and sirens within the riot area perimeter in an effort to disperse the crowd. As they did so, the rock throwing crowd dispersed, only to return as the police left the scene. Some of the older citizens in the area were inquiring, "What are those crazy kids doing?" A number of adult Negroes expressed the opinion that the police should open fire on the rock throwers to stop their activity. The police did not discharge firearms at rioters.

It was estimated that by 12:30 A.M. 70% of the rioters were children and the remainder were young adults and adults. Their major activity was throwing missiles at passing vehicles driven by Caucasians. One rioter stationed himself a block from the intersection of Avalon Blvd. and Imperial Highway, where the major group of rioters was centered, and signaled to this group whenever a vehicle driven by a Caucasian approached the intersection, so that it could be stoned.

Supervisor Kenneth Hahn and his assistant, Mr. Pennington, drove to the riot scene at about 12:35

A.M. and did not observe road blocks or policemen in the area.

Rioters continued to attack vehicles in the vicinity of Imperial Highway and Avalon Blvd. Some spectators described the crowd as having the appearance of a carnival, with persons acting with abandon and some spectators apparently enjoying the activity as if it were a sporting event.

A dozen vehicles were attacked by about 150 rioters, among them the vehicle of Supervisor Hahn and his assistant, whose automobile was struck by bricks and rocks thrown from the crowd near San Pedro St. and Avalon Blvd. The windshield and one window of his car were broken. Glass cut Mr. Hahn's head.

By 1:00 A.M. the rioters appeared to gather into about four groups of 50 to 100 persons each.

Supervisor Hahn made contact with Sheriff's deputies in the field, utilized a citizen's telephone to communicate with the watch commander at Firestone Station and then rode to that station with Sheriff's deputies. Supervisor Hahn urged action by the LAPD and the Sheriff's Department to prepare for additional trouble which might develop, based upon his view of the rioters.

About 1:30 A.M. a Sheriff's deputy was assigned to drive Supervisor Hahn and his assistant, Mr. Pennington, from Firestone Station to the Supervisor's residence, using an unmarked automobile of the Sheriff's Department. Although the driver was instructed by his superior to avoid any troubled area, Supervisor Hahn directed the driver to go through the area near Imperial

Source: Governor's Commission on the Los Angeles Riots, *Transcripts, Depositions, Consultants' Reports, and Selected Documents*, Vol. 2, *Chronology* (Sacramento, Ca., 1966), pp. 28–33, 43–45, 83–87, 168–175, 183–188.

Highway and Avalon Blvd. for the Supervisor's benefit. As they crossed Imperial Highway southbound on Avalon, they observed several Los Angeles police officers trying to disperse small groups of rioters. Suddenly, without warning, several persons ran into the street and rocks were thrown at the Sheriff's car. The driver was struck on the head and received a slight concussion.

They then proceeded to the Supervisor's residence, transferred to Mr. Pennington's car, and went to a hospital for first aid treatment. Mr. Pennington had also received a cut on the leg. It was about 2:30 A.M.

Two cars were set afire by rioters at the intersection of San Pedro Street and Imperial Highway and at 2:00 A.M. the first looted market was observed at 116th St. and Avalon Boulevard.

At about 3:30 A.M. Deputy Chief Murdock of the LAPD returned to his residence from the police action. Seventeen Los Angeles police officers had reported to Central Receiving Hospital for treatment to injuries. One officer had been stabbed in the back when attacked by the crowd he was attempting to disperse.

By 4:00 A.M. the area had become quiet as the crowd had departed. In the words of Deputy Chief Murdock, "On Wednesday night it (the crowd) dissipated itself."

Several staff members of the Los Angeles County Human Relations Commission went to the disturbed area around midnight of August 11–12. They spoke with persons in the crowd, with youths who were throwing rocks and with police officers. They attempted to get the youth to leave the streets and allow tensions to subside but were unsuccessful. Some of the staff state they observed the uniformed police officers and police cruisers at the police command post were the targets of the crowd. They state they suggested to a police command officer on the scene that the removal of police and police vehicles from the area for the purpose of eliminating the objects of attack would be advisable. They state their suggestions also included that the streets be blocked to prevent through traffic from entering the affected area, but that their suggestions were not immediately accepted. They did notice that the police moved the command post a short time later, although traffic was allowed to continue to move through the affected area and the crowd stoned passing cars. It was noted that only cars driven by Caucasian drivers were victims of the rock throwing....

Sunrise disclosed five burned automobiles amidst a large amount of rubble, broken bricks, stones, and shattered glass in the vicinity of the intersection of Imperial Highway and Avalon Blvd....

As an indication of the mood of the crowd of approximately 400 persons who had gathered on Avalon Boulevard near Imperial Highway on Thursday morning, the following comments of youth in the crowd were quoted:

"Like why, man, should I got home? These ——— cops have been pushin' me 'round all my life. Kickin' my ——— and things like that. Whitey ain't no good, he talk 'bout law and order, it's his law and his order, it ain't mine...."

"———, if I've got to die, I ain't dyin' in Viet Nam, I'm going to die here...."

"I don't have no job, I ain't worked for two years—he, the white man, got everything, I ain't got nothin'. What do you expect me to do? I get my kicks when I see Whitey running—if they come in here tonight, I'm going to kill me one...."

"Look, Brother, I ain't scared of them—what they got—a gun? I got one too, and I'm goin' to blast me a cop on that white ——— tonight—you'd better believe it...."

"If them black-and-whites (police cars) come in here tonight—they'd wish they hadn't—we are ready...."

"I got my stuff (gun) ready, and baby, I mean to use it—I'm going to get me a white ——— tonight—tell them that for me...."

"They always ——— with the Blood—beatin' them with them sticks, handcuffing women, I saw one of them ——— go up side a cat's head and split it wide open. They treat the Blood like dirt—they been doin' it for years—look how they treated us when we were slaves...."

"What I got to do with this country ——— ———? ——— Whitey ain't never done a damn thing for Blood except kill us. It's our turn now...."

"Whitey use his cops to keep us here. We're like hogs in a pen—then they come in with them silly helmets, sticks, and guns and things—who the ——— [Chief of Police] Parker think he is—God?..."

The temperature in Los Angeles at noon on August 12 was 87 degrees and because of the relative humidity of 49%, the discomfort index of the U.S. Weather Bureau shows that practically all persons would be uncomfortable under those weather conditions and that the discomfort would be acute. The discomfort index continued to rise....

August 13, 1965

State Assemblyman Mervyn Dymally of Los Angeles, accompanied by Robert Hall, co-chairman of the Nonviolent Action Committee, went to the vicinity of

Imperial Highway and Avalon Blvd. shortly after midnight on the morning of August 13th for the purpose of assisting in getting people to leave the streets and return to their homes. A group of youths were burning an information center, automobiles were being halted, overturned and burned, two liquor stores were looted, then a doctor's office and a hot-dog stand. Other fires were also started by the rioters and Assemblyman Dymally's requests to the rioters were, to a large measure, ignored.

Shortly after midnight, Colonel Quick called Colonel Turnage of the National Guard 40th Armored Division, Los Angeles, and advised Colonel Turnage that although the LAPD was experiencing considerable activity in the riot area, a call for the 40th Armored Division personnel did not appear probable at that time.

Police reported approximately 500 Negroes had gathered east of Central Avenue on Imperial Highway shortly after midnight and at 12:17 A.M. rioters were reported to have looted a hardware store in the vicinity of 109th Street and Avalon, for weapons.

The fire department attempted to respond to a rubbish fire at Imperial and Central at 12:19 A.M. but its equipment was turned back because rioters would not let firemen proceed and were throwing rocks and bottles at the vehicles. One fireman was hit on the head by a rock thrown by a rioter.

At 12:25 A.M. it was reported on a radio broadcast that the LAPD felt the riot was under control.

At 12:30 A.M. a California Highway patrolman received a minor wound from a ricocheting bullet at 108th St. and Avalon. The fire department was unable to respond to a liquor store fire at Imperial and Central because of a lack of protection. Rioters at Central Ave. and Imperial Highway were armed with bricks and police officers were instructed not to go into the area but to stay on the perimeter of the riot, for their own protection. The police reported one police officer had been hit on the arm with a brick, one officer had been hit with a bottle causing a lacerated leg, one officer had been bitten on the thumb by a rioter he was attempting to arrest, and another officer was kicked in the ribs by a rioter.

At 12:38 A.M. looters entered a war surplus merchandise store in the vicinity of 108th and Avalon....

At 1:00 A.M. Lt. Governor Anderson was informed by General Hill that Los Angeles local law enforcement officials believed the riot situation was near control.

At 1:11 A.M. several buildings were reported on fire at Imperial and Avalon and at 1:18 A.M. a Los Angeles police officer requested help at 103rd St. and Avalon because of the attacking mob. At 1:20 A.M. it was reported that stores were being looted by rioters on 103rd St. in the Watts area.

At 1:28 A.M. a church was reported on fire at Imperial Highway and Central Ave. and the fire department dispatched equipment.

By 1:30 A.M. 216 Sheriff's deputies were assigned to duty in the riot area and 40 held in reserve; 80 California Highway patrolmen were assigned to duty as were 250 LAPD officers.

At 1:45 A.M. Lt. Governor Anderson talked to Mr. John Billett, associate press secretary for the Governor, and was informed that the riot appeared to be nearing control.

At 1:54 A.M. Assemblyman Dymally was at 1237 East Imperial Highway and expressed fear for his personal safety and for the safety of his staff.

At 1:57 A.M. the Los Angeles Sheriff's deputies on perimeter control refused entry into the riot area to fire department units for the safety of the firemen.

Three cars were on fire, as well as a building, in the 1200 block of East Imperial Highway and when fire department vehicles appeared in the area they were struck by thrown projectiles.

By 2:00 A.M. the perimeter established around the riot area was dissolved, according to Deputy Chief Murdock, because of outbreaks of rioting beyond the original perimeter lines.

The owner of a liquor store in the 2000 block of East 103rd St. was reported to have barricaded himself in his store and to have shot persons attempting to break in.

At 2:16 A.M. a group of rioters proceeding north on Central Ave., on 120th Street overturned and burned automobiles in the street.

At 2:22 A.M. a Los Angeles police officer shot at a burglary suspect at 103rd St. and Beach St. A field order was issued by the LAPD to: 1) send a reserve of 60 men to 115th St. and Avalon, two officers to a unit and two cars to a team; 2) release California Highway patrolmen from duty; 3) release Sheriff's deputies from duty, and 4) begin interior control of the riot area.

By 2:25 A.M. police reported a total of 33 rioters had been booked at 77th St. Police Station on allegations of crimes arising from the riot. Local hospitals reported 74 persons were treated for injuries resulting from the riot. These were in addition to the 26 previously reported.

At 2:38 A.M. mass looting was reported by rioters in the vicinity of 103rd and Beach St. and at 2:45 A.M. Los Angeles police officers requested assistance at 102nd and Beach in a pawn shop. The owner was in the shop with a gun attempting to protect his property from the rioters.

At 2:40 A.M. Colonel Quick reported by telephone to General Hill at his residence in Sacramento the current situation in Los Angeles, and at 2:55 A.M. General Hill telephoned Lt. Governor Anderson at his home in Hawthorne, relaying the report from Colonel Quick and that there appeared to be no need for the National Guard to assist the police....

August 14, 1965

...By 12:10 A.M. thirty rioters were reported throwing bricks at passing vehicles on 7th Avenue between Brooks Ave. and Broadway in the Venice section of Los Angeles.

Moneycre Whitmore was shot and killed by police officers at 59th St. and Vermont Ave. while he was allegedly looting (the Coroner's inquest ruled this was a justifiable homicide).

At 12:38 A.M. General Hill ordered the Third Brigade, which was bivouacked in Ventura, California, returned to Los Angeles. The Brigade was to proceed to the grounds of the Hollywood Park Race Track on Century Blvd. in Inglewood.

At 12:45 A.M. the National Guard relieved the LAPD in the Watts area and 40 policemen were at the Watts police substation available to back up the National Guard in the handling of arrests.

Looters proceeded as far north as 18th St. on Broadway, Avalon Blvd., Main St. and Central Avenue, looting and burning as they proceeded northward from the areas previously struck by the rioters. Arrests in large numbers were being made by the police.

At 12:55 A.M. two suspects drove an automobile at a high speed into a National Guard skirmish line at Avalon Blvd. and Santa Barbara Ave. The vehicle struck and injured a National Guardsman. General Hill was present and observed the incident. He states the action by the driver was an obvious attempt to run down more than one of the Guardsmen, and one was seriously hurt. At that time the National Guardsmen had also been fired on by rioters in other places. Up to this point they were supplied with rifle ammunition but had been ordered not to place the ammunition in their rifles. On witnessing the incident at Avalon Blvd. and Santa Barbara Ave., General Hill personally issued the order that all National Guardsmen were to load their rifles with live ammunition. Bayonets were affixed to rifles.

The first requirement for troops in excess of those comprising the Second Brigade occurred shortly after midnight on the morning of August 14. The order was given by the office of the Adjutant General from the Los Angeles command post to the Third Brigade of San Diego commanded by Colonel Gordon M. Dawson. This complement of troops included the Brigade Headquarters Company, the Third, Fifth, and Sixth Battalions of the 185th Armored Division.

The Third Brigade, then at Ventura, returned to Los Angeles and arrived at the grounds of Hollywood Park Race Track at approximately 4:30 A.M. Arrangements were made for General Glen C. Ames, Assistant Division Commander, Colonel Taylor and Colonel Dawson to attend an early morning conference with the LAPD for the purpose of coordinating missions, areas, and liaison activities with the LAPD.

It was agreed at 1:00 A.M. by the LAPD and the National Guard Commanders that the Guard would be deployed with police personnel in coordinated missions, and that the National Guard would not engage in operations independent of the Police Department as regarded the riot.

General Hill ordered the reinforcement of National Guard troops in Los Angeles from the San Joaquin Valley. Troops of the 49th Division located in northern California were flown into the Los Angeles area by air transport. General Hill had previously alerted the Commanding General of the 49th Division so that he had made preparations leading up to the mobilization of his Division. The National Guard transported by plane more than 4,000 troops from northern California, commencing at about 1:00 A.M. on August 14. Eventually there were over 13,000 troops involved as the rioting escalated.

Approximately 100 fire department engine companies were actively fighting fires in the riot area and 54 engine companies were held in reserve. The period of maximum fire department effort was at approximately 1:00 A.M. on August 14 with nearly 58% of the engine companies working in the emergency.

Thomas Owens was shot and killed by police officers at McKinley Ave. and Vernon Ave., while he was allegedly looting. (Coroner's inquest held this to be a justifiable homicide.)

At 1:45 A.M. Carleton Elliott, an alleged looter, was killed by gunfire of police at Jefferson Blvd. and Griffin Ave. (Coroner's inquest held this to be a justifiable homicide.)

At 1:55 A.M. Deputy Police Chief Tom Reddin requested action be taken by the State to declare certain areas of Los Angeles County, affected by the riots, to be disaster areas....

By 2:00 A.M. the police department was able to supply sufficient policemen to assist the fire department in the protection of equipment and firemen. Patrolmen with riot guns were assigned to fire department vehicles and from that time forward all fire task forces responded with police protection or with National Guard protection.

At 2:10 A.M. law enforcement officers and National Guardsmen made a sweep of the main north and south thoroughfares from Pico Blvd. to Slauson Ave. between the Harbor Freeway and San Pedro St.

Albert Flores Sr. attempted to run a road block established by policemen and National Guardsmen at 102nd

St. and Compton Blvd. When he failed to stop, National Guard officers and police officers fired at his car and he was killed. (Coroner's inquest held this to be a justifiable homicide.)…

At 2:40 A.M. the fire department reported a concentration of fires on Central Ave. that were being re-set on property previously on fire. A decision was made that fire equipment would not respond to the alarms as the fire department had insufficient available personnel pending the reporting to duty of fresh fire crews.

At 3:00 A.M. the total National Guard troop commitment to Los Angeles was 3,355, all from the 40th Armored Division.

From 2:00 to 3:00 A.M. in the Pacoima area it was reported that eight or ten instances of looting and disturbing the peace had occurred.

By 3:00 A.M. the riot activity began to slow down in the south central area of Los Angeles and by 6:00 A.M. the area was fairly quiet. There had been from 35 to 40 greater alarm fires burning simultaneously in the area. The fire department was heavily involved in combatting these fires.

Andrew Huston Jr. was shot and killed at 1505 East 103rd St. by a National Guardsman, as an alleged sniper. (Coroner's inquest ruled this to be a justifiable homicide.)

By 5:00 A.M. there were 496 Los Angeles police officers, 463 Los Angeles County Sheriff's Deputies, and 47 California Highway Patrolmen on duty in the riot area.

At 5:15 A.M. Paul E. Harbin was shot and killed by police at 2004 South Central Ave., as a looter. (Coroner's inquest held this a justifiable homicide.) At 5:15 A.M. George Fentroy was killed by police at 62nd St. and South Broadway, as a looter. Police had observed two looters leaving the building with their arms full of clothing and ordered them to halt. The persons refused to heed the command. One suspect escaped. (Coroner's inquest held the killing of Fentroy was justifiable homicide.) At 5:30 A.M. Miller C. Burroughs was shot and killed by police at 6120 S. Vermont Ave., as a looter. (Coroner's inquest held this a justifiable homicide.) At 5:30 A.M. Leon Cauley was shot and killed at 6120 S. Vermont Ave. by police, as a looter. (Coroner's inquest held this a justifiable homicide.)

According to Mr. Hale Champion, he talked by telephone with Governor Brown in Athens, Greece, in the early morning hours of August 14, 1965 at which time he informed the Governor that the National Guard was on duty, that the situation in Los Angeles was very bad and chaotic, that there would need to be a larger buildup of the National Guard, which was contemplated. He believed he also reported a bit of conversa-

tion he had had with a group of Negro leaders who had come to the Governor's office on the evening of August 13. He said the substance of the conversation with the Negro leaders was that they had not been able to establish any way of communication with the Los Angeles police or the Los Angeles Mayor's office; that they were "in effect being told that they were part of the problem."

About 8:00 A.M. Mr. Champion states he talked to Governor Brown who had arrived in New York City from Athens. Mr. Champion states he had been advised that the Governor was meeting in New York City with representatives of the Federal government, including Mr. Leroy Collins, to discuss the Los Angeles situation and possible Federal assistance.

In the conversation with Governor Brown in New York, the Governor wanted to know about the curfew and the way the problem was being approached by the State Attorney General and his staff. The Governor was transported to Los Angeles from New York in a U.S. government plane which stopped in Omaha for refueling. While in Omaha, Governor Brown was again in telephone conversation with Mr. Champion who was in Los Angeles. Mr. Champion states there had been some resistance to the idea of a curfew in Los Angeles by Police Chief Parker.

The balance of the 40th Armored Division troops were ordered back to Los Angeles from Camp Roberts, California.

Between noon and 12:30 P.M. looting was occurring at 22nd St. and Central Ave., Washington Blvd. and Central Ave., Vernon Ave. and Avalon Blvd., 87th Place and Compton Ave., 41st St. and Broadway, 46th St. and Central Ave., 44th St. and Central Ave., involving markets, a department store and a furniture store. Looting was occurring at 49th and Normandie Ave. and rioters were overturning vehicles in the 700 block of East Vernon Ave.

There was a large fire in a market at 43rd St. and Crenshaw Blvd. Looters were reported in a television store at 62nd St. and Vermont Ave., at 54th St. and Central Ave., 44th St. and South Broadway, and from 200 to 300 looters were reported at 43rd St. and Central Ave. A mob was attacking police officers with bottles and rocks in the vicinity of Vernon Ave. and Central Ave. At 46th St. and Central Ave. looters were reported concentrating on a furniture store; at Washington Blvd. and Central Ave. on a drug store; at 66th St. and Menlo Ave. on a television store, and in commercial establishments in the 1100 block of East 88th St. Fires were burning in the vicinity of 43rd St. and Central Ave. and heavy looting was reported at 21st St. and Central Ave.

Between 12:30 and 1:00 P.M. a police officer at 40th Street and Central Ave. was trapped by a crowd and requested assistance; looters were in commercial establishments on the northeast corner of 48th St. and Broadway, at 21st St. and Central Ave., and at 78th St. and Hoover St.; firemen on duty were being shot at by rioters at 25th St. and Central Ave. and a large crowd of rioters was in the vicinity of 76th St. and Central Ave.; looters were in the vicinity of 46th St. and Figueroa; in a market at 80th St. and Central Ave.; and a police officer requested assistance in the vicinity of Jefferson Blvd. and Griffith Ave.

At 1:05 P.M. rioters were reported stealing guns and throwing bombs into a sporting goods store near 109th St. and Hooper Ave. At 66th St. and Denver Ave. shots were fired at a police officer who requested assistance. It was reported at 1:12 P.M. that looters were throwing fire bombs at a market at 47th St. and Broadway and three male Negroes with rifles were reported in front of 607 West Century Blvd. Looters were in a furniture store at 61st St. and Broadway, at the rear of a market and warehouse at 49th St. and Normandie Ave. and in a store at 49th St. and Broadway.

Looters were reported in a market in the 2600 block of Cimarron St. At 1:23 P.M. a market at 20th St. and Central Ave. was being looted and it was reported a group with gas bombs was gathered at 56th St. and San Pedro St.

At 1:28 P.M. at 55th St. and Broadway there was a major fire and shots were reportedly fired by suspects. At 1:35 P.M. a major fire was started at 54th St. and Broadway and snipers shot at firemen. The fire department requested police assistance. At 1:37 P.M. a store at 61st St. and Broadway was looted and a police officer at Vernon Ave. and Broadway requested assistance. At 54th St. and Broadway, it was reported that ammunition was exploding in a fire.

At 1:38 P.M. looters were reported to be holding a hostage at 757 East Vernon Ave. A bread company at Avalon Blvd. and Santa Barbara Ave. was looted and there was extensive looting in the area of 80th St. and Central Ave., and 103rd St. and Central Ave.

At 1:48 P.M. there was a report that a large truck full of male Negroes with red arm bands had been seen in the 5300 block of Cimarron St.

The fire department requested police assistance at 61st St. and Broadway at 1:57 P.M.

At 2:00 P.M. looters were in a market at 78th St. and Hoover St. and in a department store in the 1200 block of East Washington Blvd. A man was reportedly trapped inside a building at 4801 S. Broadway which was surrounded by looters.

Rioters threw rocks at cars in the 1300 block of East Adams Blvd. shortly after 2:00 P.M. and a police officer requested assistance at 41st and Broadway. New fires broke out at 52nd St. and Broadway and another police officer requested assistance at 97th St. and Main St.

By 2:15 P.M. looters were in a dress shop at Western Ave. and Exposition Blvd. and a market at 57th St. and San Pedro St. Fires were started at 44th St. and Broadway and at 113th St. and Main St.

It was reported at 2:30 P.M. that 9,958 National Guard troops had been committed to the riot area.

A doughnut shop at Vermont Ave. and Adams Blvd. was looted....

At 2:50 P.M. Los Angeles City Councilman Billy G. Mills went to the 77th St. Police Station and talked with a police lieutenant, asking that the burglary charges against Negro looters be reduced to show residents of the area that the police wanted the rioting to stop. The request was denied.

At 3:04 P.M. a fireman was injured at 55th St. and Compton Blvd. and looters were stoning vehicles at 42nd St. and San Pedro St.

At 3:08 P.M. a furniture store at 41st Place and Broadway was reported on fire and at 110th St. and Main St. a clothing store was reported on fire. At 3:30 P.M. the Los Angeles police and National Guard troops made a sweep of Central Ave. from Washington Blvd. to Slauson Ave. and there was reported sufficient manpower to control the area at the time.

From 3:30 to 4:00 P.M. liquor stores at 66th St. and Figueroa, and 42nd Place and San Pedro St., were looted....

...A market in the 4700 block of South Broadway was broken into by rioters and at another market looters were reported to have radios tuned to receive police department radio broadcasts and to have portable radio transmitters. On Main St. between 105th St. and Imperial Highway, rioters in the area started fires.

Lt. Governor Anderson states that at 4:00 P.M. he ordered the drawing up of a proclamation declaring an extreme emergency in Los Angeles.

From 4:00 to 4:30 P.M. snipers were reported in the vicinity of the 1100 block on West 29th St. Commercial establishments were being looted on Central Ave. between Vernon Ave. and Washington Blvd. by a reported mob of rioters in excess of 2,000; all north-south streets between Broadway and Central Ave. were jammed with looters. Rioting was completely out of control from the 4000 to 5000 block on South Broadway and fire department units could not enter the area. An estimated 90% to 95% of the liquor stores in the riot area had been looted....

50

The Chicago Police Riot (1968)

D A N I E L   W A L K E R

As the Democratic National Convention of August 1968, approached, opponents of the war in Vietnam grew ever more frustrated. Despite the electoral successes of antiwar candidates Eugene McCarthy and Robert Kennedy, President Lyndon Johnson's vice president, Hubert H. Humphrey, was obviously going to be the Democratic nominee. Chicago's Democratic mayor, "Boss" Richard Daley, promised that no one would be allowed to disrupt the convention. On the night of August 28, as millions of Americans watched on live television, the Chicago police, tired of being taunted by hundreds of young demonstrators, went berserk. While the crowd chanted "the whole world is watching," the police waded into the crowd, beating anyone in their path. President Johnson had already appointed a National Commission on the Causes and Prevention of Violence to examine the crisis throughout the country. A "Chicago Study Team," chaired by Daniel Walker, was sent to investigate the confrontations outside the Democratic Convention. Their report labeled events in Chicago "a police riot." Walker's summary of the riot follows.

Questions to Consider

- Why did the police beat so many people?
- What alternatives were available to the Chicago police?
- Did the demonstrators share any blame for the riot?

During the week of the Democratic National Convention, the Chicago police were the targets of mounting provocation by both word and act. It took the form of obscene epithets, and of rocks, sticks, bathroom tiles and even human feces hurled at police by demonstrators. Some of these acts had been planned; others were spontaneous or were themselves provoked by police action. Furthermore, the police had been put on edge by widely published threats of attempts to disrupt both the city and the Convention.

That was the nature of the provocation. The nature of the response was unrestrained and indiscriminate police violence on many occasions, particularly at night.

That violence was made all the more shocking by the fact that it was often inflicted upon persons who had broken no law, disobeyed no order, made no threat. These included peaceful demonstrators, onlookers, and large numbers of residents who were simply passing through, or happened to live in, the areas where confrontations were occurring.

Source: Daniel Walker, *Rights in Conflict: The Violent Confrontation of Demonstrators and Police in the Parks and Streets of Chicago During the Week of the Democratic National Convention of 1968* (Washington, D.C., 1968), pp. 1–4, 251–265, 269–274.

Newsmen and photographers were singled out for assault, and their equipment deliberately damaged. Fundamental police training was ignored; and officers, when on the scene, were often unable to control their men. As one police officer put it: "What happened didn't have anything to do with police work."

The violence reached its culmination on Wednesday....

The threats to the city were varied. Provocative and inflammatory statements, made in connection with activities planned for convention week, were published and widely disseminated. There were also intelligence reports from informants.

Some of this information was absurd, like the reported plan to contaminate the city's water supply with LSD. But some were serious; and both were strengthened by the authorities' lack of any mechanism for distinguishing one from the other.

The second factor—the city's response—matched, in numbers and logistics at least, the demonstrators' threats.

The city, fearful that the "leaders" would not be able to control their followers, attempted to discourage an inundation of demonstrators by not granting permits for marches and rallies and by making it quite clear that the "law" would be enforced.

Government—federal, state and local—moved to defend itself from the threats, both imaginary and real. The preparations were detailed and far ranging: from stationing firemen at each alarm box within a six block radius of the Amphitheatre to staging U.S. Army armored personnel carriers in Soldier Field under Secret Service control. Six thousand Regular Army troops in full field gear, equipped with rifles, flame throwers, and bazookas were airlifted to Chicago on Monday, August 26. About 6,000 Illinois National Guard troops had already been activated to assist the 12,000 member Chicago Police Force.

Of course, the Secret Service could never afford to ignore threats of assassination of Presidential candidates. Neither could the city, against the background of riots in 1967 and 1968, ignore the ever-present threat of ghetto riots, possibly sparked by large numbers of demonstrators, during convention week.

The third factor emerged in the city's position regarding the riots following the death of Dr. Martin Luther King and the April 27th peace march to the Civic Center in Chicago.

The police were generally credited with restraint in handling the first riots—but Mayor Daley rebuked the Superintendent of Police. While it was later modified, his widely disseminated "shoot to kill arsonists and shoot to maim looters" order undoubtedly had an effect.

The effect on police became apparent several weeks later, when they attacked demonstrators, bystanders and media representatives at a Civic Center peace march. There were published criticisms—but the city's response was to ignore the police violence.

That was the background. On August 18, 1968, the advance contingent of demonstrators arrived in Chicago and established their base, as planned, in Lincoln Park on the city's Near North Side. Throughout the week, they were joined by others—some from the Chicago area, some from states as far away as New York and California. On the weekend before the convention began, there were about 2,000 demonstrators in Lincoln Park; the crowd grew to about 10,000 by Wednesday.

There were, of course, the hippies—the long hair and love beads, the calculated unwashedness, the flagrant banners, the open lovemaking and disdain for the constraints of conventional society. In dramatic effect, both visual and vocal, these dominated a crowd whose members actually differed widely in physical appearance, in motivation, in political affiliation, in philosophy. The crowd included Yippies come to "do their thing," youngsters working for a political candidate, professional people with dissenting political views, anarchists and determined revolutionaries, motorcycle gangs, black activists, young thugs, police and secret service undercover agents. There were demonstrators waving the Viet Cong flag and the red flag of revolution and there were the simply curious who came to watch and, in many cases, became willing or unwilling participants.

To characterize the crowd, then, as entirely hippy-Yippie, entirely "New Left," entirely anarchist, or entirely youthful political dissenters is both wrong and dangerous. The stereotyping that did occur helps to explain the emotional reaction of both police and public during and after the violence that occurred.

Despite the presence of some revolutionaries, the vast majority of the demonstrators were intent on expressing by peaceful means their dissent either from society generally or from the administration's policies in Vietnam....

[On August 28] Just as the police in front of the Hilton were confronted with some sit-downs on the south side of the intersection of Balbo and Michigan, the police unit coming into the intersection on Balbo met the sitting demonstrators. What happened then is subject to dispute between the police and some other witnesses.

The Balbo police unit commander asserts that he informed the sit-downs and surrounding demonstrators that if they did not leave, they would be arrested. He repeated the order and was met with a chant of "Hell no, we won't go." Quickly a police van swung into the intersection immediately behind the police line, the officers opened the door at the rear of the wagon. The deputy chief "ordered the arrest process to start."

"Immediately upon giving this order," the deputy chief later informed his superiors, "we were pelted with rocks, bottles, cans filled with unknown liquids and other debris, which forced the officers to defend themselves from injury.... My communications officer was slugged from behind by one of these persons, receiving injuries to his right eye and cheekbone." That officer states: "All this debris came instantaneously, as if it was waiting for the signal of the first arrest."

A sergeant who was on the scene later said that "the hippies behind those sitting down appeared to be the ones doing most of the throwing.... Police officers were constantly being hit...and were obviously becoming anxious to do something."

A patrolman who was in the skirmish line states that "the order was given to remain in position." But then, he says, one of his fellow officers "ran into the crowd, he was surrounded and I lost sight of him." At this point, the patrolman and other officers in the line "broke into the crowd," using their batons to "push away people who had gathered around" their fellow officer.

He claims they then returned to the line. But another patrolman states that "several police officers were being knocked down by the crowd and several policemen broke formation" to help them "because groups of rioters were attempting to kick and pummel them." At this point, he said, "everything went up for grabs."

The many films and video tapes of this time period present a picture which does not correspond completely with the police view described above. First, the films do not show a mob moving west on Balbo; they show the street as rather clean of the demonstrators and bystanders, although the sidewalks themselves on both sides of the street are crowded. Second, they show the police walking east on Balbo, stopping in formation, awaiting the arrival of the van and starting to make arrests on order. A total of 25 seconds elapses between their coming to a halt and the first arrests.

Also, a St. Louis reporter who was watching from inside the Haymarket lounge agrees that the police began making arrests "in formation," apparently as "the result of an order to clear the intersection." Then, the reporter adds, "from this apparently controlled beginning the police began beating people indiscriminately. They grabbed and beat anyone they could get hold of."...

"There was just enough time for a few people to sit down before the cops charged," says the law student.... "The guys who sat down got grabbed, and the cops re-

ally hit hard. I saw a pair of glasses busted by a billy club go flying through the air."

"The crowd tried to reverse gears," a reporter for a St. Louis paper says. "People began falling over each other.... I went down as I tried to retreat. I covered my head, tried to protect my glasses which had fallen partially off, and hoped that I would not be clubbed. I tried to dig into the humanity that had fallen with me. You could hear shouting and screaming. As soon as I could, I scrambled to my feet and tried to move away from the police. I saw a youth running by me also trying to flee. A policeman clubbed him as he passed, but he kept running.

"The cops were saying, 'Move! I said, move, god dammit! Move, you bastards!'" A representative of the ACLU who was positioned among the demonstrators says the police "were cussing a lot" and were shouting, "Kill, kill, kill, kill, kill!" A reporter for the *Chicago Daily News* said after the melee that he, too, heard this cry. A demonstrator remembers the police swinging their clubs and screaming, "Get the hell out of here."..."Get the fuck out of here."..."Move your fucking ass!"...

...The crowd frantically eddied in a halfmoon shape in an effort to escape the officers coming in from the west. A UPI reporter who was on the southern edge of the crowd on Michigan Avenue, said that the advancing police "began pushing the crowd south." A cherry bomb burst overhead. The demonstrators strained against the...police's line south of the Balbo-Michigan intersection. "When I reached that line," says the UPI reporter, "I heard a voice from behind it say, 'Push them back, move them back!' I was then prodded and shoved with nightsticks back in a northerly direction, toward the still advancing line of police."

"Police were marching this way and that," a correspondent from a St. Louis paper says. "They obviously had instructions to clear the street, but apparently contradicting one another in the directions the crowd was supposed to be sent."...

"Two or three policemen broke formation and began swinging at everyone in sight," the McGovern worker says. The deputy superintendent states that police disregarded his order to return to the police line—the beginning of what he says was the only instance in which he personally saw police discipline collapse. He estimates that ten to 15 officers moved off on individual forays against demonstrators. But the McGovern worker says "this became sort of spontaneous. Every few seconds more policemen would break formation and began swinging until...all the policemen from the original line at Balbo were just swinging through the crowd."

"I turned toward the north and was immediately struck on the back of the head from behind," says the UPI reporter. "I fell to the ground...."

Thus, at 7:57 P.M., with two groups of club-wielding police converging simultaneously and independently, the battle was joined. The portions of the throng out of the immediate area of conflict largely stayed put and took up the chant, "The whole world is watching," but the intersection fragmented into a collage of violence.

Re-creating the precise chronology of the next few moments is impossible. But there is no question that a violent street battle ensued.

People ran for cover and were struck by police as they passed. Clubs were swung indiscriminately.

Two Assistant U.S. Attorneys who were on the scene characterized the police as "hostile and aggressive." Some witnesses cited particularly dramatic personal stories.

"I saw squadrols [paddy wagons] of policemen coming from everywhere," a secretary...said. "The crowd around me suddenly began to run. Some of us, including myself, were pushed back onto the sidewalk and then all the way up against...the Blackstone Hotel along Michigan Avenue. I thought the crowd had panicked."

"Fearing that I would be crushed against the wall of the building...I somehow managed to work my way...to the edge of the street...and saw police everywhere.

"As I looked up I was hit for the first time on the head from behind by what must have been a billy club. I was then knocked down and while on my hands and knees, I was hit around the shoulders. I got up again, stumbling and was hit again. As I was falling, I heard words to the effect of 'move, move' and the horrible sound of cracking billy clubs."

"After my second fall, I remember being kicked in the back, and I looked up and noticed that many policemen around me had no badges on. The police kept hitting me on the head."

Eventually she made her way to an alley behind the Blackstone and finally, "bleeding badly from my head wound," was driven by a friend to a hospital emergency room. Her treatment included the placing of 12 stitches....

Another witness said: "To my left, the police caught a man, beat him to the ground and smashed their clubs on the back of his unprotected head. I stopped to help him. He was elderly, somewhere in his mid-50's. He was kneeling and holding his bleeding head. As I stopped to help him, the police turned on me. 'Get that cock sucker out of here!' This command was accompanied by four blows from clubs—one on the middle of my back, one on the bottom of my back, one on my left buttock, and one on the back of my leg. No attempt was made to arrest me or anybody else in the vicinity. All the blows that I saw inflicted by the police were on the backs of heads, arms, legs, etc. It was the most slow and confused, and the least experienced people who got caught and beaten.

"The police were angry. Their anger was neither disinterested nor instrumental. It was deep, expressive and personal. 'Get out of here you cock suckers' seemed to be their most common cry.

"To my right, four policemen beat a young man as he lay on the ground. They beat him and at the same time told him to 'get up and get the hell out of here.' Meanwhile, I struggled with the injured man whom I had stopped to help...."

One demonstrator said that several policemen were coming toward a group in which he was standing when one of the officers yelled, "Hey, there's a nigger over there we can get." They then are said to have veered off and grabbed a middle-aged Negro man, whom they beat.

A lawyer says that he was in a group of demonstrators in the park just south of Balbo when he heard a police officer shout, "Let's get 'em!" Three policemen ran up, "singled out one girl and as she was running away from them, beat her on the back of the head. As she fell to the ground, she was struck by the nightsticks of these officers." A male friend of hers then came up yelling at the police. The witness said, "He was arrested. The girl was left in the area lying on the ground."

The beating of two other girls was witnessed from a hotel window. The witness says, he saw one girl "trying to shield a demonstrator who had been beaten to the ground," whereupon a policeman came up "hitting her with a billy club." The officer also kicked the girl in the shoulder, the witness said.

A *Milwaukee Journal* reporter says in his statement, "when the police managed to break up groups of protesters they pursued individuals and beat them with clubs. Some police pursued individual demonstrators as far as a block...and beat them.... In many cases it appeared to me that when police had finished beating the protesters they were pursuing, they then attacked, indiscriminately, any civilian who happened to be standing nearby. Many of these were not involved in the demonstrations."

In balance, there is no doubt that police discipline broke during the melee. The deputy superintendent of police states that—although this was the only time he saw discipline collapse—when he ordered his men to stand fast, some did not respond and began to sally through the crowd, clubbing people they came upon. An inspector-observer from the Los Angeles Police Department, stated that during this week, "The restraint of the police both as individual members and as an organization, was beyond reason." However, he said that on this occasion:

> There is no question but that many officers acted without restraint and exerted force beyond that necessary under the circumstances. The leadership at the point of conflict did little to prevent such conduct and the direct control of officers by first-line supervisors was virtually nonexistent.

The deputy superintendent of police has been described by several observers as being very upset by individual policemen who beat demonstrators. He pulled his men off the demonstrators, shouting "Stop, damn it, stop. For Christ's sake, stop it."

"It seemed to me," an observer says, "that only a saint could have swallowed the vile remarks to the officers. However, they went to extremes in clubbing the Yippies. I saw them move into the park, swatting away with clubs at girls and boys lying in the grass. More than once I witnessed two officers pulling at the arms of a Yippie until the arms almost left their sockets, then, as the officers put the Yippie in a police van, a third jabbed a riot stick into the groin of the youth being arrested. It was evident that the Yippie was not resisting arrest."

A witness adds: "I witnessed four or five instances of several officers beating demonstrators when it appeared the demonstrators could have been easily transported and confined to police vans waiting nearby."

"Anyone who was in the way of some of the policemen was struck," a UPI correspondent concludes in his statement, "Police continued to hit people in the back who were running away as fast as possible. I saw one man knocked to the street.... A policeman continued to poke his stick at the man's groin and kidney area. Several newsmen were struck. Individual incidents of violence were going on over the entire area at once, in any direction you might look.

"In one incident, a young man, who apparently had been maced, staggered across Michigan...helped by a companion. The man collapsed.... Medical people from the volunteer medical organization rushed out to help him. A police officer (a sergeant, I think) came rushing forward, followed by the two other nightstick-brandishing policemen and yelled, 'Get him out of here; this ain't a hospital.' The medical people fled, half dragging and half carrying the young man with them....

"Another incident I vividly recall is two policemen dragging one protester by one leg, with his shoulders and possibly his head dragging on the pavement as they ran toward a paddy wagon. So much violence was going on at one time...."

A university student who was watching the melee from a hotel window says she saw one young man attempting to flee the police. "Two or three grabbed him and beat him until he fell to the ground." Then, she says, "two or three more policemen were attracted to him and continued to beat him until he was dragged into a paddy wagon."

At another moment, the girl says, she saw another youth "felled by two or three policemen." A medic "dressed all in white and wearing a white helmet" came to aid him. When police saw him giving aid to the downed boy, "they came upon the medic and began to beat him."

"I saw a well-dressed man carrying a well-dressed woman screaming in his arms," said a *Chicago Daily News* reporter. "He tried to carry her to the Hilton Hotel front door and get in. It was secured, so it certainly would have been safe to permit them in. But the police stopped him, and he then carried her back into the crowd. She was hysterical, and I can see no reason for the police treatment of this injured woman." Also during the melee, the reporter says, he saw policemen using sawhorses as "battering rams" against the crowd.

The history professor quoted earlier says, "A number of motorcycle police drove up over the curb on the east side of Michigan and into the crowd."...

While violence was exploding in the street, the crowd wedged, behind the police sawhorses along the northeast edge of the Hilton, was experiencing a terror all its own. Early in the evening, this group had consisted in large part of curious bystanders. But following the police surges into the demonstrators clogging the intersection, protesters had crowded the ranks behind the horses in their flight from the police.

From force of numbers, this sidewalk crowd of 150 to 200 persons was pushing down toward the Hilton's front entrance. Policemen whose orders were to keep the entrance clear were pushing with sawhorses. Other police and fleeing demonstrators were pushing from the north in the effort to clear the intersection. Thus, the crowd was wedged against the hotel, with the hotel itself on the west, sawhorses on the southeast and police on the northeast.

Films show that one policeman elbowed his way to where he could rescue a girl of about ten years of age from the viselike press of the crowd. He cradled her in his arms and carried her to a point of relative safety 20 feet away. The crowd itself "passed up" an elderly woman to a low ledge. But many who remained were subjected to what they and witnesses considered deliberate brutality by the police.

"I was crowded in with the group of screaming, frightened people," an onlooker states, "We jammed against each other, trying to press into the brick wall of the hotel. As we stood there breathing hard…a policeman calmly walked the length of the barricade with a can of chemical spray [evidently mace] in his hand. Unbelievably, he was spraying at us." Photos reveal several policemen using mace against the crowd….

"Some of the police then turned and attacked the crowd," a Chicago reporter says. The student says she could see police clubbing persons pinned at the edge of the crowd and that there was "a great deal of screaming and pushing within the group." A reporter for a Cleveland paper said, "The police indiscriminately beat those on the periphery of the crowd." An Assistant U.S. attorney put it, "The group on the sidewalk was charged by police using nightsticks." A young cook caught in the crowd relates that:

> The police began picking people off. They would pull individuals to the ground and begin beating them. A medic wearing a white coat and an armband with a red cross was grabbed, beaten and knocked to the ground. His whole face was covered with blood.

"The cops just waded into the crowd," says a law student. "There was a great deal of clubbing. People were screaming, 'Help'."

As a result, a part of the crowd was trapped in front of the Conrad Hilton and pressed hard against a big plate glass window of the Haymarket Lounge. A reporter who was sitting inside said, "Frightened men and women banged…against the window. A captain of the fire department inside told us to get back from the window, that it might get knocked in. As I backed away a few feet I could see a smudge of blood on the glass outside."

With a sickening crack, the window shattered, and screaming men and women tumbled through, some cut badly by jagged glass. The police came after them.

"I was pushed through by the force of large numbers of people," one victim said. "I got a deep cut on my right leg, diagnosed later by Eugene McCarthy's doctor as a severed artery…. I fell to the floor of the bar. There were ten to 20 people who had come through…I could not stand on the leg. It was bleeding profusely.

"A squad of policemen burst into the bar, clubbing all those who looked to them like demonstrators, at the same time screaming over and over, 'We've got to clear this area.' The police acted literally like mad dogs looking for objects to attack.

"A patrolman ran up to where I was sitting. I protested that I was injured and could not walk, attempting to show him my leg. He screamed that he would show me I could walk. He grabbed me by the shoulder and literally hurled me through the door of the bar into the lobby….

"I stumbled out into what seemed to be a main lobby. The young lady I was with and I were both immediately set upon by what I can only presume were plainclothes police…. We were cursed by these individuals and thrown through another door into an outer lobby."…

There is little doubt that during this whole period, beginning at 7:57 P.M. and lasting for nearly 20 minutes, the preponderance of violence came from the police. It was not entirely a one-way battle, however.

Firecrackers were thrown at police. Trash baskets were set on fire and rolled and thrown at them. In one case, a gun was taken from a policeman by a demonstrator.

"…From the windows of the Hilton and Blackstone hotels, toilet paper, wet towels, even ash trays came raining down." A police lieutenant stated that he saw policemen bombarded with "rocks, cherry bombs, jars of vaseline, jars of mayonnaise and pieces of wood torn from the yellow barricades falling in the street."…

A patrolman on duty during the melee states that among the objects he saw thrown at police officers were "rocks, bottles, shoes, a telephone and a garbage can cover. Rolls of toilet paper were thrown from hotel windows. I saw a number of plastic practice golf balls, studded with nails, on the street as well as plastic bags filled with what appeared to be human excrement." He said he saw two policemen, one of them wearing a soft hat, get hit with bricks….

Another type of police difficulty was described by a police captain and mentioned by several other officers in their statements. The captain said that when news cameramen equipped with portable flood lights turned them toward the police, this "caused temporary blindness" and reduced the police effectiveness….

Squadrols continually drove into the intersection. "The police kept pulling as many people as they were able to get and taking them into the paddy wagons," [said] the ACLU representative…. The manner in which this was done ranged from restraint to deliberate brutality….

An Assistant U.S. Attorney who was at the battle reported later: "The arresting officers frequently used their clubs to hit the arrested person in the stomach and kidneys, even though the arrested persons were not in any way resisting arrest or struggling with the police officers." On the other hand, both police officers and a city observer who watched the loading of the paddy wagons state that no excessive force was used in placing nonresisting prisoners in the vans.

Meanwhile, more CTA buses with police reinforcements were pouring into the area.... A Chicago attorney who was near the Hilton watched one contingent unload. He says they "gave the finger" to subdued demonstrators in the vicinity and also made obscene remarks, like "Hippies eat shit." Moving quickly through the Balbo-Michigan intersection, they hurried to join their fellow officers pushing north on Michigan.

Says an ACLU representative: "The buses would discharge at the corner of Wabash and Balbo and then the men would form into a line and march down Balbo with their night sticks, chanting, "Kill, kill."

With each new police attack and flurry of arrests, the crowd dispersed farther into the park and east on Balbo....

By 8:15 P.M., the intersection was in police control. One group of police proceeded east on Balbo, clearing the street and splitting the crowd into two. Because National Guard lines still barred passage over the Balbo Street bridge, most of the demonstrators fled into Grant Park. A Guardsman estimates that 5,000 remained in the park across from the Hilton. Some clubbing by police occurred; a demonstrator says he saw a brick hurled at police; but few arrests were made.

Now, with police lines beginning to re-form, the deputy superintendent directed the police units to advance north on Michigan. He says announcements were again made to clear the area and warnings given that those refusing to do so would be arrested. To this, according to a patrolman who was present, "The hippie group yelled 'fuck you' in unison."

A police officer remembers the deputy superintendent saying, "I want this street kept completely clear. I don't want anyone except people in uniform out in the street. The objective is to get the street clean, open it to traffic and hold it."...

A priest who was in the crowd says he saw a "boy, about 14 or 15, white, standing on top of an automobile yelling something which was unidentifiable. Suddenly a policeman forced him down from the car and beat him to the ground by striking him three or four times with a nightstick. Other police joined in...and they eventually shoved him to a police van."

A well-dressed woman saw this incident and spoke angrily to a nearby police captain. As she spoke, another policeman came up from behind her and sprayed something in her face with an aerosol can. He then clubbed her to the ground. He and two other policemen then dragged her along the ground to the same paddy wagon and threw her in....

"At the corner of Congress Plaza and Michigan," states a doctor, "was gathered a group of people, number between 30 and 40. They were trapped against a railing [along a ramp leading down from Michigan Avenue to an underground parking garage] by several policemen on motorcycles. The police charged the people on motorcycles and struck about a dozen of them, knocking several of them down. About 20 standing there jumped over the railing. On the other side of the railing was a three-to-four-foot drop. None of the people who were struck by the motorcycles appeared to be seriously injured. However, several of them were limping as if they had been run over on their feet."

A UPI reporter witnessed these attacks, too. He relates in his statement that one officer, "with a smile on his face and a fanatical look in his eyes, was standing on a three-wheel cycle, shouting, 'Wahoo, wahoo,' and trying to run down people on the sidewalk." The reporter says he was chased 30 feet by the cycle.

A few seconds later he "turned around and saw a policeman with a raised billy stick." As he swung around, the police stick grazed his head and struck his shoulders. As he was on his knees, he says someone stepped on his back.

A Negro policeman helped him to his feet, the reporter says. The policeman told him, "You know, man I didn't do this. One of the white cops did it." Then, the reporter quotes the officer as saying, "You know what? After this is all over, I'm quitting the force."

An instant later, the shouting officer on the motorcycle swung by again, and the reporter dove into a doorway for safety....

A police commander says that at about this moment he received "an urgent radio message" from an officer inside the van [being rocked by demonstrators]. He radioed that "demonstrators were standing on the hood of his wagon...and were preparing to smash the windshield with a baseball bat," the commander recalled. The officer also told him that the demonstrators were attempting to overturn the squadrol and that the driver "was hanging on the door in a state of shock." The commander told the officer that assistance was on the way....

"Almost immediately a CTA bus filled with police came over the Jackson Drive bridge and the police formed a line in the middle of the street," says a witness. "I heard shouts that the police had rifles and that they had cocked and pumped them. Demonstrators began to run."

"With riot helmets and clubs raised, the police quickly cleared the street," an observer from the Chicago Legal Defense Committee states. "As one area was cleared, another contingent of police arrived with rifles raised and pointed at the people massed on the sidewalk. They pointed guns at the crowd, which responded with catcalls and slogans 'Pigs'…'Fascists' …'Shoot, go on, shoot.'…"

A political science student, who was a driver for one of the convention delegations, states: "A man about 30 or 40 approached a policeman on the corner with tears in his eyes and asked him why they were beating [the people]. The policeman responded by beating him on the side of the head. The man's glasses fell off, and as he bent to retrieve them he was beaten on the back and head until he lay huddled on the ground.

"When he tried to get up, a Green Beret of about 25 to 30, in uniform, came out of the crowd and started beating the man. The original cop was about to intervene when another cop yelled, 'Leave him alone. He just got back from Vietnam.' [It was later discovered that the man was not a Green Beret but, in fact, a deserter from the Army.]

"They left him alone and a group of officers pushed us away from the scene by advancing in a line. I saw the beaten man being arrested. I tried to get the badge numbers of the cops, but neither had them on…."

"As soon as he left, the police line on our side of the street rushed us, yelling. The crowd had nowhere to run. The masses of the people stopped us. People fell. People were trampled. Two of us tried to hide in a building. Three officers came after us. I looked around as I ran out of the doorway and was sprayed in the face and eyes with gas. The fellow with me was clubbed…. I could see only slightly. Policemen and people were running everywhere. I passed a priest leaning against a wall holding his rib cage. I tried to help him. The police rushed at me and I ran. I saw them hit the priest and he fell to the ground. I ran down a side street and got away. My face was on fire…."

"As the fray intensified around the intersection of Michigan and Jackson, a big group ran west on Jackson, with a group of blue-shirted policemen in pursuit, beating at them with clubs," says the U.S. Attorney's report. "Some of the crowd would jump into doorways, and the police would rout them out. The action was very tough and, in my judgment, unnecessarily so. The police were hitting with a vengeance and quite obviously with relish…."

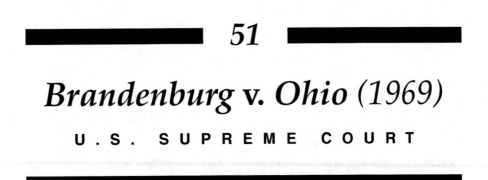

51

Brandenburg v. Ohio (1969)

U.S. SUPREME COURT

Individual states had a long history of placing restrictions on free speech. At different times, those advocating an end to slavery, the rights of workers, and birth control had all been denied their First Amendment rights. With World War I the federal government terminated the rights of those opposed to U.S. involvement in the war. This legislation was upheld by the Supreme Court in *Schenck* v. *United States* (1919). After the war, many states outlawed "criminal syndicalism," the advocacy of terrorism. In 1969 the Supreme Court heard the case of Clarence Brandenburg, the leader of a small group of the Ku Klux Klan in Ohio. A unanimous court nullified all "criminal syndicalism" laws as limitations on rights of speech and assembly, in the process overturning the court's own 1927 decision in *Whitney* v. *California*, a very rare occurrence. Justice Douglas's concurrence provides a brief review of the Supreme Court's treatment of free speech and reveals the logic of the *Brandenburg* decision.

Questions to Consider

- What exactly is the difference between advocacy and incitement?
- Should terrorists enjoy the protection of the First Amendment?

Per Curiam.[1]

The appellant, a leader of a Ku Klux Klan group, was convicted under the Ohio Criminal Syndicalism statute for "advocat[ing]… the duty, necessity, or propriety of crime, sabotage, violence, or unlawful methods of terrorism as a means of accomplishing industrial or political reform" and for "voluntarily assembl[ing] with any society, group, or assemblage of persons formed to teach or advocate the doctrines of criminal syndicalism."… He was fined $1,000 and sentenced to one to 10 years' imprisonment. The appellant challenged the constitutionality of the criminal syndicalism statute under the First and Fourteenth Amendments to the United States Constitution…. The Supreme Court of Ohio dismissed his appeal…"for the reason that no substantial constitutional question exists herein." It did not file an opinion or explain its conclusions. Appeal was taken to this Court, and we noted probable jurisdiction…. We reverse.

The record shows that a man, identified at trial as the appellant, telephoned an announcer-reporter on the staff of a Cincinnati television station and invited him to come to a Ku Klux Klan "rally" to be held at a farm in Hamilton County. With the cooperation of the organizers, the reporter and a cameraman attended the meeting and filmed the events. Portions of the films were later broadcast on the local station and on a national network.

The prosecution's case rested on the films and on testimony identifying the appellant as the person who communicated with the reporter and who spoke at the rally. The State also introduced into evidence several articles appearing in the film, including a pistol, a rifle, a shotgun, ammunition, a Bible, and a red hood worn by the speaker in the films.

One film showed 12 hooded figures, some of whom carried firearms. They were gathered around a large

wooden cross, which they burned. No one was present other than the participants and the newsmen who made the film. Most of the words uttered during the scene were incomprehensible when the film was projected, but scattered phrases could be understood that were derogatory of Negroes and, in one instance, of Jews. Another scene on the same film showed the appellant, in Klan regalia, making a speech. The speech, in full, was as follows:

> "This is an organizers' meeting. We have had quite a few members here today which are—we have hundreds, hundreds of members throughout the State of Ohio. I can quote from a newspaper clipping from the Columbus, Ohio Dispatch, five weeks ago Sunday morning. The Klan has more members in the State of Ohio than does any other organization. We're not a revengent organization, but if our President, our Congress, our Supreme Court, continues to suppress the white, Caucasian race, it's possible that there might have to be some revengeance taken.
>
> "We are marching on Congress July the Fourth, four hundred thousand strong. From there we are dividing into two groups, one group to march on St. Augustine, Florida, the other group to march into Mississippi. Thank you."

The second film showed six hooded figures one of whom, later identified as the appellant, repeated a speech very similar to that recorded on the first film. The reference to the possibility of "revengeance" was omitted, and one sentence was added: "Personally, I believe the nigger should be returned to Africa, the Jew returned to Israel." Though some of the figures in the films carried weapons, the speaker did not.

The Ohio Criminal Syndicalism Statute was enacted in 1919. From 1917 to 1920, identical or quite similar laws were adopted by 20 States and two territories…. In 1927, this Court sustained the constitutionality of California's Criminal Syndicalism Act,…the text of which is quite similar to that of the laws of Ohio. *Whitney* v. *California*…. The Court upheld the statute on the ground that, without more, "advocating" violent

---

Source: U.S. Supreme Court 395 (1969): pp. 444–457.
[1] The opinion of the court. A decision which expresses the judgment of the court without identifying a specific author.—*Ed.*

means to effect political and economic change involves such danger to the security of the State that the State may outlaw it.... But *Whitney* has been thoroughly discredited by later decisions. See *Dennis* v. *United States*...(1951). These later decisions have fashioned the principle that the constitutional guarantees of free speech and free press do not permit a State to forbid or proscribe advocacy of the use of force or of law violation except where such advocacy is directed to inciting or producing imminent lawless action and is likely to incite or produce such action. As we said in *Noto* v. *United States*...(1961), "the mere abstract teaching...of the moral propriety or even moral necessity for a resort to force and violence, is not the same as preparing a group for violent action and steeling it to such action."...A statute which fails to draw this distinction impermissibly intrudes upon the freedoms guaranteed by the First and Fourteenth Amendments. It sweeps within its condemnation speech which our Constitution has immunized from governmental control. Cf. *Yates* v. *United States*...(1957)....

Measured by this test, Ohio's Criminal Syndicalism Act cannot be sustained. The Act punishes persons who "advocate or teach the duty, necessity, or propriety" of violence "as a means of accomplishing industrial or political reform"; or who publish or circulate or display any book or paper containing such advocacy; or who "justify" the commission of violent acts "with intent to exemplify, spread or advocate the propriety of the doctrines of criminal syndicalism"; or who "voluntarily assemble" with a group formed "to teach or advocate the doctrines of criminal syndicalism." Neither the indictment nor the trial judge's instructions to the jury in any way refined the statute's bald definition of the crime in terms of mere advocacy not distinguished from incitement to imminent lawless action.

Accordingly, we are here confronted with a statute which, by its own words and as applied, purports to punish mere advocacy and to forbid, on pain of criminal punishment, assembly with others merely to advocate the described type of action. Such a statute falls within the condemnation of the First and Fourteenth Amendments. The contrary teaching of *Whitney* v. *California*...cannot be supported, and that decision is therefore overruled.

Reversed....

Mr. Justice Douglas, concurring.

While I join the opinion of the Court, I desire to enter a *caveat*.

The "clear and present danger" test was adumbrated by Mr. Justice Holmes in a case arising during World War I—a war "declared" by the Congress, not by the Chief Executive. The case was *Schenck* v. *United States*...where the defendant was charged with attempts to cause insubordination in the military and obstruction of enlistment. The pamphlets that were distributed urged resistance to the draft, denounced conscription, and impugned the motives of those backing the war effort. The First Amendment was tendered as a defense. Mr. Justice Holmes in rejecting that defense said:

"The question in every case is whether the words used are used in such circumstances and are of such a nature as to create a clear and present danger that they will bring about the substantive evils that Congress has a right to prevent. It is a question of proximity and degree."...

In the 1919 Term, the Court applied the *Schenck* doctrine to affirm the convictions of other dissidents in World War I. *Abrams* v. *United States*.... Mr. Justice Holmes, with whom Mr. Justice Brandeis concurred, dissented. While adhering to *Schenck*, he did not think that on the facts a case for overriding the First Amendment had been made out:

"It is only the present danger of immediate evil or an intent to bring it about that warrants Congress in setting a limit to the expression of opinion where private rights are not concerned. Congress certainly cannot forbid all effort to change the mind of the country."...

Those, then, were the World War I cases that put the gloss of "clear and present danger" on the First Amendment. Whether the war power—the greatest leveler of them all—is adequate to sustain that doctrine is debatable. The dissents in *Abrams*, *Schaefer*, and *Pierce* show how easily "clear and present danger" is manipulated to crush what Brandeis called "[t]he fundamental right of free men to strive for better conditions through new legislation and new institutions" by argument and discourse (*Pierce* v. *United States*...) even in time of war. Though I doubt if the "clear and present danger" test is congenial to the First Amendment in time of a declared war, I am certain it is not reconcilable with the First Amendment in days of peace.

The Court quite properly overrules *Whitney* v. *California*...which involved advocacy of ideas which the majority of the Court deemed unsound and dangerous.

Mr. Justice Holmes, though never formally abandoning the "clear and present danger" test, moved closer to the First Amendment ideal when he said in dissent in *Gitlow* v. *New York*...:

"Every idea is an incitement. It offers itself for belief and if believed it is acted on unless some other belief outweighs it or some failure of energy stifles the movement at its birth. The only difference between the expression of an opinion and an incitement in the narrower sense is the speaker's enthusiasm for the result. Eloquence may set fire to reason. But whatever may be thought of the redundant discourse before us it had no chance of starting a present conflagration. If in the long run the beliefs expressed in proletarian dictatorship are destined to be accepted by the dominant forces of the community, the only meaning of free speech is that they should be given their chance and have their way."

We have never been faithful to the philosophy of that dissent.

...In *Bridges* v. *California*...we approved the "clear and present danger" test in an elaborate dictum that tightened it and confined it to a narrow category. But in *Dennis* v. *United States*...we opened wide the door, distorting the "clear and present danger" test beyond recognition.

In that case the prosecution dubbed an agreement to teach the Marxist creed a "conspiracy." The case was submitted to a jury on a charge that the jury could not convict unless it found that the defendants "intended to overthrow the Government 'as speedily as circumstances would permit.'"...The Court sustained convictions under that charge, construing it to mean a determination of "'whether the gravity of the "evil," discounted by its improbability, justifies such invasion of free speech as is necessary to avoid the danger.'"...

Out of the "clear and present danger" test came other offspring. Advocacy and teaching of forcible overthrow of government as an abstract principle is immune from prosecution. *Yates* v. *United States*.... But an "active" member, who has a guilty knowledge and intent of the aim to overthrow the Government by violence, *Noto* v. *United States*,...may be prosecuted.... And the power to investigate, backed by the powerful sanction of contempt, includes the power to determine which of the two categories fits the particular witness. *Barenblatt* v. *United States*.... And so the investigator roams at will through all of the beliefs of the witness, ransacking his conscience and his innermost thoughts.

Judge Learned Hand, who wrote for the Court of Appeals in affirming the judgment in *Dennis*, coined the "not improbable" test,...which this Court adopted and which Judge Hand preferred over the "clear and present danger" test....

My own view is quite different. I see no place in the regime of the First Amendment for any "clear and present danger" test, whether strict and tight as some would make it, or free-wheeling as the Court in *Dennis* rephrased it.

When one reads the opinions closely and sees when and how the "clear and present danger" test has been applied, great misgivings are aroused. First, the threats were often loud but always puny and made serious only by judges so wedded to the *status quo* that critical analysis made them nervous. Second, the test was so twisted and perverted in *Dennis* as to make the trial of those teachers of Marxism an all-out political trial which was part and parcel of the cold war that has eroded substantial parts of the First Amendment.

Action is often a method of expression and within the protection of the First Amendment.

Suppose one tears up his own copy of the Constitution in eloquent protest to a decision of this Court. May he be indicted?

Suppose one rips his own Bible to shreds to celebrate his departure from one "faith" and his embrace of atheism. May he be indicted?

Last Term the Court held in *United States* v. *O'Brien*...that a registrant under Selective Service who burned his draft card in protest of the war in Vietnam could be prosecuted. The First Amendment was tendered as a defense and rejected, the Court saying:

"The issuance of certificates indicating the registration and eligibility classification of individuals is a legitimate and substantial administrative aid in the functioning of this system. And legislation to insure the continuing availability of issued certificates serves a legitimate and substantial purpose in the system's administration."...

But O'Brien was not prosecuted for not having his draft card available when asked for by a federal agent. He was indicted, tried, and convicted for burning the card. And this Court's affirmance of that conviction was not, with all respect, consistent with the First Amendment.

The act of praying often involves body posture and movement as well as utterances. It is nonetheless protected by the Free Exercise Clause. Picketing, as we have said on numerous occasions, is "free speech plus." See *Bakery Drivers Local* v. *Wohl*.... That means that it can be regulated when it comes to the "plus" or "action" side of the protest. It can be regulated as to the number of pickets and the place and hours...because traffic and other community problems would otherwise suffer.

But none of these considerations are implicated in the symbolic protest of the Vietnam war in the burning of a draft card.

One's beliefs have long been thought to be sanctuaries which government could not invade.... The lines drawn by the Court between the criminal act of being an "active" Communist and the innocent act of being a nominal or inactive Communist mark the difference only between deep and abiding belief and casual or uncertain belief. But I think that all matters of belief are beyond the reach of subpoenas or the probings of investigators. That is why the invasions of privacy made by investigating committees were notoriously unconstitutional. That is the deep-seated fault in the infamous loyalty-security hearings which, since 1947 when President Truman launched them, have processed 20,000,000 men and women. Those hearings were primarily concerned with one's thoughts, ideas, beliefs, and convictions. They were the most blatant violations of the First Amendment we have ever known.

The line between what is permissible and not subject to control and what may be made impermissible and subject to regulation is the line between ideas and overt acts.

The example usually given by those who would punish speech is the case of one who falsely shouts fire in a crowded theatre.

This is, however, a classic case where speech is brigaded with action…. They are indeed inseparable and a prosecution can be launched for the overt acts actually caused. Apart from rare instances of that kind, speech is, I think, immune from prosecution. Certainly there is no constitutional line between advocacy of abstract ideas as in *Yates* and advocacy of political action as in *Scales*. The quality of advocacy turns on the depth of the conviction; and government has no power to invade that sanctuary of belief and conscience.

52

The Watergate Investigations (1973)

R I C H A R D   M .   N I X O N

Initially, President Richard M. Nixon refused to respond to allegations about his involvement in the 1972 break-in of the Democratic headquarters at the Watergate Hotel and the ensuing coverup by the executive branch. But as the nation watched the unfolding drama of the Senate Watergate hearings, which documented a stream of crimes, major and comical, committed by the White House staff, the president felt that he had to respond. On the evening of August 15, 1973, Nixon spoke from the Oval Office, admitting the validity of many of the allegations, but insisting that he did not know about either the Watergate break-in or the coverup. Nixon also argued that "executive privilege," the need for confidentiality in presidential dealings, prevented him from turning over the tapes he kept of Oval Office conversations to the Senate investigation. Nixon hoped that these would be his last comments on Watergate. Instead, the investigation dominated the rest of his term in office, until his resignation on August 8, 1974.

Questions to Consider

- Who or what, according to Nixon, was responsible for the coverup?
- Does Nixon acknowledge any limits on presidential confidentiality?

Now that most of the major witnesses in the Watergate phase of the Senate committee hearings on campaign practices have been heard, the time has come for me to speak out about the charges made and to provide a perspective on the issue for the American people.

For over 4 months, Watergate has dominated the news media. During the past 3 months, the three major networks have devoted an average of over 22 hours of television time each week to this subject. The Senate committee has heard over 2 million words of testimony.

This investigation began as an effort to discover the facts about the break-in and bugging of the Democratic National Headquarters and other campaign abuses.

But as the weeks have gone by, it has become clear that both the hearings themselves and some of the commentaries on them have become increasingly absorbed in an effort to implicate the President personally in the illegal activities that took place.

Because the abuses occurred during my Administration, and in the campaign for my reelection, I accept full responsibility for them. I regret that these events took place, and I do not question the right of a Senate committee to investigate charges made against the President to the extent that this is relevant to legislative duties.

However, it is my constitutional responsibility to defend the integrity of this great office against false charges. I also believe that it is important to address the overriding question of what we as a nation can learn from this experience and what we should now do. I intend to discuss both of these subjects tonight.

The record of the Senate hearings is lengthy. The facts are complicated, the evidence conflicting. It would not be right for me to try to sort out the evidence, to rebut specific witnesses, or to pronounce my own judgments about their credibility. That is for the committee and for the courts.

I shall not attempt to deal tonight with the various charges in detail. Rather, I shall attempt to put the events in perspective from the standpoint of the Presidency.

On May 22, before the major witnesses had testified, I issued a detailed statement addressing the charges that had been made against the President.

I have today issued another written statement, which addresses the charges that have been made since then as they relate to my own conduct, and which describes the efforts that I made to discover the facts about the matter.

On May 22, I stated in very specific terms—and I state again to every one of you listening tonight these facts—I had no prior knowledge of the Watergate break-in; I neither took part in nor knew about any of the subsequent coverup activities; I neither authorized nor encouraged subordinates to engage in illegal or improper campaign tactics.

That was and that is the simple truth.

In all of the millions of words of testimony, there is not the slightest suggestion that I had any knowledge of the planning for the Watergate break-in. As for the coverup, my statement has been challenged by only one of the 35 witnesses who appeared—a witness who offered no evidence beyond his own impressions and whose testimony has been contradicted by every other witness in a position to know the facts.

Tonight, let me explain to you what I did about Watergate after the break-in occurred, so that you can better understand the fact that I also had no knowledge of the so-called coverup.

From the time when the break-in occurred, I pressed repeatedly to know the facts, and particularly whether there was any involvement of anyone in the White House. I considered two things essential:

First, that the investigation should be thorough and aboveboard; and second, that if there were any higher involvement, we should get the facts out first. As I said at my August 29 press conference last year, "What really hurts in matters of this sort is not the fact that they occur, because overzealous people in campaigns do things that are wrong. What really hurts is if you try to cover it up." I believed that then, and certainly the experience of this last year has proved that to be true.

I know that the Justice Department and the FBI were conducting intensive investigations—as I had insisted that they should. The White House Counsel, John Dean, was assigned to monitor these investigations, and particularly to check into any possible White House involvement. Throughout the summer of 1972, I continued to press the question, and I continued to get the same answer: I was told again and again that there was no indication that any persons were involved other than the seven who were known to have planned and carried out the operation, and who were subsequently indicted and convicted.

On September 12 at a meeting that I held with the Cabinet, the senior White House Staff and a number of legislative leaders, Attorney General Kleindienst reported on the investigation. He told us it had been the most extensive investigation since the assassination of President Kennedy and that it had established that only those seven there involved.

On September 15, the day the seven were indicted, I met with John Dean, the White House Counsel. He gave me no reason whatever to believe that any others

Source: *Public Papers of the Presidents of the United States: Richard M. Nixon, 1973* (Washington, D.C., 1974), pp. 691–698.

were guilty; I assumed that the indictments of only the seven by the grand jury confirmed the reports he had been giving to that effect throughout the summer.

On February 16, I met with Acting Director Gray prior to submitting his name to the Senate for confirmation as permanent Director of the FBI. I stressed to him that he would be questioned closely about the FBI's conduct of the Watergate investigation. I asked him if he still had full confidence in it. He replied that he did, that he was proud of its thoroughness and that he could defend it with enthusiasm before the committee.

Because I trusted the agencies conducting the investigations, because I believed the reports I was getting, I did not believe the newspaper accounts that suggested a coverup. I was convinced there was no coverup, because I was convinced that no one had anything to cover up.

It was not until March 21 of this year that I received new information from the White House Counsel that led me to conclude that the reports I had been getting for over 9 months were not true. On that day, I launched an intensive effort of my own to get the facts and to get the facts out. Whatever the facts might be, I wanted the White House to be the first to make them public.

At first, I entrusted the task of getting me the facts to Mr. Dean. When, after spending a week at Camp David, he failed to produce the written report I had asked for, I turned to John Ehrlichman and to the Attorney General—while also making independent inquiries of my own. By mid-April, I had received Mr. Ehrlichman's report and also one from the Attorney General based on new information uncovered by the Justice Department. These reports made it clear to me that the situation was far more serious than I had imagined. It at once became evident to me that the responsibility for the investigation in the case should be given to the Criminal Division of the Justice Department.

I turned over all the information I had to the head of that department, Assistant Attorney General Henry Petersen, a career government employee with an impeccable nonpartisan record, and I instructed him to pursue the matter thoroughly. I ordered all members of the Administration to testify fully before the grand jury.

And with my concurrence, on May 18 Attorney General Richardson appointed a Special Prosecutor to handle the matter, and the case is now before the grand jury.

Far from trying to hide the facts, my effort throughout has been to discover the facts—and to lay those facts before the appropriate law enforcement authorities so that justice could be done and the guilty dealt with.

I relied on the best law enforcement agencies in the country to find and report the truth. I believed they had done so—just as they believed they had done so.

Many have urged that in order to help prove the truth of what I have said, I should turn over to the Special Prosecutor and the Senate committee recordings of conversations that I held in my office or on my telephone.

However, a much more important principle is involved in this question than what the tapes might prove about Watergate.

Each day, a President of the United States is required to make difficult decisions on grave issues. It is absolutely necessary, if the President is to be able to do his job as the country expects, that he be able to talk openly and candidly with his advisers about issues and individuals. This kind of frank discussion is only possible when those who take part in it know that what they say is in strictest confidence.

The Presidency is not the only office that requires confidentiality. A Member of Congress must be able to talk in confidence with his assistants; judges must be able to confer in confidence with their law clerks and with each other. For very good reasons, no branch of Government has ever compelled disclosure of confidential conversations between officers of other branches of Government and their advisers about Government business.

This need for confidence is not confined to Government officials. The law has long recognized that there are kinds of conversations that are entitled to be kept confidential, even at the cost of doing without critical evidence in a legal proceeding. This rule applies, for example, to conversations between a lawyer and a client, between a priest and a penitent, and between a husband and wife. In each case it is thought so important that the parties be able to talk freely to each other that for hundreds of years the law has said these conversations are "privileged" and that their disclosure cannot be compelled in a court.

It is even more important that the confidentiality of conversations between a President and his advisers be protected. This is no mere luxury to be dispensed with whenever a particular issue raises sufficient uproar. It is absolutely essential to the conduct of the Presidency, in this and in all future Administrations.

If I were to make public these tapes, containing as they do blunt and candid remarks on many different subjects, the confidentiality of the Office of the President would always be suspect from now on. It would make no difference whether it was to serve the interests of a court, of a Senate committee, or the President himself—the same damage would be done to the principle, and that damage would be irreparable.

Persons talking with the President would never again be sure that recordings or notes of what they said would not suddenly be made public. No one would want to advance tentative ideas that might later seem unsound. No diplomat would want to speak candidly in those sensitive negotiations which could bring peace or avoid war. No Senator or Congressman would want to talk frankly about the Congressional horsetrading that might get a vital bill passed. No one would want to speak bluntly about public figures here and abroad.

That is why I shall continue to oppose efforts which would set a precedent that would cripple all future Presidents by inhibiting conversations between them and those they look to for advice.

This principle of confidentiality of Presidential conversations is at stake in the question of these tapes. I must and I shall oppose any efforts to destroy this principle, which is so vital to the conduct of this great office.

Turning now to the basic issues which have been raised by Watergate, I recognize that merely answering the charges that have been made against the President is not enough. The word "Watergate" has come to represent a much broader set of concerns.

To most of us, Watergate has come to mean not just a burglary and bugging of party headquarters but a whole series of acts that either represent or appear to represent an abuse of trust. It has come to stand for excessive partisanship, for "enemy lists," for efforts to use the great institutions of Government for partisan political purposes.

For many Americans, the term "Watergate" also has come to include a number of national security matters that have been brought into the investigation, such as those involved in my efforts to stop massive leaks of vital diplomatic and military secrets, and to counter the wave of bombings and burnings and other violent assaults of just a few years ago.

Let me speak first of the political abuses.

I know from long experience that a political campaign is always a hard and a tough contest. A candidate for high office has an obligation to his party, to his supporters, and to the cause he represents. He must always put forth his best efforts to win. But he also has an obligation to the country to conduct that contest within the law and within the limits of decency.

No political campaign ever justifies obstructing justice, or harassing individuals, or compromising those great agencies of Government that should and must be above politics. To the extent that these things were done in the 1972 campaign, they were serious abuses, and I deplore them.

Practices of that kind do not represent what I believe government should be, or what I believe politics should be. In a free society, the institutions of government belong to the people. They must never be used against the people.

And in the future, my Administration will be more vigilant in ensuring that such abuses do not take place and that officials at every level understand that they are not to take place.

And I reject the cynical view that politics is inevitably or even usually a dirty business. Let us not allow what a few overzealous people did in Watergate to tar the reputation of the millions of dedicated Americans of both parties who fought hard but clean for the candidates of their choice in 1972. By their unselfish efforts, these people make our system work and they keep America free.

I pledge to you tonight that I will do all that I can to ensure that one of the results of Watergate is a new level of political decency and integrity in America—in which what has been wrong in our politics no longer corrupts or demeans what is right in our politics.

Let me turn now to the difficult questions that arise in protecting the national security.

It is important to recognize that these are difficult questions and that reasonable and patriotic men and women may differ on how they should be answered.

Only last year, the Supreme Court said that implicit in the President's constitutional duty is "the power to protect our Government against those who would subvert or overthrow it by unlawful means." How to carry out this duty is often a delicate question to which there is no easy answer.

For example, every President since World War II has believed that in internal security matters, the President has the power to authorize wiretaps without first obtaining a search warrant.

An act of Congress in 1968 had seemed to recognize such power. Last year the Supreme Court held to the contrary. And my Administration is, of course, now complying with that Supreme Court decision. But until the Supreme Court spoke, I had been acting, as did my predecessors—President Truman, President Eisenhower, President Kennedy, and President Johnson—in a reasonable belief that in certain circumstances the Constitution permitted and sometimes even required such measures to protect the national security in the public interest.

Although it is the President's duty to protect the security of the country, we, of course, must be extremely careful in the way we go about this[,] for if we lose our liberties we will have little use for security. Instances have now come to light in which a zeal for security did go too far and did interfere impermissibly with individual liberty. It is essential that such mistakes not be repeated. But it is also essential that we do not overreact to particular mistakes by tying the President's hands in a way that would risk sacrificing our security, and with it all our liberties.

I shall continue to meet my constitutional responsibility to protect the security of this Nation so that Americans may enjoy their freedom. But I shall and can do so by constitutional means, in ways that will not threaten that freedom.

As we look at Watergate in a longer perspective, we can see that its abuses resulted from the assumption by those involved that their cause placed them beyond the reach of those rules that apply to other persons and that hold a free society together.

That attitude can never be tolerated in our country. However, it did not suddenly develop in the year 1972. It became fashionable in the 1960's as individuals and groups increasingly asserted the right to take the law into their own hands, insisting that their purposes represented a higher morality. Then their attitude was praised in the press and even from some of our pulpits as evidence of a new idealism. Those of us who insisted on the old restraints, who warned of the overriding importance of operating within the law and by the rules, were accused of being reactionaries.

That same attitude brought a rising spiral of violence and fear, of riots and arson and bombings, all in the name of peace and in the name of justice. Political discussion turned into savage debate. Free speech was brutally suppressed as hecklers shouted down or even physically assaulted those with whom they disagreed. Serious people raised serious questions about whether we could survive as a free democracy.

The notion that the end justifies the means proved contagious. Thus, it is not surprising, even though it is deplorable, that some persons in 1972 adopted the morality that they themselves had rightly condemned and committed acts that have no place in our political system.

Those acts cannot be defended. Those who were guilty of abuses must be punished. But ultimately, the answer does not lie merely in the jailing of a few overzealous persons who mistakenly thought their cause justified their violations of the law.

Rather, it lies in a commitment by all of us to show a renewed respect for the mutual restraints that are the mark of a free and a civilized society. It requires that we learn once again to work together, if not united in all of our purposes, then at least united in respect for the system by which our conflicts are peacefully resolved and our liberties maintained.

If there are laws we disagree with, let us work to change them, but let us obey them until they are changed. If we have disagreements over Government policies, let us work those out in a decent and civilized way, within the law, and with respect for our differences.

We must recognize that one excess begets another, and that the extremes of violence and discord in the 1960's contributed to the extremes of Watergate.

Both are wrong. Both should be condemned. No individual, no group, and no political party has a corner on the market on morality in America.

If we learn the important lessons of Watergate, if we do what is necessary to prevent such abuses in the future—on both sides—we can emerge from this experience a better and a stronger nation.

Let me turn now to an issue that is important above all else and that is critically affecting your life today and will affect your life and your children's life in the years to come.

After 12 weeks and 2 million words of televised testimony, we have reached a point at which a continued, backward-looking obsession with Watergate is causing this Nation to neglect matters of far greater importance to all of the American people.

We must not stay so mired in Watergate that we fail to respond to challenges of surpassing importance to America and the world. We cannot let an obsession with the past destroy our hopes for the future.

Legislation vital to your health and well-being sits unattended on the Congressional calendar. Confidence at home and abroad in our economy, our currency, our foreign policy is being sapped by uncertainty. Critical negotiations are taking place on strategic weapons and on troop levels in Europe that can affect the security of this Nation and the peace of the world long after Watergate is forgotten. Vital events are taking place in Southeast Asia which could lead to a tragedy for the cause of peace.

These are matters that cannot wait. They cry out for action now, and either we, your elected representatives here in Washington, ought to get on with the jobs that need to be done—for you—or every one of you ought to be demanding to know why.

The time has come to turn Watergate over to the courts, where the questions of guilt or innocence belong. The time has come for the rest of us to get on with the urgent business of our Nation.

Last November, the American people were given the clearest choice of this century. Your votes were a mandate, which I accepted, to complete the initiatives we began in my first term and to fulfill the promises I made for my second term.

This Administration was elected to control inflation; to reduce the power and size of Government; to cut the cost of Government so that you can cut the cost of living; to preserve and defend those fundamental values that have made America great; to keep the Nation's military strength second to none; to achieve peace with honor in Southeast Asia, and to bring home our prisoners of war; to build a new prosperity, without inflation and without war; to create a structure of peace in the world that would endure long after we are gone.

These are great goals, they are worthy of a great people, and I would not be true to your trust if I let myself be turned aside from achieving those goals.

If you share my belief in these goals—if you want the mandate you gave this Administration to be carried out—then I ask for your help to ensure that those who would exploit Watergate in order to keep us from doing what we were elected to do will not succeed.

I ask tonight for your understanding, so that as a nation we can learn the lessons of Watergate and gain from that experience.

I ask for your help in reaffirming our dedication to the principles of decency, honor, and respect for the institutions that have sustained our progress through these past two centuries.

And I ask for your support in getting on once again with meeting your problems, improving your life, building your future.

With your help, with God's help, we will achieve those great goals for America....

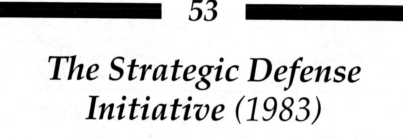

53

The Strategic Defense Initiative (1983)

R O N A L D   R E A G A N

In the following speech of March 23, 1983, President Ronald Reagan stunned the nation by proposing that the United States could prevent war by building space weapons capable of shooting down hostile missiles. That such technology did not yet exist did not bother a president famous for his complete confidence in American ingenuity. Reagan's science advisors assured him that with the proper financial support the arms industry could certainly create a foolproof system capable of targeting and destroying enemy missiles in midflight. The White House labeled this program the Strategic Defense Initiative, or S.D.I. The public quickly renamed it "Star Wars," after a popular series of movies. Congress appropriated the billions of dollars required to begin production, continuing to fund the program over the next twelve years despite doubts of its utility.

Questions to Consider

• Why does Reagan feel that current defense systems are inadequate?

• Wouldn't other nations, such as the Soviet Union, perceive S.D.I. as a threat to their security?

The subject I want to discuss with you, peace and national security, is both timely and important. Timely, because I've reached a decision which offers a new hope for our children in the 21st century, a decision I'll tell you about in a few minutes. And important because there's a very big decision that you must make for yourselves. This subject involves the most basic duty that any President and any people share, the duty to protect and strengthen the peace.

At the beginning of this year, I submitted to the Congress a defense budget which reflects my best judgment of the best understanding of the experts and specialists who advise me about what we and our allies must do to protect our people in the years ahead. That budget is much more than a long list of numbers, for behind all the numbers lies America's ability to prevent the greatest of human tragedies and preserve our free way of life in a sometimes dangerous world. It is part of a careful, long-term plan to make America strong again after too many years of neglect and mistakes....

The budget request that is now before the Congress has been trimmed to the limits of safety. Further deep cuts cannot be made without seriously endangering the security of the Nation. The choice is up to the men and women you've elected to the Congress, and that means the choice is up to you....

What seems to have been lost in all this debate is the simple truth of how a defense budget is arrived at. It isn't done by deciding to spend a certain number of dollars. Those loud voices that are occasionally heard charging that the Government is trying to solve a security problem by throwing money at it are nothing more than noise based on ignorance. We start by considering what must be done to maintain peace and review all the possible threats against our security. Then a strategy for strengthening peace and defending against those threats must be agreed upon. And, finally, our defense establishment must be evaluated to see what is necessary to protect against any or all of the potential threats. The cost of achieving these ends is totaled up, and the result is the budget for national defense....

The defense policy of the United States is based on a simple premise: The United States does not start fights. We will never be an aggressor. We maintain our strength in order to deter and defend against aggression—to preserve freedom and peace.

Since the dawn of the atomic age, we've sought to reduce the risk of war by maintaining a strong deterrent and by seeking genuine arms control. "Deterrence" means simply this: making sure any adversary who thinks about attacking the United States, or our allies, or our vital interests, concludes that the risks to him outweigh any potential gains. Once he understands that, he won't attack. We maintain the peace through our strength; weakness only invites aggression.

This strategy of deterrence has not changed. It still works. But what it takes to maintain deterrence has changed. It took one kind of military force to deter an attack when we had far more nuclear weapons than any other power; it takes another kind now that the Soviets, for example, have enough accurate and powerful nuclear weapons to destroy virtually all of our missiles on the ground. Now, this is not to say that the Soviet Union is planning to make war on us. Nor do I believe a war is inevitable—quite the contrary. But what must be recognized is that our security is based on being prepared to meet all threats....

For 20 years the Soviet Union has been accumulating enormous military might. They didn't stop when their forces exceeded all requirements of a legitimate defensive capability. And they haven't stopped now. During the past decade and a half, the Soviets have built up a massive arsenal of new strategic nuclear weapons— weapons that can strike directly at the United States.

As an example, the United States introduced its last new intercontinental ballistic missile, the Minute Man III, in 1969, and we're now dismantling our even older Titan missiles. But what has the Soviet Union done in these intervening years? Well, since 1969 the Soviet Union has built five new classes of ICBM's, and upgraded these eight times. As a result, their missiles are much more powerful and accurate than they were several years ago, and they continue to develop more, while ours are increasingly obsolete....

Another example of what's happened: In 1978 the Soviets had 600 intermediate-range nuclear missiles based on land and were beginning to add the SS-20—a new, highly accurate, mobile missile with 3 warheads. We had none. Since then the Soviets have strengthened their lead. By the end of 1979, when Soviet leader Brezhnev declared "a balance now exists," the Soviets had over 800 warheads. We still had none. A year ago this month, Mr. Brezhnev pledged a moratorium, or freeze, on SS-20 deployment. But by last August, their 800 warheads had become more than 1,200. We still had none. Some freeze. At this time Soviet Defense Minister Ustinov announced "approximate parity of forces continues to exist." But the Soviets are still adding an aver-

Source: *The Public Papers of the Presidents of the United States: Ronald Reagan, 1983*, Book 1 (Washington, D.C., 1984), pp. 437–443.

age of 3 new warheads a week, and now have 1,300. These warheads can reach their targets in a matter of a few minutes. We still have none. So far, it seems that the Soviet definition of parity is a box score of 1,300 to nothing, in their favor.

So, together with our NATO allies, we decided in 1979 to deploy new weapons, beginning this year, as a deterrent to their SS-20's and as an incentive to the Soviet Union to meet us in serious arms control negotiations. We will begin that deployment late this year. At the same time, however, we're willing to cancel our program if the Soviets will dismantle theirs. This is what we've called a zero-zero plan. The Soviets are now at the negotiating table—and I think it's fair to say that without our planned deployments, they wouldn't be there....

There was a time when we were able to offset superior Soviet numbers with higher quality, but today they are building weapons as sophisticated and modern as our own.

As the Soviets have increased their military power, they've been emboldened to extend that power. They're spreading their military influence in ways that can directly challenge our vital interests and those of our allies.

The following aerial photographs, most of them secret until now, illustrate this point in a crucial area very close to home: Central America and the Caribbean Basin. They're not dramatic photographs. But I think they help give you a better understanding of what I'm talking about.

This Soviet intelligence collection facility, less than a hundred miles from our coast, is the largest of its kind in the world. The acres and acres of antennae fields and intelligence monitors are targeted on key U.S. military installations and sensitive activities. The installation in Lourdes, Cuba, is manned by 1,500 Soviet technicians. And the satellite ground station allows instant communications with Moscow. This 28-square-mile facility has grown by more than 60 percent in size and capability during the past decade.

In western Cuba, we see this military airfield and its complement of modern, Soviet-built Mig-23 aircraft. The Soviet Union uses this Cuban airfield for its own long-range reconnaissance missions. And earlier this month, two modern Soviet antisubmarine warfare aircraft began operating from it. During the past 2 years, the level of Soviet arms exports to Cuba can only be compared to the levels reached during the Cuban missile crisis 20 years ago.

This third photo, which is the only one in this series that has been previously made public, shows Soviet military hardware that has made its way to Central America. This airfield with its MI-8 helicopters, anti-aircraft guns, and protected fighter sites is one of a number of military facilities in Nicaragua which has received Soviet equipment funneled through Cuba, and reflects the massive military buildup going on in that country.

On the small island of Grenada, at the southern end of the Caribbean chain, the Cubans, with Soviet financing and backing, are in the process of building an airfield with a 10,000-foot runway. Grenada doesn't even have an air force. Who is it intended for? The Caribbean is a very important passageway for our international commerce and military lines of communication. More than half of all American oil imports now pass through the Caribbean. The rapid buildup of Grenada's military potential is unrelated to any conceivable threat to this island country of under 110,000 people and totally at odds with the pattern of other eastern Caribbean States, most of which are unarmed.

The Soviet-Cuban militarization of Grenada, in short, can only be seen as power projection into the region. And it is in this important economic and strategic area that we're trying to help the Governments of El Salvador, Costa Rica, Honduras, and others in their struggles for democracy against guerrillas supported through Cuba and Nicaragua....

Every item in our defense program—our ships, our tanks, our planes, our funds for training and spare parts—is intended for one all-important purpose: to keep the peace. Unfortunately, a decade of neglecting our military forces had called into question our ability to do that.

When I took office in January 1981, I was appalled by what I found: American planes that couldn't fly and American ships that couldn't sail for lack of spare parts and trained personnel and insufficient fuel and ammunition for essential training. The inevitable result of all this was poor morale in our Armed Forces, difficulty in recruiting the brightest young Americans to wear the uniform, and difficulty in convincing our most experienced military personnel to stay on.

There was a real question then about how well we could meet a crisis. And it was obvious that we had to begin a major modernization program to ensure we could deter aggression and preserve the peace in the years ahead....

I know that all of you want peace, and so do I. I know too that many of you seriously believe that a nuclear freeze would further the cause of peace. But a freeze now would make us less, not more, secure and would raise, not reduce, the risks of war. It would be largely unverifiable and would seriously undercut our negotiations on arms reduction. It would reward the

Soviets for their massive military buildup while preventing us from modernizing our aging and increasingly vulnerable forces. With their present margin of superiority, why should they agree to arms reductions knowing that we were prohibited from catching up?

Believe me, it wasn't pleasant for someone who had come to Washington determined to reduce government spending, but we had to move forward with the task of repairing our defenses or we would lose our ability to deter conflict now and in the future....

Ask around today, especially among our young people, and I think you will find a whole new attitude toward serving their country. This reflects more than just better pay, equipment, and leadership. You the American people have sent a signal to these young people that it is once again an honor to wear the uniform. That's not something you measure in a budget, but it's a very real part of our nation's strength....

We haven't built a new long-range bomber for 21 years. Now we're building the B-1. We hadn't launched one new strategic submarine for 17 years. Now we're building one Trident submarine a year. Our land-based missiles are increasingly threatened by the many huge, new Soviet ICBM's. We're determining how to solve that problem. At the same time, we're working in the START and INF negotiations with the goal of achieving deep reductions in the strategic and intermediate nuclear arsenals of both sides.

We have also begun the long-needed modernization of our conventional forces. The Army is getting its first new tank in 20 years. The Air Force is modernizing. We're rebuilding our Navy, which shrank from about a thousand ships in the late 1960's to 453 during the 1970's. Our nation needs a superior navy to support our military forces and vital interests overseas. We're now on the road to achieving a 600-ship navy and increasing the amphibious capabilities of our marines, who are now serving the cause of peace in Lebanon. And we're building a real capability to assist our friends in the vitally important Indian Ocean and Persian Gulf region.

This adds up to a major effort, and it isn't cheap. It comes at a time when there are many other pressures on our budget and when the American people have already had to make major sacrifices during the recession. But we must not be misled by those who would make defense once again the scapegoat of the Federal budget.

The fact is that in the past few decades we have seen a dramatic shift in how we spend the taxpayer's dollar. Back in 1955, payments to individuals took up only about 20 percent of the Federal budget. For nearly three decades, these payments steadily increased and, this year, will account for 49 percent of the budget. By con-

trast, in 1955 defense took up more than half of the Federal budget. By 1980 this spending had fallen to a low of 23 percent. Even with the increase that I am requesting this year, defense will still amount to only 28 percent of the budget.

The calls for cutting back the defense budget come in nice, simple arithmetic. They're the same kind of talk that led the democracies to neglect their defenses in the 1930's and invited the tragedy of World War II. We must not let that grim chapter of history repeat itself through apathy or neglect....

Now, thus far tonight I've shared with you my thoughts on the problems of national security we must face together. My predecessors in the Oval Office have appeared before you on other occasions to describe the threat posed by Soviet power and have proposed steps to address that threat. But since the advent of nuclear weapons, those steps have been increasingly directed toward deterrence of aggression through the promise of retaliation.

This approach to stability through offensive threat has worked. We and our allies have succeeded in preventing nuclear war for more than three decades. In recent months, however, my advisers, including in particular the Joint Chiefs of Staff, have underscored the necessity to break out of a future that relies solely on offensive retaliation for our security.

Over the course of these discussions, I've become more and more deeply convinced that the human spirit must be capable of rising above dealing with other nations and human beings by threatening their existence. Feeling this way, I believe we must thoroughly examine every opportunity for reducing tensions and for introducing greater stability into the strategic calculus on both sides.

One of the most important contributions we can make is, of course, to lower the level of all arms, and particularly nuclear arms. We're engaged right now in several negotiations with the Soviet Union to bring about a mutual reduction of weapons....

If the Soviet Union will join with us in our effort to achieve major arms reduction, we will have succeeded in stabilizing the nuclear balance. Nevertheless, it will still be necessary to rely on the specter of retaliation, on mutual threat. And that's a sad commentary on the human condition....

...Let me share with you a vision of the future which offers hope. It is that we embark on a program to counter the awesome Soviet missile threat with measures that are defensive. Let us turn to the very strengths in technology that spawned our great industrial base and that have given us the quality of life we enjoy today.

What if free people could live secure in the knowledge that their security did not rest upon the threat of instant U.S. retaliation to deter a Soviet attack, that we could intercept and destroy strategic ballistic missiles before they reached our own soil or that of our allies?

I know this is a formidable, technical task, one that may not be accomplished before the end of this century. Yet, current technology has attained a level of sophistication where it's reasonable for us to begin this effort. It will take years, probably decades of effort on many fronts. There will be failures and setbacks, just as there will be successes and breakthroughs. And as we proceed, we must remain constant in preserving the nuclear deterrent and maintaining a solid capability for flexible response. But isn't it worth every investment necessary to free the world from the threat of nuclear war? We know it is....

I clearly recognize that defensive systems have limitations and raise certain problems and ambiguities. If paired with offensive systems, they can be viewed as fostering an aggressive policy, and no one wants that. But with these considerations firmly in mind, I call upon the scientific community in our country, those who gave us nuclear weapons, to turn their great talents now to the cause of mankind and world peace, to give us the means of rendering these nuclear weapons impotent and obsolete.

Tonight, consistent with our obligations of the ABM treaty and recognizing the need for closer consultation with our allies, I'm taking an important first step. I am directing a comprehensive and intensive effort to define a long-term research and development program to begin to achieve our ultimate goal of eliminating the threat posed by strategic nuclear missiles. This could pave the way for arms control measures to eliminate the weapons themselves. We seek neither military superiority nor political advantage. Our only purpose—one all people share—is to search for ways to reduce the danger of nuclear war.

My fellow Americans, tonight we're launching an effort which holds the promise of changing the course of human history. There will be risks, and results take time. But I believe we can do it. As we cross this threshold, I ask for your prayers and your support....

54

Support for the Contras (1984)

RONALD REAGAN

With support from the United States government, the Somoza family controlled Nicaragua as a personal fiefdom from 1934 until 1979. In that last year the Sandinista rebels overthrew Somoza and promised democratic elections. On his third day in office, President Ronald Reagan suspended all U.S. aid to Nicaragua, charging that the Soviet Union and Cuba were channeling military supplies to Communist guerrillas in El Salvador via Nicaragua. The United States immediately began supporting the "Contras," anti-Sandinista guerrillas. On May 6, 1984, Reagan called the Contras "the moral equivalent of our founding fathers." Sharply criticized for this unlikely comparison, Reagan sought to clarify his administration's policies toward Central America in this national address on May 9, 1984. Reagan's deep personal commitment to the Contras, as well as his efforts to circumvent legislation prohibiting military support for their revolution, led to a complex and often bizarre series of exchanges with the Iranian government. These latter relations, known as Iran-Contra, would seriously discredit

Reagan in his second term. The Sandinista government won the election in November 1984, but lost four years later, giving way peacefully to a conservative government.

Questions to Consider

- Why was the Contras' struggle of such importance to U.S. interests?
- What gave the U.S. government the right to intervene in Central America?

Our diplomatic objectives will not be attained by good will and noble aspirations alone. In the last 15 years, the growth of Soviet military power has meant a radical change in the nature of the world we live in. Now, this does not mean, as some would have us believe, that we're in imminent danger of nuclear war. We're not. As long as we maintain the strategic balance and make it more stable by reducing the level of weapons on both sides, then we can count on the basic prudence of the Soviet leaders to avoid that kind of challenge to us.

They are presently challenging us with a different kind of weapon: subversion and the use of surrogate forces, Cubans, for example. We've seen it intensifying during the last 10 years, as the Soviet Union and its surrogates move to establish control over Vietnam, Laos, Cambodia, Angola, Ethiopia, South Yemen, Afghanistan, and recently, closer to home, in Nicaragua and now El Salvador. It's the fate of this region, Central America, that I want to talk to you about tonight.

The issue is our effort to promote democracy and economic well-being in the face of Cuban and Nicaraguan aggression, aided and abetted by the Soviet Union. It is definitely not about plans to send American troops into combat in Central America. Each year, the Soviet Union provides Cuba with $4 billion in assistance, and it sends tons of weapons to foment revolution here in our hemisphere.

The defense policy of the United States is based on a simple premise: We do not start wars. We will never be the aggressor. We maintain our strength in order to deter and defend against aggression, to preserve freedom and peace. We help our friends defend themselves.

Central America is a region of great importance to the United States. And it is so close: San Salvador is closer to Houston, Texas, than Houston is to Washington, DC. Central America is America. It's at our

doorstep, and it's become the stage for a bold attempt by the Soviet Union, Cuba, and Nicaragua to install communism by force throughout the hemisphere.

When half of our shipping tonnage and imported oil passes through Caribbean shipping lanes, and nearly half of all our foreign trade passes through the Panama Canal and Caribbean waters, America's economy and well-being are at stake.

Right now in El Salvador, Cuban-supported aggression has forced more than 400,000 men, women, and children to flee their homes. And in all of Central America, more than 800,000 have fled—many, if not most, living in unbelievable hardship. Concerns about the prospect of hundreds of thousands of refugees fleeing Communist oppression to seek entry into our country are well-founded.

What we see in El Salvador is an attempt to destabilize the entire region and eventually move chaos and anarchy toward the American border.

As the National Bipartisan Commission on Central America, chaired by Henry Kissinger, agreed, if we do nothing, if we continue to provide too little help, our choice will be a Communist Central America with additional Communist military bases on the mainland of this hemisphere and Communist subversion spreading southward and northward. This Communist subversion poses the threat that a hundred million people from Panama to the open border of our South could come under the control of pro-Soviet regimes.

If we come to our senses too late, when our vital interests are even more directly threatened, and after a lack of American support causes our friends to lose the ability to defend themselves, then the risks to our security and our way of life will be infinitely greater. But there is a way to avoid these risks, recommended by the National Bipartisan Commission on Central America. It requires long-term American support for democratic development, economic and security assistance, and strong-willed diplomacy....

We can and must help Central America. It's in our national interest to do so, and morally, it's the only right

Source: *Public Papers of the Presidents of the United States: Ronald Reagan, 1984* (Washington, 1986), 1:659–665.

thing to do. But helping means doing enough—enough to protect our security and enough to protect the lives of our neighbors so that they may live in peace and democracy without the threat of Communist aggression and subversion. This has been the policy of our administration for more than 3 years.

But making this choice requires a commitment from all of us—our administration, the American people, and the Congress. So far, we have not yet made that commitment. We've provided just enough aid to avoid outright disaster, but not enough to resolve the crisis, so El Salvador is being left to slowly bleed to death. Part of the problem, I suspect, is not that Central America isn't important, but that some people think our administration may be exaggerating the threat we face. Well, if that's true, let me put that issue to rest.

I want to tell you a few things tonight about the real nature of the Sandinista regime in Nicaragua.

The Sandinistas, who rule Nicaragua, are Communists whose relationship and ties to Fidel Castro of Cuba go back a quarter of a century. A number of the Sandinistas were trained in camps supported by Cuba, the Soviet bloc, and the PLO. It is important to note that Cuba, the Sandinistas, the Salvadorian Communist guerrillas, and the PLO have all worked together for many years. In 1978 the Sandinistas and elements of the PLO joined in a "declaration of war" against Israel.

The Cuban-backed Sandinistas made a major attempt to topple the Somoza regime in Nicaragua in the fall of 1978. They failed. They were then called to Havana, where Castro cynically instructed them in the ways of successful Communist insurrection. He told them to tell the world they were fighting for political democracy, not communism. But most important, he instructed them to form a broad alliance with the genuinely democratic opposition to the Somoza regime. Castro explained that this would deceive Western public opinion, confuse potential critics, and make it difficult for Western democracies to oppose the Nicaraguan revolution without causing great dissent at home.

You see, that's how Castro managed his revolution. And we have to confess he fooled a lot of people here in our own country, or don't you remember when he was referred to in some of our press as the "George Washington of Cuba?"

The Sandinistas listened and learned. They returned to Nicaragua and promised to establish democracy. The Organization of American States, on June 23, 1979, passed a resolution stating that the solution for peace in Nicaragua required that Somoza step down and that free elections be held as soon as possible to establish a truly democratic government that would guarantee peace, freedom, and justice. The Sandinistas then promised the OAS in writing that they would do these things. Well, Somoza left, and the Sandinistas came to power. This was a negotiated settlement, based on power-sharing between Communists and genuine democrats, like the one that some have proposed for El Salvador today. Because of these promises, the previous U.S. administration and other Western governments tried in a hopeful way to encourage Sandinista success.

It took some time to realize what was actually taking place, that almost from the moment the Sandinistas and their cadre of 50 Cuban covert advisers took power in Managua in July of 1979, the internal repression of democratic groups, trade unions, and civic groups began. Right to dissent was denied. Freedom of the press and freedom of assembly became virtually nonexistent. There was an outright refusal to hold genuine elections, coupled with the continual promise to do so. Their latest promise is for elections by November 1984. In the meantime, there has been an attempt to wipe out an entire culture, the Miskito Indians, thousands of whom have been slaughtered or herded into detention camps, where they have been starved and abused. Their villages, churches, and crops have been burned.

The Sandinistas engaged in anti-Semitic acts against the Jewish community, and they persecuted the Catholic Church and publicly humiliated individual priests. When Pope John Paul II visited Nicaragua last year, the Sandinistas organized public demonstrations, hurling insults at him and his message of peace. On this last Good Friday, some 100,000 Catholic faithfuls staged a demonstration of defiance. You may be hearing about that demonstration for the first time right now. It wasn't widely reported. Nicaraguan Bishop Pablo Antonio Vega recently said, "We are living with a totalitarian ideology that no one wants in this country"—this country being Nicaragua.

The Sandinista rule is a Communist reign of terror. Many of those who fought alongside the Sandinistas saw their revolution betrayed. They were denied power in the new government. Some were imprisoned, others exiled. Thousands who fought with the Sandinistas have taken up arms against them and are now called the *contras*. They are freedom fighters.

What the Sandinistas have done to Nicaragua is a tragedy. But we Americans must understand and come to grips with the fact that the Sandinistas are not content to brutalize their own land. They seek to export their terror to every other country in the region.

I ask you to listen closely to the following quotation: "We have the brilliant revolutionary example of Nicaragua...the struggle in El Salvador is very advanced: The same in Guatemala, and Honduras is developing quickly...very soon Central America will be one revolutionary entity...." That statement was made by a Salvadoran guerrilla leader in March of 1981.

Shortly after taking power, the Sandinistas, in partnership with Cuba and the Soviet Union, began supporting aggression and terrorism against El Salvador, Honduras, Costa Rica, and Guatemala. They opened training camps for guerrillas from El Salvador so they could return to their country and attack its government. Those camps still operate. Nicaragua is still the headquarters for Communist guerrilla movements. And Nicaraguan agents and diplomats have been caught in Costa Rica and Honduras supervising attacks carried out by Communist terrorists.

The role that Cuba has long performed for the Soviet Union is now also being played by the Sandinistas. They have become Cuba's Cubans. Weapons, supplies, and funds are shipped from the Soviet bloc to Cuba, from Cuba to Nicaragua, from Nicaragua to the Salvadoran guerrillas. These facts were confirmed last year by the House Intelligence Committee.

The Sandinista regime has been waging war against its neighbors since August of 1979. This has included military raids into Honduras and Costa Rica, which still continue today.

And they're getting a great deal of help from their friends. There were 165 Cuban personnel in Nicaragua in 1979. Today that force has grown to 10,000. And we're being criticized for having 55 military trainers in El Salvador. Manpower support is also coming from other parts of the terror network. The PLO has sent men, and so has Libya's dictator, Qadhafi. Communist countries are providing new military assistance, including tanks, artillery, rocket-launchers, and help in the construction of military bases and support facilities....

When the Sandinistas were fighting the Somoza regime, the United States policy was hands off. We didn't attempt to prop up Somoza. The United States did everything to show its openness toward the Sandinistas, its friendliness, its willingness to become friends....

As soon as I took office, we attempted to show friendship to the Sandinistas and provided economic aid to Nicaragua. But it did no good. They kept on exporting terrorism. The words of their official party anthem describe us, the United States, as the enemy of all mankind. So much for our sincere but unrealistic hopes that if only we try harder to be friends, Nicaragua would flourish in the glow of our friendship and install liberty and freedom for their people. The truth is, they haven't....

Twenty-three years ago, President Kennedy warned against the threat of Communist penetration in our hemisphere. He said, "I want it clearly understood that this government will not hesitate in meeting its primary obligations which are to the security of our nation." And the House and Senate supported him overwhelmingly by passing a law calling on the United States to prevent Cuba from extending its aggressive or subversive activities to any part of this hemisphere. Were John Kennedy alive today, I think he would be appalled by the gullibility of some who invoke his name.

I've told you that Cuba's and Nicaragua's present target is El Salvador. And I want to talk to you about that country, because there's a lot of misunderstanding about it.

El Salvador, too, had a revolution several years ago, and is now struggling valiantly to achieve a workable democracy and, at the same time, to achieve a stable economic system and to redress historical injustices. But El Salvador's yearning for democracy has been thwarted by Cuban-trained and -armed guerrillas, leading a campaign of violence against people and destruction of bridges, roads, power stations, trucks, buses, and other vital elements of their economy. Destroying this infrastructure has brought more unemployment and poverty to the people of El Salvador.

Some argue that El Salvador has only political extremes—the violent left and the violent right—and that we must choose between them. Well, that's just not true. Democratic political parties range from the democratic left to center to conservative. Trade unions, religious organizations, civic groups, and business associations are numerous and flourishing. There is a small, violent right-wing as opposed to democracy as are the guerrillas, but they are not part of the government. We have consistently opposed both extremes, and so has the Government of El Salvador. Last December I sent Vice President Bush to El Salvador with a personal letter in which I again made clear my strong opposition to both violent extremes, and this had a positive effect....

Let me give another example of the difference between the two countries, El Salvador and Nicaragua. The Government of El Salvador has offered amnesty to the guerrillas and asked them to participate in the elections and democratic processes. The guerrillas refused. They want to shoot their way into power and establish totalitarian rule.

By contrast, the *contras,* the freedom fighters in Nicaragua, have offered to lay down their weapons and take part in democratic elections, but there the Communist Sandinista government has refused. That's why the United States must support both the elected government of El Salvador and the democratic aspirations of the Nicaraguan people....

Communist subversion is not an irreversible tide. We've seen it rolled back in Venezuela and, most recently, in Grenada. And where democracy flourishes, human rights and peace are more secure. The tide of the future can be a freedom tide. All it takes is the will and resources to get the job done....

...Meanwhile, evidence mounts of Cuba's intentions to double its support to the Salvadoran guerrillas and bring down that newly-elected government in the fall. Unless we provide the resources, the Communists will likely—to succeed....

The simple questions are: Will we support freedom in this hemisphere or not? Will we defend our vital interests in this hemisphere or not? Will we stop the spread of communism in this hemisphere or not? Will we act while there is still time?

There are those in this country who would yield to the temptation to do nothing. They are the new isolationists, very much like the isolationists of the late 1930's who knew what was happening in Europe, but chose not to face the terrible challenge history had given them. They preferred a policy of wishful thinking, that if they only gave up one more country, allowed just one more international transgression,... surely sooner or later the aggressor's appetite would be satisfied. Well, they didn't stop the aggressors; they em-

boldened them. They didn't prevent war; they assured it....

Last week, as we returned across the vast Pacific to Alaska, I couldn't help being struck again by how blessed has been our land. For 200 years the oceans have protected us from much that has troubled the world, but clearly our world is shrinking. We cannot pretend otherwise if we wish to protect our freedom, our economic vitality, and our precious way of life.

It's up to all of us—the administration, you as citizens, and your representatives in the Congress. The people of Central America can succeed if we provide the assistance I have proposed. We Americans should be proud of what we're trying to do in Central America, and proud of what, together with our friends, we can do in Central America to support democracy, human rights, and economic growth while preserving peace so close to home. Let us show the world that we want no hostile Communist colonies here in the Americas—South, Central, or North....

55

The Gulf War (1990)

GEORGE BUSH

On August 2, 1990, the Iraqi army invaded Kuwait. Iraq's dictator, Saddam Hussein, immediately announced the annexation of Kuwait. Over the next month the United States and its former Cold War opponent, the USSR, attempted to persuade Hussein to withdraw from Kuwait. The United States sent troops to Saudi Arabia within a week to protect that country from a possible Iraqi assault. On September 11, 1990, President George Bush appeared before a joint session of Congress to explain his policies on the Persian Gulf while calling for a balanced budget. On January 16, 1991, the United States and its allies launched a massive air attack on Iraq; on February 23 allied troops invaded Iraq. The ground war lasted only four days, leaving Hussein in power but no longer in possession of Kuwait.

Questions to Consider

• Why was it necessary for the United States to respond militarily to Iraq's invasion of Kuwait?

• What relationship existed between the conflict in the Persian Gulf and a balanced budget?

• Was it possible to balance the budget while increasing military expenditures?

We gather tonight, witness to events in the Persian Gulf as significant as they are tragic. In the early morning hours of August 2d, following negotiations and promises by Iraq's dictator Saddam Hussein not to use force, a powerful Iraqi army invaded its trusting and much weaker neighbor, Kuwait. Within 3 days, 120,000 Iraqi troops with 850 tanks had poured into Kuwait and moved south to threaten Saudi Arabia. It was then that I decided to act to check that aggression.

At this moment, our brave servicemen and women stand watch in that distant desert and on distant seas, side by side with the forces of more than 20 other nations. They are some of the finest men and women of the United States of America. And they're doing one terrific job....

A soldier, Private First Class Wade Merritt of Knoxville, Tennessee, now stationed in Saudi Arabia, wrote his parents of his worries, his love of family, and his hope for peace. But Wade also wrote, "I am proud of my country and its firm stance against inhumane aggression. I am proud of my army and its men. I am proud to serve my country." Well, let me just say, Wade, America is proud of you and is grateful to every soldier, sailor, marine, and airman serving the cause of peace in the Persian Gulf. I also want to thank the Chairman of the Joint Chiefs of Staff, General Powell; the Chiefs here tonight; our commander in the Persian Gulf, General Schwartzkopf; and the men and women of the Department of Defense. What a magnificent job you all are doing. And thank you very, very much from a grateful people. I wish I could say that their work is done. But we all know it's not.

So, if there ever was a time to put country before self and patriotism before party, the time is now.... So, tonight I want to talk to you about what's at stake—what we must do together to defend civilized values around the world and maintain our economic strength at home.

Our objectives in the Persian Gulf are clear, our goals defined and familiar: Iraq must withdraw from Kuwait completely, immediately, and without condition. Kuwait's legitimate government must be restored. The security and stability of the Persian Gulf must be assured. And American citizens abroad must be protected. These goals are not ours alone. They've been endorsed by the United Nations Security Council five times in as many weeks. Most countries share our concern for principle. And many have a stake in the stability of the Persian Gulf. This is not, as Saddam Hussein would have it, the United States against Iraq. It is Iraq against the world.

As you know, I've just returned from a very productive meeting with Soviet President Gorbachev. And I am pleased that we are working together to build a new relationship. In Helsinki, our joint statement affirmed to the world our shared resolve to counter Iraq's threat to peace. Let me quote: "We are united in the belief that Iraq's aggression must not be tolerated. No peaceful international order is possible if larger states can devour their smaller neighbors." Clearly, no longer can a dictator count on East-West confrontation to stymie concerted United Nations action against aggression. A new partnership of nations has begun.

We stand today at a unique and extraordinary moment. The crisis in the Persian Gulf, as grave as it is, also offers a rare opportunity to move toward an historic period of cooperation. Out of these troubled times, our fifth objective—a new world order—can emerge: a new era—freer from the threat of terror, stronger in the pursuit of justice, and more secure in the quest for peace. An era in which the nations of the world, East and West, North and South, can prosper and live in harmony. A hundred generations have searched for this elusive path to peace, while a thousand wars raged across the span of human endeavor. Today that new world is struggling to be born, a world quite different from the one we've known. A world where the rule of law supplants the rule of the jungle. A world in which nations recognize the shared responsibility for freedom and justice. A world where the strong respect the rights of the weak. This is the vision that I shared with President Gorbachev in Helsinki. He and other leaders from Europe, the Gulf, and around the world understand that how we manage this crisis today could shape the future for generations to come.

The test we face is great, and so are the stakes. This is the first assault on the new world that we seek, the first test of our mettle. Had we not responded to this first provocation with clarity of purpose, if we do not continue to demonstrate our determination, it would be a signal to actual and potential despots around the world. America and the world must defend common vital interests—and we will. America and the world must support the rule of law—and we will. America and the world must stand up to aggression—and we will. And one thing more: In the pursuit of these goals America will not be intimidated.

Vital issues of principle are at stake. Saddam Hussein is literally trying to wipe a country off the face of the Earth. We do not exaggerate. Nor do we exaggerate when we say Saddam Hussein will fail. Vital economic interests are at risk as well. Iraq itself controls some 10 percent of the world's proven oil reserves. Iraq plus Kuwait controls twice that. An Iraq permitted to swal-

Source: *Public Papers of the Presidents of the United States: George Bush, 1990* (Washington, D.C., 1991), 2:1218–1222.

low Kuwait would have the economic and military power, as well as the arrogance, to intimidate and coerce its neighbors—neighbors who control the lion's share of the world's remaining oil reserves. We cannot permit a resource so vital to be dominated by one so ruthless. And we won't.

Recent events have surely proven that there is no substitute for American leadership. In the face of tyranny, let no one doubt American credibility and reliability. Let no one doubt our staying power. We will stand by our friends. One way or another, the leader of Iraq must learn this fundamental truth. From the outset, acting hand in hand with others, we've sought to fashion the broadest possible international response to Iraq's aggression. The level of world cooperation and condemnation of Iraq is unprecedented. Armed forces from countries spanning four continents are there at the request of King Fahd of Saudi Arabia to deter and, if need be, to defend against attack. Moslems and non-Moslems, Arabs and non-Arabs, soldiers from many nations stand shoulder to shoulder, resolute against Saddam Hussein's ambitions.

We can now point to five United Nations Security Council resolutions that condemn Iraq's aggression. They call for Iraq's immediate and unconditional withdrawal, the restoration of Kuwait's legitimate government, and categorically reject Iraq's cynical and self-serving attempt to annex Kuwait. Finally, the United Nations has demanded the release of all foreign nationals held hostage against their will and in contravention of international law. It is a mockery of human decency to call these people "guests." They are hostages, and the whole world knows it....

We're now in sight of a United Nations that performs as envisioned by its founders. We owe much to the outstanding leadership of Secretary-General Javier Perez de Cuellar. The United Nations is backing up its words with action. The Security Council has imposed mandatory economic sanctions on Iraq, designed to force Iraq to relinquish the spoils of its illegal conquest. The Security Council has also taken the decisive step of authorizing the use of all means necessary to ensure compliance with these sanctions. Together with our friends and allies, ships of the United States Navy are today patrolling Mideast waters. They've already intercepted more than 700 ships to enforce the sanctions. Three regional leaders I spoke with just yesterday told me that these sanctions are working. Iraq is feeling the heat. We continue to hope that Iraq's leaders will recalculate just what their aggression has cost them. They are cut off from world trade, unable to sell their oil. And only a tiny fraction of goods gets through.

The communiqué with President Gorbachev made mention of what happens when the embargo is so effective that children of Iraq literally need milk or the sick truly need medicine. Then, under strict international supervision that guarantees the proper destination, then food will be permitted.

At home, the material cost of our leadership can be steep. That's why Secretary of State Baker and Treasury Secretary Brady have met with many world leaders to underscore that the burden of this collective effort must be shared. We are prepared to do our share and more to help carry that load; we insist that others do their share as well.

The response of most of our friends and allies has been good. To help defray costs, the leaders of Saudi Arabia, Kuwait, and the UAE—the United Arab Emirates—have pledged to provide our deployed troops with all the food and fuel they need. Generous assistance will also be provided to stalwart front-line nations, such as Turkey and Egypt....

There's an energy-related cost to be borne as well. Oil-producing nations are already replacing lost Iraqi and Kuwaiti output. More than half of what was lost has been made up. And we're getting superb cooperation. If producers, including the United States, continue steps to expand oil and gas production, we can stabilize prices and guarantee against hardship. Additionally, we and several of our allies always have the option to extract oil from our strategic petroleum reserves if conditions warrant. As I've pointed out before, conservation efforts are essential to keep our energy needs as low as possible. And we must then take advantage of our energy sources across the board: coal, natural gas, hydro, and nuclear. Our failure to do these things has made us more dependent on foreign oil than ever before. Finally, let no one even contemplate profiteering from this crisis. We will not have it.

I cannot predict just how long it will take to convince Iraq to withdraw from Kuwait. Sanctions will take time to have their full intended effect. We will continue to review all options with our allies, but let it be clear: we will not let this aggression stand.

Our interest, our involvement in the Gulf is not transitory. It predated Saddam Hussein's aggression and will survive it. Long after all our troops come home—and we all hope it's soon, very soon—there will be a lasting role for the United States in assisting the nations of the Persian Gulf. Our role then: to deter future aggression. Our role is to help our friends in their own self-defense. And something else: to curb the proliferation of chemical, biological, ballistic missile and, above all, nuclear technologies.

Let me also make clear that the United States has no quarrel with the Iraqi people. Our quarrel is with Iraq's dictator and with his aggression. Iraq will not be permitted to annex Kuwait. That's not a threat, that's not a boast, that's just the way it's going to be.

Our ability to function effectively as a great power abroad depends on how we conduct ourselves at home. Our economy, our Armed Forces, our energy dependence, and our cohesion all determine whether we can help our friends and stand up to our foes. For America to lead, America must remain strong and vital. Our world leadership and domestic strength are mutual and reinforcing; a woven piece, strongly bound as Old Glory. To revitalize our leadership, our leadership capacity, we must address our budget deficit—not after election day, or next year, but now.

Higher oil prices slow our growth, and higher defense costs would only make our fiscal deficit problem worse. That deficit was already greater than it should have been—a projected $232 billion for the coming year. It must—it will—be reduced.

To my friends in Congress, together we must act this very month—before the next fiscal year begins on October 1st—to get America's economic house in order. The Gulf situation helps us realize we are more economically vulnerable than we ever should be. Americans must never again enter any crisis, economic or military, with an excessive dependence on foreign oil and an excessive burden of Federal debt....

...Congress should, this month, enact a prudent multiyear defense program, one that reflects not only the improvement in East-West relations but our broader responsibilities to deal with the continuing risks of outlaw action and regional conflict. Even with our obligations in the Gulf, a sound defense budget can have some reduction in real terms; and we're prepared to accept that. But to go beyond such levels, where cutting defense would threaten our vital margin of safety, is something I will never accept. The world is still dangerous. And surely, that is now clear. Stability's not secure. American interests are far reaching. Interdependence has increased. The consequences of regional instability can be global. This is no time to risk America's capacity to protect her vital interests....

...Congress should, this month, enact a 5-year program to reduce the projected debt and deficits by $500 billion—that's by half a trillion dollars. And if, with the Congress, we can develop a satisfactory program by the end of the month, we can avoid the ax of sequester—deep across-the-board cuts that would threaten our military capacity and risk substantial domestic disruption. I want to be able to tell the American people that we have truly solved the deficit problem. And for me to do that, a budget agreement must meet these tests: It must include the measures I've recommended to increase economic growth and reduce dependence on foreign oil. It must be fair. All should contribute, but the burden should not be excessive for any one group of programs or people. It must address the growth of government's hidden liabilities. It must reform the budget process and, further, it must be real....

Once again, Americans have stepped forward to share a tearful goodbye with their families before leaving for a strange and distant shore. At this very moment, they serve together with Arabs, Europeans, Asians, and Africans in defense of principle and the dream of a new world order. That's why they sweat and toil in the sand and the heat and the sun. If they can come together under such adversity, if old adversaries like the Soviet Union and the United States can work in common cause, then surely we who are so fortunate to be in this great Chamber—Democrats, Republicans, liberals, conservatives—can come together to fulfill our responsibilities here....